Gettysburg– Culp's Hill and Cemetery Hill

Harry W. Pfanz

HARRY W. PFANZ

CIVIL WAR AMERICA

GARY W. GALLAGHER,

EDITOR

Gettysburg– Culp's Hill and Cemetery Hill

The University of North Carolina Press

Chapel Hill & London

The paper in this book meets the guidelines for permanence and

durability of the Committee on Production Guidelines for Book

Longevity of the Council on Library Resources.

Library of Congress Cataloging-in-Publication Data

Pfanz, Harry W. (Harry Willcox), 1921–

    Gettysburg—Culp's Hill and Cemetery Hill /

by Harry W. Pfanz.

        p. cm.

    Includes bibliographical references and index.

        ISBN 0-8078-2118-7 (alk. paper)

    1. Gettysburg (Pa.), Battle of, 1863. I. Title.

F457.53.P43 1993

973.7′349—dc20   93-3323

                                              CIP

97 96 95 94 93   5 4 3 2 1

To the memory of our parents

Harry E. and Marion Wilcox Pfanz

Donald M. and Louise Crittenden Earll

Contents

Maps

ILLUSTRATIONS

PREFACE

When Maj. Gen. Oliver Otis Howard, commander of the Army of the Potomac's Eleventh Corps, reached Gettysburg on the morning of 1 July 1863, he saw the tactical potential of Cemetery Hill should the Union forces at Gettysburg have to go on the defensive. As soon as his troops arrived, he established his headquarters on the hill and prepared to defend it as a rallying point. From the late afternoon of 1 July, when the Union First and Eleventh corps retreated to the hill, until the end of the battle, Cemetery Hill was the keystone of the Union position south of Gettysburg.

But it was not enough to occupy Cemetery Hill alone. If the Union position on Cemetery Hill was not to be turned, Union forces must also hold Cemetery Ridge to its left rear and Culp's Hill to its right. Maj. Gen. Winfield S. Hancock, whom Maj. Gen. George G. Meade sent to Gettysburg to take command of the forces there, ordered this done almost at once. Thus it was that the Army of the Potomac established its famed hook-shaped line at Gettysburg.

Gen. Robert E. Lee, who tried to hold the initiative throughout the battle, attacked the Union left and center on the afternoon of 2 July and the Union center on 3 July (in Pickett's Charge). Lt. Gen. Richard S. Ewell's corps of the Army of Northern Virginia was to support these attacks by simultaneous assaults against the Union right on Culp's Hill and Cemetery Hill. Ewell's decision not to try to seize these hills on the late afternoon of 1 July, the measures taken by Ewell's corps to cooperate with the Confederate attacks on 2 and 3 July, and the Army of the Potomac's defense of Cemetery Hill and Culp's Hill are the subject of this monograph.

The battles on Cemetery Hill and Culp's Hill were part and parcel of the battle of Gettysburg as a whole and were conceived as integral parts of the assaults on the Union left and center. Yet, as it turned out, they were essentially separate from Lee's two major thrusts and the Federal effort to repulse them. A small portion of the Twelfth Corps became briefly and actively engaged in the repulse of Longstreet's attack on 2 July. Although Eleventh Corps batteries fired at Confederate batteries prior to Pickett's Charge and briefly fired at troops on the left of the Confederate assault column, these efforts were tangential to their defense of the two important hills. Therefore, I have confined this monograph to the operations and people directly associated with the attack and defense of these hills to the exclusion of definitive discussions of the battle on other parts of the field.

The battle on the Union right had two or three rather unique qualities at the time it was fought. First of all, there was the retreat through Gettysburg and the subsequent fighting in the town. There had been some street fighting at Fredericksburg, Virginia, of course, but little of it elsewhere at this stage of the war. Secondly, although skirmishing was omnipresent throughout the war, some of the skirmishing in front of Cemetery Hill was particularly vicious. Finally, breastworks had been used since the early battles of the war, but their contribution to the defense of Culp's Hill was a harbinger of things soon to come in Virginia.

A comment on sources used might be in order. Except for those relating to the 1st Maryland Battalion (often called the 2d Battalion in later years), the accounts of operations of Confederate regiments, brigades, and divisions are skimpy. I suspect that this is due in some part to the fact that the Confederate assaults were at dusk on 2 July and that on both 2 and 3 July the Confederates on Culp's Hill fought in woods. Not only were these actions devoid of conspicuous glory, but the men involved had a very limited view and understanding of what was going on around them. It was a lonely, deadly experience that must have left unpleasant recollections that were hard to record on paper. Fortunately, Union sources, though seldom as good as they might have been, were generally helpful, and the Confederate story is often mirrored in them. It seems to me that the failure of Generals Ewell and Edward Johnson to supplement their official reports with more extensive and candid narratives is a particularly great loss to posterity.

I attempted this monograph with the intention of trying to provide a reasonably definitive account of this portion of the battle, one that has been lacking to this time. Beyond that, I hope that this effort will have one special positive result—I would like for it to increase interest in this portion of the battlefield and further its preservation. At this time, much of the area that should be preserved in its historic character is still in private hands and is subject to development that will destroy it. Some of it is lost each year; if the land not already inside the park is not protected soon, it will be gone.

Acknowledgments

This study could not have been done without the aid of many people, most of whom work in manuscript repositories and libraries throughout the eastern United States. I regret that I cannot list all the names of those who have provided assistance.

I must first acknowledge the kind help of several staff members at the Gettysburg National Military Park. They are Kathleen Georg Harrison, D. Scott Hartwig, Robert Prosperi, Paul M. Shevchuk, Karen L. Finley, and Eric A. Campbell. They helped me use the park's library and files and were the source of much useful information. More than that, they made me feel as though I was still one of the park's family.

It would be very difficult to write anything of substance about the Army of Northern Virginia without the help and advice of my friend Robert K. Krick, the chief historian at Fredericksburg and Spotsylvania National Military Park. Bob went out of his way to make sure that I had access to useful Confederate sources in his custody and provided encouragement and good advice. I owe him a great deal. I am indebted also to his son, Robert E. L. Krick, of the Richmond National Battlefield Park, who furnished me with copies of unpublished Confederate reports that I would have otherwise missed.

My son, Donald C. Pfanz, a National Park Service historian at Fredericksburg and an authority on Gen. Richard S. Ewell, was of help in many ways. He read some of the chapters, checked sources for me, and most of all shared his views on Ewell and provided me with information on him and some of his comrades that I might have overlooked.

I am indebted also to two outstanding archivist-historians known to every serious scholar in the field of military history: Michael P. Musick at the National Archives and Richard J. Sommers at the U.S. Army Military History Institute at Carlisle Barracks, Pennsylvania. Both have been of help to me on this project and in the past. Pamela Cheney, in Dr. Sommers's office, assisted me there during my most recent visits.

Many of the illustrations used also came from the Military History Institute. Michael J. Winey, as always, received me cordially there and helped me find what I needed. James Enos copied the photographs obtained at Carlisle for me, while an old friend, Walter Lane, copied those at Gettysburg.

Two persons from the Northeast graciously furnished me with useful material. Henry Roberts of Middlebury, Connecticut, one of whose ancestors served with the 9th Massachusetts Regiment, gave me material relating to that fine unit. Christian J. Heidorf of Gansevoort, New York, a fellow artilleryman who shares my interest in the Culp's Hill fight, provided me with appropriate portions of letters of Lt. Robert Cruikshank of the 123d New York Regiment. Clair P. Lyons, Junius R. Fishburne, Jr., and Mrs. C. Hughes Lyon were equally gracious in permitting me to use materials belonging to them that are currently on file in repositories listed in the bibliography.

I am indebted to staff members at various manuscript repositories for their assistance at the time of my visits to their institutions. Foremost among these was Susan Ravdin at Bowdoin College, whose knowledge of the Oliver Otis Howard Papers enabled me to explore them with some dispatch. I am greatly indebted to John E. White at the Southern Historical Collection, University of North Carolina, Pat Weber at Duke University, and William Copely at the New Hampshire Historical Society.

Other librarians and archivists who helped me include Thomas Knoles of the American Antiquarian Society, Judy Bolton at Louisiana State University, Mary Linn Bandaries at Northwestern State University of Louisiana, Julia Hodges at Tulane University, Diane B. Jacob at the Virginia Military Institute, Carl Peterson at Colgate University, J. D. Stinson at the New York Public Library, Ervin L. Jordan at the University of Virginia, Jesse R. Lankford, Jr., at the North Carolina Division of Archives and History, Christian P. Bickford at the Connecticut State Historical Society, Louise Arnold Friend at the library of the Army War College, Charles H. Gladfelter of the Adams County Historical Society in Gettysburg, and David T. Hedrick of Gettysburg College. I also appreciate the assistance given by several reference librarians of the Montgomery County, Maryland, libraries.

It was a pleasure as always to talk with my old friend and colleague Col. Jacob M. Sheads of Gettysburg about old and current times and about matters relating to this book. As always, he was generous with materials from his voluminous files. Others in Gettysburg who supplied me with information include William Ridinger and Wayne E. Motts. A fourth Gettysburgian, Arthur L. Kennell, superintendent of Evergreen Cemetery, answered a number of my questions relating to that important place.

Two North Carolinians with a special interest in Col. Isaac E. Avery and Hoke's brigade were very generous with their time and information. One of these was John R. Bass of Spring Hope, the other Fred Mende of Charlotte. Fred read my Cemetery Hill chapters, made pertinent comments regarding them, and spent some hours on the battlefield with me.

I should not forget three friends who encouraged and assisted me with their advice and counsel. They are Edwin C. Bearss, Gary W. Gallagher, and A. Wilson Greene. All are known to people with more than a casual interest in the Civil War. Gary and Will, along with Bob Krick, invited me to participate in their Mount Alto Conference of 1991, which dealt in part with the fighting on Cemetery Hill and Culp's Hill.

I cannot fail to mention the help of many people associated with the University of North Carolina Press, particularly Matthew Hodgson, Ron Maner, and Paula Wald. Paula brought a measure of order from the chaos of my drafts and saved me from much embarrassment. I deeply appreciate the good work that she has done. Eliza McClennen prepared the maps.

There were others who helped me with information and with friendly support. Some of these good folks were Vicki K. Heilig, Greg Clemmer, and Charles T. Jacobs of the Montgomery County Civil War Round Table; Roy Trimmer of Silver Spring, Maryland; Robert Weiland of Gettysburg; Arthur Eckert of Chambersburg, Pennsylvania; Dean Schultz of Littlestown, Pennsylvania; Amos C. Pearsall, Jr., of Des Moines, Iowa; L. P. Nelson of St. Paul, Minnesota; and John and Joyce Klimkiewicz of Rockville, Maryland.

No project of this scope, undertaken by a retiree at home, can fail to involve his family. I mentioned above the help given me by my son Donald; I also appreciate the help of his wife, Betty. My wife, Letitia, bore the brunt of it all. In addition to accommodating my work at home and its intrusion into her life, she traveled with me to numerous libraries where she handled logistical matters, often copied materials by machine and hand, and simply waited. Her sister, Elizabeth E. Verlie, made helpful editorial suggestions on some of the chapters. My son, Maj. Frederick W. Pfanz, who knows much about military matters past and present, favored me with his comments. Fred's wife, Carol; my daughter Marion and her husband, James E. Ake; and my five grandchildren joined the other members of my immediate family in providing the most desirable things of all: support, affection, and diversion.

1

TWO GENERALS AND THEIR ARMIES

Two generals — corps commanders — confronted one another at Gettysburg, Pennsylvania, late on the afternoon of 1 July 1863. One, a Confederate lieutenant general, whose troops had just smashed the Union Eleventh Corps and driven it in retreat through the streets of Gettysburg, sought to determine if he should push on and try to seize the high ground just south of the town where Union troops were rallying. The other, a Union major general, was on that high ground, Cemetery Hill, and was attempting to organize his badly mauled forces to meet an attack that he believed would soon come.

The generals were extraordinary fellows. Both were graduates of West Point but from classes fourteen years apart. Both were brave beyond doubt, and both had already lost limbs in battle—one a leg, the other an arm. Both were eccentric, and both had been affected by the recent battle of Chancellorsville but in very different ways. The Union general and his corps had been crushed and had suffered heavy casualties there, but worse, many people in and out of the Army of the Potomac blamed them for the Union defeat and vilified them. The Confederate general had not been at Chancellorsville himself, but his men had triumphed there, and now he commanded them in place of the mortally wounded Thomas J. (Stonewall) Jackson.

The Confederate lieutenant general was Richard Stoddert Ewell. Ewell was a Virginian and the grandson of Benjamin Stoddert, the nation's first secretary of the navy. Although Ewell had prominent family connections, he had been reared in near poverty at "Stony Lonesome," a farm near Manassas, Virginia.[1] Ewell managed to get an appointment to West Point's class of 1840, which included William T. Sherman and George H. Thomas. After graduating, he served on the frontier with the 1st Regiment of Dragoons. During the Mexican War Ewell and his company formed Gen. Winfield Scott's mounted escort, and he won a brevet. After the war, Ewell returned to the Southwest and campaigned long and actively against the Apaches. He had performed well throughout his career and had developed an enviable reputation among his peers. Then came the Civil War.

Ewell did not support secession and had much to lose by it. Nevertheless, he resigned his Old Army commission on 7 May 1861 and entered Virginia's service as a lieutenant colonel. He briefly commanded a cavalry camp of instruction at Ashland, Virginia, and on 17 June became a brigadier general. He commanded a brigade at First Manassas but saw no heavy fighting. In February 1862, now a major general, he received command of a division and led it in the Shenandoah Valley during Jackson's campaign there. He commanded his division in the Seven Days' battles, at Cedar Mountain, and at Groveton, where he was shot in the left knee. This wound led to the amputation of his left leg, and Ewell missed the battles of Antietam, Fredericksburg, and Chancellorsville.

Ewell proved to be a skillful and successful division commander, and unlike Ambrose P. Hill and others, he was able to get along with Stonewall Jackson. His bravery was legendary, and often he commanded his division as he had led his dragoon company—from the front.

Ewell was no Adonis. He was five feet, eight inches tall, thin, and had gray eyes and a fringe of brown hair on a domed bald head. Richard Taylor, who had commanded the Louisiana brigade in his division in the Shenandoah Valley, described Ewell as having "bright prominent eyes, a bomb-shaped, bald head, and a nose like that of Francis of Valois [that] gave him striking resemblance to a woodcock." In addition, he had a lisp that gave an added dimension to his pungent comments and to the blistering profanity he used when irritated.[2]

Ewell had chronic health problems associated with malaria and with his digestive system, but these ailments did not adversely affect his military performance. He rivaled Stonewall Jackson in eccentricity, but when not irritated he was pleasant and affable. He seemed devoid of vanity and had little untoward ambition. In the postwar years, when all too many former Confederate leaders sought to buttress their reputations by imputing blame for Confederate misfortunes to others, Ewell, like Gen. Robert E. Lee, remained silent. After his death in 1872, his stepdaughter Harriet Stoddert Turner wrote, "I know how much he suffered from ignorant censure & unjust criticism."[3]

Lt. Gen. Richard S. Ewell (MM)

Ewell had been a romantic in his youth and was an ardent admirer of young ladies of quality, few of whom he met on the frontier. He had wooed his cousin Lizinka Campbell without success but had not seriously pursued other ladies he admired. Then, during the recuperation from the amputation of his left leg, he got the chance to woo Lizinka again. By then she was the wealthy widow of a Mississippi planter named Brown, and Ewell won the widow's heart and hand. The new Mrs. Ewell, who curbed the general's swearing, was the mother of Maj. G. Campbell Brown, who had been on Ewell's staff since early in the war and in some measure would become his Boswell.

Ewell, at forty-six years of age and minus his left leg, returned to active duty after Chancellorsville to take command of Jackson's old corps, the Second Corps of the Army of Northern Virginia, with the grade of lieutenant general. His assignment met with wide approval. Jedediah Hotchkiss, the corps' topographical engineer, recalled that "no risk is run in asserting that the entire Second Corps desired him to be Jackson's successor, and his appointment gave general satisfaction to the officers and men of that grand body of fighters and victory winners."[4]

When Ewell accepted the corps command, he tactfully invited Jackson's staff to stay on with him. After meeting his new commander again, Maj. Alexander S. (Sandie) Pendleton, the corps adjutant, wrote: "General Ewell is in fine health and in fine spirits,—rides on horseback as well as anyone needs to. The more I see of him the more I am pleased to be with him. In some traits of character he is very much like General Jackson, especially in his total disregard of his own comfort and safety, and his inflexibility of purpose. He is so thoroughly honest, too, and has only one desire, to conquer the Yankees. I look for great things from him, and am glad to say that our troops have for him a good deal of the same feeling they had towards General Jackson."[5]

The loss of Jackson triggered a reorganization of the Army of Northern Virginia. For some time, it had had two corps commanded by Gens. James Longstreet and Stonewall Jackson plus a cavalry division commanded by Maj. Gen. James E. B. (Jeb) Stuart. After Chancellorsville, General Lee had to find replacements for ranking officers lost in the battle or found wanting and sought to obtain greater efficiency by reducing the size of his corps. His solution for the latter was to reorganize his 75,000 troops into three corps of three divisions each and a cavalry division together with supporting artillery. With two exceptions, each infantry division would have four brigades. The artillery, formed into battalions, would be assigned to the three corps and to the cavalry.

In this new organization, General Longstreet would continue to command the First Corps, Ewell would take the Second, and the Third would go to A. P. Hill, formerly commander of the famous Light Division. It is significant perhaps that General Lee had not recently worked closely with Hill and that Ewell had worked directly under Jackson and not Lee. In short, Lee would soon launch a major campaign with two new corps commanders, one of whom had not previously been his immediate subordinate. This would affect Ewell in particular, for he was accustomed to the tight-rein style of command employed by Stonewall Jackson and not the hands-off manner of General Lee.

Ewell's corps had divisions commanded by three major generals: Jubal A. Early, Edward Johnson, and Robert E. Rodes. Early's division had four brigades: a Louisiana brigade commanded by Harry T. Hays, a Georgia brigade commanded by John B. Gordon, Virginians under William ("Extra Billy") Smith, and Robert F. Hoke's North Carolinians. Hoke, however, had been wounded at Chancellorsville, and in his absence Col. Isaac E. Avery of the 6th North Carolina Regiment would lead his Tarheels.

Rodes's division underwent some change. It had been Daniel H. Hill's division, but Rodes had commanded it at Chancellorsville and had done well. Now it was his. For some reason, the division had five brigades instead of the usual four. Rodes's old Alabama brigade was commanded by Col. Edward A. O'Neal of its 26th Alabama Regiment. Brig. Gen. George Doles continued to command his Georgia brigade, and there were two North Carolina brigades under Brig. Gens. Stephen D. Ramseur and Alfred Iverson. It also had a large new North Carolina brigade under Brig. Gen. Junius Daniel.

The greatest changes had taken place in the division once commanded by Stonewall himself. It was said that Jackson had been saving the command of this division for Isaac R. Trimble, who had been wounded at Second Manassas, but Trimble had not yet recovered. Therefore, General Lee assigned it to Maj. Gen. Edward Johnson, a newcomer to the Army of Northern Virginia.[6]

But that was not all. Each of the division's four brigades needed a new commander. Elisha F. Paxton of the Stonewall Brigade had been killed at Chancellorsville; his place would be taken by James A. Walker, who had commanded other brigades at Antietam and Fredericksburg. John R. Jones was dismissed from service after having left the field at Chancellorsville; his place would be taken by John M. Jones. There was a special problem involving North Carolina–Virginia pride in the brigade once led by Raleigh E. Colston; General Lee resolved it by assigning the 1st Maryland Battalion to the brigade and placing Brig. Gen. George H. Steuart, a Marylander, in command. The final brigade, that of Brig. Gen. Francis R. Nicholls, needed at least a temporary commander for Nicholls had lost a foot at Chancellorsville. General Lee designated Col. Jesse M. Williams of the 2d Louisiana Regiment as the brigade's acting commander.[7]

Therefore, though the Army of Northern Virginia had a new and seemingly more efficient organization, two of its corps had commanders new to their assignments. Furthermore, one, Richard S. Ewell, had lost a leg and was returning to duty with whatever handicap that condition might create. The other new commander, Lt. Gen. A. P. Hill, had worsening health. We know with the benefit of hindsight that Hill would not measure up to the reputation he had gained as a division commander. Both of these generals would bear some responsibility for Confederate operations against Cemetery Hill at Gettysburg.[8]

The Army of the Potomac had suffered 17,000 casualties at Chancellorsville and had lost a number of units whose period of service had expired. Yet it was not reorganized. In June 1863 it continued to consist of seven corps of infantry, each supported by a "brigade" of artillery, most having five batteries, a cavalry corps supported by two brigades of artillery, and its Artillery Reserve—a powerful collection of twenty-one batteries formed in five brigades. It had two new corps commanders: Maj. Gen. Winfield S. Hancock of the Second Corps and Brig. Gen. Alfred Pleasonton of the Cavalry Corps.[9]

Six of the seven infantry corps were proven fighting machines, but popular opinion within the army considered one corps, the Eleventh, to be a question mark at best. Formerly the First Corps of John Pope's Army of Virginia, the Eleventh Corps, commanded by Maj. Gen. Franz Sigel, had come to the Army of the Potomac after the battle of Second Manassas. Through design or fortune, it had not taken part in the heavier fighting either at Antietam or Fredericksburg, and Sigel had left it in February 1863. Gens. Carl Schurz and Adolph von Steinwehr, two of its division commanders, were its acting commanders for a few weeks, and then Maj. Gen. Oliver Otis Howard took command.

Howard's appointment was made neither in heaven nor by angels. In retrospect, the post would seem to have called for an experienced, nononsense disciplinarian like Hancock or Maj. Gen. John F. Reynolds. Instead it fell to an officer whose demonstrated ability was balanced by his being young and rather inexperienced.

Howard was born in Leeds, Maine, on 8 November 1830, the son of a farmer who died when he was nine. He attended public schools and in

1850 graduated from Bowdoin College. Although he had taught school, he was undecided about a career, and when an uncle who was a congressman offered him an appointment to West Point, he took it. Therefore, at age nineteen, with a college degree already in hand, he entered the academy's class of 1854.[10] Howard had no problem with his studies at West Point, but he was placed in Coventry for a time during his plebe year for reasons unknown today. His classmates included W. Dorsey Pender, Stephen H. Weed, and Thomas H. Ruger, and by the time of his graduation he numbered G. W. Custis Lee and Jeb Stuart among his closer friends.[11]

After graduation, Howard married and served as a subaltern in the Ordnance Department. In 1857 he returned to West Point as an instructor in mathematics. In the years that followed, he fathered three children, conducted a Bible class for enlisted men and civilians, and studied theology with a local Episcopal priest with the idea of going into the ministry. Religion permeated his life, in much the same way that it had influenced Stonewall Jackson's.[12]

War came, and in June 1861 Howard exchanged his lieutenancy for the colonelcy of the 3d Maine Regiment. This appointment suggests that though he might not have dabbled in politics, he had support from Maine's important politicians. Howard was twenty-nine at this time. A member of the 3d Maine described him then as a "pale young man, . . . slender with earnest eyes, a profusion of flowing moustache and beard." Actually, he was about five feet, nine inches tall and had blue eyes. A later description by Maj. Thomas W. Osborn, his chief of artillery, held him to be of slight build with heavy dark hair and "undistinguished" eyes, a strong but not an impressive man. Frank A. Haskell of the Second Corps wrote that Howard was a "very pleasant, affable, well dressed little gentleman"— something that no one would have said of Ewell.[13]

Major Osborn had other things to say of Howard as he saw him in 1865. He wrote that the general "never overcame mannerisms such as fidgety gestures and a shrill voice." On the other hand Osborn termed Howard "the highest toned gentleman" he had ever known. He believed him to be neither a profound thinker like Sherman nor a man with "large natural ability." He did not "call out from his troops the enthusiastic applause that Generals Logan and Hooker do," yet, wrote Osborn, "every officer and man has unbounded confidence in him." This might have been the real Howard of 1865, but it was not necessarily the Howard of 1861.[14]

Howard took the 3d Maine to Washington, D.C., to train it. However, he received an assignment to a brigade command and led his brigade to Manassas only about two months after he resigned his lieutenancy.

Maj. Gen. Oliver O. Howard (WLM)

Howard found the battle particularly offensive because it took place on a Sunday. He became unnerved momentarily by the sights and sounds of the fight, but he responded to his fright by praying to God that he might do his duty, and he claimed that the fear left him, never to return.[15]

Howard became a brigadier general on 3 September 1861. He led a Second Corps brigade in the Peninsular campaign until he fell at Fair Oaks on 1 June 1862 with two wounds, one of which cost him his right arm. He returned to Maine to recuperate but did not dally and was back with the army and in command of another Second Corps brigade in time for Second Manassas. He led this brigade at Antietam, and when his division commander, John Sedgwick, was wounded, Howard was there to take command. He continued to command the division at Fredericksburg and became a major general on 29 November 1862.[16]

In February 1863, Maj. Gen. Joseph Hooker, commander of the Army of the Potomac, assigned his friend Daniel E. Sickles to the command of its Third Corps. Howard and Sickles shared the same promotion date to the grade of brigadier general, but Howard had ranked Sickles as a colonel. Thus, Howard had grounds for protesting that he had seniority over the bumptious Sickles and more right to a corps command than he. Hooker had to give Howard heed and on 2 April 1863 appointed him to the command of the Eleventh Corps.[17]

Howard's appointment was an unwelcome surprise to the Eleventh Corps, particularly to its Germans, for they had hoped for the return of their beloved Franz Sigel. In later years, Howard wrote that his reception by the members of the corps was outwardly cordial, but that they did not know him, and there was much dissatisfaction at the removal of Sigel. Howard and his brother and aide, Maj. Charles H. Howard, soon felt that Maj. Gen. Carl Schurz, who ranked just beneath Howard in the corps, was working against him. Truly, the corps' German element could not have felt that it had much in common with such a straitlaced fellow. For one thing, Howard did not drink; he believed alcohol to be a poison "injurious to the mental and moral life of a soldier," and such a view would have gained little support, even among the relatively few native New Englanders in the corps. Apart from that, Howard did not have the easy sense of humor and toleration that would have been helpful in developing empathy with a body of troops.[18]

But Howard gained toleration even if he did not replace Sigel in the Germans' affections. First of all, he retained much of the old corps staff for the time being, particularly Lt. Col. Charles W. Assmussen, the chief of staff, and Lt. Col. Theodore A. Meysenburg, the adjutant general, both of whom were German. Howard came to admire both, even though he wrote of Assmussen, "He drinks some but never lets me see him do so." Maj. Gen. Abner Doubleday, who developed a dislike for Howard at Gettysburg, wrote with jaundiced exaggeration that Howard's staff was made up of ministers and religious people who were looking out for their own interests. This would not have been true of Meysenburg and Assmussen.[19]

Howard did other positive things. Capt. Frederick C. Winkler wrote that the general was an active man who took note of everything. He recalled Howard's visiting a corps bakery where he heard a wagon master swearing. Howard called the man aside—he did not speak to him in front of other soldiers—and told him that it was the first such language that he had heard since coming to the corps and that he did not wish to hear any more. Later in the day another soldier, who was serving as an orderly, told Winkler that when he had held the general's horse to help him mount, Howard had said, "Thank you." The orderly commented, "Nobody said that to me before since I have been in the service."[20]

In later years at least, some of the ranking officers did not care for Howard. Hooker, who had an axe to grind, called him a fraud and deemed Maj. Gen. George Sykes, commander of the Fifth Corps, as much superior to him "as a soldier as night is to day." Brig. Gen. Henry J. Hunt wrote in a private letter, "As to the 'Christian soldier,' I have no great opinion of him, either as a soldier or as head of the Freedmen's Bureau, or as a man."[21]

People called Howard the "Christian Soldier" but not always as a compliment. This was particularly so after the war when Howard gained a high profile and became controversial. The Howard of 1863 was probably closer to the man seen by Col. Charles S. Wainwright, chief of artillery of the First Corps, an elitist from New York and something of a snob. Before Chancellorsville, he wrote, "Howard . . . is brave enough and a most perfect gentleman. He is a Christian as well as a man of ability, but there is some doubt as to his having snap enough to manage the Germans who require to be ruled with a rod of iron." After Chancellorsville, Wainwright termed the attacks on Howard as outrageous. Wrote Wainwright, "He is the only religious man of high rank that I know of in the army and, in the little intercourse I have had with him, shewed himself the most polished gentleman I have met."[22]

Stonewall Jackson smashed Howard's Eleventh Corps in a surprise evening attack at Chancellorsville, and much of it fled before the Confederate assault. This battle is often considered to be General Lee's greatest victory and was a fitting climax to Jackson's short but illustrious career. Many people, including much of the press, blamed the Army of the Potomac's defeat on the Eleventh Corps and were particularly critical of its German element, although the Germans constituted less than half of the corps' strength. Those who were more fair conceded that any corps placed in the Eleventh's position would have behaved about the same. Yet, although there was much anger within the corps for the unfair criticism its soldiers believed they had received, some of its members had doubts about the corps' capabilities. Captain Winkler of the staff of Schurz's division wrote on 11 June that he was apprehensive about the way the corps would behave in the campaign ahead. He had little confidence in it, not because of its German units as such, for he belonged to one, but because in his opinion the old regiments of the corps were rent by jealousy and intrigues among the officers and discipline was lacking.[23]

General Lee launched his Pennsylvania campaign on 3 June, eight days before Winkler penned his comment about the Eleventh Corps. Lee believed that a foray across the Potomac was the best way of defending Virginia. He could not attack the Federal army in its position near Fredericksburg with any great hope of success, and another battle in Virginia would probably be no more decisive than his victory at Chancellorsville had been. He resolved, therefore, to move the "scene of hostilities" north of the Potomac and in doing so draw the Federals from Virginia, break up their campaign plans for the summer, and possibly win a decisive victory. He wrote also of "other valuable results" that might be obtained, not the least of which were the supplies that might be garnered from the Pennsylvania countryside.[24]

Lee and most of Longstreet's and Ewell's corps and Stuart's division were in the Culpeper area on 9 June when Federal cavalry with some infantry support crossed the Rappahannock River "to disperse and destroy the rebel force assembled in the vicinity of Culpeper." The result was the cavalry battle of Brandy Station, which was a drawn fight and an embarrassment for Jeb Stuart, although his troopers finally prevailed.[25]

On the following day, 10 June, Ewell's corps set out in the van of the army for Pennsylvania. Early's and Johnson's divisions struck Maj. Gen. Robert H. Milroy's force of about 8,000 at Winchester, Virginia, on 14 June and destroyed it, capturing 23 pieces of artillery, 300 loaded wagons, and 200,000 rounds of small-arms ammunition. Stonewall Jackson could not have done better. In the meantime, Rodes's division captured Martinsburg along with five more cannons and an abundance of supplies.[26]

Ewell's corps moved on in the wake of Brig. Gen. Albert G. Jenkins's cavalry brigade. The corps crossed the Potomac on 15 June. Ewell delayed his march briefly in the Hagerstown area and then continued north up the Cumberland Valley toward Harrisburg. His troops swept the country of needed supplies as they went along. One column under Brig. Gen. George H. Steuart crossed Tuscarora Mountain to McConnellsburg and rejoined the main column near Carlisle.[27]

Jubal Early's division turned east at Chambersburg and swept through Gettysburg on its way to York and to the Susquehanna River at Wrightsville. General Lee gave a specific reason for Early's diversion; he hoped that Early's division's presence in the Gettysburg-York area would hold the Army of the Potomac east of the mountains after it crossed into Maryland and lessen its threat to the Confederates' line of communications in the Cumberland Valley. During this stage of its march, Early's division had the help of Lt. Col. Elijah V. White's 35th Cavalry Battalion (the Comanches) and the 17th Virginia Cavalry Regiment, commanded by Col. William H. French. On its way Gordon's brigade met and routed the 26th Pennsylvania Emergency Regiment. At York, Early's division picked up more booty, but the Federals burned the bridge over the Susquehanna at Wrightsville before the Confederates could seize it.

Longstreet's and Hill's corps followed Ewell at midmonth. In the meantime, General Hooker swung the Army of the Potomac north, keeping it between the Confederate positions as he knew them and Washington. There were fights at Paris, Middleburg, and Upperville on 17–21 June as Federal cavalry probed the Confederate screen. When General Lee was satisfied that Hooker's reaction was of a defensive character, he ordered Longstreet and Hill to follow Ewell across the Potomac. They crossed on 24 and 25 June.[28]

The Union army approached the Potomac in a series of halts and marches. Its Twelfth Corps took position near Leesburg on 18 June in order to support the Federal garrison at Harpers Ferry and to cover the nearby Potomac crossings. When it became apparent that the Army of Northern Virginia had crossed the river, the Army of the Potomac crossed into Maryland at Edwards's Ferry on 25, 26, and 27 June, and by 28 June was concentrated in the Frederick area.[29]

While Early marched to Gettysburg, York, and Wrightsville, Rodes's division marched up the Cumberland Valley, reaching Carlisle on 27 June. There, in the rich Carlisle area that Ewell likened unto "a hole full of blubber to a Greenlander," the Confederates found horses, cattle, flour, and grain. While some troops collected these supplies, Capt. Henry B. Richardson, Ewell's engineer, escorted by Jenkins's brigade, scouted the defenses of Harrisburg. Rodes's men "contemplated with eagerness" Harrisburg's capture on the following day.[30]

Ewell had been stationed at Carlisle Barracks just after graduating from West Point, yet he did not view the area with nostalgia. Instead, he observed that its residents "look as sour as vinegar, and, I have no doubt, would gladly send us all to Kingdom come if they could." He did send Majs. Campbell Brown and Benjamin H. Green of his staff to a family he had known to see if they were alright. The majors enjoyed both the visit and some brandy that the family served. Ewell assured some local ministers that they could hold services on the following day, a Sunday, and when asked by the Episcopal rector if they could pray for the president, he made his classic reply, "Certainly . . . he did not know anyone who needed such prayer more." Ewell's report said nothing of such things, of course. It did state that "agreeably to the views of the general commanding, I did not burn Carlisle Barracks." Jeb Stuart, three of whose brigades were stumbling along east of the Army of the Potomac and out of touch with General Lee, would reach Carlisle on 1 July. He would burn the barracks then.[31]

While at Carlisle, Ewell received a summons from General Lee to march south and join the main army in the Gettysburg-Cashtown area. Ewell had conducted a bold march, a grand raid, essentially devoid of errors even in hindsight. It seems likely that he would have captured Harrisburg had he been allowed to press ahead for another day or so. Yet more urgent matters were at hand. The Army of the Potomac had appeared north of the Potomac, and it demanded the Army of Northern Virginia's undivided attention.[32]

Howard and the other Federal corps commanders had no opportunity to distinguish themselves on the march north. Unlike Ewell, who had operated under instructions of a general nature, they worked as components of a great machine. Army headquarters prescribed their daily marches; they had the arduous task of seeing that the headquarters' orders were obeyed. On the morning of 28 June near Frederick, Maryland, they received surprising news that must have made most of them rejoice. General Hooker was gone, and Maj. Gen. George G. Meade now commanded the Army of the Potomac.[33]

Meade continued the movement north on 29 June on a broad front screened by his cavalry. He sent Maj. Gen. John F. Reynolds and the First Corps and Howard's Eleventh Corps to Emmitsburg, Maryland, where the two corps and Brig. Gen. John Buford's division of cavalry constituted the army's left. Meade knew generally of the location of Lee's army and prepared to meet it. He informed Maj. Gen. Henry W. Halleck at 11:00 A.M. on 29 June that he was trying to hold his force together in the hope that he might fall upon a portion of the Confederate army.[34]

2
THE ONLY POSITION

On the evening of 30 June, Maj. Gen. John F. Reynolds and Maj. Gen. Oliver O. Howard met in the back room of Moritz Tavern, a brick house beside the Emmitsburg Road about seven miles south of Gettysburg and a mile north of the Mason-Dixon Line. Reynolds, a Pennsylvanian and commander of the First Corps, Army of the Potomac, had been designated that day as temporary commander of the army's left wing, the three corps nearest the known locations of the enemy. His own First Corps, now under the temporary command of Maj. Gen. Abner Doubleday, commander of its Third Division, was bivouacked along the road near Marsh Creek. Howard's Eleventh Corps was at Emmitsburg, Maryland, and Maj. Gen. Daniel E. Sickles's Third Corps had moved that day from Taneytown, Maryland, to Bridgeport, a hamlet on the Monocacy River about four miles east of Emmitsburg.[1]

Schurz's division of the Eleventh Corps camped at Emmitsburg on the grounds of St. Joseph's College, a Roman Catholic school for girls. Schurz had persuaded the school's mother superior to lend him the use of one of the "nunnery's" buildings for his headquarters staff, suggesting that it would be protected better by having the headquarters party in it than it would be by having sentries posted outside. The good lady was cordial—what choice did she have—and she turned Schurz over to her chaplain, who played the gracious host and conducted some of the headquarters staff on a tour of the school. So far did hospitality extend that the sisters served dinner to Schurz and his staff, and one officer was permitted to give an impromptu recital on the school's organ.[2]

Officers and men in lower echelons received less preferential treatment. June 30 was the day of the army's bimonthly muster for pay—a burdensome task in paperwork for many company officers and noncommissioned officers. Soldiers who were Roman Catholic, and had time, received communion in the college's chapel. That evening some Germans in the corps sang "Morgenrot" and other German songs around their campfires and pondered their fate in the battle ahead.[3]

General Howard had enjoyed the comfort of a bed in the priests' quarters on the previous night and was looking forward to another night of rest when he received a message from Reynolds inviting him to Moritz Tavern for a talk. Howard, accompanied by an aide and orderly, set out for the tavern at dusk and reached it in about an hour. After dismounting, he walked to a small, sparsely furnished room at the rear of the house, on its south side, where he found Reynolds at a table spread with papers and maps. Reynolds, whom he had known when on the West Point faculty, gave him the "usual cordial greeting." Before getting down to business, Reynolds, Howard, and some staff officers had some supper and cheerful conversation.[4]

Reynolds was about ten years older than Howard, and Howard admired him. Howard remembered him in later years as an officer who governed with a steady hand, was generous and quick to recognize merit, sought to gain the confidence of his subordinates, and was foremost in battle. In later years, he likened him to Gen. George H. Thomas, the "Rock of Chickamauga," with whom Howard campaigned in Tennessee and Georgia in 1864, but Howard believed Reynolds to have been less reticent than Thomas and "not quite so tenacious of purpose."[5]

After eating, Reynolds showed Howard the order placing him in command of the army's left wing. The two generals studied maps of the locality, numerous reports on the whereabouts and doings of Confederate units, the locations of the corps of the Army of the Potomac, and General Meade's instructions. Both probably had collected rumors and bits of information during the day and had them to share, but they must have relied mostly on dispatches from Meade's headquarters and other army sources, particularly from Buford's cavalry division, which screened the army's left and was operating between Reynolds and the enemy.[6]

Buford provided two bits of information on 30 June that, in retrospect, had great significance. One was the capture of a dispatch from Jubal Early to an unnamed cavalry colonel that said that Ewell would be in Heidlersburg, ten miles north of Gettysburg. The other, sent from Gettysburg, in-

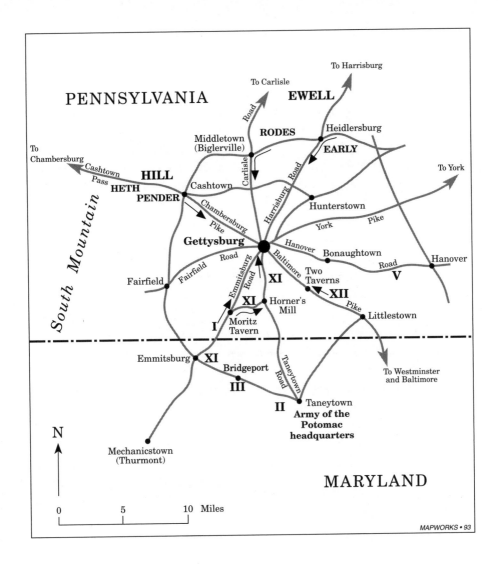

PENNSYLVANIA

To Harrisburg

To Carlisle

EWELL

RODES

Middletown
(Biglerville)

Heidlersburg

EARLY

To
Chambersburg

Cashtown
Pass

HILL

HETH

PENDER

Cashtown

Carlisle Road

Harrisburg Road

Hunterstown

To York

York Pike

Pike

South Mountain

Chambersburg
Pike

Gettysburg

Hanover

Bonaughtown

Hanover

Fairfield

Fairfield Road

Road

Emmitsburg Road

XI

Baltimore

Two
Taverns

Road

V

XI

Horner's
Mill

XII

Pike

Littlestown

I

Moritz
Tavern

Emmitsburg

XI

Bridgeport

Taneytown Road

To Westminster
and Baltimore

III

N

II

Taneytown

Army of the
Potomac
headquarters

Mechanicstown
(Thurmont)

MARYLAND

0   5   10   Miles

MAPWORKS • 93

Map 2.1. Gettysburg Campaign, 30 June–1 July

formed Reynolds and Meade that a Confederate regiment had approached the town but had retired on the approach of Buford's cavalry.[7]

The two generals conferred until nearly 11:00 P.M., expecting to get orders for 1 July from army headquarters all the while. When it became late and the orders did not come, Howard rode the rough track back to Emmitsburg and his comfortable bed. Reynolds drafted a letter to Maj. Gen. Daniel Butterfield, Meade's chief of staff. He stated that he had forwarded all of the information that he had received and then offered an opinion that he had probably developed in his conversation with Howard. If the enemy advanced on Gettysburg and the Federals were to fight a defensive battle in their present vicinity, the position that he would occupy would be just north of Emmitsburg so as to protect the plank road to Taneytown and the left of the army. If he took this position, the enemy then might be expected to try to turn his left by swinging down from Fairfield, Pennsylvania, toward the area south of Emmitsburg. That said, his evening closed with the receipt of a dispatch from Buford timed 10:30 P.M. that stated that Hill's corps was gathering near Cashtown at the entrance of the pass in South Mountain eight miles west of Gettysburg, that Longstreet was behind Hill, and that Ewell's corps was apparently approaching from the north. Reynolds digested this information and forwarded it on to army headquarters. Then he wrapped himself in a blanket and fell asleep on the tavern's floor.[8]

Howard had hardly fallen asleep in Emmitsburg when a courier awakened him with dispatches from Meade's headquarters nine miles to the east in Taneytown. He read them quickly before sending them on to Reynolds. One document was headed "Orders" and dated 30 June. Its information was not as current as that sent by Buford to Reynolds for it announced that Hill and Longstreet were believed to be "at Chambersburg, partly toward Gettysburg," that Ewell was at Carlisle and York, and that the Confederates seemed to be moving toward Gettysburg. Based on what he knew, Meade believed that his army had relieved the threat to Harrisburg and Philadelphia and that he should now "look to his own army." To that end, he ordered its various corps to move toward the enemy on 1 July in a cautious, probing manner. The First Corps was to move to Gettysburg, the Eleventh either to Gettysburg or to supporting distance of the First, and the Third to Emmitsburg to cover their left. The Second would march to Taneytown twelve miles south of Gettysburg, and the Twelfth to Two Taverns just five miles southeast of Gettysburg on the Baltimore Pike. Over to the east, the Fifth Corps was to move to Hanover, and the

Sixth to Manchester, Maryland. Since it was likely that battle was near, Meade ordered the army's empty wagons, surplus baggage, and other impedimenta back to Union Bridge, Maryland, in the army's rear. That area would become his army's supply point.[9]

A circular with later information on the enemy accompanied the orders. In it, Meade said that the army should remain in the positions designated until the situation became more clear. More to the point though, the army was to ready itself for battle. The men were to receive three days' rations, the infantrymen sixty rounds of ammunition to carry on their persons. The trains of wagons and pack animals, except for ammunition wagons and ambulances, were to go to the rear, and corps commanders were to have their commands ready to march at a moment's notice. The long campaign was approaching its climax.[10]

After Howard read the dispatches, he sent them on to Reynolds by an aide who would return with any orders that Reynolds might have for him. It seems likely that Howard prepared and sent off to his three division commanders—Francis C. Barlow, Adolph von Steinwehr, and Carl Schurz—orders regarding their trains and to prepare for an early march. Barlow's division would go directly to Gettysburg by the Emmitsburg Road, while the other two divisions would take a road that intersected the Emmitsburg Road about a mile north of Moritz Tavern and ran east from there past Horner's Mill on Rock Creek to the Taneytown Road, which they would follow to Gettysburg four miles to the north.[11]

The sun rose at about 4:30 on 1 July, but clouds covered the sky much of the day, and some Union soldiers remembered scattered showers that made marching difficult. It was a warm, sultry summer day with a slight breeze from the south—a better day for growing corn than for fighting a battle.[12]

Meade's orders for the First and Eleventh corps to move to Gettysburg reached Moritz Tavern about 4:00 A.M. Reynolds's aide, Maj. William Riddle, awakened the general reluctantly, and Reynolds stirred himself to action. He rode north to Marsh Creek, where Brig. Gen. James S. Wadsworth and his division had spent the night, and ordered the New Yorker to march his division on to Gettysburg. It is likely that he alerted Doubleday to the move before riding to see Wadsworth, and on his return to the tavern met with Doubleday there. At about 6:00 A.M., Reynolds explained the situation to Doubleday, said that he would go to Gettysburg with Wadsworth's division, and asked Doubleday to follow with his own and Robinson's divisions. The First Corps did not get off to an early start.

It was 8:00 A.M. before Wadsworth's men were collected and moving. Doubleday wrote that it was over an hour and a half before his own division was formed and on the way, and Robinson's followed Doubleday's.[13]

Reynolds did not see Howard on the morning of 1 July, but they exchanged messages at an early hour. Reynolds wrote Howard that he was going to Gettysburg and asked Howard, who would go there also, to let him know where the Eleventh Corps and its headquarters would be. He asked Howard to send a staff officer to him in Gettysburg and suggested he had better turn off north of Marsh Creek, "pretty close to the town." At 6:00 A.M., Howard informed Reynolds that he had received orders from Meade's headquarters to move to within supporting distance of the First Corps at Gettysburg, and he gave Reynolds his proposed order of march. He went on to say that unless Reynolds desired otherwise, the Eleventh Corps would "encamp" near the "J. Wintz Place" (the Peach Orchard) about a mile and a half from Gettysburg. In a later note, Capt. Edward C. Baird of Reynolds's staff cautioned Howard that the two corps would be using the road to Gettysburg and that the movement of trains would be subordinated to the movement of troops but the trains might be able to move up later. Obviously, at this time Reynolds did not foresee the enormous scope of battle that was soon to unfold and that the Third Corps would also be coming up the Emmitsburg Road. It is apparent too that he had not received the Pipe Creek Circular.[14]

As soon as his corps took to the road, Howard, some of his staff, and a small cavalry escort trotted on ahead. They followed the Emmitsburg Road, the most direct route, riding much of the way in adjoining fields in order to pass the troops and vehicles of the First Corps that struggled along the rutted and muddy road. Howard made as good time as the situation permitted and by 10:30 had reached the high ground at the Peach Orchard and was in sight of the town. From it he could hear the noise of the opening Confederate attack against Buford's cavalrymen and see First Corps infantrymen filing across the fields toward the seminary. Here, he also met one of Reynolds's staff officers, possibly Major Riddle. Riddle told him that Wadsworth's division was engaged and that Reynolds wanted him to "come quite up to Gettysburg." Howard asked Riddle where Reynolds wanted him to place his corps, and the young man replied, "Stop anywhere about here according to your judgment, at present."[15]

The divisions of the Eleventh Corps were well on the way by this time, but they would not arrive on the field for at least another hour. This gave Howard time to contact Reynolds and to become acquainted with the area. First, he sent an aide, Capt. Daniel Hall, to Reynolds to report the

Gettysburg from Cemetery Hill. Snider's Wagon Hotel is on the left. Baltimore Street runs north from it and by the courthouse, whose steeple is in the distance on the right. Note that the rails have been taken from the fence in the foreground. (O'Sullivan plate, 7 July 1863, GNMP)

progress of the Eleventh Corps and ask for orders. He then began to look around. He rode to the left, probably to Seminary Ridge west of the Peach Orchard, and found that he could see little of interest there. He rode then to what he described as "the highest point of the Cemetery Ridge," which must have been Cemetery Hill. From it he could see northwest to the seminary where the First Corps was taking position and where the battle had opened, the town at the foot of the hill, and the fields west of the town. After viewing this panorama, he turned to Lieutenant Colonel Meysenburg and, referring to the hill, said, "This seems to be a good position, colonel." Meysenburg replied, "It is the only position, general." Howard recalled later that at this moment he made up his mind "what I would do with my troops, or recommend for Reynolds's wing, or for the army, should my advice be sought, that is, use that Cemetery Ridge as the best defensive position within sight." It must have been about this time that Howard sent his brother, Maj. Charles Howard, to Reynolds for orders.[16]

As Howard rode from the hill into the town, Captain Hall returned with a message from Reynolds. Reynolds announced that he had found the enemy in force and that Howard should bring up his corps as rapidly as possible. Howard responded by sending couriers to Barlow and Schurz asking them to hurry their columns along. Hall rode with Howard for a short distance and then returned to Reynolds.[17]

Howard and his party entered the town and ascended Baltimore Street to the Adams County Courthouse in the southwest corner of the Middle Street intersection. He wanted to climb into the courthouse belfry but found no ladder there. A young man, Daniel A. Skelly, stepped forward and suggested that he try the "observatory" above his father's store in the Fahnestock building across Middle Street from the courthouse. Skelly led the general through the general merchandise store and up to the observatory. Here Howard found the view he wanted. The town lay beneath him, and its roads radiated to all directions of the compass—back southwest toward Emmitsburg, south to Taneytown, and southeast toward Baltimore. These were the roads that the Union forces would have to travel to reach the field. He also saw roads running west toward Chambersburg, north toward Carlisle, and northeast to Harrisburg, whence the Confederates were coming even then. He could make out some of Buford's troopers in the fields to the northwest, probably in the flat land north of the town, but they appeared small and few in the distance. Most remarkably of all, he could see Wadsworth's men fighting near the railroad cut and Confederate prisoners being hustled back toward the town.[18]

At this time, Howard would not have known the details of the fight. Heth's division of Hill's corps, followed by Pender's division, had marched on Gettysburg from Cashtown in a reconnaissance-in-force. The Confederates met Buford's men near Marsh Creek, they exchanged shots, and as the cavalry's resistance stiffened, the head of the Rebel column deployed into a skirmish line and advanced more slowly. Finally, as the Confederates reached Herr Ridge a mile to the west of Seminary Ridge, Federal resistance became so marked that the two leading brigades, Archer's and Davis's, prepared to move in line against the Federal position that was being established on McPherson Ridge a half mile in their front.

The Confederates attacked astride the Chambersburg Pike with two brigades and soon learned that their opponent was the infantry of the Army of the Potomac! Reynolds had arrived with Wadsworth's division of the First

Corps. The Iron Brigade smashed head-on against Archer's brigade south of the pike, and Confederates of Davis's brigade outflanked Cutler's on the Union right and drove it in. Then, with Archer gone, Cutler's men south of the pike gave all of their attention to Davis, caught some Confederates in the railroad cut, where they captured many of them, and drove the rest of the Confederate brigade back to Herr Ridge. Wadsworth's division had won the opening round, but most of the match still lay ahead. Furthermore, it had been won at enormous cost, for Reynolds had been killed early in the fight.[19]

As Howard surveyed the field from atop the Fahnestock building, Sgt. George Guinn of Cole's Maryland Cavalry drew rein in the street below, saluted, and shouted: "General Reynolds is wounded, sir." To this, Howard replied, "I am very sorry; I hope that he will be able to keep the field." There was probably more conversation, but Howard remained on the roof. A few minutes later his aide, Captain Hall, whom he had sent to Reynolds a short time before, appeared in the street and shouted up, "General Reynolds is dead, and you are the senior officer on the field." Soon afterward, Major Howard arrived with the same message.[20]

Howard knew little about the Confederate force that he faced and felt the heavy burden that was suddenly his. Yet he determined to continue the fight, saying to himself, "God helping us, we will stay here until the army comes." Dan Skelly remembered Howard's having been "perfectly calm and self-possessed." After descending from the observatory, Howard met Mrs. Samuel Fahnestock, an elderly lady who was very upset about the impending battle. He stopped and spoke a few words with her in an effort to calm her.[21]

After learning of Reynolds's death, Howard dictated orders assuming command of the left wing. Schurz was to be acting commander of the Eleventh Corps while Howard commanded the wing. Probably Howard then returned to his headquarters on Cemetery Hill and sent messages by Capt. Edward P. Pearson down the Emmitsburg Road to Barlow, Sickles, and Meade, telling of the battle and of Reynolds's death and urging Sickles to bring his Third Corps forward. Captain Hall carried messages down the Taneytown Road to Schurz, von Steinwehr, and the Eleventh Corps artillery commander, Maj. Thomas W. Osborn, saying that the First Corps was engaged and urging them to the front as rapidly as possible. Howard also informed Maj. Gen. Henry W. Slocum, commander of the Twelfth Corps, whom he believed would be at the hamlet of Two Taverns just four and a half miles back down the Baltimore Pike, that the left wing was engaged

Fahnestock building. General Howard used the observatory on its roof. (GNMP)

with Hill's corps and that Ewell's corps was advancing from York. This message itself said nothing of Reynolds's death; perhaps we may assume that the courier or staff officer would have mentioned it.[22]

Schurz's division had the lead in the column that was marching via Horner's Mill and the Taneytown Road. As it crossed the Mason-Dixon Line into Pennsylvania, its Pennsylvania regiments saluted their homeland by uncovering their colors and with music and cheers. About a half mile north of Moritz Tavern, the division turned east from the Emmitsburg Road onto the cross road leading to the Taneytown Road near Horner's Mill, two and a half miles away. Schurz was nearing the Taneytown Road at about 10:30 when he received Howard's request to hurry forward. Turning the command of his division over to Brig. Gen. Alexander Schimmelfennig, he told him to bring the column on at a double-quick and trotted ahead to find Howard. He met numerous refugees as he hurried along. Among them was a distraught middle-aged woman who carried a large bundle slung across her back and pulled a child by the hand. When she met Schurz, she tried to stop him and cried out, "Hard times at Gettysburg! They are shooting and killing! What will become of us!" Schurz had not yet heard the sounds of battle.[23]

Meanwhile, Howard had considered his options and decided that the only tenable position for the Federal forces at Gettysburg was just south of the town on Cemetery Hill. It was the site of Evergreen Cemetery, a community burial ground established in 1856.[24] The cemetery itself is on the west side of the Baltimore Pike. Its arched brick gatehouse provided access from the pike, and its grounds occupied the hill's crest west of the pike and sloped southeast 250 yards to its boundary. On its town side, the northwest slope of the hill between the pike and the road, where the Soldiers' National Cemetery is today, was covered with orchard trees. Fences and walls crossed the northwestern slope of the hill on both sides of the pike, and walls and fences bordered the pike and the Taneytown Road.

The hill's potential as a defensive position was obvious. Its 100 feet of height would provide its defenders with a view of the terrain over which attackers might approach and fields of fire, while its walls enhanced and emphasized its natural strength. Its smooth crest provided artillery positions with the visibility needed for direct fire, and its slopes, except for those to the east, were gentle enough so that they would not give defilade to an attacking enemy. The hill would be the keystone of a defensive position that had to include Cemetery Ridge to its left rear and Culp's Hill to its right rear if it was not to be turned. Cemetery Hill, with Culp's Hill and Cemetery Ridge, covered the roads to the rear over which the Army of the Potomac would approach, or, if necessary, withdraw.

Schurz and Assmussen reached the cemetery gatehouse about 11:30 and found General Howard waiting for them there. At this time, the First Corps troops west of the town were enjoying the relative quiet of the lull that separated the morning's fight from the battle of the afternoon. Schurz could hear the intermittent crackling of musketry and the thump of cannon fire and see occasional puffs of smoke out by the seminary, but this skirmishing was a mile away and was dwarfed by the broad landscape so that it seemed but a "small affair." As the officers talked, they saw an ambulance, escorted by some horsemen, pass south along the Taneytown Road. It carried Reynolds's body from the field and was an ominous portent of things to come.[25]

Howard briefed Schurz on the situation that confronted them. Schurz would command the Eleventh Corps. Howard had learned from Doubleday that the left of the First Corps seemed all right but that the corps right was hard-pressed. For this reason, Doubleday would post Robinson's small division along Seminary Ridge toward the Mummasburg Road. If the enemy was in manageable force, the Federals would continue to fight beyond the town, and Schurz would guard the First Corps right by extending it northward with his own and Barlow's divisions on to Oak Hill. On the other hand, if the enemy proved too strong, the Federal force would fall back to Cemetery Hill. In the meantime, von Steinwehr's division, after it arrived, would prepare to defend Cemetery Hill, and Major Osborn would post some Eleventh Corps batteries there.[26]

Carl Schurz's designation as acting commander of the Eleventh Corps suggested the distance he had traveled on the road of life. Schurz, age thirty-four, was the son of a schoolteacher. He was born near Cologne, Germany, and went to school there prior to studying for a doctorate at the University of Bonn. At the university, he embraced the revolutionary ideas abroad in Germany at that time. His exceptional talent as an orator propelled him into the leadership of the university's liberal faction, and he became an assistant of Prof. Gottfried Kinkel, a national leader in the revolutionary movement. Schurz was a staff officer in the revolutionary army in 1849 and took part in some of the battles of that year. His duties took him to the fortress of Rastatt just before it was surrendered to the Prussian army. Expecting execution if captured, he escaped the Prussian grasp through an unused sewer and fled to Zurich. In 1850 he returned secretly to Germany and led a daring effort that freed Professor Kinkel from Berlin's Spandau prison, where he had been imprisoned for life. The two fled in disguise to England, where Schurz became acquainted with Giuseppi Mazzini, Lajos Kossuth, and other exiled leaders of Europe's liberal movement. Schurz supported himself in England and in France by teaching German until he and his wife emigrated to the United States.

They settled finally in Wisconsin, where Schurz sampled the life of a Latin farmer. He became an ardent Republican and campaigned in 1856 for John C. Frémont. In 1858 he turned to the practice of law in Milwaukee and stumped for Abraham Lincoln against Stephen A. Douglas in the Illinois senate race. In 1860 Schurz headed the Wisconsin delegation to the Republican National Convention in Chicago, where his delegation supported William H. Seward. Nevertheless, he later made a three-hour speech at the Cooper Union in New York City in support of Lincoln, and, after taking office, Lincoln recognized Schurz's efforts and the support of the German-Americans by appointing Schurz minister to Spain. In 1862 Schurz returned to the United States to urge that Lincoln adopt a policy of immediate emancipation. In April 1862 Lincoln appointed Schurz a brigadier general of volunteers. Lincoln must have been impressed by Schurz's abilities—certainly he felt indebted to him politically—yet the appointment must be regarded as a blatant political act of the sort that was practiced all too freely by the Lincoln administration. Luckily, in

spite of Schurz's limited military experience, the appointment turned out reasonably well.

The appointment seems more cynical because Schurz's rank soon gave him the command of a division in Franz Sigel's corps. Schurz led his division at Second Manassas. Fortunately, he learned fast and was a diligent soldier. In March 1863 he became a major general, promoted over many senior brigadiers, including von Steinwehr, who had more experience and greater competence than he.[27]

When Maj. Charles Howard met Schurz in April 1863, he found him to be gentlemanly, tall, with a broad forehead, curly brown hair, reddish whiskers, and strong spectacles. To these adjectives, he might have added lanky, vivacious, charming, and of commanding presence. Charles Howard wrote that Schurz gave the "impression of being a man of ability as he undoubtedly is." Certainly Schurz was ambitious for himself and his beliefs. By the time that the Eleventh Corps reached Gettysburg, the Howard brothers were having some second thoughts about Schurz. He was causing them great anxiety because of his personal influence with President Lincoln. The major wrote, "He seems to have retained his political character notwithstanding the high hopes I first had of him and his great pretension of friendship to the General." Specifically, the Howards believed that Schurz was doing his best to have Sigel returned to the command of the corps.[28]

General Schimmelfennig led Schurz's division up the Taneytown Road and over Cemetery Hill at about 12:30. It had been a hard march since passing Horner's Mill over four miles back, but the division had moved at a double-quick much of the way. Battery I, 1st Ohio Light Artillery, Capt. Hubert Dilger's battery from Cincinnati, led the way. Its six guns, Napoleons, bronze, smoothbore twelve-pounders, headed the column and rolled into and through the town—probably by way of Washington Street. Behind it came Lt. William Wheeler's 13th New York Battery with four three-inch rifles. Four miles back along the Taneytown Road, with von Steinwehr's division, Wheeler had received an order to hurry forward because batteries were wanted at the front. Although the road was stony and the battery's wheels were in bad condition, Wheeler later wrote, the infantry moved aside and the teams trotted off, "the gun carriages rattling and bouncing in the air; feed, rations, kettles and everything else breaking loose from the caissons, the cannoneers running with all their might to keep up, for the road was so very rough, that I was afraid to have them mount."[29]

By the time Schimmelfennig reached the plain north of Gettysburg, it was obvious that Howard's first orders could not be followed. The Confederates had occupied Oak Hill in force. Instead, Schurz deployed Schimmelfennig's division in the fields facing north and below the right of the First Corps. Soon he received an order from Howard to hold where he was and push skirmishers north as far as possible.[30]

In the meantime, Howard had instructed Lieutenant Colonel Assmussen to set up corps headquarters on the highest point of East Cemetery Hill.[31] In addition, he ordered Major Osborn to plant the two reserve batteries of the corps on the hill and had von Steinwehr deploy his two brigades, Col. Charles R. Coster's and Col. Orland Smith's, in support of the batteries. Then, having sent off messages to Meade, Sickles, and Slocum, Howard set out for the front. Barlow's division happened to be passing along the Emmitsburg Road at that time, so he rode with Barlow through the town. They could hear the noise of cannon fire to the west, but the streets were quiet. There was one exception, one of those delightful vignettes that is remembered vividly in later years—a young woman who stood on a porch at a street corner and waved her handkerchief at the troops as they hurried by. She pleased the soldiers, of course, and regiment after regiment cheered her as they passed.[32]

One Gettysburg resident, Henry Jacobs, who lived in the northwest corner of the intersection of Washington and Middle streets, remembered the Eleventh Corps' passing north along Washington Street.

> Past our house came, running at the double quick, Howard's eleventh army corps. They kept the pace without breaking ranks; but they flowed through and out into the battlefield beyond, a human tide, at millrace speed. Far down the road, behind the passing regiments, a roar of cheers began. It rolled forward, faster than the running of the men who made it—like some high surge sweeping across the surface of a flowing sea. Its roar of cheering neared and neared, until we saw a group of officers coming at a brisk trot, with the mighty cheer always at their horses' heels. Among them rode one man in colonel's uniform who held his head high and smiled. He was an officer, favorite with the soldiers, who had been under arrest until the eve of the battle. Now, released he was on his way into action, and the whole brigade that knew him was greeting him with the chorus of the lungs.[33]

The officer cheered was Col. Leopold von Gilsa, commander of the First Brigade of Barlow's division. Barlow, a strict disciplinarian, had placed von Gilsa under arrest while on the march, it was said, for allowing more than one man to break ranks at a time to get water, but he had been restored to his command as the division approached Gettysburg. A few of the townsfolk shouted greetings also to Lt. Henry Hauschild of the 75th Pennsylvania as it hurried along Washington Street with Schurz's division. Hauschild had lived in Gettysburg at one time and soon would die there.[34]

Howard accompanied Barlow to the fields north of the town. He examined the position there but, unfortunately, did not meet with Schurz at this time to discuss the Eleventh Corps deployment with him. He sent Major Howard to speak with Buford and then rode left to the line of the First Corps. He passed behind Robinson's position near the Mummasburg Road and stopped to speak briefly with Wadsworth, whom he told to hold Seminary Ridge as long as possible. He noted Wadsworth's and Doubleday's divisions' positions and found Doubleday about a quarter mile beyond the seminary. Howard gained the impression that Doubleday was not worried about his left's being turned. This, however, was a special concern of Howard's; he asked Doubleday to look out for it and stated, rashly as it turned out, that he would protect the First Corps right.

Howard returned to Cemetery Hill, which von Steinwehr had strengthened as best he could. He found that Capt. Michael Wiedrich's Battery I, 1st New York Light Artillery, had unlimbered east of the pike, its six three-inch rifles under the protection of Coster's brigade. The Second Brigade of von Steinwehr's division, that of Col. Orland Smith, was west of the pike with the four Napoleons of Capt. Lewis Heckman's Ohio battery.[35] With von Steinwehr's division's arrival, all of the Eleventh Corps had reached Gettysburg. The First Corps divisions, Buford's cavalry brigades, and Schurz's and Barlow's divisions were deploying or in position in the fields north and west of Gettysburg. Howard's objective now, as he later expressed it, was to "hold Gettysburg with one wing, which only amounted, with our small corps to 'an advance guard' . . . till the army should come up."[36] He would get the chance to try.

Baltimore Pike

3

EWELL AND HOWARD COLLIDE

Lt. Gen. Richard S. Ewell, commander of the Second Corps of the Army of Northern Virginia, was testy. After a brilliant campaign into Pennsylvania, he seemed to have Harrisburg within his grasp. But, as he prepared to seize it, General Lee called him off and ordered him to assemble his corps in the Gettysburg-Cashtown area. Ewell sent off couriers to Early with orders recalling his division from York, and he started Johnson's division and the corps trains back down the Cumberland Valley toward Chambersburg. Then, in accordance with a later dispatch from General Lee, he rode south with Rodes's division, crossed South Mountain at Mount Holly Springs, and marched south to Heidlersburg, about ten miles north of Gettysburg on the Harrisburg Road. There he met Early's division coming west from York, and the two divisions bivouacked for the night, Rodes's at Heidlersburg and Early's three miles to the east.[1]

Some of Ewell's testiness could have stemmed from his disappointment at being denied an attempt to capture Harrisburg, but he was a good soldier and probably would have reconciled himself to that. It must have resulted primarily from his uncertainty of the whereabouts of the Army of the Potomac. Also, he might have experienced some irritation over the nettling presence of Maj. Gen. Isaac R. Trimble, who had recently appeared to accompany him as a volunteer aide.

Trimble, a Baltimorean, was born in 1802 and was one of the oldest men in Lee's army. He graduated from West Point but had left the army in 1832 for a successful career in railroading in the mid-Atlantic region. When war came, he cast his lot with the Confederacy, and he had been an excellent brigade commander under Ewell. Trimble had much military ambition and had once said to Stonewall Jackson that "before this war is over I intend to be a major general or a corpse." He nearly accomplished both goals for he was wounded severely at Groveton, but since it was believed that he would return soon to active service, he was made a major general and appointed to the command of Jackson's old division. Unfortunately, his wound healed slowly, and in the reorganization he lost his division to Edward Johnson. Yet, when he learned that the Army of Northern Virginia was headed into Maryland and Pennsylvania, he thirsted for action, and, though he was without a command, he hurried to Hagerstown to join General Lee.

Lee knew that the old fellow was more familiar with the geography of the campaign area north of the Potomac than just about anyone in his army and discussed it with him. He was even patient enough to listen to Trimble's foolish suggestion that a brigade, 1,500 or so men, be sent to take Baltimore! Lee quickly terminated Trimble's visit by saying, "General Ewell's forces are by this time in Harrisburg; if not go and join him, and help to take the place." Trimble liked the suggestion and hurried up the Cumberland Valley to join his old division commander.[2]

Trimble reached Carlisle on 28 June and found that Ewell had not yet taken Harrisburg. He told Ewell that it could be captured easily and that he thought that General Lee expected it. Although he must have known little about the defenses of the city and the Union forces available to man them, Trimble volunteered to do the job with a brigade! He wrote later that the capture attempt was to have taken place on 30 June but that Ewell canceled it when Lee ordered the army to concentrate near Cashtown. So on the evening of 30 June, as Reynolds and Howard conferred in Moritz Tavern south of Gettysburg, Ewell had the pleasure of Trimble's presence when he met with two of his division commanders, Rodes and Early, at Heidlersburg to the north.[3]

The generals pondered the meaning of Lee's order to Ewell that "when you come to Heidlersburg, you can move directly on to Gettysburg or turn down to Cashtown," together with a dispatch received at Heidlersburg that said that Ewell might go to Gettysburg or Cashtown "as circumstances might dictate." Ewell had learned from Hill that the Third Corps was in the Cashtown area, but he knew little beyond that. According to Trimble, Ewell fumed over the vagueness of his instructions and asked rhetorically, "Why can't a Commanding General have someone on his staff who can write an intelligible order?" It was an excellent question and a natural reaction from the excitable Ewell, who had a low fuming point and had been accustomed to receiving precise instructions from Stonewall

Jackson. After listening to what he deemed to be "unsatisfactory opinions" from Early and Rodes, Trimble stepped in. He observed that Lee had voiced the hope of falling on the enemy's advance in overwhelming force and that, since the Union First Corps was reported to be in Gettysburg, Lee would expect Ewell to go there.[4]

Ewell ordered Early and Rodes to march their divisions toward Cashtown on the following morning, 1 July. Rodes would travel directly west by Middletown (now Biglerville), and Early would go south through Hunterstown, about four and a half miles northeast of Gettysburg, then west to Mummasburg. Thus, they would approach the concentration point over parallel roads near Gettysburg and could turn south toward that town if the need arose by various roads that intersected their routes.[5]

Rodes's division resumed its march shortly after sunrise and moved at an unhurried pace toward Middletown six miles away. After two hours, according to Trimble, Ewell dismounted, hopped to a log, and sat down. He unfolded a map, looked at it, and grumbled some more about the "ambiguity of the order." Again Trimble wrote that he stepped into the breech, told Ewell that he was losing time, and urged that they march toward Middletown, from which place he could send a courier to Lee for specific orders. This is essentially what happened, although Trimble might have had less to do with the chain of events than he supposed. Rodes's division hiked to Middletown, but at about 9:00 A.M., just before its arrival there, Ewell received a dispatch from Hill stating that his corps was advancing on Gettysburg. Ewell immediately ordered Rodes to turn left at Middletown and head for Gettysburg over the Carlisle Road. At the same time, he ordered Early to march straight toward Gettysburg from Hunterstown. Then he sent Maj. G. Campbell Brown, his adjutant and stepson, to find General Lee and to inform him of the changes in his march.[6]

Brown trotted west toward Cashtown and found General Lee near there on the Chambersburg Pike. Wagons of Hill's corps clogged the road, and Brown could hear the rumble of the morning's battle to the east at Gettysburg. After receiving Brown's message, General Lee asked if Ewell had heard anything of Jeb Stuart and his cavalry. On being told that Ewell had not, Lee asked that Ewell send out scouts to the left and try to find the cavalryman. Brown recalled that "Gen. Lee then impressed on me *very strongly* that a general engagement was to be avoided until the arrival of the rest of the army."[7]

As Major Brown rode to Lee, Ewell accompanied Rodes's division south from Middletown toward Gettysburg. About four miles north of the town, Rodes's men heard the booming of a "sharp cannonade" and made immediate preparations for battle. It was probably here, south of the crossroad to Mummasburg where the road slopes down to the Gettysburg plain, that Rodes's division veered right and continued ahead on the high ground. With Iverson's brigade deployed in line, skirmishers to the front, Rodes's division pushed south toward the sound of battle. About three miles north of Gettysburg, the Confederates bumped into Union cavalrymen and became more cautious. Soon, when the ground permitted, Rodes extended his line to the left. He deployed Doles's brigade in the plain, probably astride the Carlisle Road, and O'Neal's Alabamians on its right connecting to Iverson's brigade on the ridge. Now, with three brigades in line, Rodes's troops probably moved more slowly with their artillery and the brigades of Daniel and Ramseur in the rear. Somehow, as they neared Gettysburg, all three deployed brigades must have fronted toward the low ground to the east, where troopers of the 17th Pennsylvania Cavalry provided a token resistance to their advance.[8]

After another mile of stumbling progress, the skirmishers on the right of Rodes's line broke from the woods on Oak Hill into the open ground north of the Mummasburg Road. From there, as Rodes recalled it, "the whole of that portion of the force opposing General Hill's troops could be seen." It was early afternoon, the morning's fight was over, the brigades of James J. Archer and Joseph R. Davis had been repulsed, and the combatants were preparing for more action. Ewell and Rodes could see the position of Hill's corps on Herr Ridge where the Chambersburg Pike crossed it a mile to the southwest. The Federal First Corps was nearer on McPherson Ridge and Seminary Ridge in Rodes's front. The Eleventh Corps was not yet in view, but its troops were on the way. The only action at this time was a "desultory fire of artillery" between Union batteries on McPherson Ridge and the guns of Hill's corps on Herr Ridge.[9]

Ewell and Rodes took immediate action. The three deployed brigades were not positioned to strike the Federals "properly" and had to be shifted somehow "by the right flank and to change direction to the right." After this was done, Iverson's brigade faced south down Seminary Ridge from its position atop Oak Hill. O'Neal's Alabamians were to its left down the slope and on the flat, and Doles's Georgians faced toward the town from their position in the plain astride the Carlisle Road. Daniel's large brigade was to Iverson's right and rear in a second line, and Ramseur was behind Iverson on Daniel's left.

While the infantry units filed into their positions, the four batteries of Lt. Col. Thomas H. Carter's artillery battalion hurried forward. Two batteries, those commanded by Capts. William P. Carter and Charles W.

Fry, dropped trail under Ewell's direction in front of Iverson's line and opened fire.[10]

Buford's cavalrymen had undoubtedly warned General Doubleday of the Confederates' approach from the north, and he should not have been surprised at Rodes's appearance on his right. The First Corps commander reacted quickly to it. Wadsworth pulled back Cutler's brigade, which had been on McPherson Ridge north of the railroad cut, to the woods on Seminary Ridge north of the cut. Col. Roy Stone left one regiment facing toward Heth's line and posted the other two along the Chambersburg Pike fronting toward Rodes. Then, when it became apparent that the Eleventh Corps would not be bolstering Cutler's brigade's right, Doubleday ordered the two brigades of Robinson's division, Baxter's and Paul's, from their position at the seminary north to hold the ridge line between Cutler's right and the Mummasburg Road. Now the First Corps held a crooked line over a mile long from the Mummasburg Road on Seminary Ridge out to McPherson Woods and to McPherson Ridge south of the woods. Its right flank at the Mummasburg Road was within spitting distance of Rodes's division, which was poised to strike it, and Heth's and Pender's divisions threatened its center and left from Herr Ridge to the west.[11]

Up to this time, everyone, except Trimble perhaps, would have agreed that Ewell had been a model corps commander. He had conducted a vigorous raid into Pennsylvania, he marched literally to the sound of the guns, and he had prepared to strike a blow that promised victory. Now, as Ewell and Rodes watched the shooting by Carter's battalion, Campbell Brown returned from his meeting with General Lee. Brown delivered Lee's request to Ewell—try to contact Stuart and avoid a general engagement until the arrival of the remainder of the army. Brown, tired from his hard ride, dismounted and stretched in an effort to relax. Five minutes after his return, Maj. Andrew R. Venable of Stuart's staff rode up with information from his chief! That morning Stuart had sent Venable from Dover, Pennsylvania, thirty miles to the northeast, in search of Early, while Stuart and his three brigades headed for Carlisle. Venable knew nothing of the Federal army's location except that he had met none of it on his ride from Dover. Ewell sent Venable on to report to General Lee and advised him to send his courier back to Stuart with advice to "hurry up the cavalry."[12]

Ewell and Rodes saw Robinson's two brigades shifting toward the Mummasburg Road directly in their front, and they saw Schurz's division of the Eleventh Corps debouching from the town into the lower ground to the left in front of the brigades of O'Neal and Doles, some of them shouting, "Remember Chancellorsville." Ewell decided at once that General Lee's

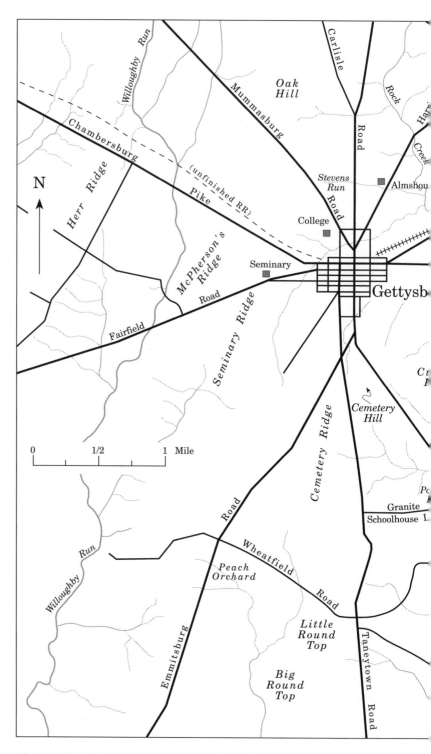

Map 3.1. Gettysburg Area

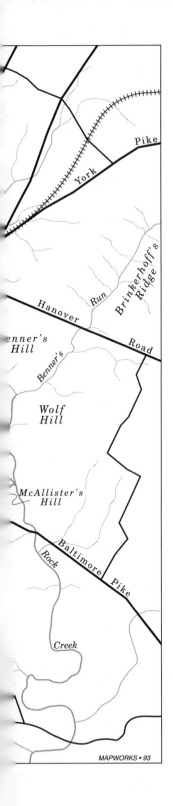

York Pike

Brinkerhoff's Ridge

Run

Hanover Road

Benner's Hill

Benner's

Wolf Hill

McAllister's Hill

Rock

Baltimore Pike

Creek

injunction against bringing on a general engagement did not apply to his particular situation—his corps was being threatened if, indeed, it was not about to be attacked. He wrote later in his report: "It was too late to avoid an engagement without abandoning the position already taken up, and I determined to push the attack vigorously." Rodes, "being thus threatened from two directions," ordered his division to attack.[13]

Having thus decided to strike the forces in his front, Ewell sent Capt. Thomas T. Turner of his staff to General Early with orders to advance on Rodes's left. Then, in keeping with his practice of sending important orders by two separate couriers, he summoned Major Brown from his rest and sent him to Early also with instructions "to hurry him up & tell him to attack at once." As Brown headed east to find Early, Rodes advanced and became sharply engaged.[14]

Early's division had not made an early start that morning; in fact, Maj. John W. Daniel, Early's adjutant, believed that it had not gotten off until about 8:00 A.M. In the meantime, Early's staff had checked out the road to Hunterstown and found it rough and winding. Early, therefore, decided to go on to Heidlersburg and turn south there onto the Gettysburg-Harrisburg Road. Gordon's brigade led, followed by those of Hays, Hoke, and Smith. While traveling south on the Harrisburg Road, and before turning west toward Mummasburg, Early received Ewell's first message. He learned that A. P. Hill was advancing on Gettysburg, that Rodes was going to Gettysburg, and that he should go there over the Harrisburg Road. Early and his staff knew little of the situation at Gettysburg, but as they marched they could hear the thudding of distant artillery fire, which grew sharper and more distinct as they advanced. At this time, there was a heavy mist, and the sky lowered with murky clouds. Yet, according to Major Daniel, the weather did not dampen the ardor of the men, who tramped on in high spirits to their expected victory.[15]

Early rode at a good distance ahead of his division with some of his staff and a cavalry escort. About two miles from Gettysburg, Captain Turner reached him with Ewell's dispatch informing him that Rodes had made contact with the enemy. Early sent Lt. Col. Elijah White forward with some of his 35th Cavalry Battalion to reconnoiter. White met Union cavalry pickets from Devin's brigade who fell back before the Confederate horsemen, but he encountered no other opposition. About a mile from Gettysburg, Early and his party reached the top of a rise, and a scenic panorama appeared before them. Gettysburg was straight ahead with Culp's Hill and Cemetery Hill rising behind it to the left, and between was a bucolic landscape of fields rich with harvest and dotted with farm

Brig. Gen. John B. Gordon (WLM)

buildings. But the view was different to the right of the town. There they could see the smoke of battle and lines of infantry exchanging fire, while along with the distant roar of gunfire they heard "the mechanical 'Hip, hip, Hurrah!' of the Federal infantry" and the Rebel yell. Early saw at once what needed to be done. "Tell Gordon, Hays, Avery, and Smith to double-quick to the front," he shouted to his staff, "and open the lines of infantry for the artillery to pass."

In response, Gordon's Georgians jogged into line on the right of the road, and three batteries of Lt. Col. Hilary P. Jones's artillery battalion, with drivers shouting and whipping their teams, rolled up in a rush and fanned into position on high ground to the left of the road. Hays's and Hoke's brigades formed in rear of Jones's gun line. Now, as if in answer to Early's bold movements, an enemy battery, Wilkeson's of the Eleventh Corps, rolled to a knoll on the west side of the road less than a half mile ahead, and a line of darkly garbed infantry, rifle barrels gleaming, deployed to protect it. Jones's guns fired, and Early sent a staff officer to Gordon. General Gordon drew his sword, and in a few minutes the Georgia line "was moving forward through a field of yellow wheat like a dark gray wave in a sea of gold."[16]

By the time that Rodes's division reached the field, Heth's division, two of whose brigades had attacked and been repulsed that morning, was re-forming on Herr Ridge. One brigade took position north of the pike, while the other three formed south of it facing the First Corps position on McPherson Ridge and in McPherson Woods. Pender's division formed in support of Heth's with two brigades on each side of the pike. Then, when Buford's cavalrymen began a vigorous demonstration near the Fairfield Road on the Confederate right, one Confederate brigade, Lane's North Carolinians, shifted from north of the pike to the right of Pender's line to confront the Union horsemen. Thus it was that Heth and Pender, with six brigades south of the Chambersburg Pike, far outnumbered the First Corps troops there and would be able to threaten their left flank.[17]

After telling Major Brown that he did not want a general engagement brought on until the arrival of the whole army, General Lee rode the five miles toward Gettysburg. He reached Herr Ridge in time to witness the deployment of Rodes's division on Oak Hill to his left. Heth's division was ready to advance, and Heth asked General Lee if he should lead it forward. "No," said Lee, "I am not prepared to bring on a general engagement today—Longstreet is not up." A bit later, when he saw Robinson's division shifting toward Oak Hill and Rodes's front and there were unmistakable signs that serious fighting would soon begin, Heth repeated his request for permission to advance. This time Lee assented, and Heth ordered his division forward.[18]

Now four Confederate divisions were advancing against defensive positions of the Union First and Eleventh corps west and north of Gettysburg. Since this battle of the afternoon of 1 July was a distinct and complex action deserving of full treatment, it will be sketched here briefly only as a prelude to the operations on Cemetery Hill and Culp's Hill. In its closing stages, though, the victorious Confederates, particularly Ewell's corps, drove and pursued the beaten troops of the First and Eleventh Union corps into the town and the Cemetery Hill arena, the purview of this monograph.[19]

The story of the assault of Heth's and Pender's divisions of Hill's corps and Rodes's division of Ewell's corps against the Union First Corps west of Gettysburg and the stubborn resistance of the First Corps ranks among the heroic epics of the Civil War. Rodes's men struck the First Corps right north of the railroad bed that paralleled the Chambersburg Pike, while Hill's men hit the First Corps formations on McPherson Ridge. Although Rodes's attack got off poorly, by weight of superior numbers and hard fighting his brigades were able to dislodge the First Corps brigades of

Baxter, Paul, and Cutler from their position on Seminary Ridge and force their retreat.

At the same time, Heth's division, advancing from Herr Ridge, was able to force the Iron Brigade from McPherson Woods and Stone's and Biddle's brigades from their adjoining positions on McPherson Ridge. They fell back to the seminary, where they and the First Corps batteries made a stand. When Heth's division reached the east arm of McPherson Ridge, it could go no farther. It was then that three brigades of Pender's division passed over it and pushed the attack home against the final Federal position on Seminary Ridge. The outnumbered, battered Federal formations were outflanked and outgunned. They had no choice but to abandon the fields west of Gettysburg, which Reynolds had selected and Doubleday had tried to hold until help from the army arrived. At Howard's order, they fell back to the Federal strong point on Cemetery Hill. As they did so, the First Corps units north of the railroad bed joined them in retreat through the streets of the town to the hill. Fortunately for the Union regiments, their hard fight had so damaged and disordered the attacking Confederate brigades of Hill's corps that only two South Carolina regiments pressed an attack east of Seminary Ridge and molested the retreat of the First Corps troops into the town.[20]

As the Confederates pressed the First Corps line west of the town, the left of Rodes's division and Early's division struck the Eleventh Corps in the fields north of Gettysburg. The Eleventh Corps position was poor and was rendered poorer still when General Barlow placed the right of his division on the knoll along the Harrisburg Road that bears his name today. Early's division, which extended beyond the Eleventh Corps right, arrived on the field in a timely fashion and crushed that flank of the unlucky corps in a manner reminiscent of Jackson's attack on the same troops two months before at Chancellorsville.

The right of the Eleventh Corps line retreated first, and the line crumbled from right to left. The units on the Eleventh Corps left fell back at about the same time that the First Corps right on the high ground above them gave way. Schurz requested reinforcements from Cemetery Hill, and Howard sent Coster's brigade to help. Schurz posted Coster's three regiments and Heckman's battery at the north edge of Gettysburg beside the Harrisburg Road. Early's brigades smashed Coster's line as they had shattered Barlow's men in the fields ahead and captured two of Heckman's four Napoleons for good measure. Some units of the corps resisted stubbornly but to no avail, and all who were able retreated to the town and to the safety of the hills beyond.[21]

So it was that by 4:00 P.M., less than two hours after Rodes's and Heth's divisions opened their attacks against the Union forces in their front, the Union formations had been crushed and were falling back to Howard's rallying place on Cemetery Hill.

Doubleday and Schurz had directed their portions of the battle as best they could. Howard rode along their lines soon after the Confederates' afternoon attacks began, and then he returned to his headquarters on Cemetery Hill. He interfered little if at all with Doubleday's and Schurz's conduct of the battle. There was really little in a constructive way that he could do. Apart from Coster's brigade, perhaps, he had no troops at hand to send them. Reinforcements would have to come from the Twelfth Corps, which had not yet reached the field. Further, although Cemetery Hill was key to the Union defense of the Gettysburg area, it was too far from the fighting west and north of the town to enable him to appreciate the needs of the troops on those fronts and respond quickly to them. After his visit to the First Corps line, Howard was concerned greatly about the Union left. In order to help the First Corps, he ordered Schurz to seize Oak Ridge on its right, but soon after, he learned of Early's approach over the Harrisburg Road and canceled the order. At 3:00 P.M., he sent another message to Slocum stating that his right was being attacked, that the Union force was in danger of being turned and driven back, and expressing the hope that Slocum would bring the Twelfth Corps to the field.[22]

Howard did intervene in one minor tactical matter that he took the trouble to mention in his report. Capt. Michael Wiedrich's New York battery was probably the last of the Eleventh Corps batteries to reach the field. Major Osborn posted it on East Cemetery Hill, and Howard spoke to its cannoneers there: "Boys, I want you to hold this position at all hazards. Can you do it?" As the boys shouted, "Yes, sir," a Confederate shell screeched close and caused some of them to duck. Soon after, Howard saw a Confederate battery near the Harrisburg Road at what he thought was a mile to the north. He asked Wiedrich to fire at it. Wiedrich opened on it with his three-inch rifles, but some of the rounds fell short among Devin's cavalry, and Wiedrich gave it up.[23]

Howard received several calls for reinforcements from Doubleday and Schurz. At 3:45 P.M., after Coster's brigade had gone to Schurz's aid, Doubleday sent Howard another plea for troops. Howard had none to send him but asked Schurz to lend him a regiment if he could. Of course, Schurz could spare no troops for Doubleday, and one can wonder if Howard really appreciated Schurz's plight or was only making a meaningless gesture. In response to this and other requests for reinforcements, Howard replied,

Maj. Gen. Abner Doubleday (WLM)

"Hold out, if possible, awhile longer, for I am expecting General Slocum every moment."[24]

At about this time, Pender's division was turning the First Corps left. Doubleday maintained that he sent Capt. Eminel P. Halstead to Howard to implore him either to send reinforcements to the First Corps or to order it back. From Cemetery Hill, Halstead, according to his account, pointed out the long Rebel lines that would soon enfold the First Corps, but Howard at first insisted that the Rebel lines of battle were fences and not men. Halstead then asked Howard to look at them through field glasses, and, possibly because this was a hard thing for a one-armed man on horseback to do, Howard asked a staff officer to look for him. The officer did so and said that the lines were men. Still, Howard, hoping for reinforcements, refused to order a retreat and instead said, "You may find Buford and use him."[25]

Matters worsened; the sound of musketry swelled. At 4:00 P.M., Howard sent Captain Hall to Doubleday with the message, "If you cannot hold out longer, you must fall back to the cemetery and take position on the left of the Baltimore Pike." He asked Buford to help Doubleday by making a show of force opposite the enemy's right. In response, Col. William Gamble, commander of Buford's First Brigade, dismounted half of his troopers and strung them behind the wall that ran along the crest of Seminary Ridge in Schultz's Woods south of the Fairfield Road. From here they stung the Rebel right with carbine fire and created an illusion of strength. However, Doubleday, whose regiments were now fighting at the seminary, claimed later not to have received the order to fall back. Howard thought that the order might not have reached him or that "cemetery" might have been mistaken for "seminary." At the same time, Howard sent his brother to Slocum to ask him to send one of the divisions of the Twelfth Corps to the left and another to the right and to come in person to the hill.[26]

Time was running out. At 4:10 P.M., Howard could see that the lines north of the town were giving way, and he knew that the positions west and north of the town were lost. He sent staff officers galloping to Doubleday and to Schurz with a "positive" order "to fall back gradually, disputing every inch of the ground." (Apparently Doubleday had no recollection of receiving this order.) They were to form the remnants of their corps on Cemetery Hill—the Eleventh Corps to the right of the Baltimore Pike, the First Corps to the left. Von Steinwehr positioned his one remaining brigade, Smith's, on Cemetery Hill to receive the enemy.[27]

It had been a hard and costly battle for both sides. Lee, Hill, and Ewell had amassed a force of seventeen brigades of infantry, over 25,000 men, to oppose twelve Federal brigades of infantry, 18,000 soldiers, counting Orland Smith's brigade on Cemetery Hill, plus two small brigades of cavalry. On the Confederate side, Rodes's division with five brigades and a strength of about 8,000 must have sustained most of its reported 2,869 casualties during the battle of 1 July. The casualties of Heth's division numbered about 2,000 and Pender's about 1,100. On the Union side, the First Corps had over 5,700 casualties, and the Eleventh Corps, 3,200. Many of the Eleventh Corps losses, its missing especially, were prisoners captured during its retreat through the town to the hill. This retreat was a unique experience in Civil War annals, and it carried the battle to Cemetery Hill and Gettysburg's hook-shaped line.[28]

4

RETREAT TO CEMETERY HILL

Capt. Fred C. Winkler stood with thirty men of the 26th Wisconsin Infantry Regiment on the Carlisle Road at the north edge of Gettysburg and watched a long, gray line of battle approaching astride the Harrisburg Road somewhat to his right. The Confederates, the brigades of Hays and Hoke, soon struck and shattered the three regiments of Coster's brigade nearby, leaving Winkler's little band almost alone to face the awful threat. Winkler saw a staff officer of the Eleventh Corps trotting near and called to him for orders. "Fall back," the officer shouted. The men of the 26th, carrying their colors, hurried back a short distance to the yard of a small white cottage where some of Schurz's troops had paused to fire a volley before continuing their retreat. Winkler's men stopped there too, delivered a volley of their own, and followed their comrades into the town.

Winkler knew that it would be useless for his little band to oppose such overwhelming Confederate strength, but having to retreat infuriated him. As he looked down Carlisle Street toward the "Diamond" or town square, he could see the troops of Barlow's division hurrying along the sidewalks while artillery vehicles, ambulances, and wagons rattled south in the street. He was ashamed. It was a northern town: "I had ridden up and down its streets from one end to the other three times that day and everywhere there were manifestations of joy; handkerchiefs were waving everywhere," he wrote, "and ladies stood in the streets offering refreshments to the soldiers as they passed. It seemed so awful to march back through those same streets whipped and beaten. It was the most humiliating step I ever took."[1]

Winkler stood in the street awhile and watched the retreating soldiers go; then he turned and saw the Rebel line coming on. They hurried along and did not pause to fire at him—why should a brigade bother with a lone man? He thought of standing there sword in hand and defying them, but common sense returned, and he followed others of his corps through the town to Cemetery Hill.[2]

The streets of Gettysburg swarmed with retreating soldiers between 4:00 and 6:00 P.M. that day. Anna Garlach, who lived on Baltimore Street, recalled that the street was so crowded with soldiers that she could have crossed it on their heads. Lt. Col. Rufus R. Dawes of the 6th Wisconsin Regiment of the Iron Brigade wrote that the streets were jammed with soldiers and vehicles and that the cellars were crowded with skulkers who waited for a chance to surrender. Dawes took some satisfaction in not seeing a First Corps badge on any of these people, but he may be pardoned for selective recall.[3]

Some generals recollected other details. Doubleday remembered that his First Corps troops passed through the town quietly and calmly without running and undue haste; Wadsworth reported that the movement was effected in good order. To Doubleday, the retreat would have been "a very successful one" if troops from the right flank of each corps had not fallen back at the same time and become entangled in the town. From the Eleventh Corps view, Schurz thought that the retreat had come off as well as could have been expected considering that the streets were cluttered with all kinds of vehicles and overrun with the men of the First Corps! He saw a good many stragglers going to the rear in a disorderly way, as often happened after a hard fight, but he saw "no element of dissolution." Schurz must have been irritated by frequent comments from First Corps partisans who blamed the Eleventh Corps for their predicament. In a private letter, he branded the charges that the Eleventh Corps gave way and uncovered the right of the First as untrue. To the contrary, he held that it was the other way around and that the men of the two corps were in the town at about the same time. He observed that when he passed through the town with the last of his troops, there were still many First Corps men about but none between him and the enemy. It was obvious to him that they had retreated before the men of the Eleventh Corps had done so, or the First Corps troops would have found the town in enemy hands.[4]

Young Henry Jacobs, who had watched Schurz's division march out Baltimore Street to battle, contrasted the bravery of its advance with the disorder of the retreat and deemed the retreat a "strange and awful spectacle." To his father, Professor Michael Jacobs, the retreating troops seemed confused and frightened, and many probably were. He thought that the First Corps soldiers, for the most part, had taken the streets in the southwest outskirts of the town, while those of the Eleventh Corps had used Washington and Baltimore streets, the main north-south routes that they had traveled earlier that day. Unfortunately, it must not have been as clear-cut as that, for the units on the right of the First Corps entered the town from the northwest and by necessity shared some streets with troops of the Eleventh Corps.[5]

Howard and Doubleday and their provost marshals might have designated practical routes of withdrawal through the town, but there is no reason for thinking that this measure, so obvious in hindsight, was ever considered. Howard had hoped for reinforcements from the rest of the army until the bitter end of the fight. In addition, the troops of the First Corps had been neither in the town nor on Cemetery Hill, and they probably did not know the best routes to follow to the hill. Col. Charles S. Wainwright, commander of the artillery brigade of the First Corps and high in its hierarchy, thought that persons referring to the "cemetery," which he had not seen, meant the "seminary," with which he was familiar, and he prepared for a stand at the seminary when he should have been readying his batteries for a retreat to the hill beyond the town.[6]

Wainwright's recollections of the retreat were similar to those of Schurz. He was on Seminary Ridge preparing for a stand there when he heard that the Rebels were advancing against the Union right. He had assumed that the advancing lines were troops of the Eleventh Corps, but it became apparent that, instead, they were driving that corps toward the town. At the same time, he saw troops of Robinson's and Wadsworth's divisions heading for the town by way of the railroad bed, a favorite path of retreat for the First Corps units north of the Chambersburg Pike. When Wainwright himself reached the town, he saw troops of both corps in the streets, the men of the First Corps tending to be on one side, those of the Eleventh Corps on the other. Units mixed, but he saw no panic; instead, most of the men seemed to be talking and joking as they passed along. He met Brig. Gen. Thomas A. Rowley of the First Corps, who insisted that he was in command of that corps. Wainwright tried to correct him but gave up when he saw that the general seemed to be drunk.[7]

Capt. Edward C. Culp of the 25th Ohio, a member of the staff of Brig. Gen. Adelbert Ames, shared Wainwright's opinion of the troops' behavior. From the vantage of horseback, Culp watched hundreds of men of both corps falling back, and, though they seemed not to be moving as units, they walked unhurriedly toward Cemetery Hill. He remembered seeing women on their doorsteps offering cups of water to fleeing soldiers and soldiers cheering them for doing so. In his view, the soldiers were defeated for the day but not greatly frightened.[8]

The experiences of the Union troops retreating through the town come down to us as episodical events having little or no immediate connection with one another. Survivors often mentioned vignettes that, in the main, were incidents they could recall with some pride. A German baron, Capt. Friederich von Fritsch, then a member of von Gilsa's staff, rode back into town in the rear of his brigade. When he paused to advise a doctor about what to do if captured, a group of Confederates rushed him. One seized the bridle of von Fritsch's horse with his left hand, threatened to jab him with his bayonet, and shouted: "Surrender! Get down you damn Yank!" The captain replied, "You be damned!," and chopped down on the Rebel's hand with his sword's sharpened blade of Damascus steel. At the same time, he spurred his horse and charged into a yard enclosed by a fence. With demands for his surrender ringing in his ears, the baron jumped his horse over the fence and got away. But not unscathed—he had a flesh wound in his left leg, a shoulder strap was shot away, a bullet damaged his saddle, and he wrenched a knee and tore off a stirrup on the fence.[9]

Captain Culp had an experience more bizarre than that of von Fritsch. Culp found himself in a street between a jam of troops blocking the street in his front and Confederates pressing him from the rear. Not wishing to abandon his horse and flee afoot, he rode onto the porch of a house, pushed open the front door, and rode into the sitting room, where a frightened family sat. He asked them if there was an alley that he could reach, and a teenaged girl beckoned for him to follow her. She led Culp and his horse to a back door and out into a fenced yard. When she started to remove some bars to let him out, he told her to hurry back into the house, jumped his horse over the fence, and saved himself "a trip to Libby Prison."[10]

Gettysburg seemed a place of blind alleys to many Union troops that afternoon. Lt. Clayton Rogers of General Wadsworth's staff gave Lt. Col. Rufus Dawes of the 6th Wisconsin an order to simply retreat to beyond the town. The 6th was in support of Stewart's battery north of the railroad cut on Seminary Ridge. Dawes looked to the rear and, seeing that the Eleventh Corps was in retreat, faced the 6th to the rear and moved it in line of battle downhill toward the college. After crossing Washington Street, the men of the 6th turned south in the apparent direction of the retreat. They came to a cross street, probably Chambersburg Street, and found it swept by rifle fire. Dawes spied a hole in the board fence on the far side of the street and decided to lead his regiment through it. Taking the colors, he dashed across, and the Badgers followed him in single file. Dawes waited for them at the hole and jerked the slower men through it, collecting his force in the yard. They somehow got into Washington Street, and when it became blocked in front of them, Dawes formed his men across it as a rear guard in order to fend off the pursuing Confederates. While the 6th was doing this, an elderly man brought them buckets of drinking water, and the men from Wisconsin responded at Dawes's call by giving three hearty cheers "for the Old Sixth and the good cause." This done, the Wisconsin men resumed firing and cleared the street behind them of Confederate pursuers. Dawes then marched his men on to Cemetery Hill.[11]

The 45th New York Infantry, a regiment of immigrant Germans, had its own experiences. After retreating from the fields north of the town, it stood on the college grounds expecting to fight there. Instead, the division bugler sounded the "Retreat" ("Schnellschritt zurueck; Rette, wer sich retten kann!"). Capt. Francis Irsch shouted defiantly that it was too late to retreat—they had only the choices of battle, imprisonment, or death. To this, the men of the regiment responded as with one voice that they would die fighting. But not right there. The 45th, with colors high, filed left-in-front into Washington Street and on into the town closely followed by the enemy.

The 45th received fire from the west at Chambersburg Street but pushed on to Middle Street. There it took more fire, which wounded Maj. Charles Koch and some others. The regiment then retraced its steps to Chambersburg Street and turned east toward the Diamond. There it ran into panic caused by the arrival of some of Early's troops. At this point, 100 or so men of the regiment with the colors managed to backtrack to mid-block, where they ran south through the passageways along the sides of Christ Lutheran Church and made their way to Cemetery Hill.

Others in the 45th were not so fortunate. They entered a passage across Chambersburg Street from the church that led into some backyards from which there was no ready exit not covered by the Confederates. They and some other troops occupied some buildings facing Chambersburg Street and prepared to fight. They refused several demands for their surrender, but at about sundown, when things became quiet, Captain Irsch accompanied a Confederate escort into the street under a flag of truce. The Confederates pointed out that they held the town in strength and that there were no other Union troops in sight. Irsch returned to his command, and the 45th's officers discussed their situation. They ordered their men to destroy their arms, ammunition, and accoutrements, dumped the debris into wells, and surrendered.[12]

When it became apparent to Colonel Wainwright that the First Corps infantry was leaving Seminary Ridge, he ordered the four Federal batteries there to limber up and go at a walk toward the town. Wainwright feared that his batteries were leaving too late, for even then the Confederates were close on them, and he could see a Rebel flag less than fifty yards from Cooper's battery. Wainwright watched as the cannoneers hooked their guns to the limbers at a deliberate speed, expecting all the while to see the Confederates shoot down or capture them all.[13]

At this time, at least three of Lt. James Stewart's six Napoleons were still on Seminary Ridge. Probably Wainwright overlooked the three north of the cut, for one of General Robinson's aides told Stewart, who was with them, that the infantry had gone and that he was on his own. Stewart ordered these three pieces to limber to the rear, and as they hurried off, he was momentarily unnerved by the beseeching looks of the wounded artillerymen whom he was forced to leave behind.[14]

Stewart led his three pieces from the ridge and tried to take them across the railroad bed at a level point east of the cut. Two guns crossed without undue trouble, but the pintle hook on the limber of the third snapped as it was crossing, and the gun's trail dropped to the ground. The crew worked feverishly to get it moving. They had to pull the limber and the gun from the bed separately and then rope the limber and gun together so that the gun could be towed off. As they worked, the Confederates closed in, some shouting, "Halt that piece." Stewart returned the two guns already across to the crossing site to cover the crew working with the damaged piece, and they opened fire. The Confederates were as close as fifty yards when the disabled piece finally moved away, so close that they killed one driver, seriously wounded another, and killed two horses of its team.[15]

As Stewart struggled with his three right pieces, the artillery with Wainwright pulled away from its positions on the ridge south of the railroad bed. Wainwright recalled having six caissons and eighteen guns with him then. They filed into Chambersburg Street and rolled down the hill three abreast. As the last of them got onto the street, Confederate skirmishers appeared from around the south side of the seminary dormitory and ran down the slope to a fence about fifty yards away. The artillery column followed slowly behind the retreating infantry and must have occupied 100 yards of road space from front to rear. It was splendid target for the Confederate riflemen and drew their fire. Yet the well-drilled First Corps batteries did themselves proud—they held to a walk even on the downslope when the temptation to increase their gait must have been exceedingly strong. When the infantry in their front ran north to the railroad

Col. Charles S. Wainwright (WLM)

bed to avoid the Confederate rifle fire, Wainwright shouted, "Trot," and then "Gallop," and the guns began to roll quickly into the limited shelter afforded by the buildings of the town.[16]

But Wainwright's column did not get away unscathed. The rifle fire killed the right (off) horse of the wheel pair of Lt. Benjamin W. Wilber's section of Capt. Gilbert H. Reynolds's New York battery, and while the crew was trying to cut the dead horse from the traces, the Confederates shot three more horses of the team plus Wilber's horse as well. Since the piece could not be moved, its crew had to abandon it to the enemy. Also at about this time, some Confederate guns reached Seminary Ridge and opened on the column, hitting at least one of the caissons of Stewart's battery.[17]

After Stewart got his three right guns off, he rode back to the ridge to look for the others. They were gone, and he was nearly captured. As he hurried toward the town, he found one of his caissons, which had some-how broken its axle and had been abandoned by all of the battery except one cannoneer who was busy destroying bags of powder. When asked if he had been ordered to stay behind, the man replied, "No; but the Rebs are following us up pretty hard, and if the caisson fell into their hands they would use the ammunition upon us." Stewart waited for the man to finish his work, and the two continued on to Cemetery Hill.[18]

The Eleventh Corps batteries had to leave three guns behind when they retreated to the hill. Confederates had captured two Napoleons from Heckman's Ohio battery when they overran it. A direct hit on one of Wheeler's pieces had dismounted its 800-pound iron barrel. The gun crew tried to move the barrel off by slinging it beneath a caisson with a prolonge, but the rope broke and the barrel had to be left behind.[19]

Lt. Christopher F. Merkle's section of Lt. Bayard Wilkeson's U.S. battery retreated to the right of the Harrisburg Road to avoid capture by Early's division. It dropped trail at the edge of the town and fired two rounds of canister before limbering up again. There it met the other two sections of the battery, and all took the time needed to fill their limber chests with ammunition from their caissons before continuing their retreat. The caissons hurried away, but the guns retired slowly by prolonge, pausing now and then to blast away at the pursuing Confederates.[20]

In the meantime, Capt. Hubert Dilger had posted a section of Napoleons from his Ohio battery and a section of three-inch Ordnance rifles from Wheeler's battery at the Washington Street entrance to the town in order to cover the retreat of Schurz's division. Later, when he tried to lead his battery through the town to the hill, he found the streets jammed. He sought to avoid congestion by taking a street to the left and led his battery around the town to the east. The Eleventh Corps batteries, like those of the First Corps, felt the enemy's pressure during their retreat, but their losses were lighter, amounting only to a broken caisson wheel and several wounded horses.[21]

Thus it was that of the forty-eight guns of the First and Eleventh corps, only four were lost on 1 July to the victorious enemy. Most of the remainder quickly prepared to defend Cemetery Hill and created a formidable presence there that discouraged attack.

Another vignette that symbolizes the Union withdrawal in a particular way involved the color-bearer of the 7th Wisconsin Regiment of the Iron Brigade. The 7th retreated in column behind Wainwright's caissons down Chambersburg Street toward the town. As it reached the town's edge, enemy artillery fire seriously wounded Color Sgt. Daniel McDermott and shattered his flag's staff into a number of pieces. McDermott's comrades halted a caisson, placed the sergeant on it, and McDermott waved his flag defiantly as he rode atop the caisson to Cemetery Hill.[22]

The retreating Federals hurried to Cemetery Hill by way of Washington and Baltimore streets. The men of the 6th Wisconsin, approaching from Washington Street, saw on the slope of the hill "the colors of the Union, floating over a well ordered line of men in blue." This was the 73d Ohio Regiment of Col. Orland Smith's brigade of von Steinwehr's division, stalwart Buckeyes from south-central Ohio. The men of the 6th walked faster, passed through the Ohioans' line, and went on to the top of the hill. There they dropped to the grass in a state of exhaustion. They saw no panic on the hill, but there was still disorder, and they could see stragglers and wounded men moving to the rear over the Baltimore Pike to their right.[23]

Many stragglers fled the field that day, and the provost guards of the various corps swept some up on their approach to Gettysburg. In later years, Pvt. Jacob Smith, an ambulance driver in the 107th Ohio Regiment, voiced a thought about the straggling. He had driven through the confusion of the retreat in the town and reached Cemetery Hill. There he saw soldiers forming on both sides of the road and for the first time realized that it was intended that the Federals rally there. He thought in retrospect that many men, like himself, believed that they had been utterly defeated on 1 July and, separated from their units, had not realized that a rally would be attempted on the hill. Yet by the time that Smith and his ambulance reached the hill, there was a provost guard of infantry and cavalry on the reverse slope of the hill halting fugitives and returning them to their regiments. The defeat north of the town had been only temporary.[24]

Captain Culp met General Howard when he reached the hill. Twenty-two years later he recalled fondly: "I linger with pride upon that interview, which in two or three minutes taught me what a cool and confident man could do. No hurry, no confusion in his mind. He knew that if he could get his troops in any kind of order back of those stone walls the country was safe."[25]

Howard and an aide were near Baltimore Street just down from the cemetery when one of the first of the retreating regiments streamed from the town, its colonel "murmuring something in German—his English was not at his command just then." As its color guard reached a spot between Howard and a wall near the edge of the town, Howard called out, "Sergeant, plant your flag down there in that stone wall!" The sergeant, not recognizing Howard, replied, "All right, if you will go with me I will!" Howard took the flag, much as he had taken one at Chancellorsville, and he and the aide led the color guard back to the wall, where they planted the colors; the regiment then formed a line.[26]

In his report of the battle, Maj. Allen Brady of the 17th Connecticut told a similar story. The 17th retreated through the town from Barlow Knoll, halting to fire occasionally, and was almost overwhelmed by the Confederates. When its survivors reached Cemetery Hill, they halted near Wiedrich's guns and formed fronting toward the town. Howard spied them there and asked Brady if he had troops brave enough to cross a small field back toward the town in order to reach a wall on the other side. Howard said that he would lead them. The men of Connecticut shouted, "Yes, the Seventeenth Connecticut will," and they went to the wall at once. They remained at the wall a few minutes before advancing again across a lot to a rail fence at the edge of the town, where they remained until evening.[27]

Most of the men of the Eleventh Corps took position behind the stone walls that crossed the forward slopes of Cemetery Hill. Barlow's division, now under Ames, formed to the right of the Baltimore Pike on East Cemetery Hill and in the fields in its front. Schurz's division rallied to the left and in front of the cemetery. Von Steinwehr's division had a special assignment: Smith's brigade guarded the northwest slope of Cemetery Hill, its right regiment, the 55th Ohio, extending down to the houses of the town. When Coster's survivors fell back, they returned to their former positions on East Cemetery Hill. The 73d Pennsylvania went forward and occupied the buildings and yards on both sides of Baltimore Street with reserve companies in Snider's Wagon Hotel at the junction of Baltimore Street and the Emmitsburg Road. They were able to cover Baltimore Street from the hotel's windows and holes punched in its roof.[28]

Colonel Wainwright reached Cemetery Hill as his first batteries were arriving, and he met Howard, who was glad to see him. Although Wainwright was a First Corps officer, Howard asked him to take charge of the batteries of both corps and to post them as well as he could. Major Osborn, Howard's chief of artillery, would take orders from him. Howard told Wainwright how he wanted the position to be organized and said that he expected to hold the hill until the rest of the army came up. Wainwright discussed the situation with Osborn, and the two artillerymen divided their work. Wainwright took charge of the batteries east of the Baltimore Pike and gave Osborn those west of it. It is likely that Wainwright elected to command the batteries on East Cemetery Hill because he believed that that was the area in greatest danger of attack.[29]

Wiedrich's battery was already on East Cemetery Hill, and Wainwright left it there, except that he aligned four of Wiedrich's three-inch Ordnance rifles "at the angle or corner of the hill" so that Wiedrich could fire from the northwest around to the northeast. Probably at General Hunt's request, Wainwright detached Lt. Christopher Schmidt's section to the left of Osborn's line, and it remained there throughout the battle. Maj. Gen. Winfield S. Hancock rode by Wiedrich's position some time later and said to Wiedrich, "Captain, you must hold your position by all means."[30]

Hancock reached the hill sometime while the Union troops were rallying there. He was already there when Schurz came from the town, and Howard associated his arrival with an attempt by the Confederates at about 4:30 to push against East Cemetery Hill. Doubleday reported that the lines had been essentially posted at the time of Hancock's coming and that the batteries were already on the summit of the hill. As Hancock himself remembered it, the Cemetery Hill position was partially occupied, but some vigorous effort was still needed in order to get the Eleventh Corps into a formidable line. Regardless of the precise time of his arrival, which we cannot determine, Hancock's presence on the hill was a tonic and inspiration for the Federal troops and will be discussed in some detail in a later chapter. He did much to bring order from confusion and to stiffen the spines of those who had to fight another day.[31]

Wainwright placed most of his batteries east of the Baltimore Pike. He posted Lieutenant Stewart's four usable Napoleons (the other two had been disabled) by the pike and near the crest of the hill just north of the cemetery gate so that they could cover the Baltimore Street exit from the town. Cooper's battery's four three-inch rifles dropped trail to the right and rear of Wiedrich in a field across from the cemetery's gatehouse. A stone wall separated Cooper's guns from Wiedrich's on their left, and Cooper's guns pointed northeast to the right of the town. Cooper made sure that his battery's ammunition chests were filled and then, at Doubleday's request, acted as a staff officer for him and worked to strengthen the Federal position.[32]

Wainwright placed the five three-inch Ordnance rifles of Reynolds's battery to the right and rear of Cooper's battery and further down the hill. Lt. George Breck now commanded this battery instead of Captain Reynolds, who had been wounded in the eye earlier in the day. Breck described his position as "a high and commanding place," and from it Breck's five guns could cover much of the area between the town and Culp's Hill to the east.[33]

A stout major general unknown to the artillerymen sat on a horse at the cemetery gate when Cooper's and Stevens's batteries reached the top of the hill. The general, in his delicate way, shouted for the captain of "that brass battery," and Capt. Greenleaf T. Stevens, who commanded the six Napoleons of the 5th Maine Battery, reported to him. Pointing toward

Culp's Hill from Cemetery Hill. The gun pits of Reynolds's battery are in the foreground. Stevens's battery's position and the left of Wadsworth's line are on the right against the trees. A segment of Brickyard Lane appears above the tent. (GNMP)

Culp's Hill, the general told Stevens to take his battery to it and "stop the enemy from coming up that ravine." "By whose order?" asked Stevens. "General Hancock's," the portly man replied.

Stevens shouted, "Fifth battery, forward!," and the battery's sections sorted themselves from the traffic on the pike and headed down to the lane at the McKnight house. They turned left into the lane, filed by the house, and swung right along a fence and wall to the knoll at the base of Culp's Hill. As the guns went into position on the bare knob, Stevens could see Confederates in the fields by the town and opened on them with a vigorous fire. Although they were mistaken, the Maine men believed that they had halted an attack.[34]

Colonel Wainwright appeared at Stevens's position and, seeing that the battery had no close infantry support, told Stevens to send some of his men to the rear of the battery to open gaps in the fences so that they could pull away in case the enemy threatened to overrun them. This was an appropriate precaution but unnecessary, for Hancock soon sent the Iron Brigade to the battery's right on Culp's Hill's west slope.[35]

Before the end of the day, Wainwright had portions of five batteries awaiting a Confederate attack on East Cemetery Hill alone—an imposing force of thirteen three-inch Ordnance rifles and ten Napoleons. Their caissons parked in the shelter of the hill, and their ammunition chests were filled with ammunition fortunately obtained from the ordnance train of the Eleventh Corps. Wainwright cautioned his battery commanders about wasting ammunition and told them not to "take orders from any man with a star on his shoulders who might choose to give them." Although Wainwright felt relief in knowing that his guns were ready for action, he hoped for darkness. Yet he saw that there would be another hour of daylight and knew that the moon would be nearly full that night. He feared that the Rebels might attack from the town and that, if they did so, they might be on the batteries almost before the artillerymen knew it. He worried too because the town was full of wounded and if his guns fired at attackers coming from it, noncombatants might be hit. But time passed and darkness fell without an attack. Wainwright somehow procured a cup of coffee and some hardtack, got his blankets, and bedded down beside Brig. Gen. Adelbert Ames in a room in the cemetery's gatehouse.[36]

As Wainwright posted his guns on East Cemetery Hill, Major Osborn set up a gun line west of the pike in and near the cemetery. He had Hall's 2d Maine Battery from the First Corps, Wilkeson's, Wheeler's, and Dilger's batteries from the Eleventh, together with a two-gun section from Wiedrich's battery east of the pike. Heckman's Ohio battery, which had been overrun and had lost two of its four Napoleons, was deemed to be in such poor condition that it was sent to the rear. Yet we may wonder why the two remaining pieces would not have been of some use in an emergency. All in all Major Osborn had a line of twelve Napoleons and eight three-inch Ordnance rifles.[37]

We cannot know the precise location of Osborn's guns. The Napoleons of Wilkeson's (Bancroft's) and Dilger's batteries were especially good for firing canister at short range. They were near Stewart's battery on the pike and could fire down toward the streets exiting from the south end of the town. The rifled pieces of Wheeler's battery and Lt. Christopher Schmidt's section of Wiedrich's battery were further west where their longer ranges would have been helpful in covering the fields west of Gettysburg and in counterbattery fire against the Rebel guns on Seminary Ridge. Capt. James A. Hall's battery took position in the cemetery. Its cannoneers leveled tombstones and the iron fences around some of the grave plots. On 2 July Lieutenant Breck in comment wrote: "A beautiful cemetery it was, but now is trodden down, laid a waste, desecrated. The fences are all down, the many graves have been run over, beautiful lots with iron fences and splendid monuments have been destroyed or soiled, and our infantry and artillery occupy those sacred grounds where the dead are sleeping. . . . It is enough to make one mourn."[38]

Since there were a few more guns east of the pike and since Wainwright commanded there, it seems likely that either Howard, Hancock, or Wainwright believed that that area was most vulnerable to Confederate attack. Future events would confirm that it was. In later years, Major Osborn recalled the nature of the position west of the pike. The troops in his front were in two lines, the most advanced being behind a fence at the foot of the hill. The position was a good one except for the area along the Baltimore Pike where the town pushed close to it. There the houses provided cover for enemy sharpshooters. Yet when troops and guns were in position, and pickets were well to the front, there was a feeling of security, and some of the soldiers were able to sleep well after their eventful day.[39]

5

THE REBELS
TAKE THE TOWN

As the Eleventh Corps fled in confusion, the slaughter was terrific, in the opinion of Maj. John W. Daniel of Gen. Jubal Early's staff. "The Federal flank had been shrivelled up as a scroll," and the men in blue were fleeing up the slight slope from Stevens's Run into the north edge of the town. The rattle of Confederate musketry blended with soul-stirring music played by a distant band of Rodes's division. It was a heady hour for the men of Ewell's corps—those who had not become casualties. John Daniel, who was riding with Early in the rear of Gordon's brigade, leaned toward the general and shouted, "General, this day's work will win the Southern Confederacy."[1]

Early did not reply; his expression did not change. Soon he sent Daniel ahead to be with Gordon and his brigade. Gordon had pushed ahead toward a Union line forming on the rise between Stevens's Run and the north edge of town by Coster's brigade, Heckman's Ohio battery, and remnants of Schurz's division. Early ordered Gordon to halt his brigade near Stevens's Run and sent Hays's and Hoke's brigades forward from the left to take care of the shaky Union line. The Georgians halted, filling their cartridge boxes, and the pursuit continued without them.[2]

As Gordon's brigade advanced, Early sent for a battery to support it, and Capt. James McD. Carrington's Charlottesville Artillery came forward with its four Napoleons. Carrington crossed the bridge over Rock Creek and turned right into a field, where he met Early. The two rode in silence at the head of the battery until Early told Carrington to give Gordon's brigade immediate support if it needed it. Soon after, when they were in the middle of the field, Early told the captain to prepare for action.

Carrington put his guns into battery, and they waited. Early rode forward slowly and stopped. Carrington cantered to him, and they watched the fighting in their front. About ten minutes later, Early trotted off suddenly, calling back to Carrington to remain where he was. Carrington watched and waited. When he heard a Rebel yell signifying that the brigades of Hays and Hoke had smashed the Federal line in front of the town, Carrington limbered his four pieces and took them forward. Soon, to his delight, he received an order to take the guns into the town itself.

The battery rolled ahead for about 400 yards when Carrington received an order to halt. There was confusion ahead. Not knowing what would happen, Carrington prepared for the worse by putting three of his pieces in position in Carlisle Street with several rounds of canister on the ground by the muzzles of each so that they could be fired rapidly. The battery waited there for nearly a half hour without firing a shot. When Carrington saw Early, Gordon, and some other officers in a field behind him, he rode back to where they were in the hope of learning what was going on. He discovered then that there would be no targets for him in the town.[3]

Maj. Harry Gilmor, who had temporary command of three companies of the 1st Maryland Cavalry, recalled the Federal retreat with pleasure. His companies had arrived during the fight, and Ewell sent them left to the support of the batteries of Jones's battalion of artillery. When he saw the Federals in retreat, Gilmor left his Marylanders in the charge of Capt. George M. Emack and dashed after the flying enemy in the company of Capt. Warner Welsh and Lt. William H. B. Dorsey. Gilmor wrote that they captured a number of Federals, whom he sent to the rear with Dorsey, and that they rode on into the town. In his opinion, he and Welsh were the first two Confederates there. As they rode along cautiously, a dismounted Union cavalryman took a shot at Gilmor that missed his ear by an inch. As the trooper walked off, Gilmor picked up a loaded rifle from the street, shot at the man, and had the satisfaction of seeing him fall. Gilmor took the man's pistol and saber before riding on.[4]

There is no way of knowing which Confederates were the first to enter the town, for it was a large place and there was much activity that day. Col. Abner Perrin, commander of McGowan's brigade, Pender's division, claimed the honor for the 1st and 14th South Carolina regiments, which had pursued fleeing First Corps troops after breaking their last line at the seminary. It was the 1st South Carolina Regiment that claimed the capture of the lost gun of Reynolds's battery and the honor of being the first to raise its flag in Gettysburg. On entering the town, these regiments broke into details and searched for stragglers. They met little resistance and suffered no casualties. "Some light-fingered persons helped themselves secretly to fowls and other dainties, of course, but even these things were not done gently." Most Gettysburg residents probably would not have made a distinction between soldiers and their minions, but the South Carolinians blamed the looting on servants who insisted on "universal pillage." In a short while, Pender recalled the two South Carolina regiments, and it was then, according to Perrin, that Ramseur's brigade filed into Gettysburg from his left.[5]

The first soldiers in the town faced real danger or had every reason to believe that such danger was lurking in wait for them. A party of unidentified Rebel soldiers pressed up Chambersburg Street toward the square. Perhaps they were aware of the peril posed by the remnant of the 45th New York in the buildings along the north side of the street, perhaps not, but their nerves were taut, and their fingers were on the triggers of their rifles as they hurried up the street. When one reached Christ Lutheran Church, which was being used as a Union hospital, he looked up its long flight of steps and saw a Union officer, and perhaps a wounded sergeant also, at the top of the steps above him. The officer, Chaplain Horatio S. Howell of the 90th Pennsylvania Infantry, wore an officer's uniform including a staff officer's sword. The soldier put a foot on the lower step, pointed his rifle toward the officer, and called for him to surrender. Instead of raising his hands at once, the chaplain launched into what probably would have been an explanation of his noncombatant status, and the soldier shot him on the spot. Soon after, a Confederate officer came up and posted a guard at the church door. When the doctors inside complained about the shooting of the chaplain, the Confederate lieutenant had only to point to the chaplain's dead body, its uniform, sash, and sword. His death was a lesson that one should heed the orders of a nervous soldier with a rifle in his hands, even when standing at the entrance of a church.[6]

There was much confusion, but in the oratory that reflected the golden glow of memory, John Daniel spoke of exulting Confederates occupying a town of closed doors and pulled blinds, few of whose citizens could be seen. The soldiers exchanged happy greetings and congratulations, asked after friends, and traded stories and boasts. Being somewhat carried away, Daniel declaimed: "All the soldiers behaved well. They were tired, but they sought no rest; they were hungry, but they seized no meat; they were in power but they were forbearing. All were gratified."[7]

Daniel also spoke of sadder things. There were numerous Union dead, and there were wounded men among the dead who moaned for aid. In the fields north of the town, many dead lay in lines where their regiments had fought, and the bodies behind these lines were more scattered. In the town, the dead and wounded lay in gardens and yards, in the mouths of alleys, and in the streets. The dead Federals, Daniel noticed, generally had been stripped almost to nakedness. "The hand that shoots from the front rank of battle is frequently first to find the pockets of the dead," he wrote, "and this pilfering of the fallen is by no means confined to the skulkers & followers in the rear." He added that if fifteen minutes after the battle line had passed on, anyone could find a Yankee with boots or pockets that had not been rifled, he had better eyes than his. He explained this by the barefooted and ragged condition of the Confederates and observed that "Conscience in thick soles & warm garments is not the same as Conscience with sore feet & shivering limbs." Yet more than shoes disappeared, and men who were robbing the dead could not be pressing an enemy that was still alive and fighting.[8]

The Confederates shot a Union soldier in front of the house of young Nellie Aughinbaugh. Soon after, the Aughinbaughs saw a Confederate soldier going through the pockets of the dead soldier, but he found nothing of value—only a photograph of the soldier, his wife, and their two small children. Not wanting the photo, the Confederate tossed it through the Aughinbaughs' open window, saying that they might be interested in it. When things quieted a bit, Nellie's grandfather stole out of the house, rolled the soldier's body in a blanket, and laid it near the house. In a few minutes, another Confederate who was going by saw the corpse, stopped, rolled the body from the blanket, and went through its pockets. After the soldier left, Nellie's grandfather rolled the body into the blanket, where it remained a short while until another prospector came along in search of wealth. The playlet continued, and Nellie's grandfather had to rewrap the body several times while it remained by the house.[9]

Michael Jacobs and his family waited out the arrival of the Confederates in the basement of their house at the intersection of Washington and Middle streets. Young Henry Jacobs tried to follow events outside from a narrow ground-level window. He saw a Union soldier run by, gasping for breath, with some Confederates in pursuit. "Shoot him! Shoot him!" one of the pursuers yelled. A rifle cracked, and the man fell dead. There was a brief lull followed by a thunderous pounding on a door. Henry ran upstairs and opened it. There was a wounded Pennsylvania soldier from a First Corps regiment attended by several comrades. They had avoided capture somehow and wanted shelter. Jacobs admitted the wounded man and two others and sent the rest on their way. A half hour later a Confederate party appeared and insisted on searching the house. They found the three Union soldiers, of course, and took off the two who were unwounded as prisoners, leaving the wounded man behind for the time being. By 5:00 P.M. Doles's brigade had occupied the area fully, and its men took down fences that might impede their movements. Jacobs found these Georgians gentlemanly and courteous and "as considerate of the townspeople as it was possible for men in their position to be."[10] Michael Jacobs remembered their being elated and anxious to talk. They boasted of themselves, their cause, and the skill of their officers and, in turn, told how poorly the Federals had conducted the battle just closed. Their confidence knew no bounds.[11]

Two blocks to the east, at the southwest corner of Baltimore and High streets, the family of Albertus McCreary had a similar experience. The McCrearys had taken refuge in their basement, where they became increasingly alarmed by the noises in the streets outside. Albertus peeked out of a window just in time to see a cannon unlimber and fire, and he was greatly impressed by the noise and dust it made. After the action seemed to move on, the slanting outer doors of the basement suddenly flew open and five Confederate soldiers jumped down among them. Everyone was frightened, and some of the women cried; they thought that their end had come. Albertus's father, David McCreary, stepped forward, asked what the soldiers wanted, and begged them not to harm them. One soldier, a dirty, sweaty fellow with a red freckled face and red hair, said that they were looking for Union soldiers. McCreary told him that there were none there. The soldiers looked around, and then they all went upstairs, where the Confederates found thirteen Federals hidden throughout the house. They assembled the thirteen in the dining room, and an officer took their names. The dining room table had been set and the McCrearys' interrupted meal was at hand. David McCreary invited the Confederates to have something to eat, and they gladly accepted his invitation. By this time the family's fear of individual soldiers had gone—along with their meal.[12]

The appearance of many of the Confederates must have engendered fear. Sarah Brodhead, who witnessed the occupation of the town from her home on Chambersburg Street, considered the Confederates that she saw a "dirty, filthy set" who were dressed in all kinds of clothes. Some were barefooted, and a few were wounded, yet in spite of their appearance, she and others agreed that by and large they were a well-behaved lot. Albertus McCreary remembered them as having been ragged and dirty and with very little to eat. The memory of one in particular stuck in his mind—a barefooted man on horseback with spurs strapped to his bare heels.[13]

When Hays's men occupied East Middle Street, some saw buckets of water that William McLean, a young attorney, had placed on the sidewalk in front of his house for retreating Union soldiers. McLean, his wife, and their small daughter, who had taken refuge in the house, felt alarm when they heard a Rebel shout, "Don't touch that water, they may have poisoned it." After a while, the McLeans decided that they were not to be molested and looked out to see tired soldiers sitting along the curb, amusing themselves by opening abandoned Federal knapsacks and reading the letters they contained. Then a fine-looking officer rode up, and when the men cheered him, he "addressed them with jubilation." McLean grew cold with fear again soon after when his five-year-old daughter leaned from a window and sang, "Hang Jeff Davis on a Sour Apple Tree," but the soldiers took no notice, and McLean calmed down.[14]

Just to the west, at the northeast corner of Baltimore and Middle streets, Hays's men searched the Fahnestock house and picked up a dozen or so soldiers who were hiding there. Mrs. Fahnestock insisted that an officer accompany the searchers, and one of them was good enough to comply. Instead of preparing for more fighting, these Louisianans took hay from the Fahnestock stable's mow and spread it on the sidewalk for better sleeping. The Fahnestock boys listened to their talk through opened shuttered windows and heard elated boasts over their victory and what they would do next day.[15]

What would they do next day? Civilian accounts have very limited value as sources of information on Confederate operations, but they suggest that the men of Doles's and Hays's brigades in the town did little to prepare to press an attack on that evening. Instead, they seemed more concerned with searching for Federal stragglers, with bedding down for the night, and with talking of what might happen next day.[16]

When Maj. Gen. Jubal A. Early followed his victorious troops into Gettysburg, he was keen for continuing the assault on Cemetery Hill. At that time, Early was but one of ten division commanders at Gettysburg, and probably many people would have rated him below several of his peers, including John B. Hood and J. E. B. Stuart and, perhaps, Lafayette McLaws, Dorsey Pender, and Richard H. Anderson. Even then, though, he was a competent general officer and was well on his way to becoming one of the many controversial generals produced by the Confederacy.

Early was born on 3 November 1816 and at forty-six was one of the older generals on the field. He graduated from West Point in 1837 with a class that included Joseph Hooker and John Sedgwick, commander of the Union Sixth Corps at Gettysburg, and like many officers of his generation, he had seen service as a subaltern in Florida. Although he was promoted to first lieutenant only a year after his commissioning, he left the army in 1838 to study law and to practice it in Rocky Mount, Virginia. Apart from his law practice, he dabbled in politics as a Whig and served in the state legislature in 1841–42. During the Mexican War he went to northern Mexico as major of the 1st Virginia Regiment, but he saw no fighting there. Early, as a Whig, opposed secession and fought it all the way, but once it was accomplished, he became an ardent supporter of the new order and entered the Confederate service as colonel of the 27th Virginia Regiment.

Early became a brigadier general on 21 July 1861 and commanded a brigade with some distinction at First Manassas. Although wounded at Williamsburg, he was back in the saddle at Cedar Mountain and at Second Manassas, where he commanded a brigade in Ewell's division. He commanded the division at Antietam and continued to command it at Fredericksburg and Chancellorsville. He had performed well on every field, and he had become a major general in April 1863. Therefore, when General Lee launched the Pennsylvania campaign, Early was a seasoned division commander who was already acquainted, perhaps too well, with Richard Ewell, his new corps commander.[17]

"Old Jube" or "Old Jubilee" Early is remembered as much for his forbidding appearance and personality as he is for his accomplishments. He was not an attractive man. He had black hair, flashing black eyes, and a rather long beard. Although he was slender and about six feet tall, he had painful rheumatism that caused him to be badly stooped and no doubt contributed to his abrasive personality. His rasping voice gave vent to a biting wit, he could be arrogant and overbearing, and he was a harsh disciplinarian. Douglas Southall Freeman described him as "unmarried, snarling and stooped, respected as a soldier but never widely popular as a man." It took a strong man, a positive personality, to stand up to Jubal Early. It must be said that Ewell relied strongly on him, too strongly perhaps, and that General Lee had something of an affection for him. Lee is supposed to have called him "my bad old man."[18]

In spite of the negative aspects of his personality, there were those who admired Early and insisted that a warm human being lived deep within his harsh exterior. John Daniel, in an oration given long after the war, extolled his supreme courage, which no one doubted, for it had been manifested on many a field. He also praised his lesser known magnanimity, generosity, and charity, together with his intellect, honesty, and genial disposition in some social situations. He cited his benevolent acts of the postwar years, when he gave generously to charities, particularly those concerned with indigent Confederate veterans and their families. Yet even

Maj. Gen. Jubal A. Early (WLM)

Daniel could recall only one instance during the war when the old warrior had betrayed a tender emotion. This was during the Battle of the Wilderness when the general learned of the death of Capt. Robert D. Early, a young cousin who had been a volunteer aide on his staff at Gettysburg. Early remarked, "Poor Robert," and Daniel saw a single tear dampen his cheek. That was all.[19]

Early wielded great power in the postwar years. He became president of the Southern Historical Society, and that society and its journal gave Early a forum through which he "upheld the manly spirit of the people, and . . . zealously . . . defended Confederate memories," especially the memory of General Lee. But woe to those who crossed Early, including James Longstreet and, insofar as this study is concerned, Walter H. Taylor. For good or bad, Early wrote of his Gettysburg experiences, and often his accounts are the only ones available and seem self-serving. His power and dogmatism no doubt inhibited the expression of views contrary to his own. Robert Stiles, whose freewheeling memoirs were not published until after Early's death, wrote that "no man ever took his pen to write a line about the late conflict without the fear of Jubal Early before his eyes."[20]

An elated Early followed Hays's troops into Gettysburg. Gordon's brigade caught its breath north of the town, and Hoke's men advanced initially only to the railroad before moving around the town to the east. One brigade, after all, was more than enough to clear the eastern half of the town. When the general saw that the town was secure and that Hays's and Hoke's brigades were ready for further action, he rode to the right in search of Ewell or Rodes or even Hill, whose troops should have been entering the town from the west. He wanted to urge an immediate advance before the enemy "should recover from his evident dismay, in order to get possession of the hills to which he had fallen back with the remnant of his forces." Then an odd thing happened.[21]

Early had ordered William ("Extra Billy") Smith to bring his brigade forward at about the time that Hays and Hoke had charged the town. But Smith's brigade did not appear. Instead, Early learned that Smith had thought it best to disregard the order "on account of a report that the enemy was advancing on the York Road." Now, as Early searched for Ewell, Rodes, or someone from Hill's corps that might help him to push forward, Lt. Frederick Smith, son and aide to the absent general, galloped to his side. In an excited manner, young Smith relayed a message from the general. Smith had taken his brigade from the division's support line to look into the report of the enemy's advance on the York Pike. His message to Early was that a large force of the enemy, including infantry, cavalry,

Brig. Gen. William Smith (WLM)

and artillery, was advancing over the York Pike and that the Confederates in Gettysburg were about to be flanked. Early's writings suggest that Smith had not consulted him about going off to the east; in fact, he had sent Smith orders on two occasions to advance in support of the attacking brigades. Early later maintained that he had no faith in Smith's report; nevertheless he not only allowed Smith's brigade to remain on the left, but he thought proper to send Gordon's brigade there also! Gordon would take charge of both brigades, which would keep watch on the York Pike and "stop any further alarm." [22]

Early's was a peculiar response to an unusual alarm. He had not yet seen Ewell and Rodes, and he thirsted to press the attack against Cemetery Hill. Still, on the basis of an alarm that he thought to be false, he depleted his division by half to guard against a threat that he believed did not exist. In hindsight, we can wonder about his untimely and immoderate response. If the flank had to be guarded awhile, would one brigade not have been enough? And what of the 17th Virginia Cavalry Regiment and the 35th Battalion? What had happened to them, and might they not have been used to screen the Confederate flank?

Several questions come to mind—we can wonder especially if General Smith might not have been much of the problem. Smith was, after all, an unusual brigadier general. First of all, at the age of sixty-five he must have been one of the oldest men in the army, and he must have had a spirit of independence that comported with his age. Like many other Confederate brigadiers, he had been a lawyer and a politician, except his career had been longer and more successful than most. He began practice in 1818 in Culpeper, where he married and started a family that would include eleven children. In addition to his law practice, he set up a "mailcoach" service that eventually was to connect Washington, D.C., with Milledgeville, Georgia. In the course of operating this service, he received extra payments from the post office that earned him the nickname "Extra Billy," a fitting sort of name for a politician. Smith's political career included service in Virginia's senate and, from 1841 to 1843, in the U.S. House of Representatives. This was followed by a term as governor of Virginia from 1846 to 1849. Then in 1849, like many others, he went to California, where he entered Democratic politics and won the party's nomination to the U.S. Senate. He declined this honor, however, for he did not wish to lose his Virginia connection, and he returned to Fauquier County in Virginia. His neighbors elected him to the U.S. House of Representatives in 1853, and he served there until 1861.

Gov. John Letcher offered to appoint Smith a brigadier general at the outset of the war, but Smith declined because he "was wholly ignorant of drill and tactics." Instead, he became the colonel of the 49th Virginia Regiment and set out to learn what he thought he needed to know. This seems not to have included a lot of military science, for he feigned, if he did not have, a contempt for "tactics" and trained officers, whom he called "West Point fellows." Although eccentric, Smith was brave and was a natural leader. He led his regiment at First Manassas and on the Peninsula and was wounded three times at Antietam while serving as acting commander of Early's brigade. In April 1863, with Stonewall Jackson's concurrence no doubt, "Extra Billy" became a brigadier general and received command of a brigade. The Army of Northern Virginia was indeed an unusual organization.

Some habits are hard to break, and Smith never gave up politics. He served in the Confederate Congress in 1861 and early 1862, while also serving as colonel of the 49th Virginia. In May 1863 he ran successfully for the governorship of Virginia. Therefore, in Smith, Jubal Early had to contend not only with an eccentric brigadier general at Gettysburg but also with the governor-elect of his state. The problem on the York Pike had to be handled with more tact, perhaps, than was sometimes exercised in Jackson's old corps.[23]

Having taken care of the emergency to the east, Early searched for Rodes, whose troops he saw in the town, and then he rode out Chambersburg Street to get a view of the field from that perspective. There he met a staff officer of Pender's division and urged him to tell General Hill that if Hill would send a division forward, they could take Cemetery Hill. There is no knowing what happened to this request.[24]

Col. Abner Smead of Ewell's staff found Early during the general's reconnaissance and brought him a question from the corps commander. Ewell expected Johnson's division to arrive shortly and wanted Early's opinion as to where it should be posted. Some Federal batteries opened at about this time, and the two officers discussed Johnson's posting as shells burst around them. Early pointed to Culp's Hill as the proper position for Johnson and urged a push toward Cemetery Hill. While Early and Smead talked, a messenger from Ewell arrived with a summons for Early from the corps commander. At this, the two officers rode off to join their chief. A new phase of the battle was at hand.[25]

6

EWELL HESITATES

General Ewell watched Rodes's division begin
its attack from Oak Ridge, and then, when the Eleventh Corps filed onto
the plain north of the town, he trotted downhill to Rodes's left. As he
passed the rifled guns of Capt. William P. Carter's King William Artillery, a shell burst close by, and one of its fragments struck and killed
his horse. The horse dropped at once and pitched the lieutenant general
to the ground. Artillerymen ran to his assistance, and soon Ewell was
mounted again. He protested that he had not been hurt, though he must
have been shaken, and he and his staff continued their ride to the left and
Early's front.[1]

Since Gordon's brigade's attack was over when Ewell reached its front,
Ewell and Gordon watched Rodes's and Early's men push into the northern edge of the town. It must have been about this time that Maj. Henry
Kyd Douglas, adjutant of Johnson's division, reported to Ewell with a
welcome message from General Johnson. Johnson and his division, with
the corps train, had been sent from Carlisle back down the Cumberland
Valley toward Chambersburg and had bivouacked on the previous night
around Scotland at the foot of the west slope of South Mountain. On the
morning of 1 July the division and the train marched for Gettysburg over
the Chambersburg Pike and had received precedence over Longstreet's
corps, a questionable decision to be sure. The soldiers of the division first
heard the sounds of battle at Cashtown Pass and soon saw couriers, probably from Ewell, gallop up to General Johnson. Now, several hours later,
Douglas found Ewell with some staff officers on what he remembered as a
hill overlooking Gettysburg. Douglas probably told Ewell of the division's

approximate location—he had left Johnson several miles west of Gettysburg and over an hour's march away. Johnson had instructed him to say that his division would be ready to attack immediately after being put into position, but Ewell knew that this could not be soon.[2]

Douglas wrote later that General Gordon, who was nearby, claimed that if he would be allowed to place his brigade with Johnson's division, they could take Cemetery Hill before dark. Such a boast from a brigadier who probably had not been within a mile of the hill that day and knew no better than Ewell when Johnson's division would arrive could be attributed to exuberance and ignored for the foolishness it was. Douglas recalled that at this time Ewell, unlike Gordon, was "unusually grave and silent," and he asked Douglas to tell Johnson that when his division "got well to the front" to halt it and wait for orders. According to the major, Ewell said, *"Gen. Lee is still in Cashtown, six miles in rear. He directed me to come to Gettysburg, and I have done so. I do not feel like going further or making an attack without orders from him."* Douglas recalled the feeling of disappointment that he and some others who had previously served on Stonewall Jackson's staff felt at Ewell's comment. One of the latter muttered, "Oh, for the presence and inspiration of Old Jack for just one hour!"[3]

Ewell and his staff followed the infantry into Gettysburg, likely by way of Carlisle Street, and paused in the square. Maj. Walter Taylor of Lee's staff found Ewell there and gave him a message from General Lee. Lee was no longer at Cashtown but was on Seminary Ridge, less than a mile away. As Taylor recalled it, Lee wanted Ewell to know that he could see the enemy retreating in confusion and that "it was only necessary to press 'those people' in order to secure possession of the heights, and that, if possible, he wished him to do this." Taylor recalled also that Ewell had expressed no objection to Lee's request or indicated any impediment to it. Instead, he had given Taylor the impression that he would execute it.[4]

That was Taylor's recollection, but his memory played him false. Ewell reported that Lee's order was for him "to attack this hill, if I could do so to advantage." In his report of the campaign, Lee himself stated that he had instructed Ewell "to carry the hill occupied by the enemy, if he found it practicable, but to avoid a general engagement until the arrival of the other divisions of the army, which were ordered to hasten forward."[5]

Although the message carried by Taylor to Ewell must not have been as Taylor recalled it, his impression that Ewell wished to renew the attack probably was correct. It would have been a natural thing for Ewell to have wanted to pursue the enemy, but it is likely that he began to have second thoughts when his ardor cooled and when, as a corps commander, he began to take stock of his situation and to consider Lee's admonition about not bringing on a general engagement until the other divisions had arrived. Ewell had willingly pitched into the Federals from Oak Hill when their movements seemed to threaten Rodes's division, but that fight was over. An assault against Cemetery Hill would be a new battle, and General Lee himself was on the field and in command.

Early and Rodes also met Ewell in the square, probably after Taylor had talked with Ewell and had returned to Lee. In answer to Ewell's question, Early suggested that Johnson's division occupy Culp's Hill. Certainly there were few alternatives; there was no room or need for it in the town or off Rodes's right. That left only the area east of the town. But Rodes and Early had other more immediate concerns. Both urged Ewell to press the attack and to tell Lee of their desire to do so. They believed that if Hill's corps could promptly occupy the high ground in front of Ewell's right, the north end of Cemetery Ridge, no doubt they could take and hold Cemetery Hill. Ewell was in sympathy with their views, particularly since they envisioned help from Hill's corps, so in response he turned in his saddle toward Lt. James P. Smith and said, "You have seen General Lee a little while ago—will you be kind enough to find him and tell him what these gentlemen say?" In response, Smith rode close to the two generals and asked them to repeat what they had said. After they had done this, Smith rode west on Chambersburg Street toward Seminary Ridge and General Lee.[6]

After Smith's departure, the generals and their staffs clattered south on Baltimore Street to get a close look at the Federal position on Cemetery Hill. They crossed High Street, and after they passed over the crest just south of the alley beyond, they presented an attractive but distant target for the skirmishers of von Steinwehr's division, marksmen who were firing from the buildings at the foot of the hill about 500 yards away. There was a fusillade, bullets zipped around the horsemen, and Major Daniel heard a thud. He thought that a ball had hit a staff officer riding at his side, but it had struck the officer's stirrup leather instead. Nevertheless, the zipping balls and the promise of artillery fire to follow made it obvious that the cavalcade was in danger, so the riders wheeled left into the cover of buildings along the alley and High Street. They could obtain some excellent views of the Federal position and Culp's Hill from the yards along High Street, but the skirmishers' fire was warning that they could do so only with risk.[7]

In the meantime, Lieutenant Smith hurried to the seminary area and

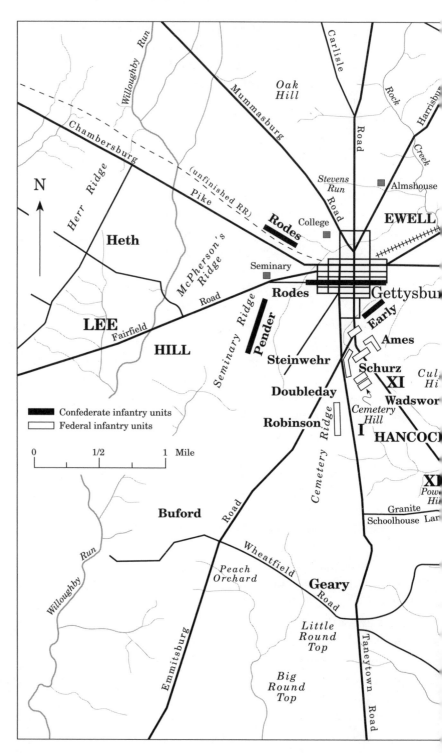

Map 6.1. Close of Battle, 1 July

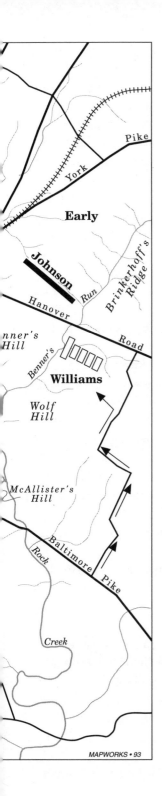

learned that General Lee had ridden south along the ridge. Smith trotted south along Seminary Ridge for about a mile until he saw some orderlies holding horses near some trees, probably McMillan's Woods. An orderly told him that Generals Lee and Longstreet were in a field to the front. Smith found them at a fence watching the Union troops to the east on Cemetery Hill and Cemetery Ridge. Both greeted Smith courteously, and Smith relayed his message. Lee lent Smith his binoculars so that he could have a close look at Cemetery Ridge and remarked, "I suppose, Captain, this is the high ground to which these gentlemen refer." As Smith studied it, Lee went on, "You will see that some of those people are there now," and Smith could see several horsemen who seemed to be making a reconnaissance. Lee went on to say that Longstreet's men were not up yet (they would not be up until next morning) and that he had no troops with which to occupy the ground. He spoke to Longstreet about the availability of his divisions and then said to Smith that on his front Ewell should do what seemed best, taking Cemetery Hill if he could. He, Lee, would direct Hill to do what he could to help. Smith returned to Ewell with Lee's message and found him still in the town. It became obvious to Ewell that, though General Lee had given him permission to attack Cemetery Hill, he could count on little significant help from Hill and none from Longstreet.[8]

Ewell had told Rodes and Early to prepare for an assault, but he suspended further action after considering his means for making one. He had been discouraged by Smith's report from Lee, and what he had learned about his own resources deterred him further. There seemed to be no really good artillery positions within his zone. There was some space on the left of Hill's corps on Seminary Ridge where guns could be positioned, but these were far off to his right, and though guns there might be of some help to Rodes, they would provide little aid to Early.[9]

Furthermore, in spite of Union fears to the contrary, Cemetery Hill did not look vulnerable to an assault from the town. Columns debouching from the confines of Washington and Baltimore streets would be extremely vulnerable to point-blank fire from Federal batteries on the hill. In order to attack the hill, the Confederate brigades would have to form between the east side of the town and the hill just in front of the Union batteries and infantrymen on the hill or attack from the fields southwest of the town. Neither option promised success without planning and the support of other Confederates on the field. In short, it would take time to prepare for a successful assault and help from Hill to make it. Neither was available to Ewell on the evening of 1 July.[10]

Also, what about the troops? Ewell must have learned that Early's men were tired, of course, but that his division was otherwise in good condition. The trouble was that it was scattered, and only two brigades, those of Hays and Hoke, were available for use in an evening attack on Cemetery Hill. Smith's and Gordon's brigades were about two miles to the east on the York Pike facing perceived threats in that area. Sometime after Lt. James Smith rode off to speak with Lee about an attack against the hill, Lt. Fred Smith, Brig. Gen. William Smith's son and aide, rode in from the York Pike to tell Ewell and Early that a heavy force was moving up in their rear. According to his postwar writings, General Early, who was responsible for Smith's and Gordon's brigades' remaining on the York Pike, said to Ewell, "Genl, I don't much believe in this, but prefer to suspend my movements until I can inquire into it." "Well," Ewell replied, "do so. Meantime I shall get Rodes into position and communicate with Hill."[11]

Ewell did not communicate successfully with Hill insofar as we know today, and he must have been discouraged by what he learned of the condition of Rodes's division when he inquired of its readiness to continue the attack. He knew that it had experienced a hard fight, yet its cost must have been sobering news. The division had lost about 2,500 officers and men—30 percent of its strength. In addition, it still had the burden of guarding about 2,500 prisoners of war. In short, the division could use some time to reorganize and get its breath if it were to attack again. When it became apparent that the pursuit would not be pressed immediately, Rodes had posted his skirmishers and brigades in "a defensive attitude." Rodes was right in doing this, but it made a resumption of the attack less practicable.[12]

Campbell Brown suggested that the reports of threats from the York Pike had much to do with Ewell's decision not to press an attack against Cemetery Hill. Because of ignorance of the whereabouts of the Union army, the false reports were taken seriously enough to gain Ewell's attention. But the reason for the rumor of the threat is a mystery. There were no organized Federal units on or near the York Pike, and Williams's division of the Twelfth Corps, which might have been considered a legitimate threat, was no closer to Smith's position than the Hanover Road a mile and a half to the south. Further, there is nothing in Confederate writings to suggest that they knew of Williams's division's being there.[13]

The accounts of Confederate participants are of no help in identifying a credible threat. They relate that the three regiments of Smith's brigade, the 31st, 49th, and 52d Virginia, received some shelling from Cemetery Hill on their way to the York Pike, but that was all. The 49th Virginia led the brigade and deployed skirmishers in such a way that there was "a general jumble," and "they advanced like a set of rabbits." Once on the left, Lt. Cyrus B. Coiner of the 52d heard General Smith instruct Fred Smith to report that the enemy was advancing and that he needed help at once. Coiner did not know the cause of Smith's alarm, and he thought that Smith mistook a distant fence marked by small trees as a line of troops. At any rate, Gordon's brigade soon approached at a double-quick, but it halted before it reached Smith's position.[14]

Ewell, Early, and Rodes, with some of their staff, rode east on the York Pike until they reached a point from which they could see that road stretching off two or three miles to the northeast and to the area posted by Smith's brigade. Early, who wrote the only account of this little diversion, stated that he (who was responsible for Gordon's brigade's being there if not Smith's) placed "no confidence in the rumor" but that Rodes was inclined to believe it and Ewell did not know what to think. As the generals surveyed the area, a line of skirmishers appeared to the right of the York Pike and Rodes exclaimed, "There they are now." Early wrote that he disagreed emphatically—Gordon's men were out there, and if what the generals saw was an enemy line advancing, there would be firing. In order to remove all doubt, Ewell and Early sent two aides forward to look into the matter—Lt. Thomas T. Turner of Ewell's staff and Robert D. Early, then a civilian volunteer. Turner and Early found that the men were from Smith's brigade and that Gordon was shifting them about. There was no enemy there. Oddly enough, in spite of there being no visible threat on the York Pike, Ewell and Early left both Gordon's and Smith's brigades out there until the following day. They did not even see fit to pull them back closer to the town where they might be more easily supported in event of a genuine threat or might be more available for use against Cemetery Hill.[15]

While Ewell, Early, and Rodes attempted to bring order from chaos in the Gettysburg area, Johnson's division continued its march toward the town. Nicholls's Louisiana brigade, Col. Jesse M. Williams of the 2d Louisiana commanding, led the way. Its men heard the sounds of battle as they crossed South Mountain, and in time there was commotion as couriers arrived from the front with news and orders. Staff officers bearing messages rode along the column, and the line officers hassled their troops with shouts: "Close up, men, close up; Hill's Corps is in." Johnson's men responded with cheers, and their step quickened, sometimes to a double-quick, as they filed down to the Gettysburg plain.[16]

Johnson's men met parties of prisoners and wounded before reaching the field of the day's battle. On the battlefield west of the town, the column swung left from the pike, filed to the bed of the unfinished railroad, and followed it into the town. By this time the artillery fire had almost stopped—the battle was over for the day. Nicholls's brigade halted near the railroad station at Carlisle Street and remained there for a time as the other brigades of the division closed up behind it.[17]

When Steuart's brigade, the third in the column, filed across a field near the railroad cut that was strewn with the dead of both armies, a barefooted Marylander broke ranks to take the shoes from a Union corpse that was lying near the line of march. As he seized a shoe, its owner raised his head and announced, "Mister, I'm not dead yet." Chastened, the startled Confederate returned shoeless to his place in the ranks. The last of Johnson's brigades reached Gettysburg shortly before dark, 6:00 P.M. or afterward. Lieutenant McKim of Steuart's staff remembered plainly that his brigade entered the town when it was still just light enough for him to read a dispatch handed him by Major Douglas. Certainly it had arrived too late to launch an attack on Cemetery Hill with or without Gordon's help.[18]

Like the activities of most division commanders, those of Johnson were not recorded well. Johnson had arrived ahead of his division and was out of sorts. It was said that his division had been delayed somehow by Longstreet's corps, though it was more likely that it was the other way around. By the time Johnson arrived, Ewell had already investigated the York Pike problem and had decided that Johnson would post his division east of Gettysburg and that it should occupy Culp's Hill. Ewell and Early met Johnson after their return from the York Pike, and Johnson told them that his troops were then about a mile to the rear and would be up within the hour. There followed an exchange between Johnson and Early in language "more forceful than elegant" over some matter regarding the posting of their divisions that, when reported, had already been blurred by time.[19]

No one said just when Ewell made the decision concerning the posting of Johnson's division; likely it was soon after it became apparent to him that he could not continue the assault against Cemetery Hill. At some point, probably after Smith's alarms from York Pike proved to be without substance, Ewell sent Lieutenant Turner and Robert Early to reconnoiter Culp's Hill. Although we do not know the time of their reconnaissance, it probably took place after the Iron Brigade and Stevens's battery took position on the hill's west slope. Turner and Early rode to the "very summit of the knoll without meeting a Federal & there saw stretched out before us the enemy's line of battle." They saw that their occupation of the hill would make the "enemy's position untenable" and rode back to report their findings to General Ewell.

Turner and young Early found Ewell sitting in a fence corner between

Rodes and Early. On hearing their report, Ewell asked Rodes what he thought of sending Johnson's division to the hill that night. Rodes, who seemed to be fatigued, replied that the men were tired and footsore and that he did not "think it would result in anything one way or the other." Ewell put the same question to Early, who replied, "If you do not go up there tonight, it will cost you ten thousand men to get up there tomorrow." Then, wrote Turner, Ewell told Johnson to move his command to the vicinity of Culp's Hill and to take possession of it, if after reconnoitering he still found the hill to be unoccupied. The order received, Johnson's division moved east while the remainder of the corps settled in for the night.[20]

Turner's reconnaissance of Culp's Hill was similar in some ways to that made by Capt. Samuel R. Johnston of Little Round Top early on the following morning. Johnston would find Little Round Top free of Union troops and miss the Third Corps bivouacked in the fields nearby. Turner and Early found no troops on the portion of Culp's Hill that they visited and failed to discover the Iron Brigade on the hill's west slope. Their failure to discover the Iron Brigade is difficult to understand. Probably they circled to the hill's east slope to avoid Union skirmishers in the fields north of the hill and climbed to a point somewhere south of its highest peak. If so, they would have been to the rear of the Iron Brigade's position, which, in the growing darkness, might have been masked by trees and the west slope's crest. Still, their report that the hill was unoccupied is puzzling.[21]

During Johnson's division's twilight march to Ewell's left, it filed along the railroad bed east from Carlisle Street, stumbling over its tracks and ties as it plodded along. Early's troops had burned the trestle over Rock Creek during their visit to Gettysburg a week before, so Johnson's men had to ford the creek. They walked the railroad bed uphill from the creek to the Hunterstown Road crossing and turned right there to the York Pike. It seems likely that they then filed from the pike into the lane leading to the George Wolf farm buildings and formed the division line in a shallow depression that cut the high ground beyond the buildings and ran southeast to Benner's Run. By the time that the division reached the Wolf farm, the moon had risen and lighted the way for Johnson's men to their new position.[22]

The division formed with Nicholls's brigade on the right 600 yards from the railroad and perpendicular to it. Jones's and Steuart's brigades and the Stonewall Brigade extended the division's line left in that order. The division's front ran roughly parallel to the Hanover Road about 500 yards in its front and faced toward Culp's Hill nearly a mile away. As soon as they reached their places in line, the brigades put pickets well to the front and slept on their arms while waiting for what was to come.[23]

Sometime late in the afternoon, Ewell received some advice from General Trimble, who was still visiting Ewell's corps. While Ewell's troops took over the town, Trimble rode to the east and saw the terrain there. When he next saw Ewell, according to his recollections in 1883, Trimble advised Ewell that, if he was not going to attack, he should "send a brigade with artillery to take possession of that [Culp's] hill," which commanded Cemetery Hill. On being queried further by Ewell, he went on to say, "If we don't hold that hill, the enemy will certainly occupy it; as it is the key to the whole position about here and I beg you to send a force at once to secure it." To this, Ewell was said to have made the "ungracious reply": "When I need advice from a junior officer I generally ask for it." In response, Trimble wrote that he warned Ewell that he would regret not following the suggestion as long as he lived. The life of a corps commander was not always a happy one.[24]

Sometime before sunset, according to Jubal Early, Lee appeared at Ewell's headquarters for a talk. Lee had not spoken personally with Ewell since the beginning of the campaign, and they had much to discuss.[25]

Lee had examined what he could see of the Union position on Cemetery Ridge and had talked extensively with Longstreet and Hill about attacking it. He had reviewed his options: to withdraw; to take a defensive position and await attack; to attempt a turning movement around the Union left as advocated by Longstreet and then take up a position that would force the Federals to attack him; or to renew an assault on the Gettysburg position on the following day—a course of action that Longstreet opposed. He deemed a withdrawal with his trains both difficult and dangerous and ruled that option out. Likewise he believed that to take a defensive posture would cost him the initiative and that his army would weaken as the enemy's forces grew stronger. He considered a turning movement impracticable, for he had too few cavalry and too little expertise present to do the necessary screening, and such a movement in the face of the enemy and in a restricted space between the enemy and the mountains would invite unacceptable risk. If he was to maintain the initiative, General Lee believed that he had no alternative but to renew the attack as early on the following morning as practicable. He had not yet developed a specific plan of attack, but it was understood that Hood's and McLaws's divisions of Longstreet's corps and Anderson's division of Hill's corps would be on the field on the following morning and ready for action.[26]

Gen. Robert E. Lee (MM)

The meeting took place, according to Early, in the arbor of an unidentified house that Ewell was using for a headquarters at that time. Present were Lee, Ewell, Rodes, and Early, who wrote the only account of the meeting and what was said. Early, who had been summoned while he was visiting Hays's brigade, arrived after the others and had no personal knowledge of what had taken place before he appeared. He reported nothing that might have been said about the battle earlier in the day—probably it had been discussed before his arrival. Nor did he report discussion about making an attack that evening, for it was already dusk and too late for that. Instead, he wrote of Lee's wanting to learn the condition of Ewell's corps, the nature of the enemy's position in its front, and what it might be able to do next day. It was a given, according to Early, that it was Lee's purpose "to attack the enemy as early as possible next day—at dawn if practicable."[27]

Lee asked Ewell, "Can't you, with your corps, attack on this flank at daylight to-morrow?" Because of the special information that he had acquired during his previous visit to Gettysburg and while posting his troops, Early replied first. He told Lee that the nature of the terrain and the enemy's position would require that the corps "go on the left of the town right up against Cemetery Hill and the rugged hills on the left of it." The result of such an attack would be doubtful, and even if successful, would entail a great loss. Early then reminded Lee of the greater chances of success by an attack on the Union left, and the advantages to be gained by seizing the Round Tops. Ewell and Rodes agreed with his views, Early wrote, and there was further conversation that convinced Lee that an attack against the Union right was not advisable. This in spite of the fact that Johnson might seize Culp's Hill.[28]

Lee observed, "Then perhaps I had better draw you around towards my right, as the line will be very long and thin if you remain here, and the enemy will come down and break through it?" This observation, wrote Early, prompted a clamorous denial from him bolstered by amens from Ewell and Rodes. A withdrawal from a position gained by fighting, Early said, would dampen the enthusiasm of his division. Furthermore, he did not like the idea of abandoning the wounded, and he did not wish to lose the captured muskets piled in the streets of Gettysburg. Early expressed the view that Lee did not have to worry that the enemy would break their line in the event that they were allowed to stay; the terrain made it more difficult for the enemy to attack Ewell's people than for the Confederates to attack the enemy.[29]

After listening to his generals' arguments against an attack from Ewell's front, General Lee remarked in the manner of someone forced to adopt a view contrary to his own, "Well, if I attack from my right, Longstreet will have to make the attack." Then, according to Early, Lee bowed his head in thought and raised it, adding, "Longstreet is a very good fighter when he gets in position and gets everything ready, but he is *so slow*."[30]

After Lee's death, Early used the latter remark about Longstreet in his vendetta against the Confederate postwar apostate, and it has received much attention. Early's other comments are more relevant to this account. He was certainly correct about the difficulties involved in attacking Cemetery Hill and Culp's Hill from the position held by Ewell's corps. Yet the whole matter of Johnson's possible occupation of Culp's Hill, if discussed, was not mentioned by Early. There was unintentional self-condemnation in the reasons given for the corps' remaining on the left. Large units are not moved by the flourish of a sword, and we do not know what matériel the Confederates would have had to remove from Gettysburg and the fields north of it. Yet it is likely that most of the trains were parked west of Seminary Ridge; there should have been comparatively few of Ewell's wounded at this time who could not have been evacuated; and the loss of weaponry in the town, if it could not be moved, was a small thing—more trivial by far than the abandonment of Stuart's celebrated captured wagons would have been when measured against Lee's loss of the use of one of his three army corps.

General Lee returned to his headquarters still undecided about what specific action should be taken on the following day. Obviously, he had been swayed by Longstreet's reluctance to attack the Federal position and his advocacy of a turning movement, even though Longstreet's accounts of their conversations did not reflect it. Furthermore, he must have been discouraged by his conversations with Ewell, Early, and Rodes. Ewell's corps seemingly could do little where it was, yet its generals did not want to move elsewhere. Their solution was that Longstreet should attack, and they would provide some diversion. That was fine except that Longstreet did not want to attack any more than they did. Lee pondered his alternatives and decided that he could not afford to squander Ewell's corps in a secondary position east of Gettysburg. Therefore, he asked Col. Charles Marshall to ride over to see Ewell and to say to him that he had found no favorable points of attack on the Cemetery Ridge position. Unless Ewell thought that he could carry the position in his front, "he intended to move Longstreet around the enemy's left & draw Hill after him, directing Genl. Ewell to prepare to follow the latter."[31]

Colonel Marshall rode down into Gettysburg in search of Ewell, but it was dark and he could not find his way. Fortunately, he met Major Gilmor, the acting provost marshal, who guided him to corps headquarters. He found Ewell resting near a roadside and relayed Lee's message to him. Ewell said that the matter was important and that he could not answer immediately. Since Rodes was also there, the two discussed Lee's message. Ewell sent for Early once again but not for Johnson, who was busy posting his division and, with his limited knowledge of the field, would have been of little help anyhow. Early answered the summons, and, if his account can be taken at face value, he must have dominated the conversation once again. He strongly urged Ewell not to abandon the idea of an attack, and, in spite of the darkness, they rode to the foot of a hill, probably Cemetery Hill, and discussed their options at great length. They wrote nothing about the content of the discussion, but since they had recently received Lieutenant Turner's report on Culp's Hill, it ought to have figured in their conversation. Finally, Marshall remarked that the hour was late and that he had to return to Lee with an answer. However, Ewell did not want to send a reply, he wanted to talk with Lee himself. The colonel and the lieutenant general set out for Lee's headquarters near the seminary.[32]

In spite of its being late, Lee and Ewell talked alone in Lee's tent for about an hour. Marshall did not hear what was said, and neither general wrote of the details of their conversation. Yet in his report Ewell stated that soon after dark Lee had ordered him to draw his corps to the right in case it could not be used where it was, Lee believing "from the nature of the ground that the position for attack was a good one on that side." Ewell countered by telling Lee that Lieutenant Turner and Robert Early had found Culp's Hill unoccupied by the enemy and that he judged that it commanded the Cemetery Hill position and made it untenable for the enemy to hold. Ewell's argument was persuasive—if by some slim chance the Federals had not occupied Culp's Hill, and Johnson's division held it at daybreak, Lee might be able to pop the Union troops from their strong position on Cemetery Hill. Then, with a united army, he could battle them successfully elsewhere. General Lee decided to allow Ewell's corps to remain east of the town.[33]

When Ewell returned to his headquarters, he awakened Tom Turner and sent him back to General Johnson with specific instructions to occupy Culp's Hill if he had not already done so. Ewell assumed that Johnson must have occupied the hill already and stated that he should hold his position until he received further orders because "Genl. Lee had determined to suspend all offensive operations until Genl. Longstreet's arrival which was momentarily expected."[34]

Turner found Johnson preparing his division for its morning assault. But Turner learned the surprising news that Johnson had not taken possession of Culp's Hill! He had sent a reconnoitering party there "with orders to report as to the position of the enemy in reference to it." On nearing the summit of the hill, the party, whose makeup is not known to us today, met a superior force of the enemy who captured some of its members and sent the rest packing. Culp's Hill was in Federal hands![35]

What had changed since Turner's reconnaissance in the early evening? One thing in particular. The 7th Indiana Volunteer Infantry Regiment of Cutler's brigade, Wadsworth's division, First Corps, had taken position on the crest of the hill. The regiment had been left in the rear that morning as train guard, had missed the battle of 1 July, and had not reached Cemetery Hill until after the Federal retreat. It was a welcome reinforcement, 400 officers and men strong and ready to fight, but by Wadsworth's order it left its exhausted comrades of Cutler's brigade on East Cemetery Hill and took position on the right of Wadsworth's line on Culp's Hill. There it extended the right of the Iron Brigade's line up the west crest to the summit of the hill. As it did so, Col. Ira G. Grover, its commander, sent Company B to the right to establish a picket line at the base of the east slope of the hill. A little later Grover pulled the company back to form a shorter line behind the right of the regiment on the south slope of the hill near the crest. It was there that Sgt. William Hussey and Pvt. A. J. Harshborger, who were on the extreme right of this picket line, heard men creeping toward them in the dark. Hussey alerted the rest of the company and set an ambush. When the officer leading the Confederate party passed by, Hussey grabbed him, and Harshborger fired at the others. Other men of Company B rushed up and blazed away, causing the Confederates to turn and flee. So ended Johnson's effort to occupy Culp's Hill and Lee's opportunity to pry the Federals from their Gettysburg position without making a full-scale and bloody attack.[36]

On their return from Culp's Hill, the survivors of the Confederate patrol intercepted a Federal courier who must have been riding toward Gettysburg over the Hanover Road. The courier carried a dispatch from Maj. Gen. George Sykes, commander of the Union Fifth Corps, to General Slocum. The message bore the time 12:30 A.M. and announced that the Fifth Corps was at Bonaughtown, now Bonneville, en route to Gettysburg and would resume its march at 4:00 A.M. Johnson turned the dispatch over to Turner, who carried it and the news that the Federals held Culp's Hill back to Ewell. This was a hard blow for Ewell. Not only had the benefits to be gained by occupying Culp's Hill without a fight been lost, but the dispatch confirmed that the Union Twelfth Corps, at least, had joined the First and Eleventh at Gettysburg and that the Fifth Corps would soon arrive.[37]

No one recorded Ewell's particular reaction to this bad news. With it, Turner relayed General Johnson's message that he would refrain from attacking the hill until he received further orders, but there seemed to be no hurry now. Ewell observed that "day was breaking, and it was too late for any change of place." The battle of 1 July was over, that day's work had been done, and the Southern Confederacy had not yet been won. Another day was about to dawn though, and the armies were already astir.[38]

7

SLOCUM AND HANCOCK REACH THE FIELD

Maj. Gen. Oliver O. Howard had ordered the First and Eleventh corps back to Cemetery Hill at 4:10 P.M.; by 4:30, he, General Doubleday, and their subordinates were rallying and deploying the retreating troops in order to make the hill secure against a Confederate attack. The hill and the stone walls that crossed it provided a strong position for its defenders, but it was defensible only so long as the enemy did not occupy Culp's Hill on its right and Cemetery Ridge to its left and rear. Should this happen, and should the enemy be able to hold his gains, the Union forces on Cemetery Hill would have to abandon their bastion and fight elsewhere some other day. Fortunately, while the Eleventh Corps manned Cemetery Hill itself, the First Corps would be able to begin the occupation of the flank positions. The two corps on the field, if attacked, could not hold their position for very long in the face of General Lee's larger and growing force. Hopefully, help for Howard would come in time; the Third Corps was marching toward Gettysburg from Emmitsburg, but it could not be expected for a while. The Twelfth Corps was much closer. How soon would it arrive?

General Slocum and his Twelfth Corps had reached the hamlet of Two Taverns on the Baltimore Pike, about four and a half miles southeast of Gettysburg, late on the morning of 1 July. They had marched only five miles from Littlestown, Pennsylvania, that morning in a leisurely fashion and, having reached their objective for the day, were looking forward to some rest. The Twelfth was the army's smallest corps; it numbered only about 9,000 officers and men for duty. Its five brigades were formed into two divisions, the First commanded by Brig. Gen. Alpheus S. Williams and the Second led by Brig. Gen. John W. Geary. Four batteries of the corps' artillery supported the two divisions instead of the usual five.[1]

General Slocum had moved his corps to Two Taverns in obedience to General Meade's orders of 30 June that had sent Reynolds to Gettysburg, but, unlike Reynolds and Howard, he had received additional instructions during the morning. Foremost among these was an Army of the Potomac circular of 1 July, the Pipe Creek Circular. In it, General Meade announced that the object of his army's recent movements had been achieved: it had relieved Harrisburg and frustrated any intention that the enemy might have had to carry his campaign beyond the Susquehanna. Now it was Meade's intention not to "assume the offensive until the enemy's movements or position should render such an operation certain of success." On the other hand, if the enemy assumed the offensive and attacked, it was his intention that the Army of the Potomac fall back to a defensive line that would be located generally along Pipe Creek in northern Maryland between Middleburg on the left and Manchester. In implementing this circular, Slocum would assume command of the Fifth Corps as well as his own, move the two back via Union Mills to the Pipe Creek position, and place his headquarters near Union Mills. The time for falling back would be "developed by circumstances."[2]

With the circular, Slocum received a dispatch from Chief of Staff Daniel Butterfield that suggested that the circular would soon be implemented. Butterfield wrote that the enemy was advancing in force on Gettysburg and that Slocum should begin moving his trains to Westminster, as stipulated by the circular. He also wrote that Slocum should be prepared to fall back to Pipe Creek with his corps as soon as Reynolds informed him that the First Corps had "uncovered" Two Taverns.[3]

Henry Warner Slocum was one of those numerous important Union generals who were deservedly prominent in their time but whose fame has paled with the passing years. He was born in Onondaga County, New York, on 27 September 1827 and attended and taught school there until 1848 when he entered West Point. He graduated seventh in the class of 1852, a year ahead of Howard, and at the age of twenty-five ought to have been more mature than most fledgling subalterns. He served in the artillery in Florida and then at Fort Moultrie, South Carolina. By this time, between 1853 and 1856, "garrison life proved irksome," and he improved on it by studying law in a prestigious Charleston law office during his abundant free hours. He resigned his lieutenancy in 1856 and returned to New York and his fiancée. In 1858 Slocum began a law practice in Syracuse. His practice allowed him time for other things, and in this brief prewar

Maj. Gen. Henry W. Slocum (WLM)

period he served as county treasurer, delegate to the New York General Assembly, and colonel and artillery instructor in the state militia.[4]

On 21 April 1861 Slocum became colonel of the 27th New York Regiment. He took his regiment to Washington and led it at Bull Run, where he received a severe wound. On 9 August he became a brigadier general, and when he had recovered sufficiently to return to duty in October, he received command of a brigade in William B. Franklin's division. Then, in May 1862, while campaigning on the Peninsula, Franklin received a corps command and Slocum took command of the division. On 4 July 1862 Slocum became a major general, and in the following September, after the death of Maj. Gen. Joseph F. K. Mansfield at Antietam, Slocum received command of the Twelfth Corps.

Slocum's rise had been a rapid one. He probably had some political backing, but, if so, it was not particularly blatant according to the standards of the time. He had served capably if briefly as a division commander, and he had received special plaudits for his performance at Gaines's Mill and Crampton's Gap. Thus, at the outset of the Pennsylvania campaign, after only four years of routine regular service as a lieutenant and two as a general officer during the war, Slocum ranked second only to Joseph Hooker in the hierarchy of the Army of the Potomac. He was senior to both Generals Reynolds and Meade.

After the battle of Chancellorsville, Slocum was among those who urged that Hooker be relieved from the command of the Army of the Potomac, and in the West in 1864 he refused to serve under him. Yet there seems to be no reason to suppose that Slocum had any ambition for the army's command or was ever seriously considered for it. After serving in the East, Slocum, like Howard, campaigned under Sherman in Georgia and the Carolinas and climaxed his war service as commander of the Army of Georgia. In the pantheon of Federal generals, Slocum would be classed among those who ranked just below the level occupied by the peers of Sherman and Meade.[5]

Slocum was above medium height, with long, wavy brown hair that he wore combed behind his ears, a heavy brown mustache, and sparkling brown eyes. Unlike many of his peers, he wore no beard. He seemed especially disposed to order and discipline and was attentive to details that he sought to master. These qualities, supplemented by high intelligence, must have been greatly responsible for his rapid promotion. Yet Gen. Alpheus Williams, a keen observer and loyal subordinate, commented after their initial meeting in October 1862, "I like our new corps commander very much so far, though he does not strike me as of wonderful capacity." Since Williams recorded no further concern about Slocum's capacity during their subsequent long service together, it seems likely that Slocum was able to grow with his challenges.[6]

Yet Slocum had a flaw or two. He could be prickly on occasion and proud, and he could be overly concerned with details and protocol. Perhaps some of the characteristics that were to make him a successful lawyer were not necessarily those most needed by a corps commander.[7]

So it was that at noon on 1 July Slocum and his corps rested in the rolling fields around the clutch of buildings at Two Taverns. In spite of the short distance and the routine nature of the march from Littlestown that morning, the troops had found the heat and humidity so oppressive that they were in great distress when they settled in for rest about noon. But some had energy. One soldier, whose brigade must have marched near the rear of the column, stopped with some comrades at a house and bought bread, apple butter, and cheese. The cheese came in balls the size of a baseball and had such an offensive odor when the balls broke open that it proved repulsive. Therefore, since the cheese balls could not be eaten, the soldiers naturally threw them at one another, thus loosing a dense odor around their company. Otherwise, the troops of the Twelfth Corps fell from ranks at Two Taverns, ate their noon meals, and napped. Meanwhile, some officers and sergeants worked on the paperwork associated with the inspection and muster held the day before.[8]

By the time that the Twelfth Corps had reached Two Taverns, the morning's battle at Gettysburg had ended and there was a noon lull. None of the Twelfth Corps people knew that there had been a battle, which suggests that the corps had no liaison with the left-wing headquarters or the First and the Eleventh corps, and it was advancing into an area that might be infested by the enemy without scouts or a screen of cavalry. Some men heard the muffled sound of distant artillery fire when at Two Taverns, but they were not alarmed by it, and some believed it to be only a cavalry action with which they had no pressing concern. It prompted such comments among those who heard it as "Hear the dogs barking," "I want to go home," "Put me in my little bed," "When will this cruel war be over," and the like. We do not know if Slocum actually heard this firing himself, but it is hard to believe that he did not know of it.[9]

Howard sent Slocum at least three messages on that fateful afternoon. He dispatched the first about 1:00 P.M., and it was identical to one sent to Sickles and forwarded by Sickles to Meade. It stated simply that "Ewell's Corps is advancing from York. The left wing of the Army of the Potomac is engaged with A. P. Hill's Corps." Since Sickles received his copy at

Emmitsburg before 3:15 P.M., in spite of the courier's difficulty in finding him, it is reasonable to suppose that the dispatch to Slocum must have been delivered by 2:00 P.M.[10]

Slocum's report and personal accounts make no mention of his receiving this message and acting on it. There is no reason to think he did not get it—perhaps he considered it merely something to be noted and filed. If Howard did not tell Slocum of Reynolds's death, he probably believed that Slocum had already learned of it. At any rate, it defies belief that the bearer of the dispatch to Slocum would not have passed such momentous news along.[11]

Slocum gave a brief account of his activities when at Two Taverns. This was done in 1875 in response to adverse comments written by Samuel P. Bates that suggested that Slocum had sat quietly with his corps at Two Taverns while the First and Eleventh corps fought at Gettysburg. Slocum replied that his corps had reached Two Taverns about noon and had rested there in readiness to move when necessary. Some firing had been heard, but it seemed to be that of a battle involving cavalry and a few pieces of artillery and had caused no alarm. It was believed later that the hills between Gettysburg and Two Taverns had created some sort of sound barrier that rendered most of the battle noise inaudible at Two Taverns.[12]

No efforts were made then to find out about the firing. Slocum's first intimation that a large battle was taking place came when a civilian arriving from Gettysburg announced that "a great battle was being fought on the hills beyond Gettysburg." This news spurred Slocum to action, and he at once sent Maj. Eugene W. Guindon of his staff forward with some orderlies to see if this was so. After Guindon had gone some distance, he was able to hear sounds of conflict that had been dampened at Two Taverns. Guindon reported back to Slocum at once, and Slocum put his corps in motion without delay.[13]

Slocum, stung by Bates's suggestion that he had not marched promptly to the field, protested: "I was not summoned by General Howard or any other person but marched at my own volition, the instant I knew help was needed." He then listed the names of some of the ranking officers of his corps and asked the rhetorical question of whether or not they would have denounced him if they had thought that the Twelfth Corps had remained idle while two other corps were in battle only five miles away. Of course they would have denounced him, he said, and had they done so, could his dereliction have remained a secret? Of course not. Since he had not been denounced by his key subordinates, he must have acted properly, Slocum replied.[14]

One reason that none of Slocum's ranking subordinates denounced him, apart from loyalty, could have been that they did not know what was happening at Slocum's level. Most of them would not have been privy to the instructions Slocum received on the morning of 1 July, and they would not have seen Howard's first dispatch. They would have been concerned with their divisions and brigades to the exclusion of most of Slocum's broader concerns. Further, they well knew that he had started the Twelfth Corps forward promptly when Guindon told him of the heavy fighting ahead. Slocum and they had answered the call. He was not tardy then, but he had not been spurred to action by Howard's first dispatch.[15]

At about 3:00 P.M., Howard sent another message to Slocum. He announced that his right flank was under attack (by Early along the Harrisburg Road) and that his force was in danger of being turned and driven back. He asked Slocum if he and his corps were moving up.[16]

Capt. Daniel Hall, who carried dispatches to Reynolds earlier in the day, carried this one. Although the road to Slocum was a turnpike and the distance short, the ride was an adventure, for Hall believed, wrongly, that Confederate cavalry had pursued him for part of the way. When he reached Slocum, Hall gave him Howard's message and briefed him on the events of the day, doubtless including the death of Reynolds. Slocum's reply to Hall is not known, but for reasons not given, Hall considered "his conduct on that occasion anything but honorable, soldierly or patriotic."[17]

Had the news of Reynolds's death not reached Slocum earlier, it certainly arrived when Capt. Addison G. Mason of Meade's staff appeared at Two Taverns between 3:00 and 4:00 P.M. with a dispatch stating that Hancock had been appointed to take Reynolds's place as commander of the left wing. It urged also that other corps commanders push forward with all possible haste. Slocum was no longer at Two Taverns at this time; he and some of the corps had already started toward Gettysburg. After showing the message to Lt. Col. Hiram C. Rodgers, Slocum's adjutant general, Mason rode on ahead to overtake Slocum with another message for both Slocum and Maj. Gen. George Sykes, commander of the Fifth Corps.[18]

It was this dispatch from Meade that probably prompted Slocum's message of 3:35 P.M. addressed to "General HANCOCK or General HOWARD." Slocum wrote simply that he was moving the Twelfth Corps to come up about one mile to the right of Gettysburg.[19]

Why did Slocum decide to take his corps a whole mile to the right of Gettysburg rather than straight up the pike toward Cemetery Hill or Culp's Hill? In his report, Slocum wrote that, "agreeably to a suggestion from General Howard," his First Division was placed on the right of the line near Rock Creek and the Second Division, pursuant to orders from Hancock, was sent to the extreme left. Yet according to Howard's report, it was not until after 4:00 P.M. that he asked that one division be sent to the right and the other to the left of Gettysburg. When Maj. Charles Howard transmitted this request to Slocum, the general replied that he had already ordered a division to the right. Therefore, had Howard somehow prompted Slocum to send a division east of Gettysburg, it must have been done through the message carried by Captain Hall at about 3:00 P.M. At 3:00 P.M., while the Eleventh Corps was still fighting north of Gettysburg, it might have made some sense for Slocum's First Division to have supported its right by coming onto the field from the east. After 4:00 P.M., when all troops available were on Cemetery Hill, such a movement would not have been reasonable.[20]

It was sometime before 4:00 P.M., therefore, that Slocum himself was approaching Gettysburg followed first by Williams's division and then by Geary's. Although a short march, it was a hard one. Sgt. Henry H. Tallman of the 66th Ohio wrote, "It was a hot day. The sun was hot. The ground was hot. The breezes that fanned our brow was hot, and the men panted like dogs on the chase and sweat and sweltered through clouds of dust." Men who were overcome by the heat left their places in ranks to rest by the roadside. Soldiers of the 13th New Jersey Regiment saw four or five local women standing by the road waving their bonnets and aprons. The women inspired the men of the 13th to wave back, then to wave their hats, and finally to cheer and to move along toward the fight in a body without straggling. Gettysburg was in Union territory after all. On the other hand, the Ohioans yelled at fleeing men: "Oh, come back; we are going to have lots of fun," "What are you going away from the picnic for," "Come . . . back and we'll show you how to cock a cannon." This banter quieted when the Twelfth Corps men met wounded from the fight.[21]

Before reaching Rock Creek, Brig. Gen. Alpheus Williams received a message from Slocum, who was somewhere to the front. Slocum asked him to turn his division right at a crossroad that led to the Hanover Road so that he could seize a commanding position east of Gettysburg. Geary's division would continue on toward the town.[22]

Williams took a road that left the Baltimore Pike a half mile southeast of Rock Creek and zigzagged a mile and a half north to the Hanover Road about a half mile east of Benner's Hill. The high wooded mass of Wolf Hill separated Williams's route from Rock Creek and Culp's Hill to the west. Williams made no mention of having used civilian guides. Instead, he sent staff officers to scout the country ahead, and his two brigades trudged along behind them. Brig. Gen. Thomas H. Ruger's brigade, the 27th Indiana Regiment in its van, had the lead, and Col. Archibald L. McDougall's brigade followed.[23]

The road was narrow and unimproved, probably no more than a rutted track; the terrain was rough; and the day was hot. Williams pushed his men hard along the slippery trace, sometimes at the double-quick. As the 2d Massachusetts Regiment passed a small farmhouse, one of the few along the way, a "hard-featured" woman with a couple of children rushed down to the column and began shaking hands with the dust-covered Bay State soldiers. She seemed delighted to see them until the regimental colors appeared. She looked at the flag with some dismay and with disgust said, "Why, I thought you were Rebs." With that, she grabbed her children and hurried back to her house.[24]

When Williams, who was riding at some distance in front of the column, reached the Hanover (Bonaughtown) Road, he turned left on it toward Gettysburg. From the high ground at Brinkerhoff's Ridge, he saw Benner's Hill ahead and how it dominated the town from the east. He learned somehow that some enemy troops were already on the hill and, wrongly, that a large Rebel force was moving to occupy it.[25]

Williams hurried back to the head of the column and turned it left from the narrow road into a lane that ran to the west, probably a lane that went near the Rosenstiel house and passed through some woods on the north slope of Wolf Hill. Ruger's brigade, now commanded by Col. Silas Colgrove, deployed in these woods about 1,000 yards east of Benner's Hill, its right at the Hanover Road and its skirmishers to the front. McDougall's brigade drew up in column behind. Williams rode down to the west edge of the woods, dismounted, and went on foot to Benner's Run at the east base of the hill. There he and the men on his skirmish line could see horsemen on the hill, but he could see no signs of a large force there.[26]

Not wishing to delay, Williams ordered Ruger to seize the hill at once. McDougall's brigade would provide support. Williams also had two batteries nearby: Lt. Charles E. Winegar's New York battery and Battery B, 4th U.S. Artillery, commanded by Lt. Sylvanus T. Rugg. They were to pace the attack from on the Hanover Road and, if necessary, fire in support of the infantry advance.[27]

Ruger's brigade advanced on Benner's Hill at the double-quick and met no opposition. The main line reached Benner's Run, and the skirmish line climbed to within 300 yards of the crest. That was all. At this time, one of Slocum's staff officers galloped up with the news that the First and Eleventh corps had been driven from the town and that the Confederates might cut Williams off. He was to return the division to the Baltimore Pike. Without further ado, Williams halted the advance, and his two brigades retraced their steps to fields about a half mile northeast of the pike, where they spent the night. As his division settled in, Williams felt uneasy because, although he was supposed to be the Twelfth Corps commander, he knew nothing of the location of Geary's division. After learning that Geary's division had been posted near Little Round Top, making sure that all was secure, and talking with some local men who were concerned about what was happening on their farms, Williams rolled himself in his "india-rubber poncho and slept most splendidly until daylight."[28]

In his 4:00 P.M. message to Slocum carried by Major Howard, General Howard told the Twelfth Corps commander of the dire situation of the Federal forces at Gettysburg and asked that Slocum, himself, come to Cemetery Hill. Major Howard met the general on the Baltimore Pike about a mile from the town—perhaps at Powers Hill, where Slocum's headquarters would be throughout the battle. Although he had sent his divisions to the left and right, Slocum told the major that he did not wish to go to Cemetery Hill and take the responsibility for the fight.[29]

Slocum explained this reluctance a short while later to Lt. Col. Charles H. Morgan of Hancock's staff, whom he met on the field. He told Morgan that he had seen so many Eleventh Corps stragglers that he feared that Gettysburg was another Chancellorsville and thought it might be prudent for him to deploy his troops in order to check the rout. Apparently he had done this by placing Geary's Second Brigade in reserve along the pike and sending the remainder of Geary's division ahead to report to Howard or Hancock. Probably Morgan told Slocum the truth of the situation, and there was further discussion about his taking command of the forces on the field. As Morgan recalled it, Slocum objected to assuming this command because Hancock had been selected to do so and had become familiar with the position. Further, Slocum did not care to assume the command "which might make him responsible for a condition of affairs over which he had no control." Who in his right mind would? However, when Morgan told him that Hancock had orders to turn the command over to him on his arrival, Slocum continued on to Cemetery Hill.[30]

Major Howard, in a private letter written eight days later, wrote that Slocum's lack of support for General Howard demonstrated the fitness of his name, "slow come." In this observation, the major voiced the feelings of many of the Eleventh Corps' staff who believed that Slocum had let them down. General Howard himself expressed a less critical view when he wrote that Slocum, to his astonishment, declined to come up to Gettysburg to participate in the action, and only sent his troops late in the afternoon at my request. He explained the course he took by showing that it was contrary to the plan and purpose of General Meade to bring on the battle at Gettysburg, he having arranged for another defensive position at Pipe Clay Creek. I think he did wrong to delay, and was hardly justified under the circumstances, even by the written orders of General Meade; still in all his previous history and subsequent lengthy service by my side in the West and South he showed himself a patriot in spirit, a brave man, and an able commander.[31]

Abner Doubleday, who was also directly affected by Slocum's fence-sitting, made two practical observations. He thought that if Slocum had concerns about whether or not Meade wanted to fight at Gettysburg, he might have sent a "swift courier" to him for orders when it became apparent that the enemy was massing on the First and Eleventh corps. Apart from that, Doubleday thought that Slocum would have been correct in interfering because "the safety of his own corps might be seriously endangered by inaction. This and a regard to the general interest of the Army would have justified him in interfering to cover the retreat."[32]

Slocum's vacillation did not lead to great controversy. Yet it did not go unnoticed. As early as December 1864, Meade wrote to his wife that he had read an Englishman's account of the battle that discussed several things not made "very public" at that time, including "Slocum's hesitation about reinforcing Howard." That Slocum's conduct did not become a public issue is probably because Meade and Howard did not choose to press it. Certainly, the Slocum who hesitated to be a bold general on 1 July seemed a different man from the pugnacious corps commander who a day later voiced the defiant appeal, "Stay and fight it out."[33]

While Howard directed the left wing's struggle to stay alive and Slocum fretted his way toward Gettysburg, Maj. Gen. Winfield S. Hancock hurried to the field. Hancock, commander of the Second Corps, was a career soldier, mature in years and service. He was thirty-eight years old, a Pennsylvanian, and an 1844 graduate of West Point. He had served in the 6th Infantry at various troubled places in the United States and in Mexico, where he had been brevetted for gallantry. Hancock was a quartermaster and a captain when the war began. In short, his background was more typical of a man of rank in the contending armies than that of Howard and Slocum.

Hancock became a brigadier general on 23 September 1861, twenty days after Howard received his star. He served as a brigade commander with

Maj. Gen. Winfield S. Hancock (NA)

distinction on the Peninsula in 1862, where Maj. Gen. George B. McClellan had referred to him as "Hancock the Superb" in tribute to his leadership at the battle of Williamsburg. He succeeded to the command of the First Division, Second Corps, after Maj. Gen. Israel B. Richardson received a mortal wound at Antietam and received his second star on 29 November 1862, the date that General Howard reached the same grade. He did not receive a corps command until after Chancellorsville when Maj. Gen. Darius N. Couch resigned command of the Second Corps out of disgust with Hooker. In summary, Hancock was a splendid officer, and both Hancock and Howard were of the same grade and commanded corps. However, Howard ranked Hancock because of his earlier promotion to the grade of brigadier general.[34]

Unlike Howard, who was relatively young and who lacked depth of experience, Hancock was an officer whose maturity and self-assurance enabled him to feel secure in his assignment and to exercise his rank with zest and skill. He was genial, outgoing, and well versed in army profanity; he had the full confidence of his subordinates and of General Meade as well. He was a model major general and would be one of the very best corps commanders produced by both the Union and the Confederacy during the war.[35]

The Second Corps had a short march on 1 July, and when it reached its destination at Taneytown, Hancock rode over to army headquarters to see Meade. Meade briefed Hancock on the army's situation as he saw it and on his plans, including his intention to fight a defensive battle at Pipe Creek if warranted. Hancock then returned to his corps.

Meade learned that Reynolds had been wounded at about 1:00 P.M. and knew that he would have to decide soon whether to implement the Pipe Creek Circular or fight at Gettysburg. Not knowing the Gettysburg area or the situation there, and deeming it important that he remain for the time being at his headquarters at Taneytown, Meade asked Hancock to go to Gettysburg in his place. If Reynolds was incapacitated, Hancock would take command of the left wing; he knew Meade's views and could exercise authority on the field. Hancock pointed out that he was junior to Howard in rank and that it was of questionable legality for Meade to detail him to a temporary position over Howard. To this, Meade replied that he did not know Howard well, but he knew Hancock to be a man that he could trust in a crisis. Meade believed that the president and Maj. Gen. Henry W. Halleck had given him authority to take such measures in emergencies, and he would not be denied by abstract questions of legality. Butterfield wrote an order to Hancock, timed 1:10 P.M., giving him authority to go to

Gettysburg and, in the event of Reynolds's death, to take command of the left wing. He was also to advise Meade if the terrain at Gettysburg was more suitable for battle than that along Pipe Creek.[36]

Hancock and Lt. Col. Charles H. Morgan, escorted by aides and some signalmen, climbed into an ambulance and rattled away. He and Morgan studied maps and orders relating to the situation ahead for a time as they bumped along. Then, their study over, they left the ambulance and went by horseback for the rest of the way. After traveling for about five miles over the rough and winding Taneytown Road, Hancock's party met the ambulance bearing the body of the lamented Reynolds to the rear. This meeting removed all doubt about Reynolds's fate and thrust Hancock into the battle of Gettysburg.[37]

As Hancock neared Gettysburg, he found the road jammed with wagons of the Eleventh Corps and he ordered them to the rear. On reaching Cemetery Hill, Hancock saw Federal forces "retreating in disorder and confusion from the town, closely followed by the enemy." He had arrived as the Union troops were coming from the town. In contrast to the confusion elsewhere, Hancock saw Col. Orland Smith's brigade of von Steinwehr's division formed along the Taneytown Road facing the enemy and ready for what might come. Hancock rode along a section of Smith's line, made some complimentary remarks about its position, and asked to see the brigade commander. Colonel Smith and Hancock exchanged greetings. Hancock said, "My corps is on the way, but will not be here in time. This position should be held at all hazards. Now, Colonel, can you hold it?" Smith replied, "I think I can." Hancock persisted, "Will you hold it?," and Smith replied, "I will."

Then, according to Smith, Hancock met Howard near the crest of the hill where Howard had been working to rally the returning troops and put them into position. There followed a conversation that later engendered one of Gettysburg's teapot-sized tempests. As Hancock recalled it, he told Howard that he had been sent by General Meade to take command of the forces present and asked Howard if he wished to see his credentials. Howard did not wish to, and Hancock did not show them to him.[38]

In his published accounts in later years, Hancock made no attempt to present this conversation in detail, but Howard did. Howard wrote that after some greetings "in his usual frank and cordial manner," Hancock said, "General Meade has sent me to represent him on the field." To this, Howard wrote that he replied, "All right, Hancock. This is no time for talking. You take the left of the pike and I will arrange those troops to the right." Then, according to Howard, Hancock "moved off in his peculiar gallant style" to put troops into position. At this time, Hancock sent the Iron Brigade to the right, without consulting Howard, but Howard wrote that he made no objection because it was just the thing to do.[39]

Hancock read Howard's account and took issue with it. He insisted that he had been in full command and not just a representative of General Meade as Howard suggested. After his arrival, Howard gave orders to only the Eleventh Corps.[40]

After their opening conversation, the generals went about their business and there was no conflict between them. Brig. Gen. Gouverneur K. Warren, Meade's chief engineer, also appeared at about this time and with his expertise assisted Hancock. Since Doubleday and Howard and their commanders and staffs were setting up the defenses when Hancock arrived, Hancock was able to give his attention to broader needs. One of the first of these was Culp's Hill, which seemed to be threatened by Confederates who had appeared south of the town. He took care of its security, as discussed above, in a temporary way and over Doubleday's objection by sending the Iron Brigade to its west slope. Then he sent Geary's division, which had just come from Two Taverns, to hold a portion of the ridge off to the left.[41]

After going over the ground with Warren, Hancock decided that "if that position could be held until night, it would be the best place for the army to fight on if the army was attacked." Hancock sent his aide, Maj. William G. Mitchell, back to Meade to tell him that he would hold the ground until night so that he could come forward and decide whether or not to fight there himself. After matters had been arranged to his satisfaction and he felt secure, Hancock sent another message back to Meade by Capt. Isaac B. Parker, another aide, with more detailed information about the field. He also ordered Brig. Gen. John Gibbon, acting commander of his own Second Corps, which was approaching over the Taneytown Road, to halt the corps two or three miles from Gettysburg to cover the Gettysburg position's rear.[42]

Howard and Doubleday had posted the retreating Federal infantry generally as Howard had prescribed. Ames's division and some of von Steinwehr's took position east of the Baltimore Pike, while Schurz's division and Smith's brigade manned walls and fences between the pike and the Taneytown Road. Hancock sent the Iron Brigade to the west slope of Culp's Hill, where Cutler's brigade joined it next day. Robinson's and Doubleday's divisions supported the left of the Eleventh Corps on Cemetery Hill and the north end of Cemetery Ridge. Lieutenant Stewart's battery must have been one of the last units to emerge from the town, and Hancock posted it near the gate of the cemetery. In Hancock-fashion, he told Stewart where to place his guns, said that the enemy would attempt to take his position, and stated that Stewart should remain there until he was relieved by Hancock's oral or written order and should take orders from no one else. There was a lot of bombast in this, of course. It is unlikely that Hancock gave Stewart's battery another thought after a few minutes passed without a Confederate attack.[43]

Carl Schurz met Hancock as he rode up the slope of Cemetery Hill from the town, and after the troops were sorted out and in position, the two sat on a wall and looked to the north and west for the Confederate attack that they feared would come. Through their binoculars they could see Confederate units moving about, but they could not discern their intentions. Schurz was nervous, but it was soothing to his pride to see that Hancock seemed nervous too. Hancock was optimistic about their being able to hold the hill until the Twelfth Corps should arrive. Their optimism about the Twelfth Corps might have been misplaced, but as time passed and the Confederates seemed not to be preparing to attack, both generals breathed more easily.[44]

In pondering Hancock's presence on the field on 1 July, Schurz thought it a fortunate thing. He believed that Hancock's arrival gave the troops new inspiration: "They all knew him by fame, and his stalwart figure, his proud mien, and his superb soldierly bearing seemed to verify all the things that fame had told about him. His mere presence was a reinforcement, and everybody on the field felt stronger for his being there." Doubleday agreed—in 1890, after he had mellowed, if not before. He still had qualms about the legality of Hancock's succeeding Howard but wrote, "He was our good genius, for he at once brought order out of confusion and made such admirable dispositions that he secured the ridge and held it."[45]

Slocum finally appeared on Cemetery Hill about 7:00 P.M. Hancock, who believed that his work at Gettysburg was over, turned command of forces on the field over to Slocum and rode back to Taneytown to report to Meade. There he learned that Meade had heeded his dispatches and other information received from the field and had already ordered the Army of the Potomac to Gettysburg. It had been a memorable six hours for Hancock, and he had acquitted himself superbly.[46]

Slocum reached Cemetery Hill at the same time as Howard's copy of the order appointing Hancock to the temporary command of the left wing. Howard was crestfallen when he read the order. He rode to Slocum and to Hancock and turned over the command to Slocum that he thought he had held since noon. Then, without delay, he sent a letter to Meade stating that he had received the order relating to Hancock at 7:00 P.M. and that he had turned the command over to Slocum, who had arrived at the same time. He went on to say that he had commanded the First and Eleventh corps from about 11:00 A.M. to 4:00 P.M., when Hancock assisted him in carrying out orders he had already issued, as well as any of Meade's commanders could have done. He closed by saying that the order had "mortified" and "disgraced" him and asked if Meade had disapproved of his conduct.[47]

At the end of the day, Howard and some other generals gathered at the gatehouse of the cemetery. It was an unusual structure consisting of two two-story red brick buildings, one on each side of the cemetery's entrance road, joined at the top to create a rather handsome arch. Each of the two buildings had a room up and down, and the one on the town side had a cellar and probably a kitchen. The gatehouse provided an office for the cemetery's caretaker. That worthy man, Peter Thorn, had entered the Union army and was then at Harpers Ferry; his wife, Catherine Elizabeth Thorn, a capable woman of German birth, served as the caretaker in his absence. Her father lived with her.[48]

Catherine Thorn had had an eventful day. In addition to her regular chores, she had baked six loaves of bread, which she gave later to soldiers, and she and her family had pumped water for them from her well. Union artillery had taken position near her gatehouse, and one battery, Wiedrich's no doubt, had fired toward "Coon (Kuhn) Town" and the "Poor Farm." Then an officer came and asked for a man to identify the roads for him. Since there was only her father, who was too old to go, she went with the officer herself to viewing points in the nearby fields. Some soldiers protested against her exposing herself to enemy fire, but she said that it did not matter. In appreciation of her sangfroid, the soldiers "gave three cheers and the band played a little piece." She told the officers what they wanted to know, and one escorted her back to her gatehouse, she walking on the opposite side of a horse from the enemy. After entering the gatehouse, she went to an upstairs room to look from the window to see what was happening around her. As she reached the room, a "shell" of some sort entered the window, "then jumped a little, then went through the ceiling." The shell and its shenanigans so frightened her that she did not go up there again that day.[49]

Soon after, a soldier asked her to make supper for General Howard. This created a dilemma for she had no bread and could only make some "cakes." The soldier said that they were good enough for wartime, and so she tried to oblige. First she walked down Baltimore Street to the nearby Myers house to borrow some meat for the meal. To her distress, she found that the house, which was practically on Schurz's line, was full of wounded, six of whom did not move. This was enough for her, and she returned to the gatehouse without the meat. In the meantime, the gatehouse had begun to fill with wounded soldiers too, and some were lying on her kitchen floor.[50]

The cemetery gatehouse, no common hostelry, had some distinguished visitors that evening. Howard, Slocum, and Sickles came to eat. In spite of there being wounded men in her kitchen, Mrs. Thorn served them "two good sized dough cakes," three pieces of meat, and coffee. Howard, who had not eaten since morning, was famished and never forgot the meal served to him by Mrs. Thorn.[51]

When the generals started to leave, she asked them if she should stay in the house. Howard, who must have been pretty tired by this time, rubbed his forehead and said, "Leave the house? Leave the house? Comrades, I say stay." But he told her to pack up her valuables and in two hours someone would help her carry them to the cellar. They thought that the fighting would begin about daybreak. She did as she was told, and when the soldier came to help her, he told her that Howard said, "When I give you the order to leave the house don't study about it but go right away." Mrs. Thorn busied herself until about 4:00 A.M. Then she went to her cellar and refuge and found seventeen people already there. Another day, like none that she had experienced before, was about to break on Cemetery Hill.[52]

8
GETTING READY FOR THE FIGHT

Cemetery Hill abounded with Union generals during the closing hours of 1 July, a sign that there were a great many men of lower rank nearby. Maj. Gen. Henry W. Slocum, now acting commander of the Federal forces on the field, was at the gatehouse, along with the commanders of the Eleventh and Third corps—Howard, Sickles, and others with stars. Warren was present, and Doubleday, who still commanded the First Corps, if not there, must have been at his headquarters not far away.

Although these generals and their staffs made an imposing force in their own right, it was the strength at their command that really counted. The Army of the Potomac had assembled rapidly; four of its seven infantry corps plus Buford's division of cavalry were on or very near the field, while the Second and Fifth corps were not far away and would be up in the early morning. Only the large Sixth Corps and the rest of the cavalry were beyond the immediate area. The Sixth Corps had been in Manchester, Maryland, on the right of the army, earlier that evening, but General Meade had ordered it to Gettysburg also, and while the generals talked, it was marching toward the town. In retrospect, Brig. Gen. Henry J. Hunt observed that "the rapidity with which the army assembled was creditable to it and its commander. The heat was oppressive, and the long marches, especially the night marches, were strenuous and caused much straggling."[1]

General Meade, who had effected this concentration, arrived at the cemetery gatehouse about midnight. He and an entourage guided by Capt. William H. Paine, an engineer, had left Taneytown, Maryland, about

10:00 P.M. and had pressed ahead so rapidly over the Taneytown Road that some of the staff and the party's civilian guide could not keep up. At times, the riders took to the fields beside the road in order to avoid Second Corps units and batteries of the Artillery Reserve that were moving on it. After an hour's wild ride, Meade and his party halted briefly at the headquarters of the Second Corps, which was located then just south of Round Top. Meade spoke briefly with Brig. Gen. John Gibbon, who commanded it in Hancock's absence, instructing him to bring the corps forward as soon as it was light. Meade rode on toward Cemetery Hill, entered the cemetery from the Taneytown Road, and followed one of its avenues to the gatehouse.[2]

General Howard greeted Meade as the commander climbed stiffly from his horse. Howard lost no time in asking for Meade's approval of the way in which he had conducted the battle of 1 July. Meade spoke in a kindly way to his apprehensive young general and lightened his heart by assuring him "that he imputed no blame." For Howard, this mild endorsement was as satisfying "as positive praise from some other commanders." Meade and the happier Howard then entered the gatehouse to confer with the other generals there.[3]

The generals had discussed their situation prior to Meade's arrival, including Meade's instructions in the Pipe Creek Circular, which Howard had not seen. General Schurz remembered the scene—six or seven generals, most of them sitting on the floor in a room lit by a solitary candle, who agreed that the battle ought to be fought on the ground they occupied. When Meade arrived, therefore, they were able to brief him on the day's fight, on Gettysburg's terrain, and on the condition of the units on the field. As Howard recalled it, he told Meade, "I am confident we can hold this position." He remembered Slocum as having been equally confident, saying, "It is good for defense," and Sickles echoing, "It is a good place to fight from, general!" To these assurances, Meade answered, "I am glad to hear you say so, gentlemen, for it is too late to leave it."[4]

Meade's response to his generals indicated that his thinking had evolved with the changing military situation. Having relieved the threat to Harrisburg, he had contemplated taking a defensive position along Pipe Creek. Then, as the day wore on, his attention focused increasingly on Gettysburg. At 1:10 P.M., after hearing of the fighting there and the rumors of Reynolds's death, he had sent Hancock to the field. More information filtered back to him during the afternoon that convinced him of the Confederate concentration there and that he should move his forces to meet it. By the time he heard from Hancock, the die had been cast. At 5:45,

Maj. Gen. George G. Meade (NA)

he approved Sickles's moving the Third Corps to Gettysburg instead of to Pipe Creek. At 6:00, Meade wrote Hancock and Doubleday, "It seems to me we have so concentrated that a battle at Gettysburg is now forced on us, and that, if we get up all our people, and attack with our whole force to-morrow, we ought to defeat the force the enemy has." At the same time, he informed Halleck that he hoped all of his corps but the Sixth were on the field and that it was moving up. He saw no other course but to "hazard a general battle"; he was committed to a major confrontation at Gettysburg.[5]

After their conversation with Meade, Slocum and Sickles left Cemetery Hill for their respective headquarters. Meade walked across the pike to East Cemetery Hill and passed among the batteries there to look at nearby Union positions and at the enemy's deployment as marked by campfires to the north and west. Then he returned to the gatehouse, and, with Generals Hunt and Howard and Captain Paine, he rode west and south along Cemetery Ridge. As the party picked its way behind the lines of sleeping soldiers, the talented Captain Paine sketched the landscape as he could see it in the dim light so that by the time they reached Little Round Top, Paine had a reasonably good sketch of Cemetery Ridge. Dawn was breaking by this time, and the party of officers rode back to Cemetery Hill. From Cemetery Hill, Meade, Hunt, and Paine rode over the Culp's Hill area and as far southeast along the Baltimore Pike as Rock Creek. When his reconnaissance was over, Meade designated the various corps sectors by markings on the sketch, and Paine hurried off to make multiple copies of his map for distribution to the corps commanders.[6]

When Meade passed along Baltimore Pike near Powers Hill, Pvt. David Mouat of the 29th Pennsylvania Infantry, whose regiment was posted there with Kane's brigade, heard that Meade was nearby. Mouat walked to the pike to have a look at the commanding general and found him there with General Geary. He saw Meade gesture in the direction of the 29th and heard him ask Geary what unit it was. On being told, Meade commented, "It is a very small one but order them up[.] We will want every man today."[7]

Whitelaw Reid, the correspondent known as "Agate," saw Meade's party during its visit to Culp's Hill and described it to his readers: "Two or three general officers, with a retinue of staff and orderlies, come galloping by. Foremost is the spare and somewhat stooped form of the Commanding General. He is not cheered, indeed is scarcely recognized. He is an approved corps General, but he has not yet vindicated his right to command the Army of the Potomac. By his side is the calm, honest, manly face of General Oliver O. Howard. An empty sleeve is pinned to his shoulder— memento of a hard fought battle before."[8]

Meade appeared later in the morning on Cemetery Hill at Schurz's position. He was on horseback, of course, and accompanied by only one staff officer and an orderly. His spectacles gave him a "magisterial look," and the turned-down brim of his hat shaded his haggard face, which appeared careworn and tired from a lack of sleep. To Schurz, there was nothing about his appearance or his conduct—no smiles or sympathetic words, nothing theatrical or posed—that might have warmed the soldiers' hearts. He was simple, cold, and businesslike and much absorbed with his own problems. Some nearby officers and soldiers gathered around him, looked at him, and then turned away, "not enthusiastic, but clearly satisfied."[9]

Meade studied the terrain and the positions of the two forces, and then he nodded as if in approval of what he saw. Schurz rode to him, and they exchanged greetings. Schurz asked how many men were up, and Meade replied, "In the course of the day I expect to have about 95,000—enough, I guess, for this business." Then, after another sweeping glance over the field, he said quietly, as if to convince himself, "Well, we may as well fight it out here just as well as anywhere else."[10]

While Meade toured the field, someone on his staff selected a small, two-room house for his headquarters. It stands beside the Taneytown Road behind Cemetery Ridge about 900 yards south-southwest of the cemetery gatehouse, and it was the home of Lydia Leister, a widow. It was a humble place, but it had a well and was as convenient to most points within the Union position as could be found. Unfortunately, it would be particularly vulnerable to Confederate shot and shell fired too high at targets on Cemetery Ridge.

At about daybreak, possibly between his visits to the Union left with Meade and before going to Culp's Hill, General Hunt was resting at the foot of a tree with Meade's staff in the cemetery when Slocum appeared to talk with Meade. Slocum was concerned about a gap in the line on the right through which the enemy might attack. Hunt did not specify the exact location of this gap—it must have been along Rock Creek in the open area near Spangler's Spring. On hearing Slocum speak, Brig. Gen. Seth Williams, Meade's adjutant general, who was resting near Hunt, stood and walked over to hear what he had to say. Meade asked Williams of Hunt's whereabouts, and Williams replied that Hunt was lying beneath a nearby tree. Meade snorted, "It is no time to sleep now," and Hunt responded, "I am not asleep, and heard all that you and Gen. Slocum said." Meade replied, "Very well, you must attend to this as it is your affair. See that the line is made good with artillery until the infantry is in position."

Hunt complied at once. He made sure that the batteries of the Twelfth Corps were positioned so that they could cover the gap and borrowed two six-gun batteries from the Eleventh Corps to help out. Major Osborn posted the Eleventh Corps guns near the pike and opposite the gap, and they remained there until the infantry of Geary's division took position on the hill. Hindsight tells us that there was no immediate threat and that

Brig. Gen. Henry J. Hunt (WLM)

the Federal commanders must have been nervous that morning. To Hunt, the event was memorable in that it signified to him that Meade expected him to be the commander of the artillery of the Army of the Potomac and not just the artillery adviser on its staff.[11]

Geary's division shifted at about daybreak from its night position on the Union left to Culp's Hill. This hill was a mass of high, rocky ground washed by Rock Creek on the east and bounded by the Baltimore Pike on the southwest. It had two peaks; the highest, 180 feet above Rock Creek, was about 800 yards southeast of Cemetery Hill and was connected to it by a sagging crest line that included Stevens's Knoll. The lower peak was 400 yards south of the taller summit and was separated from it by a narrow saddle that notched the hill from east to west. The lower peak rose about eighty feet above the creek. The south end of the hill mass was marked by a marshy meadow or swale that contained Spangler's Spring and a stream that drained to Rock Creek. It was about 850 yards from the hill's highest peak to the meadow at Spangler's Spring. The western and southern slopes from both peaks were gentle, and the northern slope of the higher peak and the eastern slope of most of the hill were steep, rocky, and wooded.

The lower hill, which would be the arena of much action, had two important features. One was a stone wall that originated at Rock Creek, ran west along the edge of the swale, and then turned northwest across the hill to the saddle. The other was a cleared field of about seven acres on the northwest slope that was surrounded by trees. This field is now called "Pardee Field."

The meadow or swale at Spangler's Spring was about 100 yards wide. The spring was about twenty-five yards from the foot of the hill and about fifty yards west of the end of the works. It was about 150 yards west of the creek and drained into a little stream that ran the length of the meadow east to the creek. Local folks had made a basin at the spring and walled it with stone so that it served a small picnic area at the site. To the south of the meadow was a low east-west ridge that connected the pike with the creek. This ridge ended at the creek in a grove, McAllister's Woods, that covered a large outcropping of granite boulders. This outcrop dominated the creekbed and formed the base of a strong bastion that would anchor the Union right. South of McAllister's Woods was a large marshy area that contained much of the pond that provided a reservoir for McAllister's Mill. The mill was on the west side of the creek about 600 yards south of Spangler's Spring.[12]

Geary's division had three brigades commanded by Col. Charles Candy, Brig. Gen. Thomas L. Kane, and Brig. Gen. George S. Greene. Geary posted his brigades in two lines. Greene's brigade, the Third, formed the left wing of the forward line with its left at the top of the higher hill near the right of Wadsworth's division. Greene's line extended along the hill's south crest about 400 yards to the saddle between the higher and lower summits. Kane's left began there, and the brigade front, following the conformation of the crest, bent left and up the north slope of the lower hill to its top. Candy's brigade, the First, massed on the reverse slope of the upper hill and, behind Greene's right, formed "double column on center." As soon as they were in position, Geary's men began to strengthen their line by erecting a breastworks of earth, logs, and rocks.[13]

The construction of field fortifications had not yet become a standard practice within all units of the Army of the Potomac at this stage of the

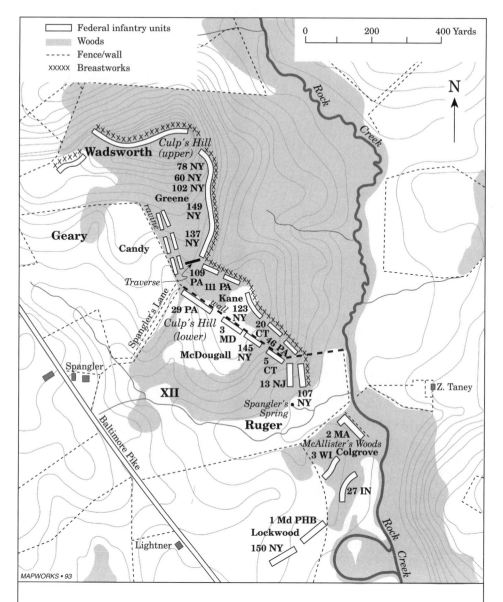

Map 8.1. Culp's Hill Defenses, Afternoon, 2 July

1. The Twelfth Corps has taken position and erected breastworks. Wadsworth's division occupies the west slope of the hill facing north.

2. Geary's division occupies the main hill. Greene's brigade mans the south slope of the hill from the peak to the saddle. It is one line.

3. Candy's brigade is in reserve in Greene's rear, probably in the ravine. Kane's brigade is on the north slope of the lower hill on Greene's right. Kane's support line is probably behind the stone wall.

4. Ruger's (Williams's) division occupies the south slope of the lower hill and McAllister's Woods. McDougall's brigade and two regiments of Colgrove's (Ruger's) brigade are on the lower hill; their front line is in the works, the support line behind the stone wall.

5. Three regiments of Colgrove's (Ruger's) brigade occupy McAllister's Woods. Lockwood's two regiments are to the right rear.

war. Although units took advantage of walls and fences when they were available, the troops of neither the Second nor Third corps, for instance, constructed defensive works when they took up their assigned positions on the center and left at Gettysburg. Greene's brigade had used breastworks only once before—at Chancellorsville. It was a matter of good fortune, therefore, that someone ordered the construction of works on the Culp's Hill line. After they had proved their worth, several officers were given credit for them, especially Generals Slocum, Williams, and Greene. Greene received credit for those in front of his brigade, and probably those of the division as well, by Capt. Lewis R. Stegman, commander of the 102d New York. Lt. George K. Collins of the 149th New York wrote that after Geary's division reached Culp's Hill, Geary conferred with his brigade commanders and gave them the option of entrenching or not. Geary said that he was opposed to doing so because he believed that it unfitted men for fighting without them. Greene replied that the saving of lives was more important than such theories and that his men would build them if they had time to do so. This story received some support from Capt. Charles P. Horton, Greene's adjutant, who wrote that there were no orders to entrench but that permission to do so was given by Geary to his brigade commanders.[14]

Nevertheless, the idea of entrenching on Culp's Hill did not originate wholly with the Twelfth Corps. As the Iron Brigade took position on its west crest on the previous night, the 6th Wisconsin's wagon joined it with a dozen spades and shovels. As soon as the regiment took its place near the right of the brigade line (toward the top of the hill), Lt. Col. Rufus R. Dawes told it to entrench and the regiment erected the first works on that slope. The 7th Indiana extended the 6th's works to the top of the hill after it arrived later in the evening. By the following morning Wadsworth's troops had constructed "a pretty good line of breastworks," and according to Dawes, the Twelfth Corps continued those of the 7th Indiana to the right.[15]

Fortunately for the Union troops on the hill, there was material for the works at hand. Rocks and trees abounded as supplements to the shallow earth. There was also some cordwood there already cut and ready for use. Capt. Jesse H. Jones of the 60th New York recalled that "right and left the men felled the trees and blocked them up into a close log fence. Piles of cordwood near by were forthwith appropriated. The sticks set on end and leaning against the outer face of the logs, made excellent battening." They incorporated the boulders already there when possible and topped the barricade with a head log. They blocked the log up so that it would protect the

Brig. Gen. James S. Wadsworth (WLM)

soldiers' heads while allowing them to fire from the slit between the log and the body of the works. Only the regiments' pioneers carried entrenching tools then, and Capt. Joseph Moore of the 147th Pennsylvania Regiment lamented that "as usual in the hasty preparations for defense, the pioneer corps was not at hand, and bayonets, tin pans, tin cups etc. were improvised as implements in the construction of earthworks." Yet the men worked with a will, and in three or four hours the job was done. Geary's men who were not on the skirmish line rested behind their handiwork and waited for what would befall them. Many would call the earthworks "rifle pits" or simply "pits." [16]

General Greene described his position on the taller peak: "Our position and the front were covered with a heavy growth of timber, free from undergrowth, with large ledges of rock projecting above the surface. These rocks and trees offered good cover for marksmen. The surface was very steep on our left, diminishing to a gentle slope on our right. The Second

Brigade was on our right, thrown forward at a right angle to conform with the crest of the hill."[17]

At 5:00 A.M., as Geary's division occupied the higher peak of Culp's Hill fronting east, General Williams was with his own division east of Wolf Hill. Williams had awakened at daybreak and had put his division "in better order than the dark permitted" on the previous evening. He then borrowed some coffee from an orderly and made "an excellent breakfast" of it and a piece of hardtack. It was still early when General Slocum visited him in order to give him some general directions about the position that the corps was to occupy.[18]

Slocum's orders for Williams were to return the First Division to the Hanover Road area. That division, with Brig. Gen. Thomas H. Ruger in temporary command and with Ruger's brigade in the lead, hurried back toward the Hanover Road. There it deployed in line of battle facing north, threw a long line of skirmishers forward and to the left, and engaged skirmishers of the Stonewall Brigade. Soon after, the Fifth Corps arrived from the east over the Hanover Road and took position on Ruger's right.[19]

The Fifth Corps, which had marched from Frederick, Maryland, to the Hanover, Pennsylvania, area via Liberty and Union Mills, had spent a few hours in rest along the Hanover Road east of Bonaughtown and had resumed its march at daybreak. It was only three miles from Bonaughtown to Brinkerhoff's Ridge, east of Gettysburg, and Barnes's division, which led the corps, should have reached the fields off the Twelfth Corps right by 6:00 A.M. At the time of Barnes's arrival, Twelfth Corps skirmishers, including those of the 27th Indiana, the 2d Massachusetts, and the 3d Wisconsin regiments, were already exchanging fire with the Virginians who guarded the Confederate left. Ayres's and Barnes's divisions of the Fifth Corps deployed to join the fight, with Ayres on the left in contact with the Twelfth Corps and Barnes on the right. The Fifth Corps deployed south of the Hanover Road and facing it, and its skirmishers, including men from the 9th and 18th Massachusetts regiments and the 2d and 10th U.S. Infantry regiments, moved to the front. The 18th Massachusetts supported Capt. Frank C. Gibbs's Ohio battery, which had taken position in a wheat field 100 yards in front of the main line.[20]

The skirmish firing beyond Brinkerhoff's Ridge east of Gettysburg was an overture without an opera. After a short while, at 8:00 A.M., Slocum ordered Williams to withdraw his division from the Hanover Road and place it to the right of Geary's division on Culp's Hill. General Sykes received similar orders: he was to march the three divisions of his Fifth Corps from Hanover Road and mass them west of the Baltimore Pike behind the Union right, where they would constitute the army's reserve. Although these divisions moved from the Hanover Road, the Union forces did not abandon it. The 27th Indiana Regiment remained for a short while as a rear guard for Ruger's withdrawal. The burden of maintaining a picket line until the cavalry arrived fell to the 9th Massachusetts Infantry Regiment of Barnes's division, Fifth Corps. More of it later.[21]

We do not know whether or not Meade asked that the three divisions of Sykes's corps be deployed along the Hanover Road early on 2 July or if it was Slocum's idea. However, their presence in that area was symptomatic of Meade's concern for the security of the right flank of his army early on 2 July and of the Baltimore Pike behind it. Meade did not address the matter later, but Hancock testified that Meade believed that the enemy would make a formidable attack there, a belief that might have been strengthened by Slocum's opinion that artillery was needed to plug the early morning gap near Rock Creek.[22]

The Baltimore Pike was the Army of the Potomac's lifeline to its wagon trains and the railhead at Westminster twenty miles to the southeast. Should Lee somehow be able to turn Meade's army's right and seize the Baltimore Pike, the consequences could be dire indeed. Not only might Lee pry Meade from his Gettysburg position, but Meade would have to pull back over the Taneytown and Emmitsburg roads, both of which were in poor condition and led to the left of the Pipe Creek line and Westminster. Furthermore, if the Confederates could seize the Baltimore Pike, they would separate Meade's force at Gettysburg from the Sixth Corps, which, even then, was approaching over that very road. Since Meade and most other officers of rank in the Army of the Potomac believed that the Army of Northern Virginia was comparable in size to their own forces if not larger, they would consider the loss of the services of the 13,000 officers and men of that corps, even for a few hours, to be a serious matter indeed.

Meade also manifested concern about his right during the early morning hours of 2 July in other ways. When the Second Corps arrived behind the Union center by way of the Taneytown Road, it did not take its well-known position on Cemetery Ridge immediately. Instead, Meade ordered General Gibbon to mass it along the Taneytown Road fronting east toward Culp's Hill as if in support of the Twelfth Corps, and it remained there about an hour before moving on to Cemetery Ridge.[23]

After a while, when an early Confederate assault did not come, Meade contemplated the possibility of launching an attack from his right against the Confederates east of Gettysburg. The attack would be made by the

Twelfth and Fifth corps, which were already available, and by the Sixth Corps, which would be coming in from the right rear and be in a position to help out. To this end, in a message sent at 9:30 A.M., Meade asked Slocum to examine the ground in his front and give him his opinion of the advisability of making an attack from that quarter. A half hour later he ordered Slocum to prepare to make an attack on his front with the Twelfth Corps, supported by the Fifth. Meade would order the attack as soon as the Sixth Corps arrived and was able to cooperate in the proposed assault. At the same time, Meade sent Warren over to consult with Slocum about the attack. Slocum replied without delay that he had already made such an examination, and both he and Warren advised Meade that such an attack would not be practicable. Further, Slocum told Meade that the ground held by the Confederates in his front did not possess any advantages for them. As it turned out, of course, the attack could not have been made anyhow—the Sixth Corps was still far from Gettysburg and would not arrive until late that afternoon.[24]

Slocum did not say how the examination of the ground in his front was made. Perhaps he studied it from Culp's Hill, perhaps someone from his or Warren's staff actually went into the area, at least to the extent that the Confederate skirmishers would have allowed. However, Slocum did have one reconnaissance made that day, an amateurish effort that strains credulity.

A remnant battalion of the 10th Maine Regiment, three companies of 170 officers and men, served as provost guard for the Twelfth Corps. It provided sentries for corps headquarters, guards for prisoners, and men to do a myriad of other chores. At some time during the morning of 2 July, General Slocum asked Capt. John D. Beardsley, the battalion's commander, for "six volunteers for dangerous duty." They would not be armed but would carry canteens and haversacks. Their job was to go out to the right of the army, to the east and northeast, and find the enemy. Their main task was "to learn if the enemy was attempting to flank the right of Meade's army." In addition, they were to record the locations of houses and springs they saw and to get the residents' names for use on a map being made of the field. If captured, they were to say that they were hunting food and water.

The Maine volunteers went off in two or three parties, through the corps skirmish line and into the woods that covered Wolf Hill. In due course, they met some Confederates. First Sgt. James F. Tarr's party found some Rebels at some farm buildings. It was apparent that the Rebels had seen them, so the Maine men feigned ignorance of being seen until they could make a dash for it. They ran, the Confederates fired at them but missed, and the Maine men escaped capture.

In the meantime, two others, Pvt. Henry F. Cole and Pvt. Sidney W. Fletcher, had a similar experience. With the help of a civilian, they found some Confederate pickets near a barn, drank from a spring nearby, and returned to the Union lines. No more. Two others, 1st Sgt. H. Henry Kallock and Sgt. Charles R. Anderson, also visited a farmyard near the Hanover Road, which they thought to be that of E. Deardorff. They believed that Ruger's men had been there that morning and that Sergeant Tarr had been there too. Although Confederates fired at them, they also got away.[25]

All of the Maine men returned unscathed and received General Slocum's thanks. Their reconnaissance must have had little value. They found no signs of a turning movement for none was being made, and they were beyond the zone of that made later in the day. Nor did they see the Union troops on the skirmish line in the area they patrolled. In hindsight, this looks like a foolish exercise conceived by someone with more imagination than sense. Yet General Sickles might have profited by ordering one no better than it in front of the Union left that very afternoon.

When it became apparent that an attack could not be made from his right, and when Slocum informed him that the ground there held no "particular advantages" for the enemy, General Meade turned his attention to other matters. The Twelfth Corps sector would soon be secure, but there had been lively skirmishing in front of the Union center, and he had learned that General Sickles had not placed his corps in its designated position. Clearly there was need for his attention on those fronts. At 3:00 P.M., Meade dictated a dispatch to General Halleck in Washington in which he reviewed the day's events. He announced that his army was in a strong position and had awaited the enemy's attack. The Sixth Corps was just arriving on the field, very tired after eighteen hours of marching. In fact, the whole army was fatigued after its exertions to reach Gettysburg. He was still in doubt as to the enemy's position and intentions, but he was expecting battle and had sent his trains to the rear. If he was not attacked and could justify making an attack himself, he would make one. Should he find such an attack to be too risky and discover that the enemy was trying to get between the Army of the Potomac and Washington, he would then fall back on his supplies at Westminster—the Pipe Creek line. Therefore, though Meade intended to fight at Gettysburg, he still thought it possible that under certain circumstances he might find it necessary to fight elsewhere.[26]

Meade's indecision that morning was mirrored by that of General Lee. Although Meade expected an attack and hoped to fight a defensive battle, Lee knew that he had to maintain the initiative either through maneuver or assault. Since maneuver seemed out of the question, he had to attack. His hopes for an early morning assault had died for, of his fresh troops, only Johnson's division was in position, but Ewell did not want to make the main attack from his front. Anderson's division of Hill's corps, as it turned out, would not be in position on Seminary Ridge until nearly noon, and Longstreet's two divisions, Hood's and McLaws's, were behind Anderson. Nevertheless, Lee had ordered a reconnaissance of the Union left at daybreak and had developed a tentative plan of attack against that flank to be aided by an attack against the right.[27]

Like Meade, Lee seemed interested in launching some sort of an attack east of Gettysburg. Perhaps he sensed that a successful attack there would expose the enemy's jugular, though he could hardly have known that the Baltimore Pike led to Meade's principal supply point. It seems likely that he was more interested in finding an alternative to an attack against Cemetery Ridge. Lee's talks with Ewell had raised questions, and the news that Culp's Hill had been occupied by Union forces before Ewell could seize it must have been a disappointment to him. Therefore, at about sunrise, when Capt. Samuel R. Johnston, his engineer, rode off to examine the ground in front of the Union left, Lee sent Maj. Charles S. Venable of his staff to ask Ewell once again "what he thought of the advantages of an attack on the enemy from his position." Lee told Venable that the question was whether he "should move all the troops around on the right and attack on that side."[28]

Ewell welcomed Venable; probably he felt the need to have a daylight look at the enemy's positions. In answer to Venable's question, Ewell "made" Venable ride from point to point along his lines. They could see that the enemy had many guns on Cemetery Hill and that the Union infantry had recovered from the shock of the previous day and seemed ready to fight. The tour must have taken much longer than Venable wished. Perhaps the extended survey was an admission that Ewell himself had no firm opinion on what course of action he should recommend. At any rate, before the two had finished their reconnaissance, General Lee would appear on the scene.[29]

Before Venable's arrival, Ewell, who had been up all night and was ready to attack, had become impatient. He had sent Major Brown to see General Lee. Johnson's division and Hays's and Hoke's brigades of Early's division were ready to advance at the expected sound of Longstreet's guns, but it was nearly an hour after sunrise and even a longer time after daybreak and they had heard nothing. Ewell wanted Lee to know that his men were ready and waiting and, without doubt, to learn the cause of the delay. When Brown reached Lee's headquarters, he found that the general had gone to see Longstreet. Brown rode after him. By this time Longstreet's corps had moved from its bivouac near Marsh Creek and was gathering in the fields between Lee's headquarters and Herr Ridge. Lee pointed to Hood's division, which was nearby, as evidence that there would be considerable delay and repeated to Brown his former orders about Ewell's coordinating his movements with Longstreet's. That would have to do for the time being.[30]

Lee's wishes were clear enough, but Longstreet was not yet acting on them. He was to form on Anderson's right, but Anderson was still moving into position so Longstreet bided his time, possibly hoping for a change in orders and awaiting the arrival of Law's brigade of Hood's division, which had not yet reached the field. Whether Lee suffered Longstreet's inactivity or whether there was a misunderstanding at this critical hour can never be known. Perhaps Lee believed that, since he had indicated his desire for an early attack, Longstreet and Hill would prepare to make one. But, as Lee knew, it takes time to ready large units for battle, and he had given no specific hour for the attack. It appears too that Lee was not certain of the efficacy of his plan for, since Venable had not yet returned with Ewell's answer to his question, Lee himself rode to the left to see Ewell.[31]

It was said that General Lee started for Ewell's headquarters at 9:00 A.M., but perhaps it was earlier than that. It is likely that he rode east on West Middle Street to Baltimore Street, turned right at the courthouse, and proceeded south to High Street and the Presbyterian church. He turned east onto High Street, where he would have had a good view of Cemetery Hill, went downhill to Stratton Street, and from there rode to Ewell's headquarters. When he arrived, he found that Ewell was still out touring the lines with Major Venable.[32]

Although Ewell and Venable were away, General Trimble was there and ready to be of help. While someone went to fetch Ewell, Trimble took Lee to the cupola of the Adams County almshouse so that he might get a view of the enemy's position. As Lee gazed at the formidable array, he remarked to Trimble: "The enemy have the advantage of us in a shorter and inside line and we are too much extended. We did not or we could not pursue our advantage of yesterday, and now the enemy are in a good position."[33]

When Ewell appeared, he and Lee talked again. They concluded that an attack against the Union right, in itself, gave little promise of success and that one could be useful only if made in concert with assaults against the Union left and center. Lee would have to make do with the plans made earlier that morning. While the two generals talked, Col. Armistead L. Long of Lee's staff, who had been scouting for artillery positions on Ewell's front, appeared and accompanied his chief back through the town to Seminary Ridge.[34]

Ewell and Lee would not meet again before the attack was made. Ewell spent the rest of the morning examining his position and planning his assault. Lee's orders called for him to make a diversion in favor of Longstreet's corps when Longstreet attacked and to convert his demonstration into a full-scale assault if a favorable opportunity arose. According to Major Brown, the attack, which had been delayed until 9:00 A.M., was postponed a second time until 4:00 P.M. This postponement was an unfortunate thing; many of Ewell's soldiers had to pass the day in perilous idleness under a broiling sun while pondering an attack against enemy positions that were becoming stronger by the hour.[35]

Most of the men of Johnson's division spent a rather quiet morning. Except for its skirmishers and the Stonewall Brigade, which was busy with the protection of the Confederate left, the division rested in line north of the Hanover Road, separated from the enemy on Culp's Hill by Benner's Hill in its immediate front and by Rock Creek beyond. It is likely that some of its men spent time discussing their new division commander, General Johnson, and comparing him with some of his illustrious predecessors. Unlike Early, Johnson left no personal account of his opinions and actions on that fateful day. It may be presumed that he made one or more careful inspections of his line. It may be surmised too that he went out the Hanover Road to see what was taking place on Brinkerhoff's Ridge and that he spent a lot of time studying Culp's Hill in his front.

Edward Johnson was a character in an army that had more than its full share of eccentric general officers. Yet the bare bones of his career were prosaic enough. He was born in 1816 just west of Richmond, Virginia, in Chesterfield County, but his parents moved to Kentucky when he was very young. He entered West Point from Kentucky and graduated in 1838, thirty-second in a class of forty-five. None of Johnson's classmates served at Gettysburg with either army, but Ewell was in the class of 1840, and the two were likely acquainted. Johnson went to the 4th Infantry after graduation and served against the Seminoles in Florida. He campaigned with Winfield Scott's army in Mexico, where he received brevets for bravery displayed at Molino del Rey, Chapultepec, and in the capture of Mexico

City, along with presentation swords from both Richmond and Chesterfield County. Between wars, Johnson served at various western posts and in the Utah Expedition. He became a captain in 1851 and was a captain when he resigned from the Old Army in June 1861 to enter the Confederate service.[36]

Johnson became colonel of the 12th Georgia Infantry and was promoted to brigadier general on 11 December 1861. It was at this grade that he commanded the "Army of the Northwest," a brigade-size force in western Virginia with a grand name that fell under the command of Stonewall Jackson. Johnson commanded his little army at the battle of McDowell on 8 May 1862 and suffered a bad wound in the ankle. More importantly, he impressed Jackson favorably in an indelible way that reaped reward a whole year later.

Johnson's recuperation from his ankle wound took longer than expected, but it was not unpleasant because it took place in Richmond, where he had property, relatives, and friends. Johnson was a large, rough-hewn bachelor with a scant amount of sandy hair, a booming voice, and an eye that winked uncontrollably. He was not a handsome man, but his photograph suggests that Mary Chesnut exaggerated when she described his head as "strangely shaped, like a cone or an old fashioned beehive. . . . There are three tiers of it; like a pope's tiara." While recuperating in Richmond, the hero whose bravery on the field and in the parlor knew no bounds wooed various ladies with gusto and in an audible way that set fans aflutter and created much comment and amusement.[37]

But all good times pass. Johnson had never served with the Army of Northern Virginia, but he was slated for service with it as soon as his wound permitted. Jackson had urged his promotion to the command of D. H. Hill's division, but Rodes had commanded it well at Chancellorsville and secured a firm claim to it. Therefore, when Trimble was unable to take the field with Jackson's old division after Chancellorsville, it fell to Johnson instead. Thus it was that Johnson, an outsider with limited experience as a general officer, was catapulted into the upper echelons of the Army of Northern Virginia.[38]

Johnson's ability to command a division received an early test at Winchester on the march north, and he passed with flying colors. Over a year later, believing that Johnson's services at Winchester and elsewhere had not been fully appreciated, Ewell wrote the secretary of war to extol Johnson's boldness and decisiveness in battle. He stated also that while Johnson was under his command in later battles "he was uniformly distinguished for hard and successful fighting." Therefore, on 2 July at Gettysburg, John-

Maj. Gen. Edward Johnson (WLM)

son had the confidence of Ewell and a short but successful record as a battlefield commander.[39]

No one in Johnson's division could have denied his success as a commander at Winchester, but they did not hold him in affection and awe. A former orderly sergeant of the 27th Virginia, Charles A. Rollins, termed

Johnson "irascible" and wrote that the Stonewall Brigade had not taken kindly to him from the start. His troops gave him several nicknames: he was "Allegheny Johnson," "Allegheny Ed," and "Old Allegheny," all in recognition of his service in the mountain theater that had culminated at McDowell. Because of his wound and the stiff ankle that resulted from it, Johnson walked with the help of a heavy wooden staff that many likened unto a fence rail. This gained him the names "Old Clubby," "Fence Rail Johnson," and probably others too. The soldiers saw him as a heavyset, "large rough looking man," who hobbled along with the help of his rail. He was profane enough to cause comment, and one soldier, Pvt. Tedford Barclay, described him as being a good general and a brave man but one of the "wickedest men I ever heard of." Another called him a "brute." After his Gettysburg experience, Barclay observed that Johnson "had none of the qualities of a general but expects to do everything by fighting." Johnson could be a rough customer for friend and foe alike.[40]

While the division's skirmishers screened its front, the men back on the line of battle waited "in anxious anticipation" and wondered why their attack was delayed. In his postwar writings, Lt. Col. David Zable, commander of the 14th Louisiana Regiment in Nicholls's brigade, remembered dissatisfaction at their failure to attack on the evening of 1 July in "Stonewall Jackson's way" and their restlessness on the following day as they heard chopping on Culp's Hill and their skirmishers reported (wrongly) that there was no force in their front. Zable remembered also seeing a wagon train on the hill—another instance of error that colored Confederate views in the postwar years. What he saw might have been limbers and caissons and possibly some regimental wagons and ambulances—signs of combat troops, not a wagon park. But there was no attack in the morning and early afternoon, and Johnson's men waited for the sound of Longstreet's guns.[41]

If most of the men waiting on Johnson's line were anxious, they were probably idle too. Some went off with water details and in search of food, no doubt, to farmhouses nearby. John O. Casler wrote of a farmstead that provided the Stonewall Brigade with several barrels of flour, a smokehouse full of bacon, a springhouse with butter and milk, and a garret full of apple butter. Was there ever such bounty in July? The Virginians cooked and baked on its stoves and a privileged few milked some Pennsylvania cows.[42]

Lt. Randolph H. McKim, aide to General Steuart, conducted religious services for those of his brigade able and willing to attend. A few, probably a very few, wrote letters to their loved ones. Sgt. David Hunter of the 2d Virginia wrote his mother:

We are in all probability on eve of a terrible battle. The two contending armies lie close together and at any moment may commense the work of death. Great results hang upon the issue of this battle. If we are victorious peace may follow if not we may look for a long and fierce war. We trust in the wisdom of our Gens. and the goodness of our Father in Heaven who doeth all things well. He has time and again vouchsafed to give us victory and I know He wil [*sic*] not forsake us in the hour of trial. Although we may be victorious many must fall, and I may be among that number. If it is the Lord's will I am, I trust, prepared to go.[43]

Some of Johnson's Confederates might have had religious services, but there is no reason to believe any were conducted on Culp's Hill for the soldiers of the Union Twelfth Corps. Yet most of Geary's men had little to do but rest after they had finished with their entrenchments at mid-morning and might have profited from some common prayer. The men of Williams's division, however, who were returning from their adventure beyond Wolf Hill, would hardly have started with the construction of their works by that time.

Williams's two brigades, now under Ruger's command, took position on the right of Geary's division and extended the Twelfth Corps line into McAllister's Woods south of the swale. Col. Archibald L. McDougall's brigade was on the left, its flank abutting the right of Kane's brigade on the lower peak of the hill. Its forward line continued over this lower hill and far enough down its south slope to leave space for just one regiment in the forward line between McDougall's right and the meadow. In the meantime, its support line formed behind the stone wall about 200 feet in the rear.[44]

Lt. Robert Cruikshank of the 123d New York Volunteer Infantry Regiment described the works constructed by McDougall's brigade. His account suggests that the 123d had experience in this work. First the men of the brigade cut down trees, trimmed the branches from them, and piled the logs breast high. They fixed the heavy logs in place with smaller timbers, notched and laid crossways to the pile. Then they topped the pile with a head log wedged three inches above the logs beneath. Behind the line of logs they dug a ditch deep enough so that men standing in it, or on a fire step in it, could fire their rifles through the slot beneath the head log. They threw the dirt from the trench over the forward face of the works to absorb some of the enemy's fire and reduce the splintering of the logs. They strengthened the work by entwining the branches trimmed from the logs in front of the works to form an abatis. All in all, it seemed to create a strong position.[45]

Ruger placed two regiments of his own brigade between McDougall's right and the swale: the 107th New York in the forward line and the 13th New Jersey in a double column behind it. Ruger's three other regiments formed south of the swale among the rocks and trees of McAllister's Woods. The 2d Massachusetts on the left fronted north toward the meadow of the swale, and the 3d Wisconsin and 27th Indiana faced east across the creek. Ruger's brigade erected works in extension of those in McDougall's line, and, though they constructed none in the low, wet meadow, they positioned those on its shoulders so that the troops manning them could cover it with fire. Ruger's men on the right among the rocks did what they could to improve their natural cover. In addition, they tore down some walls to their front that might prove useful to the enemy.[46]

Rodes's division and half of Early's passed the day to Johnson's right confronting the defenders of Cemetery Hill. Having been told that the Confederate attack would begin early in the morning, Early had posted Hays's and Hoke's brigades east of Baltimore Street in the ravine of Winebrenner's Run. Hoke's brigade, 900 strong, probably formed with its left about thirty yards west of the Culp springhouse and its right in the ravine 300 yards to the west. Hays's brigade, with 1,200 men, continued the line west toward Baltimore Street. We will probably never know just where Hays's brigade formed and what its position was like. Nearly 100 years later, local school officials placed three large school buildings and some roads on the site. Col. Isaac E. Avery, commander of Hoke's brigade, and some of his staff tied their horses to a fence behind his line and spent the night under an apple tree there. They awakened next morning expecting to launch an attack, but they would hold their position the rest of the day.[47]

Early's troops, the brigades of Hays and Hoke, spent a miserable day in their ravine. It was deep enough to cut off cooling breezes, its slopes were bare of trees, and the July sun warmed the Confederates in it without mercy. It was a debilitating and dangerous place. General Ewell wanted to pull Hays's brigade back when it became apparent that the attack would be delayed, but he could not do so without the risk of great loss. But staying there was not much better because, as Lt. William Seymour observed, it was almost death for a man to stand upright.[48]

While Early's two brigades awaited daylight and the signal for their attack, they could hear the enemy "chopping away and working like beavers," strengthening their hilltop bastion, and when daylight came, they saw Cemetery Hill crowned with field works—lunettes at the gun positions—and "bristling with a most formidable array of cannon." In accordance with the best practice of that day, both brigades sent out skirmishers, even on the restricted right, and settled down to await the order to advance.[49]

To Early's right, Doles's, Iverson's, and Ramseur's brigades of Rodes's division occupied Middle Street west from Baltimore Street to the edge of town. O'Neal's brigade was along the railroad bed to the right and rear, and Daniel's brigade occupied the ridge at the seminary. Daniel's brigade supported three batteries of the 1st Virginia Artillery Battalion that were posted on the ridge.[50]

Rodes's division had skirmishers across its front. One battalion of the 5th Alabama Regiment, sharpshooters commanded by Maj. Eugene Blackford, occupied houses in the town, and perhaps some of it was in the fields west of the town as well. Skirmishers of Ramseur's and Doles's brigades were in the fields between the town and Seminary Ridge and no doubt connected with the right of the skirmish lines of Pender's division. This Confederate skirmish line was a strong one that pushed forward until it made firm contact with the enemy who had moved down from Cemetery Hill. Their contest will be discussed below in chapter 9.[51]

There was intermittent artillery fire throughout the day, of course, as Union batteries shot at Confederates moving about in the distance. Troops received ammunition, and a few were able to get some hardtack. But sniper fire blanketed Cemetery Hill, and the soldiers there found it dangerous to move about.[52]

The planning of the generals, the skirmishing, sniping, and the desultory barking of batteries, were mere preliminaries—the tuning up before the overture of the great work that was to follow. General Howard, whose headquarters were on the high point of East Cemetery Hill in sight of all that went on there, saw fit to report that "very little occurred while the other corps were coming into position until about 4 P.M." He added that a little before that time he had issued orders to division commanders to make ready for battle as the enemy was reported to be advancing on the left. When the men of Lieutenant Wheeler's New York battery heard cannonading off to their left, they stood on tiptoe in an attempt to see what was going on. Just then Howard rode by and cautioned them, "Never mind the left boys, look out for your own front." A few minutes later they saw puffs of smoke at the positions of the enemy's batteries opposite them, and in an instant they heard the boom of the distant guns and Confederate shells burst around them. The Army of Northern Virginia was about to show what it thought General Lee intended when he ordered a demonstration against the Union right.[53]

9
Skirmishers, Sharpshooters, and Civilians

There was firing somewhere at Gettysburg throughout the battle's daylight hours. Even in the periods of relative calm, a soldier who bothered to listen might have heard the bark of cannon, the more frequent cracking of rifles, and occasional flurries of shots that marked a firefight somewhere in the no-man's-land between the armies.

There were some actions that seemed to demand the response of a cannon shot or two, such as the appearance of a sizable body of enemy troops or the threatening fire of an enemy battery, but prudent battery commanders kept their gun crews in check. Artillery ammunition was too precious to be wasted by the gunners of either army. On 3 July General Meade took time from his major concerns to demand the name of a battery commander of the Eleventh Corps who "shamefully wasted" ammunition by firing all of his battery's guns at a reconnoitering Confederate officer. There is no knowing if Meade ever got the culprit's name (in theory at least it could only have been one of four men), but the request in itself was a warning against waste and might have done some good for a while.[1]

But infantry fire during lulls in battle was quite another thing. Both armies used skirmishers and pickets (small outpost guards) as a matter of course, and they seem not to have limited the amount of ammunition that they might expend. The War Department drill manual, *U.S. Infantry Tactics*, defined a skirmish as a "loose, desultory kind of engagement, generally between light troops thrown forward to test the strength and position of the enemy." Both armies used essentially the same manuals and deployed infantrymen as skirmishers as their texts prescribed. Skirmishers screened and protected the main positions on front and flank from enemy harassment by holding enemy marksmen at a distance. On the other hand, skirmishers preceded their own attacking lines to brush away their enemy counterparts, to uncover enemy positions, and to prevent premature contact by the enemy with their main line. Although skirmishing required a degree of flexibility and individuality not usually exercised in the more rigid lines of battle, officers and noncommissioned officers exercised a firm control over the men in their skirmish lines and held them to their work.[2]

Soldiers on the skirmish line deployed in groups of four men each so that the men would "be careful to know and sustain each other." Several groups of four operated in an extended line, a "chain of skirmishers," and were expected to remain within forty paces of one another. The men within the groups of four in turn would stay five paces apart. Officers and noncommissioned officers controlled the line from behind, where they could see both their men and the enemy. When necessary, they used bugles to relay commands. Chiefs of section, twenty paces to the rear of a skirmish line, each had a reserve group of four and possibly a bugler at their disposal, and there was a reserve platoon about 150 paces behind the segment of line it was to support. Although the line was carefully controlled, the men in it were expected to use their own initiative in taking advantage of terrain and nearby cover.[3]

Johnson's division east of Gettysburg put out skirmishers early on 2 July to feel the enemy in its front. Among them was a detachment from the 25th Virginia Regiment under Maj. Robert D. Lilley, and most of the 1st North Carolina Regiment also spent some time on the skirmish line that day. Confederate accounts had little to say of this, but Col. Warren W. Packer of the 5th Connecticut Regiment recorded in his diary that they annoyed the Twelfth Corps a great deal.[4]

At about 8:00 A.M. on 2 July, Lt. Col. John C. O. Redington of the 60th New York took a force of seven officers and 170 enlisted men from Greene's brigade to the east of Culp's Hill, where they relieved two companies from Wadsworth's division. Redington deployed his men east of Rock Creek, with the left of his line about 700 yards north of Greene's left and opposite Benner's Hill. The line extended south probably as far as the bend in the creek just south of the lane that ran from the creek up to Benner's farmyard. Redington's men must have taken full advantage of the tree cover east of the creek when engaged with the Confederates on the hill above them. Later in the day, they sallied toward batteries on the hill. At General Geary's request, Colonel Candy sent the entire 28th Pennsylvania Regiment of his brigade down to the west side of Rock Creek on the

Footbridge near McAllister's Mill (NA)

morning of 2 July, and its men traded shots with the enemy throughout the day.[5]

Skirmishers from Williams's division deployed to the right of Redington's line, but little was written about their work. Capt. George W. Reid took Company K, 145th New York, east of Rock Creek, and Capt. Daniel Oakey led two companies of the 2d Massachusetts beyond the creek to "watch the enemy lest he should come upon us unawares." Oakey thought that Rock Creek in front of his regiment's position was too deep to ford, so he took his force south to McAllister's Mill and crossed it on a footbridge there. After crossing, Oakey's party returned north and deployed in a field to the front of Ruger's brigade and in plain sight of the enemy high on Benner's Hill. Things were relatively quiet there for most of the day, but late in the afternoon Oakey's men saw a gathering of horsemen near the Benner farmyard who seemed to be watching them through field glasses. Oakey thought that the mounted party was a general and his staff and considered it an ominous portent of things to come.[6]

By the morning of 2 July Howard's Eleventh Corps seemed strongly posted on Cemetery Hill, and the men of two of its three divisions—Barlow's, now commanded by Brig. Gen. Adelbert Ames, Schurz's, and von Steinwehr's—became heavily involved in their own peculiar battle with troops of Early's and Rodes's divisions south and east of the town.

The men of Ames's division wrote little of their experiences on the skirmish line. They would have been deployed in front of Cemetery Hill in a line that arced from north to northeast and faced the brigades of Hays and Hoke. They must have connected with the line of Wadsworth's division on the right, and their left joined with other Eleventh Corps skirmishers south of the town.[7]

There was brisk skirmishing between Ames's men and the North Carolinians of Hoke's brigade all day long. Col. Isaac Avery, commander of Hoke's brigade, his aide, Lt. John A. McPherson, and Capt. James M. Adams, a brave man of "high moral character," spent most of that day, like others in the brigade, lying on the slope of the ravine containing Winebrenner's Run. According to McPherson, "the enemy sharpshooters kept us uneasy all the time balls hissing all around us." Avery chuckled about their uncomfortable situation and said that they had better move, but there was no place for them to go. McPherson went on to observe that it had always been the colonel's wish that if he ever fell in battle, the battle would be a great one. Obviously, death from a skirmisher's bullet while lying in a ravine on a Pennsylvania farm was not quite what Avery had in mind.[8]

The skirmishers of Ames's division closest to the town had the disadvantage of sparring with Confederates who had some cover. Lt. J. Clyde Miller of the 153d Pennsylvania Regiment commanded two companies of skirmishers deployed in front of Hays's line. Miller and his men received fire from the brickyard that was east of Baltimore Street and in front of Hays's right. The Confederates in the brickyard were too well supported by Hays's main line for Miller to drive them out, so the lieutenant sent a corporal back to Cemetery Hill to ask the batteries there to give him some help. After the artillerymen dropped some shells into the brickyard, Miller advanced his line far enough so that he could see Confederates lying in the ravine. During this skirmishing, a projectile that made an unusual sound as it passed through the air crashed into the branches of a tree under which Miller and Lt. Henry R. Barnes were standing. They thought that the missile was a piece of iron (some Federal infantrymen believed wrongly that the Confederates fired all sorts of metal junk from their guns), but likely it was a bolt fired from a Whitworth gun (Whitworth projectiles were commonly called "bolts") posted in Schultz's Woods on Seminary Ridge.[9]

Artillerymen made fine targets for sharpshooters on the skirmish line or elsewhere, often because they had no cover while firing their guns and because officers, sergeants, and drivers were on horseback. Skirmishers, probably from Hoke's brigade, annoyed Stevens's battery on its knoll between the hills, and the Federals did not seem to have much luck in squelching their fire. Their greatest success came on 2 July at 4:00 P.M. when one of them shot Captain Stevens through both of his legs.[10]

The fighting among the buildings in the south end of Gettysburg, though limited, was rather distinctive in the annals of the armies that fought there. Similar fighting had taken place in Fredericksburg, of course, but hardly anywhere else in the East. It was continuous during the daylight hours and episodical, marked by small and temporary victories and defeats and many personal tragedies.

The men of the Eleventh Corps bore the brunt of this action. Col. Orland Smith's brigade was in position on the left along the Taneytown and Emmitsburg roads, Schurz's division occupied walls west of the Baltimore Pike, and Ames's two brigades were east of the pike. Coster's brigade's position is an enigma. It had been east of the pike before it went into Gettysburg to reinforce Barlow's division during the fighting north of the town. After its return, its regiments spent some time in the cemetery, and later some of it had positions east of the pike and in the buildings along the pike at the edge of the town.[11]

After the 73d Pennsylvania Regiment of Coster's brigade returned to Cemetery Hill, a general officer, probably von Steinwehr, ordered Capt. Daniel F. Kelly, commander of the 73d, to take his regiment forward and find out how much of the town was occupied by the enemy. Captain Kelly formed his 300 Pennsylvanians and gave them their instructions. Three companies would push through the gardens and alleys east of Baltimore Street, two would go up Baltimore Street, three others would go west of Baltimore Street and sweep a wheat field there, while the two remaining companies, G and I, would constitute the reserve and occupy Snider's Wagon Hotel at the junction of the Baltimore Pike and the Emmitsburg Road.

Kelly signaled the start of the advance by firing his pistol, which suggests that the 73d had spread beyond the range of his voice. The companies stepped off, but they did not go far. Not long after their line passed one of the two tanneries at the south end of the town, the Confederates greeted them with a well-directed volley and drove them back to the foot of Ceme-

Col. Charles R. Coster (WLM)

tery Hill. If there was any doubt about the Confederates' occupying the town in front of Cemetery Hill, that doubt was dispelled.[12]

From the high point just south of the intersection of Baltimore and High streets, the town buildings lined Baltimore Street downhill for about 500 feet and a drop of forty feet in elevation to the base of Cemetery Hill. Houses and their outbuildings, two tanyards, and a brickyard sat along Baltimore Street near Winebrenner's Run. Snider's Wagon Hotel dominated the area. It was a large two-and-a-half-story brick house, with an ell and outbuildings behind, that stood in the sharp angle of the Emmitsburg Road and Baltimore Pike. Its left or west side was along the Emmitsburg Road, and it had a large yard for parking wagons along the Baltimore Pike. Although near the foot of Cemetery Hill, it was still twenty feet above Winebrenner's Run 100 yards to the north. Because of its elevation and height, it must have loomed like a small castle above the other buildings nearby and provided a vantage point for the skirmishers who manned it. Yet it was not prominent enough to be singled out as a target by Confederate artillerymen on Seminary Ridge, although at least three solid shots struck it during the great artillery preparation on 3 July.[13]

The south end of Gettysburg—the portion of the town 300 or so yards north of Cemetery Hill and the Wagon Hotel—was something of an industrial area. John Rupp's house stood about 100 yards north of the hotel

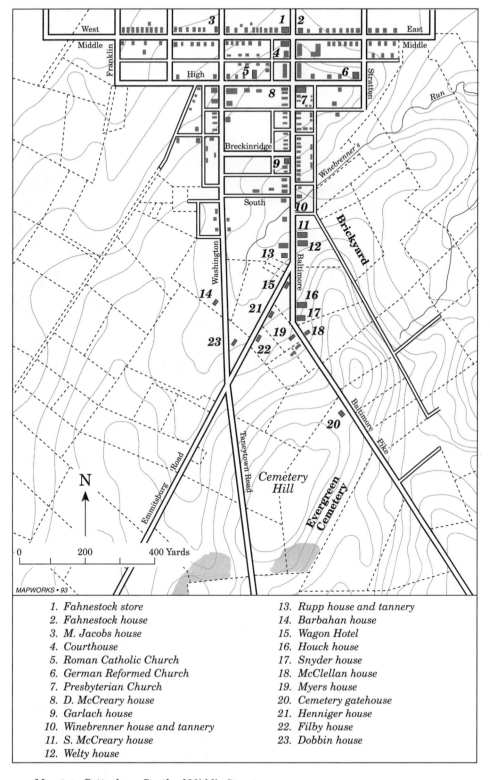

West Middle

East Middle

Franklin

High

Stratton

Run

Breckinridge

South

Winebrenner's

Brickyard

Baltimore

Washington

Emmitsburg Road

Taneytown Road

Baltimore Pike

Cemetery Hill

Evergreen Cemetery

N

0   200   400 Yards

MAPWORKS • 93

1. Fahnestock store	13. Rupp house and tannery
2. Fahnestock house	14. Barbahan house
3. M. Jacobs house	15. Wagon Hotel
4. Courthouse	16. Houck house
5. Roman Catholic Church	17. Snyder house
6. German Reformed Church	18. McClellan house
7. Presbyterian Church	19. Myers house
8. D. McCreary house	20. Cemetery gatehouse
9. Garlach house	21. Henniger house
10. Winebrenner house and tannery	22. Filby house
11. S. McCreary house	23. Dobbin house
12. Welty house	

Map 9.1. Gettysburg South of Middle Street

Snider's Wagon Hotel. The Baltimore Pike and Study house are on the left, the Emmitsburg Road on the right. This is a postwar photograph; the houses on the left were not there during the battle. (NA)

on the west side of Baltimore Street. It was a long brick building with its east end to the street, and on its south side, facing the hotel, it had wide upper and lower porches. Rupp's tannery was just north of his house and to its rear and might have imparted a certain aroma. There was some open space north of the tannery and then a tract containing structures of a waterworks. The brick house of Harvey Sweeny was a bit north of the waterworks at the south side of what is now South Street, and the house of John Swope began the block beyond South Street to the north. Beyond Swope's, the houses, mostly brick, stood side by side and extended uphill toward High Street and the center of town. The double house of Henry Garlach was about midway up the block from South Street and contained the Garlach home and carpentry shop.[14]

Just east of the Wagon Hotel on the east side of the Baltimore Pike was a brick one-and-a-half-story double house shared by the McClellan family and Mrs. Isaac McLean. Two more houses stood north of McClel-

Baltimore Street north from the base of Cemetery Hill. The Rupp house and tannery are on the left, the Garlach house midway up the hill on the left. The Welty, S. McCreary, and Winebrenner houses are on the right. (NA)

lan's beyond the bend in the road. These were the homes of John Houck and Mrs. Conrad Snider. Beyond them down the slope and in front of the hotel were three large widely spaced houses on large lots. Like the Rupp house across the street, their ends abutted Baltimore Street, and each had upper and lower porches on their south sides. The first two were the homes of Samuel McCreary and Solomon Welty. The third, that of John Winebrenner, stood beyond Winebrenner's Run and a lane that led east to the brickyard and house of John Kuhn. This brickyard, which hosted sharpshooters or skirmishers of Hays's brigade, was about 100 yards east of the street and at the foot of the hill.[15]

Like John Rupp, John Winebrenner had a tannery with a bark shed along Baltimore Street just north of his house. There was an alley north of the tanyard, and houses lined the street to the top of the hill and to the center of the town beyond. Most of these houses are there today, along with some additional houses that filled gaps that were there in 1863 or replaced the tannery structures that were later removed. Unfortunately, the McCreary and Welty houses, which figured so prominently in the battle, are gone, a school building stands on the brickyard site, and a large motel is just south of the McClellan house. The Wagon Hotel has long gone; a

north ? [handwritten annotation]

Probably the Holiday Inn [handwritten annotation]

service station stands on a portion of its site, and the open spaces that once graced the area are covered with houses and commercial buildings.

The terrain behind the houses on the east side of Baltimore Street was relatively open then, as now, to High Street and the top of the hill. Washington Street, which parallels Baltimore Street to the west, had only scattered houses, and there were open fields west of it. Uphill, behind the hotel on the Baltimore Pike, there were two houses between the hotel yard and the cemetery's gatehouse. That of Dr. David Study stood at the bend of the road, and John Myers's large brick house was just beyond. There were two houses along the Emmitsburg Road behind the hotel, those of John Heninger and Samuel Philby. Although these buildings stood on or in front of the Union line, their presence received little attention in the accounts of those who fought around them.[16]

After the 73d Pennsylvania re-formed following its abortive push into the town, its Company B occupied the hotel. Soldiers manned its windows and punched holes in its roof, from which they could fire down on houses occupied by Confederates in the south end of the town. Company B remained in the hotel through the night and was relieved on the following morning, probably by another unit from Coster's brigade.[17]

As some of von Steinwehr's men occupied the hotel and other buildings on the north slope of Cemetery Hill, the Confederates occupied the brickyard, the McCreary house, and those north of it, including Winebrenner's house and tannery. They were also in Rupp's tannery on the west side of the street and the buildings north of it. John Rupp wrote that there were Union soldiers on the south porch of his house at the same time that the Confederates were on its north side. He complained too that the Confederates had broken out the windows of his tannery's shop and used it for a fort. From it, they shot across the street at Union soldiers in the Welty house, and they killed a man beneath the large oak tree that stood between the Rupp house and the street. John Rupp spent a lot of time in his cellar. Some Union soldiers knew that he was there, but the Confederates did not. After the battle, Rupp picked up a double handful of minié balls from inside his house.[18]

Other Rebels, probably Hays's men, fired from the McCreary house. Cpl. William H. Poole of the 9th Louisiana Regiment pushed a table across the doorway facing Cemetery Hill and knelt behind it, resting his gun upon it. The table top covered the door well enough, but its top was too thin to stop a bullet. A minié ball pierced the table top and struck Poole, killing him on the spot. Union soldiers picked off other Confederates too, one as far away as the Shriver house on Breckinridge Street to the north.[19]

The 8th Louisiana Regiment of Hays's brigade had two companies on the skirmish line during the night of 1 July and on the following day. These were the two most miserable days of Lt. J. Warren Jackson's life. The Federals commanded his position and raked it with a galling fire. On 2 July Company I had a line of skirmishers to the front and Jackson was with the reserve behind a plank fence. "There we had to stay," wrote Jackson; "if anyone showed himself or a hat was seen above the fence a volley was poured into us." But the Federals wounded only two men there. Later, in order to return to the regiment's main line, Jackson had to crawl sixty yards through some bushes and make a dash of thirty yards from there.[20]

Hays's skirmishers accomplished more than they knew. Those in the brickyard inflicted numerous casualties on the men of Ames's division. Anna Garlach watched the Louisianans around the Winebrenner house from her own house across Baltimore Street. They put up a barricade on the pavement, perhaps the sidewalk of Baltimore Street. One man behind it would raise a hat on a stick to draw Union fire. After the Union soldiers emptied their rifles firing at the hat, the Louisianans stood up quickly and shot back.

Anna also saw that some Confederates, probably from Doles's brigade, had taken over the house adjoining hers on the north. They knocked some bricks from the wall of its second floor, which rose above the Garlachs' roof, and shot from the holes made there. Union soldiers returned this fire, of course, and some of their bullets hit the Garlach house.[21]

Capt. William W. Blackford, Jeb Stuart's engineer, visited General Lee on 2 or 3 July. After his business was ended, Blackford rode into Gettysburg in search of his brother, Maj. Eugene Blackford, the commander of a battalion of sharpshooters in Rodes's division. He found the major in the middle of a block of houses on "Main Street" on the side facing Cemetery Hill. Major Blackford and some of his officers were "lolling on the sofas of a handsome parlor" with a decanter of wine and all sorts of delicacies on a marble-top table nearby. After the captain had eaten of the bounty, the major took him on a tour of that part of his position. According to the captain, the Alabamians occupied the second floor of a block of houses, and they had connected them by cutting holes in the party walls. The back windows of these houses overlooked Cemetery Hill, and they had been closed up with furniture and mattresses, except for loopholes there and in the walls through which the sharpshooters could fire toward Cemetery Hill. There was "a constant rattle of musketry by men stripped to the waist and blackened with powder," while those not firing rested on sofas and carpets. He saw some pools of blood that marked where wounded men had lain, and he saw some bodies that had not been removed. But, all in all, duty there must have been a lot better than being on the skirmish lines in the fields west of the town.[22]

The German Reformed Church at High and Stratton streets was used in the constant sniping between Cemetery Hill and the town. In spite of its containing Union wounded, its nave and steeple provided a view of Cemetery Hill that Confederate marksmen could not pass up. Pvt. Reuben S. Ruch of the 153d Pennsylvania Infantry was among the walking wounded stranded there during the battle. Ruch watched some of the fighting from a church window and saw a Rebel soldier climb to the roof of a two-story house nearby and fire from behind one of its chimneys. Ruch thought it a bad place to be, for if the sniper was hit, the fall from the roof alone might kill him. The man fired four shots, and as he looked for another target, a bullet struck him and tumbled him from the roof. After the battle, Ruch examined the man and found that he had been shot in the forehead.[23]

Sharpshooters in the church were a deadly threat to the soldiers on Cemetery Hill nearly a half mile away. They were probably the snipers who shot Lt. Nicholas Sahm and Lt. Christian Stock of Wiedrich's battery and a number of battery horses also. Wiedrich's third piece fired at the church's steeple, and the batterymen believed that they stopped the sniping from it even though they did little, if any, damage to it. Sometime on 2 July, Captain von Fritsch, then serving as an aide to General Ames, complained to Ames about the firing from the steeple. Ames suggested that he speak to General Howard about it. He did so, and Howard ordered a detail of twelve sharpshooters sent to deal with the problem. Von Fritsch said the men were Swiss and were armed with rifles with telescopic sights. They fired from behind a wall at the top of the hill and in twenty shots sent the Rebel snipers running from the church.[24]

These Swiss sharpshooters were not identified, but they might well have been from the 82d Illinois Regiment, commanded by Lt. Col. Edward S. Salomon, which contained companies of men of several nationalities. On 2 July General Schurz told Salomon to send some men through a peach orchard and take some houses on the south edge of town from the Confederates who held them. Salomon selected Capt. Joseph B. Greenhut to lead the storming party of about 100 men. Greenhut, a native of Austria, was twenty-one at the time, but he was a veteran soldier who had been wounded at Fort Donelson before joining the 82d. Greenhut asked for volunteers to do the job and got them. His detail worked its way forward in full view of the troops on Cemetery Hill, seized the houses, and held them.[25]

Greenhut wanted one soldier in particular to go with him—Pvt. John Ackermann. But Ackermann, who had been something of a daredevil, begged off. He had a premonition of death and was afraid. Greenhut ordered him to go anyhow, and Ackermann obeyed. Five minutes later, Ackermann returned to the main line, pale and shaking with fright. Someone told him to lie down, and he did so. Soon afterward, a shell whistled in, exploded near the frightened soldier, and killed him. There were no safe spots on the forward slope of Cemetery Hill that day.[26]

Rifle fire from Cemetery Hill and the Union skirmish lines southeast and southwest of the town proved dangerous as far into town as Middle Street. Henry Jacobs wrote that Rodes's men, who used Middle Street as the position for their main line, erected a stone wall across Washington Street at the intersection by the Jacobs house. From inside the house, Jacobs could hear the pickets firing outside, and bullets from Union soldiers somewhere to the south struck the house and killed a Confederate soldier at its cellar door. William McLean, who lived on East Middle Street next door to the Methodist church, became tired of sitting with his wife and daughter in their cellar and on 2 July went up to the back bedroom on the second floor to have a look toward Cemetery Hill. He opened the shutter slightly, peeked out, and then, realizing that it was probably unsafe to stand at the window, stepped back. No sooner had he done this than a bullet smashed through the shutter, punched through the footboard of the bed behind him, and lodged in its mattress.[27]

Some of the larger houses had trapdoors in their roofs, and several civilians risked their lives by looking from them. Albertus McCreary, whose house was in the southwest corner of the intersection of Baltimore and High streets, could see Cemetery Hill and the field of Pickett's Charge from his trapdoor—he remembered seeing a cannoneer shot on Cemetery Hill and saw the charge. Once while looking out, he saw a neighbor peering from his own trapdoor until a bullet zipped by the neighbor's head and knocked a brick loose from a chimney behind him. Albertus and his brother were enjoying this when two bullets struck shingles in their own roof not far from Albertus's head. Not to be daunted by the good shooting, the boys fixed a board across their hole that would hide them while they peeked out. On another occasion they saw Confederates shooting from a house on a side street. There were several of them, and each time they shot there was a flash and a puff of smoke. Finally, some guns on Cemetery Hill opened on the house, hit it, and drove the Confederates out.[28]

John Will, son of the proprietor of the Globe Hotel on York Street just east of the square, climbed partway through the hotel's trapdoor. While standing on a ladder with his chest above the roof, he could see Confederate batteries over on Benner's Hill. Soon he heard a shout, "Get off that roof!," and looking down, he saw a soldier pointing a rifle at him. Feigning innocence, Will asked the soldier if he was speaking to him, and the man replied, "I am talking to *you*, and I want you to get *off that roof*." Will saw him turn to speak to two other soldiers and slipped down out of sight. He could still see a battery firing and was enjoying the spectacle when a Confederate officer on horseback appeared in the street below, pistol in hand, and announced that General Early wanted to see him. By now the family was aroused and frightened, and his mother begged him to come down. The officer took Will from the hotel along with the barkeeper and a couple of other men who happened to be there. Accompanied by Cassatt Neeley, a lawyer friend, they all went off to see Early. They found him sitting on a marble slab behind the John Cannon Marble Works on a rear lot near the intersection of Baltimore and Middle streets. Early asked him who he was, where his father was, and then gave him some advice. He said that Will might have been picked off by some Union sharpshooters on Cemetery Hill and observed with some exasperation, "Your people are on the streets; they are at their *garret* windows and on the roofs. I sent Guards from door to door on your streets to tell them to go into their cellars or at least to remain within their houses, the only safe place for them. If your people would but take my advice, I want to save your people." Early ended by telling him that he could go home and said that the Confederates would not molest citizens and that they would protect private property. Early then fell into conversation with lawyer Neeley. An officer walked back to the hotel with Will, and during their walk, they saw a Confederate soldier struck by a ricocheting bullet.[29]

In retrospect, the Gettysburg civilians were fortunate in their contacts with Confederate soldiers, even those who were actively skirmishing with the Union troops on Cemetery Hill. On 3 July the Garlach women were in their cellar when they heard someone enter their front door. Mrs. Garlach hurried up the stairs in time to see a soldier going up to the second floor. She caught him by the coat and asked him what he was doing. He told her that he was going to do some shooting from the house. She held on to him and said, "You can't go up there. You will draw fire on this house full of women and children." He maintained that he must go about his shooting; she insisted that he should leave the house. He began to waver and said that it would be instant death for him to go outside. To this, Mrs. Garlach, who was far from helpless, replied that he could stay but that he could not fire the gun while he was in the house. The soldier obeyed her and waited awhile. Then, feeling that he had to get on with the battle, he opened the door, fired his rifle, and, covered a little by the smoke of the discharge, dashed across the street into Winebrenner's Alley, leaving Mrs. Garlach mistress of her home.[30]

Albertus McCreary, who must have enjoyed the excitement once his fear of the Confederates had gone, recalled a couple of them with pleasure. One was a fellow who braved the bullets that flew across the McCreary yard to feed their rabbits for them. The other was a soldier who climbed a tree in their yard to eat its cherries. He sat in the tree eating in a most unconcerned manner that Albertus deemed truly heroic. He endeared himself further by teaching Albertus how to identify various bullets and shells by the noises they made.[31]

William McLean cultivated the friendship of the Confederates around his house on East Middle Street. He recalled that one of the Louisianans' principal concerns was the route and distance to Baltimore. On the night of 2 July he treated the sore throat of one of them with a dose of Ayer's Wild Cherry Pectoral, and on 3 July the McLeans had a North Carolina captain to supper. They found the captain a perfect gentleman, and the captain promised the McLeans his protection. Perhaps the promise eased their minds, but it likely had little other real value.[32]

The bullets and the damage they caused could be viewed philosophically—Gettysburg was in the middle of a battle after all. But Albertus McCreary remembered one especially sour note. As the bullets whizzed in the air about him, a boy stood in the middle of Baltimore Street hurling stones at windows and laughing loudly every time he broke one. The flying bullets had no terror for him; when one zipped close he would duck, laugh, and return to throwing stones. Soldiers said that this devil had followed them up from the South.[33]

If the sniping and firefights among the buildings of Gettysburg was a unique experience for the soldiers involved, the skirmishing along Washington Street and in the fields between Cemetery Hill and Seminary Ridge must have been familiar stuff. Here, the soldiers of von Steinwehr's division confronted not only Rodes's men but skirmishers of Pender's division as well. Pender's division had a "select battalion of sharpshooters" from McGowan's South Carolina brigade, commanded by Capt. William T. Haskell. Their part in the battle would not be one of grand assaults but rather relentless dueling in the hot July sun.[34]

Orland Smith's brigade of von Steinwehr's division manned the Federal skirmish line in the fields just southwest of the town. Their division commander, the Baron Adolph Wilhelm August Friedrich von Steinwehr,

Brig. Gen. Adolph von Steinwehr (WLM)

was a native of Blankenburg in the north German duchy of Brunswick. Von Steinwehr's grandfather, a general in the Prussian army, had served against Napoleon, and his father had been in the ducal service. The baron himself was born in 1822, was educated at Göttingen and at the duchy's military school, and served briefly as a lieutenant in the ducal army. In 1847 he secured a year's leave and journeyed to the United States in the hope of getting a commission in its regular army. Although he did not accomplish this goal, U.S. topographical engineers hired him to help with a survey of the new border with Mexico and later to work on a survey in the Mobile Bay area. There he met and married an Alabama woman who returned with him to Brunswick. In 1854, however, he severed his ties with his native land and returned to the United States, where he settled in Connecticut and took up farming.[35]

After the war began, von Steinwehr became the colonel of the German 29th New York Regiment and led it to battle. He served with it at Manassas in the Reserve Division. In October 1861 he became a brigadier general and commanded a brigade in Louis Blenker's division, which campaigned in the Shenandoah Valley under John C. Frémont; after Cross

Keys, he led the division. When Sigel's corps joined the Army of the Potomac and became the Eleventh Corps, von Steinwehr retained command of its Second Division. His division was on the corps left at Chancellorsville. Although it was not struck by the onset of Jackson's assault, it experienced hard fighting, and Howard described von Steinwehr's bearing as "cool, collected and judicious." Thus, by Gettysburg, von Steinwehr had been a brigadier general for nearly two years and a division commander in two major battles.[36]

Many people thought highly of von Steinwehr. After spending a couple of hours with him over dinner, Gen. Alpheus Williams described him as being a "remarkably intelligent and agreeable person." In the postwar years, a man who had served under him in the 55th Ohio Regiment recalled that he was "an officer of great merit, trained in the German school and possessing the confidence of his superiors." Unlike many high-ranking officers of the Army of the Potomac, he was a political liberal. Such sentiments would have been approved by many politicians, but if they had any political value, von Steinwehr failed to exploit it.[37]

In contrast, Col. Orland Smith, whose brigade would bear the brunt of the skirmishing, was of New England stock, born in 1825 in Lewiston, Maine. Smith had no military background of note; he was a railroader by profession and, until 1852, was station agent at Lewiston. In that year, Smith moved to Ohio, and at the outbreak of the war, he was an official of the Marietta and Ohio Railroad and was living in Chillicothe. He became colonel of the 73d Ohio Regiment in late 1861 and led it at McDowell, Cross Keys, and Second Manassas. He received command of the Second Brigade, Second Division, Eleventh Corps in September 1862 and had commanded it at Chancellorsville. He would continue to lead the brigade during the Chattanooga area battles until the army reorganization in 1864 when it was abolished. Smith reverted then to the command of the 73d Ohio Regiment.[38]

When Smith's brigade reached Cemetery Hill on 1 July, von Steinwehr ordered it to the left of the pike, while Coster's brigade took position on the right and in the buildings at the foot of the hill. After Coster's brigade went forward to aid the troops north of the town, von Steinwehr shifted two of Smith's regiments to East Cemetery Hill to support Wiedrich's battery until Coster's brigade returned to the hill. In the meantime, the 136th New York Regiment waited in the cemetery; its soldiers loaded and capped their pieces, and one of every twelve of them took twelve canteens and went for water. This done, they stood "amid the tombs of the dead awaiting orders," and even the "dullest could see that danger was on every

Col. Orland Smith (WLM)

hand." Late in the day Smith's brigade deployed along the Taneytown Road and along that part of the Emmitsburg Road northwest of the hill. That night portions of the brigade pulled back to the cemetery, possibly to be in close support of the batteries that had gone into position there, and it spent a moonlit night among the tombstones. One soldier of the 55th Ohio heard the shouts of men, the tread of horses, and the ominous but reassuring rumbling of caissons, limbers, and guns throughout the night as the Union forces strengthened their position on the hill.[39]

After some changes in position during the night, the regiments of Orland Smith's brigade formed along that part of the Taneytown Road in front of the cemetery and to the right along the Emmitsburg Road. The 55th Ohio was on the right with its center near the intersection of the two roads, the 73d Ohio was along the Taneytown Road to the 55th's left, and the 136th New York was on the left of the 73d Ohio. The 136th New York was the left regiment of the Eleventh Corps and connected with the Second Corps at Ziegler's Grove. The other regiment of Smith's brigade, the 33d Massachusetts, went across Cemetery Hill to reinforce Ames's division and stayed there for the remainder of the battle. The main line of Smith's brigade, particularly the 136th New York on its left, rested under the muzzles of the artillery pieces on the high ground at the cemetery in their rear—a perilous area when Union shells burst prematurely or passed close above their heads or when Confederate rounds intended for the Union batteries might strike.[40]

The right of Smith's skirmish line rested near the straggling houses at the south end of the town and ran across the fields west of the Emmitsburg Road. The brigade manned this area for the remainder of the battle, with the limit of its advance being a fence that paralleled the Emmitsburg Road on rising ground about 300 yards to the west. Confederate skirmishers had a line about 150 yards beyond the fence, probably just beyond a small rise there. The Confederate reserve must have occupied the lane to the Bliss farmhouse (now Long Lane) downslope to the rear. The opposing lines exchanged shots throughout the daylight hours. The fire seemed heaviest at the close of 1 July, while the armies were taking up their new positions and before the pattern of the battle in that area was established. Smith's brigade tended to force the fight then, but it became more passive later when it became apparent that General Meade wanted to invite an attack rather than make one. The 136th New York kept three or more of its companies forward at all times and sustained heavy losses. Casualties seemed greatest when troops from the main line relieved those to the front.[41]

Perhaps it was at such a time that Pvt. George Metcalf of the 136th New York first saw a man killed and became aware of the deadliness of war. The man had just returned from a turn on the skirmish line and was telling Metcalf about the fighting to the front. Metcalf heard a bullet thud into the man's head and saw him drop backward without moving a muscle. Metcalf believed, probably wrongly, that the shot had come from a church steeple in the town.[42]

The sun on 2 July baked the soldiers lying in the road and fields so that by noon the heat became almost unbearable and men were overcome by it. The water most convenient to the New Yorkers was at a spring to their front. They took turns going to the spring, each man carrying as many canteens as he could manage. The Confederates, who were equally bad off, shot at the water bearers and wounded several of them.[43]

Orderly Sgt. Lucian Smith complained that his company, and at least one other, went forward on the morning of 2 July without adequate preparation. But they advanced rapidly, drove the enemy before them, and as they neared the fence that crossed the field in their front, they suddenly confronted a reserve of the Confederate skirmish line that had been waiting in the lane. It was a strong body that seemed the size of a regiment. It charged to the aid of its comrades and fired a volley at the New Yorkers, who began a hurried retreat. The volley killed several men of the 136th New York, and one was captured. The Confederates, who knew their limits, did not push beyond the fence, and Smith's company fell back to its original position. This sort of push and shove highlighted the endless sparring on the skirmish lines.

The commander of the relieving company saw that one of the men shot was still alive, and he and another man dashed forward to rescue him. The Confederates understood what was happening and did not fire on them. As a detail carried the wounded man to the rear, he said to Sergeant Smith, "I am sorry for you. . . . It is over with me, but you little know what you have to go through with."[44]

It was on this day that Private Metcalf and his comrades crowded close to the wall along the Taneytown Road in front of the cemetery. They had piled rails on top of the wall and planted their flag among its rocks so that it stood proudly above them. Suddenly there was a flurry of screeching artillery shells that thudded and exploded around them. One hit the wall, severed the colors staff, and sent rails flying. Some rails fell on Metcalf, men were mortally wounded behind him and to his right, and a limb from a locust tree fell on a man to his left. It was a good shot. After receiving this hit, the regiment shifted 100 feet, probably to the right, to a safer segment of the wall.[45]

The battle warmed up toward the end of the day when General Pender ordered McGowan's and Lane's Confederate brigades forward to occupy the lane in force and to push the Federal skirmish line back to the Emmitsburg Road. Haskell's provisional battalion of sharpshooters from McGowan's South Carolina brigade, supported by 100 men of the 1st South Carolina Regiment under Maj. Comillus W. McCreary, and a body of men from Lane's brigade under Maj. Owen N. Brown of the 37th North Carolina "executed the order handsomely," and the men of the 136th New York and 73d Ohio fell back before them. The Confederates gained the fence, and from it they peppered the artillerymen serving the batteries on Cemetery Hill. The Federals could not tolerate this, of course. Smith's skirmishers, probably reinforced heavily from the reserve, counterattacked and followed the retreating Rebels too far. The Confederates re-formed and pushed again, driving the Union skirmishers back with a heavy loss. Finally, the equilibrium was reestablished, and the Confederates settled into the sunken lane behind their skirmish line. They would have use for the lane a little later that evening.[46]

Captain Haskell led the sharpshooters in their "intrepid charge," boldly walking in front of his line encouraging his men. He made an excellent target, and one of Smith's men shot him, inflicting a wound from which he soon died. Haskell was one of those gallant, well-favored, and socially prominent young men who are so cherished in the lore of the "Lost Cause." Col. Abner Perrin, his brigade commander, wrote in his report that Haskell was "educated and accomplished, possessing in a high degree every virtuous quality of the true gentleman and Christian. He was an officer of most excellent judgment, and a soldier of the coolest and most chivalrous daring."[47]

The fighting on the right of Smith's line was much like that on the fronts of the 55th Ohio and 136th New York, but the men of the 55th had to deal with Confederates both in their front and in buildings to their right. The skirmishing began at daylight, and at mid-morning Company H, which was on the line, fell back, its commander saying that "no man in God's world could stand it on that hill," meaning the rise west of the Emmitsburg Road.

Someone had to stand it though, so Col. Charles B. Gambee, the 55th's commander, ordered Capt. Frederick H. Boalt to take Company D forward. First Sgt. Luther B. Mesnard formed the company, Boalt drew his sword, and, in the words of Mesnard, "we were out there in a jiffy, but my how the lead did fly." Company D drove the Confederates from the fence that had once been manned by Company H. This placed them under the lethal fire that had driven Company H from the field. Pvt. Charles Stacey, who had earned a reputation as a marksman, volunteered to go to a vantage point to their right front and to locate the deadly enemy marksmen.

Stacey, followed closely by Mesnard, crept along a fence that ran toward the Confederate line. At some point, they removed a rail, and Stacey crawled through the hole and snaked twenty or so feet to some brush sprouting from the roots of an old stump. From there he could see the source of their special trouble—two sharpshooters who were in a cut beyond a small wheat field. Stacey shot at them, and the Rebels fired back at him, one shot splintering a rail on the fence sheltering Sergeant Mesnard and driving some splinters into his face.

Stacey stayed in his sniper's nest for two or three hours, long enough to fire twenty-three carefully aimed shots, and left it when Company D returned to the main line. The Confederates captured Stacey later in the day and sent him to Belle Isle prison. Thirty years later, he received a Medal of Honor for his valor at Gettysburg.[48]

The 55th Ohio's line must have arced around to Washington Street, and some of its men could see up the street into the town. Late in the afternoon, a large party of Confederates took over a house between the lines—

perhaps the one-and-a-half-story stone house of Frederick Barbahan on Washington Street about 300 yards north of the 55th's position. When the fire from the house became so deadly that something had to be done about it, Colonel Gambee called for volunteers to take care of it, and Captain Boalt offered to lead them.

Boalt led the force of about twenty men along Washington Street, the party crawling partway to avoid being seen. Some Confederates spotted them, but before those in the house could react to the threat, Boalt and his men rushed the building and captured it. The 55th held the house during the rest of the battle. Unlike Haskell, Boalt survived the war. In later years, Boalt's comrades recalled his having been "modest and brave" and a "brave and warm hearted gentleman."[49]

In their recollections, the men of the 55th Ohio complained more about the shots received from their right than those from their front. The Confederates pressed them hard late in the afternoon, probably in conjunction with their attack on Smith's left, and Company D went forward to bolster the right of the 55th's line—"the worst place," according to Mesnard. They could not hold the fence because the Rebels could enfilade it from left and right. They fell back closer to the Emmitsburg Road, a "bad place" where they "laid close and fired as fast as possible." Here a bullet hit Mesnard in the arm, and after the shock of the blow had eased, the sergeant ran back to the main line along the road just ahead of the bullets that seemed to "criss cross from every way." Since the regiment expected an attack, Gambee sent Mesnard farther to the rear. Mesnard dashed up Cemetery Hill between batteries that were "belching war" and was nearly trampled by a regiment changing position on the hill. "Dear me," Mesnard wrote in later years, "that was a terrible place just at that time."[50]

The bravery of individuals was more obvious on the skirmish line than in a regiment's line of battle. On 3 July some Confederates in a small brick building on Washington Street became such a nuisance that General Howard asked that they be removed. Gambee again called for volunteers, and five men responded. They made ready to attack and were supposed to rush the building when a signal was given. But at the signal, only one man, Pvt. Benjamin Pease, dashed forward. Pease reached the building, pounded its door with the butt of his rifle, and demanded the surrender of those within. Five men came out, chagrined soldiers who learned too late that they had surrendered to just one man.[51]

Musician Richard Enderlin of Company B, 73d Ohio Volunteer Infantry Regiment, a German immigrant and drummer for his company, also received a Medal of Honor for a deed of bravery in these fields. Like the other regiments of Smith's brigade, the 73d had been skirmishing all day on 2 July and had taken heavy casualties. At dusk, the Confederate threat was so great that Lt. Col. Richard Long, the 73d's commander, increased the strength of the skirmish line to half that of the main line, and the opposing skirmish lines were less than 200 yards apart. Between them was a trodden field of wheat strewn with dead and wounded. The moans of one of the wounded men, Pvt. George Nixon of Company B, 73d Ohio, were so distinct and so heartrending that Enderlin resolved to try to bring him in. Enderlin asked his company commander for permission to try to do this, but he refused—it was too dangerous. Enderlin persisted, and the officer relented.

By this time it was dark. Enderlin removed his equipment and unneeded clothing and crawled forward into the wheat, taking advantage when he could of the dark periods that came when clouds covered the bright moon. Finally, Enderlin reached the wounded man, who was lying only a short distance in front of the Confederate picket line. Slowly and quietly he dragged his wounded comrade back toward the Union line, his presence obscured by the distraction of the constant fire that crossed the field around him. When nearer to the Union line than to the Confederate, Enderlin stood with Nixon in his arms and dashed for the Union line. It was an impressive feat. Enderlin's company commander promoted him to the rank of sergeant on the spot. Unfortunately, the story's ending was not a happy one. George Nixon's painful wound was mortal; he died at Gettysburg and is buried on the hill he fought to hold. Still, George Nixon had a destiny none of his comrades would have suspected—his great-grandson would be a president of the United States.[52]

Col. Orland Smith's brigade, apart from its 33d Massachusetts Regiment, was the only brigade on the hill engaged solely in skirmishing. It sustained unusually heavy casualties for fighting of this sort. The three regiments involved had a combined strength of about 1,300 officers and men and suffered 303 casualties. This high figure is a tribute to Union courage and Confederate marksmanship.[53]

In his report of the battle, Colonel Smith remarked that his men were engaged for three days and exposed to enemy fire not only from the front but also from sharpshooters in the town off to the right. He remarked that his main line, though posted behind a stone wall, was constantly annoyed by fire from the same source. In a sense, the report is almost as complimentary to the enemy as it is to his own men. Von Steinwehr, who

10

BRINKERHOFF'S RIDGE

The skirmishing in front of Cemetery Hill was deadly, but that along the Hanover Road at Brinkerhoff's Ridge on 2 July might well have been decisive. On the east slope of Brinkerhoff's Ridge, two and a half miles east of Gettysburg, infantrymen of the Stonewall Brigade guarded the left of the Army of Northern Virginia. They sparred with a series of units of the Army of the Potomac—troops of the Twelfth and the Fifth corps and finally squadrons of Brig. Gen. David McM. Gregg's division of the Cavalry Corps.

The skirmishing began at daybreak when troops of the Stonewall Brigade exchanged shots with Hoosiers of the 27th Indiana Regiment from Ruger's brigade of the Twelfth Corps. Ruger's brigade, now under the temporary command of Col. Silas Colgrove of the 27th Indiana Regiment, had spent the night south of Wolf Hill near the Baltimore Pike. It returned to the fields near the Hanover Road early in the morning behind a screen formed by Company F of the 27th Indiana. When the Indiana soldiers reached the north slope of Wolf Hill, they found elements of the Stonewall Brigade in the woods in their front and in a stone house and its barn to their right. The Virginians attempted to seize another house and barn to Colgrove's left, but the Hoosiers beat them to it. The Rebels shot from the cover of the buildings on Colgrove's right and the woods, and the Twelfth Corps men replied from the buildings just seized and from the open fields to their right.[1]

Not long after this fighting began, the Fifth Corps filed into the area by way of the Hanover Road from the east. The First and Second divisions of the corps massed briefly south of the road behind a screen of their own skirmishers that included the 9th Massachusetts Infantry Regiment. No one described the 9th's position, but it was probably near the farm buildings on the right of Colgrove's men at first, and then its commander, Col. Patrick R. Guiney, swung it left across the road so that it faced the Confederates to the west.

Soon after the Fifth Corps arrived, the Twelfth Corps units received orders to rejoin their corps on Culp's Hill, leaving the area along the Hanover Road to the care of the Fifth. Shortly thereafter, Colonel Guiney, who was directing the fight of the 9th Massachusetts, saw the Fifth Corps "with-drawing from its position and passing over to the left." This withdrawal came as a surprise to him, and he asked for orders. In response, he learned that his regiment was to stay where it was, and soon he found that the 9th was alone with both flanks "unconnected and exposed." Guiney felt uneasy having only the 470 officers and men of the "Irish Ninth" to face a Confederate force of unknown size and intentions. The 9th was not alone long, however, for Union cavalry appeared along the Hanover Road in its rear. But, to Guiney's disgust, the cavalrymen made no effort to relieve them so that they could move to the left and rejoin their brigade. Instead, the horsemen rested, and Guiney growled that the Massachusetts men were "merely protecting an inactive cavalry force large enough, and assuredly brave enough to take care of its own front."[2]

The reports of the Stonewall Brigade record that there was skirmishing on its front throughout the day, but they say little more about it. Sgt. Charles Rollins of the 27th Virginia wrote of watching some Confederate skirmishers at work. Those whom he saw from his place at the edge of a piece of woods were in the open. They were in full sight of the enemy and "resorted to the 'lie down' process." They lay flat on the ground, heads toward the enemy, loaded their rifles while lying on their backs, and then rolled to their stomachs to shoot. From time to time, the Confederate skirmish line would advance with a yell, and then there would be relative quiet. Rollins complained that screening flanks was the job of the "absent, truant, cavalry" but that since the cavalry was elsewhere, the Stonewall Brigade had to do it. The soldiers of the brigade held the cavalry in low esteem, and "playing cavalry" was not to their liking.[3]

The commander of the Stonewall Brigade, Brig. Gen. James A. Walker, enjoyed a rare distinction. Of all the generals in the armies of the Confederacy, he was the first to have had a major confrontation with Stonewall Jackson. Walker was a Virginian from Augusta County, born in 1832, and he had been a cadet at the Virginia Military Institute until the spring of 1852. It was during a class session that he exchanged sharp words with

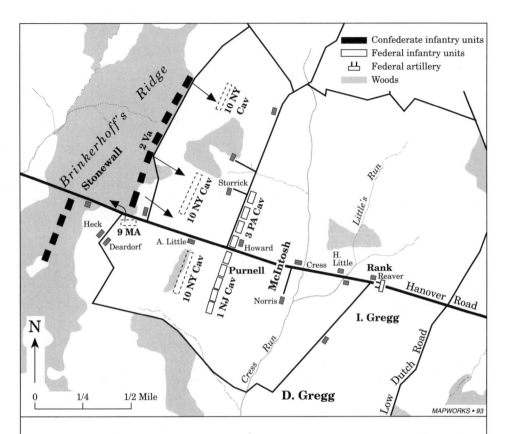

Confederate infantry units
Federal infantry units
Federal artillery
Woods

Brinkerhoff's Ridge

Stonewall

2 Va

10 NY Cav

10 NY Cav

Storrick

3 PA Cav

Heck

Little's Run

9 MA

Howard

A. Little

Deardorf

10 NY Cav

Purnell

McIntosh

Cress

H. Little

Rank
Reaver

Hanover Road

1 NJ Cav

Norris

I. Gregg

N

Cress Run

Low Dutch Road

0   1/4   1/2 Mile

D. Gregg

MAPWORKS • 93

1. The 9th Massachusetts Regiment, on picket near the Deardorf house, skirmishes in the area until late afternoon.

2. The 10th New York Cavalry relieves the 9th Massachusetts, forms on both sides of the Hanover Road, and skirmishes with the Stonewall Brigade.

3. The 2d Virginia Infantry Regiment deploys north of the road and advances to clear the fields in its front.

4. At 7:00 P.M. the 10th New York is relieved by two squadrons of the 3d Pennsylvania north of the road and two squadrons of the 1st New Jersey Regiment and the Purnell Legion troop south of it..

5. The 2d Virginia and two squadrons of the 3d Pennsylvania Cavalry fight for a fence. Aided by Rank's guns, the Pennsylvanians seize the fence and hold it. The fight ends at dusk.

Map 10.1. Brinkerhoff's Ridge, 2 July

Jackson. Walker believed that Jackson had insulted him, and he challenged the professor to a duel. The duel did not take place; instead Walker was expelled from the school.

Walker worked for a time in railroad construction, read law, and attended law school at the University of Virginia. He established a practice in Pulaski County, Virginia, and was living there at the time of John Brown's raid on Harpers Ferry. The raid prompted him to form a militia company, the "Pulaski Guard," which, as its captain, he took into the Confederate service at the outbreak of the war. The company became part of the 4th Virginia Regiment and served in Jackson's command at Harpers Ferry. There and later, Walker's relations with Jackson were amicable. Walker became lieutenant colonel of the 13th Virginia Regiment, which was commanded by A. P. Hill, and when Hill became a general, Walker succeeded to the 13th's colonelcy. Walker took part in the Valley campaign and at various times in 1862 served as acting brigade commander for Gen. Arnold Elzey's and Gen. Isaac Trimble's brigades. He was wounded while commanding Early's brigade at Antietam. Thus, it was only right that when the army had its major reorganization after Chancellorsville, this capable officer, who was "as brave and gallant as he was positive," received his own brigade. His appointment to the command of the Stonewall Brigade, however, was a shock to its colonels, who resented him as an outsider and offered their resignations. Somehow the matter was settled, and Walker led the Stonewall Brigade to Gettysburg.[4]

Late in the afternoon, the men of the "Irish Ninth" could hear the sounds of the battle on the left and were more anxious than ever to join their brigade in the fight. Finally, Lt. T. Corwin Case, aide to Brig. Gen. James Barnes, their division commander, appeared and led the 9th to the left. It was time for the cavalry to face the Virginians alone.[5]

The cavalry had plenty of reasons to need rest. It had been on "incessant duty" since the outset of the campaign on 9 June, and since crossing the Potomac on 27 June, it had been constantly on the move. Gregg's division had screened the right of the Army of the Potomac and had traveled north through Frederick, New Windsor, and Westminster to Manchester, Maryland, about thirty-five miles southeast of Gettysburg. It was while the division was near Manchester on 1 July that Gregg learned that the Confederates were concentrating at Gettysburg and that he should take his division there without delay. Gregg and his division set out for Gettysburg, but when passing through Hanover Junction, he received orders to send one brigade back to Manchester to cover the supply point being established at Westminster. Gregg detached Col. Pennock Huey's brigade

Brig. Gen. James A. Walker (WLM)

for this service and continued on to Gettysburg with his First and Third brigades commanded by Col. John B. McIntosh and Col. J. Irvin Gregg.[6]

David McMurtrie Gregg was one of the Union's more mature and modest cavalry leaders and, therefore, has received less notice than upstarts like George Custer, Judson Kilpatrick, and others of their ilk. He was born in 1833 in Huntington County, Pennsylvania, and was reared in prosperous circumstances. While attending what became Bucknell University, he received an appointment to West Point and became a member of its class of 1854. Brig. Gen. Alexander S. Webb, whose brigade held the Union center at the Copse of Trees, was a classmate, and Stuart, Ruger, and Pender, of the class of 1853, must have known him.

After graduation, Gregg served as a subaltern in the West until he received a captaincy in the 3d Cavalry in May 1861. He transferred to the 6th Cavalry in August and in January 1862 became colonel of the 8th Pennsylvania Cavalry. Gregg led his regiment during the Peninsular campaign and in November received a promotion to brigadier general and commanded a brigade at Fredericksburg. He led the Third Division of the Army of the Potomac's Cavalry Corps on the Richmond raid during Chancellorsville, at Brandy Station, Aldie, Middleburg, and Upperville, and finally north of the Potomac to Gettysburg. One of Gregg's biographers described him as

having been "endowed with a rare combination of modesty, geniality, and ability . . . universally liked and respected." He might have added "nearly forgotten" as well. It was Gregg who commanded the Union cavalry on the right on 3 July. With less than three brigades, Gregg halted General Stuart's four when Stuart moved against the Federal right, and Gregg was victor on that field. Yet even among those who know something of the battle of Gettysburg, few would recognize his name.[7]

Gregg's regiments were in poor condition indeed when they approached the Gettysburg area over the Hanover Road late on the morning of 2 July. Lt. William Brooke Rawle of the 3d Pennsylvania Cavalry, the unofficial scribe for Gregg's division, in the postwar years wrote that the column had been without food and forage for many days, the heat had been almost unendurable, and the dust had been nearly impenetrable. The men were so begrimed as to be unrecognizable. Some troopers whose horses had collapsed plodded afoot carrying their cumbersome saddles and bridles, while those with horses often led them to conserve their strength. On 30 June, for instance, the 3d Pennsylvania Cavalry had 384 men but only

322 serviceable horses, and by the time it reached Gettysburg, even that number had declined. It is not surprising then that when Gregg's regiments reached the fields east of Gettysburg at the intersection of the Hanover and Low Dutch roads, the troopers were eager to let their horses graze and get a little rest. Yet even then Gregg had work for them to do; he ordered them to remove fences along the Hanover Road so that they would not obstruct the division's movements.[8]

After a short while, Col. Irvin Gregg received an order to take his brigade toward the Union left by way of the Low Dutch Road. The brigade followed that country road nearly to the Baltimore Pike and then it received an order to return to the Hanover Road. When it did so, it turned into the fields south of the road near the Reever farm buildings and sought some rest. From there, its men could hear the sound of rifle fire to the west, which told them that infantrymen were enjoying a firefight on the skirmish line. When General Gregg learned that Colonel Guiney's infantrymen would soon be leaving for the left, he asked Colonel Gregg to replace them with troopers of the 10th New York Cavalry Regiment. The general wanted not only to occupy the ground vacated by the 9th Massachusetts Regiment but also to establish a picket line that would cover the right of Meade's army.[9]

By the sort of coincidence that was so common during the Civil War, the 10th New York Cavalry had returned to familiar ground. After entering Federal service in 1861, it spent the winter of 1861–62 at Gettysburg learning the rudiments of soldiering and creating a Federal military presence close to the Mason-Dixon Line. Its camp that winter had been on the Wolf farm, about a mile and a half to the northwest of its 2 July position, and many in the regiment had acquaintances in the community. Now they would fight for the possession of their old stomping ground.[10]

Gregg's division was in poor condition for a fight. Although the Order of Battle shows that his two brigades had a paper strength of nine cavalry regiments, an independent cavalry company, and a stray section of artillery, his available usable force consisted only of the 10th New York and 16th Pennsylvania Cavalry regiments in Irvin Gregg's brigade and the 1st New Jersey and 3d Pennsylvania regiments and one Maryland cavalry troop in McIntosh's brigade plus the section of artillery. Gregg placed the 16th Pennsylvania Cavalry Regiment on a picket line to the left, leaving only the three other weakened regiments for the work on Brinkerhoff's Ridge. Had push come to shove, they would hardly have been a match for the Stonewall Brigade.[11]

Gregg had two excellent brigade commanders with him. Col. John B.

Col. John B. McIntosh (WLM)

McIntosh was the son of Lt. Col. James S. McIntosh of the 5th Infantry, who had been killed during the war with Mexico. McIntosh had served during that war as a midshipman and afterward had gone into business in New Brunswick, New Jersey. He was scandalized when his brother, Capt. James McQ. McIntosh of the U.S. Army, entered the Confederate service, and, in spite of his age, he secured a commission as a second lieutenant in the 2d Cavalry. A year later, he became a first lieutenant in the 5th Cavalry. This was on-the-job training for bigger things. After this experience, he received command of the newly formed 3d Pennsylvania Cavalry Regiment. His time as a regimental commander was short for by the time of the battle of Kelly's Ford in March 1863, he was an acting brigade commander, and in the Gettysburg campaign, he commanded his own brigade.

McIntosh played a signal role in the fight at Gettysburg and received a brevet for his service in the battle of 3 July. According to Gen. William W. Averill, for whom he had served previously, McIntosh was a brigade com-

Col. J. Irvin Gregg (WLM)

mander second to none. A biographer described him as a "born fighter, a strict disciplinarian, a dashing leader, and a polished gentleman."[12]

Col. John Irvin Gregg, a "distant relative" to the general, was also a Pennsylvanian. He had had some service in the war with Mexico, and when the Civil War began, he secured a captaincy with the 3d U.S. Cavalry Regiment. He soon transferred to the 6th Cavalry and served with it on the Peninsula. After this apprenticeship, he became colonel of the 16th Pennsylvania Cavalry Regiment in November 1862. A member of the regiment at that time recalled Gregg as having been a "very tall, quiet, soldierly captain." The recruits of the 16th Regiment were impressed by his height and nicknamed him "Long John." Like McIntosh, he soon received a brigade command and led the Third Brigade of Gregg's division north during the Gettysburg campaign.[13]

The cavalry entered the fight on Brinkerhoff's Ridge when the 9th Massachusetts Infantry Regiment departed for the left. The 10th New York Cavalry Regiment went into position astride the Hanover Road, and the 16th Pennsylvania extended its line toward Wolf Hill and the left. Colonel Gregg and Maj. M. Henry Avery, commander of the 10th, deployed two squadrons of the 10th (there were two companies in a squadron) under Maj. Alvah D. Waters south of the Hanover Road. At the same time, Avery sent another squadron, composed of Companies H and L, under Maj. John L. Kemper into the fields north of the road. Kemper's men advanced on foot west along the Hanover Road, crossed Little Run and Cress Run, and then deployed to the right in the fields north of the road. From Cress Run, the ground slopes up about fifty feet in a half mile to the Howard buildings on the south side of the road and to a cross road (Hoffman Road today) that ran north from the Hanover Road along the east slope of the ridge and for practical purposes marked the ridge's crest. Kemper left a portion of his squadron at the John Cress house in the low ground beside Cress Run and advanced toward the crest of the ridge through a field of tall, ripe wheat on the north side of the Hanover Road. There, below the cross road and between the Hanover Road and a grove of trees, Kemper deployed a skirmish line that remained essentially undisturbed for nearly an hour, while in the rear the remainder of the troopers in the regiment groomed their horses and tried to rest.[14]

As Kemper's squadron went forward, its troopers saw the Cress family fleeing their house, the father carrying a bag of foodstuffs, the women bearing bedding, and the children loaded with items of clothing. Some of the soldiers foraged at the Cress property, of course, but took later satisfaction in having taken only some "mackerel" from a tub of water and leaving some chickens that were running in the yard.[15]

When the cavalry took over the skirmish line, Colonel McIntosh posted the two guns of Capt. William D. Rank's battery at a high point on the Hanover Road near the Abraham Reever house. From their position, Rank's two three-inch Ordnance rifles could cover the ground to their front as far as the crest of Brinkerhoff's Ridge. Rank's guns were at Gettysburg only by chance. The section had been guarding the railroad bridge over the Monocacy River at Frederick until Lee's army crossed the Potomac. In the face of such an overwhelming threat, it had been ordered back to Relay House near Annapolis and was on its way there with Company A of Maryland's Purnell Legion when the two units were nearly captured near Cooksville by Stuart's cavalry. Next day the fugitive units met McIntosh's brigade, which they accompanied to Gettysburg. Both the gun section and the cavalry troop were unlikely candidates for field service with the Army of the Potomac.[16]

As the cavalrymen deployed on the Union right, Longstreet's corps was attacking the Union left and General Johnson was preparing for his assault on Culp's Hill. In order to secure his exposed flank, Johnson ordered the Stonewall Brigade to shift left to cover it better. This shift placed the 2d Virginia Regiment immediately north of the Hanover Road. General Walker ordered Col. John Q. A. Nadenbousch of the 2d Virginia to "clear the field"—the wheat field containing a Union skirmish line—advance into the woods there, and ascertain what force was in his front. Nadenbousch obeyed, collapsed Kemper's squadron's line, and drove its men south across the Hanover Road, where it would have the support of the squadrons commanded by Major Waters.[17]

When Colonel Gregg saw Kemper's squadron giving ground before the Virginians, he asked Major Avery to feed another fifty men into the fight north of the road. Avery turned to Capt. Benjamin F. Lownsbury, who was cleaning his pistol nearby, and asked him to take in his squadron, Companies E and K. Each company was small and was commanded then by a sergeant. After every fourth trooper left ranks to hold horses, Lownsbury had only twenty-seven men on line. Lownsbury's little force climbed uphill to a rail fence on the ridge about 100 yards east of the cross road. The sun was low at this time (it must have been after 6:00 P.M.), and it shone directly in the New Yorkers' eyes. Lownsbury posted his men along the fence until the sun dropped behind some trees in their front and did not shine in their eyes. Soon after, another squadron composed of Companies B and D and commanded by Lt. Truman White came forward to reinforce Lownsbury's line on the right and drive the Rebels from a grove of trees at the Storrick house.[18]

Even with two squadrons on line north of the road, the New Yorkers, who were armed with Sharps carbines, were at a disadvantage. Sgt. Alfred J. Edson of Company D recalled that they had to lie as flat as possible to protect themselves from the Virginians' rifle fire and that every enemy shot made them flatten more. Pvt. Hiram Hadden, who wore a large white hat, became a particular target. After being shot at several times, Hadden became so angry that he stood, fired off all of his cartridges, and walked away. Another man in Edson's squad was such a "constitutional coward" that Edson placed him in the care of two troopers who were told to keep him in his place. As soon as the shooting began, the nervous fellow fired straight into the air. "Hold on there!" shouted one of his keepers, "there ain't any rebs up there; you'll kill yourself an angel!"[19]

The 10th New York's line did not hold long, for soon after his arrival at the fence, Lownsbury saw some mounted men heading for the rear along the Hanover Road and he "concluded that they had found something they didn't want." The enemy confirmed this suspicion when what seemed to be two enemy regiments charged the men of the 10th from the front and the right. Lownsbury's bugler sounded the "Recall" but not quite soon enough. In spite of a rapid retreat by Lownsbury's men, the 2d

Virginia captured Lownsbury and Sgt. Edmund G. Dow of Company K. After their capture, the Virginians took both men to see General Walker at the Shriver farm west of the ridge. Dow recalled Walker as having been gentlemanly, even when sitting on a rail fence. Walker asked them some questions about the forces in his front and expressed the belief that the Confederates would win the impending battle.[20]

Major Avery made a final effort to get control on the north side of the road when he saw the three squadrons there in retreat. He sent in Company F under Lt. James Matthews, the only one left in reserve. Matthews and his company went in mounted and rode to the top of the ridge, "where the bullets flew very thick." Matthews wheeled his company around and sought shelter from the fire beneath the brow of the ridge. A few minutes later, according to Matthews, Avery rode up in a rage and demanded to know who had ordered the company back. Matthews said that he had done so, and before Avery could reply, the Confederates fired a volley at them. Avery dodged a bit, and when he could speak, he shouted, "You should have done it before."[21]

In the meantime, Major Waters, who commanded the two squadrons south of the road, had deployed Company C in a picket line that extended south to the base of Wolf Hill. Company G on its right carried the line to the Hanover Road, and Waters held Companies A and M to their rear in support. Sometime after they had deployed, Waters asked Sgt. John M. Freer of Company M and four volunteers to find out if the enemy in their front was there in force. The five cavalrymen went through the woods to a seven-rail fence on the edge of an open field. From there, they could see a large Confederate formation in the field. Freer left his comrades at the fence and hurried back to report what he had seen to Major Waters. Freer told him that the Confederates had a division there, at least!

Freer rejoined his party in time to witness the approach of about thirty Virginians who seemed to want to remove the fence that sheltered Freer's party. As the Rebels approached, Freer's "boys" became anxious and wanted to open fire, but Freer made them wait until they came to within fifty yards; then he yelled the order, "Give them h—l." The crack of Union carbines surprised the Confederates, and they scampered in such a way that Freer thought "that they had struck the open door to sheol and found everyone at home." The Confederates recovered quickly, however, and advanced "with their celebrated 'Ki-yi.'" Freer and his party skedaddled back to Cress Run, far behind Waters's skirmish line, and the Confederates did not press. They had bigger fish to fry elsewhere.[22]

When it was relieved by the regiments of McIntosh's brigade, the 10th

New York rallied east of Cress Run and licked its wounds before taking its position for the night. On the following morning, Pvt. Charles Cutter of Company G got into a quarrel with another soldier identified as an infantryman. They argued about which of them had the right to "plunder" a dead Confederate soldier whom Cutter had already gone over with some thoroughness. The infantryman scolded Cutter for having robbed the man before he was dead. An insulted Cutter ended the conversation by ascending to a high moral plane and replying, "Well, you may rob a dead man, but I'll not disgrace myself by doing it; I think it's bad enough to rob a live one!"[23]

The horsemen whom Captain Lownsbury saw hurrying to the rear before his capture as the fight on Brinkerhoff's Ridge was heating up might have included either hospital steward Walter Kempster of his own regiment or Assistant Surgeon Theodore T. Tate of the 3d Pennsylvania Cavalry Regiment. Both had fled on horseback that day. Kempster, who seemed to have no casualties to care for, was watching the skirmishing south of the Hanover Road when a line of Confederate infantry appeared on his right and fired a volley in his direction. Kempster wheeled his horse around and galloped off Indian-style, hanging on with his left arm and leg. Rank's guns started firing as he fled, and he rode to them. Captain Rank congratulated him on his escape. Kempster wrote that the skirmish line had fallen back to their horses but went forward again when they saw the enemy give way before the cannon fire.[24]

Tate, whose home was in Gettysburg, had a different story. Tate had been especially helpful to the division by acting as its guide as it approached Gettysburg. After reaching the fields east of the town, he had gone on ahead in the hope of seeing his family. Instead, he ran into Confederates who chased him at a gallop out the Hanover Road, across Brinkerhoff's Ridge, and into Gregg's lines. A body of mounted Confederates appeared on the road where it crossed the ridge a moment after Tate's wild ride. This group of horsemen looked important enough to merit some attention, so General Gregg asked Captain Rank to send them a "feeler."[25]

Rank's two guns sat in the road by the Reever house and were admired by some local civilians who gathered near them to see what was going on. Nearby was an elderly woman with a crutch under one arm and a cane, who was observing the excitement from the Little house downhill and in front of the guns. When Rank's guns banged at the party of mounted Rebels, firing over the woman's head, they so startled her that she fell over backward. Then getting to her feet, without cane and crutch she ran off across the fields and into history like a young woman, shrieking with all of her might, much to the amusement of the cannoneers and cavalrymen nearby.[26]

These were the first shots fired by Rank's battery in battle, and they were lucky ones, bursting in the midst of the party and scattering it like "chaff in a wind storm." At the same time that the shots were fired, General Gregg ordered McIntosh to take his brigade forward, and forward it went—two squadrons of the 3d Pennsylvania Cavalry Regiment to the right of the road toward the area vacated by Kemper's squadrons and two squadrons of the 1st New Jersey Regiment and Company A of the Purnell Legion to the south of the road where Waters's men had been. All started mounted but dismounted in due course, leaving their horses in the care of horse holders so that they could fight afoot.[27]

The troops on the left of the road formed with Capt. Robert E. Duvall's company of the Purnell Legion on the right abutting the road and New Jersey squadrons under Maj. Hugh H. Janeway and Capt. Robert N. Boyd south of it. It was a thin line; there were only 150 New Jerseymen and less than half that many Marylanders. Janeway rode behind the line cheering it on as it pushed forward for about 100 yards. The New Jersey troopers used all of their carbine ammunition and, as the fighting wound down, faced the Virginians with their pistols until the 3d Pennsylvania Cavalry Regiment relieved them.[28]

On the north side of the road, the 3d Pennsylvania Cavalry had formed in the woods behind the Cress house and sat on horseback waiting for orders to join the fight. After Rank's guns fired their opening rounds, two squadrons, those of Capt. Frank W. Hess and Capt. William E. Miller, went forward, Hess's men on the left beside the road, keeping pace with Janeway's line south of the road. They splashed through Cress Run and hurried up the slope. They could see the wall or fence in their front that had sheltered the squadrons of the 10th New York just a short while before. Beyond, though, was a field of ripe wheat, and in that field was a line of Confederate infantry making for the wall. Rank's two guns blazed away at the Virginia line, slowing its advance, while the Pennsylvanians panted as they dashed toward the wall. The race for the wall was a near thing, but the Pennsylvanians reached it first. They opened fire with their Sharps carbines at the Virginians, who were still about twenty feet away. Although the Confederates made several attempts to drive the Pennsylvanians from the wall, the squadrons of Hess and Miller held on. Later, after dark, the Virginians turned the right of the cavalry's line, but the cavalrymen reestablished their line, and the fighting north of the road died.[29]

By dusk the skirmishing was essentially over for the day on Brinkerhoff's Ridge. Measured by casualties, the fighting east of the town was trivial, more noisy than deadly—for instance, the 2d Virginia Regiment had only three men wounded. On the Union side, the 3d Pennsylvania Cavalry had only one man wounded and three captured; the 10th New York Regiment had two killed, four wounded, and three captured; and the 16th Pennsylvania had two killed and four wounded. These were paltry figures in a battle as bloody as Gettysburg.[30]

Yet this skirmishing had results that probably were highly significant. General Walker, in his report, wrote that after the fight, the 2d Virginia had fallen back to the edge of the woods and that Colonel Nadenbousch reported that the enemy in its front was a large force composed of two regiments of cavalry, two regiments of infantry (!), and a battery. Walker sent this information to General Johnson, who replied that the division was about to advance but that Walker should hold his brigade on the flank if he thought it necessary.

Walker did think so. He believed that the army's flank and rear would be entirely uncovered and unprotected if his brigade left its position in order to advance with the division. Further, if done before dark, its departure would be in full view of the enemy—an invitation for it to exploit the brigade's departure. Therefore, he deemed it prudent for the Stonewall Brigade to stay where it was until dark. Thus, Johnson's division began its attack on Culp's Hill without the Stonewall Brigade in line and without the strength and flexibility it could have provided. It would be sorely missed and could have pushed all the way to the Baltimore Pike.[31]

After dark, Walker posted a picket line to guard the Hanover Road and marched his brigade off to join Johnson's division, but too late to be of help in its assault. At about the same time, Gregg's division also pulled away and spent the night along the Baltimore Pike at White Run. Gregg's division and the Stonewall Brigade would both fight again next day but not each other.[32]

11

THE ARTILLERY, 2 JULY

Maj. Joseph W. Latimer was a military prodigy. At the beginning of the war, as a seventeen-year-old cadet at the Virginia Military Institute, he had served as a drillmaster for a green, untutored battery of Virginia artillery. Amid this verdure, he had so impressed those in high places that he received a commission as a first lieutenant in September 1861, just after turning eighteen, and assignment to Virginia's Courtney Artillery. Latimer became the battery's captain during the summer of 1862 and a major in March 1863 when only nineteen. In spite of his age, Latimer's performance at First Winchester, at Cedar Mountain, and on other fields had elevated him to the peerage of the likes of John Pelham and William Pegram. Ewell called him the "Young Napoleon," and after his recent promotion, soldiers referred to him as "The Boy Major." Campbell Brown wrote that Latimer "was small & slight of his age . . . but one of those born soldiers whose promotion is recognized by all to be a consequence of their own merit." While serving as an acting battalion commander at Gettysburg in place of the wounded Lt. Col. R. Snowden Andrews, Latimer had captains in his charge who were many years his senior and was "liked by them and idolized by his own men & the Infantry of his Division as well." Sometimes the infantrymen cheered him when he rode by them—a distinction usually reserved for General Lee, Stonewall Jackson, and scampering rabbits.[1]

Latimer led Andrews's battalion to Gettysburg, marching with Johnson's division, and had arrived on 1 July just before dark. Shielded by darkness from the sight of the gunners on Cemetery Hill, he parked the battalion in a wheat field east of town for the night. After a march of over

Maj. Joseph W. Latimer (NA)

twenty miles, those men not on guard duty slept soundly in spite of their concerns over the battle that they knew must come.

On 2 July the men of Andrews's battalion awakened to a damp and overcast morning. Throughout the day, they heard the occasional bark of a cannon and the popping of skirmish firing near the hills to their front. At about 4:00 A.M., when light permitted, Major Latimer searched for a position for his guns. He found that he had to settle for Benner's Hill south of the Hanover Road for there was no better position to be had on the Confederate left. Yet the guns posted there would be so vulnerable to enemy fire that it would be folly to occupy the hill prematurely.[2]

Benner's Hill overlooked Gettysburg from astride the Hanover Road just to the east of Rock Creek and the town. The hill's broad crest extended about 300 yards south-southwest from the Hanover Road and 500 yards north-northeast of it. The crest loomed 100 feet above Rock Creek at the hill's west base and sloped rather steeply to the west, the south, and the east. The crest and the slopes from it were mostly bare of rocks and trees, there being only a small clump of trees just southwest of a small rocky rise at its southern end and another clump just to the east. At the time of the battle, the hill's crest south of the road and its west slope were covered with a field of ripe wheat. Much of the wider crest north of the road was planted in knee-high corn. There was no cover either to impede the movement of batteries or to shield them.[3]

The south end of the crest of Benner's Hill was about 1,000 yards northeast of Culp's Hill and 1,500 yards east-northeast of East Cemetery Hill. These distances increased to points on the hill toward the Hanover Road and beyond. All batteries to be posted on Benner's Hill could fire effectively at Union guns on Cemetery Hill, but it was only practicable for the left battery in the Confederate line to fire toward Culp's Hill. In turn, any batteries on Benner's Hill were potential targets for batteries on East Cemetery Hill, Stevens's Knoll, and the highest point on Culp's Hill.

Sometime early in the morning, the Rockbridge Artillery, commanded by Capt. Archibald Graham, took position on Benner's Hill north of the Hanover Road. Although one of its veterans remembered it as having been about 200 yards from the right of Latimer's battalion later in the day, its exact position was not recorded. The battery had six twenty-pounder Parrott rifles, which could fire effectively at targets on Cemetery Hill. It may be assumed that it shot a few rounds toward the hill early in the day in order to get its range. Otherwise it was quiet. At one time early in the morning before the battery had fired, General Ewell and his staff rode by. Maj. Sandie Pendleton, of Lexington in Rockbridge County, left the general's party momentarily to say hello to his neighbors and to deliver a couple of letters to Pvt. Edward Moore, a cannoneer in the battery. To Moore, receiving two letters at any time was "an event," but to have them delivered on a battlefield by a general and his staff was "quite something."[4]

Col. Charles S. Wainwright, commander of the artillery of the Union First Corps, was in charge of the Union guns on East Cemetery Hill—that portion of the hill east of the Baltimore Pike. All of Wainwright's batteries had dropped trail there late in the afternoon of 1 July, and the cannoneers had improved their positions by erecting lunettes of earth and fence rails in front of their pieces. Wainwright had Stewart's U.S. battery posted beside the Baltimore Pike near the cemetery gate, its four serviceable Napoleons pointing down the road toward the town. Wiedrich's New York battery, an Eleventh Corps outfit, was on the hill's crest just northeast of Stewart's guns; its four three-inch Ordnance rifles could fire north toward the town and northeast toward Benner's Hill as well. Cooper's Pennsylvanians were on Wiedrich's right in the narrow field just south of the crest, and Reynolds's New York battery, now commanded by Lt. George Breck, was in the field below. Both of these batteries had three-inch Ordnance rifles, Cooper four and Breck five, and both could fire at targets on Benner's Hill. Wainwright's other battery was the 5th Maine, commanded by Capt. Greenleaf T. Stevens. From its knoll on the west slope of Culp's Hill, its six Napoleons enfiladed the fields east of East Cemetery Hill, but they could also swing around to the northeast far enough to shoot at Benner's Hill. All told, Wainwright had twenty-three guns under his immediate charge. The ten Napoleons were especially useful in firing canister, but they could hurl twelve-pound balls for more than a mile; the thirteen three-inch Ordnance rifles were more accurate than the smoothbores and could be especially useful in counterbattery fire. All but Stewart's Napoleons could fire at Benner's Hill.[5]

Maj. Thomas W. Osborn, artillery chief for the Eleventh Corps, had more space for fieldpieces on Cemetery Hill west of the pike than Wainwright had east of it. Osborn asked General Hunt for additional batteries from the Artillery Reserve on 2 July, and Hunt was pleased to provide the few batteries that he could use. By 4:00 P.M. on 2 July Osborn had over forty guns on his portion of the hill, including ten rifled pieces set parallel to the pike to the right and rear of the cemetery gate. These pointed primarily toward Benner's Hill. The remaining guns were west of the gate and fired to the north and northwest.[6]

No one recorded the precise position of these batteries; their having been in the Evergreen and Soldiers' National cemeteries might have discouraged their accurate marking on the ground in later years. By late afternoon the three Napoleon batteries were closest to the Baltimore Pike, where their special effectiveness with canister could be put to good use in case of an attack from the town. In spite of their hard fight north of the town, Dilger's battery, which was nearest the pike, and Wilkeson's (Bancroft's) on its left each had six Napoleons ready to fire. Battery H, 1st U.S. Artillery, commanded by Lt. Chandler P. Eakin, came up from the Artillery Reserve late in the afternoon and went into position on Bancroft's left. These eighteen Napoleons must have occupied a line that extended about 150 yards west from the Baltimore Pike.[7]

Wheeler's battery, now with only three three-inch Ordnance rifles, came next. Battery C, 1st West Virginia Light Artillery, commanded by Capt. Wallace Hill, with four ten-pounder Parrott rifles, was on Wheeler's left, and four three-inch Ordnance rifles of Hall's battery were on Hill's left. Hall's 2d Maine Battery, a First Corps unit, had reached Cemetery Hill with only three usable guns after the fight of 1 July, but Captain Hall had "rehorsed" one of the disabled guns and was able to have four in line on

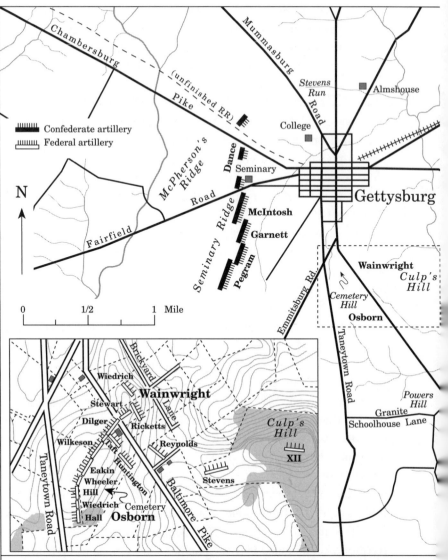

Confederate artillery

Federal artillery

N

Chambersburg
(unfinished RR)
Pike
Mummasburg Road
Stevens Run
Almshouse
College
McPherson's Ridge
Dance
Seminary
Gettysburg
McIntosh
Road
Seminary Ridge
Garnett
Fairfield
Pegram
Emmitsburg Rd.
Wainwright
Cemetery Hill
Culp's Hill
Osborn
Taneytown Road
Powers Hill
Granite
Schoolhouse Lane

0   1/2   1   Mile

Brickyard Lane
Wiedrich
Wainwright
Stewart
Dilger
Ricketts
Wilkeson
Taft
Reynolds
Huntington
Culp's Hill
XII
Taneytown Road
Eakin
Wheeler
Hill
Stevens
Baltimore Pike
Wiedrich
Hall
Cemetery
Osborn

1. To support his evening attack, Ewell has sixteen guns of Latimer's battalion on Benner's Hill together with four of the Rockbridge Artillery. He has twelve pieces of Dance's battalion on Seminary Ridge north of the Fairfield Road.

2. Hill's corps has forty-one guns of McIntosh's, Garnett's, and Pegram's battalions facing Cemetery Hill from Seminary Hill south of the Fairfield Road.

3. Major Osborn commands forty-three Union guns in and near Evergreen Cemetery. Thirty-three face Seminary Ridge, and ten face Benner's Hill.

4. Colonel Wainwright has twenty-five guns east of the Baltimore Pike facing Benner's Hill. Ricketts's battery of six pieces replaces Cooper's battery of five after the duel with Latimer.

5. Five guns of the Twelfth Corps on Culp's Hill exchange fire with Latimer's battalion. They leave the hill at dusk.

Map 11.1. Artillery Positions, Late Afternoon, 2 July

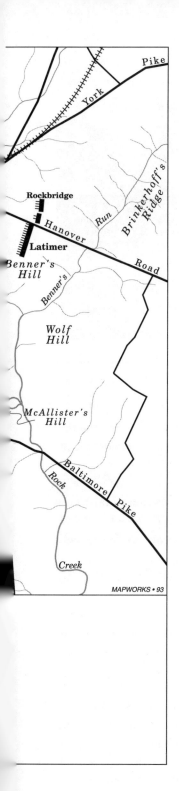

Pike

York

Brinkerhoff's
Ridge

Rockbridge

Run

Hanover

Latimer

Benner's
Hill

Benner's

Road

Wolf
Hill

McAllister's
Hill

Baltimore

Rock

Pike

Creek

MAPWORKS • 93

A Federal battery in the cemetery. The limbers and caissons are with the guns on the left. Sketch by Edwin Forbes. (GNMP)

the afternoon of 2 July. Hall's battery would be relieved later in the day by the 1st New Hampshire Battery, commanded by Capt. Frederick M. Edgell. The New Hampshire battery had six three-inch rifles.[8]

Lt. Christopher Schmidt's section of Wiedrich's battery was probably near the left of this line by the Taneytown Road. A position so far to the left seems likely if its two rifles assisted in the repulse of Pickett's Charge on 3 July. Major Osborn overlooked this section's presence on his line both in his report and in his other writings.[9]

The shape of Cemetery Hill provided an opportunity for posting two lines of guns fronting toward Benner's Hill. Cooper's and Reynolds's batteries were so placed east of the pike and under Wainwright's command. Sometime during the afternoon of 2 July, Major Osborn posted two batteries in a second line, higher than the first, in the cemetery, southwest of the cemetery gate. He placed Capt. Elijah D. Taft's 5th New York Battery, which was armed with six twenty-pounder Parrotts, in position to the rear of Dilger's battery. Four of its guns pointed toward Benner's Hill, but its two left pieces faced toward the northwest along with Dilger's and Bancroft's. Taft's guns were the largest Federal pieces on the field; they were assigned to the Artillery Reserve. No one said so, but it seems likely that Hunt placed them on Cemetery Hill to confront the twenty-pounders of the Rockbridge Artillery. After posting Taft's Parrotts, Osborn placed the six three-inch rifles of Battery H, 1st Ohio Light Artillery, under Lt. George W. Norton, to Taft's right rear. They also fired toward Benner's Hill, probably to the right of Reynolds's battery, which was in their left front.[10]

Wainwright and Osborn were both New Yorkers, both were carried on the rolls of the 1st New York Light Artillery Regiment, and both were excellent artillerymen. That was about all they had in common. Charles S. Wainwright, born in 1836, was a patrician, a wealthy farmer from the Hudson Valley, a Democrat and no admirer of President Lincoln, and something of a snob. He entered the service as major of the regiment and by April 1862 was its colonel. However, since the regiment did not operate as a unit, his assignments were elsewhere. From September 1862 to March 1864, he served as chief of artillery of the First Corps. When that corps was abolished, he received command of the artillery of the Fifth Corps and held this assignment until the end of the war. He received a brevet to brigadier general as of August 1864. A bachelor, Wainwright kept a personal journal that was published in 1962 under the title, *A Diary of Battle*, which must rank with the better personal accounts of the war.[11]

Thomas W. Osborn was born in 1836 in New Jersey. His father, a farmer, moved the family to Jefferson County, New York, near Watertown, when Osborn was young, and there he grew to manhood. He studied law in Watertown and was there when the war began. He had no interest in military matters—in fact, he found the idea of military service repulsive. Nevertheless, after Bull Run he decided to serve and set about to raise a company of artillery from the counties near Watertown. This he did with the aid of George Winslow, a merchant in the area. The company became Battery D, 1st New York Light Artillery, and Osborn commanded it on the Peninsula and in subsequent battles through Chancellorsville. He was promoted then to the grade of major and given command of the artillery of the Eleventh Corps. Osborn served as Howard's chief of artillery from that time until the end of the war and during the campaign through Georgia and the Carolinas was chief of artillery of the Army of the Tennessee. After the war, he served for a time with the Freedmen's Bureau in Tennessee. Writing during the Gettysburg campaign, Lieutenant Wheeler described Osborn as "a gentleman and a soldier, a most energetic and gallant man."[12]

While the batteries of the First and Eleventh corps prepared for action on Cemetery Hill, the four batteries of the Twelfth Corps waited quietly behind its infantry's lines. Early on the morning of 2 July, General Hunt deployed them to cover the gap at Spangler's Spring from its right side,

Maj. Thomas W. Osborn (WLM)

but this was a temporary assignment. Lt. Edward Muhlenberg, the assigned and nominal commander of the Twelfth Corps' artillery brigade, believed that the heavy woods and rough terrain in the corps sector rendered it impractical for his batteries to take position along the infantry line, and so they waited in the rear. Hindsight suggests that better use might have been made of this quiet time and that they might have taken positions occupied later, but that was not so apparent then. Apparently neither General Hunt nor Lt. Col. Clermont L. Best, now on Slocum's staff but formerly the commander of the Twelfth Corps artillery and likely still its supervisor, inspired, ordered, or perhaps permitted Muhlenberg to take more positive action. Thus the artillery waited "in reserve and readiness to answer all calls which might be made upon it by the future movements of the opposing forces."[13]

The reticence of those in command to post the Twelfth Corps batteries before mid-afternoon on 2 July was mirrored on the Confederate side of the field. Col. J. Thompson Brown could find employment on the afternoon of 2 July for only two of the battalions of Ewell's corps, those of Andrews and Capt. Willis J. Dance. He saw no good places at which to post the other three. Some of Jones's battalion was used to support the troops guarding against the feared movement from the York Pike. Carter's battalion, which had performed well on 1 July, parked near the seminary in readiness but was not used. Lt. Col. William Nelson's battalion awaited a summons near the college.[14]

On the morning of 2 July, though, Brown placed three batteries of Dance's battalion (the 1st Virginia Artillery Regiment) on Seminary Ridge. Capt. David Watson's battery took position north of the railroad cut a mile and a half from the target area on Cemetery Hill and too far away for accurate shooting. Brown placed Capt. Benjamin H. Smith's 3d Richmond Howitzers near the seminary dormitory and the Powhatan Artillery under Lt. John M. Cunningham just south of the Fairfield Road about a mile from Cemetery Hill. In sum, Ewell's corps had twelve guns on Seminary Ridge that might fire on Cemetery Hill.[15]

Cemetery Hill was directly opposite and closer to the left battalions of Hill's corps and was their natural target. The guns of these battalions were on the ridge between McMillan's Woods and the Fairfield Road. Lt. Col. David G. McIntosh's battalion was on the left. It occupied the edge of Schultz's Woods and had the cover of a stone wall there. McIntosh had three batteries on line: those commanded by Capt. William B. Hurt, Capt. Marmaduke Johnson, and Lt. Samuel Wallace. Capt. R. Sidney Rice's battery was in reserve. Hurt's Hardaway Artillery (Alabama) had the army's two Whitworth rifles, English pieces with hexagonal bores and great range whose bolts made a peculiar whistle when passing through the air that created fear and gained them excessive attention. The axle of one broke on 2 July and put it out of action. The battery's smith fixed it that night, but it broke down again from its own recoil when on Oak Hill the following day. McIntosh's battalion had twelve pieces aimed at Cemetery Hill.[16]

Lt. Col. John J. Garnett's battalion was on McIntosh's right and on the ridge line south of Schultz's Woods. Because of a lack of space or because Garnett's two howitzers and four Napoleons lacked the effectiveness of rifled guns in counterbattery fire, Garnett put only his nine rifled pieces in position under the command of Maj. Charles Richardson. Richardson's nine pieces would have been aimed at Osborn's batteries on Cemetery Hill, their rounds arcing over the skirmish lines in the fields to their front.[17]

Maj. William J. Pegram's battalion was on Garnett's right near McMillan's Woods between the McMillan house and the site of the present North Carolina memorial. It had five batteries on line: Capt. T. A. Brander's Letcher Artillery was on the left, Capt. Joseph McGraw's Purcell Artillery was next in line, Lt. William E. Zimmerman's Pee Dee Artillery was beside McGraw, Andrew B. Johnson's Crenshaw Battery was to Zimmerman's right, and the Fredericksburg Artillery, commanded by Capt. Edward A. Marye, was on the battalion's right. Pegram's battalion was the last of those of Hill's corps confronting Cemetery Hill. The guns of the battalions of Majs. John Lane and William T. Poague were too far to the right to have given much attention to the batteries on Cemetery Hill; their efforts would have been directed toward the guns of the Second Corps on Cemetery Ridge.[18]

There was only sporadic firing by the batteries of both forces prior to 4:00 P.M. Neither side could afford to waste ammunition, and there were few really good targets to shoot at. Major Osborn wrote of an hour's fire from the right at sunrise. This must have come from the Rockbridge Artillery, which was ranging in on Cemetery Hill and was answered by some of his guns. The Confederate batteries on Seminary Ridge fired also to get the range to Cemetery Hill. Some of their shells cleared the crest of the hill and fell into Cooper's battery, killing and disabling some of its horses. Col. R. Lindsay Walker, commander of Hill's artillery, reported that his batteries fired at intervals during the day, "enfilading the enemy's guns when they were attempting to be concentrated," but they also fired in support of skirmishers.[19]

Union batteries also fired to determine ranges and at occasional targets such as bodies of troops seen passing toward the right. Most of this shooting was probably ineffective, yet a shell fragment from a round fired from Cemetery Hill about noon on 2 July seriously wounded Brig. Gen. Albert G. Jenkins of the cavalry in the head. At that time, Jenkins was on Barlow Knoll and on his way to the Confederate left.[20]

Firing associated with skirmishing has already been mentioned. Major Osborn wrote of Confederate skirmishers who took over a house in the south of Gettysburg late in the afternoon of 2 July. From it, snipers busily fired at Union infantrymen and artillerymen on Cemetery Hill. When it became apparent that the infantry could not deal with them, General Howard suggested that Osborn see what his guns could do. Although there was concern about the house's containing civilians, Osborn had several guns fire on the building. Their rounds riddled its brick walls and drove the sharpshooters from it. Unfortunately, Osborn wrongly believed that the family had been in the house and that they had killed a girl.[21]

The artillery's sporadic firing ended late in the afternoon when Longstreet opened his assault and when, to support Longstreet's attack, General Johnson sent word for Major Latimer to post his battalion on Benner's Hill and "open fire with all of his pieces." Maj. William W. Goldsborough of the 1st Maryland Infantry Battalion related a curious story concerning Latimer's occupation of the hill. At some time before Latimer was ordered to move his guns there, General Johnson summoned Goldsborough, said that he wished to post some artillery on the hill, and suggested that Goldsborough reconnoiter it. Johnson stressed that this was not an order but that he was asking Goldsborough to do the job because he understood that, as a Baltimorean, he was familiar with the Gettysburg area. According to the major, Johnson's division was still in line north of the Hanover Road at this time.[22]

In accord with Johnson's request, Goldsborough rode toward the crest of the hill seeking what cover he could find along the way. Strangely enough, he did not know if the enemy held the other side of the hill. This, of course, was several hours after the skirmishing on the west slope of the hill had begun, and Johnson should have known the exact location of the enemy skirmish line in his front. The major reached the crest of the hill without trouble, found it free of the enemy, of course, and saw that it provided a fine view of the Federal position on Cemetery Hill. He saw too that the enemy's guns on Cemetery Hill commanded Benner's Hill and thought that Johnson would not place guns there after receiving Goldsborough's report of the situation. But before he could leave the hill, Johnson himself rode up with some of his staff and, after surveying the scene, sent an aide to Latimer with the order to bring up his guns. The order sickened Goldsborough, as he recalled in later years, because the Chesapeake Artillery, a battery of Marylanders well known to him, would be coming to the hill. Goldsborough feared the worse for them.[23]

At Johnson's order, Latimer led his batteries to the crest. They passed in front of the position of the Rockbridge Artillery on the way. Marylanders of Steuart's brigade recalled that their arrival was "a splendid sight. Sixteen guns, sixteen caissons, with their attending cavalcade of company and field officers, streaming over the field in bustle and busy speed and enveloped in clouds of dust." One section of Capt. C. I. Raine's Lee Battery went into position on the left at the south end of the crest, that closest to the enemy. Capt. William F. Dement's 1st Maryland Battery was next in line, Capt. J. C. Carpenter's Alleghany Artillery was on Dement's right, and Capt. William D. Brown's Chesapeake Artillery went in on the right of the line nearest the Hanover Road. One of Raine's battery's sections was armed with twenty-pounder Parrotts. Since it would have been folly to have placed those long-range guns closer to the enemy than necessary, Latimer posted them north of the Hanover Road with the Rockbridge Artillery. Therefore, south of the road Latimer had five ten-pounder Parrotts, three three-inch rifles, and six Napoleons, and north of the road there were six twenty-pounder Parrotts.[24]

Latimer's batteries opened the artillery duel on the Federal right. Cannoneer Jacob F. Cook of the Chesapeake Artillery wrote that Latimer, the "Young Napoleon," rode to the front and with sword aloft called the battalion to attention and ordered it to fire. Yet John Hatton of Dement's battery recalled that the batteries rolled up, dropped trail, and fired as soon as they were in position. The Federal batteries replied at once, and "Benner's Hill was simply a hell infernal." Hatton recollected that a storm of shells greeted Dement's battery as soon as the first shot was fired, and it seemed that the enemy already had their range. Solid shot whistled by them, some rounds tore up the ground, and shells exploded above their heads. The firing produced "a continuous vibration like a severe storm raging in the elements." Some horses were killed outright, while others reared and kicked from wounds and fright.[25]

Behind Benner's Hill in Johnson's line along the Hanover Road, the air around men of Steuart's brigade seemed full of "exploding, crashing, screaming shells." Every man fell flat to the ground at the order, "Lay Down." Sgt. William J. Blackistone of Company A of the 1st Maryland Battalion climbed a tree to watch the duel, shouting down an account of the damage that he could see. Nicholls's brigade on Steuart's right was more in line with the artillery fire and seemed to suffer severely. Major Goldsborough expressed what soldiers in the Peach Orchard were experiencing at about that very time: "Perhaps nothing in battle is so trying to an infantryman's nerves and patience as the preliminary artillery fire."[26]

It was little if any better in the Federal gun positions across the fields. They were taking a pounding from Confederate batteries on Seminary Ridge as well as from those on Benner's Hill. A war correspondent in the cemetery wrote: "Then came a storm of shot and shell; marble slabs were broken, iron fences shattered, horses disemboweled. The air was filled with wild, hideous noises, the low buzz of round shot, the whizzing of elongated balls and the stunning explosion of shells overhead and all around. In three minutes the earth shook with the tremendous concussion of two hundred pieces of artillery."[27]

General Howard wrote that many of the Confederate projectiles flew high, fell in the rear among the ambulances and wagons, and sent "a host of army followers into rapid motion farther to the rear." Others were short and did no harm, and some exploded, "throwing out their fragments to trouble the artillery men and horses, or to rattle among the tombstones." He saw a cannoneer who ran back and forth between his caisson and gun carrying ammunition, singing and whistling all the while. He would dodge if a shell fell near and help to straighten out the teams when the horses became frightened; this done, he would return to his work. Then a solid shot struck him in the thigh; "he gave one sharp cry, and was no more."[28]

One of Cooper's battery's first shots struck and exploded an ammunition chest on Benner's Hill. Lieutenant Stewart saw it blow and called for his men to give three cheers for Cooper's men. The sound of their cheers carried all the way to the Rockbridge Artillery. It had hardly died when a Confederate round hit one of Stewart's caissons, and the Confederates returned the cheer. In Stewart's opinion, this hit "was the cleanest job I ever saw. The three chests were sent skyward and the horses started off on a run toward the town, but one of the swing team got over the traces, throwing him down and causing the rest of the team to halt. The men ran after them and brought them back; every hair was burnt off the tails and manes of the wheel horses." Stewart asked about the drivers and learned that none of them were badly hurt. A few minutes later, one of his battery's limber chests exploded. This time, two men and two horses were lost. A piece of a jacket was all that could be found of one driver; yet Stewart learned later that the man had somehow survived, was completely blind, and was a patient in a Detroit hospital.[29]

Colonel Wainwright, who had no guns to serve, sat on the wall between Wiedrich's and Cooper's batteries and watched the inferno around him with a detached, professional eye. In time, he became indifferent to the missiles flying nearby, even to the point of feeling that they were harmless. In his opinion, the Confederate fire that afternoon was the most accurate he had seen. He marveled, in retrospect, that it did not kill more horses, considering that the Federal limbers were parked just behind their guns and the caissons were just behind the hill. From his seat on the wall, he saw a twenty-pound shot plow through two or three yards of infantrymen lying behind a wall, killing or wounding a dozen or so. He was pleased that it was not an explosive shell for it landed so near to him that its impact covered him with dust.

At another time, he was standing by Wiedrich's battery when a shell from a rifled piece burrowed into the ground and stopped almost beneath his feet. He had become so inured to the pounding by this time that he stood quietly waiting for the shell to explode and wondering if it would blow out the hole it entered when it burst or if it would blow straight up. It blew out its entrance hole, and he escaped unharmed.[30]

Wainwright saw another shell burst under Cooper's left piece. It killed one man, wounded three, and "blew another all to pieces" so that he died soon after. Wainwright jumped from his perch on the wall and told Cooper to man the piece with other men from the battery and that he would get some infantrymen to take care of the wounded. The men of Cooper's battery had often vexed him with their unsoldierly behavior, but they made him proud that afternoon. Five men came to the gun immediately (possibly they were drivers), and they fired it before the dead and wounded were taken from beneath their feet. Infantrymen carried the mortally wounded man to a well near the cemetery gate. According to Wainwright, the wounded man's brother would not leave his post in the battery to be with him without Cooper's permission, and Cooper would not let him do so without Wainwright's approval.[31]

Another shell broke the axle of Cooper's second piece. The carriage did not collapse, so the crew continued to fire the gun until it collapsed shortly before the end of the fight. In later years, Lt. James A. Gardner remembered the scene at Cooper's position:

> The shots of the enemy came thick and fast, bursting, crushing, and ploughing, a mighty storm of iron hail, a most determined and terrible effort of the enemy to cripple and destroy the guns upon the hill. Situated as we were in the center of this artillery line, our battery received the full force of the enemy front, oblique and flank fire. Against the batteries on Seminary Ridge we [Wainwright's batteries] were powerless; but upon the batteries of Latimer on Benner's Hill, and upon Graham and Raine to our left, an accurate and most telling fire was opened from the batteries on this hill and continued for about two hours.[32]

Not everything went well on Cemetery Hill. In Wainwright's opinion, Reynolds's and Cooper's batteries fired beautifully but not Wiedrich's. The Germans seemed overly excited to him, and they forgot how to set their fuses. Even Wiedrich, "the old man," was of little help. Wainwright saw one gun firing shells with fuses set at fifteen seconds at five degrees in elevation, while another was using fuses set at eighteen seconds at four degrees. The colonel went to each of the four guns, set the pendulum hausse of each, and showed the crews what time to cut their fuses.[33]

From their position on Stevens's Knoll at the base of Culp's Hill, the men on the left of the 5th Maine Battery viewed the deployment of Latimer's battalion with intense interest. It was like watching a performance in an arena—an "almost unexampled spectacle of a Confederate battery in full view, thrown into 'action front' as deliberately as on parade." To them, Latimer's guns seemed crowded together on the crest, although the fourteen pieces there ought to have had plenty of room. Stevens's men could also.see the six twenty-pounder Parrotts of Raine's and Graham's bat-

"The Runaway Limber." Oil painting by William H. Shelton. The scene is at the position of Reynolds's battery on East Cemetery Hill. (GNMP)

teries to Latimer's right and rear as the big guns opened fire with those on Latimer's line. Those of Stevens's guns that could be brought to bear on the enemy's guns opened in reply, firing fast enough that the bronze guns became so hot that it was an hour after the fight before a cannoneer could place a bare hand on their cascabels. Yet, being partially concealed and less obvious to the Confederate gunners than the batteries on Cemetery Hill, Stevens's guns received less attention than they warranted. Lt. Edward N. Whittier believed that no more than six or eight Confederate projectiles struck their knoll during the fight.[34]

Latimer's batteries received some dangerous fire from Culp's Hill. General Geary became concerned about the effect of the Rebel fire from Benner's Hill on the infantry, particularly that on the left of his own division, and he called for some Twelfth Corps guns to combat it. In response, Muhlenberg sent a ten-pounder Parrott from Lt. Charles A. Atwell's (Knap's) Pennsylvania battery to the summit of the hill. An hour and a half later, he sent up two more of Atwell's Parrotts plus a section of Napoleons from Lt. David H. Kinzie's U.S. battery to join them. Lt. Edward R. Geary, son of the general, commanded the three guns from Atwell's battery, and Lt. William E. van Reed those from Kinzie's battery. Since the north slope of Culp's Hill was wooded, we may well wonder how these guns secured a field of fire. Probably in the hour and a half interval between the arrival of the first gun and that of the remaining four, Twelfth Corps pioneers cut enough trees to provide the needed gap. The Culp's Hill batteries exchanged fire with the Confederates for about a half hour. It was a vicious little fight, characterized on the Federal side by a "remarkable coolness exhibited under a very galling fire," which left one Union cannoneer dead, two mortally wounded, and five wounded less severely. In the eyes of the Twelfth Corps artillerymen, the Confederate fire ceased after a caisson exploded. The Federal guns then left the hilltop for other positions.[35]

Lieutenant Geary, in a letter to his mother, wrote that the five guns had disabled an enemy battery 800 yards to their front that was planted in a wheat field. They had blown up two of its caissons, dismounted one of its pieces, and killed twenty-five of its horses. It was not without cost, for three of his men were wounded. In Geary's words:

One had a piece of his head knocked off, all the flesh between his shoulder and neck taken away, and his right hand almost knocked off, he was still living when we left Gettysburg. He was a terrible sight when first struck, and when I had him carried to the rear, it almost turned my stomach, which is something that, as yet, has never been done. The other two were not so severely wounded. I made one very narrow escape from a shell. One of the gunners, who saw the flash of one of the rebel guns, hallowed to me to "look out, one's coming," and I had just time to get behind a tree before the shell exploded within a foot of where I had been standing.[36]

Capt. William D. Brown, commander of the Chesapeake Artillery, was one of the first casualties on Latimer's line. In keeping with the practice of the time, Brown had ridden to the front of his battery at the beginning of the fight and urged his men to stand manfully to their guns for the honor of Maryland. The words had scarcely passed his lips when a solid shot hit his right leg, passed through his horse, and shattered his left leg. The horse fell, of course, and pinned the captain to the ground, breaking three of his ribs. After some men were able to pull Brown from beneath the horse, litter bearers carried him to the rear. As they passed the 1st Maryland Battalion, some of its officers went to the stretcher to see who was on it. Brown, whose face was as pale as death, smiled at them and, speaking to Capt. John W. Torsch, said, "Captain, if you should get home, tell my poor father I died endeavoring to do my duty." Then he added, "We are making out badly up there."[37]

Brown's fall was just the beginning of what was to come. For a time, a short time, the Union batteries tended to fire high, and the Confederates cheered, thinking that they were getting the best of their enemies. It was a cruel delusion. The Federal gunners ranged in, and Confederate casualties began to mount. When no ammunition was brought to his gun, Pvt. Jacob F. Cook of Brown's battery, who was serving as a Number 1 cannoneer, leaned his rammer staff against his gun and ran to the limber to see what had gone wrong. He found Sgt. Robert A. Crowley, the chief of piece, there, and when he asked where the other crewmen were, Crowley showed him. Cpl. Daniel Dougherty was cut in half, Pvt. Frederick Cusick's head was torn off, Doctor Jack Brian had lost his head, and there were other wounded lying nearby. As they spoke, another shell hit the ground in front of Pvt. Thaddeus Parker, driver of the limber's lead pair, who stood at their heads holding them and the rest of the team in place. The shell exploded, disemboweling Parker and killing both lead horses. Crowley and Cook carried the dying Parker to the side, ignoring his pleas to be put out of his misery.[38]

Cannoneer John Hatton of Dement's battery wrote that during the shelling, Cpl. Samuel Thompson was dealing out ammunition from the caisson of his piece. Sam was a friendly, carefree fellow who often spoke longingly of returning to his home in Baltimore after the victory that he knew would come. Sam was careless that day about closing the lid on the ammunition chest after removing rounds from it. Another cannoneer warned him that he was running a risk, but Sam replied, "Oh, nothing's going to hurt Sam! Sam's going to Baltimore!" A few seconds later a shell exploded near Sam's caisson, scattering sparks so that some fell into Sam's open ammunition chest. The chest exploded in "a sheet of flame, a terrible report." Then, as the smoke drifted aside, wreckage appeared—spindles of twisted axles, shattered wheels, and ammunition boxes reduced to splinters. The caisson's horses were frantic with pain and fear; some were wounded, and all were becoming tangled in their harness. No one reported wounded, but one man did not report.

Hatton wrote that a silent form was lying nearby on the ground: "Clothes scorched, smoking and burning, head divested of cap and exposing a bald surface where use [sic] to be a full suit of hair, whiskers singed off to the skin, eye-brows and eye-lids denuded of their fringes, and the eyes set with a popped gaze, and facial expressions changed to a perfect disguise. Was he breathing? No! The body was warm and flaccid, but the spirit had flown from the care and scenes of strife to seek his 'Baltimore.' It was the body of Sam Thompson, the jovial soul."[39]

There was a lull in the shelling, a busy time spent by the Confederate cannoneers in removing bodies and the wounded and moving debris away from the gun sections as drivers straightened out their damaged teams. Lt. Walter S. Chew now commanded the Chesapeake Artillery in Captain Brown's stead; he saw that it was in poor condition, but they had to make do. Personnel were shifted around—Private Cook went to Sgt. Philip H. Brown's piece, the only one still firing, to take the place of Brown's Number 2 cannoneer, who had been wounded. By now the lull was over and Chew, in a ringing voice, called "Resume Firing." The whole battalion fired almost in unison, and "the ground trembled from the jar." Wainwright's batteries replied so promptly that it seemed to Latimer's battered Confederates that their own projectiles were boomeranging against them. The enemy seemed to fire more furiously than before.[40]

Cannoneer Cook had just inserted the first charge when another shell exploded against the piece's right wheel, knocking it apart, wounding Sergeant Brown, mortally wounding Pvt. Philip Oldner, and severely injuring two other members of the crew. By this time Lt. Benjamin G. Roberts, who commanded the section, had been mortally wounded, and the fight was not yet over.[41]

During this cannonade, Private Hatton, in Dement's battery, was passing ammunition from a caisson chest, being careful to close its lid after removing the individual rounds. As he did so, a shell exploded above him, spraying hot fragments in every direction. One struck the copper-sheathed lid of the chest he had been using and spun around on it like a top before flying to the ground. Had the chest been open, there would have been reason for another cheer on Cemetery Hill.[42]

When it became apparent to Latimer that his battalion was being wrecked, that his men were exhausted, and that his ammunition was running low, he sent his sergeant major to General Johnson to say that he could no longer hold his position on Benner's Hill. In response, Johnson said that he should haul off all but four pieces; these should be left there to support the advance of the infantry.[43]

Latimer ordered all but four pieces of his battalion from the hill. Lieutenant Chew managed to remove his guns by fitting them with spare wheels from the caissons. Later, burial details returned to the hill to inter the dead but found the ground so stony that they had to carry the bodies some distance before the graves could be dug.[44]

After directing most of his battalion from the crest, Major Latimer rode back to the four guns left on the hill. Unfortunately, the battalion's report does not identify these guns. The four pieces opened fire on the enemy in support of Johnson's attack and immediately drew a "terrible fire" upon themselves. A shell exploded near the gallant major, killing his horse and wounding him severely in the arm. The horse fell upon him, pinning him to the ground. Pvt. Joseph Hatton, who was carrying a shell to his gun, got rid of it and ran to Latimer. He grasped the horse by the neck in an attempt to raise the animal's shoulders, while others tugged on Latimer to pull him free. It must have been a painful ordeal for the wounded major, but they freed him from his horse, and stretcher-bearers bore him to the rear. The "Boy Major's" wound was mortal; he bore the pain of the return to Virginia, but he died on 1 August. At Latimer's fall, Captain Raine took command of the battalion.[45]

The gallant but futile fight of Andrews's battalion on Benner's Hill inspired hyperbole. Robert Stiles wrote:

> Never, before or after, did I see fifteen or twenty guns in such a condition of wreck and destruction as this battalion was. It had been hurled backward, as it were, by the very weight and impact of metal from the position it had occupied on the crest of the little ridge, into a saucer-shaped depression behind it; and such a scene as it presented—guns dismounted and disabled, carriages splintered and crushed, ammunition chests exploded, limbers upset, wounded horses plunging and kicking, dashing out the brains of men tangled in the harness; while cannoneers with pistols were crawling around through the wreck shooting the struggling horses to save the lives of wounded men.[46]

Although Stiles's description seems much too turgid, it was bad enough on Benner's Hill, especially while the Federal batteries were pounding it. Yet Lt. Col. R. Snowden Andrews, who must have talked with Major Latimer and others before he prepared his report, wrote the battalion's report in a calm and dispassionate way that did not accentuate its losses. Even according to Lt. John M. Gregory, Jr., the Ordnance officer for Ewell's corps, after repairs were made and wheels replaced, the condition of the battalion's matériel was better than might be supposed. He counted only two caissons blown up, a limber chest shot through, and the lid of a caisson's ammunition chest torn off. He found the carriage of one of Raine's twenty-pounder Parrotts damaged and a wheel smashed on a ten-pounder Parrott. Other damage included twenty-seven horses killed or permanently disabled. Apparently he did not count wheels that had been smashed and replaced, and there were a number of horses wounded that were still fit for service. The battalion's serious human casualties totaled ten killed and forty wounded—a large figure for an artillery battalion. Latimer's sixteen guns had fired 1,147 rounds—a lot of ammunition.[47]

Nevertheless, the Federal batteries prevailed. Colonel Brown, chief of artillery of Ewell's corps, reported that the Federal fire was well directed and effective and that the enemy's position was so good and the Federal guns so numerous that they forced Latimer to withdraw. All of this was true.[48]

The Confederate artillerymen on Seminary Ridge wrote practically nothing of their duel with the Federals on Cemetery Hill except that McIntosh's battalion found the Union fire extremely warm. Their casualty numbers are not so readily available. On 2 July Pegram's battalion lost two men killed, seven wounded, and twenty-five horses killed. In the three days, McIntosh's battalion had thirty-two casualties and Garnett's two, but it would not be safe to assume that a third of them took place on 2 July.[49]

In their reports of the artillery exchange between Benner's Hill and Cemetery Hill, both Hunt and Wainwright wrote of a duel between thirteen Federal guns and ten Confederate pieces, all rifled, thus ignoring Andrews's six Napoleons and the six Napoleons of Stevens's battery. They mentioned the remarkable accuracy of the Confederate fire and the twenty-eight dead horses counted afterward on Benner's Hill. Hunt regretted that he had left two batteries of 4.5-inch guns in Westminster, for they could have been used advantageously in the fight.[50]

Infantrymen in front of the Union guns suffered from the Confederate fire, receiving the short rounds fired at the batteries behind them. Capt. Hartwell Osborn of the 55th Ohio Regiment wrote of one round that somehow killed and wounded twenty-seven men. Sergeant Mesnard of the same regiment recalled that the guns on Cemetery Hill fired over their heads and that Confederate shells struck between two trees the size of a wagon box at a rate of three rounds per minute. Mesnard's statement suggests that there was a lot of shooting going on, but his memory of its accuracy is suspect.[51]

In his recollections in later years, Major Osborn wrote that if it had been General Lee's intention to drive the Federal artillery from Cemetery Hill, the Confederate shelling had been "useless." He summed it up by writing that "no impression was made on the artillery beyond the loss of a very few men killed and wounded, a few horses killed, and a caisson or two blown up. The batteries were in no way crippled or the men demoralized."

Osborn made an observation about one aspect of artillery practice at that time. He wrote that they gauged the effect of their own fire by the accuracy of the enemy's fire. If their own was bad, the enemy would soon find their range and hold it. On the other hand, the "bad range" of their adversaries meant that their own fire was accurate. On the afternoon of 2 July, the Confederate batteries had fired much more rapidly than his own and with "comparatively little effect." Therefore, Osborn and others concluded that the Federal fire had been more accurate and effective than that of the Confederates. He believed that that opinion was borne out by the wreckage later found on the field.

Osborn mused that the Federal batteries had accomplished two other things that afternoon. Because of their effectiveness, they had attracted Confederate fire to themselves, where it did comparatively little damage, and had kept it from being directed at the infantry. Had it been turned on the infantry, he wrote, it would have done "material injury." They also compelled the enemy to exhaust its ammunition. Osborn and others believed that the Union artillery had more ammunition available than the Confederates did, and if they could make the Confederates expend theirs, the results would be in the Federals' favor.[52] The first accomplishment seems less believable than the second. A battery should have made an easier target than a line of infantry lying down.

When the firing died, the Federal batteries prepared for further action. Stevens's guns had to be cooled and cleaned and the battery had to replenish its supply of ammunition. Cooper's battery, which had experienced two days of hard fighting and had had one gun dismounted on 2 July, turned over its position to Capt. R. Bruce Ricketts's battery (F and G, 1st Pennsylvania Light Artillery Regiment), which had six three-inch rifles. Both Wheeler's and Hall's batteries went to the rear, also worn from two days of fighting. In addition, Wheeler's battery was out of ammunition and one of Hall's guns had broken an axle in recoil. Osborn replaced the two worn batteries with batteries from the Artillery Reserve. Soon there were more guns on Cemetery Hill than there had been before. They would see more action presently.[53]

12

BLUNDER ON THE RIGHT

The command structure of the Twelfth Corps at Gettysburg was an awkward thing, justifiable for a brief time, perhaps, but beyond that a mischief-making incongruity. The immediate problem went back to the Pipe Creek Circular. In order to implement its provisions, General Meade had appointed General Slocum to command both the Twelfth and Fifth corps, the army's "right wing" as Slocum saw it. Although the circular's provisions were never implemented insofar as the withdrawal of the army to Pipe Creek was concerned, Slocum considered himself to be a wing commander throughout the battle. If every echelon of the corps was to have a commander then, four officers in the chain of command had to step up one rank in an acting capacity. General Williams, who ranked second to Slocum in the corps, became its acting commander in Slocum's stead. Brig. Gen. Thomas H. Ruger, commander of the Third Brigade of the First Division, moved up to Williams's place as commander of that division, Col. Silas Colgrove of the 27th Indiana Regiment took command of Ruger's brigade, and Lt. Col. John R. Fesler received temporary command of the regiment.[1]

As it happened, the Fifth Corps remained under Slocum's command for only a short time before passing from Slocum's control on the afternoon of 2 July, if not before, when Meade ordered it from reserve behind the right to the battle on the Union left. Yet Slocum's "wing" organization continued in effect, even though the wing consisted of only the Twelfth Corps and units sent to its assistance. This meant that Williams, Ruger, and Colgrove continued in their acting assignments throughout the battle. This added echelon in the Twelfth Corps command was to increase awkwardness in the management of the corps and place an extra burden on Williams and the First Division. Ironically enough, General Meade and his staff apparently were unaware all the while that a "right wing" existed.[2]

This cumbersome command arrangement within the Twelfth Corps created some embarrassment on the morning of 2 July when Brig. Gen. Henry H. Lockwood reached Gettysburg with two large regiments from the defenses of Baltimore and southern Maryland (a third regiment of Lockwood's brigade would arrive on 3 July) and reported for duty with the corps. Since Williams's First Division had only two brigades while Geary's division had three, it was only logical that Lockwood's be assigned as a third brigade of Williams's division. Yet Lockwood, who had no experience in field command, outranked Ruger, as he did Geary and, if assigned to the First Division, would have to be given temporary command of it. To avoid this, Williams adopted a transparent subterfuge and retained the neophyte brigade as a separate unit outside of the First Division until he stepped down from acting corps command.[3]

General Williams had only four months of seniority over Lockwood, no more. Such was the difference in rank between an acting corps commander and the inexperienced brigade commander who had been sent to his assistance. Yet, even at this stage of the war, Williams was deserving of much more recognition for his service than he received. Alpheus Starkey Williams, who was born in Connecticut in 1810, graduated from Yale in 1831. He traveled extensively in Europe and North America and settled in Detroit in 1836. There, in the years preceding the Civil War, he was involved in many things, including practicing law, serving one term as a probate judge, being president of a bank, and owning a Whig newspaper. In addition, Williams joined a militia unit, the Brady Guards, and was its captain at the time of the outbreak of the war with Mexico. He served in that war with the 1st Michigan Regiment. From 1849 to 1853 he was postmaster of Detroit, and afterward he became president of the Michigan Oil Company. He also held other public posts, including the presidency of the state's military board, and was a major in the Detroit Light Guard. On the domestic side, Williams married a woman from a prominent family and fathered five children, two of whom died young.

When the Civil War began, Williams commanded Michigan's camp of instruction at Fort Wayne. He left the state service and became a brigadier general of volunteers in August 1861, a grade that he held throughout the war, although he was brevetted a major general in January 1865. He commanded a brigade under Nathaniel P. Banks in 1861 and early 1862 and served as a division commander thereafter in the parent units of the

Brig. Gen. Alpheus S. Williams (WLM)

Twelfth Corps. He continued to serve as a division commander in the Twelfth Corps after it was established in September 1862 and later in the Twentieth Corps. He commanded the Twelfth Corps at both Antietam and Gettysburg and the Twentieth Corps from time to time during its campaigns in Georgia and the Carolinas.[4]

In a letter requesting a promotion for Williams to the grade of major general, Slocum described him as "a most valuable and efficient officer" who was at his post constantly during the Chancellorsville campaign. This was faint praise, but he also wrote that Williams had not followed a common custom in the army—that of calling the press to his aid and employing reporters to sound his praise. Gen. William T. Sherman, in 1865, described Williams as an "honest, true, and brave soldier and gentleman. One who never faltered or hesitated in our long and perilous campaign." At the time of his death, another officer eulogized Williams as "one of the finest commanders in the eastern army," who, had he been fairly treated, "would have found his place at the head of it." He went on to observe that the general was as brave as a lion, was thoroughly versed in the art of war, and had a genius that inspired him when others failed in a pressing emergency.[5]

"Old Pap," as the soldiers called their heavily bearded general, wrote long informative letters to his children, even when on the march and under adverse conditions. These letters reveal him to have been a man of sensitivity who could find beauty in landscapes and romance even in the appearance of his camp. They spoke of a yearning to be home with his family and a felt need, if not a fondness, for a good night's sleep.

"Old Pap" had his complaints. Early in the war when under the command of General Banks, he wrote critically of West Point graduates and praised Banks, whom he believed was a victim of discrimination. Perhaps he felt this way because both he and Banks were not West Pointers and had that bond between them. Later he expressed much frustration over not being promoted to the grade of major general, citing seeming inequities in the system. In January 1863 he growled about a promotion list that included a major general, whom he did not name, who had served under him as a captain six months before and observed that he had been a division commander longer than anyone on the list. He was annoyed, he explained, not because he was not promoted but because others were promoted over him. He complained that "every such promotion over me, as Carl Schurz and twenty others in the last list, is an insult." He mentioned that Meade wondered about his not being promoted and mused that somehow the fault lay with Banks. Williams himself thought that it stemmed from a lack of prestige and from his having been in the Shenandoah Valley in 1862 rather than on the Peninsula. In October 1864, still a brigadier general, he wrote with understandable bitterness: "There is something, especially in military life, where the gradations of command are violated and the shirking junior is foisted over the heads of long-serving and faithful officers, that falls with especial weight upon one's pride and self-respect. It can't be denied nor concealed, and he who does not feel it is not fit to hold a commission."[6]

Early in the evening of 2 July, both Williams and Lockwood were to be involved in one of the most curious chains of events of the battle. In accordance with General Lee's plan, Longstreet had opened his attack against the Union left at about 4:30 P.M. Longstreet smashed the Union Third Corps' line, driving that corps and the Fifth and Second corps units sent to support it back to Cemetery Ridge. After ordering the Fifth Corps and portions of the Second into this fight, Meade summoned assistance from the Sixth Corps, which was just arriving on the field, and from the Twelfth Corps, which, until then, had been undisturbed in its works on Culp's Hill.

How much help did Meade want from the Twelfth Corps? Meade himself did not say, either in his report or otherwise, but one Meade biographer wrote that he had asked for a division. When the matter was discussed in later times, Slocum insisted that Meade had ordered him to "remove the entire 12th Corps from its position on the right, to one on the left." Williams, who executed the order, wrote in one letter that he was ordered, presumably by Slocum, to "detach all I could spare—at least one Divn to support our left." In another letter, Williams stated simply that he received an order from Slocum to send a division to reinforce the left. He explained that Meade had asked for all of the troops that Slocum could spare, but that Slocum had approved of his own suggestion that at least one division was required on Culp's Hill to hold the corps' line and works.[7]

After ordering the First Division, including Lockwood's brigade, to the left, Slocum sent Lt. Col. Hiram C. Rodgers of his staff to Meade. Rodgers was to tell Meade that the enemy was in Slocum's front and that Slocum deemed it hazardous to leave the corps' position undefended. He was to ask permission to retain at least one division on Culp's Hill. In a while, Rodgers returned from his talk with Meade with the message that Meade believed that the left was the point of real danger, which it then was, but that if Slocum deemed it absolutely essential, he could retain not a division on the right but a brigade.[8]

Slocum accepted this decision; there seems to be no reason to believe that he made a further appeal to Meade. Meade's order for the detachment of the whole corps was ill-considered, and hindsight suggests that it should not have been given. At the time that it was given, Meade could see that his left and center were in great danger, there had not been a serious threat to his right, and Slocum had not made a case for holding more than a brigade there. Still, it was an injudicious order.

Slocum's partisans praised him for managing to retain one brigade of the right. In later years, when the New York Monuments Commission dedicated the Slocum memorial at Gettysburg, Lt. Col. William F. Fox, its historian and a former officer of the 107th New York Regiment, held that Meade had ordered the entire corps to the left and that it was only by "Slocum's resolute insistence" that Greene's brigade was left to guard the hill. General Howard was obliging enough to say that this was so, and others agreed. They failed to question why Slocum, the second-ranking officer in the Army of the Potomac, had not been more adamant about retaining a division on his line and had not gone to see Meade personally on such a vital matter.[9]

When Slocum received criticism from Samuel P. Bates, the Pennsylvania historian, for his too ready compliance with Meade's order without making a vigorous protest, he commented:

> The first duty of a subordinate is to obey the orders of his superior; and this is particularly true when an army is engaged, and is in the very crises of a great struggle. Under such circumstances I can hardly conceive of any excuse that would justify a subordinate in remonstrating, protesting, or even delaying for an instant any order for the transfer of troops from one point of danger to another, when directed to do so by his commander. That it was my duty *while obeying the orders* of Gen. Meade, to place him in possession of any information I deemed important, and *while executing orders*, to make suggestions as to the situation of my own portion of the line, I fully admit, and I claim, that, this is precisely what I did do.[10]

When General Williams received an order from Slocum to send a division to the left, he ordered the First Division and Lockwood's brigade to march there by way of Granite Schoolhouse Lane along the south base of Powers Hill. He rode then to Slocum's headquarters on that hill to speak with the general. Williams told Slocum that he feared that the Rebels would seize the vacated position as soon as the Twelfth Corps troops moved away. He said that he had told Geary to extend his line to cover the vacated works and that they "could not safely spare more troops from that position." Slocum replied that the call was for all of the troops that he could spare, but he approved of Williams's suggestion that at least one division was necessary to hold the Culp's Hill line. With the understanding that Geary would remain on Culp's Hill, Williams rode to the head of the column marching to the left.[11]

The soldiers on the Twelfth Corps right had watched what they could see of the fight on the Union left with great interest. They had heard the sounds of a fierce battle, one that seemed to threaten their rear, and believed that the firing became more intense as the Confederate attacks spread toward the Union center. From south of Spangler's Spring, the men of the 2d Massachusetts Regiment could see back across the fields toward Cemetery Ridge. They could see portions of the vast artillery park beyond the Baltimore Pike with its batteries and wagons of the Artillery Reserve's ammunition train. As the battle progressed, they saw batteries "bounding away to the support of the fighting lines, with the horses at full run." Their anxiety grew as they saw wounded men and stragglers streaming to the rear, and they feared that the Confederate attacks had broken the Union line. They also saw units of the Fifth Corps filing toward the left from their reserve position beyond the pike and heard the sound of battle increase in intensity as the Fifth Corps units collided with the Confederates and contested their advance. It was then that they saw the staff officers and orderlies ride from the direction of Slocum's headquarters on Powers Hill and knew that soon they would be marching west.[12]

Lockwood's brigade on the corps right and the First Division were nearest to the enemy and farthest from the Confederate threat. Lockwood's brigade led the Twelfth Corps column and was the first away. Williams directed it to cross the pike and to march to the Union left around the base of Powers Hill by way of Granite Schoolhouse Lane. It was an exciting, proud, and scary time for these unbloodied defenders of the Union. Since Lockwood's regiments had not been worn down by field service, they were among the largest on the field. One, the 1st Maryland, Potomac Home Brigade, which led the column, numbered over 700 officers and men, and the 150th New York Regiment had only 100 less. Their uniforms were almost new, their packs were full, and they marched four abreast with bedrolls slung across their shoulders. Yet the day was warm, shot and shell flew nearby, and in the excitement of the hour, many soldiers carelessly discarded their bedrolls and packs along the way.[13]

It was a heady time for these heroes. The men of the 150th New York remembered that wounded men and others they met along the way shouted greetings such as "Go in Dutchess County! Give it to them, boys! Give it to them!" As the 123d New York of McDougall's brigade neared the

Brig. Gen. Henry H. Lockwood (WLM)

Taneytown Road, its men saw what they thought was a battery on the run. Instead, it was a sergeant hurrying back to the ammunition train with several caissons with empty chests to fill. As the caissons rumbled and jounced past, the "Dutch sergeant" in charge yelled, "Dis ish nod a retread, dish is nod a retread!," and the Twelfth Corps boys were glad to hear that it was so.[14]

An officer of Slocum's staff rode with Williams for a while at the head of the column, but he did not know where Williams was to go. After crossing the Taneytown Road and climbing the east slope of Cemetery Ridge, Williams met "large gatherings of our troops swarming in confusion" who yelled for the Twelfth Corps men to "go in and give them Jessie," but none of them offered to go along. It seems likely that these men had been driven from their positions at the front and had not yet re-formed. Williams followed the best route that he saw to the crest of the ridge and soon found himself in a large field surrounded by woods. There he met Lt. Col. Freeman McGilvery, commander of the Artillery Reserve's First Volunteer Brigade, whom he knew. McGilvery, "in great excitement," told him that the batteries in the gun line that he was trying to set up were threatened, that they had no infantry support, and that the Rebels had already captured some of his guns. That was all that Williams needed to know. Displaying an "intense anxiety in both manner and in tone" unusual for him, Williams ordered Lockwood to charge into the woods in his front where the captured cannon had been taken. Lockwood, whose men were already loading their rifles, quickly formed his regiments with the Marylanders in front, and Williams ordered them to charge.[15]

The two large regiments charged with a shout in heroic style that probably reflected their excitement and inexperience more than their bravery. Lockwood reported that they advanced a mile, but less than half that distance seems more likely. Fortune favored them. The gallant 21st Mississippi, the only force in their immediate front, had run out of steam and was already falling back toward the Peach Orchard. It offered little resistance as Lockwood's brigade swept down to the Trostle buildings and beyond. The 150th New York, in support, did not even have to fire a shot. Lockwood's men recovered the three Napoleons captured from Bigelow's battery and swept the Confederates from that portion of the field. It had been a great time for Lockwood's rookies—it was battle at its best.[16]

After sending Lockwood's men forward, Williams turned his attention to the First Division. It had followed Lockwood to the left, its Third Brigade in the lead. As the brigade neared Weikert's Woods, its men could hear yelling there, perhaps from Brig. Gen. William T. Wofford's Georgia brigade, "which sounded, as it came out of the dark woods, more devilish than anything that *could* come from human throats." At this point, an old woman—Maj. Charles F. Morse of the 2d Massachusetts called her a "crone"—stood by the lane and called repeatedly to the soldiers as they passed, "Never mind, boys, they're nothing but MEN." In Morse's recollection, her words seemed "sublime" under the circumstances, and he thought that nothing better could have been said to calm the soldiers' nerves.[17]

At Williams's instructions, General Ruger formed the two brigades of his division in two lines and entered Weikert's Woods. Williams halted them there until he could find out more about what was going on in the area, and there in the dusk and behind a heavy line of skirmishers, the division awaited the order to advance. Before such an order came, Lt. Robert P. Dechert, Ruger's aide, whom Ruger had sent ahead to report the division's approach, returned with word from both Generals Sykes and Sedgwick that the enemy had been repulsed and that the division's services were not needed. At about the same time, Ruger received orders from General Williams to return the division at once to its works on Culp's Hill. Ruger started his division back as rapidly as possible.[18]

After halting Ruger's division in the woods, Williams had searched for someone who could tell him what was happening. At what was likely the George Weikert house, he met Brig. Gen. Joshua Owen, who was between assignments. Owen was able to tell him only that the enemy had fallen back. At sunset, Williams received orders from Slocum to return his force to Culp's Hill.[19]

After giving Ruger and Lockwood further instructions, Williams rode north along the ridge "well into the dusk of evening." Near the Union center, he found General Meade with a large number of general and staff officers who were exchanging congratulations and discussing the events of the afternoon. In the fields around them, officers were calling for the men of their regiments in an effort to reassemble and re-form them. He paused there only long enough to hear the results of the day's fight up to that time, for he was anxious to get back to Culp's Hill. It was dark when he reached the Baltimore Pike on the rear slope of Cemetery Hill. Somehow one of General Meade's staff officers found him there and told him that he was wanted at army headquarters. Apparently Williams did not get back to his corps, and, strangely enough, he remained unaware of what had taken place on the hill in his absence and what, in fact, was still going on there.[20]

The staff officer guided Williams to the Leister house along the Taneytown Road behind the Union center. "Old Pap" found the corps commanders there. He remarked to General Slocum that it probably was not necessary that he attend the meeting and asked General Meade if he should leave. Meade asked him to stay but wrote later that he was puzzled by his being there, since Slocum was there and he did not know that Williams was the acting commander of the corps. Nevertheless, Meade wrote that he "refrained from courtesy to him from asking any explanation" and invited him to stay.[21]

Brig. Gen. John Gibbon, acting commander of the Second Corps, wrote an account of this meeting in which he noted that two corps were "doubly represented," the Second by himself and Hancock and the Twelfth by Slocum and Williams. The meeting opened with a general discussion during which those present made comments on the fight and on what they knew of the army's condition. Then Major General Butterfield, Meade's chief of staff, asked three questions: Should the army remain at Gettysburg or retire to another position nearer its base of supplies; if the army remains at Gettysburg, should it attack or await attack; and if it awaits attack, how long?

In reply, Williams, who ranked only Gibbon, spoke second. He said that the army should remain in its present position rather than retire; he advised that the army await an attack rather than make one; and he stated that the army should wait one day. The other corps commanders answered in a similar way—all were in favor of holding their position at Gettysburg and awaiting an attack for at least another day. When Slocum's turn came to reply (being the ranking officer under General Meade, he was the last to do so), he said simply that the Army of the Potomac should "stay and fight it out." This epigram was one of the finest of the war; it represented Slocum at his best.[22]

Williams explained the reason for his answers to Butterfield's questions in a letter to his daughters. He regarded the question of remaining at Gettysburg a good one for one practical reason if not for others. The army, he said, had but one day's rations at Gettysburg at best; in fact, many corps did not have even that. Yet the generals thought that with the beef cattle and flour they could possibly "get together," they might be able to "eke out a few half fed days." Thus they voted to hang on for another day.[23]

The departure of the two brigades of the Second Division, Geary's, from the hill was a botched job. In his report, Slocum wrote only that the division had been ordered to the left and that "by some unfortunate and unaccountable mistake, did not follow the First Division, but took the road leading to Two Taverns, crossing Rock Creek." Williams reported that "by direct orders from Major-General Slocum" Geary had been directed to follow him, leaving Greene's brigade to hold the breastworks, and that "by some mistake" Geary had taken his division, perhaps by a roundabout route, down the Baltimore Pike toward Littlestown.[24]

Geary provided a few more details in his report. He stated that at 7:00 P.M. he had received orders from one of Slocum's staff officers to move his division by the right flank and to follow the First Division, leaving one brigade behind to occupy the works of the entire corps. By this time, he wrote, the First Division had been gone for nearly a half hour. In obedience to the order (he made no mention of protesting it), he left Greene's brigade in the works and marched Candy's and Kane's brigades down the Baltimore Pike. After they crossed the Rock Creek bridge, they halted and he reported their position back to corps (presumably Slocum's) headquarters. Then, at 7:30 P.M., probably in answer to his report to corps headquarters, Geary received instructions to "hold the position down to the creek at all hazards." With that, he formed a line with the right of Candy's brigade "resting on the turnpike, near the bridge, and my left on Rock Creek." He would have found few hazards there unless the Army of the Potomac was routed—he was far in its rear.[25]

Geary sought to explain what had happened by observing that when ordered away he received no instructions as to the object of the move, the direction he was to take, or the point to be reached—only that he should follow the First Division. Since that division had gone beyond sight and hearing, he went in the direction being taken by some men who seemed to be going the right way. Why he did not receive or did not seek the necessary information, Geary did not say. Perhaps he believed that he would come up with Williams somehow, a foolish assumption since Williams was far ahead, the field was a place of confused activity, and it was dusk. Williams, of course, would not have been expecting Geary, for he believed that his division was holding the corps line. It seems that someone on Slocum's staff should have seen Geary's column passing his headquarters in the wrong direction, but no one did. They eventually found Geary along the Baltimore Pike and told him to hold his position there instead of returning to Culp's Hill. Indeed, several people had blundered.[26]

Anyone looking at a résumé of John White Geary's life would never suspect that he would commit such a blunder. Few men at Gettysburg or elsewhere in the war had backgrounds that could match Geary's. He was born in 1819 in Westmoreland County, Pennsylvania, and spent some time at Jefferson College before his father died, leaving him the head of the family. As such, young Geary had to assume responsibility for his father's debts. He left school and worked at a number of local jobs and then went as a surveyor to Kentucky. There he speculated successfully in land and amassed fortune enough to enable him to return to Pennsylvania and to college, where he studied engineering. After he graduated, he worked as an engineer in the construction of the Allegheny Portage Railroad.

Geary was a natural leader—at least he had the physique for one. He was over six feet, five inches tall and weighed over 200 pounds. Furthermore, he was a "zealous cold water man." He had been active in militia affairs, and when the Mexican War came, he was elected to the lieutenant colonelcy of the 2d Pennsylvania Regiment and served with it in Scott's army in Mexico. He led his regiment in the assault on Chapultepec, was wounded five times, and became the regiment's colonel before returning home. Few other Civil War generals had accomplished so much in Mexico.

During the Polk presidency, Geary went to San Francisco to serve as postmaster, but when the administration changed, he lost the appointment. He then served briefly in some local offices and became the city's first mayor. This too did not last long because his wife's ill health prompted their return to Pennsylvania. After her death, Pres. Franklin Pierce offered Geary the governorship of the Utah Territory, which he declined, but in 1856 he became governor of the Kansas Territory. He held this position for less than a year; he had taken an antislavery position, and when

Brig. Gen. John W. Geary (WLM)

he believed that the administration in Washington was not supporting his authority, he resigned and returned again to Pennsylvania. By this time Geary was a man of wealth and strongly pro-Union in outlook.

When war came, Geary raised the 28th Pennsylvania Regiment and what became "Knap's Battery" and became a colonel of volunteers. Like others in the future Twelfth Corps, he served in the Shenandoah Valley with Banks and in April 1862 became a brigadier general. He led his brigade at Cedar Mountain, where he was wounded. Still a brigadier general and lower in rank than Alpheus Williams, he received command of the Second Division of the Twelfth Corps in October 1862 and led it at Chancellorsville and to Gettysburg.

Geary was a fearless sort of fellow. In Panama on his way to San Francisco he single-handedly attacked and routed thirteen soldier-policemen who had stolen some of the Geary family's food. In Kansas he turned his back in disdain on a man who was threatening to shoot him. In addition to being courageous, he seemed to enjoy conflict. In writing of the battle of Wauhatchie, where Geary's son was killed, General Howard described Geary as having been "vigorous, strong, hearty, and cool headed." At Peach Tree Creek, Howard compared him with France's Marshal Michel Ney because of his size and mentioned his "cheerful deportment, and his unfailing energy. . . . He reconnoitered without regard to personal Safety."[27]

Geary had some trouble in getting his two brigades from their trenches and on the march. It was nearly dark, and they had to gather their gear, which they had probably stowed in the expectation that they would be in their positions for a while. Candy's brigade was the first away. When its turn came to go, the 29th Pennsylvania of Kane's brigade must have been a little slow in moving for Geary rode up to it and ordered, "Follow me!" Col. William Rickards, Jr., would have none of that. He immediately protested the command and demanded that any orders to the 29th be given through him. Rickards was right, Geary apologized, and Rickards started the 29th Regiment for the pike.[28]

In later years, comments were made about the march that suggested confusion. Capt. William L. Stork of the 29th Pennsylvania Regiment wrote of marching cross-country to the Third Corps rear and of the stragglers encountered there. A captain of the 147th Pennsylvania spoke of going to the rear and of taking a position near Ziegler's Grove! The memory of Pvt. Joseph A. Lumbard of the same regiment was closer to the mark, for he wrote of their getting lost but of winding up near McAllister's Mill. Artillery fire, "overs" fired at batteries on Cemetery Ridge, raked the column when it was near Rock Creek and mortally wounded Sgt. Maj. Charles Letford of the 29th Pennsylvania. For some reason not given, the 29th forded Rock Creek instead of crossing it by the bridge. Night marches can be confusing—this one certainly must have been.[29]

Geary halted the division when Candy's brigade crossed Rock Creek. By this time some of them realized that they had taken the wrong road, and Geary sought to make the best of it. He told Candy to post his brigade near the creek with its right near the bridge and its left at the creek. Candy did so and put out a strong line of skirmishers to the front. In this position, Candy's men would have been on the hill southwest of the pike fronting toward the Musser farm across the creek and the day's battle, which should have been almost over. It might have been an excellent position for covering a retreat from the field, but the army did not retreat and the artillery park was in its front instead of the enemy.[30]

No one gave a lucid account of what happened to Kane's brigade. After reaching the creek area, Kane reported that he rode ahead to "learn what was expected of his command." Then, having decided that there was no justification for his brigade's being on the left, he returned it to Culp's Hill. Col. George A. Cobham, Jr., reported simply that before they had gone a mile to the left, the order was countermanded and he was directed to return to his position. The 29th forded the creek; the 109th Pennsylvania spent some time in a field. Whether some or all of Kane's little brigade crossed the creek or not is open to question, and it makes no difference now. In spite of what Kane wrote in his report, it seems likely that Kane's brigade would have moved along the pike behind Candy's brigade until the halt and that even Kane would not have moved his brigade back to Culp's Hill without either Geary's or Slocum's assent.[31]

It is plain that at 8:00 P.M. on the evening of 2 July the Union right was depleted and vulnerable. Only one brigade, Greene's, was on Culp's Hill and guarding nearly a half mile of Twelfth Corps works. The remaining two brigades of Geary's division had marched off to the right away from the fight, and for a while no one knew where they had gone. The First Division had gone to the left and would soon start back, but it would have to march a mile in the darkness to reach its old position. And Slocum and Williams? Slocum must have known something of what was happening on the left, but Williams seems not to have known the extent of the peril there. Neither General Lee nor General Ewell dreamed of having such good fortune; it remained to be seen if they would be able to take advantage of it.

13

JOHNSON ATTACKS!

The roar of the Federal artillery subsided to the occasional bark of individual shots and then to relative silence. Mounted officers trotted along the line of "Maryland" Steuart's brigade, and as they passed along the fronts of its regiments of Virginians, North Carolinians, and Marylanders, the soldiers grasped their rifles, stood, stretched, and, at the urging of sergeants and officers, formed a long double-ranked line. Lt. Col. James R. Herbert of the 1st Maryland Battalion called to his major and his staff, "Mount your horses quickly for we are going in." Herbert cantered to the front of his battalion's line and after a pause, as if to echo the distant protracted shouts from other commanders along the brigade's front, bawled in stentorian tones, "Forward—guide center! March!"[1]

Johnson's advance came after a day of preparation and waiting. The division had not seized Culp's Hill during the previous night because the enemy had occupied it first. Contrary to the expectations of Ewell and his generals, General Longstreet made no morning advance on the Confederate right. Before dawn, General Lee had told Ewell to delay his attack until he heard Longstreet's guns open on the _left_. Then, early in the morning, the assault time was postponed to late afternoon; Lee instructed Ewell to make a diversion in favor of the attacking troops on the Confederate right, "to be converted into a real attack if an opportunity offered."[2]

In later years, with the advantage of hindsight, many Confederates remarked on their inactivity, expressing surprise and disapproval of it. Lt. Col. David Zable, commander of the 14th Louisiana, recalled that "all were looking for the command to advance" and that there was restlessness as

left of union
rt of Conf

the day passed and the Federals improved their position. Lt. Randolph H. McKim, General Steuart's aide-de-camp, wrote that they marveled as the day passed in inaction while the enemy, "as we well knew," was "plying axe and pick and shovel in fortifying a position which was already sufficiently formidable." Major Goldsborough agreed almost word-for-word with McKim: "Greatly did officers and men marvel as the morning, noon, and afternoon passed in inaction—on our part, not on the enemy's." They might have assumed that the enemy was entrenching but had no way of knowing the extent until they saw the product of its labor.[3]

Ewell began his diversion with artillery fire from Dance's battalion on Seminary Ridge and from the batteries on Benner's Hill. At the same time that Johnson ordered Latimer to place his guns on Benner's Hill, he told Brig. Gen. John M. Jones to advance his brigade from its position in the division's line to the support of Latimer's battalion. Jones provided this close support by posting Lt. Col. Logan H. N. Salyer's 50th Virginia Regiment on the south slope of Benner's Hill immediately to the left of Latimer's line of guns. The artillery exchange was in "full play" by the time that the Virginians arrived, and Salyer soon saw that the men in the batteries were suffering and that they could not stay long upon the hill. Yet some infantrymen of the 50th helped Latimer's cannoneers at the guns, and the regiment had three casualties while in Latimer's support.[4]

Brig. Gen. John Marshall Jones's unusual career merits some attention here. It is doubtful that Jones was known to many soldiers in the Army of Northern Virginia in 1863. Even his name would have helped little in his recognition for he shared most of it with John R. Jones, his predecessor, who, by virtue of his rank, would have been better known than he. John M. Jones was born in Charlottesville, Virginia, in 1820 and graduated from West Point in 1841 with John F. Reynolds and Horatio G. Wright on the Union side, a year behind his corps commander, Ewell, and a year before Generals Longstreet, McLaws, and Anderson. At the time that Jones was posting his brigade on Benner's Hill, the latter were preparing to strike the Union left and center.

Jones's military career had been routine. He did not serve in Mexico during that war, but he was on the frontier. He taught tactics at West Point for seven years, and he participated in the Utah Expedition. He had been a captain in the 7th Infantry for six years before he resigned from the Old Army at the outset of the Civil War. Then, while many of his juniors became brigade and division commanders, Jones served in staff assignments at division level under John B. Magruder, Ewell, and Early—lastly as a lieutenant colonel. Finally his break came after Chancellors-

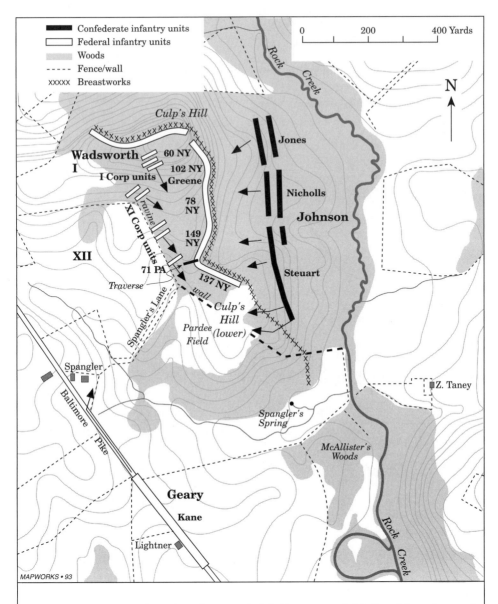

1. After other Twelfth Corps brigades go to the left, Greene extends his line right to the top of the lower hill.

2. At dusk, Jones's brigade attacks Greene's left, Nicholls's attacks his center, and Steuart's attacks his right.

3. Steuart's left regiments occupy works vacated by McDougall on the lower hill and wheel left to strike Greene's right.

4. Greene's right is reinforced, but the 137th New York and others are driven back to the traverse and the main hill.

5. After the fighting dies, Kane's and Candy's brigades return to the main hill, and Ruger's division returns to McAllister's Woods.

Map 13.1. Johnson's Division Attacks, Evening, 2 July

Brig. Gen. John M. Jones (WLM)

ville when capable brigade commanders were in short supply and General Lee appointed him to the command of the brigade he led to Gettysburg. It is pleasant to think that Ewell might have had something to do with this appointment, but it is doubtful that he did. At the same time that General Lee recommended Jones's appointment to Pres. Jefferson Davis, Lee wrote, "Should he fail in his duty, he will instantly resign." This suggests that Jones had made a pact with Lee. Freeman believed that Jones had a drinking problem and "failure" might have meant a return to it. If that was the case, Jones triumphed, for in spite of wounds at Gettysburg and Payne's Farm, he retained command of the brigade until he fell while trying to rally it during the Battle of the Wilderness.[5]

Four companies of the 25th Virginia had been on the skirmish line since dusk the evening before. In late afternoon, to foil an attempt by Federal skirmishers to harass Latimer's cannoneers with rifle fire, Jones ordered the rest of the regiment forward, and Col. John C. Higginbotham took command of the skirmish line. The skirmishing now increased in tempo and spread along the 25th's front when the assault began.[6]

The remaining four regiments of the brigade—the 21st, 42d, 44th, and 48th Virginia regiments—took position to the left of the artillery line and about 300 yards to its rear. A portion of this line rested near the Benner house and barn, which were about 500 yards southeast of the crest— about two-thirds of the way downslope toward the foot of the hill. The four regiments remained there during the artillery duel, but when the Union skirmishers seemed to threaten the artillery remaining on the hill, they moved to form on the left of the 50th Virginia and prepared to do battle. It was probably about this time that a couple of shells struck near the Benner house. Mrs. Benner, who was there with a twelve-year-old boy, hurriedly left the house for the shelter of the nearby woods. Some Rebels shouted, "The fun's getting too hot for you old lady." To this, she turned and replied, "Fun's fun, but this ain't no fun."[7]

Johnson rode to the top of the hill after most of Latimer's guns had gone to the rear. It was time for the second phase of his demonstration—the infantry attack. He directed Jones to form his brigade in line and advance when Nicholls's brigade came up on his left. Col. Jesse M. Williams of the 2d Louisiana Regiment, who commanded the Louisiana brigade in Nicholls's absence, had been ordered to bring his men forward from the right of the line north of the Hanover Road and to form on Jones.[8]

Neither Johnson nor Jones revealed the details of Johnson's order. Neither of them would have known much about the Union position on Culp's Hill for the trees there would have screened it from their view. They might have learned a little about the hill from the reconnaissance party that had been on the hill the evening before, but that seems doubtful. They could hardly have known that the boulders strewn thickly on its north slope would have rendered an assault from that direction impractical and would have confined Jones's approach to that portion of the hill facing Benner's Hill.

There was another reason for Jones to advance in a direct manner from his position on the south slope of Benner's Hill. A rail fence ran southwest down the hill from a point near its crest. This fence ended at a cross fence along the eastern edge of the woods and marshy ground beside Rock Creek but, if extended, would have crossed Culp's Hill near its summit and the right of Greene's line. Therefore, it seems quite likely that the fence would have been a convenient guide for the right of Jones's line in the brigade's advance on Culp's Hill.

What formation did Johnson's division use? Johnson reported that Jones's brigade led off, followed by Nicholls's and Steuart's brigades, and that he ordered the Stonewall Brigade (Walker's), which was then engaged with Union cavalry on Brinkerhoff's Ridge, to "repulse them and follow as soon as possible." The three brigades present numbered about 4,000 and, if formed in a single line, would have occupied a front of about that many feet. Yet the width of the open space between the fence line on Benner's Hill and the woods on the slope of Wolf Hill to the southeast and south was only about 2,700 feet. It seems likely then that in addition to advancing in echelon, the brigades must have gone forward on narrow fronts in two or more lines in order to avoid extensive entanglement in the woods and to conform to the Union position on the hill.[9]

General Jones wrote that his brigade advanced in good order, and Lieutenant Colonel Salyer reported that his regiment did so "in handsome order." Yet the commander of the 44th Virginia wrote of halting several times; perhaps the 44th was in the support line and had to pause to maintain an interval. Shells fired from Ricketts's battery on Cemetery Hill fell among the men on Jones's right soon after the advance began, but they did little damage and soon the brigade descended far enough down the slope of Benner's Hill to be out of the gunners' sights. The fire from Federal skirmishers increased as the Virginians advanced and proved troublesome. Jones's line reached Rock Creek about dusk and paused there to re-form before pushing across it and up the slope of Culp's Hill.[10]

Nicholls's brigade went forward on Jones's left at 7:00 P.M. Nothing was said of the nature of its formation in the early stages of its advance. Before starting, Pvt. Sykes Phillips of the 2d Louisiana Regiment had a premonition of misfortune and exchanged his position in the front rank for Cpl. R. C. Murphy's in the rear. Murphy advised Phillips to stay as close to him as possible.[11]

Steuart's brigade's advance to Rock Creek was not an easy one. To reach its place on the left of Johnson's line, it had to wheel clockwise to the southwest, the 3d North Carolina Regiment on its right coming up to connect with Nicholls's brigade. The 3d's efforts to close on Nicholls separated it and the 1st Maryland Battalion from the 23d Virginia and the brigade's left wing. The wheel to the right and the rough terrain in its path caused the left of the brigade to tail back and not reach Rock Creek until after the units on its right had crossed.

The 23d Virginia was far below strength, and its commander, Lt. Col. Simeon T. Walton, was displeased. Two companies were serving as "brigade guard," and four had been detailed to some unnamed area as skirmishers. As it prepared to go forward, one of its men, Pvt. Benjamin A. Roberts, wished that Stonewall Jackson was in command. He believed it against Jackson's policy to attack a stronghold like Culp's Hill—"he always found a way to move the enemy, and at the same time save his own men." Unfortunately, many commanders at Gettysburg had a hard time fighting the battle in a manner that many thought of as "Stonewall Jackson's way."[12]

Reaching Rock Creek had been easy enough for Johnson's three brigades. Unfortunately for the Confederate cause, they knew nothing about the Twelfth Corps position on Culp's Hill or that Greene's brigade manned the hill alone. With the possible exception of Col. Strong Vincent on Little Round Top, no brigade commander at Gettysburg rendered more decisive service than Brig. Gen. George Sears Greene, and few, if any, men on the field were older. Greene was born in 1801 in Rhode Island and graduated from West Point in 1823, six years before Robert E. Lee. He received a commission in the artillery and spent his early years in the service as an instructor of mathematics at West Point and at the artillery school at Fort Monroe. He left the army in 1836, as a first lieutenant, to embark upon a career as a civil engineer. In this profession, he achieved eminence in the construction of railroads, reservoirs, and aqueducts. He did not participate in the Mexican War, but in January 1862, at the age of sixty, he became colonel of the 60th New York Volunteer Infantry Regiment. Greene was promoted to brigadier general in April 1862 and served under Nathaniel P. Banks in the Shenandoah Valley. He led his brigade at Cedar Mountain and commanded the Second Division, Twelfth Corps, at Antietam. He reverted to the command of his brigade at Chancellorsville and led it to Gettysburg. After Gettysburg, he went to Tennessee with the Twelfth Corps and suffered a severe facial wound at Wauhatchie on 15 October 1863 that kept him from the field until Sherman's march through the Carolinas. Greene was described as a disciplinarian and an officer with a rigid sense of justice.[13]

Greene's five New York regiments, 1,350 strong, occupied the crest of the south slope of Culp's Hill, from the hill's highest peak, where the observation tower stands today, downhill to the south some 400 yards to the saddle that divides the hill mass into upper, or higher, and lower hills. The brigade's position, like that of the remainder of the corps, had been fortified. Its breastworks, or pits as the soldiers called them, followed the crest of the upper hill south to the saddle, where they joined the works constructed by Kane's brigade. Initially, Greene's works angled back on the right along the north side of the saddle, but when the direction of the line changed to connect with Kane's, the refused works became a traverse that fronted the saddle and the lower hill beyond. This short traverse would come in handy later in the day.[14]

Lt. Col. John C. O. Redington of the 60th New York had been in command of the skirmish line in front of Geary's division since eight o'clock that morning. Redington had a force of 7 officers and 170 enlisted men from Greene's brigade, and the 28th Pennsylvania Regiment of Candy's brigade, 300 strong, stood in support along the west bank of Rock Creek at the foot of the hill. Redington and his skirmishers sparred with their

Brig. Gen. George S. Greene (WLM)

Confederate counterparts throughout the day, but the tempo of their fire increased toward evening as Johnson's division deployed for its attack. It was at this time that General Geary pulled Candy's and Kane's brigades from their positions on Greene's right and rear and marched them from the field. Unfortunately, the 28th Pennsylvania Regiment left its position along Rock Creek at this critical time and marched off with the rest of Candy's brigade.[15]

Soon after, as Kane's brigade vacated its position, Greene began to extend his line to the right in order to occupy as much as he could of Kane's vacated works. First he shifted the 137th New York on its right beyond the base of the saddle to the lower hill's north slope. But before more could be done in a deliberate manner, Redington's bugler sounded a call for assistance. The Confederates were attacking; Jones's brigade and the skirmishers in its front "came booming." Greene immediately ordered Lt. Col. Herbert von Hammerstein and his 78th New York Regiment from the left of his line at the top of the hill to Redington's assistance as a substitute for the departed 28th Pennsylvania Regiment. Hammerstein's 200 men passed to the right behind the line of the 60th New York on the hill's steep slope and to the rear of the 102d New York. He led the 78th through the 102d's ranks and down to Rock Creek 400 yards to the front.[16]

In the meantime, Greene's remaining four regiments extended to the right to occupy the division's works as best they could. The result was a "thin line of separate men" fully a foot apart, a wide interval in a Civil War–period formation that meant a significant loss in firepower.[17]

At 7:00 P.M., when the attack began, Greene sent for aid to Wadsworth who was close by and to Howard on Cemetery Hill. Both responded. Wadsworth sent him the 6th Wisconsin Regiment of the Iron Brigade and the 14th Brooklyn and 147th New York regiments of Cutler's brigade. Each had fought valiantly on 1 July. Howard sent four good regiments from Schimmelfennig's brigade of Schurz's division. A First Corps staff officer led the 61st Ohio and the 157th New York to Greene's front, and Lt. Col. August Otto of Schurz's staff also took the 82d Illinois and the 45th New York there. It seems likely that the Eleventh Corps regiments were the first to reach Greene, for they left Cemetery Hill prior to Early's attack. Probably Wadsworth did not send his regiments until somewhat later when it became apparent that Early's attack would not strike his front.[18]

The deeds of the Eleventh Corps regiments were not recorded well. Otto's two regiments had difficulty reaching Greene. Their march into dark woods was bad enough, but they also met staff officers who gave them contradictory orders that made for countermarching and confusion.

The four regiments probably supported Greene's line and helped the New Yorkers in the breastworks. Apparently the 157th New York, at least, went to Greene's right, for its casualties included its color-bearer, who lost his flag, probably to Sgt. Thomas J. Betterton of the 37th Virginia Regiment of Steuart's brigade. The Eleventh Corps regiments returned to Cemetery Hill after the fighting died that night.[19]

Schurz believed that his four regiments had behaved well while helping Greene and related a story about the 82d Illinois. After it had repulsed an attack on the works that it held for one of Greene's regiments, an unknown officer commented on how well it had done and then said, "If you had been here yesterday instead of that d—d 11th Corps, we would not have been driven back." At this, Lt. Col. Edward S. Salomon, to whom the man spoke, reared back in righteous indignation and replied, "You are a miserable hound, sir, I and my regiment belong to that same 11th Corps you are speaking of, and we did no worse fighting yesterday." At this, the unknown officer vanished without a word.[20]

As Greene prepared to defend the hill with his own regiments and those sent to his aid, Redington withdrew his skirmishers as slowly as possible ahead of the heavy line of advancing Confederates. In his opinion, his men behaved "in a truly splendid manner." Redington intended at this time to set up a line about 100 yards west of Rock Creek from which his men could pepper the Confederates as they forded the creek and tried to re-form on its west bank. He requested that the 28th Pennsylvania come up to his aid and learned only then that it was leaving with Candy's brigade for the Union left. The 78th New York had not yet come down from the works, so, instead of halting, Redington's force continued its withdrawal. By this time it was dark among the trees—so dark that Redington's men could not see the enemy. Yet the Rebels continued to press after his retreating line, firing occasional volleys in its direction. Redington's men returned fire by shooting toward the flashes of the enemy rifles and fell back from one bit of cover to another. When within fifty yards of the Union works, Redington's men scurried for the cover of Greene's line. They had been in such close contact with the enemy that they had taken a dozen prisoners. In the meantime, Hammerstein's men had reached the 28th's position with the intention of relieving it, but it had gone and the enemy was pressing forward. The 78th New York exchanged several volleys with the Confederates and fell back to the Union works, taking position behind the right wing of the 102d New York.[21]

Greene's New Yorkers awaited the Confederate attack with nervous concern. For over two hours, they had heard the roar of artillery and musketry behind them on Cemetery Ridge. They were well aware that the rest of the Twelfth Corps had left the hill. From their position on the crest of the main hill, they could follow the fights of Redington's and Hammerstein's men in their front by the muzzle flashes of the opposing forces and the growing sound of the Rebel yell. Bullets zipped by their heads with increasing frequency and heightened their anxiety. Some men were eager to shoot back and clamored to do so, and a few nervous ones fired. But they had to wait until their own skirmishers cleared their front and were safely behind their line. Some of the skirmishers realized that they might be shot by their comrades behind the works and "cried out in an agonizing and beseeching manner" as they hurried toward the shelter of Greene's line. As one rolled over the parapet sheltering the 60th New York Regiment, "Z-z-z-t, a line of sound cuts through the air . . . and ends in that body, which rolls back and is silent."[22]

It was a frightening time: "Moments passed which were years of agony. The pale faces, starting eyeballs, and nervous hands grasping loaded muskets, told how terrible were those moments of suspense." Then firing began here and there and spread along the whole line. After the first halting shots, the Twelfth Corps veterans regained some of their composure and fired steadily, if not with accuracy. Soon the smoke under the trees became so heavy that the men behind the works could no longer see their targets and shot at what they heard rather than at what they saw. At one point in the fight, Capt. Jesse H. Jones of Company I, 60th New York, stood behind a small tree just to the rear of his company's place in the rifle pits and directed its fire. Jones had found a pair of steel breastplates and wore them beneath his blouse. As he watched the muzzle flashes in his front, he felt a hard blow. A minié ball had struck the edge of one plate where it overlapped the other, bending it before glancing to strike the other plate and making a dent a half inch deep. The blow left only a bruise on Jones's chest, and in his opinion, the breastplates had been "God's hand to me reached down out of Heaven to save my life."[23]

The right of the Confederate line waded Rock Creek without great difficulty; certainly it would have been harder had Redington's line been able to make a stand there. Yet as it was, Colonel Higginbotham of the 25th Virginia noticed an increased resistance as the Federal skirmish line fell back on some supports west of the creek. Although the Virginians were able to dislodge the Federal skirmishers with one rush, they sustained significant casualties, including the colonel himself.[24]

The Virginians of Jones's brigade on the right of Johnson's line pressed up the hill in the darkness, a difficult thing to do in the daylight but a hellish feat at night when the steep slope's brush and rocks tripped up the attackers and disordered their lines. They loaded and fired as they went and drove the Federal skirmishers before them. Jones's brigade became jumbled on the left and had to be realigned. To Capt. Thomas R. Buckner of the 44th Virginia, as they pressed near the enemy's works, "all was confusion and disorder." Pvt. Benjamin A. Jones of the 44th remembered the enemy's works as "a ditch filled with men firing down on our heads." He recalled that they had fallen back a few hundred yards and charged again, three times, without success. Here General Jones received a flesh wound in the thigh that brought on excessive hemorrhaging, and he had to turn command of his brigade over to Lt. Col. Robert H. Dungan of the 48th Virginia and leave the field.[25]

After crossing Rock Creek, Colonel Williams pushed Nicholls's brigade forward without delay. It dealt summarily with the Union skirmishers in its front and rushed forward with a yell "as best they could up the steep hill side over rocks and through the timber up to the enemy's line of works." Although some believed that the 1st Louisiana Regiment pierced the Union line, the brigade actually halted about 100 yards below the Federal works, where it exchanged fire with the enemy and attempted further assaults throughout the night. Sgt. Charles Clancy, color-bearer of the 1st Louisiana, advanced so far that he knew that he would be captured. Under the cloak of darkness, he removed the flag from its staff and wrapped it around his body. Although he was captured, he was able to keep the flag concealed until his exchange that winter, and he returned with it to the regiment. Sometime during the night, the fears of Private Phillips of the 2d Louisiana were realized when a bullet struck him in the groin. Being in the rear rank behind Corporal Murphy had not negated his premonition.[26]

Steuart's brigade on the left of Johnson's line had its own experiences. The 3d North Carolina Regiment and the 1st Maryland Battalion in the brigade's right wing had a shorter distance to cover before reaching the creek and easier terrain to cross than did their comrades on the left. The three left regiments had to pass down the wooded slope of Wolf Hill on the south side of the Benner farm. There the trees and rocks forced field and staff officers to leave their horses and proceed over the rough ground with their regiments on foot.[27]

The 3d North Carolina and the 1st Maryland passed through a cornfield and reached the creek considerably ahead of the units on their left. They waded the creek, which here was a waist-deep millpond, and pushed up the slope, inclining toward the right into the broad depression that led into the saddle at the left of Greene's line. As they climbed Culp's Hill's east slope, they met little resistance, but their skirmishers fell back to their line of battle and the attacking regiments groped blindly in the darkness toward the enemy works. Perhaps Steuart's right approached the Union line as Jones's and Nicholls's brigades were regrouping between attacks, for when they neared the Federal position, there was no firing to warn them that they were treading on very perilous ground. Suddenly there was a flash in their front of what seemed like thousands of rifles, and their column "reeled and staggered like a drunken man" from Union fire on front and flank. The 3d North Carolina exchanged shots with the 149th New York in its front and initially received a heavy oblique fire from the 137th New York on the lower hill to its left. The 1st Maryland then attacked the 137th New York, after which the flank fire against the 3d North Carolina ceased. Like the brigades to their right, Steuart's men had struck a line that would not be easily driven.[28]

The Confederates did not know it, but this contact with the right of Steuart's brigade meant that Johnson's three brigades had engaged the entire Union line on the hill, first Greene's brigade and later Greene's men and the troops sent to assist them. Jones's brigade struggled against Greene's left, the 60th New York at the top of the hill; Colonel Williams's Louisianans (Nicholls's brigade) in the center fought the 78th and 102d New York regiments on the crest of the hill above the saddle, and Steuart's right in the draw faced both the 149th New York on the north shoulder of the saddle and the 137th New York in Kane's works south of it. Any further extension of the Confederate line to the left that evening would encounter only vacated works.[29]

As his right battled Greene's right, Steuart brought up his left regiments. Although some members of these units later wrote of resistance, it seems likely that it was scattered for there were no Union troops except some stray skirmishers, perhaps, to provide it. They climbed the slope of the lower hill to the south of the Marylanders, where they were separated from them by a bulge in the hill's northeast slope. The 23d Virginia somehow reached the empty works vacated by McDougall's brigade and occupied them. The 23d's fifty men immediately worked their way to the right toward the lower hilltop and that portion of the pits manned by troops already engaged with the 1st Maryland Battalion. There, just below the lower summit and above the point where Kane's works turned to the northwest, the 23d swung into line facing the right of Greene's line and prepared to attack. Steuart's remaining regiments maneuvered to join in. Of Johnson's brigades, only Steuart's had the option of making anything but a frontal assault on the Federal line.[30]

After Steuart's regiments crossed the creek, Lt. Randolph McKim, Steuart's aide, guided eight companies of the 1st North Carolina Regiment from the left rear to the assistance of the 3d North Carolina Regiment and the 1st Maryland Battalion. Mistakes are all too common in battle, and here McKim made a big one. He led the 1st North Carolina up the draw behind the forward units until he came abreast of some muzzle flashes to the right. He could also see firing in his front and hear the bullets zipping through the air around him. After positioning the 1st North Carolina to fire toward the flashes to the front, he shouted, "Fire on them, boys; fire on them!" The 1st fired until Maj. William M. Parsley, commander of the 3d North Carolina, rushed up from the right and shouted, "They are our own men." They were shooting at the 1st Maryland Battalion, McKim's own unit. McKim took some solace later in the belief that only a few men of the 1st North Carolina had heard his command and fired, but perhaps that was wishful thinking.[31]

When reinforced by the 1st North Carolina, the 1st Maryland and 3d North Carolina were engaged warmly with the right of Greene's line, receiving not only fire from works on the northwest slope of the lower hill but also enfilading fire from the pits on the north shoulder of the saddle. The 3d North Carolina was in a particularly vulnerable position but fought gamely in spite of heavy losses. Many were shot; among them was Pvt. Charles F. Futch, who was hit in the top of the head while loading and firing prone. His brother carried him from the firing line and stayed with him until he died a few hours later. Lieutenant Colonel Herbert, commander of the 1st Maryland, also received a serious wound. Although staggered for a moment, the 1st Maryland, aided by the regiments arriving on its left, pressed its attack against the Union forces on the lower hill.[32]

When the 23d Virginia reached the top of the lower hill on the flank of Greene's line, its commander, Lt. Col. Simeon Walton, did not know what troops were in his front. In order to make sure that they were Federals, he called for a volunteer to go forward to see. Lt. Charles A. Raines offered to go, and Walton ordered a cease-fire. Raines, a big fellow, went to within less than twenty paces from the people he was to identify and saw that they were Yankees. He fired his pistol at one and dashed back to report their identity to Walton.[33]

Knowing that the 1st Maryland was nearby, Walton walked around the hill to the right and found Major Goldsborough, who was commanding the 1st Maryland's left wing. At this time, the battalion was hotly engaged, and the noise was so loud that commands could not be heard above it. The Marylanders were lying down and in the moonlight could see the Federals

Lt. Randolph H. McKim (McKim, A Soldier's Recollections)

in their front rising to fire down at them. The men in blue fought so stubbornly that some optimists thought that they must be Longstreet's men who had pushed their way through from the Confederate right. The Maryland men returned their fire, but in retrospect, at least, Goldsborough thought that it must have had little effect on the enemy, who was protected by breastworks. It was a hot place; Goldsborough wrote, "To stand there was certain death, and therefore, why not sell our lives dearly as possible?" Walton was of a similar mind and asked Goldsborough what he thought they should do.[34]

Goldsborough answered that since he was not in command of the 1st Maryland, he could do nothing. To this, Walton replied, "Well, I shan't wait for orders any longer but will charge the works if I lose every man in my regiment. Take the responsibility and charge with your left at the same time." Goldsborough agreed with Walton's proposal and hastily shifted his three left companies to advance with the Virginians. Without further ado, the men of the two units charged the breastworks and cleared them in a moment with a loss in the 1st Maryland of only three men. The Maryland men then wheeled right, enfiladed the works on the north slope of the lower hill, and cleared them of Union troops. In the lull that followed, Goldsborough walked to the right and learned that Lieutenant Colonel Herbert had been shot and that he was in command of the battalion.[35]

At some time, probably during this lull, a stranger rode up to Goldsborough and asked, "How's the fight going?" Goldsborough replied, "I don't know," and walked to the man on horseback. He seized the horse's bridle. The mounted man asked, "What corps is this?" Goldsborough pointed his pistol at him and replied, "A Confederate corps, and you are my prisoner, sir!" With that, the officer, Lt. Harry C. Egbert of the staff of the Union First Corps, climbed from his horse and surrendered his sword and pistol to Goldsborough.[36]

At 8:00 P.M., when Col. David Ireland of the 137th New York detected the presence of Confederates on his right, he ordered Company A, his right company, to face its line to meet the new threat. It was at this time that Ireland received some help from beyond his corps.[37]

Greene had not asked Hancock for reinforcements, but Hancock sent some anyhow. After dispatching Carroll's brigade to Howard, Hancock heard firing on Slocum's front and, fearing that the Twelfth Corps troops sent to Cemetery Ridge had left Slocum weak, he directed General Gibbon to send two more regiments to the Union right. Gibbon sent them from Webb's brigade at the Union center—the 71st and 106th Pennsylvania. The 106th reported to Howard on Cemetery Hill as the Confederates were driven off, but the 71st Pennsylvania went to Culp's Hill to assist Greene.

The 71st's visit to the Twelfth Corps is a puzzling thing. After Carroll's brigade moved off and as darkness was settling over the Cemetery Hill area, Col. R. Penn Smith led the 71st to the right and somehow met Capt. Craig W. Wadsworth of the First Corps, who, like Hancock, seemed to be everywhere. Wadsworth led the 71st to Greene's position and turned it over to Capt. Charles P. Horton, Greene's adjutant. Horton led the 71st to the right and posted it on the right of the 137th. As Horton recalled, the 71st was slow in moving to the position, but when they reached the works, its men gave three loud cheers that were answered by rifle fire from the front and right.[38]

The 71st arrived in time to help the 137th meet Steuart's assault and was attacked frontally and from the right, probably by the 1st Maryland Battalion and the 23d Virginia. In Horton's recollection, the 71st stayed while a few shots were fired and then simply left its place in line without panic or disorder. Colonel Smith might have agreed with Horton's assessment for he reported that after being fired on, he and his regiment left immediately. Sgt. William J. Burns of Company G thought differently. He wrote in his diary that the 71st had been caught up in a blunder "that came near costing us dear." While in its position, he wrote, the 71st experienced "the heaviest and wickedest musketry firing for about a half an hour that I ever lay under." When the 71st left its place in line, Horton protested to Colonel Smith, who said that he would not have his men murdered and that he had orders to return to his corps. Smith had no such orders. The men of the regiment seemed brave enough to Horton and, he thought, were mortified by Smith's action. Colonel Smith reported that in its brief stay on Culp's Hill the 71st lost three officers and eleven enlisted men. As far as Greene was concerned, the 71st's withdrawal had left his right in a critical condition. Colonel Ireland mentioned the 71st's falling back but wrote no more about it.[39]

After driving the 71st Pennsylvania beyond the saddle, Steuart's brigade, minus the two North Carolina regiments that remained on the hill's east slope, slowly occupied Culp's Hill's lower mass. It was dark even though the moon should have been rising at about this time, and the Confederates were in unknown and enemy country. They formed in some way between the works and the stone wall and fired across the saddle at Greene's right. This was a halting sporadic effort for they had the gnawing fear that they might be firing on fellow Confederates. Steuart asked Col. Edward T. H. Warren of the 10th Virginia Regiment, on the brigade left, to find out who was in his front. At this time, the 10th was formed perpendicular to the wall, which was on its right. Warren brought the left up to the wall and then filed left along it down toward the saddle. When it reached what Warren thought was the enemy rear, the 10th opened fire and drove the enemy, possibly the 137th New York, from its front. From what happened a short time later, it seems likely that some of the Virginians crossed the saddle and entered the Union works on the main hill.[40]

After the 71st Pennsylvania's departure, the 137th New York received fire from the front, from the right, and from the 10th Virginia in its rear. The 137th took heavy casualties, and Colonel Ireland ordered it back north of the saddle to the traverse that had marked the left of Greene's original line. It was possibly during the 137th's withdrawal that Pvt. George Pile pursued some of the retreating Yankees at a "swift run." He captured one man by seizing him by the knapsack and a lieutenant by catching hold of his sword belt. Later, Capt. Joseph H. Gregg led a sortie from the 137th's position against Confederates who were harassing them. Gregg fell mortally wounded while cheering on his men.[41]

By this time matters must have become thoroughly confused in the saddle area. Not only was it dark, but what moonlight there was would have been filtered by powder smoke. Still, units groped their way into the area and tried to distinguish friend from foe.

The 6th Wisconsin, the 14th Brooklyn, and 147th New York, all of Wadsworth's division, were among the new arrivals. What the 147th New York did on its arrival is quite clear. It went into the rifle pits on the left of the 149th New York and fought there until the evening's battle ended. Lt. Henry H. Lyman wrote of its adventures in his diary in staccato terms: "14th & 147th go among 12th corps to help drive back the charging Rebs. Hot work from ½ past 5 to ½ past 9. Lie in the pits all night on our arms. No pickett [sic] in front." The other regiments might have experienced a little more variety.[42]

When the 14th Brooklyn entered the Twelfth Corps sector, Lt. John J. Cantine, one of Greene's aides, met it and conducted Col. Edward B. Fowler and the regiment to a position on the right of Greene's line. As Cantine led Fowler by some trees, a soldier stepped from the darkness and demanded Cantine's surrender. Cantine dismounted, Fowler drew his pistol, and there were a dozen or so shots from the nearby woods. Fowler hurried back to the 14th and formed it facing the woods. Then, thinking that the woods might be occupied by Union troops, he called for volunteers to scout it out. Two men, musician John Cox and Sgt. James McQuire of Company I, responded and slipped into the woods "in the teeth of flank fire" to find out who was there. The 14th waited for an interminable period until Cox returned with the word that McQuire had been wounded and that the troops in their front belonged to the 10th Virginia Regiment! Colonel Fowler ordered the 14th to fire and to charge the woods, which it did, driving the Virginians from it. Yet so great was the confusion at this time that the Virginians believed they had repulsed a bayonet attack. What happened next is not certain, but one account holds that the 14th relieved the 137th New York, which then fell back to the rear to rest and to make ready for the morning's fight. The 14th spent the night in the 137th's position and returned to Wadsworth's line in the morning. In later years, as they pondered the evening's battle, some veterans of the 14th's action claimed that their chance meeting with the 10th Virginia frustrated General Johnson's plans and had "probably" saved the army's ammunition train and the army from a disastrous flank movement![43]

Lt. Col. Rufus Dawes of the 6th Wisconsin Regiment watched Early's attack on Cemetery Hill, and when the firing swelled on Culp's Hill behind him, he received an order to report with his regiment to General Greene.

Dawes did not know the general, but he started off at once toward the firing that was only a short distance in Wadsworth's rear. Fortunately, Greene was the first mounted officer that Dawes met. Greene wrote his name and command on a card that he gave to Dawes and ordered him to occupy some breastworks to the right and hold them.[44]

Dawes led the 6th off to the right at a double-quick, if that was possible in the woods. As Dawes approached, there were Rebels in the works. Both parties were surprised; some of the Virginians fired, and, being in no position to face Dawes's onslaught, they faded back into the darkness. The 6th remained at this position at or near the traverse until midnight, when Twelfth Corps troops, probably of Kane's brigade, relieved it.[45]

Steuart's attack was over for the evening, but the Confederates continued to try to learn what was happening around them. They were uneasy in their position on the lower hill. Major Goldsborough, who was somewhat familiar with the Gettysburg area, thought that the Baltimore Pike should be near. To find out, he asked Capt. John W. Torsch to take someone with him and to feel his way through the darkness until he found the enemy or the road. Torsch left and returned later saying that he had reached the pike and had seen wagons moving on it and parked beside it. Goldsborough passed this information along to General Johnson personally a short while later when Johnson and General Steuart visited his position. Johnson listened for a while to the rumbling of wheels on the turnpike about 600 yards to the west and observed that the noise "would indicate the enemy was retreating." That said, he went elsewhere.[46]

If Johnson believed that the sound of wheels on the pike signaled a retreat, he was wrong. Although ambulances used the road and wagons and caissons went to the rear for rations and ammunition, there was no retreat. The most significant traffic was that of returning units of the Twelfth Corps to Culp's Hill. It would be idle to speculate which division returned first, for the leading elements of each arrived at about 10:00 P.M., shortly after Greene's fight ended, and their return continued until after midnight.[47]

The arrival of Kane's small brigade would have been of greatest assistance to Greene and his valiant men. Kane's three regiments left the McAllister's Mill area shortly after 9:00 P.M., and Candy's brigade, which was beyond the creek, followed a short time later.[48]

These two brigades had three commanders at Gettysburg. Col. Charles Candy of the 66th Ohio Volunteer Infantry Regiment commanded the First Brigade. Candy, who was born in Kentucky in 1832, had served two enlistments in the Old Army, one in Ewell's regiment, the 1st Dra-

goons, and the other in the 1st Infantry. He entered the volunteer service as a captain in September 1861 and served temporarily on the staff of Brig. Gen. Charles P. Stone at Ball's Bluff. Candy became a colonel in the newly organized 66th Ohio in December 1861. He led the regiment in the Shenandoah Valley and in the battles of Port Republic and Cedar Mountain. He succeeded to the command of the brigade in August 1862 and commanded it in subsequent campaigns in Pope's Army of Virginia and in the Twelfth Corps. After Gettysburg, he would lead his brigade in the West in the Twelfth and Twentieth corps and be awarded a brevet to the rank of brigadier general in March 1865.[49]

Unlike Candy, Thomas L. Kane, commander of the Second Brigade, had an illustrious civilian background. Kane was born in wealth in Philadelphia in 1822 and as a young adult spent some time in Europe. Although he studied law, he rarely practiced it. Instead, he held some appointed offices

and dabbled. He was an active abolitionist and, though not a Mormon, was a friend of Brigham Young who worked to avoid the "Mormon War." Then, shortly before the Civil War, he founded the town of Kane in northwestern Pennsylvania.

When war came, Kane helped organize the 13th Pennsylvania Reserves, which became the original "Bucktails," and he became their lieutenant colonel. Kane was wounded at Dranesville and captured by Ewell at Harrisonburg but soon released. He became a brigadier general in September 1862 and commanded his brigade at Chancellorsville. He was sick with pneumonia when the Gettysburg campaign began, but after an arduous journey by railroad and buggy and contact with Stuart's cavalry, he finally caught up with General Meade and the army at Taneytown. It was said that he delivered Meade a highly sensitive message at Taneytown concerning possession of a Confederate cipher. Kane reached his brigade finally

Col. George A. Cobham, Jr. (WLM)

on the morning of 2 July but was so incapacitated that he had to share its command with Col. George Cobham, who had led it to Gettysburg. Kane was an unusual man; General Williams described him as being small and precise and full of "pluck and will."[50]

Therefore, to all intents and purposes, Col. George A. Cobham, Jr., commanded Kane's brigade. Cobham, a native of England, entered the service as a lieutenant colonel of the 111th Pennsylvania Regiment in January 1862 and became its commander in November. Cobham commanded the 111th during its garrison at Harpers Ferry and at Chancellorsville and later in Kane's absence. He commanded it in his own right after Kane left the army in November 1863 and did so in the grade of colonel until he was killed at Peach Tree Creek. The veterans of the 111th remembered Cobham as "a modest, brave and meritorious officer," and, in his report for Gettysburg, Kane recommended Cobham for promotion. The promotion came finally in the form of a posthumous brevet to the grade of brigadier general to date back to the day before his death. The promotion did not help Cobham in the command of his brigade, but it might have pleased his family. Maybe it was proof that the leaders of the Republic did not confine their generosity to prominent men like Kane![51]

Thus, it was under these three men and General Geary that Geary's two prodigal brigades returned to Culp's Hill. The 29th Pennsylvania Regiment of Kane's brigade led the march back up the Baltimore Pike, followed by the 111th and 109th Pennsylvania in turn. The 29th left the pike somewhere southwest of the brigade's old position, entered the woods there, and made its way toward its works on the lower hill, oblivious to the presence there of Steuart's brigade. As the men of the 29th moved into the woods on the hill's west slope, someone called for a good Union "hurrah" to announce to Greene's brigade that they were returning to its flank. The cheer was of great interest to Greene and to Steuart's men as well. The Confederates answered it with a volley from behind the stone wall just about twenty-five paces in the 29th's front.[52]

Colonel Rickards believed that Greene's men had fired on the 29th by mistake and ordered his men not to return the fire. Instead, the 29th collected its fourteen dead and wounded, faced about, and hurried 100 yards back toward the pike. Once the regiment was safe, Rickards rode back toward the wall, shouted his identity, and received another volley. Still not understanding the reason for this shooting, the regiments of Kane's brigade continued along the pike, with the 111th in the lead, to the Spangler farmyard.[53]

The brigade left the pike at the farmyard and followed Spangler's Lane for about 300 yards to Greene's right and the saddle between the main and lower hills. From the point opposite the end of the stone wall, the 111th continued on another 100 yards to an angle in the works where its left had been earlier in the day. Somehow the officers in charge still could not comprehend that the Confederates were on the lower hill just to their right, and they seem not to have spoken with anyone in Greene's brigade about it. At Cobham's order, Lt. Col. Thomas M. Walker, acting commander of the 111th, began to deploy the regiment behind the works. Two companies had taken position there when the 111th received a volley at a range of only thirty yards. Walker quickly aligned his remaining eight companies to face the fire and sent out scouts to make sure that the people shooting at his men were Confederates. When he confirmed that this was so and reported it to Cobham, Cobham told him to occupy the works. Finally, when Walker protested that to do so would subject the regiment to an enfilading fire, Cobham relented and left the 111th where it was.[54]

The 109th and 29th followed the 111th into the saddle area. When the column halted, the 29th, now in the rear, was at the end of the stone wall that crossed the lower hill. It was now clear that the Confederates were on the hill's top, but Kane wanted to know more about them. At his request, Colonel Rickards, who must have become leery of such assignments, sent a party of skirmishers led by Capt. George E. Johnson up the hill to locate the enemy's position. Johnson and his party disappeared into the darkness, and some of them returned but not Johnson. The Confederates had allowed Johnson and five of his men to enter their lines and had captured them. Kane could not have learned much, but there was no doubt that the enemy was on his right. Thus, he faced his brigade in that direction; it occupied the low ground in the saddle, its left at the works, its right in the open field southwest of the wall.[55]

Kane's brigade stayed in its vulnerable position through much of the remainder of the night, protected from Steuart's brigade by a little tree cover and the darkness. Yet in the moonlight the Pennsylvanians could see the Confederates moving about on the hill above them. When some Confederates began firing, Kane and Cobham realized that "there was nothing to be done but to connect with Greene, fold down to the right along the best ground offering, and strengthen the right flank as much as possible." They withdrew the brigade from the saddle itself and placed it behind the traverse and among some rocks on the lower slope of the main hill. Here it relieved the 14th Brooklyn and 6th Wisconsin regiments and took over the flank position of the 137th York. It formed in two lines that had some natural protection and could dominate the slope of the hill in their front.[56]

But even this adjustment was not easily done. The 111th was so close to the Confederates that Lieutenant Colonel Walker feared that the movement would draw their fire. To avoid this, he attempted to move the regiment back one man at a time, "with utmost caution," but it did not work. The enemy detected the move and opened fire. The 111th returned the fire until the enemy fire was silenced, and then they formed their new line.[57]

Kane's brigade put out a picket line that must have been very close to the main line behind it. During the quiet hours before dawn, Private Mouat of the 29th Pennsylvania heard someone out front carrying a lot of clanking canteens. A picket challenged the noise maker, got no reply, and fired. Someone then called, "Did you fetch him[?]," to which the picket replied, "You bet I did[,] there he lays." When daylight came, Mouat saw a dead Confederate in front of the 29th's position with a lot of canteens scattered around him. Probably he had lost his way in the dark, and he had paid the price for doing so.[58]

The return of Candy's brigade to the Twelfth Corps front was less difficult than Kane's had been. It followed Kane's brigade along the pike, but Geary held it there until Kane's brigade was in place. Geary posted Candy's regiments in double line of battle on Kane's right, behind Spangler's Lane, with their right in the orchard north of the Spangler house. In Geary's words, "All of these dispositions were made with the utmost silence and secrecy and within a few yards of the enemy's lines."[59]

Capt. Joseph A. Moore of the 147th Pennsylvania Regiment remembered Candy's march as a meandering exercise, a "slow, tiresome, roundabout manoeuvering," that on its return included a halt on the pike, during which some men fell asleep, and then a walk over rough terrain until the regiment finally reached its position. The 7th Ohio ended its march in a "hollow," the draw. There a volley from the enemy wounded one man. Soon after, the 7th moved to the right and to a position behind a wall, and Col. William R. Creighton sent out twenty men as skirmishers. Candy's brigade then settled down to await developments.[60]

As Geary's division was returning to its position on the main hill, General Ruger tried to place the First Division in its old works in McAllister's Woods and on the lower hill. On the march back, one of Slocum's staff officers told him that Geary's division had gone to the left and that only Greene's brigade had remained behind. However, the Second Division had been ordered back and was supposed to have returned to its old position. Sometime soon after, Ruger may have received additional information from a more reliable source. Captain Oakey and his skirmishers from the 2d Massachusetts had fallen back before Johnson's advancing Confederate lines and had recrossed the bridge at the mill. Oakey told his superiors that he believed that the enemy had occupied the division's works.[61]

Thomas Howard Ruger, the First Division's acting commander, was one of those capable officers who has received far less attention than he deserves. He was born in April 1833 in New York but was reared in Janesville, Wisconsin. He graduated third in West Point's class of 1854, where he was a classmate of the Confederates W. Dorsey Pender and J. E. B. Stuart and of Oliver O. Howard, who ranked just below him in the class. Ruger received a commission in the engineers but soon resigned from the army to study and practice law in Wisconsin. He returned to the army in 1861 as lieutenant colonel of the 3d Wisconsin Regiment and became its colonel in September. He and his regiment served in the Shenandoah Valley under Banks and at Cedar Mountain. He commanded his brigade at Antietam and became a brigadier general in November 1862. He led his brigade at Chancellorsville and then to Gettysburg.[62]

General Williams, Ruger's division commander, described him in August 1862 as being as "modest as a girl but of most thorough and sterling character." In later years, Howard remembered Ruger as having been "de-

Brig. Gen. Thomas H. Ruger (WLM)

liberative, cautious, and yet fearless; persistent, and, if unfairly pressed, obstinate to the last degree." Howard concluded that "it was a good thing that a division fell to him at Gettysburg."[63]

It is likely that the division's Third Brigade led Ruger's column on its return to Culp's Hill, followed by McDougall's brigade, the First, and Lockwood's brigade, which brought up the rear. Since Lockwood's brigade had not been in the works prior to going to the left, it played no part that evening in their recovery.[64]

After crossing the turnpike, the cautious Ruger ordered his brigade commanders, McDougall and Colgrove, to send skirmishers forward to see whether or not the enemy was in their works. If not, they were to occupy them at once. Each brigade commander proceeded separately to carry out his orders. McDougall led his brigade toward the woods on the south slope of the lower hill, halted, and deployed in the open fields south of the hill. He formed the brigade in a double line of battle and sent two companies forward as skirmishers into the woods—one from the 123d New York, the other from the 5th Connecticut. They were to approach the works cautiously to determine whether or not they were occupied.[65]

Since the 123d New York had been on the left of McDougall's line and near the top of the lower hill, it seems likely that it moved on the left. The

5th Connecticut, in turn, had been on the right of McDougall's line and behind the stone wall. Whether or not the two companies operated under one commander we do not know—reports suggest that they did not.

Col. Warren W. Packer of the 5th Connecticut detailed Capt. Alfred A. Chinery and thirteen soldiers to represent his regiment. He ordered them not to fire or otherwise alarm the enemy but merely to determine his strength and position. Chinery did as he was told; he found the works in Confederate hands and lost five men as prisoners.[66]

Lt. Col. James C. Rogers of the 123d New York sent Lt. Marcus Beadle forward with Company I to see if the Confederates were on the hill. Before starting off, Beadle heard that Confederates had been at Spangler's Spring, and, though he did not believe the report, it made him cautious. As Beadle and his men approached the woods, Lieutenant Beadle shouted a challenge. A voice replied, "Come on, it's all right." Beadle walked forward in front of his line and was taken prisoner. But as the Confederates seized him, he yelled, "Fall back men." At this warning, Company I began shooting, and the Confederates shot back.[67]

When the bullets began to fly, confusion developed within the brigade. McDougall had formed it on a rise between McAllister's Woods and the Baltimore Pike in a column of regiments, one behind another, each regiment having a regimental front. The 145th New York was about thirty-five feet behind the 123d's main line. When Beadle's skirmishers retreated to the main line in the face of Confederate fire, the 123d was told to fall back to the crest of the rise. As it tried to do so, the 145th, thinking that the 123d was the enemy, opened fire on it and fell back rapidly, leaving its colors and some knapsacks behind. The rest of the brigade held firm, and the 145th settled down. One man, Pvt. Nelson A. Thayer of the 123d New York, was shot in the head and died without a word. The brigade spent the remainder of the night lying in line of battle on the high ground beyond the marshy meadow from the lower hill with its front screened by a line of skirmishers.[68]

When the Third Brigade, on the division's right, reached the fields east of the Baltimore Pike, its people could not see if its old position had been occupied by the enemy. Its works in McAllister's Woods were concealed by darkness. In obedience to General Ruger's orders, Colonel Colgrove sent a company of the 2d Massachusetts forward to see if the works were clear. They found them vacant, and the brigade reoccupied them at once. Before going on to their works north of the meadow, Lt. Col. Charles R. Mudge sent a few skirmishers forward, and somewhere in the darkness they captured a lone Confederate.[69]

The situation on the lower hill was confusing, and Ruger's men were feeling their way in the darkness. They must have heard the musketry on Geary's front not far away, and Ruger and his two brigade commanders should have known something of what each was doing. Yet their reports and other accounts suggest that each brigade operated separately.

The capture of the Rebel soldier, coupled with Captain Oakey's account of the Confederate assault, must have increased the caution of Mudge and Maj. Charles F. Morse, who was directing the 2d Massachusetts's skirmishers. Rather than take the whole regiment across the meadow, Mudge sent Company F forward into the dark woods on the hill to find out who was there. "Some slight confusion" followed, and Company F returned with a Confederate captain and twenty-two captured soldiers and the news that Jones's and Steuart's brigades occupied the works. Mudge reported what had been accomplished, but the "proper authorities"—Colgrove and perhaps Ruger—thought that the captured Rebels might be stragglers. They were reluctant to believe that an enemy force was in the Union position and told Mudge to send out another party of skirmishers followed by his whole regiment. In addition, they told Col. Nirom M. Crane of the 107th New York to advance in Mudge's support. To Major Morse, "matters now began to look serious."[70]

Mudge and Morse discussed their problem, and Mudge decided that he would hold his regiment on the north edge of the meadow, while Morse, Capt. Thomas B. Fox, and Company K went ahead to reconnoiter. Company K's men "crawled along cautiously and quietly" and after a while heard talking to their front. They had been warned that Geary's division might be moving toward them, so Morse had to find out what troops were there. Fox sent two men forward. They walked ahead to the men who were talking, and one asked, "Boys, what regiment do you belong to?" "Twenty-third," someone replied. "Twenty-third what?" the Massachusetts man queried. "Twenty-third Virginia," a voice in the darkness retorted. But the ignorance implied by the last question raised suspicions. Another voice cried, "Why, they are Yanks," and the Virginians seized one of the scouts while the other bolted back to Morse. Morse told Mudge what had happened, and Mudge withdrew the regiment's main line to the south side of the meadow.[71]

Morse and Fox decided that a bluff was in order; they would act in a noisy, forthright manner and see what would happen. Fox ordered, "Forward!," and almost immediately there was a challenge, "Who goes there?" Fox shouted, "Surrender, or we fire!" From ahead someone shouted, "Battalion, ready—fire!," and there was a line of muzzle flashes that extended far beyond the flanks of Company K. Fortunately, the Massachusetts men were downslope from the Virginians, probably from the 10th Regiment, who could not really see them in the darkness, and most of the balls went over their heads. The Confederate force then advanced, and Company K took to its heels. In Morse's opinion, they had done enough "skylarking" for one evening, and he sent Company K back across the meadow to the regiment. In this last foray, Morse captured three Confederates, but three men of Company K were wounded.[72]

While Morse probed toward the summit of the lower hill, Colonel Crane and the 107th New York pushed into the woods to Morse's left. He halted the regiment under the trees and walked about sixty yards in its front. There he found what seemed to be a Confederate regiment. Crane returned to the base of the hill and found Major Morse. Morse told him that he was withdrawing, and Crane moved the 107th back across the meadow and reported to Colonel Colgrove. There had been enough skylarking that night for everyone.[73]

By midnight both Geary and Ruger recognized that the Confederates had occupied their old works on the lower hill and that the penetration would have to be sealed off and removed. To do so would require preparations, and the work would have to be done in the daylight. Their acting corps commander, Alpheus Williams, returned from the council-of-war at Meade's headquarters at about midnight. It was only then, after his return, that he learned "this state of affairs." It did not surprise him greatly that the enemy had penetrated his works, but he was astonished to learn that Geary had been ordered away from the hill, leaving only Greene's brigade to defend it. Williams rode to see General Slocum and told him "the condition of affairs." Slocum's reply was a brief one: "Well, drive them out at daylight."[74]

14

EARLY ATTACKS CEMETERY HILL

Ewell's demonstration in support of Longstreet's assault was to start at about 4:00 P.M. and was to be made by all three divisions of his corps. Johnson's division was to attack the Federals on Culp's Hill. When Early and Rodes heard the roar of musketry that told them that Johnson's men had struck the enemy's main line, they were to hurl their divisions against Cemetery Hill. Since there were no significant natural obstacles in their paths, they hoped to be able to strike Cemetery Hill without undue delay.

When he learned the time of the attack, Early summoned Gordon's brigade from the York Pike east of the town, but he left Smith's there with some of Stuart's cavalry to guard the road. Early posted Gordon's Georgians along the railroad track on the east side of the town a quarter mile behind his main line. Obviously, he believed that the Georgians would be close enough to support his forward line when the attack began and, perhaps, would be able to march quickly from there to the aid of Smith's brigade in case their help was needed on the York Pike.[1]

The artillery fire ended, and Johnson's men advanced. Toward sunset, clouds of smoke billowed above the dark trees on Culp's Hill, and Early could hear a roar "like that of a sea lashed in fury." Johnson's brigades had struck the Union position on Culp's Hill, and it was time for Early's line to attack. Early and one of his staff officers rode from the town, probably down from the foot of Stratton Street, to Hays's position on Winebrenner's Run. Puffs of dust that spurted from the slope around them as they approached the infantry line showed that the Federal skirmishers had spotted the two riders and sent them greetings. But light was failing, the marksmanship was lacking, and they rode unscathed to General Hays. Hays would command his and Hoke's brigades in their advance, and he had received his instructions during the afternoon. Now that Johnson was engaged, Early asked Hays if he was ready to go and, being assured that he was, told him to take his brigades forward and "carry the works on the height in their front." It was Hays's understanding at this time that a general attack on Cemetery Hill would be made and that Rodes's division would be advancing on his right from beyond the town. Having given Hays the order to attack, Early and his staff officer, probably Major Daniel, passed along the line of the Louisianans and North Carolinians, who stood, stretched, and formed lines to go forward.[2]

After speaking to Early, Hays, "who was no man to deceive his men," rode along his line in the growing dusk. Hays tried to encourage his Louisianans by telling them that Early said that they should silence the guns on Cemetery Hill and that Gordon's brigade would be up to reinforce them and to hold on to their gains. Yet Lt. J. Warren Jackson, who had been on the skirmish line most of the day, was not assured; he felt as though his doom was sealed.[3]

Harry Thompson Hays, like many other Confederate brigade commanders, had been a lawyer before the war. He was born in 1820 in Tennessee near Andrew Jackson's "Hermitage" and was a little older than many of his peers. Orphaned at an early age, he was reared by an uncle in Wilkeson County, Mississippi. A Roman Catholic, he was sent to Saint Mary's School in Baltimore and, after leaving school, studied law in that city. He practiced law in New Orleans, taking time out for service in a Mississippi cavalry unit during the Mexican War. He furthered himself politically, perhaps, by being an active Whig.

When the Civil War began, Hays became the colonel of the 7th Louisiana Regiment, the "Pelican Regiment," which had been recruited primarily from New Orleans. Hays led his Pelicans with distinction at First Manassas and in the Shenandoah Valley until he was wounded at Port Republic. He became a brigadier general while recovering from his wound and received command of the brigade in July 1862 when Gen. Richard Taylor was promoted to the command of the District of Western Louisiana. Hays led his brigade, nicknamed the "Louisiana Tigers," at Antietam and in subsequent battles until he received a wound at Spotsylvania Courthouse in 1864 that ended his career with the Army of Northern Virginia. In May 1865, before the official end of the war in the Trans-Mississippi Department, Lt. Gen. Edmund Kirby Smith promoted him to the grade of major general.[4]

Brig. Gen. Harry T. Hays (WLM)

Although Hays's brigade contained five Louisiana regiments, the 5th through the 9th, it numbered only about 1,200 officers and men. Most of the members of the brigade had been recruited from the New Orleans area, but the 9th Regiment had been formed from companies obtained elsewhere. The brigade contained a large proportion of native-born Americans, many of whom were undoubtedly of French ancestry, and Irish immigrants seem to have been the most numerous of its foreign-born. Hays did not describe his brigade's formation along Winebrenner's Run in his report or give the order of its regiments in line when the attack began. However, the Bachelder maps for 2 July show the brigade in a single line with the 5th Regiment on the right and the 6th, 9th, 7th, and 8th regiments in turn to its left.[5]

Hoke's brigade, which formed on Hays's left in the ravine, had three regiments but only about 900 officers and men. The 6th North Carolina was on its right, the 21st occupied the center of the line, and the 57th was on the left near the stone springhouse of the Culp farm. The brigade had spent the day under the hot sun, harassed by skirmishers' fire, and hailed the command to go forward with relief.[6]

Robert F. Hoke was the brigade's assigned commander, but he had been wounded at Chancellorsville and Col. Isaac E. Avery served in his place.

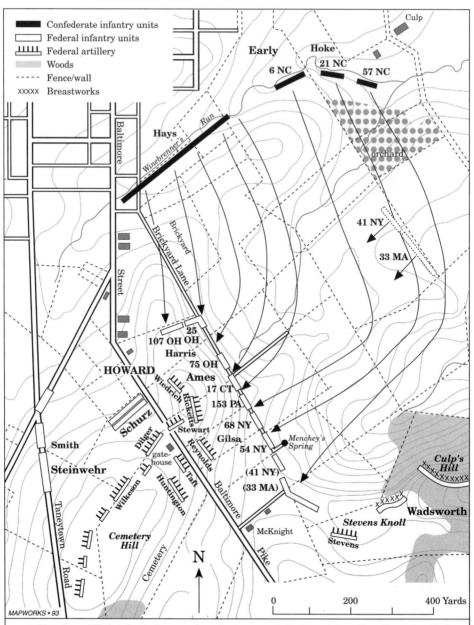

Legend:
- Confederate infantry units
- Federal infantry units
- Federal artillery
- Woods
- Fence/wall
- xxxxx Breastworks

Culp

Early   Hoke
        21 NC
6 NC   57 NC

Hays

Winebrenner's Run

Baltimore

orchard

41 NY

33 MA

Brickyard Lane

Street

25
107 OH OH
Harris
75 OH
HOWARD   Ames
17 CT
153 PA

Wiedrich
Ricketts
68 NY
Schurz   Stewart   Gilsa
Dilger   54 NY   Menchey's
Smith   gate-   Reynolds   Spring   Culp's
       house   (41 NY)   Hill
Steinwehr   (33 MA)   xxxxx
       Taft
Wilkeson Huntington
                Baltimore   Wadsworth
Taneytown   xxxxx
                         McKnight   Stevens Knoll xxxxx
Cemetery   Stevens
Hill   Cemetery   N

MAPWORKS • 93   0   200   400 Yards

1. Hays's and Hoke's brigades attack at dusk, toward the batteries on East Cemetery Hill.

2. Ames, concerned about an attack by Johnson, has posted two regiments in Culp's Meadow to the east and has shifted the 17th Connecticut right to bolster von Gilsa's line. This leaves a gap in Harris's line.

3. Hays and Hoke advance; the forward Federal units fall back to von Gilsa's position.

4. Hays strikes Harris's left and the gap and drives toward Wiedrich's battery.

5. Hays's and Hoke's regiments smash the center of von Gilsa's line. Portions of each brigade charge up the hill.

6. The 75th, 17th, 41st, and 33d regiments hold to their positions at the base of the hill.

Map 14.1. Early's Division's Assault, 7:30 p.m., 2 July

Col. Isaac E. Avery (Avery Papers, NCDAH)

Avery was born in Burke County, North Carolina, in December 1828, the scion of a distinguished family of the Old North State. He studied for a year at the University of North Carolina but left it in 1847 to manage a family farm. About ten years later he went into business with Charles F. Fisher and Samuel McD. Tate to take part in the building of the Western North Carolina Railroad. The partners were working in Burke County when the war began. Fisher received authorization to organize what became the 6th North Carolina Infantry Regiment, and both Tate and Avery raised companies for it.

Fisher fell at First Manassas, and Dorsey Pender was given command of the regiment and remained with it until he went on to a brigade command after the battle of Seven Pines. Isaac Avery, who was promoted to the grade of lieutenant colonel on 1 June 1862 and colonel ten days later, succeeded Pender in the command of the 6th. Avery had been wounded at Manassas and was wounded again severely at Malvern Hill. The 6th fought in Hoke's brigade at Chancellorsville, and when Hoke was wounded, Avery became acting brigade commander in his place. Thus it was that Avery commanded at Gettysburg instead of the wounded Hoke.[7]

In later years, Capt. John A. McPherson described Avery as always having been with his regiment and always cheerful and in good spirits. He was a large and powerful man, weighing over 200 pounds—not the sort to be trifled with. In recalling Avery's conduct at Manassas, McPherson wrote that "there was no fall back in Capt. Avery." Others would write of his "high moral worth," "genial nature," "stern inflexible fortitude," and "chivalrous bearing."[8]

The North Carolinians did not write of Early's visiting their front, but one recalled seeing aides riding rapidly from one command to another and there were shouted commands. Colonel Avery ordered, "Forward, Guide Right," and regimental and company commanders repeated it along the length of the North Carolina line. In the 57th Regiment, at least, the oral command received emphasis from the blaring of a bugle. At the commands of Hays and Avery, Early's second assault at Gettysburg got under way.[9]

Avery had led his brigade on horseback in the previous day's attack, but that was a different situation—the fields were open and level, and it was practicable for a commander to have a horseman's view of things. This time he elected to go in afoot and summoned a courier to take his and McPherson's mounts. But after McPherson had dismounted and walked off to the left, Avery changed his mind, kept his horse, and rode forward with his brigade, one of the few mounted men along the line.[10]

Early's advance came as a surprise to the Federals in his front. Col. Andrew L. Harris of the 75th Ohio, acting commander of Ames's brigade, termed it a "complete surprise." He expected no assault from that quarter and could not have been more astonished "if the moving column had raised up out of the ground amid the waving timothy grass of the meadow." Yet toward sundown Lt. J. Clyde Miller of the 153d Pennsylvania Regiment of von Gilsa's brigade, who had spent much of the day on the skirmish line, saw the enemy skirmishers move forward followed by two lines of battle. Obviously the Confederates were up to something. Miller ordered his men to commence firing and to fall back on the main line at the base of Cemetery Hill.[11]

The force manning Cemetery Hill at this time was not so formidable as it might have appeared to be. The Eleventh Corps had three divisions of two brigades each, but all but one brigade had been handled roughly by the Confederates on 1 July. Orland Smith's brigade was the freshest of the lot, yet all but one of its regiments, the 33d Massachusetts, had been heavily engaged in deadly skirmishing the entire day. Further, it had its hands full guarding Cemetery Hill from an attack from the west, not from an assault from the northeast. Von Steinwehr's other brigade, Coster's, on the other hand had no sector of its own; its four regiments, or what

Col. George von Amsberg (WLM)

remained of them, rested near the crest of Cemetery Hill. If Howard had a corps reserve, it was the four regiments of Coster's brigade.[12]

Schurz's division's main line was in an orchard and behind a wall to the west of the Baltimore Pike and about 100 yards north of the cemetery. By this time, according to Schurz, the division numbered only about 1,500 officers and men and was the size of an average brigade. To avoid capture, General Schimmelfennig, commander of the division's First Brigade, had hidden in an outbuilding behind the Garlach house on Baltimore Street a rifle shot away, and Col. George von Amsberg of the 45th New York commanded in his place. Amsberg's five regiments were in the first line behind a wall located where the northwest wall of the Soldiers' National Cemetery stands today. The Second Brigade under Col. Wladimir Krzyzanowski formed behind the First in a support line. Schurz's men were heavily involved in the skirmishing in the town to their front, but because the town was a poor place from which to launch an attack, it would be spared a frontal assault on its position.[13]

Brig. Gen. Adelbert Ames (WLM)

The First Division, Eleventh Corps, now commanded by Brig. Gen. Adelbert Ames, protected that portion of the hill east of the pike. It had been mauled badly on 1 July and, like other units of the Eleventh Corps, was much weaker than it had been. In total, according to Ames, the division's First Brigade numbered no more than 650 rifles on 2 July and the Second had about 500. Yet, in spite of its casualties, Ames did poorly by the division's reputation after the Cemetery Hill fight. His report contains only five lines concerning the division's activities on 2 and 3 July, a time when the Confederate artillery subjected it to heavy poundings, when it was engaged in almost constant skirmishing, and when it bore the brunt of Early's 2 July attack.[14]

Adelbert Ames was a native of Maine, born in Rockland in 1835. He had gone to sea before enrolling in West Point's class of 1861. After graduating in May, he joined Battery D, 5th U.S. Artillery, in time to command a section at Bull Run. Ames suffered a serious thigh wound there but continued to command his section from a perch on a caisson until he was too weak to do so, for which he received a Medal of Honor in 1893. After a short recuperation, Ames returned to the field and commanded Battery D during the Peninsular campaign. Ames's bravery and ability, together with his Maine connections, no doubt, paid handsome dividends in August 1862 when he received the colonelcy of the 20th Maine Regiment. Ames trained and commanded this soon-to-be-distinguished unit until May 1863 and led it in the battle of Fredericksburg. Then he received a promotion to the grade of brigadier general—without having first commanded a brigade, as many colonels were doing—and was appointed to command the Second Brigade, First Division, Eleventh Corps, which was no longer dominated by regiments of German immigrants.

When Ames became an acting division commander at Gettysburg, therefore, he was twenty-eight years old, two years out of West Point, and had commanded the 20th Maine in one battle and his own brigade in the fighting north of Gettysburg, where it had been outflanked and driven from the field.[15]

Wainwright became acquainted with Ames while they awaited an attack on East Cemetery Hill. He found him "the best kind of a man to be associated with, cool and clear in his own judgment, gentlemanly and without the smallest desire to interfere." Wainwright went on to observe that Ames was a gentleman and "a strange thing in this army, I did not hear him utter an oath of any kind during the three days!" Shortly after the battle, Lt. Oscar D. Ladley of the 75th Ohio wrote that Ames was a young man of good judgment "and far superior to any Dutchman in the army."[16]

Ames's brigade, the Second Brigade, First Division, Eleventh Corps, was the remnant of the "Ohio Brigade" that had campaigned in western Virginia and the Shenandoah Valley. It still had three Ohio regiments and, with Ames's temporary elevation, was commanded by Col. Andrew L. Harris of the 75th Ohio Regiment. Harris was born near Oxford, Ohio, in 1835, was reared on a farm, and attended nearby Miami University, from which he graduated in 1860. He began reading law in Eaton, Ohio, but when war came, he entered the 20th Ohio Volunteer Infantry, a three-month regiment in which he served as a lieutenant. In October 1861 he recruited and became captain of Company C, 75th Ohio Volunteer Infantry. After leading his company at McDowell, where he was wounded severely in the arm, Cedar Mountain, and Second Bull Run, he became the regiment's major in January 1863. After the 75th Ohio's commander was killed at Chancellorsville, Harris received command of the regiment, going directly from the rank of major to colonel. Although a new colonel

Col. Andrew L. Harris (MM)

at Gettysburg, Harris ranked second to Ames in the brigade at that time, and when Ames stepped up to division command, Harris took his place.[17]

On 2 July the main line of the Ohio Brigade, which included the 17th Connecticut Regiment, occupied the wall east from the bend at Baltimore Street and to Schurz's right front. (The wall ran from the rear of Snider's Wagon Hotel almost east across the hill and down to the lane known as Brickyard Lane or Winebrenner's Lane and now as Wainwright Avenue.) The brigade skirmished throughout the day, with Confederates firing from the brickyard and the houses in the south of the town.[18]

The First Brigade, von Gilsa's, was scattered. Its 54th and 68th New York regiments were to the right and rear of the Second Brigade behind a low wall along Brickyard Lane. Except for two companies on the skirmish line, the 153d Pennsylvania was at the top of Cemetery Hill. The 41st New York, which was about 200 strong and had missed the 1 July fighting, had two companies on the skirmish line and seven on top of the hill. Somehow, on 1 July von Gilsa had become separated from his troops, which had rallied on Cemetery Hill, and when he reached them during the night of 1 July, Captain von Fritsch pointed to the flags of its regiments and the small number of soldiers sleeping around them and said, "You can now command your Brigade easily with the voice, my dear Colonel, this is all that is left." [19]

The brigade's three New York regiments dated back to 1861 and were composed primarily of German immigrants. They bore the names "DeKalb Regiment," "Lutzow's Schwarzer Jaeger," and the "Cameron Rifles," after the former secretary of war. All had served in the Shenandoah Valley in 1862 and had joined the Army of the Potomac with Sigel. The 41st had been von Gilsa's first command, and it had contained numerous veterans of the Schleswig-Holstein conflict. It was said that twenty-three of its thirty-three officers were veterans of European wars. The 68th was particularly unfortunate, for its colonel, Gotthilf Bourry, a former Austrian officer, drank heavily and would be cashiered the following October for drunkenness. The brigade's other regiment, the 153d Pennsylvania, was not a German regiment but had a lot of men of German descent within its ranks. The 153d was a nine-month unit that had fought at Chancellorsville and would be mustered out three weeks after the battle of Gettysburg.[20]

Leopold von Gilsa, commander of the brigade, was one of the Union army's many unsung and unrewarded brigade commanders. He had been a major in the Prussian army during the Schleswig-Holstein conflict. He then emigrated to the United States, where he became a teacher. At one period, he fell on hard times and lived by working as a pianist in music halls and dance halls (such as "Tingletangles" and "Polkakneipen") on New York's Bowery.

The Civil War provided von Gilsa with new opportunities, and in June 1861 he became colonel of the 41st New York Volunteer Infantry Regiment, which he did much to organize. He led the 41st in the Shenandoah Valley, where he was wounded at Cross Keys, and he served as Sigel's chief of staff at Second Bull Run. He received command of his brigade just prior to Chancellorsville, where it had the misfortune of being on the right of the Eleventh Corps line and the first unit struck by Jackson's onslaught. When he saw that his brigade was outflanked and that no reinforcements were at hand, he sent two officers with orders for the brigade to pull back. After both were shot, he rode forward himself thundering, "Wollt ihr denn all' in die Hoelle sein? Zurueck!" Von Gilsa was strict about observing the Articles of War, it was said, but incapable of observing the regulation forbidding the use of profanity. Perhaps this resulted from the baleful

Col. Leopold von Gilsa (WLM)

influence of Prussian service and the Bowery's Tingletangles. When a thoroughly irate von Gilsa met General Howard during the withdrawal from Chancellorsville, and when Howard sought to assuage his anger by reminding him to depend on God, the Prussian responded with such a stream of profanity that Howard thought him insane.

Yet Howard described von Gilsa as "a German officer, who at parades and drills makes a fine soldierly appearance"—faint praise if that was all the good that could be said. Schurz, whose standards probably differed from Howard's, said the Prussian was "one of the bravest men and an uncommonly skillful officer." General Barlow wrote that he was "personally brave." Wilhelm Kaufmann, the biographer, termed him valiant and prudent. His soldiers expressed their opinion with cheers as he rode past their column during their march through Gettysburg. After Gettysburg, von Gilsa continued for a time as brigade commander after the division had been assigned to the Tenth Corps in the Carolinas and then reverted to commander of the 41st New York. In June 1864, when the 41st New York's enlistment expired, von Gilsa, still a colonel, left the army and returned to New York. He had joined as a colonel, had commanded a brigade in two major battles, and left the service without even the sop of a brevet. One biographer blamed his lack of promotion on the influence of the Princess Salm-Salm, a celebrity with unmerited influence over politicians, whose husband, a German princeling, was described as an old enemy of the colonel. Perhaps service with the Eleventh Corps and his German oaths, coupled with a peculiar promotion system, created a combination that could not be overcome.[21]

One additional regiment was on Ames's front. The 33d Massachusetts Volunteer Infantry Regiment of Smith's brigade had spent the night of 1 July in the Taneytown Road on the left of Smith's line. Sometime on the morning of 2 July, Col. Adin B. Underwood was ordered to report with it to General Ames. Ames posted it at one of the stone walls on the crest of East Cemetery Hill in support of the artillery there. At this time, one of its wings was in the road, the other behind a stone wall. There it remained during the afternoon's artillery duel, under a fire that came from several directions. Two or three times during this shelling, Underwood moved his men from one side of the wall to the other to avoid incoming rounds.[22]

Late in the afternoon, presumably after Latimer's guns fell silent, Ames ordered Lt. Col. Detleo von Einsiedel and Underwood to take their regiments, the 41st New York and the 33d Massachusetts, out to Culp's Meadow beyond Brickyard Lane. Underwood posted the 33d in front of the "valley" between Cemetery Hill and Culp's Hill, probably at the fence line that ran where East Confederate Avenue is today, and pushed skirmishers to the front. Stevens's battery on its knoll to the 33d's right and rear was not firing then for it had no target, it was low on ammunition, and its guns were hot and fouled.[23]

It seems likely that Ames's attention, if not Howard's, focused on Johnson's attack on Culp's Hill and that Ames prepared to counter what he deemed to be a threat posed by Johnson to Cemetery Hill. This he sought to do by posting a strong force in front of Cemetery Hill and by shifting the troops of his division to the right to strengthen his line at the northeast base of the hill. It was then, perhaps, that, speaking of one of his brigades, he is alleged to have said to Capt. R. Bruce Ricketts, the battery commander, "Captain, three times I have sent orders to that brigade to advance to the support of our men on Culp's Hill, and they will not advance one step."[24]

Thus it was that the shift of the 41st New York and the 33d Massachusetts to Culp's Meadow was part of a large redeployment. Ames ordered Colonel Harris to move most of the Second Brigade from along the wall facing the town and from the crest of the hill to a position along the lane on

View toward Gettysburg from East Cemetery Hill. The German Reformed Church is on the far right. The 107th Ohio Regiment manned the wall marked by the tall trees on the evening of 2 July when struck by Hays's brigade. (GNMP)

von Gilsa's left. After the shift, the 107th Ohio Regiment was still on the left behind a wall facing the town, its line extending from the crest toward the base of the hill. The 25th Ohio formed on the 107th's right, the 17th Connecticut was next fronting northeast along Brickyard Lane, and the 75th Ohio was on the right of Harris's line. Unfortunately, Harris's line did not reach von Gilsa's left. To give von Gilsa's brigade support, Ames ordered that the 17th Connecticut join it. Maj. Allen G. Brady, the 17th's commander, took his regiment from its place in Harris's line, moved it to the right, and reported with it to the commander of the First Brigade. At von Gilsa's suggestion, Brady posted the 17th on the First Brigade's left, along the wall at the lane and facing another lane that led to the northeast. He sent two companies forward as skirmishers toward a grain field, probably the one southwest of the orchard through which Hoke's brigade was already advancing toward the meadow. Brady reported that he strengthened his own line with 300 stragglers whom he compelled to join him. Where these stragglers came from and who they were, Brady did not say. Certainly stragglers would not have been lollygagging at the base of

Cemetery Hill. If there were such men, they were probably skirmishers falling back from the front to join their regiments on the hill.[25]

Why did Ames pluck the 17th Connecticut from its place in the center of Harris's line and place it under von Gilsa's command when essentially the same thing could have been accomplished by shifting it and the 75th Ohio to the right? No one said. Perhaps Ames regarded the 17th Connecticut more highly than the Ohio regiments and thought that placing it under von Gilsa's command would do the most to strengthen his line.[26]

The removal of the 17th from the right center of his line left Harris with a gap that had to be closed even as the enemy pressed toward it. Harris tried to do this by ordering that the left of the 107th Ohio hold its place while the remainder of the regiment and the 25th Ohio extended right toward the gap. As Harris observed, "This left my line very thin and weak. All the men could get to the stone wall, used by us as a breastwork, and have all the elbow room he wanted."[27]

While Harris tried to patch up his line in the face of Hays's advance, the 41st New York and the 33d Massachusetts, which were threatened by Early's advance, fell back to the base of the hill. The Union line there, the one that would meet Early's attack, was somewhat as follows. The 17th Connecticut was to the left center opposite the mouth of the lane that ran into the fields to the northeast. The 153d Pennsylvania was on its right, followed to the right by the three remaining regiments of von Gilsa's brigade—the 68th, 54th, and 41st New York. The 33d Massachusetts was to the right of von Gilsa's line, covering the lane that led by the McKnight house to the Baltimore Pike. The 68th and 54th New York were near Menchey's Spring. It was said that a Rebel sharpshooter in a hidden perch in a tree shot several men from the 54th New York as they went to the spring. If so, they must have been long and lucky shots.[28]

Harris, in turn, had the 75th Ohio on the left of the 17th Connecticut, the 25th beyond the gap to its left at the junction of the walls, probably fronting northwest, and the 107th along the wall running to the west with its left near the top of the hill. We have only rough estimates of the strengths of these Ohio regiments. Harris thought that their combined strength at this time did not exceed 500 men. Lt. Peter F. Young, adjutant of the German 107th Ohio, wrote that the 107th had gone into battle with 434 muskets but had only 171 on Cemetery Hill on the evening of 1 July. He believed that the other Ohio regiments had less than 100 men each. The line was very thin, therefore, no more than one rank deep in the sector manned by the 27th and 75th regiments, but the weakness would not matter if the brunt of the attack fell elsewhere.[29]

The troops on the skirmish lines were naturally the first to know of Early's attack. Those of the 33d Massachusetts saw the Confederates approaching in two lines and began firing. When Colonel Underwood realized that the Confederates were advancing in strength, he ordered his skirmishers back. They "formed companies deliberately and with great steadiness," and then they retired. Lieutenant Miller on the skirmish line of the 153d Pennsylvania saw the Confederate skirmishers advancing, followed by what looked like two lines of battle in their rear. He ordered his companies to fire and fall back. Miller's men halted three times to fire during their retreat, and then, at Miller's command, the men of the two companies ran toward the wall at the base of the hill.[30]

The Confederates pressed their attack; when "Old Harry" Hays shouted "Forward," Lieutenant Jackson started his skirmish line off in the lead with great reluctance, but it moved ahead followed by the main line. To Major Tate of the 6th North Carolina, the start of Hoke's brigade's advance was a time to be remembered: "Every man in the line knew what was before him." They knew something of the enemy's preparations for them, and that was bad enough, yet their fears might have made it worse. Both brigades hurried over the little rise that formed the south wall of the ravine and had sheltered them all day. Hays's men descended into the low ground at the base of the hill and into the swale draining it. There they met "a considerable body of the enemy," a skirmish line, no doubt, and there was a brisk exchange of shots.[31]

It was while they were in this low ground that Hays's men received their first artillery fire, probably from Wiedrich's battery. Capt. William J. Seymour of Hays's staff wrote that the enemy had anticipated their advance and opened on them right away with musketry and artillery fire. Capt. Neill W. Ray of the 6th North Carolina, however, recalled that the enemy's "sharpshooters" emptied their rifles at them and then fell back to their main line. Probably each was essentially correct. Ray's account coincides with those of the enemy, and it is likely that the left of Hays's line became the target of the batteries not long after it hove into the gunners' view.[32]

There are no lucid descriptions of the routes followed by the two brigades, and it is unlikely that they can be known with great certainty. It seems probable, however, that the right of Hays's line followed along the east side of Brickyard Lane for about 250 yards, skirting the steep slope of Cemetery Hill. When it approached the 107th and 25th Ohio regiments on the left of Harris's brigade's line, it wheeled right and climbed the hill to strike them. Had Hays's right been moved closer to Baltimore Street,

Officers of the 153d Pennsylvania Regiment. Lts. William Beidelman and H. R. Barnes are fourth and fifth from the left, Lt. William Simmers stands behind them, and Lt. J. Clyde Miller is on the right. (Kiefer, One Hundred and Fifty-third Regiment*)*

it would have been slowed by the buildings and fences there and by the Union troops who occupied them.[33]

As Hays's brigade advanced, its left, which would have been as much as 400 yards east of its right, would have tried to stay on line but probably would have found it difficult to do so. It would have passed over the knoll about 200 yards south of its starting point, where a school building sits today, and, as the right struck the Union line at the base of Cemetery Hill, it would have descended from the knoll into the swale that drains from the base of Cemetery Hill below Wiedrich's battery—in front of that portion of the wall formerly held by the 17th Connecticut Regiment. Here, at the present site of a school athletic field, as Hays's right pushed against the left of the Ohio Brigade, Hays's left would have swung right, climbing the fold of high ground in front of the center of the Union line at the base of Cemetery Hill.

Hoke's brigade advanced on Hays's left, probably moving astride the fence line that ran where East Confederate Avenue is today. The brigade's left probably remained on the southwest or near side of the lane that connected the Culp farmyard with the fields near Culp's Hill. About 200 yards south of the farmyard, its left wing passed through an orchard that encompassed a segment of the stream draining down from Cemetery Hill. Once through this orchard, it would have entered the two large open fields known as Culp's Meadow. By the time that the North Carolinians debouched from the orchard into the open fields, Hays's line would have been wheeling toward the hill. It was here that the Tarheels dressed their lines and had a full view of their objective—Cemetery Hill. They saw that the batteries they had been ordered to take were "considerably to the right of our right flank" and in front of Hays's brigade. This meant that Hoke's brigade would have to swing to the right at once in order to strike the hill.[34]

The Federal batteries opened on Early's men almost as soon as their advance began. Captain Seymour wrote that "Yankee missiles" hissed, screamed, and hurtled over their heads while they were in low ground in front of the hill and did them little damage. Hays believed that a horrible slaughter had been avoided because the darkness of the evening and the heavy smoke concealed the Confederates from the enemy gunners' view. Perhaps he was right.[35]

Yet, of all the guns on Cemetery Hill, only those of Wiedrich's, Ricketts's, and Reynolds's batteries, together with Stevens's battery on its knoll, could be brought to bear on Early's infantry. Wiedrich's four guns would have been shooting at Hays's line in the low ground northeast of their position; Ricketts's and Reynolds's batteries would have fired on Hoke's brigade and perhaps the left of Hays's line as they moved onto the high ground of the meadows in their front. Stevens's battery would have fired at Hays's left and the North Carolinians as they crossed Culp's Meadow and passed up the low ground toward Ames's division's right.[36]

Ricketts's battery had been sent from the artillery park to the back side of Cemetery Hill, where it awaited a call to the front. General Hunt, who had been on the hill for a while during the afternoon's artillery exchange, figured that Wainwright might need a fresh battery and sent Ricketts's six three-inch Ordnance rifles to him. Wainwright recalled that the Pennsylvanians approached his position on the hill as if "moving onto a parade ground"—an ultimate compliment. Everything about the battery was in beautiful order, so much so that General Ames assumed that it was a regular battery, an observation that "tickled Ricketts greatly." Wainwright used Ricketts's six rifles to replace Cooper's battery's four, and Ricketts occupied Cooper's position, placing four of his guns in Cooper's lunettes. Cpl. Eugene C. Moore, the gunner on Ricketts's second piece, found the severed hand of one of Cooper's men and buried it in the top of the lunette in front of his gun. Soon after Ricketts's guns were in place, Colonel Wainwright stopped at the battery and said, "Captain, this is the key to our position on Cemetery Hill, and must be held[,] and in case you are charged here, you will not limber up under any circumstances, but fight your battery as long as you can." Ricketts repeated this order to his officers and men.[37]

The men of Stevens's battery were probably among the first artillerymen to fire on Early's attacking lines. From their position on the knoll at the base of the west slope of Culp's Hill, they could see across the east face of East Cemetery Hill to the town and to the right from there to Rock Creek east of the Culp buildings. At sundown, the Maine men were resting from their labors even though they could hear the roar of musketry from the east face of Culp's Hill just 500 yards to their right. Some of the cannoneers had finished sponging the bores of their six Napoleons to clean and cool them, while others had transferred the ammunition remaining in their caissons to the gun limbers so that the caissons could be refilled at the artillery park. Now the sun had gone down behind South Mountain and Cemetery Hill; "the dusk of evening was creeping down the valley of Rock Creek and shutting out the town from view, and there was abundant promise of a peaceful night." After all, Civil War–period battles usually sputtered out with the setting sun.[38]

The officers of the battery had done a wise thing during the day. Using a range finder that they called a "French 'ordnance' glass," they had measured the ranges to various key points within their field of fire, including the Culp buildings. Then, with the approval of General Hunt, they had checked their findings by firing a few rounds of solid shot. Thus, the battery's officers and chiefs of piece were ready to do some reasonably accurate shooting if the need arose.[39]

A sergeant, who was keeping an eye toward the front, interrupted this tranquillity by shouting, "Look! look at those men!," as he pointed off toward the left front and the Culp buildings. There, in the growing dusk, they could see Confederate infantry climbing fences and forming a long line. Undoubtedly, the Confederates were Colonel Avery's North Carolinians and Louisianans on the left of Hays's brigade. They had left the ravine, had clambered over the fence on the northwest side of the fields of Culp's Meadow, and were forming for their push against Cemetery Hill.[40]

The sergeant's cry brought the cannoneers to their posts, Lt. Edward Whittier shouted, "Case 2½ degrees, 3 seconds time," and with that the cannoneers threw open the lids on the limber chests, took out the ordered rounds, and carried them to their pieces. The cannoneers rammed them into the bores of the waiting guns. Then Whittier gave the command to "Fire by battery." Colonel Underwood, who had just posted the 33d Massachusetts behind a wall 100 yards to the battery's left and did not realize that the guns were so close, was startled by "a flash of light, a roar and a crash as if a volcano had been let loose" above his head. The crash of Stevens's battery's opening rounds settled into a continuous thunder as it was joined by its fellow batteries on East Cemetery Hill.[41]

Wiedrich's battery probably fired canister almost from the beginning. The battery was Hays's prime objective, and the right of the Louisiana line had only a short distance to march along the northeast base of the hill before it could make its charge. When the charge came, it was "sudden and violent."[42]

Lt. Charles B. Brockway of Ricketts's battery described Hoke's brigade as a "heavy line of infantry" that came from behind a grassy knoll. The artillerymen thought that the Confederates intended to strike Wadsworth's position on Culp's Hill, for their line seemed to be moving in that direction. Ricketts's guns opened with solid shot and case shot. When the Confederates in their sights reached a cornfield, the line wheeled right toward Cemetery Hill and Ricketts's men switched from case to single canister. The battle was taking a personal turn for the artillerymen.[43]

Ames's line at the base of the hill plus the refused 107th and 25th Ohio regiments to its left rear measured no more than 500 yards from flank to flank; the assaulting Confederate line, if tightly formed, need not have been more than 700 yards in width, less if part of the two brigades was in a support line. When Hays's right struck the 107th and 25th on Harris's left, his line would have pivoted right to hit the Union line along Brickyard Lane. The right of the Louisiana brigade would have been exposed to rifle fire from the infantry in its front, but its left might have marched almost unscathed until it crossed the rise opposite von Gilsa's left. There, though Ricketts's guns could have pelted it with canister and Stevens's Napoleons with spherical case, Hays's left would have been safe from infantry fire until within 120 yards of the Union line.

Colonel Avery might well have tried to hold his North Carolinians to Hays's left at the beginning of the right wheel, but he soon would have found it an impracticable, if not impossible, thing to do. Had the North Carolina brigade continued as an extension of Hays's line, its arc would have carried it to the rugged slopes of Culp's Hill rather than its objectives on Cemetery Hill. It seems logical then that Avery would have wheeled his brigade separately into a supporting line behind Hays's left wing. Such a maneuver would have taken the 57th North Carolina on the left perilously close to Stevens's Napoleons, but it would have brought the Tarheel brigade directly against von Gilsa's line and the northeast face of Cemetery Hill in a timely manner. This was a vital action—if Hays's men punched through Harris's line, the North Carolinians would have to deal immediately with those units still on Hays's left. Such a movement might have been accomplished in different ways: Avery might have shifted his brigade by the right flank for 200 yards prior to making the right wheel, or he might simply have made a tight turn from the dressing point along the fence.[44]

Therefore, as Early's brigades wheeled, their formation changed from the single line that they started out in into at least two lines. This was how Union soldiers recalled it. Lieutenant Whittier saw the North Carolinians change front toward the hill after becoming separated from Hays—"a movement which none but the steadiest veterans could execute under such circumstances." As the Confederates neared the position of the 153d Pennsylvania at about the center of Ames's line, Sgt. Maj. Charles Bornemann of the 153d remembered their approaching in three lines with intervals between of 500 or so feet. Lieutenant Miller recollected that the first Rebel line, presumably Hays's, went over the wall to the left of the 153d and that a second, probably Hoke's, struck the 153d itself.[45]

As the Confederates approached the hill, Stevens's Napoleons poured it to them. Ricketts's battery fired single and then double canister. When it used up its canister, it fired "rotten shot"—spherical case loaded without fuses. When fired, the shell burst at the muzzle, giving something of a canister effect.[46]

After the skirmishers, the 41st New York, and the 33d Massachusetts fell back, Stevens's battery had no Union infantry in its front and could fire without hitting its comrades. Further, the battery could cover the "dead space" in front of Cemetery Hill that the batteries on the hill could not reach. To do this, when the Confederate lines neared the base of the hill, the cannoneers on the battery's left three guns had to swing their muzzles hard to the left, and those on the three right pieces had to limber to the rear and take them to the battery's left. On the other hand, Reynolds's battery was bothered less by dead space in his front than by the Federal infantry it might hit if it fired at Confederates within 200 yards of the Union line.[47]

Colonel Harris saw the Louisianans come on, moving steadily to the assault. Soon his infantry opened fire on them, but they never faltered.

The field of Hoke's brigade's attack. Its right would have been near the top of the far rise, its left just beyond the wall. The 33d Massachusetts Regiment manned the wall toward the left, von Gilsa's brigade occupied Brickyard Lane where the tall trees stand, and Stevens's battery was to the right of the place from which the photo was taken. Menchey's Spring drains into the low area beyond the first rise. (GNMP)

"They moved forward as steadily, amid this hail of shot and minnie ball, as though they were on parade far removed from danger." Harris rode along his line, trying to encourage his Buckeyes, telling them of the importance of their position and that they must hold it at all hazards. As he did so, Wiedrich's battery barked above him, and his troops loaded and fired as fast as they could, keeping up a galling fire that seemed to cause the Rebel line to veer to the right. There was hand-to-hand fighting, "obstinate and bloody," that spread to the right along the lane and included the 17th Connecticut. But Harris's line was too thin; the Rebels hit it hard on the refused flank at the juncture of the 107th and 25th Ohio regiments and at the fatal gap between the 25th and 75th Ohio that had not yet been well closed.[48]

The Louisianans forced the Ohioans on the left back up the hill toward Wiedrich's battery. Lieutenant Jackson of the 8th Louisiana wrote that

The assault of Hays's brigade on East Cemetery Hill. Sketch by Edwin Forbes. (GNMP)

they "fotched up" at a stone wall manned by Yanks that did not wish to leave, but with bayonets and "clubbed guns," they drove them back even though by this time it was so dark that they could not tell whether they were shooting their own men or not. Sgt. George S. Clements of the 25th Ohio remembered the Johnnies charging down the hill from the left and toward him. They "put their big feet on the stone wall and went over like deer, over the heads of the whole . . . regiment, the grade being steep and the wall not more than 20 inches high."[49]

Capt. John M. Lutz, the commander of the 107th, and Lt. Peter F. Young, its adjutant, maintained that the 107th was ordered from its position behind the wall. The "Tiger Brigade" had charged toward them, whooping a Rebel yell, had broken through to their right, and were pouring up the slope behind them when the 107th received the order to fall back on the battery and to hold it at all hazards. The Rebels shot Color Sgt. Christian Taifel as he flaunted his flag in their faces, but Lieutenant Young seized the flag before the Rebels could capture it and carried it up the hill to the wall at the left of Wiedrich's battery.[50]

The 75th Ohio and the 17th Connecticut had better positions than their comrades to the left. Their part of Brickyard Lane ran across the bulge of the hill that made for an abrupt rising slope in their rear, a short slope in their front, and a good field of fire along the perpendicular lane and down the swale that drained toward the Culp farmhouse. In addition, on its left the 75th had the flank protection of the wall that led uphill to Wiedrich's battery and a clump of trees that would probably have impeded the attackers. From their somewhat elevated positions, the 75th and 17th regiments, together with whatever "stragglers" Major Brady impressed, saw in the gloaming some enemy advancing on their right and what they deemed to be a full brigade heading at the oblique toward their left. When the Confederates got to within 150 paces, the 17th and 75th opened a destructive fire that thinned the Rebel ranks and checked their advance. The Federals fired several volleys at the Confederates, whom they saw by the light of their muzzle flashes, but the Confederates closed to hand-to-hand combat. Although a small force pushed its way between the 17th and the 75th and there was a melee, Hays's men lost momentum here. One man, indeed, had gone too far—close enough for a Connecticut captain to grab him and pull him over the wall as a prisoner. In the meantime, small streams of Confederates flowed by this strong point toward the top of the hill and another fight.[51]

The North Carolinians recorded little about their advance on the Union line, perhaps thinking that there was little to say. The accounts of members of the 6th North Carolina mentioned artillery fire, particularly from Stevens's Napoleons, which raked them from the left, yet according to Pvt. Thomas E. Causeby, most of its missiles passed over their heads (perhaps to strike the ranks of Hays's men, who were higher up the slope) and the 6th proceeded in good order. Over to the North Carolina left, in the course of the turn, Col. Archibald C. Godwin recalled crossing three walls and rocky and uneven ground that "prevented that rapidity of movement and unity of action which might have insured success." He remembered also that when near the base of the hill he saw that its slope receded before his left, and a right wheel by his left seemed to be in order if his regiment, the 57th, was to go forward with the regiments on his right. He gave the command for the movement, but it must have been futile. By this time the 57th was being blasted by artillery and infantry fire from front and rear.[52]

Sometime after he had given orders for the brigade to wheel right, a ball struck Colonel Avery at the base of his neck on the right side and knocked him from his horse. It was a mortal wound. From this time until their attack was over, Hoke's North Carolinians were without a commander. Avery fell alone; probably in the smoke and darkness no one even saw him

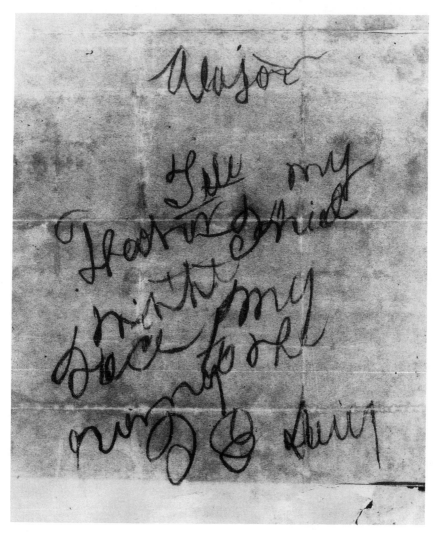

Colonel Avery's last message (Avery Papers, NCDAH)

fall. He knew that his wound was mortal and that he was out of the fight. In his last moments of consciousness, his thoughts turned to his family, and with his waning strength, he took a pencil and a piece of paper from his pocket. On the paper he scrawled a last message to his friend, Major Tate. Its jumbled words read: "Major: Tell my father I died with my face to the enemy," and he signed it, "I. E. Avery." A hero had fallen.[53]

The Eleventh Corps troops on the right wing of Ames's line saw the Confederates approaching in the growing darkness. The 33d Massachusetts waited behind the stone wall that connected Menchey's Spring with Stevens's Knoll. The 33d had fallen back at the onset of the attack and had re-formed there while the Union batteries pounded Hoke's brigade in its front. Colonel Underwood, a Harvard man who would become a general, described the inferno. As he recalled it, the darkness "lighted up with the flames from the cannons' mouths, that seemed to pour down in streams" on the North Carolinians. "The roar and shriek of the shot and shell that plough through and through their ranks is appalling. The gaps close bravely up and still they advance. Canister cannot check them." When the North Carolina line, Colonel Godwin's 57th Regiment, was fifty yards from their front, the 500 men of the 33d opened on it. The Tarheels wavered but pushed doggedly on. The men of the 33d clinched their teeth and waited. In the light of the flaming muzzles, they saw the 57th's color-bearer seeming to wave his flag almost above them. There was another blast from Stevens's double-shotted Napoleons, the colors went down, and all that was left of these "brave traitors" were groans and shrieks and the windrows of dead and dying. "Good for Maine!" shouted the men from Massachusetts in tribute to the artillerymen on their right. Their part of the line had held.[54]

But not all of the 57th had fallen before the blasts of canister and the 33d's fire. Colonel Godwin crossed the wall somewhere to the left of the 33d. The wall's defenders there were melting away, but one large man rushed at Godwin with his musket clubbed. He swung his piece at the colonel, a large man himself, and Godwin deflected the blow to the ground with his left arm. At the same time, Godwin chopped down with his sword and clove the man's head in two.[55]

It was von Gilsa's brigade's position between Menchey's Spring and the lane in front of the 17th Connecticut that proved vulnerable to the North Carolina assault. The position was not a good one: like the rest of the positions along the lane, it was a remote spot, separated from the batteries that supported it on the hill fifty feet above it and 100 yards in its rear. In addition, it offered few advantages to the Union regiments defending it. Not only was this part of the lane not elevated, but the troops on the left there faced gently rising ground that culminated in a knoll about 120 yards in their front. This knoll dominated the Union position and gave cover to the attackers behind it from frontal fire if not from the guns of Stevens's battery 400 yards to the south. This rising ground fell off rather abruptly into low ground to the south so that advancing troops in the low area were concealed and had cover from frontal fire as close as fifty yards from the Union line. In short, the terrain in front of this portion of von Gilsa's line favored the attackers.

The attacking Confederates appeared first to von Gilsa's troops as gray shadows emerging from the darkness and forming for their push against the Union line. Lieutenant Miller of the 153d Pennsylvania, who had just returned to the Union line with his skirmishers, saw von Gilsa standing behind the 153d. As Miller approached the colonel, he heard him shout, "Cease fire, they are our own men!" (He must have thought that they were the troops who had been to the front.) Miller protested to the colonel that this was not so, it was the enemy, and that he had been watching them for some time. Miller then started for his place in the line. As he reached his company, he saw skirmishers followed by a line of battle advancing toward it, yet von Gilsa withheld the command to fire. As the Rebels neared the wall, Lt. William Beidelman of Company F shouted, "Ready—aim—fire!," and above the roar of Company F's rifles, von Gilsa again shouted, "Cease firing!" Miller yelled for his company to fire, and the firing became general along the line.[56]

The Confederates—Hays's left wing, the 6th and 21st North Carolina regiments, and the right of the 57th—charged from the darkness with a yell and with bayonets fixed. The attack on the two weak New York regiments in the center of the line was one of great violence. The New Yorkers had been struck similarly at Chancellorsville and again the day before at Gettysburg and were probably shaky—if so, with reason. The Tarheels shot and killed Sgt. Heinrich Michel, color-bearer of the 54th, almost immediately and wounded his two successors severely. Soon the surviving members of the 68th and 54th regiments retreated up the hill, probably the first troops in von Gilsa's line to go.[57]

The 41st New York had better luck. It was tied to the 33d Massachusetts on its right, and its right wing was able to help the 33d hold the 57th North Carolina at bay. Yet the 41st's left fell back along with the other New York regiments toward the top of the hill.[58]

The 153d Pennsylvania met the attack head-on. There must have been two or more distinct Rebel lines visible from its front, possibly the lines of individual regiments belonging to either Hays's or Hoke's brigades. Lieutenant Miller saw one "pass over," probably on the left, and head for the batteries. The second struck the 153d. There was a melee; "clubs, knives, stones, fists,—anything calculated to inflict death or pain was resorted to." A Rebel color-bearer, rifle in one hand and flag in the other, jumped on the wall and shouted, "Surrender you Yankees," and in an instant a Pennsylvanian jabbed him with his bayonet and fired his rifle into him at the same time. Lieutenant Miller remembered long after how the ball tore shreds from the back of the color-bearer's blouse. The man fell backward, holding both his rifle and the colors. The flagstaff rested briefly across the wall. A Union soldier grabbed for it, and a Confederate grasped its other end. There was a tug-of-war, and the Confederate won.[59]

The pressure grew as more Confederates piled in, crowding Lieutenant Miller and his company back up the hill with the New Yorkers, back toward Ricketts's battery and another stand. Ames's line at the base of the hill had been smashed, yet in the darkness some of its regiments hung on. The 33d Massachusetts and the right of the 41st New York, its line refused behind a wall, formed a shoulder where the right of the line had been, while the 75th Ohio and the 17th Connecticut retained a strong point at the center. From atop the hill, Colonel Wainwright looked down in the darkness at the base of the hill. He wrote, "The night was heavy, and the smoke lay so thick that you could not see ten yards ahead; seventeen guns vomiting it as fast as they can will make a good deal of smoke." He went on then to remark that he pitied General Ames—"his men would not stand at all, save one. I believe not a single regiment of the Eleventh Corps exposed to the attack stood fire, but ran away almost to a man." Obviously, the colonel could not see everything that took place at the base of the hill.[60]

Men of the 21st North Carolina remembered going through Ames's line at a double-quick and with a cheer. Some of the "maddened column rushed on" into continued enemy fire toward the batteries at the top of the hill. Many men of the 21st North Carolina had already fallen. Maj. Alexander Miller had picked up its colors after the first bearer fell and was soon shot. Pvt. Jerry W. Bennett carried the flag next, followed by Capt. James F. Beall, who turned it over to Cpl. Eli Wiley. "The hour was one of horror," yet the batteries and success were only a few yards away.[61]

15

CEMETERY HILL–
THE REPULSE

Generals Howard and Schurz, from where they paused behind Schurz's division's position near the cemetery, heard a shrill and ominous cry from the direction of Ames's division. It was the yell of the Tigers who were striking Ames's line, and soon the attackers and defenders would be "tumbling back together." The generals did not ride to the sound of the guns—not yet. At Howard's request, Schurz hurried to his two nearest regiments, the 58th and 119th New York of Col. Wladimir Krzyzanowski's brigade, and ordered him to take them across the road to the aid of Wiedrich's battery. Schurz and his staff also rode toward the threatened point, swinging their swords at stragglers met along the way in an effort to return them to the fight.[1]

Of course, these were not the first troops recently taken from Howard's center and left to bolster the Union right. The 33d Massachusetts Regiment was already fighting on Ames's line, and a few minutes earlier four regiments of Schimmelfennig's (von Amsberg's) brigade had been sent to the right to assist Greene's brigade on Culp's Hill. These detachments left the defense of Cemetery Hill, the keystone of the Union line, to three regiments of Smith's brigade, which were heavily engaged in skirmishing out toward Seminary Ridge, to the seven weak regiments of Krzyzanowski's and Coster's brigades, and to the batteries behind them.

Howard could weaken his line further only at his peril for other attacks might be coming out of the gloaming. He sent for help. General Hancock responded at once by suggesting to General Gibbon, then commanding the Second Corps, that he send the First Brigade of the First Division to Howard's aid. The attack on the Second Corps front was over by this

Col. Wladimir Krzyzanowski (WLM)

time, and three regiments of this brigade, commanded by Col. Samuel S. Carroll, were free to go. At General Hancock's order, Gibbon also sent the 71st and 106th Pennsylvania regiments of Brig. Gen. Alexander S. Webb's brigade to report to General Howard. The 71st found its way to Slocum's front, and the 106th reported to Howard on Cemetery Hill after the fighting there was over for the evening.[2]

Samuel Sprigg Carroll was a descendant of Charles Carroll of Carrollton and was born in the District of Columbia in 1832. He graduated from West Point in its class of 1856, two years behind General Howard. Carroll served on the frontier with the 10th Infantry and was quartermaster at West Point, where he and his family shared a double house with the Howards. Carroll and Howard might have been close at that time, for when Howard became seriously ill in Washington in 1861, Carroll's mother took him into her home and nursed him back to health.[3]

Col. Samuel S. Carroll (WLM)

Carroll, like Howard, was a lieutenant when the war began, but he did not become a captain until November 1861. Then, somehow, he received the colonelcy of the 8th Ohio Regiment in December 1861. The colonelcy led to a brigade command in James Shields's division in the Shenandoah Valley. Carroll fought in the valley battles, including Port Republic, where he was injured when his wounded horse fell on him. He fought at Second Manassas, was shot near the Rapidan River in August 1862, and commanded his brigade at Fredericksburg and Chancellorsville, all in the grade of colonel. We can wonder what he thought of Howard's meteoric rise to the command of a corps. Carroll's men called him "Brick Top" because of his red hair; he had an ample temper and was a good fighter. Howard described him as being, in 1863, "a young man of great quickness and dash" and wrote that "for fearless and energetic action Col. Carroll had not a superior." One of his subordinates remembered him as "a thorough

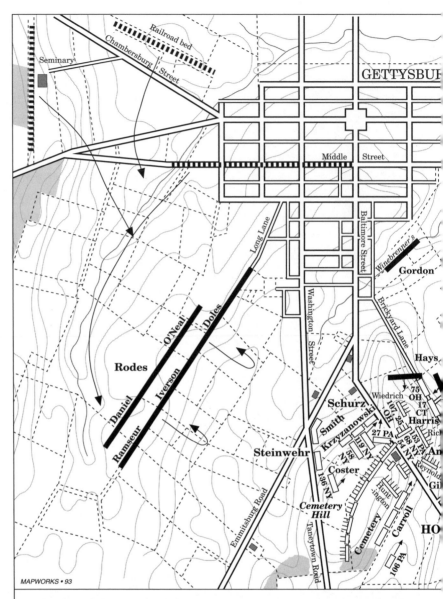

1. *Portions of Hays's and Hoke's brigades smash through Ames's line and push toward Wiedrich's and Rickett's batteries at the top of the hill near the cemetery gatehouse.*

2. *Four of Ames's regiments hold their positions along Brickyard Lane. Many of the troops driven back rally at the top of the hill and help defend the guns.*

3. *Eleventh Corps regiments west of the Baltimore Pike hurry to the aid of Wiedrich's battery. Carroll's brigade marches to Ricketts's battery's aid from Cemetery Ridge.*

4. *Hay's and Hoke's brigades are driven from the hill and form near Gordon's brigade.*

5. *Rodes's division files from the town tardily and forms to attack Cemetery Hill from t northwest. It advances after Early's attack has failed but halts and forms along Long La*

Map 15.1. *Early and Rodes Fail to Take Cemetery Hill, 2 July*

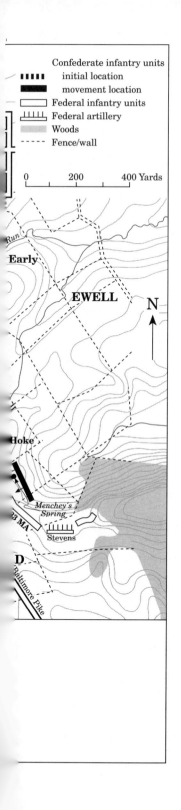

Confederate infantry units
▪▪▪▪▪ initial location
▬▬▬ movement location
☐ Federal infantry units
⊞⊞⊞ Federal artillery
▨ Woods
- - - - Fence/wall

0   200   400 Yards

Run

Early

EWELL   N

Hoke

Menchey's
Spring

33 MA

Stevens

D

Baltimore Pike

soldier and unsurpassed commander of men." This was the man, then, who led his brigade to the aid of the Eleventh Corps at dusk on 2 July.[4]

When Carroll received his orders, at least two of his three available regiments were resting along the Taneytown Road near Ziegler's Grove. Guided by a staff officer, Carroll led them off in column through the cemetery toward East Cemetery Hill. Known as the "Gibraltar Brigade," they hustled at a double-quick, moving so fast that many men had to discard their knapsacks and blankets in order to keep up. The moon had not yet risen, and the cannon smoke lay heavy around the batteries on the hill. Some men recalled later that they heard the splat of minié balls against tombstones as they passed the cemetery, but they probably had active imaginations. The 14th Indiana Regiment marched in the lead, followed by the 4th Ohio and the 7th West Virginia regiments.[5]

While Howard's staff officers were seeking help and Krzyzanowski formed his regiments to take them to the right, the attacking Confederates were climbing toward the batteries on the hill. It seems likely that their attack was made in two columns, moving more in swarms than in lines, for it was dark and linear formations would have been almost impossible to maintain. Hays's units composed one column. These were the men who had plunged through the gap created when the 17th Connecticut shifted to von Gilsa's left and those who had driven in the 107th Ohio on Harris's left. This swarm made for Wiedrich's battery on the hill above them. Those who followed the retreating 107th and 25th Ohio up the hill would have a stone wall to cross before they reached the guns.

The men from Hoke's brigade and those from the left of Hays's line, who had punched the large gap in von Gilsa's line, would have climbed the hill toward Ricketts's battery. They would have been separated from Hays's men to their right by the 17th Connecticut and the 75th Ohio regiments, which still held their positions along Brickyard Lane, by the bulge in the hill, and by the stone wall that separated Wiedrich's and Ricketts's batteries. According to Major Tate of the 6th North Carolina, this cluster of Confederates numbered about seventy-five men of his regiment and a dozen from the 9th Louisiana. Likely there were others too who approached the crest without Tate's knowing it. (He wrote that the attack had failed because Hays's brigade had not supported Hoke's.) Yet the number must have been comparatively few. In his report for Hoke's brigade, Colonel Godwin observed that the command had become separated during its charge against the wall and that it had become impossible to concentrate more than forty or fifty men at any one point in order to make a further advance. Therefore, it seems likely that only a few of the attacking force in either brigade pushed forward far enough to strike the batteries. The rest, who were not seriously wounded and still had some sense of discipline and loyalty to their regiments, would have tried to re-form at the base of the hill for what work might lie ahead.[6]

Although the Confederates wrote and spoke of occupying the crest of the hill and capturing the batteries there, Union accounts concede less Confederate success. The sparse accounts of Wiedrich's battery say that the Confederates attacked suddenly and violently and entered the battery's position but insist that they were there only briefly. Maj. Harry Gilmor, a Maryland cavalryman, having nothing better to do, rode with Hays's brigade into the attack—in fact, he wrote that he was the only mounted man with that command. When the Louisianans reached Wiedrich's position, he saw in the dusk a color-bearer climb upon a gun, wave his flag, and fall. Then another man, said to have been an Irishman, seized the flag and with a shout also climbed upon the gun. He too was shot down. A small captain took the flag next, and, like the others, he mounted the gun only to be shot in the arm that held the flag. At that, he dropped his sword, took the flag in his right hand, and waved it above his head seemingly oblivious to his pain and the lead that was flying around him. As the captain gave his third cheer, a ball struck him in the chest, and he also fell. Some of those whom he had tried to lead forward carried him back beyond the wall where Gilmor watched the fight from his horse. They placed him on the horse in front of Gilmor, and the major carried him back down the hill.[7]

Wiedrich's men had some help in their epic fight. Von Fritsch, General Ames, and two other officers pitched in. Von Fritsch was injured, not by a Tiger, but by the gun butt of a Union infantryman who was fleeing to the rear. Stewart's cannoneers helped in a special way. Since they had no targets to fire at, Stewart strung them along the pike with fence rails as a barrier to stop frightened soldiers from running to the rear. When artillerymen knocked fleeing men down, they took food from the men's haversacks for themselves. Wiedrich's men defended their guns with courage. Colonel Wainwright had thought poorly of the way that Wiedrich's men had served their guns, but he admitted that they "fought splendidly" to protect them and finally, with help, drove the Confederates from their position.[8]

One of the repeated stories that came out of this fight told of a Confederate leading Hays's charge who threw himself across the muzzle of a cannon and shouted, "I take command of this gun." To this, a cannoneer holding its lanyard replied, "Du sollst sie haben!," yanked the rope, and blew the Confederate to Kingdom Come.[9]

Ricketts's battery faced less pressure than Wiedrich's, but none of its members, especially Ricketts, would have admitted it. Lt. Charles B. Brockway, in his account, stated that the infantry in the battery's front had fled at the first volley, which was not true, and that Wiedrich's battery had retired, permitting the enemy to occupy the wall just to the Pennsylvania battery's left and to pour in "a most galling fire" upon it. In short, as Brockway saw it, Ricketts's battery bore the brunt of the attack alone.[10]

Some of the enemy did get into the battery's left section, capturing and attempting to spike its left piece. Many fugitives from the line at the base of the hill, no doubt, fled back past the battery with the Confederates following them as far as the guns. Cpl. William H. Thurston wrote that he was "handling cannister" when the Confederates struck and was severely wounded. They captured three men and hustled them off, but he escaped capture by lying next to a gun and letting the fight go on above him.[11]

A Rebel lieutenant made for the battery's guidon, which was standing in the dirt of a lunette in front of one of the guns. As he grasped it, Pvt. James H. Riggin, the guidon-bearer, rode up and shot him with his revolver. Riggin took the pennant, but as he turned his horse away, someone shot him and the bullet broke the staff in two. Somehow Riggin got off his horse and staggered up to Ricketts, saying, "Help me captain." By the time that the fight was over, Riggin was dead.[12]

During the melee, Lieutenant Brockway saw a Confederate pointing his rifle at one of the battery's sergeants and demanding his surrender. Brockway bashed the Confederate in the head with a rock and knocked him to the ground. As the man fell, the sergeant grabbed a rifle and shot the Confederate in the stomach. Then for good measure he clubbed the gun and broke the poor fellow's arm with it, causing him to cry for quarter. Brockway explained the sergeant's excess zeal by observing that the darkness made him unsure of the injury he had done to the man.[13]

The fight in Ricketts's left section must not have lasted long. Yet, in spite of the fracas there, the right guns of the battery continued to fire canister to their front, their drivers helping to serve the pieces. No doubt their fire did much to hold some of the 21st and 57th North Carolina regiments at bay. Ricketts had a fine battery, though he and some of his men were overcritical of others. Their casualties testified to their fighting spirit: six were killed, fourteen wounded, and three captured. Yet the men of the battery held their position until help came, obeying the order, "Die on the soil of your State, but don't give up your guns."[14]

The focus of the fight at the top of the hill centered on the two batteries, but their cannoneers did not fight alone. Sgt. Frederick Nussbaum wrote that the 107th fell back in some disorder to the rear of Wiedrich's battery. When Lt. Peter F. Young, its adjutant, reached there, he saw some Louisianans who had gotten around the regiment's right and were already at the battery, "yelling like demons at the supposed capture." Young saw that it was of the utmost importance that they be driven back and feared that the day would be lost if they captured and held the gun position. At this time, Nussbaum called Young's attention to a Louisiana color-bearer, possibly Capt. Charles DuChamp of the 8th Regiment, who was waving a flag near the battery while several soldiers rallied around him. Young ordered the Ohioans near him to fire at the knot of Confederates, and they did so, scattering them and wounding the color-bearer, who dropped to one knee while still holding to the flag. Wanting to inspire the men of the 107th Ohio to a "glorious effort," Young rushed forward, shot the man with his revolver, and sprang for the "vile rag." At this time, a Louisianan, possibly Cpl. Leon P. Gusman, seized the flag but fell back to the ground with it. Young wrested the flag from Gusman. Then, with the flag in one hand and his revolver in the other, Young turned back toward his men. The Confederates shot him in the shoulder, but he was able to stumble to the safety of the 107th's line, where Sgt. Henry Brinker caught him and kept him from falling. A Rebel lieutenant followed Young with a drawn sword, seeming intent on getting the colors back, but Lt. Fernando C. Suhner intercepted the Confederate and downed him with a sword cut to the shoulder. The colors of the 8th Louisiana Regiment remained in Federal hands. In looking back on his fight in later years, Young called it "a hot time in old Gettysburg."[15]

Later, some Confederates believed that they had captured Wiedrich's guns because there was silence on the hill. Hays reported that his Louisianans captured "several pieces of artillery, four stand of colors, and a number of prisoners" and that every piece of artillery that had been firing had been silenced. Major Tate, whose little force was probably near Ricketts's battery, sent back for reinforcements and waited in hopes that they would come. To Tate's right, the Louisianans attempted to re-form their lines during the lull and waited for expected help. Soon they heard and dimly saw a line of infantrymen approaching through the darkness from the direction of the cemetery.[16]

Hays and his men waited expectantly as the line of infantry approached. It came to within 100 yards of Hays's men and fired a volley, but Hays held his fire as von Gilsa had done only a few minutes before, for Early had cautioned him to expect help from Rodes's division on his right. The line continued to advance and fired a second volley and a third. The light from the muzzle flashes of the last volley revealed that the advancing line was a Union force instead of Confederates coming to Hays's aid. Hays quickly ordered his men to fire, and they did so. The Confederate fire seemed to check the enemy line, which seemed to melt away in the darkness, but only briefly. Hays saw another line in the rear of the first and two more coming up behind it. He quickly ordered his troops to fall back to the wall at the base of the hill.[17]

Capt. Neill W. Ray of the 6th North Carolina called the regiment's charge a "success that did not succeed." A small party of men from the 6th waited for help behind a stone wall, probably the one between Wiedrich's and Ricketts's batteries. They could hear the sounds of an enemy rally— perhaps from the 153d Pennsylvania or another of von Gilsa's regiments. As the enemy approached, the North Carolinians drove the rallied line back with a volley. This happened twice, and when no reinforcements came, Major Tate ordered his men to "break and to risk the fire."[18]

Who were the troops that approached Hays and his valiant troops? At Howard's order, Colonel Krzyzanowski, aided by General Schurz and his staff, led the 119th and 58th New York regiments at a double-quick the short distance across the Baltimore Pike to Wiedrich's battery. It is likely that the New Yorkers trotted forward in two lines, bayonets fixed, the 119th in the forward line and the 58th in support behind it. The 119th New York, less than 200 strong but joined by Captain von Fritsch, made a "vigorous rush" against the Louisiana interlopers and swept them down the hill. When they reached its base, Krzyzanowski's men flopped down and Wiedrich's guns belched canister at the fleeing Confederates.[19]

Von Steinwehr sent the 27th and 73d Pennsylvania regiments of Coster's brigade from their position in or near the cemetery and summoned the 136th New York of Smith's brigade from over along the Taneytown Road. No one really described the advance of Coster's brigade and what they did. Pvt. Andrew Diembach of the 73d Pennsylvania remembered that the fight at Wiedrich's battery, as they approached, made for a sight of "awful sublimity," whatever that might have meant. Lt. Walter S. Briggs, adjutant of the 27th, fell in this fight. In the meantime, the 136th was double-quicking toward East Cemetery Hill. When it neared the Baltimore Pike, it halted and its men dropped to the ground. Acrid powder smoke filled the air, and "bullets from ten thousand rifles" whizzed by. The flash of rifles in the dark, the cheers and shrieks were overpowering to Pvt. George Metcalf. He placed his rifle, frying pan, and canteen between himself and the fighting and lay flat behind the pile saying to himself,

"What a fool you were to enlist. You need not have come. You were only eighteen years old and could not have been drafted."[20]

As Schurz's troops smashed into the Confederates around Wiedrich's battery and rushed them down the hill, Carroll's three regiments hurried through the cemetery toward the Baltimore Pike in the area to the right of the gatehouse. The men of Huntington's Ohio battery in the cemetery could hear the sounds of the brawl in Ricketts's battery across the pike, and then they heard the deep base voice of Colonel Carroll calling for Captain Huntington. Huntington, who commanded the artillery brigade to which Ricketts's battery belonged, told Carroll that the battery was in Confederate hands, and Carroll took measures to get it back. In the meantime, as the infantry passed through the Ohio battery, with which they had served before, they "exchanged chaff" with its cannoneers. As the 14th Indiana approached Ricketts's battery, one of the cannoneers shouted, "Glory to God! We are saved!"[21]

When the head of the brigade reached the pike to the right of the gatehouse, Carroll formed his regiments for the attack facing obliquely to the left and uphill toward Ricketts's battery. Because of the artillery horses and matériel spread across the hill behind the battery, he deemed it impossible to advance with more than a regimental front, and so we may assume that his front was that of the 14th Indiana—about seventy-five yards wide. Once the brigade was formed, Carroll waited until the battery fired, and then, "in his clarion voice," he commanded, "Halt! Front face! Charge bayonets! Forward, double-quick! March! Give them ——!," and the brigade dashed forward with a cheer. It advanced in column; the 14th Indiana led, followed by the 7th West Virginia and the 4th Ohio.[22]

Carroll's brigade charged through Ricketts's battery and probably through Reynolds's as well, sweeping the Confederates from Ricketts's guns and driving them down the hill. The Hoosiers advanced at a double-quick as rapidly as they could in the darkness, some of them probably stumbling over the bodies of wounded and dead men that must have been in their path. The charge went over the crest of the hill and down its east slope until the Indiana line reached the wall along the lane at the base of the hill. The Hoosiers halted there and fired two or three volleys into the darkness. When there was no return fire and it seemed that the enemy had disappeared from their front, Carroll ordered them to cease fire.[23]

During the charge, the brigade received a brisk fire from behind the wall to its left. Col. John Coons of the 14th Indiana rushed toward the wall and shouted, "Who are you?" Someone answered "Union" from out of the darkness, but there were more shots. Coons emptied his revolver in the direction of the voice, and his regiment went on. Colonel Carroll turned the 7th West Virginia toward these attackers and drove whatever enemy that was there away.[24]

When the brigade reached Brickyard Lane at the foot of the hill, it fanned out into a line, the 4th Ohio moving up to the right of the 14th Indiana, while the 7th West Virginia remained for a time at the wall to the brigade's left rear. The 4th fired after the retreating enemy until from out of the darkness its men heard the voice of an Irishman. He shouted, "Hould on byes, I'm wan ov yoursilves. Don't shoot me." They told him to jump over the wall in their front, which he did, and then he commented, "Thank Jasus, I'm in the Union again."[25]

After the charge was over, Carroll wondered about the nature of his position, which he had not seen in the daylight. He wondered also what other troops ought to be in the area, for he saw none. Therefore, he sent Capt. James E. Gregg of his staff back to General Howard to ask that the Eleventh Corps make some connection with his brigade for he felt uncomfortable about his position and would leave it unless he was "connected with." Gregg did not find Howard but met General Ames instead. Ames sent Capt. John M. Brown of his staff down to see Carroll with the request that Carroll stay where he was because Ames had no confidence in his own troops. Carroll told Brown to go back to Ames with the message, "Damn a man who had no confidence in his troops."[26]

After sending his comments to General Ames, Carroll rode back in search of Howard himself. He found the general in the cemetery. To Carroll, Howard seemed worried. He thanked Carroll warmly and, according to Carroll, begged him to hold his brigade where it was "as he could not rely on his troops and had not any . . . he could trust to the front." Therefore, Carroll returned to his brigade at the base of East Cemetery Hill. He sent skirmishers to the front, made connection with troops on his left and right, and prepared to spend the night.[27]

Carroll's brigade had had a heady experience, and its men were in the "happiest mood" with good reason. The brigade had made an exhilarating and successful counterattack and had captured two field officers of the 21st North Carolina Regiment plus an assortment of Confederates of other ranks. Furthermore, its men believed that they had saved the Army of the Potomac from the results of the cowardice and bungling of others, a belief that they would hold and broadcast for the rest of their lives.[28]

Carroll's brigade had performed to perfection, but later some of its veterans, like some from Ricketts's battery, claimed too much. Perhaps there were some men from Hays's Louisiana brigade who, when at Wiedrich's battery, had seen Carroll's line in the dark distance and were influenced by it, but they were driven back primarily by units of the Eleventh Corps. In their elation, Carroll's troops ignored or deprecated the fighting done by others and forgot that they had met a spent assault that had crested and needed only a nudge to send it ebbing down the hill.[29]

General Hays formed what he could of his brigade at the base of the hill. This was only a temporary measure, taken in the hope that he could collect those of his brigade who had become scattered in the darkness. As he prepared to take his men back to a better position, Capt. John G. Campbell of his staff told him that Gordon's brigade was coming to his support. Hays sent an officer back to Gordon immediately to see if this was true, but the officer returned without having seen the general. Hays then went back himself to look for the Georgia brigade that was to have given his brigade support and found it "occupying the precise position in the field occupied by me when I received the order to charge the enemy on Cemetery Hill, and not advancing." It was obvious to Hays that any help from Gordon's brigade would come too late, so he gave up all thought of further offensive action. He placed his Louisianans beside Gordon's Georgians for the night and, when morning came, received an order from Early to take them back to their old position along Middle Street. These Tigers would roar no more at Gettysburg.[30]

A bitter Major Tate and his 6th North Carolina Regiment reassembled with Hoke's brigade along Winebrenner's Run. Colonel Godwin now commanded the brigade in place of the mortally wounded Avery. At daylight, by Early's order, the North Carolinians fell back to a "railroad cut," certainly one east of the town. As soon as he rejoined the brigade, Tate demanded to know why his troops had not been supported "and was coolly told that it was not known that [they] were in the works." The angry Tate on 30 July fumed in a letter to North Carolina's governor that he had no doubt that the major general, Jubal Early, would report that the works on Cemetery Hill could not be taken, and Tate complained about the injustice of it all.[31]

Tate misjudged Early for, though brief and devoid of hyperbole, the comments in his report about the assault were accurate enough. After ordering the advance, Early had returned to what was likely the end of Stratton Street where he could watch its progress. (Ewell also watched the assault and probably was nearby.) At his order, Gordon's brigade started forward from its position along the railroad tracks at the same time that Hays's and Hoke's brigades began their assault. In some way, no one said how, Gordon moved his brigade from the railroad down to Winebrenner's Run, where Hays's and Hoke's brigades had been, and aligned it there. By this time wounded men were coming back. They said that the attack was going splendidly, and Early's staff could "see the line rolling rapidly up the hill." However, Early could detect no action to his right—Rodes's division was not yet in the fight! Early ordered Gordon to hold his brigade where it was along Winebrenner's Run, for it had become apparent that the hill could not be held by Early's two brigades alone. In Early's opinion, sending Gordon forward then would only be a "useless sacrifice." Early would hold Gordon along the run for the other two brigades to fall back on.[32]

With the advantage of hindsight, we can wonder what might have happened had Gordon's brigade advanced closely behind Hays. Would the six Georgia regiments have provided enough of an edge to have enabled the assaulting brigades to take and hold the batteries on East Cemetery Hill? Did Early, by holding Gordon's people so far in the rear and then halting their advance, forfeit whatever opportunity for a successful assault he might have had? It seems likely that he did, yet the keys to real success remained with Generals Johnson and Rodes.

Early had been concerned about the support that Rodes's division might give his brigades and, during their advance, had sent a staff officer to urge Rodes forward. The assault had been under way for a half hour, and Early saw no sign of help from Rodes. Before the officer returned, the roar of musketry swelled again on Cemetery Hill, an indication that the enemy had been reinforced, and soon it moved down the hill, a sign that Hays's and Hoke's brigades were falling back. What had happened to Rodes and the support on the corps right?[33]

Robert Emmett Rodes (1829–1864) was one of the bright stars in the Confederate firmament. He was a native of Virginia, and, though he was the only one of Lee's division commanders who was not a graduate of West Point, he had special credentials—a diploma from the Virginia Military Institute, class of 1848. After his graduation, Rodes worked in Alabama as a civil engineer and had a brief stint as a professor at his Virginia alma mater just before the war began. At the war's outbreak, Rodes became colonel of the 5th Alabama Infantry Regiment and returned with it to Virginia, where he displayed great talent as a commander. He became a brigadier general on October 1861 and led his brigade in the Peninsular campaign in 1862, suffering a wound at Fair Oaks. He received another wound at Antietam but led his brigade again at Fredericksburg. He commanded D. H. Hill's division at Chancellorsville and even commanded

Jackson's corps there for a brief time. In every instance, he had performed well and had added to his enviable reputation.[34]

Unlike Ewell, Early, and Johnson, Rodes looked the part of a heroic general. Douglas Southall Freeman described him as having been over six feet tall, blond, with a sandy mustache—a "Norse God" with a "fiery imperious manner," a character out of the Beowulf saga. After Chancellorsville, Rodes was "the personification of the new type of Confederate leader." But not at Gettysburg on 1 July. His division had attacked in a disjointed manner, but perhaps that performance was an anomaly.[35]

In his report, Rodes wrote of orders given in the afternoon, after Longstreet's attack began on the right, requiring him "to co-operate with the attacking force as soon as any opportunity of doing so with effect was offered." When Longstreet's attack began, Rodes detected a "stir" on Cemetery Hill and thought the opportunity for an attack had come. He found Early, and the two agreed to act in concert. This done, he informed someone in Pender's division on his right that he would attack at dark and proceeded to make arrangements to do so. All of this belated coordination must have taken time.[36]

In preparing for his assault, Rodes learned something that he should have known earlier in the day—moving his brigades from the streets of Gettysburg to the west of the town and forming them for an attack to the east against Cemetery Hill was a time-consuming task. In comparison, Early had only to move half the distance and without a change in front. Why did Rodes not deploy his division sooner? He did not explain, but perhaps he wanted to shield his men as long as possible from artillery fire, perhaps he misjudged the time that the movement would take, or perhaps he was simply slow.[37]

Brig. Gen. Stephen Dodson Ramseur became the central figure in the division's subsequent actions. Ramseur, a North Carolinian, was born in 1837 and was one of the youngest and most promising officers of his grade on the field. A graduate of West Point, class of 1860, he served briefly in the Old Army but resigned his lieutenancy in April 1861 and entered the Confederate service as a lieutenant of artillery, rising to the grade of major within a year. In April 1862 he became the colonel of the 49th North Carolina Infantry Regiment and led it on the Peninsula, where he was seriously wounded at Malvern Hill. He became a brigadier general in November 1862 and commanded a brigade in D. H. Hill's division at Chancellorsville, where he was wounded again. He would be wounded once more at Spotsylvania a year later, become a major general in June 1864, and suffer a mortal wound at Cedar Creek in October 1864 while commanding what at Gettysburg had been Early's division.[38]

During most of 2 July, Ramseur's, Iverson's, and Doles's brigades had been resting along West Middle Street in Gettysburg. The street provided the three brigades cover close to the Union defenses but was a poor place from which to launch an assault. Therefore, in order to attack Cemetery Hill, the three brigades had to move by the right flank west of the town far enough to be clear of its buildings and, after facing left, move forward in line of battle over open terrain toward the hill. When clear of the town and formed, the division consisted of, from the right, Ramseur's, Iverson's, and Doles's brigades in the first line and Daniel's and O'Neal's brigades in a support line in their rear. Here the men of Ramseur's brigade learned that they were to take Cemetery Hill at the point of a bayonet and that when they reached its crest they might encounter confusion in the darkness. At such time, in order to identify friend from foe—and perhaps be shot by one of the latter—they were to shout, "North Carolina to the rescue."[39]

What was Rodes doing during the deployment? Often the specific ac-

Brig. Gen. Stephen D. Ramseur
(WLM)

tivities of individual commanders are hard to discern, and Rodes's are no exception. Yet at this time there was a special arrangement between Rodes and his brigade commanders that suggests that if Rodes was with his division, he was commanding it only in a passive way. Before the advance began, Rodes told Ramseur that the other brigades of the division would be governed by his movements. In short, insofar as the attack was concerned, Ramseur was in command.[40]

The moon was rising as the advance began. One North Carolina participant was astounded by the order to advance on the hill. He thought his leaders mad or ignorant for, as he saw it, they were preparing to attack a hill crowned with thickly packed artillery and crossed by at least two stone walls manned by infantry. Others shared his misgivings, including General Iverson, who believed that they were going to certain destruction. Many men gave wallets and messages to the surgeons and others who would not be going forward. In spite of their forebodings, the North Carolinians of Ramseur's brigade had confidence in their "noble commander." When, in his "characteristically clear, ringing voice," Ramseur gave the command, "Forward!," they stepped out, nervously clutching their rifles.

The line wheeled to the left as it advanced, crossed the dirt road that is now Long Lane, passed the Confederate skirmish line, and pushed against the skirmishers of Smith's brigade, driving them back toward the Union line. There was a cost to this, for the Union skirmishers shot several of Rodes's men. Although the enemy skirmishers had found them out, officers told their men to make as little noise as possible. After going about 300 yards beyond Long Lane, the Confederate line halted and the troops lay down.[41]

Ramseur himself continued forward in a cautious manner to see what awaited them. He saw batteries in position "to pour upon our lines, direct, cross, and enfilade fires" and two lines of infantry behind stone walls. Back on the division's line, the soldiers waited as their "great hearts thump and beat within our bosoms as if they would leap out." Some of the men could hear commands being shouted by Union officers on the hill in their front, but they would not have heard the clamor of Early's assault; it was over.[42]

Ramseur returned to his line and had a hurried conversation with Doles and Iverson. They agreed to tell Rodes what they had learned about the enemy's position and await further instructions. In response to the information given him, Rodes sent them an order to fall back to Long Lane. He had learned that Early's assault had failed and believed that their continuing the attack would result in a useless sacrifice of life. The three brigades of the forward line would wait in the lane, which Rodes described as a sunken road. It would be a position from which he thought they might launch a later attack without confusion.[43]

With that decision and with relief, the three brigades fell back to Long Lane as quietly as they had advanced. There they strengthened their position by piling up fence rails in front of it and digging in with their bayonets, swords, tin cups, and any other tools they could find. These three brigades—Iverson's, Doles's, and Ramseur's—would remain in this exposed position throughout the following day, ready to advance again if opportunity arose.[44]

It seems apparent that Rodes's division had not been prepared for an attack in a timely way. Why? Were Ewell's instructions not clear? Perhaps. Yet Rodes had seen much of Ewell and Early prior to the assault and must have known what was expected of his division. If not, he could have asked.

Rodes's report suggests that he was greatly concerned with cooperation with Pender's division on his right and rightly so. Ewell shared this concern, perhaps belatedly, and had sent a staff officer to see Pender, not corps commander Hill, and find out what his division was to do. He had learned that Pender had been wounded and that Brig. Gen. James H. Lane was serving in his place. Lane replied to Ewell merely that he was to attack if a "favorable opportunity presented." Ewell advised Lane that his corps was attacking and asked him to cooperate. Ewell heard nothing more from Lane, and Pender's division did not advance with Rodes. Such a lack of cooperation was not unique in the Army of Northern Virginia. There had been little or none between Hill's and Ewell's corps on 1 July and between Longstreet's and Hill's corps that afternoon. Hindsight suggests that cooperation between corps should have been handled on the army and corps level—it was an army problem.[45]

In retrospect, we can wonder why the advance, once started, had to be halted so that Ramseur could go forward and examine the position he was to attack. Rodes's skirmishers had been in front of Cemetery Hill all day and must have been quite familiar with the nature of the Federal defenses on the hill. Yet the information that they might have provided seems not to have been pondered and put to use by those in command. Nor, apparently, had Rodes or anyone else of rank and authority prepared for the attack by taking a close look at the hill and its defenses ahead of time. The hill was no better defended that evening than it had been before Ramseur and his troops left Middle Street. The only difference was that Early's attack had failed, and Rodes should have known that before his men approached the threshold of extreme peril.

Rodes's failure to support his attack angered Jubal Early, and he did not mince words about it. In his report, Early complained: "No attack was made on the immediate right, as was expected, and not meeting with support from that quarter, these brigades could not hold the position they had attained." In the postwar period, when veterans' tempers sometimes soared, he was even more explicit. In an article in the *Southern Historical Society Papers*, Early stated that he and Johnson had attacked together but that Rodes did not attack at all. In his opinion, the failure of Rodes to attack was "the solitary instance of remissness on the part of any portion of the corps in the battle." This was an exaggeration, of course. There was also the performance of Rodes's division on 1 July, Early's own detachment of Smith's and Gordon's brigades on 1 July, and finally his own failure to have Gordon's brigade in practicable supporting distance of Hays's and Hoke's brigades that very evening.[46]

Ewell was a fair man who did not blame others for his own errors. In his report, he dismissed Rodes's flawed generalship on 2 July by remarking only that "Major-General Rodes did not advance, for reasons given in his report"—nothing more. For additional information about Ewell's opinion, we must rely on Campbell Brown. Brown wrote with some bias, perhaps, that Ewell's attack on Cemetery Hill had been "admirably timed & failed because of Rodes' failure to co-operate. For this Ewell always thought Rodes fairly censurable & implies as much in his report. . . . Ewell & Early both thought Rodes had been too slow."[47]

In his report, Rodes explained his tardiness by writing that he had to move his troops from the town, align them for the attack, and then advance 1,200 to 1,400 yards, while Early had "to move only half that distance without a change in front." No reason was given for his not having started the movement sooner. Even Norse gods have bad days perhaps, and no one involved offered a better reason for Rodes's delay on 2 July. A comment published fifty years after the battle suggests an explanation, but the source of the information and the long interval before it was offered diminish its credibility. John C. Early, Jubal's nephew, who, as a teen-age boy, was present at his headquarters during the battle, wrote that on 4 July, when some Confederate soldiers saw his father, Capt. Samuel Early, riding in a buggy after having been slightly wounded, they chaffed him by shouting, "There goes General Rodes." Early then explained: "This officer [Rodes] had been so sick that he was compelled to ride in an ambulance, whenever practicable, during the fight." If this was so, it might explain Rodes's lapses and was added reason for both Ewell and Early to act with caution and be alert for problems on the right.[48]

Hays lost over 300 men in the evening assault, and Hoke's brigade lost a similar number. Maj. John Daniel saw survivors of these two brigades in the town soon after their attack was over. Some were "groaning piteously"; others, who had been helped back by their comrades, lay bleeding on the sidewalks. Officers and men were looking for their regiments and asking for their friends. To Daniel, "all was in confusion, distress." Yet, he mused, it was one thing to make such a charge during the daylight when flags were waving and men were under the eyes of their comrades, but it was another to do so when it was dark and when individuals were cloaked in anonymity. Then "it is manhood indeed which faces danger & does not shrink."[49]

After the fighting died that evening, Catherine Thorn and her father returned to their home at the cemetery's gatehouse to look after the hogs they had left in a pen there. Union pickets stopped them on their way but, after their explanations, allowed them to pass. They found many wounded men around the gatehouse but went first to look after the hogs. Hungry soldiers and hogs do not coexist for long, and the hogs were gone. The Thorns had a soldier escort them to the cellar of the gatehouse, where, at General Howard's suggestion, they had stored their valuables. They found six wounded men there "crying and going on" and her bedclothes scattered about. She had hoped to get a pillow and a quilt but trudged back down the Baltimore Pike with only her mother's shawl. The cemetery gatehouse was no longer her castle.[50]

That night, when the smoke had cleared and the moon shone on Cemetery Hill "as peaceful-faced as ever and the stars looked down unchanged," Rowland B. Howard, the general's civilian brother, stood on Cemetery Hill and reflected on the carnage about him. Quietly he said to himself and to the Lord, "O God, the moon and stars Thou hast made, but not the miserable murder and mangling of men"—the politicians and the armies had seen to that.[51]

16
Culp's Hill–
Johnson's Assault,
3 July

"Drive them out at daylight"—Slocum's order for eliminating the Confederate bulge at Culp's Hill was clear enough, but in Gen. Alpheus Williams's opinion, it was an order "more easily made than executed." Orders are usually that way, especially in battle, but Williams immediately took measures to prepare for the bloody work ahead.[1]

The Federal push could not start right away, of course. Plans and preparations had to be made. Geary's division and its position were the key to the Federal effort. The Confederates could not exploit their penetration so long as Geary's division held the main hill, and since most of Johnson's force faced Geary's front, Geary's men would have to bear the brunt of the fight. The First Division would deal with the Confederate left on the lower hill, but even that was a strong position. The Confederates there had the cover of the stone wall, the captured Union breastworks, and the trees and boulders that covered the hill. In addition, the marshy meadow around Spangler's Spring provided a deadly field of fire for the Confederates that strengthened their position on the lower hill.

With these considerations in mind, General Ruger deemed it unwise to attack the lower hill soon after the First Division returned because of the darkness, the difficult terrain, and their lack of knowledge of the Confederate deployment in their front. General Williams wanted to take advantage of the firepower of the Federal artillery. As he saw it, the Confederates had no nearby positions from which they could bring their guns to bear on the hill except at a long and inaccurate range, while the Twelfth Corps had a few excellent sites at hand.[2]

After considering these matters and others, no doubt, Williams and his people developed a plan. Some members of the 27th Indiana Regiment later claimed to have overheard a discussion held by a knot of ranking officers near the 27th's position soon after their return from the left. Although the officers could not be seen in the darkness, the Hoosiers could identify Williams, Colgrove, and some others by their voices. Colgrove urged an immediate attack against the interlopers, but others, probably including Ruger, dissented. Their prolonged discussion closed when Williams announced, "We will hold the position we now have until morning. Then, from those hills back of us, we will shell hell out of them." Williams summarized his plan simply in his report. He wrote, "I made such arrangements for a heavy artillery fire, with infantry feints upon the right, followed by a strong assault by Geary's division from Greene's position on the left, as I judged would speedily dislodge the enemy." Two years later, Williams wrote that he planned that after the batteries shelled the Confederates for fifteen minutes at daybreak, Geary's division would press forward from Greene's position while the First Division would be held in readiness to support Geary or to "push the extreme rebel left, should opportunity offer."[3]

Some of the batteries were already in position. Lt. Charles E. Winegar's New York battery had two ten-pounder Parrotts on McAllister's Hill about 800 yards south of Spangler's Spring and two more on Powers Hill about 700 yards south-southwest of it. Knap's Battery, commanded by Lt. Charles A. Atwell, had six ten-pounder Parrotts on Powers Hill also. They were to the right of Winegar's section and not far from Slocum's headquarters. Battery A, 1st Maryland Light Artillery, a battery from the Artillery Reserve commanded by Capt. James H. Rigby, was also on Powers Hill. It had six three-inch Ordnance rifles. We can wonder if these Marylanders had any friends or relatives in the 1st Maryland Battalion that must have been at the bull's-eye of their target. All three of these batteries had been in place since the afternoon or evening of 2 July.[4]

The two other batteries of the Twelfth Corps had been parked along the Baltimore Pike until they went into position at 1:00 A.M. on 3 July. Slocum reported that Lt. Col. Clermont Best posted them, Williams probably had something to say about where they would be placed, Geary wrote that he trained the guns of at least Knap's Battery, and Hunt testified that he had taken charge of the artillery on the Twelfth Corps line! We can feel sorry for the commanders of the Twelfth Corps batteries for all of the attention they received that morning. Nevertheless, Battery E, 4th U.S. Artillery, now nominally under the command of Lt. Sylvanus T. Rugg, and Battery K, 5th U.S. Artillery, under Lt. David Kinzie, took position on a rise just

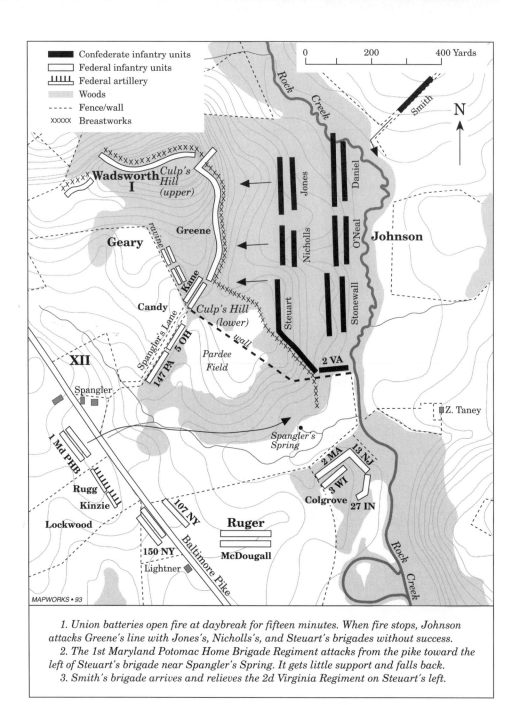

Legend:
- ■ Confederate infantry units
- □ Federal infantry units
- ⊥⊥⊥⊥ Federal artillery
- ▓ Woods
- - - - Fence/wall
- xxxxx Breastworks

0 — 200 — 400 Yards

N

Smith

Rock Creek

Wadsworth I

Culp's Hill (upper)

Jones

Daniel

Greene

Nicholls

O'Neal

Johnson

Geary

ravine

Kane

Stonewall

Steuart

Candy

Culp's Hill (lower)

Spangler's Lane

5 OH

XII

147 PA

Pardee Field

wall

2 VA

Spangler

Z. Taney

1 Md PHB

Spangler's Spring

Rugg

Kinzie

2 MA

13 NJ

Lockwood

3 WI

107 NY

Colgrove

27 IN

Ruger

150 NY

McDougall

Baltimore Pike

Lightner

Rock Creek

MAPWORKS • 93

1. Union batteries open fire at daybreak for fifteen minutes. When fire stops, Johnson attacks Greene's line with Jones's, Nicholls's, and Steuart's brigades without success.

2. The 1st Maryland Potomac Home Brigade Regiment attacks from the pike toward the left of Steuart's brigade near Spangler's Spring. It gets little support and falls back.

3. Smith's brigade arrives and relieves the 2d Virginia Regiment on Steuart's left.

Map 16.1. Johnson's Division Attacks at Daybreak, 3 July

west of the pike 300 or so yards southeast of the Spangler buildings. From their position, the ten Napoleons of these two batteries had a clear field of fire down the meadow toward Spangler's Spring only 700 yards to the east and into the woods on the lower hill occupied by Steuart's brigade and its supports. Should the enemy push up the meadow toward the pike or attack it from the woods on the lower hill, the Napoleons would be able to blast them with canister.[5]

The infantry went into position as described in chapter 12. Greene's brigade held the hill, and, on their return, Candy's and Kane's brigades of Geary's division took up a line connecting Greene's right with the pike. Their line ran from the saddle between the larger and smaller hills along Spangler's Lane to the Spangler farmyard at the road. Williams placed Lockwood's brigade along the pike, where it would be able to support the regular batteries and act as a reserve for the corps. Ruger's brigade occupied McAllister's Woods by Rock Creek, and McDougall's faced the lower hill from the high ground between McAllister's Woods and the Lightner buildings on the pike. By deploying the two divisions in this way, Williams had sealed off the Confederate penetration of the night before and was ready to make Confederates pay dearly for their trespass.[6]

This planning and the orders to go with it took much of the short summer night. At about 3:30 A.M., when his duties permitted, Williams stretched out on a flat rock beneath an apple tree near the pike and had a half hour's sleep. He could look forward to an interesting day ahead.[7]

While Slocum, Williams, and their subordinate commanders prepared for action at daybreak, the nearby Confederates were also busy. General Lee's plan remained essentially unchanged from that of the afternoon before: Longstreet would resume his assault at daybreak, and Ewell's corps would assail the Union right at the same time. Since an attack on Johnson's front offered Ewell his only hope of success, he decided to reinforce Johnson's division and exploit the gains already made on Culp's Hill. The Stonewall Brigade rejoined the division during the night, and Ewell sent Johnson additional help from the divisions of Early and Rodes. These reinforcements consisted of two regiments from Smith's brigade of Early's division (the 31st Virginia arrived later in the morning) and O'Neal's and Daniel's brigades from Rodes's division. In effect, Ewell doubled the Confederate force on Culp's Hill in size.[8]

Although not surprising, it is highly regrettable that there is so little specific information in the Confederate reports of the Culp's Hill fight and in the few personal accounts that are available. Those that are extant tell us that Jones's, Nicholls's, and Steuart's brigades remained in the positions they held at the close of the fighting on the previous evening. Lt. Col. Robert H. Dungan, who now commanded Jones's brigade in the absence of the wounded Jones, re-formed the brigade after its unsuccessful attack of the evening before. He posted it again on the slope of the hill behind its line of skirmishers. Its main line was about 300 yards in front of and about 100 feet lower than the Twelfth Corps works and, therefore, was not far from the creek. The Union works above the Virginians were all but impregnable; aggressive action on Jones's front promised casualties without success.[9]

Nicholls's brigade stayed about 100 yards in front of the enemy works. It faced the center and right of Greene's brigade's position. The crest was lower there, probably no more than thirty or forty feet above Nicholls's line. The Louisianans were so close to the enemy line that they had to speak in whispers during the night so as not to disclose their location. In the meantime, they could hear commotion in the enemy ranks as Greene's brigade prepared to fight them on the following day.[10]

Steuart's brigade was at the saddle and on the lower hill in what Steuart believed was an admirable position even though it would prove vulnerable to enemy artillery fire and his troops would have no artillery support of their own. Its regiments contended with probes from Twelfth Corps units whose positions they had occupied, and throughout the night, its officers remained on the alert while the brigade's pickets kept a watchful eye toward the enemy. There was much tension elsewhere along the division's line, but it must have been extreme on the lower hill. Steuart's men could hear vehicles on the pike 500 yards in their front, and they ought to have been aware that a steel cordon was forming around them. Yet there was optimism, for even Johnson and Steuart, when they visited that front, voiced the opinion that the vehicle sounds meant that the enemy was pulling back rather than preparing for another fight![11]

The outline of Williams's plan for the morning of 3 July seems relatively plain, but Johnson's is obscure. It is obvious that he would have expected no artillery support. Shells fired into the Culp's Hill woods from the positions available to the Confederate batteries would have endangered friends as much as enemies. Johnson's successes would have to be gained by the skill, courage, and musketry of his infantry alone.

Probably the Stonewall Brigade was the first of Johnson's reinforcements to arrive. Johnson placed it behind and in support of Steuart's brigade. It would be there before daybreak and in time for the opening of the battle.[12]

General Daniel led his and O'Neal's brigades to the left and reported

Brig. Gen. Junius Daniel (WLM)

to Johnson at about 4:00 A.M. Johnson placed Daniel's brigade in support of Jones's. At some point while it was approaching the hill, the 32d North Carolina Regiment received artillery fire, probably from Cemetery Hill. Daniel found Jones's men skirmishing with Greene's at long range and concluded that the enemy position on the crest above them "could not have been carried by any force." Daniel's brigade remained in support of Jones's for what Daniel estimated as two or three hours.[13]

When O'Neal's brigade reached Johnson's front, Daniel turned it over to Johnson for orders. Neither Daniel nor O'Neal mentioned where the Alabamians deployed, but if Daniel was with Jones and the Stonewall Brigade supported Steuart, O'Neal's brigade must have formed in support of Nicholls's brigade. O'Neal recalled that the enemy was posted behind "a log fort on the spur of the mountain." The works on the right of Greene's line, and perhaps those elsewhere, could well have had that appearance when viewed from below. Fortunately for the Alabamians, they did not have to attack until 8:00 A.M. [14]

"Extra Billy" Smith came to Johnson's aid with his 49th and 52d regiments after daybreak and the fighting began. It is likely that they approached Johnson's front from behind Benner's Hill and down the valley of Benner's Run. Maj. Henry Kyd Douglas of Johnson's staff rode to meet Smith's two regiments and hurry them on their way. Douglas found Smith "cool and deliberate" and full of questions about the situation ahead. Not wishing to take the time for conversation, Douglas told Smith that if he would permit it, Douglas would lead Smith's regiments to their place in line.

Smith assented, and Douglas led the regiments to the southeast slope of the lower hill where the stone wall runs west from Rock Creek. There, at about 7:00 A.M., they relieved the 2d Virginia Regiment, which was posted on the left of the Stonewall Brigade. Douglas sent skirmishers forward, and as he rode into the smoky area, the infantrymen called for him to get down from his horse. Since he believed it improper for a staff officer to dismount at such a time, Douglas stayed in the saddle and, with his sword, directed Smith's regiments to their positions. Suddenly, he spied Federal skirmishers who were pointing their rifles at him, and he "fancied . . . they [the rifles' barrels] were large enough to crawl into." He saw puffs of smoke, felt a tremendous blow, and slumped in his saddle. Some officers held him to keep him from falling, and, as they did so, Smith's line and the general passed him on the way to their position. Soldiers lifted Douglas from his horse, placed him on a stretcher, and carried him to the rear. He would be hospitalized at the seminary and be left there after the battle to become a prisoner of war.[15]

Johnson intended to attack at daybreak, but neither Johnson nor his brigade commanders recorded the orders given for the assault. At daybreak, all the brigades in the front line, at least, were poised to advance as far as they could, in accordance with the plan of General Lee. The deployment of the Confederate brigades suggests that Johnson intended a direct assault all along his line but particularly in the more promising zones of Nicholls and Steuart. It would be a slugfest, for Johnson's brigades had no other choice but to strike straight ahead. Early had demonstrated that there was nothing to be gained from a movement to the right, and the terrain to the Confederate left—the rocky wooded slope of Wolf Hill and the pond of McAllister's Mill—discouraged a flanking movement in that direction. Therefore, Johnson's attack of Friday morning would be a continuation of that of Thursday evening inspired by the hope that his increased strength would enable the division to either smash its way through a weak point in the Union line or create a diversion that would help Longstreet. Whatever Johnson's plans might have been, they had to be changed a bit, for before the Confederates could advance, the Twelfth Corps handed them an unpleasant surprise.[16]

At daybreak, about 4:30 A.M., Williams gave Lieutenant Muhlenberg the order to open fire, and "the woods in front and rear and above the breastworks held by the rebels were filled with projectiles from our guns." It was a furious, short-range pounding by the twenty-six guns of the Twelfth Corps and Rigby's battery, magnified by the noise and confusion made by shells ricocheting and exploding among the trees and rocks. Major Goldsborough, whose Maryland battalion was near the summit of the lower hill, found the artillery fire, and some of the musketry from Geary's division that accompanied it, awful—"the whole hillside seemed enveloped in a blaze." It riddled the trees above them, "and the balls could be heard to strike the breastworks like hailstones upon the roof tops." Fortunately for the Confederates, most of Johnson's force was sheltered from much of the shelling by being on the east slope of the hill and behind the captured wall and works. The Confederates beyond the wall on the lower hill would have been in grave peril, however. Three companies of the 1st Maryland were beyond this shelter, and Goldsborough withdrew them hastily to cover. The major wrote later that he believed that had it not been for their cover, scarcely a man from Steuart's brigade would have survived.[17]

The Confederates were not the only ones harassed by this artillery fire. Some "friendly" rounds fell among McDougall's regiments during the morning's fight. McDougall sent Capt. Edward Rice of his staff to complain to Ruger and to the battery commanders involved. When the short rounds continued to fall among the brigade, killing and wounding some of its men, Col. Edward Livingston Price of the 145th New York and Col. James L. Selfridge of the 46th Pennsylvania became angry. Selfridge, drawing his pistol, told McDougall that he was going to speak with the battery commander and if another round fell short, he would shoot him. Selfridge and Price spoke to the unnamed battery commander and to Slocum. After that, some of McDougall's regiments were pulled back a little and suffered no more from the Federal fire.[18]

The artillery fire continued at intervals for the next six hours. Muhlenberg reported that it "was of essential service, and did excellent execution." So long as the Confederates held the crest of the lower hill and part of the west slope, the Union batteries would have a target to shoot at. Once this target was eliminated, its work would be done.[19]

The burden of the Culp's Hill battle would fall on the infantry of the two armies. The fight divided itself rather neatly into two fronts. Until late in the morning, the combat on the Twelfth Corps right, the sector of the First Division, would be limited mainly to skirmishing and probes up the southwest slope of the lower hill. The main action was on the left where Johnson's forces assaulted Geary's line. In the course of the morning, the Confederate brigades there made three assaults according to Johnson's reckoning. The first, a renewal of the attack of the evening before, took place at daybreak all along his line. It seemed in response to the Federal artillery fire and musketry that opened Williams's effort to squeeze the Confederates from the hill. The second was an attack against Greene's center and right involving O'Neal's brigade and those of Johnson's division, and the third was a final push by Steuart's brigade from the lower hill against Geary's right and by the Stonewall Brigade and Daniel's brigade against Greene's line. There was a special tragedy to this battle on Culp's Hill. A half hour after Johnson's attack began, Ewell learned that Longstreet would not advance until after 9:00 A.M. Lee's plan had broken down; Johnson was attacking alone.[20]

If any of Geary's troops attempted to advance after the artillery fire ended, they soon gave it up in favor of fighting on the defensive behind their works. On the other hand, Johnson reported that his assault "was renewed with great determination." Steuart, whose brigade should have delivered the knockout blow, wrote that the fire was heavy on his right but little more, and the remarks of the commanders of Jones's and Nicholls's brigades were very brief. Lt. Col. David Zable, commander of the 14th Louisiana Regiment, recalled that before daybreak and the beginning of the morning's fight, officers and men of Nicholls's brigade, which was in front of Greene's center and right, conferred and decided to mask their weakness; they would get the jump on the Federals by opening fire first. In later years, seemingly ignorant of General Williams's plan to drive them from the hill, Zable expressed the belief that the ruse had worked because the enemy reply was "the most terrific and deafening that we ever experienced." The smoke became so heavy on their front that their position was marked at times only by muzzle flashes, and the accompanying roar of musketry was so intense that commands had to be shouted into the soldiers' ears.[21]

General Walker wrote that the Stonewall Brigade supported Steuart's brigade, which was hotly engaged in its immediate front. Walker's men were engaged along their whole line after moving up to Steuart's support. The 2d Virginia on the left fought along with the 1st North Carolina in order to protect the Confederate left. Company D of the 2d Virginia crossed the creek, and two other companies took position by the creek, the better to assail the flank of an enemy force pressing Steuart's front.[22]

The reports of William and Ruger say nothing about this attacking force that so engaged the attention of the 2d Virginia Regiment. However, General Lockwood's report mentions a puzzling action that seems to dovetail with the brief Confederate accounts. Very early in the morning, while Lockwood's brigade rested in support of the artillery along the pike, Williams told Lockwood to deploy a regiment and attack the enemy in the woods in his front. Lockwood selected Col. William P. Maulsby's regiment, the 1st Maryland, Potomac Home Brigade, for the job. Possibly Lockwood selected this regiment because it was more experienced than the 150th New York and was a strong unit, numbering over 700 officers and men.

Maulsby formed his men along the pike and began his advance from there. At Maulsby's command, "Forward, double quick!," the Marylanders charged at a trot toward the woods. The left of the regiment under Maj. John A. Steiner passed through a tongue of woods that extended into the meadow, while the right under Maulsby's direction advanced in the meadow itself. Enemy skirmishers in the woods fired "from behind every tree and rock," and sharpshooters from across the creek, men of the 2d Virginia Regiment, peppered them. The regiment pushed ahead "with energy," however, and, in spite of "a severe musketry fire," approached the stone wall. Maulsby halted the regiment when about twenty yards from the wall and ordered it to fix bayonets for a charge. Maulsby's men saw enemy soldiers fleeing from the wall, but information reached Lockwood that other troops were advancing on his right and that the 1st Maryland's fire would interfere with their advance. Then, in the words of General Lockwood, "having already lost in killed and wounded some 80 men, and our ammunition being short, I withdrew the regiment, and returned to the turnpike." There was no other advance, and, if the Marylanders' account is accurate, their withdrawal could have been one of the major mistakes made that morning on the hill.[23]

Steuart reported a "terrific fire of artillery" and "a very heavy fire of musketry" on his right, and the troops there would have agreed. Sgt. J. William Thomas of the 1st Maryland Battalion wrote of firing at a range of 150 yards toward troops on the "main hill" and of "hot work" and heavy losses. The 3d North Carolina Regiment, the right of the 1st Maryland Battalion, and the right of the Stonewall Brigade in their rear were on the slope that ran up to the saddle and did not have the protection of a wall or works. Sometime well after the morning's fight began (he recalled it as being 8:00 A.M.), Major Goldsborough walked to the right of his line and saw that the troops there had suffered "dreadfully" from the enemy's fire, which even then was taking its toll. He found Capt. William H. Murray,

Confederate skirmishers on Culp's Hill. Sketch by Edwin Forbes. (GNMP)

commander of Company A and the right of the Marylanders' line, and Maj. William M. Parsley of the 3d North Carolina sharing the shelter of a large rock. He asked Parsley if the 3d had suffered much, and Parsley replied, "Very much indeed. I have but thirteen men left," and then, as another North Carolinian fell, Parsley added, "and now I have but twelve." Parsley could not have been referring to the regiment's strength for it was many times larger than that.[24]

At this time, a ball struck Goldsborough's forehead and stunned him. When he had shaken off his dizziness, Goldsborough cautioned Sgt. William J. Blackistone about exposing himself too much, and as he spoke, a bullet tore through the sergeant's arm, inflicting a mortal wound. Captain Murray, "one of the bravest of the brave, a thorough disciplinarian, brave as a lion, calm and collected," reported that his men were out of ammunition and were dispirited. Beyond that, as Sergeant Thomas observed, their guns were clogged so as to be useless, and the men had not eaten for two days. Murray asked permission to take Company B from the line for an hour so that its men could clean their guns and get some ammunition and water. Goldsborough granted him this, and Company C relieved them.[25]

After leaving Murray, Goldsborough learned that his other companies were also low on ammunition. He feared that getting more would be difficult, for it might involve pulling his battalion from its works and somehow obtaining the ammunition, which he thought was a half mile away. He went to see Steuart about the problem and found him and his staff behind another rock on the hillside. After listening to Goldsborough, Steuart suggested that the major call for volunteers to go for the ammunition. (Had the brigade no system for keeping the troops supplied?) Lieutenant McKim, who had led the battalion in prayer before the fight began, interrupted their conversation. McKim said, "General, do not ask one of your officers or privates to volunteer to perform this duty whilst you have a staff officer left. I will bring the ammunition, if I live." McKim secured the help of three men and walked with them to some ammunition wagons that he recalled as being over a mile away. They got two boxes of cartridges and carried them to the front. There they emptied the boxes into blankets, swung the blankets from rails, and carried them to the hill. Goldsborough observed that "the noble fellow made the venture, and succeeded in his mission."[26]

The Confederates pressed their attack against Geary's division. There was extremely heavy musketry and little movement—in some ways it was a harbinger of warfare soon to come. Geary's front had two sectors. On the left, Greene's brigade and those troops who relieved its regiments in the course of the morning's fight faced down the hill's east slope. Geary's right was the refused line that faced the saddle and Steuart on the lower hill. Because it was quieter on the right, regiments were taken from Candy's brigade to reinforce Greene's center and left. Yet the firing was almost constant along the entire line.

The 66th Ohio Volunteer Infantry Regiment, commanded by Lt. Col. Eugene Powell, was the first of Candy's regiments to go to the left. It had a very special assignment. Sometime in the dark early morning hours of 3 July, Powell received orders to take the 66th to the top of the hill, cross the line of works there, face right so as to enfilade the enemy on Greene's front, and do what the 66th could to help in regaining the lost entrenchments. No one wrote of the origins of the order, but it must have come from Geary.[27]

Powell reached the top of the hill while it was still dark, halted the 66th so that its men could rest, and reported to the "commanding officer" there. It was still too dark for them to see one another well, and Powell did not know who the other officer was. Powell told the officer, probably General Greene, the substance of his orders, and the officer replied, "My God, young man, the enemy are right out there. I am expecting an attack every moment; if you go out there with your regt. they will simply swallow you." He told Powell also that the enemy was right up to his works. Greene thought that the 66th would be annihilated, as did Powell.[28]

Powell replied by repeating his orders. He returned then to his regiment and called it to attention. "Instantly there was the jostle of soldiers arousing themselves from rest, together with the suppressed hum of voices, followed by the clatter of canteens and other utensils which were then carried by soldiers, in addition to that of their arms, as these clashed together in the efforts of the men to get into ranks and go none knew where: forward meant into instant deadly conflict with the enemy, but to a man the regiment stood at attention and ready."[29]

When the artillery opened fire, Powell led the 66th across the crest between Greene's left and the right of the First Corps. So near and alert were Jones's Virginians that they shot some of the Buckeyes immediately, including Lts. John F. Morgan and Charles E. Butts, each of whom was hit twice. After a "close hot fight," the Ohioans drove Jones's Virginians from their tenuous position near the crest. The 66th took up a line with its right in front of, at right angles to, and below Greene's left and facing south across Greene's front. Its left rested on a shelf that towered like the prow of a ship above the steep slope that fell away from it to the east. The Buckeyes held this position throughout the morning. Powell wrote that Greene's brigade directed its fire at the enemy to its right. Although the 66th Ohio fired in that direction too, raking the slope across Greene's front, it was more concerned with the Confederates downhill toward the creek, Jones's and Nicholls's brigades, and particularly some sharpshooters behind a fence. That Powell could take and hold such a position at the cost of only seventeen casualties tells us that Jones's brigade did not press hard toward the Federals at the top of the hill. One of those killed in the 66th was Maj. Joshua G. Palmer, who had been a dentist in Urbana, Ohio, before the war. Palmer's position near the regiment's left made him an especially inviting target for the Virginians down the slope.[30]

The left regiment of Greene's brigade, the 60th New York from New York's "North Country," shared the summit of the hill with the 66th Ohio, and both regiments held their positions for the entire morning. At early dawn, its 250 men saw a large number of dead Virginians scattered just in front of their works, their harvest from the attack of the evening before. The New Yorkers fired in earnest when the Federal batteries opened, and Johnson's infantry began shooting in reply. Jones's brigade did not press the New Yorkers closely, probably because its men were intimidated by the steep slope and the breastworks near its top and because there was an easier slope nearby in front of Greene's right. Regimental accounts spoke of heavy firing by these two regiments at the summit of the hill but of nothing else.[31]

During this fight, Capt. Edward D. Camden of the 25th Virginia was forward with Jones's brigade's picket line. Sometime during the morning, he attempted to eat some corn bread, and as he took a bite, a minié ball struck him in the face, knocking the bread from his mouth along with some upper teeth and a piece of jawbone. The impact stunned Camden briefly, then came the pain, and in his pain and shock he stood and ran around crazily on the hill. Others calmed him, and when sanity returned, he started to the rear. Although the Union soldiers above him had had no interest in winging a crazed man who might soon die, when they saw him walking off in a sane manner, he "drew the fire of the whole army." Nevertheless, he made less of a target as he descended the hill and got away. That night, with a face swollen as large "as a half bushel measure," Camden left the hospital to walk alone back to Virginia. In many ways, he was one of the most fortunate members of his brigade.[32]

The fight on the 60th New York's right was more intense down where the elevation of the crest was forty feet lower and the forward slope gentler. It was characterized by a continuous roar of musketry, an unremitting fire that consumed vast quantities of ammunition, fouled rifles, and begrimed and fatigued the men who shot them. General Meade heard this roar on the Twelfth Corps front with skepticism and concern; after all, ammunition was a precious commodity that had to be carted long distances in wagons over bad roads, and it was not to be wasted. General Wadsworth led Meade to believe that Geary was wasting ammunition. Meade told Slocum that he should suggest to Geary that he might reserve his ammunition for a time when it might be needed more. In truth, a lot of ammunition was being fired that day, and most of the balls fired went into trees, splattered against rocks, or buried themselves into the earth. But even Meade became satisfied that its expenditure had to be tolerated.[33]

When the morning's battle opened, four of Greene's regiments were in the works downhill and to the right of the 60th New York. They held their positions of the previous evening, although they would leave and return to them in the course of the morning's fight. The 78th New York was on the 60th's right, the 102d beyond it, followed by the 149th New York, and Col. David Ireland's 137th Regiment held the right by the traverse above the saddle. The three regiments on the left were locked in battle with Nicholls's Louisiana brigade and with O'Neal's brigade, which supported it. The 137th on the right continued its fight with the 3d North Carolina

Regiment and the 1st Maryland Battalion on Steuart's right and with the right of the Stonewall Brigade, which was formed in Steuart's support.[34]

The three regiments of Kane's brigade—the 29th, 109th, and 111th Pennsylvania regiments—commanded by Colonel Cobham during most of the morning's battle, were behind Greene's right and faced the lower hill. A portion of the left regiment, the 29th or the 111th, in turn, had the partial shelter of the traverse; the line to its right had to rely on the cover afforded by rocks there. The 109th occupied Kane's right, and whatever regiment was not in line rested in support in the rear. Kane's regiments faced Steuart's brigade at the top of the lower hill and could enfilade that portion of the stone wall north of the smaller hill's peak.[35]

Geary recognized the slope up to the saddle as the likely path of Johnson's assault on 3 July, and it was on that front that he concentrated his strength, leaving only two regiments, the 147th Pennsylvania and the "Cincinnati Regiment," the 5th Ohio, in the space between Kane's right and the pike. Each regiment had a strength of about 300 officers and men, enough to cover the 400 yards of front left to them with a thin line. Soon after the artillery opened fire, Candy advanced the 147th Pennsylvania down the slope from the lane to the ravine, the term used by Capt. Joseph A. Moore to designate the low ground along the rivulet at the base of the hill. In its new position at the edge of the tree line, the 147th had its back to a long rock ledge and faced the small open field, later named Pardee Field in honor of the 147th's commander, that ran uphill to the wall occupied during the night by Steuart's brigade. From this position and from the woods to its right, the 147th could cover some of the wall occupied by Steuart as well as the no-man's-land between Steuart and the works occupied by Greene's right and Kane.[36]

The men of the 147th Pennsylvania and the 5th Ohio, which had come forward on its left, fired throughout the morning at the Confederates they could see and into the woods at the top of the lower hill. Sometime after this fight began, Col. John H. Patrick of the 5th Ohio saw the opportunity to give the enemy a cross fire by advancing a company of skirmishers to a stone wall. Patrick did not indicate the part of the wall manned, and none of it seems to be clearly suited for such a purpose. Yet Patrick's instructions to Lt. Henry C. Brinkman were to "fret the enemy as much as possible." Patrick was pleased to report that Brinkman and Company F did this so well that they drew and repelled Confederate attacks. Brinkman, "a brave and gallant officer," fell during the action.[37]

Three of Candy's regiments—the 28th Pennsylvania and the 7th and 29th Ohio—collected in the hollow to Candy's left rear and behind the crest held by Greene's four regiments. This ravine ran north from Kane's position and was fifty yards behind the works occupied by Greene. It served as a place of rest and resupply for the regiments on Greene's front throughout the morning, and there were frequent mad and perilous dashes between it and the works. A soldier of the 137th New York wrote: "Just back of the brest work [sic] was a hollow where the reinforcements stayed. A regiment would use up their ammunition in about two hours, when another one would relieve them and they fall back to the hollow where the balls would whistle over their heads. They would clean their guns and get some more ammunition and be ready to relieve another regiment. They would all rather be in the trenches than in the hollow. In this way we could have stood as long as the rebs chose to show themselves below, which was until 11 A.M., but few were seen after this."[38]

The veterans of Greene's brigade believed that they had saved the Army of the Potomac from defeat on the evening of 2 July and considered that fight their best. In their Gettysburg recollections, most concentrated on the evening's battle rather than that of the following morning. Most of their accounts of the 3 July action were brief, being confined to remarks on the intensity of the fighting and the times when they left the rifle pits to renew their ammunition supply and returned to fire it away. The veterans of the 149th New York were an exception.

The 149th had an excellent position. Its works crowned a low escarpment that dominated the slope in its front. The regiment (also called the "Fourth Onondaga") had been organized in Syracuse in September 1862. Col. Henry A. Barnum, who had gone to war first with the 12th New York Regiment, had been wounded and captured at Malvern Hill. Before it was known that he was a prisoner, a body believed to have been his was given a funeral and buried back in New York. Barnum led the 149th to Gettysburg and during the battle on 2 July, but then he became ill and turned the command over to Lt. Col. Charles B. Randall, another Syracuse lawyer, who led it into the fight on the morning of 3 July.[39]

The 149th spent a few early morning hours in the hollow behind its position, but Randall returned it to the works before daylight of 3 July. It was probably before it left the hollow that Randall spoke to the officers about the necessity of caring for their men and preserving them from injury. Apart from reasons of humanity and compassion, Randall observed that the government could not afford casualties because of expenses accrued in replacing losses, caring for the wounded, and paying pensions! Randall was serious in his views and called officers to account when he saw their men overly exposed to danger. After the 149th returned to the pits, and while it awaited daybreak, Randall passed along its line in order to give each of his officers a drink of whiskey. It was rather like a "last supper," for Randall observed to each that it was probably the last drink they would take together and that he hoped it would sustain them in their duty. At about the time that the last officer had his swig, the Twelfth Corps batteries opened fire and the fight began.[40]

The fight was a hard one. Colonel Ireland of the 137th New York, whose regiment faced the regiments on Steuart's and Walker's right, wrote that the enemy advanced with a yell and opened on them. Colonel Barnum described the charges of Nicholls's and O'Neal's brigades as "most impetuous" and their fire as terrific. Capt. Lewis R. Stegman, commander of the 102d New York, wrote that prior to its relief at 9:00 A.M. the regiment had held its position "in the face of fearfully destructive fire."[41]

O'Neal's brigade would have faced the right of Greene's line from about 8:00 to 10:00 A.M. Lieutenant Colonel Zable of Nicholls's brigade remembered that his brigade's relief, presumably O'Neal's brigade, came up with a yell that served "no other purpose but to intensify a more galling fire in our front." As Nicholls's men looked behind them and saw soldiers of their relief being shot down, they regretted that they were being relieved at all. The troops coming in were more exposed to enemy fire than those already on the hill, who were so close to the enemy line that the Union soldiers fired over their heads. It was in falling back that they had quite a large number killed and wounded. Yet the Alabamians 'came on and took up the fight. Col. Cullen A. Battle of the 3d Alabama described the fighting as "furious combat." Col. Samuel B. Pickens of the 12th Alabama wrote that his regiment attacked with great spirit. Colonel O'Neal agreed, and they all wrote that they were exposed to a murderous fire for three hours.[42]

Capts. William H. May and William T. Bilbro and Ens. Hendrik Harding, the 3d Alabama's color-bearer, reached a place on the hill from which they could look back and see their regiment deployed behind them. While there, they witnessed a "most ludicrous affair" involving Pvt. Tom Powell. Powell had taken cover behind a rock about two feet square that was home to a nest of yellow jackets. To May, Bilbro, and Harding, the rock seemed "the most contested point on the whole line." Powell could not leave the rock's cover, and the yellow jackets made him pay a price to stay. The wasps attacked, and Powell jumped up "slapping, stamping, and cursing." When fear of the bullets flying near overcame his dislike of the yellow jackets, he would dive for the cover of the rock. This double fight lasted for several minutes, with Powell cursing all the while, until somehow he

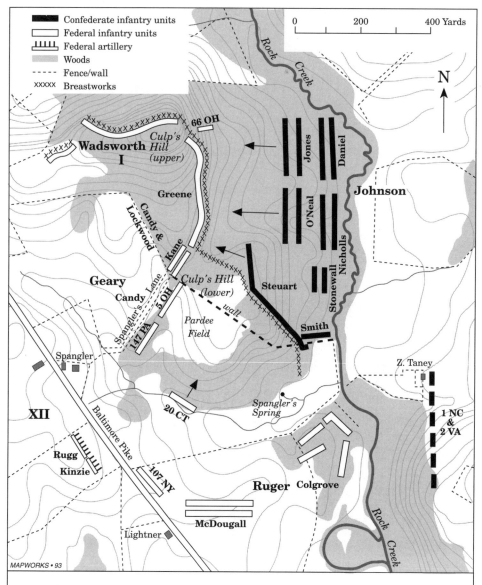

1. The 2d Virginia and a portion of the 1st North Carolina Regiment deploy as skirmishers east of Rock Creek.

2. O'Neal's brigade replaces Nicholls's in the forward line opposite Greene's center. The Stonewall Brigade leaves the forward line for ammunition.

3. Lockwood's brigade joins Candy's in Greene's support. Units of the three brigades serve at the breastworks as needed.

4. The 5th Ohio and 147th Pennsylvania regiments face Steuart's brigade across Pardee Field.

5. The 20th Connecticut Regiment begins a morning of skirmishing with units on Steuart's left.

6. O'Neal and Steuart's right attack Greene without success.

Map 16.2. Johnson's Second Attack, 3 July

Col. Edward A. O'Neal (WLM)

emerged victorious as well as stung. May could not think of it in later years without laughing.[43]

While they watched Powell, it became apparent that the men of the 3d Alabama were being picked off one by one. They could not advance, and they could not stay. May and Bilbro went back and told Colonel Battle "the utter impossibility of accomplishing a thing." Yet the brigade did not fall back until ordered to do so by General Johnson.[44]

The 149th New York measured the intensity of the enemy's fire, in part, by the damage to its colors. Confederate fire knocked the flag from its place on the breastworks twice, and Confederate balls ripped through its folds eighty times during the course of the battle and twice broke its staff. After each break, Color Sgt. William C. Lilly spliced the staff together with wood splints and knapsack straps and returned it to its place on the works. Lilly was wounded while doing this. Twenty-nine years after the battle, the 149th erected a memorial where it had fought. The memorial has a bronze bas-relief that depicts a portion of the regiment behind the works and Sergeant Lilly kneeling in the foreground splicing the colors' staff.[45]

The 137th New York held its position about two hours before the 29th Ohio relieved it. Capt. Edward Hayes, acting commander of the 29th Ohio, dashed forward to the works and discussed the relief with Colonel Ireland. He returned then to the hollow, explained the movement, and ordered the

"Mending the Flag." Sgt. William C. Lilly splices the flagstaff of the 149th New York Regiment. Note the absence of a head log on the works. Sketch by Edwin Forbes. (Collins, 149th Regiment*)*

regiment forward. At his signal, the 300 officers and men of the 29th went over the crest by the hollow at a run without pausing to fire until they reached the shelter of the works. Then, covered by the fire of the 29th, the 137th ran back to the hollow. Another regiment relieved the 149th at about the same time. The men of the 149th ended their first stint behind the works that morning by firing and then falling back quickly as their relief rushed in with a deafening cheer. Once back in the hollow, they were safe except from balls that ricocheted from the trees above them. Lieutenant Colonel Randall began their rest by calling for three cheers for their tattered colors, which the men of the 149th gave "with a tiger." Someone called for three cheers for Randall, and the men responded again with enthusiasm. These preliminaries over, the men were told to tear pieces from their shirts to clean their rifles, which had become so fouled that they could hardly be loaded and so hot that they were painful to the touch. In the meantime, someone doled out ammunition, and the 149th prepared to go back into its works.[46]

The 137th New York sustained the heaviest casualties in Greene's brigade—40 killed, 87 wounded, and 10 missing, for a coincidental total of 137. This number tells us that the 137th's position was a perilous one. It was low, easy to attack, and dominated by the top of the lower hill about 150 yards to the southeast. The 149th on its left had fifty-five casualties all told, and the 60th at the top of the hill and longest in line had fifty-two. Colonel Barnum wrote that the 149th's casualties were so light because of the "excellent management of its officers, the substantial character of our works, and the advantage of our position." Most of the wounded of the 149th were hit in the upper body because the lower body areas were protected by the works. Some were hit in the legs when they crossed the rise between the works and the hollow; some were wounded by balls that glanced off the head logs, through the slit between the logs and the works beneath them, and struck the men the head logs were to protect.[47]

There was less pressure on the right of Geary's line. Confederate prisoners told General Kane that they had tried to advance at daybreak in three lines, but the Federals saw them only dimly as yelling Confederates "closed in mass." Kane's and Candy's short line met the attack with "an unswerving line of deadly fire," in the view of the 109th, or a "smothering fire of bullets," as the men of the 111th saw it. They forced the Confederates back to the shelter of the rocks at the top of the hill. From time to time, according to Kane, his troops would hold their fire for a minute or two in the hope that Steuart's men would expose themselves and be shot. Apart from such breaks, there was a steady fire throughout the morning, punctuated by limited relief of the regiments on line. Only two regiments on the right had relief—the 29th Pennsylvania was relieved once, the 111th twice to clean their guns and get more ammunition. Neither the 109th Pennsylvania of Kane's brigade nor the 5th Ohio and 147th Pennsylvania of Candy's brigade reported having been relieved in this way, suggesting that the firing on their front—the right of Geary's line—was not nearly as heavy as that on the left.[48]

Perhaps Candy's regiments had ammunition brought to their positions. According to Private Mouat of the 29th Pennsylvania, Lt. Col. Orrin Crane of the 7th Ohio issued ammunition to the 29th and, perhaps, to the rest of the division as well. As Mouat stepped up for his sixty rounds, Crane said, "Help yourself White Star and make good use of it for the prisoners say that Ewell is going to break through here if it takes every damn man he has." To this, Mouat replied, "If he comes we will give him the best we have in the shop."[49]

During the morning's firing, the men of the 111th from northwest Pennsylvania, who prided themselves on their marksmanship, enjoyed sniping at the enemy. First Sgt. Castor G. Malin saw puffs of smoke from some rocks down the slope. He aimed and fired carefully at the source of the smoke several times, but the puffs of smoke continued to appear. The sergeant, a deer hunter, was annoyed with his shooting until after the battle when he walked down to the rock pile and found five dead soldiers there. They had followed each other in turn until the last man shot had fallen dead upon his gun and closed the gap through which they had fired.[50]

Colonel Cobham also tried his hand. While he spoke with another officer, a bullet passed between them, and soon after, another zipped by his head. The colonel saw that the last one had come from a rock shelter down the hill. He forgot that he was a brigade commander long enough to borrow a rifle, watch the rocks patiently, and finally take a shot. After the fight, like Sergeant Malin, he walked down the hill, and there he found a dead Confederate behind the rocks with a bullet hole in his head.[51]

Three regiments of Candy's brigade, apart from the 66th Ohio, shared Greene's works with his regiments on the morning of 3 July. The 7th Ohio went into the works early in the morning, fell back to the hollow, and returned to the works again about 9:30, remaining for most of the rest of the day. The 7th must have been near the right of Greene's position, but the identity of the regiment it relieved was not recorded. It sustained only eighteen casualties. The only man killed, Cpl. Charles Carroll, was a tall fellow whose head showed above the rise between the hollow and the works as the regiment formed to go into the works the second time. His head made a good target, and a Confederate shot him.[52]

The 29th Ohio relieved the 137th New York "in splendid style" about an hour after the fighting opened. The 28th Pennsylvania Regiment relieved the 29th, but it returned to the works in time to be on hand at the climax of the fight. When in position, the men of the 28th, like other units along the line, contended with Confederate snipers firing from the shelter of the boulders in its front. Each sniper's shot was advertised by a puff of smoke that invited a reply.[53]

The 14th Brooklyn and the 147th New York regiments of Cutler's brigade, Wadsworth's division, First Corps, were unique in one respect— of all of the infantry regiments on the field, only they had taken part in hard fighting on each of the three days of the battle. Both had sustained heavy casualties on 1 July, yet for reasons not known today, both were detached from the brigade line to points of special risk on 2 and 3 July while other regiments in their brigade remained on the quieter line just 500 yards away.[54]

On 3 July the 147th New York, commanded by Maj. George Harney, spent much of its day on the left of the 149th New York; it was to the left of the boulder on which the monument of the 149th was later placed. Lt. Henry Lyman wrote in his diary that the men of the regiment were up and blazing away at 3:30 A.M. and were hard-pressed all day. Lyman later wrote that the men of the regiment had each fired 200 rounds by 10:00 A.M. and that it was relieved four times to clean its guns, get more ammunition, and obtain rations. New troops were sent in, but in Lyman's view they "made bad work." He summed up his diary entry with the nota-tion, "A noisey day on the whole." The regiment had "beef & gunpowder for supper" and picket duty that night.[55]

The 14th Brooklyn would have been an obvious addition to Greene's line. Before entering Federal service in 1861, the 14th was a militia unit and had adopted a distinctive chasseur-style uniform that it wore throughout its Federal service. This garb, often mistaken for a Zouave uniform, was dis-tinguished by many nonregulation items, including a red cap, a short blue jacket, a red vest, and red pantaloons. It was said that the men wanted to wear their distinctive uniform into battle so that their dead could be easily recognized. The regiment had spent the night on Greene's line but was relieved early in the morning and returned to its brigade on the north slope of the hill. The men from Brooklyn were there just long enough to get something to eat before being sent back to Greene's line for more fighting. Colonel Fowler wrote that when they entered the trenches, they did so with a shout, and they remained there until their ammunition was all but exhausted. According to Fowler, the casualties while in the rifle pits were light but the colors, which rose above the works, were riddled by bullets, and the staff of their state flag was shot through.[56]

The 14th's position on 3 July was somewhere near that of the 149th New York—Fowler remembered its being halfway up the hill. The 149th and the 14th were in the hollow at the same time once; the men of the 149th had heard that the 14th was "a bully fighting regiment" and studied its warriors closely. They saw that it was composed mostly of young men with a tidy and smart appearance. As they waited there, a ball ricocheted down from a tree and struck one of the Brooklyn boys. He gave a piercing scream and was carried away quickly "lest his condition made cowards of them all."

When the troops of the 14th were ordered back into the line, the men of the 149th observed their behavior:

They were nearly all young boys, and as they took their places in line and waited the direction of their commander, their pale faces and ashy lips told how great was the conflict within. Most of them trembled like an aspen leaf from head to foot, and as they looked at each other and tried to laugh[,] the very smile they gave had impressed upon it the inward agony they endured. It was feared, so great was their trepidation, they would be unable to go forward, but when the word of command came the lips tightened, the eyes flashed, every nerve was strained, and they moved forward with almost mechanical ease and firmness. As they advanced, a thousand men, observing their heroic conduct in sympathy and admiration, rose in their places and cheered, while their prayers ascended to God that he would spare those young men possessed of so much courage and manliness.[57]

Williams placed the three regiments of Lockwood's brigade at Geary's disposal. The 150th New York, over 500 strong, was the first to march from the artillery position along the Baltimore Pike to Geary's front. Led by a staff officer, it went up the pike, turned off toward Culp's Hill, and passed through some woods. Soon it deployed from column into line, and Col. John H. Ketcham ordered it forward. The men gave a cheer, went off at a double-quick, and passed over the crest and down the slope toward the line of breastworks. There they relieved a regiment, probably the 78th New York, and spent the next hour or so shooting up their 150 rounds of ammunition. The woods in their front was so dense that they seldom saw a target, but they fired anyhow.[58]

The 150th New York had relieved the 78th New York at 7:40 A.M., the 102d New York at 9:00 for about twenty minutes, and the 102d again at about 10:30. It would seem logical for the 150th to simply have extended from the works of the 78th into those of the 102d, but no one wrote that it happened that way. The 150th had only eight fatalities in the course of its adventure on Culp's Hill. Pvt. Charles Howgate was one of the first. As he stepped back from the works for some ammunition, a ball tore through the top of his head. The same bullet struck two other men, Pvts. John P. Wing and Levi Rust, and killed them too. Wing was standing behind Rust, and they both dropped at the same time. The 150th had pulled easy duty in Baltimore, but from Gettysburg to the end of its service, it would share the hardships of the Twelfth Corps.[59]

The 1st Maryland Regiment, Eastern Shore, which had reached Culp's

Hill only that morning, went to Geary's aid soon after the 150th New York did so. The Eastern Shore Regiment had over two years of service at that time, all in the occupation of the Delmarva Peninsula and none in a combat situation. It was unique in the Army of the Potomac in that its colonel, James Wallace, and some other members were slaveholders and a few had brought servants to the field with them. In addition, it was a troubled regiment. Some of its former soldiers who had been mustered out after they had objected to the regiment's being ordered from Maryland to Virginia's Eastern Shore counties had gone south and apparently had joined the 1st Maryland Battalion of Steuart's brigade. In fact, it was said that the color-bearers of the two opposing Maryland units were cousins.[60]

The Eastern Shore Regiment marched hurriedly to Culp's Hill by way of Spangler's Lane. On the hill somewhere, it halted briefly so that its men could drop off their blankets and packs. Then, at the urging of staff officers, it climbed the hill, receiving fire from the right as it did so. At this point, the regiment "rushed toward the front yelling like mad" and there was a foul-up: while the five companies on the right pressed straight ahead under Wallace's eye, the remaining four, under Lt. Col. William H. Comegys, veered left and out of touch with the right. When the right wing reached the crest behind the works, it saw the Rebels attacking! Without waiting, the Marylanders fired a volley over the heads of what Wallace believed was a Pennsylvania regiment, possibly the 111th, in the works in his front. This shooting from the rear created consternation among the men already in the works, and their commander demanded that the firing stop. The attack had been checked, however, and the Marylanders entered the works as the regiment it relieved pulled out.[61]

No one reported what happened to the four companies to the left under Comegys. Apparently they went in on the left of the 150th New York, which was then behind the works. Wherever they were, the Eastern Shore men experienced heavy musketry that would wax and wane during their stay in the works. After they had fired most of their ammunition, some of them on the left began to drift away from their works to the rear. In spite of the effort of some officers to stop it, the drift continued. Fortunately, the 150th New York was at hand and able to take over the Marylanders' place in the line.[62]

The 1st Maryland Regiment, Potomac Home Brigade, was the last of Lockwood's regiments to go to Geary's aid that morning. About 9:00 A.M., after some rest from its attack above Spangler's Spring, it followed the Eastern Shore Regiment to Geary's front and went into the trenches, relieving the 29th Pennsylvania, which had run out of ammunition. There these Marylanders fought well for perhaps three hours until the end of the morning's fight when the regiment pulled back, some said without permission. After the battle, Colonel Maulsby took issue with such an accusation by Captain Stegman, commander of the 102d New York, and vigorously insisted that he had been given permission to leave by one of Greene's staff officers.[63]

Lockwood's brigade gained little glory on Culp's Hill. It would have been surprising had it done so considering the inexperience of its commanders and of the regiments themselves. In his report, General Greene mentioned the brigade's presence and its "efficient service." He made a point of commending the 150th New York and the 1st Maryland Regiment, Potomac Home Brigade, but had nothing to say of the men from the Eastern Shore. Lockwood made no distinction between his regiments when he praised them for their "coolness and firmness" in spite of their inexperience. He could find fault only with "a too rapid fire and a too hasty and inconsiderate advance." The advance that he criticized, perhaps with tongue in cheek, must have been on the Union left on 2 July and not something that had taken place on Culp's Hill.[64]

In his report of the battle, General Geary disposed of the "efficient service" of Lockwood's brigade with five lines. Shaler's brigade, which followed it onto Culp's Hill, received nearly fifty. Shaler's brigade from the Sixth Corps would be the last reinforcement sent to the Twelfth Corps and would arrive in time for Johnson's final assault.[65]

17
THE LAST ATTACKS

It was mid-morning. Maj. Gen. Edward Johnson had sent his brigades forward twice in an effort to seize Culp's Hill, and they had been repulsed. Now, perhaps at Ewell's suggestion, he ordered a third attack. This time Walker's Stonewall Brigade and the brigades of Steuart and Daniel would make the push.[1]

Steuart's brigade would attack from the lower hill. The 3d North Carolina on the brigade right had been facing the draw leading up to the saddle between the hills and, having little cover, had suffered terribly during the evening's and early morning's battles. Now only a small portion of it was able to continue the fight. Like the 3d North Carolina, the right companies of the 1st Maryland Battalion had also been outside of the works and facing the deadly draw, but its left companies had been at the breastworks at the top of the lower hill. The remainder of the brigade stretched to the left behind the stone wall that led to the position of the 1st North Carolina Regiment beside the meadow east of Spangler's Spring. In forming for Johnson's attack, the right of the brigade would shift left so that the 3d North Carolina would be between the breastworks and the stone wall south of the crest of the lower hill. The brigade would wheel right from the stone wall and into the woods and would form on the left of the 3d North Carolina facing the open field.[2]

The brigade commander, Brig. Gen. George Hume Steuart, was one of the few Maryland generals in the Confederate army. He was born in Baltimore on 24 August 1828 and graduated from West Point in 1848 near the bottom of his class. He had been a classmate of the Union cavalry general, John Buford. Steuart missed service in the war with Mexico but

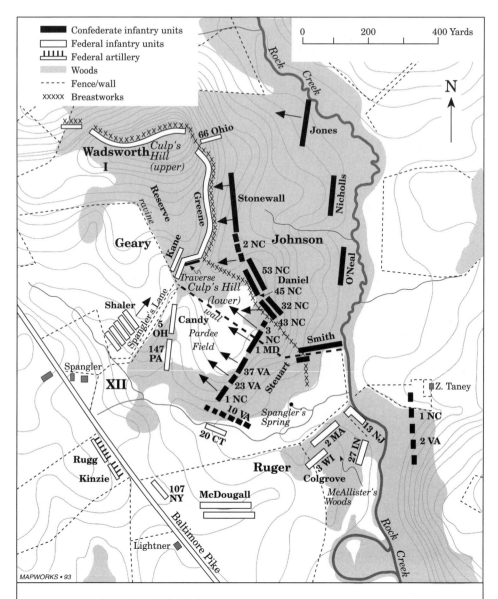

Confederate infantry units
Federal infantry units
Federal artillery
Woods
Fence/wall
xxxxx Breastworks

0   200   400 Yards

N

Rock Creek

Jones

66 Ohio

Wadsworth
I

Culp's
Hill
(upper)

Stonewall

Nicholls

Greene

Reserve ravine

Geary

Kane

2 NC

Johnson

O'Neal

53 NC
Daniel
45 NC

Traverse
Culp's Hill
(lower)
wall

32 NC

Shaler

5
OH

Candy
Pardee
Field

147
PA

43 NC

3
NC
1 MD

Smith

37 VA

Spangler

XII

23 VA

1 NC

10 VA

20 CT

Steuart

Z. Taney

1 NC

2 VA

Spangler's
Spring

13 NJ

2 MA

Rugg

Kinzie

107
NY

McDougall

Ruger

Colgrove

3 WI

27 IN

McAllister's
Woods

Lightner

Baltimore Pike

Rock Creek

MAPWORKS • 93

1. Steuart's brigade is shifted left to the top of Pardee Field. Five regiments are in line, and the 10th Virginia guards their left.

2. The Stonewall Brigade with four regiments relieves O'Neal and faces Greene's center. Daniel's brigade occupies Steuart's old position.

3. Greene's line and the reserve in its rear are occupied by units from Greene's, Candy's, and Lockwood's brigades. Kane's brigade is between the works and the wall, and the two regiments of Candy's brigade face Pardee Field.

4. The Stonewall Brigade and Steuart's brigade attack dead ahead. Their attacks fail.

5. Shaler's brigade comes up during the fight. Its 122d New York Regiment goes into line on Greene's right at the close of the fight.

6. The 20th Connecticut and the 10th Virginia skirmish.

Map 17.1. Johnson's Final Attack, 3 July

Brig. Gen. George H. Steuart (WLM)

campaigned on the Texas frontier with the 2d Dragoons and on the central plains with the 2d U.S. Cavalry Regiment. He was still a lieutenant when he resigned from the Old Army in April 1861 and entered the cavalry of the Confederacy in the grade of captain. He soon became lieutenant colonel of the 1st Maryland Infantry Regiment, fought at Manassas, and became its colonel on that day. He was promoted to brigadier general in March 1862 and commanded brigades of cavalry and infantry in the Shenandoah Valley. Steuart's career received a black mark at the battle of Winchester on 25 May 1862. When Stonewall Jackson wanted to order in his cavalry to exploit his victory there, Steuart and his horsemen were not at hand. When a staff officer did find him, Steuart bridled about accepting the order because it did not come through General Ewell, his immediate commander. Although this incident and other lackluster performances as a cavalryman did not result in disciplinary action, he was reassigned to an infantry brigade, which he commanded at Cross Keys. After recuperating from being wounded there, he returned to active service in time for the Gettysburg campaign.[3]

Steuart must have been something of an eccentric—at least the men of the 1st Maryland Regiment thought so. They did not like him at first because he was a very strict disciplinarian and ran the 1st Maryland by the letter of the army's regulations. It was said that he once even had them sweep the floor of some woods in which they bivouacked down to the bare earth. In addition, the former Indian fighter would test his sentinels by trying to infiltrate the regiment's picket line and shouting "Indians!" As the war went on and the men of the regiment mellowed, many credited him with the regiment's "fine state of discipline." Fifty years after Gettysburg, in the glow of the Lost Cause, one of the Maryland veterans said of him, "No one in the war gave more completely and conscientiously every faculty, every energy that was in him to the southern cause."[4]

Daniel's brigade moved from its position in Jones's zone to take position in two lines at Steuart's brigade's right and rear. Its two larger regiments, the 43d and 45th North Carolina, manned the works vacated by Steuart's brigade when it shifted position for its attack; however, the right companies of the 45th extended beyond the works and formed on the dangerous slope where Steuart's right had been. The 2d North Carolina Battalion deployed on the right as skirmishers.[5]

Junius Daniel, born in 1828, was the son of a prominent North Carolina politician who was a congressman and an attorney general for the state. He graduated from West Point with its class of 1851 and served as an infantry officer until 1858, when he left the army to run one of his father's plantations near Shreveport, Louisiana. In June 1861 he entered the Confederate service as colonel of the 14th North Carolina Regiment. He and his regiment took part in the Peninsular campaign, and on 1 September 1862 he received a promotion to brigadier general. Daniel then left the Army of Northern Virginia for less eventful service at Drewry's Bluff and in North Carolina, but he and his brigade joined Lee's army and Rodes's division in time for the Gettysburg campaign. The brigade and its commander acquitted themselves nobly on 1 July in the fields northwest of Gettysburg. After Gettysburg, Daniel and his brigade continued to serve in the Army of Northern Virginia. Unfortunately, Daniel's career came to an abrupt end on 12 May 1864 when he was wounded at the Mule Shoe at Spotsylvania. He died the following day.[6]

Daniel's orders from General Johnson were to "charge the enemy works, in conjunction with General Steuart." Daniel viewed his brigade's mission with foreboding, for he had witnessed the failure of the first attacks that day and several of his men had already been shot while going into position. Lieutenant McKim noted in his diary that both Steuart and Daniel "strongly disapproved of making the assault."[7]

The Stonewall Brigade, which had supported Steuart's brigade earlier that morning, had been sent to the rear so that its men could clean their rifles and replenish their supply of ammunition. Pvt. Charles Rollins wrote that Johnson came up to the brigade and asked, "What brigade is this?" "Stonewall, sir," was the reply. To this, Johnson responded, "Where is your commander? What in the ——— are you doing here?" Someone pointed the way to Walker, and the two generals talked. Johnson told Walker to take his brigade to the right and renew the attack. Since Colonel Nadenbousch's 2d Virginia Regiment was across Rock Creek skirmishing with Neill's brigade and with the Twelfth Corps troops in McAllister's Woods, only four of Walker's regiments—the 4th, 5th, 27th, and 33d Virginia— less than 1,000 men, would take part in the assault.[8]

The four Virginia regiments shifted beyond Daniel's right into the zone of Nicholls's brigade where it and O'Neal's brigade had already attacked Greene's line without success. The Virginians confronted the seemingly impregnable position above them. The slope was gradual, but it was interrupted by trees and rocks. The works of Greene's brigade defied them from the crest. Yet there were occasional dead spaces that would give them a little shelter. The regiments of the Stonewall Brigade deployed for their attack. No one mentioned their order in line or exactly where they were. It seems likely that their left was in the depression leading up into the saddle, and their line extended no more than 300 yards north from there, far enough to confront Greene's line to the point where the hill's crest rose steeply to its summit.

Johnson's third attack would be two separate and loosely coordinated assaults. That of the Stonewall Brigade would be a continuation of the earlier assaults up the slope of the main hill against the works erected by Greene's and Kane's brigades—heavy firing and a push. In contrast, the attack by Steuart's brigade would be a charge of 200 yards down the northwest slope of the lower hill, much of it across an open field.

Major Goldsborough, now commander of the 1st Maryland Battalion, was near the right of its line when he learned of the coming attack. Capt. George Williamson of the brigade staff approached him with the order from General Steuart. The major was to move his battalion by the left flank, file to the right, and join the right of the line formed by the Virginia regiments in the woods west of the wall. Goldsborough saw the intent of the order at once and told the captain that "it was nothing less than murder to send men into that slaughter pen." Williamson agreed with him and said that Steuart shared his opinion but that the order had come from General Johnson and was "imperative." Goldsborough sent for Captain Murray, who was resting Company A behind some large boulders on the right, and asked that the company take its place in line.[9]

The Marylanders filed quietly southeast along the wall and turned to the right to cross to their place in the new line. All the Maryland men knew what was in store for them and seemed to "feel the solemnity of the occasion." Pvt. D. Ridgely Howard of Company A remembered it as a "terrible and trying time for all." He prayed for strength to do his duty "and not to bring disgrace and shame upon a name that had been honored in the State from its earliest history." After the battalion took its place in line astride the wall, Goldsborough told Murray, its senior captain, to command the companies on the right in the assault; he would oversee the left, which included the battalion's newer companies.[10]

Steuart therefore formed that portion of his brigade available for the attack in a space that must have been no more than 300 yards from the breastworks on the right to the tree line on the southwest side of Pardee Field. He placed the 3d North Carolina on the right with its flank against the works. Its numbers here were small at best—McKim and Goldsborough said just eighteen men. The 1st Maryland Battalion was on the left of the 3d with two companies on the right side of the wall and five on its left extending into the woods at the southeast end of the field. The 23d Virginia, no more than fifty strong, was next in line, followed by the 37th Virginia and possibly six companies of the 1st North Carolina Regiment. Major Goldsborough wrote that Steuart's brigade had only 900 men in line, less than half of the number it had brought to the field but just about the right amount for the space available in its zone.[11]

Steuart still had to protect his left from harassment from the 20th Connecticut and others that might attack it. He did this by sending the whole 10th Virginia Regiment into the woods on the lower hill with orders to clear the woods of the enemy's skirmishers. The 10th pushed into the woods until it found the enemy drawn up in a line of battle about 350 yards west of the stone wall. The west slope of the hill was sliced in a north-south direction by a small ravine. It seems likely that the 10th would have held the Federal forces in the area beyond this ravine. After the charge, the 10th pulled back to the breastworks, and according to Col. Edward T. H. Warren, its commander, it did not have more than fifty men at this time.[12]

When the line formed, the command to fix bayonets was given quietly, and there was a momentary clicking noise along the line. General Steuart, who was on the right behind Company A, 1st Maryland Battalion, unsheathed his sword, raised it high, and commanded, "Attention! Forward, double-quick! March!" The brigade started off promptly, rifles at right shoulder shift. Steuart accompanied the brigade on foot. Just as they stepped off, Private Howard heard an officer, probably Captain Murray, say, "Use your bayonets, boys; don't fire." [13]

When Steuart's brigade advanced, Daniel's line moved to support it. Col. Thomas S. Kenan started the left wing of his 43d North Carolina Regiment over the breastworks and through the trees in front of it. The 43d, and probably others of Daniel's brigade, would advance in Steuart's support. [14]

The Union position that Steuart was to strike was at the far side of the field, about 200 yards to the northwest. The 5th Ohio and 147th Pennsylvania regiments, 600 strong, waited there among the trees in the marshy saddle between the main and lower hills. Kane's brigade also waited at the junction of the stone wall and Spangler's Lane. It had the cover of boulders there and, from them, faced the right of Steuart's line. [15]

If the Confederates started off at a double-quick, their pace must have slowed soon. The soldiers of the 147th Pennsylvania saw them approaching with "astonishing deliberation" and held their fire. Yet some men in the gray line remembered catching a blistering cross fire from batteries and infantry as soon as they left the shelter of the trees. The 147th Pennsylvania and the Cincinnati Regiment opened with a vengeance at a range of 100 yards. "The death shriek rends the air on every side," wrote one Marylander. There was disorder and confusion, wrote another; "there seemed no commander, or his orders were not forwarded." In truth, for reasons not given, Steuart and his staff were advancing with the Marylanders on the right of the brigade rather than with its center. [16]

Sgt. George Pile, Company A, 37th Virginia Regiment, who was advancing just to the left of the Marylanders, wrote that they had pushed on "a considerable distance" when the enemy hit them with a murderous fire that seemed to nearly wipe out the Maryland battalion and left only him and another man from his company standing. Someone ordered the 37th to fall back, and it retired slowly. As Pile obeyed, his orderly sergeant called pitifully to him, "For God's sake, Pile, don't leave me." Pile and musician John Stokes grasped the wounded sergeant by his hands and dragged him back to the breastworks. The charge was over for Sergeant Pile and the 37th. Lt. Col. Simeon Walton of the 23d Virginia found the enemy fire "terrible," and his small band also had to retire. [17]

After the war, some of the Maryland veterans wrote disparagingly of the failure of the Virginians to continue to press ahead. Goldsborough complained that they threw themselves to the ground and refused to heed the pleadings and curses of their officers to advance. "Never," wrote Golds-

"The 29th Pennsylvania Regiment on Culp's Hill." Drawing by William L. Sheppard. (GNMP)

borough, "shall I forget the expressions of contempt on the faces of the men of the left companies of the Second [First] Maryland as they cast a side glance upon their comrades who had proved recreant in this supreme moment."[18]

Their expressions would change soon. Goldsborough felt a "violent shock" and toppled to the ground. Feeling no immediate pain, he raised himself on an elbow and watched his battalion shatter before his eyes. He saw those who were still standing seek the cover of the woods pursued by "a merciless storm of bullets" that struck more of them down. By this time the left and center of Steuart's brigade were out of the fight.[19]

The two Maryland companies and the North Carolinians advancing between the wall and the works had some cover and still forged ahead. The soldiers of the 29th Pennsylvania, from their position in the saddle opposite the space between the wall and works, saw Steuart's men coming. They had been shooting at Confederates on the hill all morning and needed no command to take the charging column under fire. They could see the

Confederates advancing steadily, partially concealed by foliage and rocks until they got to within 100 paces of the Federal position. Pvt. David Mouat wrote that the 29th did not open fire until their attackers were within fifty yards of them and seemed ready to charge; then the 29th's "whole line up and let them have it." Colonel Rickards saw from the number of leaves falling above the Confederates that his men were firing too high. He shouted for them to aim at the Confederates' knees, and the effect "was noticeable at once." Yet the Confederate column continued on until at about a distance of sixty yards it seemed to waver.[20]

General Steuart, Captain Williamson, and Lieutenant McKim were still with the troops on the right, with swords drawn, cheering them on. The colors of the 3d North Carolina and 1st Maryland Battalion were still going forward, although it was said, probably incorrectly, that only about eight North Carolinians were with them. Sgt. James W. Thomas of Company A, 1st Maryland, thought that their safety lay in charging, but the officers thought it was too soon. Officers urged, "Steady, boys, steady," again and again, as the bullets cut them down. Thomas wrote that they advanced slowly until they were within forty paces of the enemy, and then someone shouted for them to retreat! Thomas fired, turned, and took a bullet in his hip that exited in front of his stomach.[21]

There had been no disorder in the companies on the right, but it began at this time. Captain Murray, who was now in command of the Marylanders, waved his sword, perhaps as a signal for them to fall back. A bullet struck Murray in the neck. Murray's fall, if not the wave of his sword, signaled that the attack was over for the men from Maryland. The survivors staggered back, leaving the ground strewn with their dead and desperately wounded.[22]

At about this time, Private Howard looked to the right and saw Company A going back. He became angry and dashed forward after 1st Sgt. Robert H. Cushing of Company C. Cushing stopped suddenly to shoot, and Howard also stopped to fire at a Union color-bearer whom he saw to his front waving the "gridiron" and cheering. Howard fired but missed. He attempted to reload, but before he could get a cartridge from his box, he felt a stinging in his hip and pitched forward. Soon he was sitting on the ground.[23]

The 1st Maryland had done its best, and its remnants were fleeing for cover, their faces free of expressions of disdain. The men of the 3d North Carolina were alone. In the calm of later years, a North Carolinian wrote, "We found our regiment alone moving to the front, unsupported, when the officers and men were ordered to withdraw, which was done slowly and

Capt. William H. Murray (McH. Howard, Recollections*)*

without confusion." He mused, "That last . . . charge was a cruel thing for the Third."[24]

General Kane watched Steuart's men advancing toward his position. With admiration, he recalled their steady approach, rifles at right shoulder shift, dressing and redressing their lines as men went down. Then the column seemed to waver, and its men broke into a double-quick, then a run, toward the Union line. As the column fell apart, some of its more impetuous soldiers dashed against the Union line, some who were wounded doing so with their last breath.

At the climax of the charge, a dog broke from the Confederate ranks and raced to the front. It

came in among the Boys in Blue as if he supposed they were what in better days they might have been, merely the men of another noisy hose or engine company, competing for precedence with his masters in the smoke of a burning building. At first—some of my men said, he barked in valorous glee; but I myself first saw him on three legs between our own and the Men in Gray on the ground as though looking for a dead master, or seeking on which side he might find an explanation of the Tragedy he witnessed, intelligible to his canine apprehension. He licked someone's hand, they said, after he was perfectly riddled.

Kane ordered the dog to be honorably buried "as the only Christian minded being on either side."[25]

The great drama of Steuart's charge disintegrated into tragic vignettes. The Confederates who were able fell back to the refuge of the wall and works, where they formed to meet a Federal counterattack. Steuart was distraught; he wrung his hands repeating, "My poor boys! My poor boys!," as tears coursed down his cheeks.[26]

As Steuart's brigade began its advance, Colonel Kenan led the 43d North Carolina in its wake, but not far. Before his right wing could get over the works and form a line, Steuart's men were coming back. The best thing that the North Carolinians could do was to cover their retreat.[27]

Lt. J. Winder Laird, adjutant of the 1st Maryland Battalion, found Goldsborough as Laird walked to the rear. He picked up the major and carried him to shelter. The major, who was weak from loss of blood, dozed off but was awakened soon by Lt. Thomas Tolson, who asked if he could do anything for him. Goldsborough asked him to have Captain Murray take command of the battalion, and he learned only then that Murray was dead. Captain Torsch of Company E took command until relieved by Capt. J. Parran Crane.[28]

Back down the slope, the helpless wounded awaited their fate. The firing around them continued for a while, and Sergeant Thomas received two more wounds, one in the left elbow, another in the left thigh. Thomas was a tough fellow; he dragged himself ten feet down the hill, and during a lull in the firing, two Union soldiers were brave and compassionate enough to pick him up and carry him behind their line. General Kane talked with him there, and Lt. Thomas J. Leiper of Kane's staff gave him three dollars and had him taken to a hospital. Thomas grieved for Murray and others who had fallen. He remained convinced that had the brigade been "properly conducted and supported" its losses might have been small and there would have been a chance for victory.[29]

Private Howard, who must have been near Thomas, made a tourniquet with his handkerchief and bayonet and applied it to his broken leg. The firing around him continued for a while; another ball struck him in the hip, giving him a minor wound. He could hear the sounds made by the balls striking around him. Those that hit bodies made different sounds from those that hit the ground, and Howard was convinced that Union soldiers were deliberately firing at the wounded. A man near him writhed in agony and then died. Howard expected every moment to be his last, and he prepared to die. He straightened himself out as much as he was able, folded his arms across his chest, and waited for death, hoping that it would come without a struggle. He wanted those who found him to see that he died content "in the consciousness of duty faithfully performed." *Dulce et decorum est pro patria mori.*

Many minutes passed, the shooting stopped, and Howard still lived. He saw several Union soldiers down the slope beckoning the Confederates to come into their lines. Now determined to live, he pulled himself in their direction until two soldiers dashed out, took him by the arms, and dragged him to their line, his broken leg "swaying from side to side every step they took." One of the first things they said to him was, "What made you so brave?" There were other questions. They asked the identity of his unit, and he told them. They then said, "Do you know that you are fighting your own men?," meaning fellow Marylanders, and Howard replied, "Yes, and we intend to fight them."[30]

The soldiers who questioned Howard must have been from the 1st Maryland Regiment, Eastern Shore, of Lockwood's brigade. They had been recruited on the Eastern Shore and had served there and in Baltimore— service that would not have endeared them to Howard and to the other Confederate Marylanders. Yet according to the regiment's commander, Col. James Wallace, they "sorrowfully gathered up many of our old friends & acquaintances [from the Confederate battalion], & had them carefully & tenderly cared for."[31]

The musketry of Steuart's charge and repulse had just died when the soldiers of the 147th Pennsylvania Regiment viewed a tragedy that symbolized the sad event. In the sloping field, littered with wounded and dead Confederate soldiers, they saw a Maryland soldier who seemed to have a wound in his abdomen and was lying on his back. The wounded man struggled wearily to load his rifle. They watched him; some men who were wary of his intentions even covered him with their own loaded guns, but Maj. John Craig told them to hold their fire. They watched fascinated as he finished loading. He removed the ramrod laboriously, cocked the hammer, drew the muzzle of the piece beneath his chin, and with the ramrod pushed the trigger.[32]

This one shot that so clearly symbolized the futility of the Confederate attacks on the morning of 3 July would not have been noticed by either

Union or Confederate soldiers contending on the slope of the hill about 250 yards away to the east. There the battle's roar would have been deafening and would continue so for a little while.

No one from either Daniel's brigade or the Stonewall Brigade left an adequate account of that assault. In his report, General Daniel wrote only that the attack of his brigade "was made in a most gallant manner" and that some of the enemy was driven from their works. General Walker reported even less. The Stonewall Brigade had little to show but casualties for its "five hours of incessant firing" over to the left on Steuart's front earlier that morning, and this attack was made with "equally bad success as our former efforts." In fact, the Federal fire became so destructive that Walker pulled his brigade back "to a more secure position, as it was a useless sacrifice of life to keep them longer under so galling a fire."[33]

To the Union soldiers who were generally unaware of the shifting of brigades in their front, the morning's battle was a continual fight, punctuated by Confederate pushes that caused the fighting to swell, subside, and swell again. As the fighting continued through Johnson's first two assaults, the regiments of Greene's and Kane's brigades, which bore the brunt of the Confederate attacks, were given short respites when their ammunition was gone and their guns were fouled. Regiments of Candy's brigade, the 14th Brooklyn and 147th New York regiments, and then the three regiments of Lockwood's brigade took turns in the rifle pits, so there was frequent movement to and from the hollow fifty or so yards behind the works on Greene's line. Because of the nature of the slope, the Union regiments opposite the Confederates in front of the eastern approach to the saddle were especially vulnerable to Confederate fire. General Daniel, who seems not to have understood these shifts, wrote, "I obtained through a gorge between their lines of intrenchments a most destructive fire with the whole of the Forty-fifth [North Carolina] Regiment for five minutes upon a crowd of the enemy who were disorganized and fleeing in great confusion."[34]

Pvt. Louis Leon of the 53d North Carolina Regiment had his own view of the morning's fight. The 53d had been in a support role initially, but it soon became involved with the attacks from the slope of the lower hill against Greene's and Kane's positions at the saddle. Its troops charged down the hill several times and each time fell back, leaving casualties behind. The 53d "melted away." Leon's company, Company B, went into the fight with about sixty men and left with sixteen. Leon recalled that one man's head was shot off, another was cut in two, one soldier's brains oozed out, and so forth. Some wounded begged for water, others for someone to kill them. Men with leg wounds lying between the lines called for someone to carry them out, but they could not be reached. General Daniel sent a staff officer to bring the 53d from the hill, but he was killed, as was the next man sent. Finally, Lt. W. Edward Stitt, an acting aide from the 43d Regiment, reached them and led them back.[35]

This final assault lasted no more than an hour. Because of their shuttling in and out of the rifle pits throughout the morning, we cannot be certain which Union regiments were in them at a given time and where they were in line. The 66th Ohio and 60th New York were probably in place at the top of the hill throughout the fight, and it seems certain that the 149th New York was in the works. The 149th New York was firing in an intermittent fashion in obedience to Lieutenant Colonel Randall's instructions not to waste ammunition—its men were to shoot only after aiming deliberately at specific targets. A soldier near Randall aimed and fired. Randall went to the man and asked if he had seen anything to fire at. "Yes," said the soldier. "Where?" asked Randall. "Right there," the man replied, pointing to the front. Randall stared through the smoke and saw the Stonewall Brigade headed for his position. He shouted, "Give them h—l boys, give it to them right and left." The Onondaga County boys did so.[36]

The 7th Ohio, sent from Candy's brigade earlier in the morning, was also in Greene's rifle pits when the Stonewall Brigade attacked. They watched the Virginians, formed in more than one line as they saw it, begin their charge from far down the slope. The men of the 7th held their fire until the first line was well within their range. Col. William R. Creighton ordered them to open, firing by rank, first the front rank then the rear. The gray line melted away before their solid volleys, many Confederates taking cover behind the numerous rocks and trees on the slope. The Virginians fired from this cover as they could, and the Union riflemen replied, shooting at any patch of clothing that protruded from behind the dark boulders. Cpl. Gilbert D. Bertholf recalled that the Confederates worked their way up the slope until some were no more than fifteen yards from the Union works. One orderly sergeant reached the works in front of the flag of the 149th New York, seemingly intent on seizing it. The New Yorkers shot him there, and there he stayed. Lt. George Collins wrote that the sergeant "was a large noble-looking man, and no one who afterwards saw him lying with his head and arm against the works, could help admiring his manly appearance and evident courage."[37]

Geary was convinced that the enemy was attempting to carry his division's position on the hill "at all hazards." He saw that his whole line was engaged and was concerned that some of his troops, Lockwood's brigade

in particular, might not stand the gaff. He asked Slocum for reinforcements, an interesting request considering that by this time he must have had a half dozen regiments that were not on the firing line. Slocum sent Shaler's brigade to him; it was on loan to the Twelfth Corps from the Third Division, Sixth Corps.[38]

Shaler's brigade had reported to Slocum at 8:45 A.M., and its five regiments—the 65th, 67th, and 122d New York and the 23d and 82d Pennsylvania—had been held in reserve along the Baltimore Pike near the Spangler house since its arrival. Geary had been instructed not to use Shaler's people unless absolutely necessary. Johnson's third attack seemed reason enough to send in Shaler's brigade. Geary and Shaler rode forward to examine conditions on his front. Soon Shaler returned to his regiments and spoke to Col. Silas Titus of the 122d New York Regiment, or the "Third Onondaga." (It, like the 149th New York, had been raised in Onondaga County, New York.) Shaler said to Titus, "Col., things are a little mixed up in there, go in and report to me, I will support you with the balance of the brigade."[39]

The 400 officers and men of the 122d New York made their way to the hollow and formed. At the signal to advance, they scrambled up the side of the ravine and dashed for the shelter of the works. "O! how the balls whistled," wrote Cpl. Sanford Truesdell. It seemed impossible to reach the rifle pits alive, but almost all of them did. Each of them had sixty

"Patent Cartridges," which Truesdell claimed they could load and fire as "fast as you could count." The enemy attempted to charge them but could not "stand the storm"; the Rebels were in what Truesdell called "a tight fire" and could neither advance nor retreat. Finally, the Confederates ceased firing, but the New Yorkers could still see some of them behind a "wall" and popped away at them. These unfortunates raised a white flag, and the 122d stopped firing. Colonel Titus ordered the Rebels to come forward. A few did so while others watched. Then, when the first of them reached the Union line in safety, the remainder followed. All told, there were seventy-five Confederates who surrendered to the 122d. After about two hours in the rifle pits, the Onondaga boys were out of ammunition, and their fight was over. They had sustained forty-four casualties, most of them while crossing from the hollow to the works. All were so black from powder smoke that they were scarcely recognizable.[40]

The men of the 149th New York welcomed the 122d to the section of the works on their right. There was mutual joy at their meeting, and the men of the two Onondaga regiments cheered so loudly that, in warm recollection, they drowned out the noise of battle and might have intimidated the enemy. It would be the only time that the regiments would meet in the course of the war. There was a dark side to the reunion, sad to say. Capt. James E. Doran of the 149th went down the line to visit the newcomers and, while waving his cap in jubilation, was shot in the arm and crippled for life. To make matters worse, Lieutenant Colonel Randall, who had been directing the 149th's fire from behind a bullet-scarred tree, went over to tend to Doran and took a bullet in the shoulder as he bent over the wounded captain.[41]

The Stonewall Brigade and Daniel's North Carolinians had done their best and failed. When the Confederate tide ebbed away from the Union works, it left many Confederates stranded in dead spots under the brow of the hill and behind boulders close to the enemy works. Perhaps there were several like Lt. John H. B. Jones who, rather than surrender, chose to run for it. Jones bounded down the slope away from the Union line and took refuge behind a rock. In doing so, he lost his sword, no great catastrophe perhaps, but also three bullets had passed through his clothes during his wild dash, and Union soldiers splattered lead balls against the boulder that sheltered him. Others could or would not run to the rear, and they surrendered.[42]

Several makeshift white flags appeared in front of the Union position. Seventy-eight soldiers surrendered to the 7th Ohio, five to the 29th Ohio, and fifty-two to the 137th New York; Greene's brigade as a whole captured about 130 prisoners. The Liberty Hall Volunteers, a company of the 4th Virginia, had sixteen men captured, including its captain. As he pulled prisoner Pvt. John McKee over the breastworks, a Union soldier said, "Gim-me-your hand, Johnny Reb; you've give' us the bulliest fight of the war." In addition, Cpl. John Pollack somehow acquired the flag of the 4th Virginia Regiment. It and two other colors were captured by Geary's division on Culp's Hill. Out in front of the 122d New York, a man waved a white handkerchief in token of surrender, but one of his own officers "rose up, and split his head open with his sword." The New Yorkers, in turn, shot the officer seven times.[43]

It was at the time of these surrenders that those on the right of Greene's line witnessed a dramatic and memorable act of heroism. Colonel Creighton of the 7th Ohio wrote in his report, "At the time the white flag was raised, a mounted rebel officer (Major Leigh, assistant adjutant-general to General Ewell [actually to Edward Johnson]), was seen to come forward and endeavor to stop the surrender, when he was fired upon by my men and instantly killed."[44]

B. Watkins Leigh was a brave and valued officer. He had been on Gen. A. P. Hill's staff during the battle of Chancellorsville and was one of the three officers who had carried Stonewall Jackson from the field after he was wounded. Once when the party came under fire, Leigh and the others placed Jackson's stretcher on the ground and shielded it with their own bodies. Now Leigh was in an even more deadly fight. When he saw part of the Stonewall Brigade surrendering, he spurred his horse up the slope in the very face of the Union infantry and tried to stop them. Union soldiers shot him, of course; it was as simple as that. Leigh and his horse went down, both pierced by several balls, and there they lay in front of the Union line, a dead major and his dead horse. Lieutenant Collins of the 149th described him there as a man of small stature with a "smart and intelligent look."[45]

Major Leigh's heroism did not go unappreciated. General Johnson in his report wrote, "Maj. B. W. Leigh, my chief of staff, whose conscientious discharge of duty, superior attainments, and noble bearing made him invaluable to me, was killed within a short distance of the enemy's line."[46]

Generals Geary and Greene and Colonel Creighton also wrote of Leigh's death in their reports. Greene forwarded some papers taken from Leigh's pockets to a higher headquarters, and scroungers took some of Leigh's possessions. In a letter to his brother, Sgt. Fergus Elliott of the 109th Pennsylvania included a piece of cloth cut from Leigh's pocket with the notation, "i cut it off myself, we killed him on the 3d of July 1863." Nevertheless, in spite of these abuses, "struck with admiration at his gallantry," Greene ordered a "soldier's burial" for the gallant major. They buried him near the graves of the dead defenders of the Union. Leigh might have appreciated the honor if not the company.[47]

After the third attack failed, Johnson yielded to failure and, according to Ewell, to reports from the cavalry that heavy columns of infantry were moving to turn his left. Ewell sent Campbell Brown to look into the reports of the turning movement and found them false. But the reasons at hand were persuasive enough. Johnson wrote, "The enemy were too securely entrenched and in too great numbers to be dislodged by the force at my command." Then he noted that the enemy, Colgrove's brigade perhaps, had made an assault on his left and rear that had been checked by the 2d Virginia Regiment and by Smith's brigade. His attacks were over: "all had been done that it was possible to do."[48]

Walker drew the Stonewall Brigade back to avoid "a useless sacrifice of life," but an hour or so later it went forward again, not in an attack, but to discourage any counterattacks by the enemy on the hill. At Johnson's order, Daniel's brigade fell back to the creek, but it left skirmishers behind to screen its position there. The 2d Virginia Regiment continued its skirmishing on the east side of Rock Creek opposite McAllister's Woods until evening—obviously Johnson wanted no Union soldiers harassing his left flank. Also on the left, Johnson removed Smith's brigade from its position near Spangler's Spring and sent it across the creek, but after some rest, it returned to the west side, where it remained until after dark. After rallying at the stone wall when its attack failed, Steuart's brigade remained there for another hour or so. Before it withdrew to the creek bottom, it was "exposed to a fire of artillery and infantry more terrific than any experienced during the day, although less disastrous." Randolph McKim remembered the brigade's retreat from Culp's Hill, "marching steadily down that hill of death, while the heroic Capt. Geo. Williamson and another staff officer [probably McKim himself], with drawn swords, walked backwards (face to the enemy) to steady them,—never breaking into a run, never losing their order,—and I say, 'Then and there was the supreme exhibition of their soldierly qualities!'"[49]

18

COUNTERATTACKS NEAR SPANGLER'S SPRING

John Wesley Culp returned to his native Gettysburg on 1 July 1863, not with other Gettysburg men in Company K of the 1st Pennsylvania Reserves but as a private in Company B, 2d Virginia Infantry! Wesley was the son of Jesse Culp and the great-grandson of Christobel Kolb, who had owned the Culp farm and Culp's Hill. Now Wesley's cousin, Henry Culp, owned the farm, but Wesley would probably have felt at home there if only because Gettysburg's swimming hole was nearby at Rock Creek.

Wesley and his brother William had worked for a Gettysburg carriage maker who had moved his business to Shepherdstown, Virginia. Wesley had gone with his job, but William remained behind. After living in Shepherdstown awhile, Wesley joined the local militia company, probably for social reasons as much as any other, but when war came, he had to make a choice. For his own reasons, the twenty-two-year-old carriage maker abandoned his allegiance to his native Pennsylvania and, with his Shepherdstown militia comrades, entered Virginia's service at Harpers Ferry as a member of Company B, 2d Virginia Infantry, commanded by Henry Kyd Douglas. There the diminutive Pennsylvanian (he was about five feet tall) with a cut-down musket must have created some comment.

Probably Wesley spent 2 July on Brinkerhoff's Ridge with his regiment. Sometime after his arrival and before the morning of 3 July, he managed to visit his sister Julia and some other relatives. Local lore holds that at this time he told of having seen another Gettysburg man, Cpl. Johnston H. Skelly of the 87th Pennsylvania Regiment, at Winchester a couple of weeks before. Skelly had been mortally wounded in the battle there

Pvt. John Wesley Culp (GNMP)

and had given a message to Wesley to deliver to Mary Virginia Wade in Gettysburg. Unfortunately, the message would not be delivered.[1]

At about 2:00 A.M. on 3 July, the 2d Virginia and the Stonewall Brigade left Brinkerhoff's Ridge and crossed to the west bank of Rock Creek, where they joined Johnson's division on the slope of Culp's Hill. General Johnson sent the brigade to the base of the lower hill to support Steuart's brigade, which now occupied the captured Union works and the stone wall beyond them. The 2d Virginia took its place on the left of the Stonewall Brigade's line, about thirty yards from the captured works, with its left near Rock Creek. It was in position there at daybreak when the artillery opened, and it felt the wrath of the enemy's "heated fire, of shot, shell, grape, and musketry." The regiment advanced to the works in its front for it seemed that the enemy, probably the 1st Maryland, Potomac Home Brigade, was trying to turn and enfilade the Confederate left.[2]

In order to meet the perceived threat against the Confederate flank, General Walker moved Colonel Nadenbousch and his 2d Virginia Regiment further left to the support of the 1st North Carolina Infantry. Six companies of the 1st North Carolina occupied a large cluster of boulders at the base of the southeast slope of the hill near the stone wall. From this place, they could cover a portion of the meadow east of Spangler's Spring and guard the Confederate left. At this time, four other companies of the North Carolina regiment were on a picket line east of Rock Creek. The six companies would remain among the boulders until relieved by Smith's brigade; then they would rejoin Steuart's brigade higher on the hill.[3]

After the 2d Virginia took position by the meadow between the creek and Spangler's Spring, Nadenbousch sent Lt. John S. Harrison and Company D across the creek so that it could distract the enemy by firing into his flank. Nadenbousch then advanced his remaining eight companies toward the meadow, where they poured an oblique fire at a Union force that was attacking there. When the Federals refused to give way, Nadenbousch moved two companies to his left and rear at the bend of the creek, where, he said, they were at the head of the meadow and had a full view of the enemy. He also sent some other companies across the creek. Troops in these new positions could sweep the lower meadow with fire and make it hot for the Federals in McAllister's Woods. After Nadenbousch made these dispositions, the Confederates repulsed the presumed Federal attack.[4]

The Federal troops opposite the Confederate left, of course, were those of the First Division, Twelfth Corps. McDougall's brigade was between McAllister's Woods and the Baltimore Pike, and its 20th Connecticut Regiment was in the woods on the lower hill pressing Steuart's left from the west. The Third Brigade, now under Colonel Colgrove, was in McAllister's Woods itself, where it was separated from the Confederates on Culp's Hill by the soggy meadow. The opposing lines were not on the edge of the meadow but were on higher ground well into the trees.

Colgrove's brigade had four regiments in McAllister's Woods: the 2d Massachusetts, the 3d Wisconsin, the 13th New Jersey, and the 27th Indiana. The 107th New York was now in support of the batteries along the pike. The 2d, 3d, and 27th regiments had been in the woods the day before and had erected breastworks there that faced Rock Creek just to the east and afforded cross fire over the meadow just to the north. At daybreak on the morning of 3 July, as the light grew stronger, the regiments facing the meadow realized their vulnerability to the Confederates about 100 yards away and tactfully moved to higher ground back in the trees. The 13th New Jersey faced Rock Creek with two of its left companies refused to face the meadow. The 2d Massachusetts and 3d Wisconsin regiments fronted toward the meadow, and the position of the 27th Indiana cannot be known with certainty. Colgrove recalled that the Hoosiers faced the meadow, but others placed them to the right or rear of the 13th New Jersey. The 3d Wisconsin, whose line was about thirty yards to the left and rear of that of the 2d Massachusetts, had two companies scattered as skirmishers along the edge of the woods throughout the morning, and the 2d Massachusetts had at least one company there.[5]

The 3d Wisconsin's skirmishers exchanged fire with the Confederates in their front. Capt. Julian W. Hinkley recalled that the Twelfth Corps line was strong and active but that the Confederates did not seem to be in strong force. The companies of the 3d Wisconsin, which traded places on the skirmish line from time to time, were on the left of the brigade line and directed their fire obliquely to the right. Hinkley had a "field glass" that he used for spotting targets for his riflemen.[6]

The 2d Massachusetts, to the right front of the 3d Wisconsin, rested above the meadow under cover of trees and rocks in the woods. Because they had some shelter, the enlisted men were able to eat some of their scarce rations, but many officers, who had to provide their own food, could not leave the area to get it and had to go hungry. Probably the men of Company E under Capt. Thomas R. Robeson went hungry too. Their skirmish line was so close to the Rebels beyond the meadow, and they had such little cover, that they had to be very careful. The Confederates shot several of them, and one who was in an exposed position was wounded so badly that he was helpless. Robeson, "a brave officer and true gentleman," stepped from the cover of the tree line, exposing himself to the Confederate marksmen, took the wounded man in his arms, and carried him to shelter.[7]

The 13th New Jersey and the 27th Indiana near Rock Creek had a special problem on the morning of 3 July. Skirmishers from the 2d Virginia and 1st North Carolina sniped at them from across the creek. They shot from behind rocks and trees on the hillside above Rock Creek and from the cover of the ⁁Z.⁝ Taney house. It was a small stone building about 200 yards from the creek on a nose of the hill that pushed into the floodplain opposite McAllister's Woods. These marksmen proved quite a problem for the Twelfth Corps troops who could not cross the creek and get at them. The men of the 13th New Jersey became especially irate when one of the snipers shot a stretcher-bearer who had gone to help a wounded man. Someone, probably Col. Ezra A. Carman of the 13th New Jersey, sent for Lt. Charles Winegar, whose New York battery had sections of Parrott

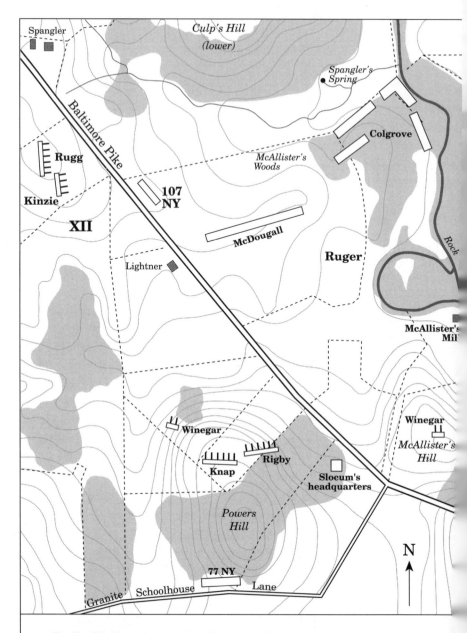

Culp's Hill (lower)

Spangler

Spangler's Spring

Baltimore Pike

Colgrove

McAllister's Woods

Rugg

107 NY

Kinzie

XII

McDougall

Ruger

Lightner

Rock

McAllister's Mill

Winegar

Winegar

McAllister's Hill

Rigby

Knap

Slocum's headquarters

Powers Hill

N

77 NY

Granite Schoolhouse Lane

1. The Twelfth Corps batteries fire throughout the morning at areas occupied by Confederate infantry.

2. Slocum sends Neill's brigade to guard the Federal right. Neill posts the 7th, 43d, 49th, and 61st regiments on the hill near the J. Taney house. They skirmish there with companies of the 2d Virginia Regiment.

3. Slocum's headquarters is on Powers Hill, about 200 feet west of Baltimore Pike. The 77th New York is posted nearby in support of the batteries on the hill.

Map 18.1. The Union Far-Right, 3 July

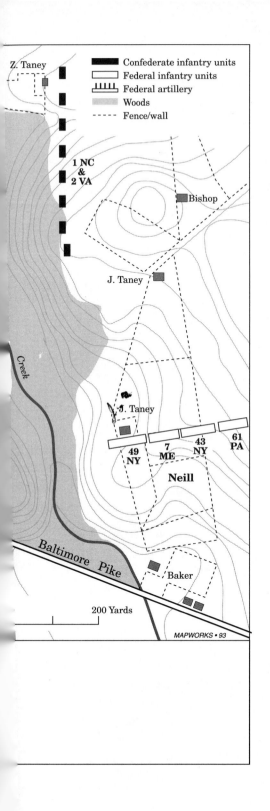

Z. Taney

Confederate infantry units
Federal infantry units
Federal artillery
Woods
Fence/wall

1 NC
&
2 VA

Bishop

J. Taney

Creek

J. Taney

49
NY

7
ME

43
NY

61
PA

Neill

Baltimore Pike

Baker

200 Yards

MAPWORKS • 93

Col. Silas Colgrove (WLM)

rifles on both McAllister's Hill and Powers Hill. Winegar came down and studied the site. He moved one of his guns from Powers Hill west across the pike to a place where it could get a good shot at the house. The gun fired a few shots and hit it. The Jerseymen cheered the lucky shots that drove the Rebels from the building. Unfortunately, the Rebel snipers returned to it again after the firing ceased.[8]

At 7:00 A.M., according to Nadenbousch's report, Smith's brigade relieved the 2d Virginia west of the creek, and Nadenbousch shifted his entire regiment to the east side of the creek, where it was to spend the day in brisk skirmishing. The troops in McAllister's Woods held most of the 2d's interest for a while, but, in the course of the morning, a brigade of the Sixth Corps also demanded some of Nadenbousch's attention.[9]

On the evening of 2 July, shortly after its arrival on the field, the Third Brigade, Second Division, Sixth Corps, commanded by Brig. Gen.

Thomas H. Neill, was sent to Slocum's aid. It went at once to Powers Hill, "a height crowned by a battery," which, Neill understood, General Meade had ordered held "at all hazards." At this time, Neill's men saw stragglers from Cemetery Ridge and heard the sounds of Johnson's attack on Culp's Hill, but the Union right seemed to be holding. To the Sixth Corps men, "the scene on the field at this hour was terrible." There was a cloud of smoke over some "slight eminence" in their front, perhaps Cemetery Hill, and "upon the black linings of this cloud continually played the flashings of a battery which was thundering at the enemy from the summit of the knoll." While waiting there, Neill received orders from Slocum to go to Geary's and Wadsworth's support, and he moved his brigade closer to Culp's Hill. When the fighting died, Neill returned his brigade to Powers Hill, where it remained for the rest of the night.[10]

On the following morning, Slocum ordered Neill to take two regiments

Brig. Gen. Thomas H. Neill (WLM)

to the extreme right of the army to keep the enemy from turning that
flank. Neill had five regiments: the 7th Maine, the 43d, 49th, and 77th New
York, and the 61st Pennsylvania. He led the 7th Maine and 43d New York
back to the Baltimore Pike, crossed Rock Creek, then turned left through
the Baker farmyard and climbed the steep slope behind it. Neill and Lt.
Col. Selden Connor of the 7th Maine rode ahead to the top of the hill and
saw the J. Taney house ahead. Neill suggested that they occupy the house,
but as he spoke, some Confederate skirmishers already there fired a fusillade in their direction. At this, Neill told Connor to use his own discretion
about taking the house and went back for the rest of the brigade. Connor
led the two regiments at hand in a rush for a wall near the house that was
about 100 yards to their front and took position there. In the meantime,
Neill brought up the 49th New York and the 61st Pennsylvania regiments.
The four regiments established a line behind a wall that ran from the brow
of the hill overlooking Rock Creek on the left, east across an open field to
some woods about 200 yards away. It is something of a commentary on
the practices of the time that the 77th New York Regiment, 400 strong,
remained at Powers Hill, where there was no immediate threat, to guard
Slocum's headquarters and to support the batteries there.[11]

There was skirmishing in the open fields and woods in front of Neill's line but no heavier action. Colonel Nadenbousch described the 2d Virginia's part in it: "I advanced some distance on the left, driving the enemy's skirmishers from and taking possession of the heights at this point, where I remained during the day, skirmishing with and inflicting some injury on the enemy by killing, wounding, and taking some prisoners, and keeping the left flank clear." Of his brigade's part in the battle, Neill reported simply that it was sent to the right to prevent the enemy "from turning us." He went on to say that "upon taking position, I felt the enemy strong in sharpshooters, and put my whole brigade in position there, and stopped them from going any farther." Connor wrote that the 7th Maine had had "smart skirmishing" but was not heavily engaged.[12]

In later years, some of Neill's veterans took satisfaction in the exaggerated belief that they had prevented Ewell from turning the Federal right. One man wrote that they had poured a heavy volley into the enemy, who, thinking that they had a heavy force on their left, withdrew. We know today that Neill's brigade was dealing with just a portion of the 2d Virginia Regiment and maybe some of the 1st North Carolina who were screening Johnson's left flank and that Neill's presence probably did not influence events on Culp's Hill.[13]

Neill's brigade did what it had been ordered to do, but there were those who wondered why it did not do more. Some soldiers of the 27th Indiana Regiment who, like others in McAllister's Woods, were harassed by Confederate fire from east of Rock Creek throughout 3 July wondered why Neill's brigade had not driven the Virginians from their front. The brigade, which had 1,400 officers and men, certainly had the strength to try it. Perhaps the reason lies in the explanation that the 7th Maine, and the brigade, was "to hold the line thus taken but not to force the fighting, as General Meade intended only to hold the line in this place."[14]

During the early hours of 3 July, when Johnson launched two assaults against Geary's division, there was only limited action on the Twelfth Corps right in the Spangler's Spring area. The 20th Connecticut continued its battle among the trees on the south slope of the lower hill. Pvt. Horatio D. Chapman recalled advancing through the dead and wounded left in the wake of the Confederate counterattack of early morning, the withering fire delivered by Rebels from behind the wall, and the advances and retreats. When the Rebels forced the Connecticut men back, the artillery along the pike opened fire again, "the shell passing just over the heads of our men and exploding in the rebel ranks." A Connecticut soldier recalled "the sharp and almost continuous reports of the twelve pounders, the screaming, shrieking shell that went crashing through the tree tops;

the deadened thud of the exploding shell; the whizzing sound of the pieces as they flew in different directions; the yells of the rebels when they gained a momentary advantage; the cheers of the men when the surging tide of battle turned in our favor."

The 20th Connecticut continued its battle until about 10:00 A.M., when it pushed close to the stone wall. At this time, momentous events took place in the meadow to the 20th's right and on the hill's west slope. The latter events and the 20th's part in them will be covered below.[15]

Over the hill to the east of the 20th Connecticut there was another phase of the action. When Smith's brigade arrived to relieve the 2d Virginia and guard the left of the Confederate position on the hill, Lt. Robert W. Hunter of General Walker's staff watched the 49th and 52d Virginia regiments take position along the wall near Rock Creek. These Virginians had formed first behind Johnson's left and then moved down to the wall between the creek and the hill. There they claimed to have dislodged "a large body of the enemy near the left flank of that division" from its position. The identity of the body of the enemy forced from its position is concealed by the fog of war, for only the 1st Maryland Regiment, Potomac Home Brigade, and the 20th Connecticut were on the north side of the meadow that morning. Hunter saw the Virginians approach their new position with a rush. General Smith led them in, "taking the highest pos. he could find, reckless of shot and shell, with bare head & sword in hand, pointing to the enemy." In response to the general's leadership, the Virginians shouted, "Hurrah for Governor Smith," a shout that "went along the lines like an electric current, mingling with the sullen roar of the enemy's cannon." It was all very glorious in the memory of some.

Lt. Cyrus Coiner of the 52d Virginia, however, recalled it a bit differently. As he saw it, Smith had led them into battle without orders, they were badly cut up, and they accomplished nothing. The enemy was hidden by rocks and trees, no doubt those of McAllister's Woods, and Smith had taken them too far forward. Lt. Col. John D. Ross of the 52d asked that they either charge or drop back to cover, for they could not stay where they were. Coiner believed that they should have charged, but, as later events would prove, making a charge would not have been the thing to do.[16]

If there was an illusion of a heavy fight, it might have stemmed from the artillery fire that poured in on Smith's brigade. Sgt. Osborn Wilson of the 31st Virginia wrote of the 31st's coming from the York Pike and joining the other regiments while the artillery fire was coming in. Wilson thought it terrible, the most fearful that they had ever experienced. They could only lie close to the ground and pray. Capt. Robert D. Funkhouser thought it was "the most deadly fire of musketry and cannon I was ever under." Pvt. James E. Hall found it to be "a very trying place, as the grape shot and minie balls came to us at right angles." Something struck him on the knee, and he considered himself lucky to get out of the battle alive.[17]

General Ruger echoed these Confederate comments about the fighting that morning, except that from his perspective it was the Confederates who were "maintaining the attack with great constancy, throwing forward fresh troops from time to time, suffering severely, but gaining no advantage, while our own loss was comparatively slight." Ruger knew little of what was taking place on Geary's front (described in chapter 17) because the lower hill and its trees screened it from his view. Yet the constant roar of musketry there, rising and falling throughout the morning, would have told him that Geary's division was bearing the heavier burden of the fight. At about 10:00 A.M., according to Ruger's recollection, he received a direct order from Slocum, not through Williams, to attempt to carry that portion of his original line on Culp's Hill then occupied by the enemy. This was to be done with two regiments. Along with the order came the observation that the enemy seemed to be "becoming shaky" or words to that effect. Instead of complying with the order immediately, Ruger questioned it. He believed that the enemy still held the position to be attacked in force and that to assault it would only result in heavy losses. He asked instead that he be allowed first to determine the strength of the enemy there; whether or not he attacked would depend on what he learned by this reconnaissance. General Slocum accepted the suggestion.[18]

The order then, as Ruger described it, was "to try the enemy on the right of the line of breastworks, to the left of the swale, with two regiments, and, if practicable, to force him out." All in all, considering what was happening on Geary's front, the order had some logic. Certainly, if Ruger's people could get a lodgment on the southeast slope of the lower hill to Johnson's left and rear, they might assist Geary immeasurably. Yet the Confederate position still seemed to be a strong one, and the attempt promised to be costly.[19]

After Slocum's order was modified, Ruger sent Lt. William M. Snow of his staff to Colonel Colgrove with his instructions. Colgrove was to advance skirmishers against the enemy beyond the meadow, and if he found the Rebels "not in too great a force," he was to "advance two regiments, and dislodge him from the breastworks." After sending Colgrove these orders, Ruger rode out to the right of McDougall's line where he could watch Colgrove's advance and send support from McDougall's brigade if Colgrove's effort promised success.[20]

Snow carried the order to Colonel Colgrove. Snow spoke only to Colgrove, and he insisted later that he had repeated the order to Colgrove as Ruger had given it to him. Some members of the 27th Indiana Regiment saw the two officers converse but did not hear most of what was said. They believed that Colgrove, their colonel, took special pains to be sure that he understood the order and that he had doubts about being able to carry it out. In fact, a sergeant of the 27th Indiana remembered seeing Colgrove tug on his nose, something he did when pondering a problem, and hearing him say, "It cannot be done, it cannot be done." Then he added, "If it can be done, the Second Massachusetts and the Twenty-seventh Indiana can do it." However, if Colgrove had qualms, he did not take his concerns to Ruger.[21]

Col. Silas Colgrove was forty-seven years old at this time, a native of western New York, and a resident of Westminster, Indiana. He was a lawyer and, like many of his colleagues, had been active in politics and had served in the state legislature and as a prosecuting attorney. When war came, he became a captain in the 8th Indiana, a three-month regiment, in spite of his age and served with it in western Virginia. After the 8th was mustered out in August, he became colonel of the 27th Indiana Regiment, a post that he held until the regiment was mustered out in November 1864. He was brevetted a brigadier general in August 1864. Colgrove was a feisty fellow. General Ruger termed him "not only a brave officer but also impetuous." One veteran of the corps described him as "a brave and sagacious officer" who "possessed to an extraordinary degree the confidence and affection of his men."[22]

What was it that Colgrove feared could not be done? As Colgrove recalled, Lieutenant Snow arrived at a time when he had heard cheering on Geary's front that indicated to him that Geary had dislodged the enemy and retaken his works. Also at this time, he discovered that the First Brigade had advanced into the woods, presumably those on the lower hill, and had formed a line at a right angle to his own. In short, as Colgrove understood it, the corps was driving the enemy to his left. Snow gave him the order, "The general directs that you advance your line immediately." Since he had room for only two regiments in line, this meant to Colgrove that he was to open the attack with only two regiments. Furthermore, as he saw it, he could not send the regiments forward behind a skirmish line. Why? The meadow was open, there was no cover, and it was only about 150 yards across. The enemy was on the far side sheltered by rocks, trees, and the wall and would cut down the skirmishers as soon as they left the cover of the trees. Colgrove believed that his only hope of carrying the enemy position was by storming it.[23]

Colgrove selected the 2d Massachusetts and the 27th Indiana to make the attack. He did not say why, but perhaps he chose the 2d Massachusetts because it faced the meadow and could simply start across it. The 3d Wisconsin was to the 2d Massachusetts's left and rear, perhaps back far enough for it to constitute a second line. The 13th New Jersey had two companies to the right of the 2d Massachusetts fronting the meadow, while its remaining eight companies faced the creek and the Confederates on the other side. The position of the 27th Indiana has not been described clearly, but it is likely to have been to the right of the 13th New Jersey and, perhaps, to its rear and fronting toward the creek.[24]

Therefore, he selected the 2d Massachusetts because it was a good regiment and was in position to advance. He probably selected the 27th Indiana because it was his regiment and he knew it. In addition, it seems likely that it was freer to leave its position than was the 13th New Jersey, which was busy skirmishing with the Confederates across the creek. It is also tempting to believe that he might have selected the 27th to avoid probable charges of favoritism that would be levied if he allowed it to sit behind while others made the dangerous attack.[25]

Colgrove ordered Lt. Col. Charles Mudge of the 2d Massachusetts to charge the enemy's line in front of the regiment's position. He told Lt. Col. John R. Fesler of the 27th to attack at an oblique to the right in order to "carry the position held in the ledges of rock." Therefore, it appears that Colgrove directed the assault toward the area between the works on the lower hill and the boulders and wall between the works and the creek.[26]

Colonel Colgrove sent the order to attack to Mudge by a "messenger" who was not named. Lt. John A. Fox, Mudge's adjutant, was with him when the messenger arrived. In his presence, Mudge asked the man, probably a staff officer, to repeat the order a second time and then asked some questions.

"Are you *sure* that is the order," asked Mudge.

"Yes," the man replied.

"Well," said Mudge, "it is murder, but it's the order."

There was no time for delay; the regiment was formed well enough to go forward. Mudge turned to face his men and shouted, "Up men, over the works! Forward, double quick!"

The men of Massachusetts gave a Yankee cheer, sprang over their wall, and "with bayonets unfixed" trotted forward at a double-quick into the

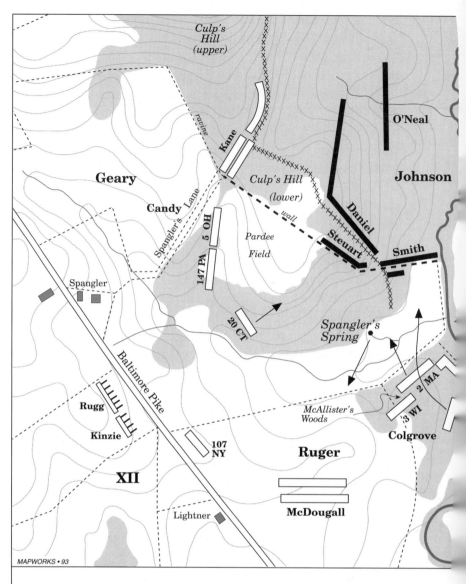

1. Johnson's last attack has failed. Steuart's brigade has fallen back to the shelter of the wall and works on the south slope of the lower hill.

2. Colgrove is ordered to attack the Confederate left across the meadow from his position in McAllister's Woods. It is manned by Smith's brigade .

3. Colgrove orders the 2d Massachusetts and 27th Indiana regiments to attack.

4. The 2d Massachusetts advances northwest toward Spangler's Spring. It is repulsed and retreats to the left.

5. The 27th Indiana advances north against Smith; it reaches a point midway across the meadow and is driven back.

Map 18.2. Counterattack at Spangler's Spring, 3 July

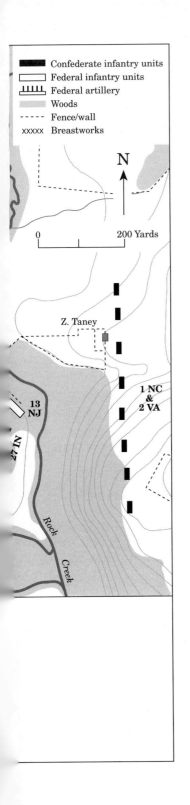

Confederate infantry units
Federal infantry units
Federal artillery
Woods
Fence/wall
xxxxx Breastworks

N

0   200 Yards

Z. Taney

1 NC
&
2 VA

13
NJ

27 IN

Rock

Creek

Lt. Col. Charles R. Mudge (MM)

meadow, moving as fast as good order and the soggy ground would allow. Captain Robeson's Company E joined the main line as it passed into the meadow but without Robeson—he fell with a mortal wound, one of the first in the regiment to fall in the charge.[27]

It was much more difficult for the 27th Indiana to get under way. Colgrove was near the 27th when Ruger's order came, and he told Lieutenant Colonel Fesler to go forward. Fesler reported that the 27th advanced immediately, but the unofficial accounts of what happened state that there was more to it than that. It was necessary for the 27th to change front for it was facing Rock Creek at a right angle to the direction it was to charge. Fesler faced the regiment about and started it off, at double-quick time, in a right half wheel—through the trees. Hardly had it started though when the 27th Indiana and the 13th New Jersey "ran plump into each other." For a brief time, there was confusion, and a heated exchange of insults and profanity, no doubt. Colgrove was on the spot though and gave orders to both regiments. As soon as the 27th was back in line, "in shrill, piercing tones"

Colgrove commanded, "Twenty-seventh, charge! Charge those works in your front." Fesler and other officers repeated Colgrove's commands and with "a wild, prolonged shout" the men leaped over the breastworks of the 2d Massachusetts and were off.[28]

Only the unofficial accounts of the 27th mention the collision, and, of course, they blamed it on wrong commands given by officers of the 13th New Jersey. A New Jersey man wrote only that the 13th's companies that were fronting on Rock Creek were moved around to the breastworks vacated by the 2d Massachusetts at Colonel Colgrove's orders. At the same time, the 3d Wisconsin advanced from its position to the edge of the meadow so that it would be better able to support the 2d Massachusetts.[29]

Colgrove's account of the charge suggests that the 2d Massachusetts and the 27th Indiana advanced at the same time, but this was not so. The 2d Massachusetts started several minutes ahead of the 27th Indiana, and, though the 27th passed through the 2d Massachusetts's position to reach the meadow, their paths diverged. Undoubtedly, the difference in their starting times stemmed from the Hoosiers' difficulty in changing front and their need to follow the 2d Massachusetts into the meadow.[30]

Confederate skirmishers opened a scattered fire when the 2d Massachusetts debouched from the trees and began to cross the "mowing." The 2d advanced in a straight line to the northwest that took it across the front of the 3d Wisconsin and between the 3d and the Confederates. The first Confederate fire, which was felt even before the Massachusetts men entered the meadow, was bothersome only to the few whom it happened to hit. The 2d's line moved onto the field, then halted and fired a volley that caused the Confederate skirmishers to beat a hasty retreat to the cover of the woods and works behind them on the hill. The Bay Staters moved forward again, pressing closely after the retreating skirmishers. As they neared the Confederate position, within a few rods of it in the memory of one soldier, the Confederates blasted them and their "thin line melted away under that withering fire as the dew does under the scorching rays of the summer's sun." From where they were, all that the Massachusetts men could see of their enemies were heads above the rocks and rifles blazing away. Then a party of Rebels moved out toward the Massachusetts right in a seeming attempt to close around their flank and capture them. It was a tight spot. It was at this point that the 27th Indiana appeared off to the right and provided some distraction to help the Massachusetts men.[31]

In such a circumstance as this, the 2d Massachusetts's color-bearers were an obvious and inviting target. Color Sgt. Levitt C. Durgin received a "death wound" before the regiment had gone fifty yards; Cpl. Rupert J.

Sadler took the flag from him, and a bullet killed him a moment later; then Cpl. James Hobbs took his turn and received a wound that he survived. Pvt. Stephen A. Cody seized the color from Hobbs before it hit the ground, and, springing onto a rock in front of the Confederate position, he flaunted the flag in their faces until they shot him dead. Pvt. James Murphy seized the flag from the heroic Cody and finally bore it from the field.[32]

When the men of the 2d Massachusetts vaulted their works to advance, the men of the 3d Wisconsin shouted, "See there goes the 2d." Col. William Hawley cautioned his officers to be ready to follow the 2d in, but the orders to do so did not come. As the Wisconsin men watched the drama before them, they heard the loud crash of Confederate rifles and saw their Massachusetts comrades "being cut down in our front like grass before a prairie fire," an analogy the easterners in the Army of the Potomac would not have used. About this time, they saw the 27th Indiana move onto the meadow off to their right. In the words of Sgt. A. Sheridan Jones, "It was an awful moment."[33]

At Colgrove's shrill command, the good soldiers of the 27th Indiana Regiment hustled down the short wooded slope to the meadow with a cheer. The 2d Massachusetts had stirred up a hornet's nest beyond the meadow so that bullets flew into the Indiana ranks even before they left the cover of the trees. The men on the regiment's left wing were sobered by the sight of bodies of several Massachusetts soldiers at the edge of the woods—men who had been killed not too long before. After the 27th's line reached the meadow, it quickened its pace and veered somewhat to the right into the wider portion of the field. Now they could see the enemy's position more clearly, and there was a tendency to rush toward it, the officers cheering on their men, all hurrying ahead to close with the enemy and bring their punishment to an end.[34]

No one recorded whether or not the field and staff officers of the two regiments went forward on horseback. It seems likely somehow that those of the 2d Massachusetts went in on foot, but at least Maj. Thomas F. Colgrove of the 27th was mounted, up where he could be seen and present a target. At about mid-field, the major, who was with the left wing, pointed with his sword to the left. There, Lt. John Rankin, who would be wounded and become a quarrelsome veteran, saw a body of troops about 100 yards away and facing in their direction. They did not know it at the time, but it was the remnant of the 2d Massachusetts Regiment re-forming after being driven from in front of the Rebel position. All had gone as well with the Hoosiers as could be expected until they were halfway across the meadow. By this time they were in good range of the North Carolinians concealed among the boulders near the base of the hill and of Smith's Virginians behind the wall. Suddenly there was "a terrific volley . . . one of those well-aimed, well-timed volleys which break up and retard a line, in spite of itself." To Major Colgrove, who was still astride his horse, it seemed as though the volley had knocked down the three right companies. To others, it seemed as though the earth had opened and swallowed the regiment.[35]

Then, as the Rebels paused to reload, the able men of the 27th touched elbows and pushed ahead. The enemy now fired at will, a more scattered fire but still heavy. "The air was alive with singing, hissing and zipping bullets." At this time, instead of charging, the 27th paused to fire, advanced a little, and fired again. It was a recipe for disaster! The Confederates in their front had cover; they had none. Lt. William W. Dougherty, the adjutant, saw the futility of the advance and suggested a withdrawal.[36]

Like their Massachusetts counterparts, the men who bore the colors of the 27th Indiana suffered heavily. Only one or two of the nine in the color guard survived the heavy volley unscathed, and these men fell soon after. Color Sgt. John L. Files and Pvt. Christopher Melker were the only men of this select group whose names were later recalled, and neither was killed. Lieutenant Dougherty took a turn at carrying the flag. He picked it up at about the time that the regiment's forward movement stalled and waved it to inspire the regiment to move forward again, but when the line did not move and Dougherty saw that he was needed elsewhere, he planted the flagstaff in the soft soil. Then, when the regiment was ordered back, he returned for the flag and was carrying it off when Pvt. Alonzo C. Burger volunteered to carry it instead.[37]

On the Confederate side of the meadow that morning, probably at this time, Pvt. William O. Johnson of the 49th Virginia saw a Union officer on a black horse. The officer carried a large flag and was calling for his men to advance. Was it Lieutenant Colonel Fesler, Major Colgrove, Lieutenant Dougherty, or someone else? No one said if Dougherty was mounted or not—he might have been. Johnson wrote that he took deliberate aim at the officer with his rifle, he pulled the trigger, and it did not fire. He recapped the nipple, took aim, and pulled the trigger again, and it did not fire. He looked at the piece and found that a chain on the "tube protector" was blocking the hammer. He took aim for a third time, but before he could fire, a bullet struck the rifle, passed through his left hand, and buried itself in his chest. The fighting was over for Private Johnson.[38]

The 27th had advanced, had caught hell, and was ordered back by Colgrove himself. Lieutenant Colonel Fesler reported that the regiment fell back in good order to the works it had previously occupied. Not so the 2d Massachusetts—not quite yet. When its attack stalled in front of the enemy's position in the brigade's old works, it had the cover of some large rocks, particularly on its left, and was separated from the enemy in the captured works by a fringe of trees. At this time, Major Morse was near the regiment's left, but he was able to see that the 27th was falling back. Not having heard from Mudge, Morse walked toward the regiment's right in search of him and met other officers who were doing the same. Mudge had been shot through the throat and killed during the attack, and Morse was now in command. The regiment was in a tight spot. It was under the enemy's guns and had been fighting there for about ten minutes. Yet it could get little help from the brigade because the 3d Wisconsin could not fire at the Confederates without endangering the men from Massachusetts.[39]

Morse decided that the 2d Massachusetts must fall back. He faced it around and started away. The regiment exchanged a few shots with the small force that had come out to flank it and brushed it aside—Morse thought that he himself had passed a few feet from a Rebel soldier. The regiment did not retrace its steps, which would have kept it under Rebel guns all the way back to McAllister's Woods. Instead, it veered toward the pike and to a point on the low stone wall on the south side of the meadow about 200 yards west of its old position. The color company halted at the wall and the remainder of the regiment formed on it. An officer who saw the 2d's retreat remarked, "I never saw a finer sight than to see that regiment, coming back over that terrible meadow, face about and form in line as steady as if on parade."[40]

General Smith, waving his hat above his graying head, sent the 49th Virginia, supported by the 52d, into the meadow against the rear of the retreating Hoosiers. Portions of the 13th New Jersey, the 3d Wisconsin, and the 27th Indiana fired on them from McAllister's Woods, and the 2d Massachusetts shot at them from its temporary position behind the low stone wall. They drove the Confederates from the meadow without difficulty, and both sides settled down to potting at one another across the meadow again. The 2d Massachusetts, though secure enough behind its wall, was running low on ammunition, and Major Morse thought it time to take action. Pvt. Amos L. Madden volunteered to carry a message from Morse to Colgrove asking for ammunition and orders. Madden trotted off in a nonchalant fashion across the open ground to the woods, carrying his rifle at right shoulder shift. The Rebels shot at him, of course, and one

The meadow from McDougall's brigade's position. McAllister's Woods begins on the right, and Spangler's Spring is left of the lone tree right of center in the distance. The 2d Massachusetts Regiment fell back to the wall in the middle distance. (Tyson Brothers stereopticon, GNMP)

ball punctured his canteen, but Madden reached Colgrove safely. A little later, Madden returned with Colgrove's order for the 2d to return to its old position in the woods.[41]

Before venturing across the open ground to the woods, Morse asked for a demonstration by a nearby regiment, undoubtedly one from McDougall's brigade, to distract the Confederates, but none was made. No one explained why not. However, by this time the division had begun to loosen up, and two companies of the 3d Wisconsin Regiment under Capt. George W. Stephenson had swung from McAllister's Woods around to the left and had entered the woods on the south slope of the lower hill near Spangler's Spring, not far from where the 20th Connecticut would have been. Probably Stephenson's men gave Morse's some support.[42]

Morse called the 2d Massachusetts to attention, faced it about, and, when its officers had taken their places in the line, started it off for McAllister's Woods at a double-quick. It was only a short trot, done with precision, and soon the 2d was back in the woods. Even then, there was danger, for several men were wounded as they returned to their works. When the Bay Staters settled in, those men not on the skirmish line stacked arms and there was a roll call. The adjutant reported that after their harrowing experience all men were either present or accounted for. Most of the latter were dead or wounded in the meadow to their front.[43]

The firing continued from across the creek for the rest of the day. Worse, though, there were still wounded from both regiments lying in the bloodied meadow. Stretcher-bearers retrieved some of them, but others lay where they had fallen and cried for help. There were men who tried to bring them in, but it was dangerous work and they were forbidden to go. The wounded would have to wait.[44]

Colonel Colgrove's order to attack became controversial. General Ruger looked into the matter and concluded that he could not affix blame for the lamentable error—the order "was one of those unfortunate occurrences that will happen in the excitement of battle." It was a hard thing for the men of the 27th, of course, but they were Colgrove's men and would close ranks to support him. Most of the 2d Massachusetts's survivors were also understanding when all was said and done. Mudge's adjutant, Lt. John A. Fox, commented some fourteen years after the battle: "Where the mistake was made I never knew and don't care to know. . . . We never had any hard feeling towards Gen. Colgrove. He sent his own Regt. in with us, and they stood as long as brave men could be expected to."[45]

The charge at Spangler's Spring was a dramatic climax to the battle on the lower hill, but Steuart's brigade had been vexed throughout the morning by a more sustained effort. No one wrote of a direct correlation between it and Colgrove's attack, but each must have helped the other in the closing stages of the morning's fight. Early in the morning, the 20th Connecticut Regiment of McDougall's brigade deployed as skirmishers in the woods on the southwest slope of the lower hill to watch Steuart's brigade and to frustrate any attempts it might make to turn the right of Geary's division. From his vantage point, Col. William B. Wooster, the 20th's commander, kept Colonel McDougall apprised of the enemy's movements. He also sent runners to the nearby batteries asking them to "elevate & sometimes to hold up" their fire, thereby enabling them to "more accurately obtain the range of the enemy and to greatly increase the effectiveness of our shells." The Connecticut men and the Virginians had a seesaw fight. At times, the 20th advanced its left wing to deal with the advances of the enemy; at other times, Colonel Wooster had to pull the regiment back to keep it from being shelled by the Federal artillery.[46]

This tug-of-war continued until late morning, probably until the repulse of Steuart's attack across Pardee Field and Colgrove's attack at Spangler's Spring. Then the 20th was able to push all of the way to the stone wall and to the works beyond. The Confederates had abandoned the works, but their snipers still fired at the Connecticut men from the tops of trees not far away. Like most other regimental commanders, Colonel Wooster saw the battle from a restricted perspective and, oblivious to other factors, announced that with the help of the artillery his regiment had expelled the Confederates from the works. There were other reasons for the Confederate withdrawal, of course, but the 20th had fought gamely and effectively for several hours, more than any other regiment of the division, and had earned the right to boast.[47]

When the 20th Connecticut pushed to the wall and works, according to Wooster, "the last living, unwounded rebel within our lines had disappeared." Finding that his men were low on ammunition and fearing the return of the enemy before they could get more, Wooster asked Colonel McDougall for relief. It was a reasonable request, and McDougall sent the 123d New York, his own regiment, now under the command of Lt. Col. James C. Rogers, forward to take the 20th's place. In his report, Rogers wrote that "the enemy having been driven from the breastworks, it moved forward and occupied them." McDougall passed this information on to General Ruger, who ordered additional regiments into the vacated works.[48]

Lt. Robert Cruikshank had more to say of this. At McDougall's order, Lieutenant Colonel Rogers led the 123d to the rear of the 20th Connecticut. After artillery fire ceased, Rogers ordered the New Yorkers to fix bayonets and charge. The 123d rushed forward, bayonets bristling before them, and the enemy (whatever enemy there was) fell back. Rogers posted pickets immediately, and the Union soldiers moved the tree limbs that had served the Confederates as an abatis from the west side of the works to the east. Cruikshank noticed that dead soldiers lay on the ground all along the line.[49]

The works on Culp's Hill were in Twelfth Corps hands once again, and the Union right had been restored. It had been a hard fight for officers and men of both armies, but the weight of the defense of the Union right had fallen on George Greene and his brigade. Though others had fought well and had done their full duty, Greene's brigade more than any other had foiled Confederate attacks and had held the line. After the battle, Greene tallied the score. On his front alone, 3,105 officers and men of his and other brigades, including 1,350 of his own brigade, had been engaged, but no more than 1,300 at any one time. After the fight, they found 391 dead in front of his line, and they estimated that there were another 150 across the creek. They took 130 prisoners and picked up 2,000 rifles, 1,700 of which must have belonged to the enemy.[50]

General Geary gave the most astounding figure. He reported that in the fight the 3,900 officers and men of his division had fired 277,000 rounds of ammunition! This figure would not have included those fired by troops of the First Division and by Shaler's brigade. Yet in spite of the long fight and the ammunition expended by both sides, the Union victory was a cheap one in Civil War terms. The Twelfth Corps casualties numbered only 1,082, only 204 of whom were killed. Many of the others would return to fight another day.[51]

The Culp's Hill fight was a disaster for the Army of Northern Virginia. Its casualties far exceeded the 1,823 reported for Johnson's division (Daniel's, Smith's, and O'Neal's brigades were not included in this figure), and nothing was gained. When the fighting ended late on the morning of 3 July, the Union line was intact and held more strongly than before. Further, the fight had contributed little, if anything, to Confederate efforts elsewhere on the field. Through no fault of either Ewell or Johnson, the Culp's Hill battle on 3 July had begun and ended long before General Longstreet was ready to launch the attack (Pickett's Charge) against the Union center on Cemetery Ridge. Neither would aid the other. Hindsight tells us that the Confederate assault of 3 July on Culp's Hill was a tragic waste.[52]

19

3 JULY, MOSTLY AFTERNOON

In the late morning, after his last attack, General Johnson ordered his brigades back from their forward positions on Culp's Hill to the low marshy ground along the west bank of Rock Creek. A soldier of the 37th Virginia Regiment returning from the rear found them there, "sheltered behind rocks, trees or anything that would protect them." There they waited behind their skirmish lines until darkness, when they could recross the creek free from the harassment of the men in blue on the hill above them. A Marylander jotted in his diary, "At the foot of the hill, along whose crest lie so many of our dead, we sleep—poor, worn out, powder stained soldiers, our guns grasped that we may be ready to rise at a moment's notice."[1]

Colonel Nadenbousch and the 2d Virginia Regiment returned from the skirmishing on the Confederate left and rejoined the Stonewall Brigade. There were company roll calls, and when the sergeant major tallied up the companies' reports, he discovered that one man had been killed, sixteen had been wounded, and three were missing. Nadenbousch should have rejoiced at these figures, for his regiment's casualties were only a third of those of the other regiments of the brigade. The dead soldier, sad to say, was Pvt. John Wesley Culp.[2]

There had been some late morning action on Geary's front apart from the usual skirmishing. After repulsing the third Confederate assault, Geary attempted to push his picket line forward, perhaps to Rock Creek. In the works, he replaced the 122d New York of Shaler's brigade with the 82d Pennsylvania Regiment. In addition, at Geary's request, Shaler ordered five companies of the 23d Pennsylvania into the works as well. The Con-

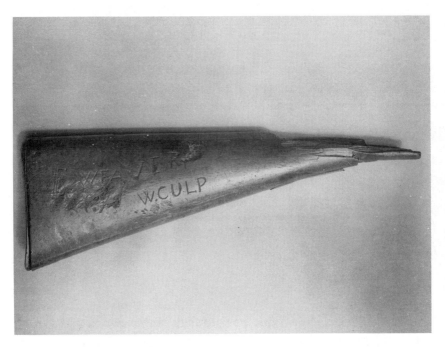

Wesley Culp's rifle stock (GNMP)

federates greeted the 23d with a heavy fire, and when it subsided, two men from each of its companies went forward to see if the enemy was still on the hill and ready to fight. They advanced only a few yards before a fusillade drove them back to the cover of the works. Within a little while, after the remaining two regiments of the brigade had spent a short time in the works, Slocum informed Meade that he could spare a brigade or two. In reply, Meade asked him to return Shaler's brigade to the army's reserve.[3]

The Union forces on the hill did not know that Johnson was abandoning the offensive and prepared to continue the battle. General Kane sat in a corner of his works, where the men of the 29th Pennsylvania busily watched the hillside and trees for Rebel snipers. Kane allowed them to use a "spyglass" that had once belonged to his brother, Elisha Kane, the Arctic explorer. Geary sent skirmishers forward under Lieutenant Colonel Redington, and there was lively sparring until sunset. On the lower hill, soldiers prepared for further action by gathering abandoned rifles, loading them, and placing them in the works ready for use.[4]

At 1:00 P.M., as if to render a coda to the heavy musketry of the morning's battle, the Confederate artillery on Seminary Ridge and at the Peach

Orchard opened the massive shelling to pave the way for Pickett's Charge. Although the troops on Culp's Hill were 1,000 yards from the target areas on Cemetery Ridge, numerous rounds fired high fell in the Twelfth Corps position, providing its soldiers with a lasting memory. Geary, in his florid manner, wrote that his troops were subjected to a galling fire "as the missiles thickly swept over and into the position occupied by us, causing a number of casualties." Sgt. John E. Anderson of the 2d Massachusetts believed that such a sound would never be heard again until "the heavens should be rolled together as a scroll." The demonic shrieking frazzled nerves, and tree limbs came crashing down. In the 29th Pennsylvania, "every man laid very close to the ground while it lasted, [and] it sounded as if all the fiends of Hell were having a whistling and shrieking match over us." The troops of the 149th New York wondered if it was better to be on the west side of the works and trees and be protected from snipers or on the east side and protected from the artillery fire.[5]

Yet, as Sergeant Anderson remarked, the guns firing at them were a mile and a half away and the shells reaching Culp's Hill were so nearly spent that some could be seen falling to the ground, where they would ricochet away, most of them not exploding. One did hit an ammunition wagon along the pike, setting it on fire and creating a "great explosion followed by the scattering [of the] wreck of that wagon as it rose in the air and then fell to the ground."[6]

When the artillery fire ceased, Slocum alerted his corps to be ready to reinforce the Union center. As it turned out, only McDougall's and Lockwood's brigades went to the center. One of Meade's staff officers met McDougall's brigade and led it to the vicinity of the Leister house. The brigade halted in column and awaited the order to deploy, but it never came. Lockwood's brigade accompanied McDougall's and halted near the cemetery. However, the Second Corps and other units repulsed Pickett's Charge without their help. After the repulse, Slocum ordered the two brigades back to Culp's Hill.[7]

When darkness came and the sniper fire ceased, the men of the Twelfth Corps relaxed behind their picket line. Lieutenant Cruikshank of the 123d New York removed his sword belt and shoes for the first time in three days and stretched out on a rubber blanket. All around him, tired soldiers slept. Suddenly, there was a rifle shot, followed by others that "all at once came rolling down the line" as the pickets opened fire. Cruikshank grabbed his sword and rushed barefoot with others of the 123d to the works. None of them had a target in the darkness, but they opened fire anyway, and each man fired a couple of rounds before the officers could bring the shooting to

Damaged trees on Culp's Hill (GNMP)

an end. When the musketry ceased, some pickets came in accompanied by some Rebel soldiers who had crawled close to the Union line and surrendered because they believed they would not be able to escape. The Rebels told Cruikshank the farfetched story that they had been sent forward to surprise, capture, and drive back the Union troops and that, had they been successful, a large force was ready to charge and turn the Union right. There were similar strikes elsewhere along the Union line that were easily beaten off; perhaps they were diversions made to cover Johnson's retreat to the east side of Rock Creek.[8]

One raid was simply a deed of daring. At about midnight, a Confederate sergeant stole up to the position of the 7th Ohio Regiment and approached its colors, which were propped against the works. The sergeant was downslope and could not reach over the head log, so he attempted to capture the colors by reaching through the slot beneath the log and raising the flag until it was high enough to topple over the parapet and into his arms. The

Confederate awakened the sleeping color sergeant, who shot and killed him. The shot aroused other sleeping Buckeyes who assumed that there was an attack and blazed away into the darkness. At daybreak of 4 July, the men of the 7th found that they had been alarmed by only one man.[9]

As the fighting of 3 July climaxed and faded on Culp's Hill, the troops on Cemetery Hill prepared for further action. The soldiers of the Eleventh Corps awakened at dawn on 3 July to the fierce rattle of musketry on Culp's Hill. They heard it swell to a great roar and saw clouds of white smoke billowing above the hill. Colonel Wainwright looked, listened, and concluded that two-thirds of the ammunition expended there must have been wasted, which spoke "badly for the pluck of the men, and cannot ever be necessary with good troops." The men of the Twelfth Corps would not have agreed.[10]

The Eleventh Corps skirmishers were busy all day long. After repulsing Early's attack on the night of 2 July, Colonel Harris formed his brigade along the wall to the left of Wiedrich's battery and facing the town. Before daybreak, Ames ordered him to move the brigade right along the wall until it abutted von Gilsa's brigade and to send a strong line of skirmishers to the front. At daybreak, his men opened a heavy fire on Gordon's skirmishers, which the Georgians returned with "vigor," and, according to Harris, this firefight continued all day long.[11]

At about noon on 3 July, General Ewell and his engineer, Capt. Henry B. Richardson, rode down Liberty Street past the left of Hays's brigade toward Gordon's position along Winebrenner's Run. Hays's men warned him that it was dangerous to ride there because the enemy's sharpshooters had the foot of the street covered with their long-range Whitworth rifles and telescopic sights. Ewell made light of their warning; he said that they were 1,500 yards off and could not shoot with accuracy at that distance. Actually, it must have been closer to 1,000 yards, and he and the captain had not gone more than twenty yards before bullets began to fly about them. One ball struck Richardson in the body, and another hit Ewell's wooden leg. When Gordon asked Ewell if he was hurt, " 'No, no,' he replied; I'm not hurt. But suppose that ball had struck you: we would have had the trouble of carrying you off the field, sir. You see how much better fixed for a fight I am than you are. It don't hurt a bit to be shot in a wooden leg."[12]

Skirmishing continued among the buildings along Baltimore Street in the south end of the town. One of these houses was the story-and-a-half brick double that stands on the northeast side of the street just north of the bend. Its northern unit was the home of John L. McClellan and his family.

Mrs. McClellan had just given birth and was bedridden. Her sister, Mary Virginia (Jennie) Wade, a woman of twenty, and her mother were staying with the McClellans to help out during her confinement.

Because Mrs. McClellan could not leave her bed, the three women remained in the house after the Union forces fell back to Cemetery Hill and the Eleventh Corps' skirmish line deployed nearby. It was a very dangerous place to be; a shell had already entered the upper floor and had punched a hole in the party wall between the McClellans' and Mrs. Isaac McLean's half of the house. It is not surprising then that on 3 July, when Jennie was kneading dough for bread, a bullet smashed through the closed door on the north side of the house, passed through an inner door that was standing ajar, and struck Jennie in the back. Nearby soldiers who heard the screams of Mrs. McClellan came to the family's aid. They moved Mrs. McClellan through the hole in the upper story into the south half of the double. Then on 4 July they buried Jennie in a temporary grave beside the house. In January her body was moved to the cemetery of the German Reformed Church and in November to its present location in the Evergreen Cemetery about 400 yards from the McClellan house. Jennie Wade was the only Gettysburg civilian killed during the battle.[13]

Cemetery Hill on 3 July was an artillery platform, a "Grand Battery." Colonel Wainwright had the same four batteries on East Cemetery Hill that were there on the evening of 2 July, but there were some changes west of the pike.

Major Osborn started the day with Dilger's Ohio battery on the right of his line near the cemetery's gatehouse. Wilkeson's (Bancroft's) U.S. battery was on Dilger's left, and Eakin's battery, now commanded by Lt. Philip D. Mason, was next in line. Each of these batteries had six Napoleons, and all were positioned to cover the town and the fields to the northwest. Taft's New York battery, with six twenty-pounder Parrotts, had two guns west of the cemetery's gatehouse firing west, while the other four were south of the gatehouse pointing toward the Rockbridge Artillery on Benner's Hill north of the Hanover Road. Huntington's (Norton's) Ohio battery faced east until the artillery duel began at 1:00 P.M.; then it changed front to the west and occupied the space on Eakin's left that had been vacated by Wheeler's guns, which had gone to the rear. Hill's West Virginia battery, whose officers and men were Ohioans, had four ten-pounder Parrotts and was facing west, and Wiedrich's section of three-inch rifles was somewhere on the left of the line. All told, Osborn started the day with thirty-six guns on the hill firing at targets in an arc from northeast to west. Later in the afternoon, Edgell's New Hampshire battery, with four three-inch Ordnance rifles, would relieve Norton's, and McCartney's Massachusetts battery from the Sixth Corps would relieve Hill's at the very close of the fight.[14]

Major Osborn wrote that his gun line followed the crest of the hill between his two flank batteries and that nearly all of the guns and caissons were "among the graves." He claimed, with probable exaggeration, that "each battery was in position as in park." This meant that there would have been a fourteen-yard interval between his guns and limbers and caissons at proper distances in the rear. The horses were hitched, and the men stood or rested at their posts "as at rest on parade." They had no earthworks in front of the pieces (why he did not say), and the reverse slope of the hill was too steep for the guns to use in order to secure cover behind the crest. Therefore, Osborn's guns stood on the crest in plain view of the enemy.[15]

There were also a few changes in the Confederate artillery opposing the Federal batteries on Cemetery Hill. The two Whitworth guns in Captain Hurt's Hardaway Artillery moved from Schultz's Woods south of the seminary to Oak Hill. This gave them a clear, though long, shot at the batteries on Cemetery Hill and removed them from the danger of fire from the Federal batteries. The guns of Watson's and Smith's batteries of Dance's battalion moved from the seminary to south of the Fairfield Road, where they could be used more effectively against the Union center. Two rifled pieces of the Salem Artillery joined them there. Ten rifled pieces from Carter's battalion went into Dance's old position astride the railroad cut. It was hoped that they would attract some of the shelling that otherwise might be poured on the advancing infantry and on Dance's guns, which were closer to the enemy. Graham's battery, the 1st Rockbridge Artillery, remained in its position north of the Hanover Road. Some guns of Nelson's battalion joined it there for a brief period, just long enough to fire twenty or so rounds.[16]

In the memories of the artillerymen on Cemetery Hill, the signal for the artillery preparation preceding Pickett's Charge came not from the Washington Artillery of New Orleans at the Peach Orchard but from the bark of a Whitworth gun that fired at them from Oak Hill. The Whitworth's bolt, making a distinctive sound, passed over their heads. According to Major Osborn, the artillery of both armies then fired very fast, he believed in excess of three shots a minute. He kept his guns supplied with ammunition by sending caissons back to the artillery park for more as soon as they were emptied. Osborn also wrote that he sent back to the Artillery Reserve for more batteries, enough to increase the number of guns on his line to sixty. Unfortunately, he did not identify the batteries that were sent to him, and we know of only one, McCartney's, which relieved Edgell's at the end of the fight.[17]

Wainwright remembered the cannonade as a roar, "as continuous and loud as that from the falls of Niagara." General Schurz said that the noise was deafening, so loud that he had to cup his hands and shout into the ears of those to whom he wished to speak. He ordered his infantrymen to lie down, but he, being a general, walked back and forth behind the infantry line, smoking a cigar. Like other generals of his time, he believed that such posturing had a good effect upon the soldiers of his division. He was so convinced of this that he encouraged some regimental officers to do the same. In the meantime, he saw that some of the troops were using this time to mend their clothes and clean their rifles. Schurz's stroll, and whatever good it did, almost ended when a solid shot struck the ground within inches of his left foot, whirling him around and covering him with dust. This near miss only confirmed his view of the value of conspicuous bravery, for nearby troops responded to his survival with cheers.[18]

Captain von Fritsch carried a message from General Ames to Schurz, and on the way back to East Cemetery Hill, he stopped to see Captain Dilger, whose battery was blazing away at a distant target. Von Fritsch pointed out enemy troops who were forming behind a fence some 1,200 yards away. Dilger aimed some guns in their direction and fired, and the fence disappeared. When von Fritsch returned to East Cemetery Hill some soldiers yelled, "Look Out! Look Out!," and he jumped to one side barely in time to escape a shell that was ricocheting in his direction.[19]

General Howard and his staff were in the middle of it all at his headquarters on the hill. He wrote:

Shells burst in the air, on the ground, at our right and left, and in front, killing men and horses, exploding caissons, overturning tombstones, and smashing fences. The troops hugged their cover, when they had any, as well as they could. One regiment of Steinwehr's was fearfully cut to pieces by a shell. Several officers passing a certain path within a stone's-throw of my position were either killed or wounded. The German boy holding our horses under the cover of Cemetery Hill, on the eastern slope, near a large rock, had his left arm clipt off with a fragment of shell. Men fell while eating, or while the food was in their hands, and some with cigars in their mouths. As there seemed to be actually no place of safety, my staff officers sat by me nearly in front of four twelve-pound Parrott guns that played over our heads, almost every available space being covered with artillery.

Howard went on to say that sabots from guns behind him sometimes hit them. To prevent this, some of the staff officers stacked some hardtack boxes between Howard and the guns as he continued to watch the Confederate lines. After an hour, Howard sent a message to General Meade saying that the enemy fire was having no great effect; the batteries on the enemy's right were not reaching them, and those in the center overshot them.[20]

Whitelaw Reid, the war correspondent "Agate," wrote that during this artillery fire he saw Howard "calmly reclining against a hillock by a gravestone, with his staff about him." He had one or two of them constantly watching the "right" and occasionally sweeping the whole Rebel position with field glasses. Reid had seen many men in action but never one so "imperturbably cool" as Howard. A minié ball whizzed overhead; Reid dodged, but he was confident that Howard had not moved a muscle.[21]

Pvt. George Metcalf of the 136th New York Regiment sweated out the artillery fire behind a wall along the Taneytown Road about seventy-five yards in front of a battery on the left of Osborn's line. He heard the firing of the Union batteries as a constant roar. Sabots and other debris fired from the guns often flew down to the infantry line and struck some soldiers hard enough to cause pain. In addition, occasional muzzle bursts were potentially lethal. As the infantrymen huddled close to the stone wall, they could look skyward and see black specks fly toward them at half-minute intervals. The specks first seemed stationary; then they would come tearing through the air with the noise of a skyrocket but "ten thousand times louder." Metcalf's knowing comrades said that the Rebels were firing pieces of train rails. The screeching Whitworth bolts (we can assume that was what they were) would hit the ground and tear out a "dozen bushels of earth, and then go bounding through the fields, something after a run, hop, skip, and jump fashion." Whitworth shells contained little powder and had limited explosive potential, but shot or shell, their peculiar noise was unnerving, and in Metcalf's words, "it frightened the whole regiment every time it came, for no live man could tell where it would hit next."[22]

Fifteen minutes after the cannonade began, Confederate shells whistled toward Cemetery Hill from the east. The twenty-pounder Parrotts of the Rockbridge Artillery and the smaller projectiles from Nelson's battalion raked the Union position on the hill. Osborn saw one round pass through six horses. Four of Taft's big guns replied to this fire along with the rifled pieces on East Cemetery Hill. The Union rounds fell closer and closer to the Virginia guns. One shell plowed into the ground beneath Lt. William B. Brown, exploded, and made a large crater into which Brown sank but emerged unhurt. Another shell burst at the trail of one gun. It wounded two cannoneers, and a fragment sliced off the leg of Captain Graham's horse. It also spooked the limber team, and as the horses turned to run, another shell struck one of them and exploded, killing all six horses, stunning a cannoneer who had grabbed their bridles, and wounding another cannoneer. In attempting to reach Graham's battery, one of Taft's guns blew off its muzzle and became useless. Taft's big guns fired 557 rounds at Gettysburg.[23]

When the cannonade was at its height, General Meade rode into the cemetery and called for Osborn. In contrast with Howard and most other high-ranking officers whom Osborn knew, Meade, like Maj. Gen. Edwin V. Sumner, had an excitable manner. He asked Osborn about his drawing ammunition from the train and seemed satisfied when Osborn told him that Hunt had authorized his doing so. He asked, "Can you stay here? Are your men thoroughly in hand?" The major assured him that his officers and men were in good condition and that they would stay. Osborn commented later that the fire was fearful then and that he was not surprised that Meade was anxious. In spite of his nervous manner, Meade seemed "cool and collected in his judgment" and showed a full appreciation of everything around him.[24]

At one point during the cannonade, Capt. Craig W. Wadsworth of the First Corps staff rode up to Osborn with a message. The two officers sat on their horses side by side, their horses head to tail and at right angles to some of the incoming artillery fire. Each horse stood quietly. As the officers talked, a percussion shell struck the ground beneath the horses and exploded. Fortunately, the shell's momentum carried its fragments away from the horses, and they escaped unharmed. Neither Osborn nor Wadsworth flinched, but, to his regret, Osborn glanced down toward where the shell had exploded while Wadsworth did not. Osborn believed that Wadsworth was the only man in the entire army who could have a ten-pounder shell explode beneath him and not glance down to see where it had struck.[25]

After the cannons had thundered for over an hour, General Howard and Osborn received a visit from General Hunt. Hunt was searching for General Meade. The ammunition supply at the Federal batteries was running low, and Hunt wanted Meade to approve an order to cease fire while they still had enough ammunition to meet the infantry assault that he believed would soon be launched. The three officers discussed this; Hunt assured them that Meade would welcome an infantry attack, and they decided to try to trigger it. In Howard's words, "At half past two P.M. we ceased to reply. We had ammunition and were not silenced, but we knew that this cannonade preceded an attack, and we thought it possible the enemy would conclude that we had been stopped by their effective shots, and would proceed to the contemplated assault; then we should need batteries in readiness, and plenty of ammunition."[26]

In the course of their conversation, Hunt asked Osborn if he could control his men if he ordered a cease-fire while the enemy fire was so heavy. Osborn assured him that "the men were under perfect control by their officers and nothing was to be feared from the order." Howard observed that a cease-fire would produce the desired effect—if the enemy intended to attack, they would do so at once. With that, Hunt said that he would order a cease-fire himself and would report what he had done when he saw Meade. Hunt rode off to Cemetery Ridge to stop the firing there, and Osborn walked his gun line from the right, ordering the cease-fire. He instructed his battery commanders to have their men take cover until the enemy fire ceased and then to be ready for any emergency. Within a short while, the Union batteries on Cemetery Hill and on Cemetery Ridge beyond the Second Corps fell silent, and soon after the enemy infantry appeared.[27]

Private Metcalf remembered that when the guns in his rear stopped firing, the silence was "awful." It was so still that he could almost hear his heart beat. Then Metcalf and his comrades saw long lines of Confederate infantry forming in front of the tree line on Seminary Ridge. He thought this martial array would have been a beautiful sight had it not been for its intent. Howard saw it too—or at least the left quarter of the mile-long line. He likened what he saw to an "extensive parade; the flags were flying and the line steadily advancing." The officers of Smith's brigade ordered their men to lie down. After they did so, "Boom! went one cannon from Cemetery Hill, and the shell went tearing through the air over our heads and burst just over the heads of the advancing column."[28]

The Federal batteries on Cemetery Hill that were able to do so concentrated on the Confederate infantry rather than the southern batteries. When firing at long range, the Napoleons used solid shot and the rifles fired shells with percussion fuses. Osborn saw that a solid shot or a shell that did not explode might cut two men out of the Confederate line but that a percussion shell that exploded in front of the line might cut down four or more men and create a gap in the enemy's line. Twice he saw the Rebel lines halt, dress, and close the gaps. After dressing their lines a second time, the infantry column passed from the view of the gunners behind the trees of Ziegler's Grove and into the embrace of the Second Corps. When seen again from Cemetery Hill, the Confederates were falling back, formations broken. The grand charge was over. "A deep sigh of relief wrung itself from every breast," remembered General Schurz. There were tremendous cheers along the Eleventh Corps line, the men began to sing "John Brown's Body," and the "song swept weirdly over the bloody field."[29]

Generals Early and Hays and some of their staff officers were napping in the town when the artillery fire began. They heard its roar and felt the ground shaking as though there was an earthquake. A courier from General Ewell galloped up with a dispatch that read, "Longstreet & A. P. Hill are advancing in splendid style—if you see an opportunity—strike." The cannons continued to roar and the ground to quiver, and then the fire seemed to slacken. Another courier appeared, this time riding slowly. Someone asked him, "What's the news?" He replied, "Longstreet & Hill have been driven back." At that news, Major Daniel felt that "the clock of the Confederacy had gone back ten years—Whipped in Pennsylvania! driven back! 'What will they think of us at home?'"[30]

20

EPILOGUE

The battle was all but over. General Lee and the Army of Northern Virginia would return to Virginia. In retrospect, Lee wrote, "The severe loss sustained by the army and the reduction of its ammunition, rendered another attempt to dislodge the enemy inadvisable, and it was, therefore, determined to withdraw." So, on the night of 3 July, at Lee's orders, General Longstreet abandoned his hard-fought gains on the Confederate right and posted Hood's and McLaws's divisions in defensive positions on the extension of Seminary Ridge from which he had launched his attacks on 2 and 3 July. Hill's corps remained in the center, and Ewell ordered his corps to leave its positions in front of Cemetery Hill and Culp's Hill and in Gettysburg, which once had been deemed so vital to hold, and deploy on the army's left on Seminary Ridge near the Chambersburg Pike. The Confederates would remain on the ridge for only another day; on 4 July Lee would start a wagon train of wounded back to the Potomac crossings south of Hagerstown, and Early's division, the rear guard of the army, would leave the Gettysburg area late in the morning on 5 July.[1]

In accordance with the orders of Lee and Ewell, Johnson's division abandoned its bridgehead west of Rock Creek sometime after 10:00 P.M. on 3 July and marched via "the rear" of the town to Seminary Ridge. Early's division left its position about 2:00 A.M. after Johnson's division had cleared the area to its left, and Rodes's division deployed on the ridge astride the railroad bed. Although Ewell's corps had to leave some of its wounded behind, and there were stragglers enough, the movement came off in a quiet and orderly way that did not attract the attention of the Union forces on Culp's Hill and Cemetery Hill. At daybreak, Henry Jacobs saw that most of the Confederates had gone from his neighborhood on West Middle Street, and the only ones still to be seen there were half-drunken stragglers who were hurrying west to the shelter of the new Confederate line on Seminary Ridge.[2]

When the order came to move from Gettysburg back to Seminary Ridge, some soldiers believed that Ewell's corps was merely shifting its position before making another attack, but most must have realized that the movement was the beginning of a retreat.[3] Ewell's men found their new positions west of Gettysburg, the arena of the battle of 1 July, a desolate place. There was a heavy mist, and a dark sky added to the gloom. The fields had been trampled, the fences were gone, and the bodies of dead soldiers lay scattered about. Certainly there must have been a number of Rodes's division's dead still lying in the fields north of the railroad bed. Burial details from Daniel's brigade, and probably others, performed their gruesome chore. The corpses had been lying in sun and rain for three days and had an awful odor. Private Leon of Daniel's brigade thought it odd that "all" of the Yankees corpses had turned black. Lieutenant Jackson of the 8th Louisiana passed a "miserable" time. The battle of Gettysburg had been a series of such experiences for him.[4]

Although some Confederates believed that the battle was a draw and found encouragement in General Meade's not attacking them, even they could not avoid reality. Lt. Green B. Samuels of the 10th Virginia wrote his wife that Maryland was lost forever, and thousands of brave men had perished needlessly. Pvt. Ted Barclay of the 4th Virginia confided later to his sister that so many of his friends had been killed that he felt lonesome but did not cry.[5]

In retrospect, Maj. John Daniel, recalling the emotions of 4 July, wrote that "every ingredient that could add to the poignancy of their grief was mingled in the cup." They had experienced the height of anticipation until 2 July and then had plunged into the depths of despair; he feared that they would disappoint their friends at home and that their hard marches and hard fighting had gained nothing. Furthermore, they would be moving off leaving hundreds of their dead unburied and their wounded in the care of the enemy. He believed that they had made a fatal mistake in not charging Cemetery Hill on 1 July and, afterward, in continuing to fight at Gettysburg. He was not alone in having second thoughts, for soon after the battle, many Confederate soldiers looked for reasons for their defeat. They were certain that Stonewall Jackson would have brought them victory. Therefore, Ewell, and perhaps Hill, were responsible for their defeat. Lt.

Micajah Woods voiced the views of many in the army. He criticized Hill for not supporting Longstreet, but his greatest criticism was of Ewell for not following up his "magnificent success" on 1 July and seizing Cemetery Hill and Culp's Hill before the Yankee army fortified them.[6]

When daylight came on the Glorious Fourth, a dismal, rainy morning, Union soldiers on the skirmish lines in front of Cemetery Hill and Culp's Hill soon noticed an unusual quiet in their front. A Union soldier, who had just escaped captivity in the town, told Capt. George B. Fox, commander of the 75th Ohio Regiment, that the Confederates had left the town, and Union skirmishers elsewhere pushed forward and found their adversaries gone. The departure of the Confederate skirmishers prompted an immediate and seemingly uncoordinated response from Union commanders. Scouting parties from at least three corps went into Gettysburg, and they must have gotten in each other's way.[7]

General Ames told Colonel Harris to take his brigade into the east side of the town. A veteran of the 107th Ohio wrote that those of the brigade who entered Gettysburg pushed their way through alleys, with their left on Baltimore Street. They expected to be shot by Rebel soldiers concealed in the houses. After working their way to the town square, they went by twos to search houses for Confederate stragglers and bring those whom they found back to the square. On the other hand, Lt. Oscar D. Ladley of the 75th Ohio Regiment wrote that though it was raining hard, "they went like a set of devils," encouraged by residents who smiled and waved handkerchiefs. The 75th Ohio had only thirty men in the town that morning, and he took half of them on a sweep through the area east of Baltimore Street while Captain Fox took the other half to the west. After completing his sweep, he posted his men as pickets and accepted an invitation to breakfast with gratitude, for he was very hungry. Harris's men captured a few Confederates, and the colonel claimed that his brigade was the first to enter Gettysburg.[8]

Very early in the morning, perhaps at 4:00 A.M., Lt. Paul Bachschmid and the skirmishers of von Gilsa's brigade—forty-six men from the 153d Pennsylvania and the 54th and 68th New York regiments—were told to feel out the enemy and see what was going on in Gettysburg. They pressed ahead against some light opposition and entered the town. There they took 290 prisoners and collected 250 rifles. While there, they met troops of an unnamed brigade, perhaps Harris's, which had entered the town by another route, and heard a band playing in the town square! Whose band it was, they did not report. At an early hour, young Dan Skelly had awakened in his home on Baltimore Street just south of the town square to the music of fifes and drums (field music) and had seen a squad of soldiers bearing regimental colors marching by. Perhaps it was the same band.[9]

Schurz also sent units into the town. A ten-man patrol from the 58th New York Regiment, which was posted east of Baltimore Street on the left of Wiedrich's battery, went forward at daybreak, probably by way of Baltimore Street. With the help of Gettysburg civilians, it captured several sleeping soldiers, stragglers from Gordon's brigade no doubt. Soon after, Lt. Frederick Lauber took two squads into the town and brought back 200 prisoners. Later Colonel Krzyzanowski led the 119th New York and the 26th Wisconsin regiments two miles to the east out the York Pike and returned with forty-seven prisoners.[10]

At mid-morning, Col. J. William Hofmann led the 7th Indiana and 56th Pennsylvania regiments into the northeast portion of Gettysburg, which had already been cleared of the enemy. General Wadsworth accompanied them into the town. Hofmann was to collect Union wounded who had been left in the area. He marched his regiments into the town by way of Baltimore Street and turned right on York Street at the square. As the 7th Indiana filed through the square, a bullet fired from the Confederate lines to the west struck and killed one of its men. Hofmann believed that he was the last Union soldier killed at Gettysburg. Hofmann and his men were in Gettysburg for only a half hour before he was ordered to return with his regiments to the position of Cutler's brigade on Culp's Hill.[11]

General Slocum ordered, and perhaps participated in, the longest reconnaissance of the day. At his order, General Ruger's brigade plus the 46th Pennsylvania, the 5th Connecticut, and the 123d New York assembled on the Baltimore Pike, marched southeast along it for about two miles, and then turned left on the Salem Church or Low Dutch Road. They followed this road northeast to the Hanover Road and filed west along it into Gettysburg. They left the town by way of Baltimore Street and marched along the pike back to their position on Culp's Hill. It was a long, uneventful hike of nearly ten miles on a hot, rainy day. With the advantage of hindsight, we can wonder why the men were ordered to make such a march. They had marched to their rear away from the enemy and then into the area of cavalry operations on the Union right, which had been controlled by Gregg's division of cavalry. From the scene of the cavalry battles on 2 and 3 July, they moved west into Gettysburg, which, by this time, was in the hands of the First and Eleventh corps. Perhaps the movement's greatest benefit was that it took the troops involved away from the filth and odors of Culp's Hill.[12]

The stench was everywhere that fighting had taken place. It welled up from human excrement, from the bodies of thousands of sweating men encased in wool uniforms on a hot and wet summer's day, but mostly from the corpses of men and horses. Maj. Philo B. Buckingham of General Williams's staff remembered the dead men, "some sitting up against trees or rocks stark dead with their eyes wide open staring at you as if they were still alive—others with their heads blown off with shell or round shot[,] others shot through the head with musket bullets. Some struck by a shell in the breast or abdomen and blown almost to pieces, others with their hands up as if to fend off[f] the bullets we fired upon them, others laying against a stump or stone with a testament in their hand or a likeness of a friend, as if wounded and had lived for some time. O it was an awful sight, Terrible! Terrible!" Private Mouat also thought it terrible to see the dead lying in heaps, "and as it was very warm the bodies were swollen and commenced to turn black in the face . . . froth issuing from the mouths and nose."[13]

It was desirable then that, as soon as the Confederates disappeared from the front of Cemetery Hill and Culp's Hill and it was safe to do so, burial parties bury the dead. Sgt. Sherman R. Norris of the 7th Ohio Regiment wrote in his diary of having been a "'pall bearer' to the largest funeral I ever attended, having been detailed to help bury the rebel dead in front of our brigade; and we dug a trench, into which we piled about 200 and carried off 2,000 stand of arms." Norris wrote that they gathered bodies from "perfect lines of battle," dragged them from behind rocks, and found them behind logs and scattered everywhere in their front from a few feet of their breastworks down to the foot of the hill.[14]

Lieutenant George Collins remarked that Union burial parties often wrapped the Union dead in blankets and placed them in single graves, about two feet deep. After all, on Culp's Hill there were not too many of them, and they could be given individual attention. The burial parties marked the graves with boards taken from cracker and ammunition boxes. Confederate dead, of course, were far more numerous, and most had fallen close to the Union line where their Confederate comrades could not reach them. Union burial parties, who knew none of them as individuals, interred them in long trenches near where they had fallen. Insofar as the 2d Massachusetts Regiment's dead were concerned, two men from each company remained behind to bury them while the rest of the regiment went elsewhere, perhaps on the march to the east mentioned above.[15]

One of the first orders of business for the Army of the Potomac was getting rations for the troops, many of whom had had little or nothing to eat since their arrival at Gettysburg. Some men of the Twelfth Corps had not eaten in two days, but the conditions around them were so sickening that they had difficulty keeping down whatever food they could get. The quartermaster of the 33d Massachusetts, like many others, perhaps, was able to bring up a wagon load of hardtack on the night of 3 July. It was welcome because the 33d had had nothing to eat during the battle except wheat stripped from stalks in the fields in which they fought. Some soldiers foraged and learned that civilians did not have the same "spirit of Liberality" after the battle as before it. Pvt. William Tallman of the 66th Ohio did not blame them greatly, for soldiers had helped themselves to their milk, butter, and chickens to the extent that "there was not a rooster left to tell them when to get up in the morning."[16]

Lieutenant Cruikshank of the 123d New York wrote that on 4 July the excitement of battle was over and they were nearly starved. They had not been entirely without food, for on 2 July the commissary had brought fresh beef to the field and had thrown it from wagons onto a grassy spot, where it had been in the sun for two days. Those who were hungry enough would cut slices from it, place them on a stick, broil them over a fire, and eat them without salt. Cruikshank did not eat any of the meat, for the stench of the dead men and horses took away his appetite. He wrote nothing of flies; perhaps the soldiers took them for granted.[17]

Although troops of the Eleventh and Twelfth corps made forays into Gettysburg, their reports fail to say which of them occupied the town. They also do not indicate if any troops other than skirmishers went into the fields north of the town on 4 July while the men of Ewell's corps looked down on the area from Seminary Ridge. Henry Jacobs wrote of Union troops skirmishing near his house on 4 July. When a detail of them first approached Middle Street via Washington Street, his teenage sister, Mary, stood in the shelter of the doorway of their house and warned them that Rebel soldiers had Washington Street covered from a position in Stevens's Run just west of the town. After a time, the Union soldiers made the Washington Street crossing somewhat safe by placing a barricade of barrels filled with rocks across it. Union soldiers skirmished near the Jacobs house, and a captain from Philadelphia who was in charge of them spent some of his time conversing with the Jacobs family through a parlor window on Washington Street. Once when Mary played the piano in the parlor, "her notes were accentuated by the crack of rifles a few feet away."[18]

Gettysburg was a tragic place, its public buildings brimming with wounded soldiers. After its streets became relatively safe, it must have been visited by many others on one pretext or another. General Schurz and some staff officers rode into the town on the way to the fields to the north to ascertain whether or not there were any wounded there. As he passed up Baltimore Street, he saw his old friend General Schimmelfennig, who had emerged from his hiding place in the Garlach's backyard, waving to him from the doorway of a house. Schimmelfennig invited Schurz to a breakfast of fried eggs, and Schurz enjoyed the meal before riding on to view the horrors of the battlefield.[19]

The adventurer, von Fritsch, a campaigner in the European tradition, visited Gettysburg, escaping the stench of Cemetery Hill. After spending some time that day visiting wounded officers in the hospitals, he rode into town in search of a shave and a photographer! Why he needed the photograph taken then, he did not say, but he had one snapped of himself in a uniform composed of trousers with gold stripes on the seams of the legs and a braided jacket with "extra richly gilded buttons." The jacket also displayed two golden half-moons, the insignia of the Eleventh Corps, on the collar and a pair of "rich and large" shoulder straps given to him by Kate Chase, the Washington belle.[20]

Early's division, the rear guard of the Army of Northern Virginia, left Gettysburg on the morning of 5 July, marching out the Fairfield Road on its way to Hagerstown. The Sixth Corps followed Early's people, and Howard and the cavalry assigned to his headquarters also saw them off. Howard wrote General Meade that the Confederate rear guard had been found two miles west of Gettysburg. In the course of this exercise, Howard's aide, Capt. James J. Griffiths, was mortally wounded. At 5:30 P.M., Howard received orders for the Eleventh Corps to march to Middletown, Maryland, in two days via Emmitsburg, and he started it off that afternoon. The corps marched down the Taneytown Road to the Horner's Mill area along Rock Creek and bivouacked there. It did not go far, but at least it got away from the pestiferous battlefield.[21]

On the afternoon of 5 July, the Twelfth Corps left Culp's Hill for Littlestown by way of the Baltimore Pike. After companies formed for the march, their battle losses were more apparent than they had been before. Lieutenant Collins of the 149th New York recalled that the survivors of one regiment, probably the 137th New York, whose casualties were the most numerous in the corps, looked sad and mournful as they marched away; many had eyes filled with tears. When the 2d Massachusetts passed by Slocum and his staff as it left the field, the general and his staff bared their heads to the Yankees in well-earned respect.[22]

By 6 July both armies were on the march toward the Potomac crossing south of Hagerstown. General Meade left the Gettysburg area to army personnel who were to salvage usable government property from the de-

Cemetery gatehouse with lunettes of Stewart's battery in the foreground.
(GNMP)

bris that cluttered the area, care for the wounded, and see to the burial of the dead. Gettysburg's civilians worked to restore their lives and property and to deal with the host of strangers who came in search of loved ones, living and dead, and to see the sights. Catherine Thorn returned from her refuge in the country on the "fifth day" of her flight, probably 6 or 7 July. On her way back to her home on Cemetery Hill, she met David McConaughy, president of the Evergreen Cemetery Association, who said, "Hurry on home, there is more work for you than you are able to do." When she arrived and saw the cemetery's gatehouse, she could only say, "Oh my!" Many of its windows were gone, and even some of the sashes had been knocked out, probably to fuel soldiers' cooking fires. Fifteen soldiers' graves crowded near her pump shed, and thirty-four dead and bloated horses lay nearby. It was a shambles.

She went down into the gatehouse's cellar, where she had left some chests containing linens and other valuables that she could not take with her in her flight. Almost everything was gone. All that remained were three featherbeds, valued items for people with meager resources, but they had been used by wounded soldiers and were soiled with blood and grime. After she dragged them from the house, she asked an officer who was riding by whether the government would reimburse her for such damage. He told her no. Mrs. Thorn and three other women washed the beds for four days before they were clean.

Soon after returning to the cemetery, she learned from David McConaughy that she would have to bury some soldiers in Evergreen Cemetery. He instructed her to lay out lots and dig graves as fast as possible. She, her aged father, and two hired men began the work. It was awful labor amid filth, rotting horse flesh, odors, and flies. One of the two hired men became deathly sick after two days and left; the other stayed five days before becoming too ill to continue. By this time they had dug forty graves and had presumably buried forty soldiers whose friends or relatives had purchased plots for them. Mrs. Thorn and her father had buried 105 soldiers before official burials began in the Soldiers' National Cemetery just to the north. Three months after all of this work, Mrs. Thorn gave birth to a baby girl.[23]

Two things of special importance happened in the postbattle years on Cemetery Hill and on Culp's Hill. The hills became focal points of two simultaneous projects that gave added emphasis to the significance of the battle and resulted in the preservation of much of the battlefield. David Wills was a Gettysburg attorney who had been working to remove the bodies of Pennsylvania soldiers from the battlefield to their home cemeteries. After conferring with John F. Seymour and Theodore S. Dimon, agents of New York State, and with others concerned with the wounded and dead at Gettysburg, Wills proposed to Gov. Andrew G. Curtin of Pennsylvania that there be a common burial ground for the Union dead at Gettysburg. He recommended that this cemetery be created on eight acres of East Cemetery Hill, "the key to the whole line of our defences, the apex of the triangular line of battle." Pennsylvania would take the lead in this project and would seek the cooperation of other northern states whose soldiers had fought at Gettysburg. The governor approved Wills's recommendation and appointed him Pennsylvania's agent for the project, and Wills began his work.[24]

When Wills attempted to buy the eight acres on East Cemetery Hill, he learned that they had already been purchased by David McConaughy, the president of the Evergreen Cemetery Association. McConaughy had bought this land not for the cemetery but with his own funds. He explained, "Immediately after the Battle of Gettysburg, the thought occurred to me that there could be no more fitting and expressive memorial of the heroic valor and signal triumphs of our Army . . . than the Battle-field itself, with its natural and artificial defences preserved and perpetuated

Procession to Soldiers' National Cemetery, 19 November 1863 (GNMP)

in the exact form & condition they presented during the Battles." To this end, by mid-August McConaughy had purchased Stevens's Knoll, East Cemetery Hill, the west face of Little Round Top, portions of Round Top, and portions of Culp's Hill.[25]

After these acquisitions, McConaughy proposed to several leading citizens of Gettysburg that they establish the "Gettysburg Battle-field Memorial Association." He obtained the needed support, and Pennsylvania incorporated the association on 30 April 1864. (The state later reimbursed McConaughy $6,000 of the money he had spent to purchase the land turned over to the association.) Although the association would have its ups and downs, this landmark pioneer effort in historical preservation would secure 600 acres of the Gettysburg battlefield that in 1894 would, with its 300 memorials and markers, be conveyed to the U.S. government as the nucleus of the Gettysburg National Military Park.[26]

When David Wills learned that he could not secure the tracts on East Cemetery Hill for the proposed military cemetery, he turned his attention to Cemetery Hill west of the Baltimore Pike where Schurz's and von Steinwehr's divisions and Osborn's batteries had been located. He described that area as the "centre of our line of battle" and "one of the most prominent and important positions on the whole battle field." Although McConaughy had hoped that the Evergreen Cemetery Association would manage the grounds in which the soldiers would be buried, Governor Curtin and the representatives of the various northern states involved wanted a separate and distinct cemetery for the Union dead. Therefore, Wills bought twelve acres on the hill from the Evergreen Cemetery Association and five adjoining acres for the new cemetery.[27]

The dedication of the Soldiers' National Cemetery took place on 19 November 1863, even though all of the Union soldiers buried on the field would not be interred there until March 1864. The story of the dedication ceremony and Pres. Abraham Lincoln's Gettysburg Address is a familiar one. The address gave meaning and a measure of dignity to the vast carnage that had taken place at Gettysburg (and was occurring elsewhere at the time) and has become a classic of the English language. It is ironic though that these few quiet words have overshadowed the events and people on Cemetery Hill that Lincoln intended to honor. Visitors to the battlefield remember this bastion of the Union line, which General Howard termed the "*only* position," less as the keystone of the Union defenses at Gettysburg and a place of struggle "of brave men living and dead" than as the site of the Gettysburg Address. Actions do not always speak louder than words.

Appendix A

Spangler's Spring

Spangler's Spring has long been one of the landmarks of the battlefield, although it is one of several springs in the area. It is located at the south base of the lower peak of Culp's Hill, about 150 yards west of Rock Creek. It drains into a small stream that flows around the south base of the hill, the origins of which include other springs near the McKnight house west of the hill and in the saddle between the two peaks of the hill. The stream that drains these springs flows through the marshy meadow or swale between Culp's Hill and McAllister's Woods to Rock Creek.

Gettysburg lore credits a Gettysburg resident, Henry J. Stahle, with discovering the spring in about 1847. Stahle and others were picnicking nearby, and Stahle went to search for water. He saw some wet leaves, and when he stirred them with a stick, water bubbled forth. Stahle later secured permission from the farm's owner, Mr. Spangler, to clear out the spring and wall it up, and thereafter the spring provided water for the picnic grounds nearby.[1]

When Williams's division occupied the area on the late morning of 2 July, some of its soldiers erected breastworks on the hill not far from the spring. A soldier of the 2d Massachusetts Regiment recalled being on the picnic grounds and remembered "the pellucid waters of the spring refreshingly cool."[2]

The spring gained prominence in the postwar years. A story grew that both Union and Confederate soldiers drank from it during the battle on the night of 2 July, and it is sometimes implied that they did so in a fraternal way, as they are reputed to have done on occasion between campaigns in Virginia. Such a story has had great appeal for many visitors to the battlefield.

Soldiers from three brigades were in the Spangler's Spring area on the night of 2 July. They would have been from Ruger's and McDougall's brigades of the Twelfth Corps and Steuart's Confederate brigade. Any creditable accounts of the joint use of Spangler's Spring must come, then, from soldiers of these brigades. Other sources should be viewed with skepticism.

Steuart's brigade of Johnson's division occupied the lower hill on the evening of 2 July while Williams's division was on Cemetery Ridge. When Ruger's and McDougall's brigades of Williams's division returned, they discovered that Confederates had occupied a portion of their old position and took measures to learn where the Confederates were. As the Union commanders sent patrols or skirmishers forward to gain this information, there were firefights and men were shot and captured. One account of this activity tells of the capture of twenty-three Confederates by soldiers of the 2d Massachusetts Regiment near the spring. The men taken carried canteens and "appeared to be straggling about looking for water." No other members of Ruger's brigade mention the spring in this connection. I have seen no mention of the spring in Confederate accounts.[3]

Yet three different members of McDougall's brigade tell of the spring in what seem to be credible stories. Capt. Alexander W. Selfridge of the 46th Pennsylvania Regiment later spoke of taking some of his men forward to fill canteens from where McDougall's brigade had halted on its return (perhaps it was in the meadow west of the spring). Selfridge found "Johnnies" there filling their canteens. He "backed out with the best grace he could command" and reported their presence to Colonel McDougall.[4]

Horatio D. Chapman of the 20th Connecticut Regiment recorded another account in his diary. After their return from Cemetery Ridge, Chapman and some others took canteens to the spring for water. They found other men at the spring whom they did not recognize in the darkness. Somehow Chapman "knew" that they were Rebels, and he believed that they knew that Chapman and his comrades were Yankees. According to Chapman, they filled their canteens and returned to the regiment "to the joy of our thirsty comrades."[5]

Lt. Robert Cruikshank of the 123d New York reported a similar incident. Some members of the 123d went to the spring and found other men there. Because of the darkness, the New Yorkers did not at first recognize the other men as Rebels. After filling their canteens, they returned to the regiment and reported that they had seen Confederates to Lieutenant Marcus Beadle, who was about to lead a patrol to their old position on the hill. Although Beadle did not believe the account, the information made him cautious.[6]

These three accounts indicate that Union soldiers saw men at the spring whom they believed to have been Confederates and that in the darkness a few men of each side filled canteens there at the same time. Yet they do *not* suggest that there was fraternization. Instead, they imply that there was embarrassment and tension and that the Union soldiers were glad to get away unscathed.

No one knows what the Confederates thought or felt or if they even suspected that they were in the presence of Union soldiers. It is probable that they did not. We do not know if the men going for water were armed; possibly they were not, for they were carrying canteens for others as well as themselves and were not expecting a fight.

It seems apparent from the accounts of Selfridge and Cruikshank that the visits to the spring took place immediately after the return of Williams's division and before patrols went out to learn if there were Confederates in the area and where they were. We may assume that once the soldiers of both sides learned that the enemy was nearby and blood was being shed, the visits to the spring ended until after the Confederates pulled away on 3 July.

APPENDIX B
TWO CONTROVERSIES

The battle of Gettysburg engendered several controversies. Three of the better known ones were those between Generals Longstreet and Early, between General Sickles and General Meade and his partisans, and between Generals Hancock and Hunt. None of these spats were to the credit of the participants and are significant principally because they prompted the preparation of accounts of portions of the battle that might not have been written otherwise.

Two lesser controversies relate to the subject of this monograph. One involved Generals Howard and Hancock. The battle of Gettysburg was a high point in the life of each, and each man was jealous of his reputation and did not wish to see it diminished. Howard wrote Samuel P. Bates in 1875 that he had taken "especial pride in Gettysburg, and am therefore perhaps unduly sensitive at adverse criticism."[1]

The controversy began with the mischievous action of Congress. That august body, in gratitude for the victory of the Army of the Potomac at Gettysburg, passed a resolution on 28 January 1864 thanking three officers by name for their contributions to the victory. The first was General Hooker for shielding Washington and Baltimore from the "meditated blow" of General Lee; the second and third were Generals Meade and Howard for the victory at Gettysburg. Had the solons confined their expressions to Hooker and Meade, there would have been no hard feelings, but it was foolish and invidious of them to single out Howard from his peers for this honor.[2]

The resolution prompted criticism that surfaced in a letter to the editor written by "TRUTH" on 20 February 1864 in the *Army and Navy Journal.* "TRUTH" gave an account of the battle and asked why Howard had been singled out for thanks over Hancock. "One Who Knows" replied on 19 March with an account extolling Howard's activities and saying that Hancock did not assume command when he arrived on the field. "TRUTH" could not let this pass and replied that Hancock had taken command and that many people had seen him do so.[3]

The central issue then became whether Howard or Hancock commanded on the field after Hancock's arrival. That Hancock was in command could not be disputed since General Meade had so ordered. The question was whether Hancock exercised this command over Howard and which officer should be credited for the rallying of Union forces on Cemetery Hill.

The two principals exchanged views on the matter. On 25 February Howard wrote to Hancock regarding an article in the *Philadelphia Evening Bulletin* that spoke favorably of Hancock and critically of him. Howard said that he hoped that the article did not express Hancock's views, and he wrote in a complimentary way of Hancock's services on 1 July. He went on to say that he had had no prior knowledge of the resolution by Congress and did not know even then who was behind it.

He observed that one of his friends had told him that Hancock himself had spoken in high terms of Howard's services that day.[4]

If Howard hoped to mollify Hancock, he did not succeed. In a stiff, formal response, Hancock claimed that he was not aware of the article Howard had referred to, that he had not written anything, that he did not intend to do so, and that he had seen many unjust things in the papers. He stated that he thought Howard had been singled out for special mention because "of a desire on the part of the Administration to make you prominent, to have an Effect in case it should be thought wise or advisable" to use Howard's name and reputation in the next presidential election.[5]

In reference to the above articles, Howard also wrote to a Prof. Henry Coppee. He reviewed the events of 1 July briefly and insisted that he had been in command of the forces on the field until he turned the command over to Slocum at 7:00 P.M. and that he had not recognized Hancock's having been in command. He went on to say that the judgment of Reynolds and Hancock might have coincided with his own that day and that it was unfair of their friends to charge him with folly in order to enhance their reputations.[6]

There was another spirited exchange in 1876. The *Atlantic Monthly* published an account by Howard of his part in the battle. In it, he wrote of Hancock's arrival on the field at what he said was 4:30 P.M., but he did not recognize Hancock's having been in command until his receipt of Meade's order at 7:00 P.M., when he turned the command over to Slocum. However, he also said that when he saw the order at 7:00 P.M. he was mortified and asked Hancock to "represent to General Meade how I had performed my duty on that memorable day." Such sniveling probably did not please Hancock. Howard added that Hancock had told Vice Pres. Hannibal Hamlin that "the country will never know how much it owes to your Maine general, Howard."[7]

Hancock replied to Howard's writings in the *Galaxy*. He gave his time of arrival wrongly as 3:30 P.M. and said that Howard, without looking at the order giving him command, relinquished command to him at this time. Hancock went on to buttress his claim to have been in command by describing measures he had taken and the recognition by others of his command status. In a letter written at this time to General Hooker, Hancock observed that he had never praised Howard to Hamlin or anyone else as Howard had suggested. He stated that he had never held such laudatory opinions of Howard; on the contrary, he had always believed that Howard claimed too much for himself at Gettysburg and that he had received greater honor than he deserved.[8]

Hancock died in 1886 and probably never altered his opinion of Howard and the events of 1 July 1863. As late as 1888, Howard maintained that he had "really" exercised command during all of the fighting on the afternoon of 1 July and that he was not aware of Meade's order until he received a copy of it that evening. He repeated the story in his autobiography, which was published in 1902. Howard was constant in his views.[9]

Howard had his faults, as many were quick to note, but it is hard to believe that he was a liar. It is possible that in the excitement and confusion on Cemetery Hill, he did not understand that Meade had actually placed Hancock, his junior, in command. He was not in the mindset later to believe that such a thing had happened, and it pleased him to continue to think that he had really been in command until 7:00 P.M. It was his finest hour, and he did not want to lose it.

The second controversy was of short duration and involved Generals Meade, Slocum, and Williams. Prior to the battle, these officers had been on friendly terms; in fact, in a letter written to a friend on 17 July, Slocum wrote, "I think well of Meade & do most earnestly hope that he will continue to do as well as he has thus far. Please don't believe the newspapers when they tell you we could have captured (bagged) the rebel army. Our best officers think everything was done for the best."[10]

In September 1863 the Eleventh and Twelfth corps were sent west to the Army of the Cumberland, and in April 1864 they were merged into the Twentieth Corps under General Hooker. In the meantime, General Meade prepared his report of the battle. He based his report on those of the corps commanders, using Slocum's report as the source of Twelfth Corps operations and not that of Williams. The result was that Meade's report of 1 October 1863 did not do justice to the Twelfth Corps. Williams described it as "botched" and wrote that it "beats all in blunders and partiality."[11]

On 30 December 1863, Slocum wrote a letter of transmittal to Meade to accompany General Ruger's report, which had been submitted late. With it, he enclosed a letter from Williams that called Slocum's attention to errors in Meade's report. Although Slocum's letter to Meade was businesslike, he was clearly unhappy. On 2 January, before his letter would have reached Meade, Slocum wrote a letter to a friend in Syracuse in which he said that his first impulse on reading Meade's report was to request a court of inquiry. However, he did not do this, he said, because it would not promote the interests of the service. He then referred to a "secret history" of the campaign, a history that would have revealed Meade's alleged timidity and hiding behind the opinions of his officers when at Hagerstown. It was a different tune than he had sung in July.[12]

What had Meade done? Williams pointed out that he had credited Lockwood's brigade and its accomplishments to the First Corps. He had also omitted the great fight by Greene's brigade on the night of 2 July and had ignored the operations of Williams's division. In addition, he had disregarded statements made by Williams as commander of the corps and the fact that Williams had commanded the corps.[13]

Meade replied to Slocum's letter on 25 February 1864. He acknowledged that he had erred insofar as Lockwood's brigade was concerned but stated that he did not believe he was in error for failing to mention Greene's brigade because his report covered many brigades and the work of Greene's had not been emphasized as a "pointed manner" in Slocum's report. Had he, Meade, appreciated Greene's work at the time that he wrote his report, he would have given it credit for special service. (This might have been considered a criticism of Slocum's report.) Insofar as Williams's being a corps commander was concerned, Meade wrote that he was not aware that he had been. He said that he had been puzzled by Williams's attendance at the council-of-war on 2 July but had refrained out of courtesy from asking him why he was there.

The latter comment must have been a blow to Slocum. Meade had not known that Williams was a corps commander because he had believed that Slocum served in that capacity. This meant that Meade had not been aware that Slocum had considered himself to be a wing commander and that Meade "did not expect or design him to be so."[14]

Meade dismissed two remaining criticisms. He maintained that he could not mention every unit in his report and pointed out that Geary's division had received the most prominent mention in the corps report. He disclaimed blame also for confusing Wheaton's brigade with Shaler's since he had received that information from the Sixth Corps report.[15]

Meade's reply was not as gracious as it might have been—he could have expressed more admiration for the work of Greene's brigade and more sympathy with Williams as commander of the Twelfth Corps. Much of the criticisms, however, were addressed in corrections to his report that he forwarded with Ruger's report on 25 February. Sad to say, however, in the *Official Records*, Meade's initial report was published unchanged and the corrections appeared as separate correspondence. In the meantime, Meade had talked with Greene and had expressed much regret for his oversights. He told Greene that he had not read Williams's report when he made his own. Still, Meade's efforts to atone for his omissions would not have pleased Slocum. Meade had not mentioned Slocum's name in the corrections; although Meade referred to Williams as a temporary corps commander, he still did not credit Slocum with the command of the right wing![16]

Appendix C
Order of Battle: Army of the Potomac and Army of Northern Virginia, 1–3 July 1863

The Order of Battle is reproduced from U.S. War Department, *The War of the Rebellion: A Compilation of the Official Records of the Union and Confederate Armies*, 128 vols. (Washington, D.C.: U.S. Government Printing Office, 1880–1901), series 1, 27 (1):155–68, (2):283–91.

No. 9.

Organization of the Army of the Potomac, Maj. Gen. George G. Meade, U. S. Army, commanding, at the battle of Gettysburg, July 1–3, 1863.

GENERAL HEADQUARTERS.

COMMAND OF THE PROVOST-MARSHAL-GENERAL.

Brig. Gen. MARSENA R. PATRICK.

93d New York,* Col. John S. Crocker.
8th United States (eight companies),* Capt. Edwin W. H. Read.
2d Pennsylvania Cavalry, Col. R. Butler Price.
6th Pennsylvania Cavalry, Companies E and I, Capt. James Starr.
Regular cavalry (detachments from 1st, 2d, 5th, and 6th Regiments).

SIGNAL CORPS.

Capt. LEMUEL B. NORTON.

GUARDS AND ORDERLIES.

Oneida (New York) Cavalry, Capt. Daniel P. Mann.

ARTILLERY.†

Brig. Gen. HENRY J. HUNT.

ENGINEER BRIGADE.‡

Brig. Gen. HENRY W. BENHAM.

15th New York (three companies), Maj. Walter L. Cassin.
50th New York, Col. William H. Pettes.
United States Battalion, Capt. George H. Mendell.

FIRST ARMY CORPS.§

Maj. Gen. ABNER DOUBLEDAY.
Maj. Gen. JOHN NEWTON.

GENERAL HEADQUARTERS.

1st Maine Cavalry, Company L, Capt. Constantine Taylor.

FIRST DIVISION.

Brig. Gen. JAMES S. WADSWORTH.

First Brigade.	*Second Brigade.*
Brig. Gen. SOLOMON MEREDITH. Col. WILLIAM W. ROBINSON.	Brig. Gen. LYSANDER CUTLER.
19th Indiana, Col. Samuel J. Williams.	7th Indiana, Col. Ira G. Grover.
24th Michigan:	76th New York:
Col. Henry A. Morrow.	Maj. Andrew J. Grover.
Capt. Albert M. Edwards.	Capt. John E. Cook.
2d Wisconsin:	84th New York (14th Militia), Col. Edward B. Fowler.
Col. Lucius Fairchild.	95th New York:
Maj. John Mansfield.	Col. George H. Biddle.
Capt. George H. Otis.	Maj. Edward Pye.
6th Wisconsin, Lieut. Col. Rufus R. Dawes.	147th New York:
7th Wisconsin:	Lieut. Col. Francis C. Miller.
Col. William W. Robinson.	Maj. George Harney.
Maj. Mark Finnicum.	56th Pennsylvania (nine companies), Col. J. William Hofmann.

---

* Not engaged.
† See artillery brigades attached to army corps and the reserve.
‡ Not engaged. With exception of the regular battalion, it was, July 1, and while at Beaver Dam Creek, Md., ordered to Washington, D. C., where it arrived July 3.
§ Maj. Gen. John F. Reynolds, of this corps, was killed July 1, while in command of the left wing of the army; General Doubleday commanded the corps July 1, and General Newton, who was assigned to that command on the 1st, superseded him July 2.

Brig. Gen. JOHN C. ROBINSON.

First Brigade.	Second Brigade.

First Brigade.

Brig. Gen. GABRIEL R. PAUL.
Col. SAMUEL H. LEONARD.
Col. ADRIAN R. ROOT.
Col. RICHARD COULTER.
Col. PETER LYLE.
Col. RICHARD COULTER.

16th Maine:
    Col. Charles W. Tilden.
    Maj. Archibald D. Leavitt.
13th Massachusetts :
    Col. Samuel H. Leonard.
    Lieut. Col. N. Walter Batchelder.
94th New York:
    Col. Adrian R. Root.
    Maj. Samuel A. Moffett.
104th New York, Col. Gilbert G. Prey.
107th Pennsylvania:
    Lieut. Col. James MacThomson.
    Capt. Emanuel D. Roath.

Second Brigade.

Brig. Gen. HENRY BAXTER.

12th Massachusetts:
    Col. James L. Bates.
    Lieut. Col. David Allen, jr.
83d New York (9th Militia), Lieut. Col. Joseph A. Moesch.
97th New York:
    Col. Charles Wheelock.
    Maj. Charles Northrup.
11th Pennsylvania:*
    Col. Richard Coulter.
    Capt. Benjamin F. Haines.
    Capt. John B. Overmyer.
88th Pennsylvania:
    Maj. Benezet F. Foust.
    Capt. Henry Whiteside.
90th Pennsylvania:
    Col. Peter Lyle.
    Maj. Alfred J. Sellers.
    Col. Peter Lyle.

THIRD DIVISION.

Brig. Gen. THOMAS A. ROWLEY.
Maj. Gen. ABNER DOUBLEDAY.

First Brigade.	Second Brigade.

First Brigade.

Col. CHAPMAN BIDDLE.
Brig. Gen. THOMAS A. ROWLEY.
Col. CHAPMAN BIDDLE.

80th New York (20th Militia), Col. Theodore B. Gates.
121st Pennsylvania:
    Maj. Alexander Biddle.
    Col. Chapman Biddle.
    Maj. Alexander Biddle.
142d Pennsylvania:
    Col. Robert P. Cummins.
    Lieut. Col. A. B. McCalmont.
151st Pennsylvania:
    Lieut. Col. George F. McFarland.
    Capt. Walter L. Owens.
    Col. Harrison Allen.

Second Brigade.

Col. ROY STONE.
Col. LANGHORNE WISTER.
Col. EDMUND L. DANA.

143d Pennsylvania:
    Col. Edmund L. Dana.
    Lieut. Col. John D. Musser.
149th Pennsylvania:
    Lieut. Col. Walton Dwight
    Capt. James Glenn.
150th Pennsylvania:
    Col. Langhorne Wister.
    Lieut. Col. H. S. Huidekoper.
    Capt. Cornelius C. Widdis.

Third Brigade.

Brig. Gen. GEORGE J. STANNARD.
Col. FRANCIS V. RANDALL.

12th Vermont,† Col. Asa P. Blunt.
13th Vermont :
    Col. Francis V. Randall,
    Maj. Joseph J. Boynton.
    Lieut. Col. William D. Munson.
14th Vermont, Col. William T. Nichols.
15th Vermont,† Col. Redfield Proctor.
16th Vermont, Col. Wheelock G. Veazey.

---

* Transferred, in afternoon of July 1, to the First Brigade.
† Guarding trains, and not engaged in the battle.

Col. CHARLES S. WAINWRIGHT.

Maine Light, 2d Battery (B), Capt. James A. Hall.
Maine Light, 5th Battery (E):
    Capt. Greenleaf T. Stevens.
    Lieut. Edward N. Whittier.
1st New York Light, Battery L:*
    Capt. Gilbert H. Reynolds.
    Lieut. George Breck.
1st Pennsylvania Light, Battery B, Capt. James H. Cooper.
4th United States, Battery B, Lieut. James Stewart.

SECOND ARMY CORPS.†

Maj. Gen. WINFIELD S. HANCOCK.
Brig. Gen. JOHN GIBBON.

GENERAL HEADQUARTERS.

6th New York Cavalry, Companies D and K, Capt. Riley Johnson.

FIRST DIVISION.

Brig. Gen. JOHN C. CALDWELL.

First Brigade.

Col. EDWARD E. CROSS.
Col. H. BOYD MCKEEN.

5th New Hampshire,Lieut. Col. Charles
    E. Hapgood.
61st New York, Lieut. Col. K. Oscar
    Broady.
81st Pennsylvania :
    Col. H. Boyd McKeen.
    Lieut. Col. Amos Stroh.
148th Pennsylvania, Lieut. Col. Robert
    McFarlane.

Second Brigade.

Col. PATRICK KELLY.

28th Massachusetts, Col. R. Byrnes.
63d New York (two companies) :
    Lieut.Col. Richard C. Bentley.
    Capt. Thomas Touhy.
69th New York (two companies) :
    Capt. Richard Moroney.
    Lieut. James J. Smith.
88th New York (two companies), Capt.
    Denis F. Burke.
116th Pennsylvania (four companies),
    Maj. St. Clair A. Mulholland.

Third Brigade.

Brig. Gen. SAMUEL K. ZOOK.
Lieut. Col. JOHN FRASER.

52d New York:
    Lieut. Col. C. G. Freudenberg.
    Capt. William Scherrer.
57th New York, Lieut. Col. Alford B.
    Chapman.
66th New York:
    Col. Orlando H. Morris.
    Lieut. Col. John S. Hammell.
    Maj. Peter Nelson.
140th Pennsylvania:
    Col. Richard P. Roberts.
    Lieut. Col. John Fraser.

Fourth Brigade.

Col. JOHN R. BROOKE.

27th Connecticut (two companies) :
    Lieut. Col. Henry C. Merwin.
    Maj. James H. Coburn.
2d Delaware:
    Col. William P. Baily.
    Capt. Charles H. Christman.
64th New York:
    Col. Daniel G. Bingham.
    Maj. Leman W. Bradley.
53d Pennsylvania, Lieut. Col. Richards
    McMichael.
145th Pennsylvania (seven companies) :
    Col. Hiram L. Brown.
    Capt. John W. Reynolds.
    Capt. Moses W. Oliver.

---

* Battery E, 1st New York Light Artillery, attached.

† After the death of General Reynolds, General Hancock was assigned to the command of all the troops on the field of battle, relieving General Howard, who had succeeded General Reynolds. General Gibbon, of the Second Division, assumed command of the corps. These assignments terminated on the evening of July 1. Similar changes in commanders occurred during the battle of the 2d, when General Hancock was put in command of the Third Corps, in addition to that of his own. He was wounded on the 3d, and Brig. Gen. William Hays was assigned to the command of the corps.

SECOND DIVISION.

Brig. Gen. JOHN GIBBON,
Brig. Gen. WILLIAM HARROW.

First Brigade.

Brig. Gen. WILLIAM HARROW.
Col. FRANCIS E. HEATH.

19th Maine:
    Col. Francis E. Heath.
    Lieut. Col. Henry W. Cunningham.
15th Massachusetts:
    Col. George H. Ward.
    Lieut. Col. George C. Joslin.
1st Minnesota:*
    Col. William Colvill, jr.
    Capt. Nathan S. Messick.
    Capt. Henry C. Coates.
82d New York (2d Militia):
    Lieut. Col. James Huston.
    Capt. John Darrow.

Second Brigade.

Brig. Gen. ALEXANDER S. WEBB.

69th Pennsylvania:
    Col. Dennis O'Kane.
    Capt. William Davis.
71st Pennsylvania, Col. Richard Penn Smith.
72d Pennsylvania:
    Col. De Witt C. Baxter.
    Lieut. Col. Theodore Hesser.
106th Pennsylvania, Lieut. Col. William L. Curry.

Third Brigade.

Col. NORMAN J. HALL.

19th Massachusetts, Col. Arthur F. Devereux.
20th Massachusetts:
    Col. Paul J. Revere.
    Lieut. Col. George N. Macy.
    Capt. Henry L. Abbott.
7th Michigan:
    Lieut. Col. Amos E. Steele, jr.
    Maj. Sylvanus W. Curtis.
42d New York, Col. James E. Mallon.
59th New York (four companies):
    Lieut. Col. Max A. Thoman.
    Capt. William McFadden.

Unattached.

Massachusetts Sharpshooters, 1st Company:
    Capt. William Plumer.
    Lieut. Emerson L. Bicknell.

THIRD DIVISION.

Brig. Gen. ALEXANDER HAYS.

First Brigade.

Col. SAMUEL S. CARROLL.

14th Indiana, Col. John Coons.
4th Ohio, Lieut. Col. Leonard W. Carpenter.
8th Ohio, Lieut. Col. Franklin Sawyer.
7th West Virginia, Lieut. Col. Jonathan H. Lockwood.

Second Brigade.

Col. THOMAS A. SMYTH.
Lieut. Col. FRANCIS E. PIERCE.

14th Connecticut, Maj. Theodore G. Ellis.
1st Delaware:
    Lieut. Col. Edward P. Harris.
    Capt. Thomas B. Hizar.
    Lieut. William Smith.
    Lieut. John T. Dent.
12th New Jersey, Maj. John T. Hill.
10th New York (battalion), Maj. George F. Hopper.
108th New York, Lieut. Col. Francis E. Pierce.

---

*2d Company Minnesota Sharpshooters attached.

Third Brigade.

Col. GEORGE L. WILLARD.
Col. ELIAKIM SHERRILL.
Lieut. Col. JAMES M. BULL.

39th New York (four companies), Maj. Hugo Hildebrandt.
111th New York:
    Col. Clinton D. MacDougall.
    Lieut. Col. Isaac M. Lusk.
    Capt. Aaron P. Seeley.
125th New York, Lieut. Col. Levin Crandell.
126th New York:
    Col. Eliakim Sherrill.
    Lieut. Col. James M. Bull.

ARTILLERY BRIGADE.

Capt. JOHN G. HAZARD.

1st New York Light, Battery B:*
    Lieut. Albert S. Sheldon.
    Capt. James McKay Rorty.
    Lieut. Robert E. Rogers.
1st Rhode Island Light, Battery A, Capt. William A. Arnold.
1st Rhode Island Light, Battery B:
    *Lieut. T. Fred. Brown.
    Lieut. Walter S. Perrin.
1st United States, Battery I:
    Lieut. George A. Woodruff.
    Lieut. Tully McCrea.
4th United States, Battery A:
    Lieut. Alonzo H. Cushing.
    Sergt. Frederick Fuger.

THIRD ARMY CORPS.

Maj. Gen. DANIEL E. SICKLES.
Maj. Gen. DAVID B. BIRNEY.

FIRST DIVISION.

Maj. Gen. DAVID B. BIRNEY.
Brig. Gen. J. H. HOBART WARD.

First Brigade.

Brig. Gen. CHARLES K. GRAHAM.
Col. ANDREW H. TIPPIN.

57th Pennsylvania (eight companies):
    Col. Peter Sides.
    Capt. Alanson H. Nelson.
63d Pennsylvania, Maj. John A. Danks.
68th Pennsylvania:
    Col. Andrew H. Tippin.
    Capt. Milton S. Davis.[?]
105th Pennsylvania, Col. Calvin A. Craig.
114th Pennsylvania:
    Lieut. Col. Frederick F. Cavada.
    Capt. Edward R. Bowen.
141st Pennsylvania, Col. Henry J. Madill.

Second Brigade.

Brig. Gen. J. H. HOBART WARD.
Col. HIRAM BERDAN.

20th Indiana:
    Col. John Wheeler.
    Lieut. Col. William C. L. Taylor.
3d Maine, Col. Moses B. Lakeman.
4th Maine:
    Col. Elijah Walker.
    Capt. Edwin Libby.
86th New York, Lieut. Col. Benjamin L. Higgins.
124th New York:
    Col. A. Van Horne Ellis.
    Lieut. Col. Francis M. Cummins.
99th Pennsylvania, Maj. John W. Moore.
1st United States Sharpshooters:
    Col. Hiram Berdan.
    Lieut. Col. Casper Trepp.
2d United States Sharpshooters (eight companies), Maj. Homer R. Stoughton.

*Transferred from Artillery Reserve, July 1; 14th New York Battery attached.

Third Brigade.

Col. P. REGIS DE TROBRIAND.

17th Maine, Lieut. Col. Charles B. Merrill.
3d Michigan:
    Col. Byron R. Pierce.
    Lieut. Col. Edwin S. Pierce.
5th Michigan, Lieut. Col. John Pulford.
40th New York, Col. Thomas W. Egan.
110th Pennsylvania (six companies):
    Lieut. Col. David M. Jones.
    Maj. Isaac Rogers.

SECOND DIVISION.

Brig. Gen. ANDREW A. HUMPHREYS.

First Brigade.

Brig. Gen. JOSEPH B. CARR.

1st Massachusetts, Lieut. Col. Clark B. Baldwin.
11th Massachusetts, Lieut. Col. Porter D. Tripp.
16th Massachusetts:
    Lieut. Col. Waldo Merriam.
    Capt. Matthew Donovan.
12th New Hampshire, Capt. John F. Langley.
11th New Jersey:
    Col. Robert McAllister.
    Capt. Luther Martin.
    Lieut. John Schoonover.
    Capt. William H. Lloyd.
    Capt. Samuel T. Sleeper.
    Lieut. John Schoonover.
26th Pennsylvania, Maj. Robert L. Bodine.
84th Pennsylvania,* Lieut. Col. Milton Opp.

Second Brigade.

Col. WILLIAM R. BREWSTER.

70th New York, Col. J. Egbert Farnum.
71st New York, Col. Henry L. Potter.
72d New York:
    Col. John S. Austin.
    Lieut. Col. John Leonard.
73d New York, Maj. Michael W. Burns.
74th New York, Lieut. Col. Thomas Holt.
120th New York:
    Lieut. Col. Cornelius D. Westbrook.
    Maj. John R. Tappen.

Third Brigade.

Col. GEORGE C. BURLING.

2d New Hampshire, Col. Edward L. Bailey.
5th New Jersey:
    Col. William J. Sewell.
    Capt. Thomas C. Godfrey.
    Capt. Henry H. Woolsey.
6th New Jersey, Lieut. Col. Stephen R. Gilkyson.
7th New Jersey:
    Col. Louis R. Francine.
    Maj. Frederick Cooper.
8th New Jersey:
    Col. John Ramsey.
    Capt. John G. Langston.
115th Pennsylvania, Maj. John P. Dunne.

---

*Guarding corps trains, and not engaged in the battle.

ARTILLERY BRIGADE.

Capt. GEORGE E. RANDOLPH.
Capt. A. JUDSON CLARK.

New Jersey Light, 2d Battery:
    Capt. A. Judson Clark.
    Lieut. Robert Sims.
1st New York Light, Battery D, Capt. George B. Winslow.
New York Light, 4th Battery, Capt. James E. Smith.
1st Rhode Island Light, Battery E:
    Lieut. John K. Bucklyn.
    Lieut. Benjamin Freeborn.
4th United States, Battery K:
    Lieut. Francis W. Seeley.
    Lieut. Robert James.

FIFTH ARMY CORPS.

Maj. Gen. GEORGE SYKES.

GENERAL HEADQUARTERS.

12th New York Infantry, Companies D and E, Capt. Henry W. Rider.
17th Pennsylvania Cavalry, Companies D and H, Capt. William Thompson.

FIRST DIVISION.

Brig. Gen. JAMES BARNES.

First Brigade.	*Second Brigade.*
Col. WILLIAM S. TILTON.	Col. JACOB B. SWEITZER.

18th Massachusetts, Col. Joseph Hayes.
22d Massachusetts, Lieut. Col. Thomas Sherwin, jr.
1st Michigan:
  Col. Ira C. Abbott.
  Lieut. Col. William A. Throop.
118th Pennsylvania, Lieut. Col. James Gwyn.
	9th Massachusetts, Col. Patrick R. Guiney.
	32d Massachusetts, Col. G. L. Prescott.
	4th Michigan :
	  Col. Harrison H. Jeffords.
	  Lieut. Col. George W. Lumbard.
	62d Pennsylvania, Lieut. Col. James C. Hull.

Third Brigade.

Col. STRONG VINCENT.
Col. JAMES C. RICE.

20th Maine, Col. Joshua L. Chamberlain.
16th Michigan, Lieut. Col. Norval E. Welch.
44th New York :
    Col. James C. Rice.
    Lieut. Col. Freeman Conner.
83d Pennsylvania, Capt. Orpheus S. Woodward.

SECOND DIVISION.

Brig. Gen. ROMEYN B. AYRES.

First Brigade.	*Second Brigade.*
Col. HANNIBAL DAY.	Col. SIDNEY BURBANK.

3d United States (six companies):
  Capt. Henry W. Freedley.
  Capt. Richard G. Lay.
4th United States (four companies), Capt. Julius W. Adams, jr.
6th United States (five companies), Capt. Levi C. Bootes.
12th United States (eight companies), Capt. Thomas S. Dunn.
14th United States (eight companies), Maj. Grotius R. Giddings.
	2d United States (six companies):
	  Maj. Arthur T. Lee.
	  Capt. Samuel A. McKee.
	7th United States (four companies), Capt. David P. Hancock.
	10th United States (three companies), Capt. William Clinton.
	11th United States (six companies), Maj. De Lancey Floyd-Jones.
	17th United States (seven companies), Lieut. Col. J. Durell Greene.

Third Brigade.

Brig. Gen. STEPHEN H. WEED.
Col. KENNER GARRARD.

140th New York:
Col. Patrick H. O'Rorke.
Lieut. Col. Louis Ernst.
146th New York:
Col. Kenner Garrard.
Lieut. Col. David T. Jenkins.
91st Pennsylvania, Lieut. Col. Joseph H. Sinex.
155th Pennsylvania, Lieut. Col. John H. Cain.

THIRD DIVISION.*

Brig. Gen. SAMUEL W. CRAWFORD.

First Brigade.	*Third Brigade.*
Col. WILLIAM MCCANDLESS.	Col. JOSEPH W. FISHER.
1st Pennsylvania Reserves (nine companies), Col. William C. Talley.	5th Pennsylvania Reserves, Lieut. Col. George Dare.
2d Pennsylvania Reserves, Lieut. Col. George A. Woodward.	9th Pennsylvania Reserves, Lieut. Col. James McK. Snodgrass.
6th Pennsylvania Reserves, Lieut. Col. Wellington H. Ent.	10th Pennsylvania Reserves, Col. Adoniram J. Warner.
13th Pennsylvania Reserves: Col. Charles F. Taylor. Maj. William R. Hartshorne.	11th Pennsylvania Reserves, Col. Samuel M. Jackson.
	12th Pennsylvania Reserves (nine companies), Col. Martin D. Hardin.

ARTILLERY BRIGADE.

Capt. AUGUSTUS P. MARTIN.

Massachusetts Light, 3d Battery (C), Lieut. Aaron F. Walcott.
1st New York Light, Battery C, Capt. Almont Barnes.
1st Ohio Light, Battery L, Capt. Frank C. Gibbs.
5th United States, Battery D:
Lieut. Charles E. Hazlett.
Lieut. Benjamin F. Rittenhouse.
5th United States, Battery I:
Lieut. Malbone F. Watson.
Lieut. Charles C. MacConnell.

SIXTH ARMY CORPS.

Maj. Gen. JOHN SEDGWICK.

GENERAL HEADQUARTERS.

1st New Jersey Cavalry, Company L, } Capt. William S. Craft.
1st Pennsylvania Cavalry, Company H, }

FIRST DIVISION.

Brig. Gen. HORATIO G. WRIGHT.

Provost Guard.

4th New Jersey (three companies), Capt. William R. Maxwell.

First Brigade.	*Second Brigade.*
Brig. Gen. A. T. A. TORBERT.	Brig. Gen. JOSEPH J. BARTLETT.†
1st New Jersey, Lieut. Col. William Henry, jr.	5th Maine, Col. Clark S. Edwards.
2d New Jersey, Lieut. Col. Charles Wiebecke.	121st New York, Col. Emory Upton.
3d New Jersey, Lieut. Col. Edward L. Campbell.	95th Pennsylvania, Lieut. Col. Edward Carroll.
15th New Jersey, Col. William H. Penrose.	96th Pennsylvania, Maj. William H. Lessig.

* Joined corps June 28. The Second Brigade left in the Department of Washington.
† Also in command of the Third Brigade, Third Division, on July 3.

Third Brigade.

Brig. Gen. DAVID A. RUSSELL.

6th Maine, Col. Hiram Burnham.
49th Pennsylvania (four companies), Lieut. Col. Thomas M. Hulings.
119th Pennsylvania, Col. Peter C. Ellmaker.
5th Wisconsin, Col. Thomas S. Allen.

SECOND DIVISION.*

Brig. Gen. ALBION P. HOWE.

Second Brigade.	Third Brigade.
Col. LEWIS A. GRANT.	Brig. Gen. THOMAS H. NEILL.
2d Vermont, Col. James H. Walbridge.	7th Maine (six companies), Lieut. Col. Selden Connor.
3d Vermont, Col. Thomas O. Seaver.	
4th Vermont, Col. Charles B. Stoughton.	33d New York (detachment), Capt. Henry J. Gifford.
5th Vermont, Lieut. Col. John R. Lewis.	43d New York, Lieut. Col. John Wilson.
6th Vermont, Col. Elisha L. Barney.	49th New York, Col. Daniel D. Bidwell.
	77th New York, Lieut. Col. Winsor B. French.
	61st Pennsylvania, Lieut. Col. George F. Smith.

THIRD DIVISION.

Maj. Gen. JOHN NEWTON.†
Brig. Gen. FRANK WHEATON.

First Brigade.	Second Brigade.
Brig. Gen. ALEXANDER SHALER.	Col. HENRY L. EUSTIS.
65th New York, Col. Joseph E. Hamblin.	7th Massachusetts, Lieut. Col. Franklin P. Harlow.
67th New York, Col. Nelson Cross.	10th Massachusetts, Lieut. Col. Joseph B. Parsons.
122d New York, Col. Silas Titus.	
23d Pennsylvania, Lieut. Col. John F. Glenn.	37th Massachusetts, Col. Oliver Edwards.
82d Pennsylvania, Col. Isaac C. Bassett.	2d Rhode Island, Col. Horatio Rogers, jr.

Third Brigade.

Brig. Gen. FRANK WHEATON.
Col. DAVID J. NEVIN.

62d New York :
    Col. David J. Nevin.
    Lieut. Col. Theodore B. Hamilton.
93d Pennsylvania, Maj. John I. Nevin.
98th Pennsylvania, Maj. John B. Kohler.
102d Pennsylvania,‡ Col. John W. Patterson.
139th Pennsylvania:
    Col. Frederick H. Collier.
    Lieut. Col. William H. Moody.

ARTILLERY BRIGADE.

Col. CHARLES H. TOMPKINS.

Massachusetts Light, 1st Battery (A), Capt. William H. McCartney.
New York Light, 1st Battery, Capt. Andrew Cowan.
New York Light, 3d Battery, Capt. William A. Harn.
1st Rhode Island Light, Battery C, Capt. Richard Waterman.
1st Rhode Island Light, Battery G, Capt. George W. Adams.
2d United States, Battery D, Lieut. Edward B. Williston,
2d United States, Battery G, Lieut. John H. Butler.
5th United States, Battery F, Lieut. Leonard Martin.

---

* No First Brigade in division.
† See foot note (§), p. 155.
‡ Guarding wagon train at Westminster, and not engaged in the battle.

ELEVENTH ARMY CORPS.*

Maj. Gen. OLIVER O. HOWARD.

GENERAL HEADQUARTERS.

1st Indiana Cavalry, Companies I and K, Capt. Abram Sharra.
8th New York Infantry (one company), Lieut. Hermann Foerster.

FIRST DIVISION.

Brig. Gen. FRANCIS C. BARLOW.
Brig. Gen. ADELBERT AMES.

First Brigade.	*Second Brigade.*
Col. LEOPOLD VON GILSA.	Brig. Gen. ADELBERT AMES.
	Col. ANDREW L. HARRIS.
41st New York (nine companies), Lieut. Col. Detleo von Einsiedel.	17th Connecticut:
	Lieut. Col. Douglas Fowler.
54th New York:	Maj. Allen G. Brady.
Maj. Stephen Kovacs.	25th Ohio:
Lieut. Ernst Both [?].	Lieut. Col. Jeremiah Williams.
68th New York, Col. Gotthilf Bourry.	Capt. Nathaniel J. Manning.
153d Pennsylvania, Maj. John F. Frue- auff.	Lieut. William Maloney.
	Lieut. Israel White.
	75th Ohio:
	Col. Andrew L. Harris.
	Capt. George B. Fox.
	107th Ohio:
	Col. Seraphim Meyer.
	Capt. John M. Lutz.

SECOND DIVISION.

Brig. Gen. ADOLPH VON STEINWEHR.

First Brigade.	*Second Brigade.*
Col. CHARLES R. COSTER.	Col. ORLAND SMITH.
134th New York, Lieut. Col. Allan H. Jackson.	33d Massachusetts, Col. Adin B. Underwood.
154th New York, Lieut. Col. D. B. Allen.	136th New York, Col. James Wood, jr.
27th Pennsylvania, Lieut. Col. Lorenz Cantador.	55th Ohio, Col. Charles B. Gambee.
73d Pennsylvania, Capt. D. F. Kelley.	73d Ohio, Lieut. Col. Richard Long.

THIRD DIVISION.

Maj. Gen. CARL SCHURZ.

First Brigade.	*Second Brigade.*
Brig. Gen. ALEX. SCHIMMELFENNIG.	Col. W. KRZYZANOWSKI.
Col. GEORGE VON AMSBERG.	
	58th New York:
82d Illinois, Lieut. Col. Edward S. Salomon.	Lieut. Col. August Otto.
	Capt. Emil Koenig.
45th New York:	119th New York:
Col. George von Amsberg.	Col. John T. Lockman.
Lieut. Col. Adolphus Dobke.	Lieut. Col. Edward F. Lloyd.
157th New York, Col. Philip P. Brown, jr.	82d Ohio:
61st Ohio, Col. Stephen J. McGroarty.	Col. James S. Robinson.
74th Pennsylvania:	Lieut. Col. David Thomson.
Col. Adolph von Hartung.	75th Pennsylvania:
Lieut. Col. Alexander von Mitzel.	Col. Francis Mahler.
Capt. Gustav Schleiter.	Maj. August Ledig.
Capt. Henry Krauseneck.	26th Wisconsin:
	Lieut. Col. Hans Boebel.
	Capt. John W. Fuchs.

* During the interval between the death of General Reynolds and the arrival of General Hancock, on the afternoon of July 1, all the troops on the field of battle were commanded by General Howard, General Schurz taking command of the Eleventh Corps, and General Schimmelfennig of the Third Division.

ARTILLERY BRIGADE.

Maj. THOMAS W. OSBORN.

1st New York Light, Battery I, Capt. Michael Wiedrich.
New York Light, 13th Battery, Lieut. William Wheeler.
1st Ohio Light, Battery I, Capt. Hubert Dilger.
1st Ohio Light, Battery K, Capt. Lewis Heckman.
4th United States, Battery G:
    Lieut. Bayard Wilkeson.
    Lieut. Eugene A. Bancroft.

TWELFTH ARMY CORPS.

Maj. Gen. HENRY W. SLOCUM.*
Brig. Gen. ALPHEUS S. WILLIAMS.

PROVOST GUARD.

10th Maine (four companies), Capt John D. Beardsley.

FIRST DIVISION.

Brig. Gen. ALPHEUS S. WILLIAMS.
Brig. Gen. THOMAS H. RUGER.

First Brigade.	*Second Brigade.*†
Col. ARCHIBALD L. McDOUGALL.	Brig. Gen. HENRY H. LOCKWOOD.
5th Connecticut, Col. W. W. Packer.	1st Maryland, Potomac Home Br
20th Connecticut, Lieut. Col. William	gade, Col. William P. Maulsby.
B. Wooster.	1st Maryland, Eastern Shore, C .
3d Maryland, Col. Jos. M. Sudsburg.	James Wallace.
123d New York:	150th New York, Col. John H. Ketcham.
Lieut. Col. James C. Rogers.	
Capt. Adolphus H. Tanner.	
145th New York, Col. E. L. Price.	
46th Pennsylvania, Col. James L. Sel-	
fridge.	

Third Brigade.

Brig. Gen. THOMAS H. RUGER.
Col. SILAS COLGROVE.

27th Indiana:
    Col. Silas Colgrove.
    Lieut. Col. John R. Fesler.
2d Massachusetts:
    Lieut. Col. Charles R. Mudge.
    Maj. Charles F. Morse.
13th New Jersey, Col. Ezra A. Carman.
107th New York, Col. Nirom M. Crane.
3d Wisconsin, Col. William Hawley.

SECOND DIVISION.

Brig. Gen. JOHN W. GEARY.

First Brigade.	*Second Brigade.*
Col. CHARLES CANDY.	Col. GEORGE A. COBHAM, Jr.
5th Ohio, Col. John H. Patrick.	Brig. GEN. THOMAS L. KANE.
7th Ohio, Col. William R. Creighton.	Col. GEORGE A. COBHAM, Jr.
29th Ohio:	29th Pennsylvania, Col. William Rick-
Capt. Wilbur F. Stevens.	ards, jr.
Capt. Edward Hayes.	109th Pennsylvania, Capt. F. L. Gimber.
66th Ohio, Lieut. Col. Eugene Powell.	111th Pennsylvania:
28th Pennsylvania, Capt. John Flynn.	Lieut. Col. Thomas M. Walker.
147th Pennsylvania (eight companies),	Col. George A. Cobham, jr.
Lieut. Col. Ario Pardee, jr.	Lieut. Col. Thomas M. Walker.

* Exercised command of the right wing of the army during a part of the battle.
But see Slocum to Meade, December 30, 1863, p. 763, and Meade to Slocum, February 25, 1864, p. 769.
† Unassigned during progress of battle; afterward attached to First Division, as
Second Brigade. The command theretofore known as the Second (or Jackson's)
Brigade had previously been consolidated with the First Brigade.

Third Brigade.

Brig. Gen. GEORGE S. GREENE.

60th New York, Col. Abel Godard.
78th New York, Lieut. Col. Herbert von Hammerstein.
102d New York:
    Col. James C. Lane.
    Capt. Lewis R. Stegman.
137th New York, Col. David Ireland.
149th New York:
    Col. Henry A. Barnum.
    Lieut. Col. Charles B. Randall.

ARTILLERY BRIGADE.

Lieut. EDWARD D. MUHLENBERG.

1st New York Light, Battery M, Lieut. Charles E. Winegar.
Pennsylvania Light, Battery E, Lieut. Charles A. Atwell.
4th United States, Battery F, Lieut. Sylvanus T. Rugg.
5th United States, Battery K, Lieut. David H. Kinzie.

CAVALRY CORPS.

Maj. Gen. ALFRED PLEASONTON.

FIRST DIVISION.

Brig. Gen. JOHN BUFORD.

First Brigade.	*Second Brigade.*
Col. WILLIAM GAMBLE.	Col. THOMAS C. DEVIN.

8th Illinois, Maj. John L. Beveridge.
12th Illinois (four cos.), ⎰ Col. George H.
3d Indiana (six cos.), ⎱   Chapman.
8th New York, Lieut. Col. William L.
  Markell.
	6th New York, Maj. Wm. E. Beardsley.
	9th New York, Col. William Sackett.
	17th Pennsylvania, Col. J. H. Kellogg.
	3d West Virginia (two companies),
	  Capt. Seymour B. Conger.

Reserve Brigade.

Brig. Gen. WESLEY MERRITT.

6th Pennsylvania, Maj. James H. Haseltine.
1st United States, Capt. Richard S. C. Lord.
2d United States, Capt. T. F. Rodenbough.
5th United States, Capt. Julius W. Mason.
6th United States:
    Maj. Samuel H. Starr.
    Lieut. Louis H. Carpenter.
    Lieut. Nicholas Nolan.
    Capt. Ira W. Claflin.

SECOND DIVISION.

Brig. Gen. DAVID McM. GREGG.

Headquarters Guard.

1st Ohio, Company A, Capt. Noah Jones.

First Brigade.	*Second Brigade.*‡
Col. JOHN B. McINTOSH.	Col. PENNOCK HUEY.

1st Maryland (eleven companies), Lieut.
  Col. James M. Deems.
Purnell (Maryland) Legion, Company A,
  Capt. Robert E. Duvall.
1st Massachusetts,* Lieut. Col. Greely S.
  Curtis.
1st New Jersey, Maj. M. H. Beaumont.
1st Pennsylvania, Col. John P. Taylor.
3d Pennsylvania, Lieut. Col. E. S. Jones.
3d Pennsylvania Heavy Artillery, Sec-
  tion Battery H,† Capt. W. D. Rank.
	2d New York, Lieut. Col. Otto Harhaus.
	4th New York, Lieut. Col. Augustus
	  Pruyn.
	6th Ohio (ten companies), Maj. William
	  Stedman.
	8th Pennsylvania, Capt. William A. Cor-
	  rie.

---

*Served with the Sixth Army Corps, and on the right flank.
†Serving as light artillery.
‡At Westminster, etc., and not engaged in the battle.

Third Brigade.

Col. J. IRVIN GREGG.

1st Maine (ten companies), Lieut. Col. Charles H. Smith.
10th New York, Maj. M. Henry Avery.
4th Pennsylvania, Lieut. Col. William E. Doster.
16th Pennsylvania, Lieut. Col. John K. Robison.

THIRD DIVISION.

Brig. Gen. JUDSON KILPATRICK.

Headquarters Guard.

1st Ohio, Company C, Capt. Samuel N. Stanford.

First Brigade.	*Second Brigade.*
Brig. Gen. ELON J. FARNSWORTH. Col. NATHANIEL P. RICHMOND.	Brig. Gen. GEORGE A. CUSTER.
5th New York, Maj. John Hammond. 18th Pennsylvania, Lieut. Col. William P. Brinton. 1st Vermont, Lieut. Col. Addison W. Preston. 1st West Virginia (ten companies): Col. Nathaniel P. Richmond. Maj. Charles E. Capehart.	1st Michigan, Col. Charles H. Town. 5th Michigan, Col. Russell A. Alger. 6th Michigan, Col. George Gray. 7th Michigan (ten companies), Col. William D. Mann.

HORSE ARTILLERY.

First Brigade.	*Second Brigade.*
Capt. JAMES M. ROBERTSON.	Capt. JOHN C. TIDBALL.
9th Michigan Battery, Capt. Jabez J. Daniels. 6th New York Battery, Capt. Joseph W. Martin. 2d United States, Batteries B and L, Lieut. Edward Heaton. 2d United States, Battery M, Lieut. A. C. M. Pennington, jr. 4th United States, Battery E, Lieut. Samuel S. Elder.	1st United States, Batteries E and G, Capt. Alanson M. Randol. 1st United States, Battery K, Capt. William M. Graham. 2d United States, Battery A, Lieut. John H. Calef. 3d United States, Battery C, Lieut. William D. Fuller.*

ARTILLERY RESERVE.

Brig. Gen. ROBERT O. TYLER.
Capt. JAMES M. ROBERTSON.

Headquarters Guard.

32d Massachusetts Infantry, Company C, Capt. Josiah C. Fuller.

First Regular Brigade.	*First Volunteer Brigade.*
Capt. DUNBAR R. RANSOM.	Lieut. Col. FREEMAN McGILVERY.
1st United States, Battery H: Lieut. Chandler P. Eakin. Lieut. Philip D. Mason. 3d United States, Batteries F and K, Lieut. John G. Turnbull. 4th United States, Battery C, Lieut. Evan Thomas. 5th United States, Battery C, Lieut. Gulian V. Weir.	Massachusetts Light, 5th Battery (E),† Capt. Charles A. Phillips. Massachusetts Light, 9th Battery: Capt. John Bigelow. Lieut. Richard S. Milton. New York Light, 15th Battery, Capt. Patrick Hart. Pennsylvania Light, Batteries C and F, Capt. James Thompson.

* With Huey's Cavalry Brigade, and not engaged in the battle.
† 10th New York Battery attached.

Second Volunteer Brigade.

Capt. ELIJAH D. TAFT.

1st Connecticut Heavy, Battery B,* Capt.
  Albert F. Brooker.
1st Connecticut Heavy, Battery M,* Capt.
  Franklin A. Pratt.
Connecticut Light, 2d Battery, Capt.
  John W. Sterling.
New York Light, 5th Battery, Capt.
  Elijah D. Taft.

Third Volunteer Brigade.

Capt. JAMES F. HUNTINGTON.

New Hampshire Light, 1st Battery, Capt.
  Frederick M. Edgell.
1st Ohio Light, Battery H, Lieut. George
  W. Norton.
1st Pennsylvania Light, Batteries F and
  G, Capt. R. Bruce Ricketts.
West Virginia Light, Battery C, Capt.
  Wallace Hill.

Fourth Volunteer Brigade.

Capt. ROBERT H. FITZHUGH.

Maine Light, 6th Battery (F), Lieut. Edwin B. Dow.
Maryland Light, Battery A, Capt. James H. Rigby.
New Jersey Light, 1st Battery, Lieut. Augustin N. Parsons.
1st New York Light, Battery G, Capt. Nelson Ames.
1st New York Light, Battery K,† Capt. Robert H. Fitzhugh.

Train Guard.

4th New Jersey Infantry (seven companies), Maj. Charles Ewing.

No. 124.

Organization of the Army of Northern Virginia at the battle of Gettysburg, July 1–3.*

FIRST ARMY CORPS.

Lieut. Gen. JAMES LONGSTREET.

M'LAWS' DIVISION.

Maj. Gen. LAFAYETTE McLAWS.

Kershaw's Brigade.

Brig. Gen. J. B. KERSHAW.

2d South Carolina:
    Col. J. D. Kennedy.
    Lieut. Col. F. Gaillard.
3d South Carolina:
    Maj. R. C. Maffett.
    Col. J. D. Nance.
7th South Carolina, Col. D. Wyatt Aiken.
8th South Carolina, Col. J. W. Henagan.
15th South Carolina:
    Col. W. D. De Saussure.
    Maj. William M. Gist.
3d South Carolina Battalion, Lieut. Col. W. G. Rice.

Barksdale's Brigade.

Brig. Gen. WILLIAM BARKSDALE.
Col. B. G. HUMPHREYS.

13th Mississippi, Col. J. W. Carter.
17th Mississippi:
    Col. W. D. Holder.
    Lieut. Col. John C. Fiser.
18th Mississippi:
    Col. T. M. Griffin.
    Lieut. Col. W. H. Luse.
21st Mississippi, Col. B. G. Humphreys.

Semmes' Brigade.†

Brig. Gen. P. J. SEMMES.
Col. GOODE BRYAN.

10th Georgia, Col. John B. Weems.
50th Georgia, Col. W. R. Manning.
51st Georgia, Col. E. Ball.
53d Georgia, Col. James P. Simms.

Wofford's Brigade.

Brig. Gen. W. T. WOFFORD.

16th Georgia, Col. Goode Bryan.
18th Georgia, Lieut. Col. S. Z. Ruff.
24th Georgia, Col. Robert McMillan.
Cobb's (Georgia) Legion, Lieut. Col. Luther J. Glenn.
Phillips (Georgia) Legion, Lieut. Col. E. S. Barclay.

Artillery.

Col. H. G. CABELL.

1st North Carolina Artillery, Battery A, Capt. B. C. Manly.
Pulaski (Georgia) Artillery:
    Capt. J. C. Fraser.
    Lieut. W. J. Furlong.
1st Richmond Howitzers, Capt. E. S. McCarthy.
Troup (Georgia) Artillery:
    Capt. H. H. Carlton.
    Lieut. C. W. Motes.

---

*The actual commanders are indicated as far as practicable.

†No reports on file for this brigade. Bryan was in command July 7, and was probably Semmes' immediate successor. The commanders of the Tenth, Fifty-first, and Fifty-third Georgia are given as reported for June 22 and July 31. Manning reported in command of Fiftieth Georgia, June 22. No commander reported on return for July 31.

Maj. Gen. GEORGE E. PICKETT.

Garnett's Brigade.

Brig. Gen. R. B. GARNETT.
Maj. C. S. PEYTON.

8th Virginia, Col. Eppa Hunton.
18th Virginia, Lieut. Col. H. A. Carrington.
19th Virginia:
    Col. Henry Gantt.
    Lieut. Col. John T. Ellis.
28th Virginia:
    Col. R. C. Allen.
    Lieut. Col. William Watts.
56th Virginia:
    Col. W. D. Stuart.
    Lieut. Col. P. P. Slaughter.

Kemper's Brigade.

Brig. Gen. J. L. KEMPER.
Col. JOSEPH MAYO, Jr.

1st Virginia:
    Col. Lewis B. Williams.
    Lieut. Col. F. G. Skinner.
3d Virginia:
    Col. Joseph Mayo, jr.
    Lieut. Col. A. D. Callcote.
7th Virginia:
    Col. W. T. Patton.
    Lieut. Col. C. C. Flowerree.
11th Virginia, Maj. Kirkwood Otey.
24th Virginia, Col. William R. Terry.

Armistead's Brigade.

Brig. Gen. L. A. ARMISTEAD.
Col. W. R. AYLETT.

9th Virginia, Maj. John C. Owens.
14th Virginia:
    Col. James G. Hodges.
    Lieut. Col. William White.
38th Virginia:
    Col. E. C. Edmonds.
    Lieut. Col. P. B. Whittle.
53d Virginia, Col. W. R. Aylett.
57th Virginia, Col. John Bowie Magruder.

Artillery.

Maj. JAMES DEARING.

Fauquier (Virginia) Artillery, Capt. R. M. Stribling.
Hampden ((Virginia) Artillery,Capt. W. H. Caskie.
Richmond Fayette Artillery, Capt. M. C. Macon.
Virginia Battery, Capt. Joseph G. Blount.

HOOD'S DIVISION

Maj. Gen. JOHN B. HOOD.
Brig. Gen. E. M. LAW.

Law's Brigade.

Brig. Gen. E. M. LAW.
Col. JAMES L. SHEFFIELD.

4th Alabama,Lieut. Col. L. H. Scruggs.
15th Alabama:
    Col. William C. Oates.
    Capt. B. A. Hill.
44th Alabama, Col. William F. Perry.
47th Alabama:
    Col. James W. Jackson.
    Lieut. Col. M. J. Bulger.
    Maj. J. M. Campbell.
48th Alabama:
    Col. James L. Sheffield.
    Capt. T. J. Eubanks.

Robertson's Brigade.

Brig. Gen. J. B. ROBERTSON.

3d Arkansas:
    Col. Van H. Manning.
    Lieut. Col. R. S. Taylor.
1st Texas, Lieut. Col. P. A. Work.
4th Texas:
    Col. J. C. G. Key.
    Maj. J. P. Bane.
5th Texas:
    Col. R. M. Powell.
    Lieut. Col. K. Bryan.
    Maj. J. C. Rogers.

Anderson's Brigade.

Brig. Gen. GEORGE T. ANDERSON.
Lieut. Col. WILLIAM LUFFMAN.

7th Georgia, Col. W. W. White.
8th Georgia, Col. John R. Towers.
9th Georgia :
    Lieut. Col. John C. Mounger.
    Maj. W. M. Jones.
    Capt. George Hillyer.
11th Georgia :
    Col. F. H. Little.
    Lieut. Col. William Luffman.
    Maj. Henry D. McDaniel.
    Capt. William H. Mitchell.
59th Georgia :
    Col. Jack Brown.
    Capt. M. G. Bass.

Benning's Brigade.

Brig. Gen. HENRY L. BENNING.

2d Georgia :
    Lieut. Col. William T. Harris.
    Maj. W. S. Shepherd.
15th Georgia, Col. D. M. DuBose.
17th Georgia, Col. W. C. Hodges.
20th Georgia :
    Col. John A. Jones.
    Lieut. Col. J. D. Waddell.

Artillery.

Maj. M. W. HENRY.

Branch (North Carolina) Artillery, Capt. A. C. Latham
German (South Carolina) Artillery, Capt. William K. Bachman.
Palmetto (South Carolina) Light Artillery, Capt. Hugh R. Garden.
Rowan (North Carolina) Artillery, Capt. James Reilly.

ARTILLERY RESERVE.

Col. J. B. WALTON.

Alexander's Battalion.

Col. E. P. ALEXANDER.

Ashland (Virginia) Artillery :
    Capt. P. Woolfolk, jr.
    Lieut. James Woolfolk.
Bedford (Virginia) Artillery, Capt. T. C. Jordan.
Brooks (South Carolina) Artillery, Lieut. S. C. Gilbert.
Madison (Louisiana) Light Artillery, Capt. George V. Moody.
Virginia Battery, Capt. W. W. Parker.
Virginia Battery, Capt. O. B. Taylor.

Washington (Louisiana) Artillery.

Maj. B. F. ESHLEMAN.

First Company, Capt. C. W. Squires.
Second Company, Capt. J. B. Richardson.
Third Company, Capt. M. B. Miller.
Fourth Company :
    Capt. Joe Norcom.
    Lieut. H. A. Battles.

SECOND ARMY CORPS.

Lieut. Gen. RICHARD S. EWELL.

Escort.

Randolph's Company Virginia Cavalry, Capt. William F. Randolph.

EARLY'S DIVISION.

Maj. Gen. JUBAL A. EARLY.

Hays' Brigade.

Brig. Gen. HARRY T. HAYS.

5th Louisiana :
    Maj. Alexander Hart.
    Capt. T. H. Biscoe.
6th Louisiana, Lieut. Col. Joseph Hanlon.
7th Louisiana, Col. D. B. Penn.
8th Louisiana :
    Col. T. D. Lewis.
    Lieut. Col. A. de Blanc.
    Maj. G. A. Lester.
9th Louisiana, Col. Leroy A. Stafford.

Smith's Brigade.

Brig. Gen. WILLIAM SMITH.

31st Virginia, Col. John S. Hoffman.
49th Virginia, Lieut. Col. J. Catlett Gibson.
52d Virginia, Lieut. Col. James H. Skinner.

Hoke's Brigade.

Col. Isaac E. Avery.
Col. A. C. Godwin.

6th North Carolina, Maj. S. McD. Tate.
21st North Carolina, Col. W. W. Kirkland.
57th North Carolina, Col. A. C. Godwin.

Gordon's Brigade.

Brig. Gen. J. B. Gordon.

13th Georgia, Col. James M. Smith.
26th Georgia, Col. E. N. Atkinson.
31st Georgia, Col. Clement A. Evans.
38th Georgia, Capt. William L. McLeod.
60th Georgia, Capt. W. B. Jones.
61st Georgia, Col. John H. Lamar.

Artillery.

Lieut. Col. H. P. Jones.

Charlottesville (Virginia) Artillery, Capt. James McD. Carrington.
Courtney (Virginia) Artillery, Capt. W. A. Tanner.
Louisiana Guard Artillery, Capt. C. A. Green.
Staunton (Virginia) Artillery, Capt. A. W. Garber.

JOHNSON'S DIVISION.

Maj. Gen. Edward Johnson.

Steuart's Brigade.

Brig. Gen. George H. Steuart.

1st Maryland Battalion Infantry:
  Lieut. Col. J. R. Herbert.
  Maj. W. W. Goldsborough.
  Capt. J. P. Crane.
1st North Carolina, Lieut. Col. H. A. Brown.
3d North Carolina, Maj. W. M. Parsley.
10th Virginia, Col. E. T. H. Warren.
23d Virginia, Lieut. Col. S. T. Walton.
37th Virginia, Maj. H. C. Wood.

Stonewall Brigade.

Brig. Gen. James A. Walker.

2d Virginia, Col. J. Q. A. Nadenbousch.
4th Virginia, Maj. William Terry.
5th Virginia, Col. J. H. S. Funk.
27th Virginia, Lieut. Col. D. M. Shriver.
33d Virginia, Capt. J. B. Golladay.

Nicholls' Brigade.*

Col. J. M. Williams.

1st Louisiana, Capt. E. D. Willett.
2d Louisiana, Lieut. Col. R. E. Burke.
10th Louisiana, Maj. T. N. Powell.
14th Louisiana, Lieut. Col. David Zable.
15th Louisiana, Maj. Andrew Brady.

Jones' Brigade.

Brig. Gen. John M. Jones.
Lieut. Col. R. H. Dungan.

21st Virginia, Capt. W. P. Moseley.
25th Virginia:
  Col. J. C. Higginbotham.
  Lieut. Col. J. A. Robinson.
42d Virginia:
  Lieut. Col. R. W. Withers.
  Capt. S. H. Saunders.
44th Virginia:
  Maj. N. Cobb.
  Capt. T. R. Buckner.
48th Virginia:
  Lieut. Col. R. H. Dungan.
  Maj. Oscar White.
50th Virginia, Lieut. Col. L. H. N. Salyer.

Artillery.

Maj. J. W. Latimer.
Capt. C. I. Raine.

1st Maryland Battery, Capt. William F. Dement.
Alleghany (Virginia) Artillery, Capt. J. C. Carpenter.
Chesapeake (Maryland) Artillery, Capt. William D. Brown.
Lee (Virginia) Battery:
  Capt. C. I. Raine.
  Lieut. William W. Hardwicke.

---

*The regimental commanders are given as reported for June 14,

Maj. Gen. R. E. RODES.

Daniel's Brigade.

Brig. Gen. JUNIUS DANIEL.

32d North Carolina, Col. E. C. Brabble.
43d North Carolina :
    Col. T. S. Kenan.
    Lieut. Col. W. G. Lewis.
45th North Carolina :
    Lieut. Col. S. H. Boyd.
    Maj. John R. Winston.
    Capt. A. H. Gallaway.
    Capt. J. A. Hopkins.
53d North Carolina, Col. W. A. Owens.
2d North Carolina Battalion :
    Lieut. Col. H. L. Andrews.
    Capt. Van Brown.

Iverson's Brigade.

Brig. Gen. ALFRED IVERSON.

5th North Carolina :*
    Capt. Speight B. West.
    Capt. Benjamin Robinson.
12th North Carolina, Lieut. Col. W. S.
    Davis.
20th North Carolina :†
    Lieut. Col. Nelson Slough.
    Capt. Lewis T. Hicks.
23d North Carolina :‡
    Col. D. H. Christie.
    Capt. William H. Johnston.

Doles' Brigade.

Brig. Gen. GEORGE DOLES.

4th Georgia :
    Lieut. Col. D. R. E. Winn.
. Maj. W. H. Willis.
12th Georgia, Col. Edward Willis.
21st Georgia, Col. John T. Mercer.
44th Georgia :
    Col. S. P. Lumpkin.
    Maj. W. H. Peebles.

Ramseur's Brigade.

Brig. Gen. S. D. RAMSEUR.

2d North Carolina :
    Maj. D. W. Hurtt.
    Capt. James T. Scales.
4th North Carolina, Col. Bryan Grimes.
14th North Carolina :
    Col. R. Tyler Bennett.
    Maj. Joseph H. Lambeth.
30th North Carolina :
    Col. Francis M. Parker.
    Maj. W. W. Sillers.

O'Neal's Brigade.

Col. E. A. O'NEAL.

3d Alabama, Col. C. A. Battle.
5th Alabama, Col. J. M. Hall.
6th Alabama :
    Col. J. N. Lightfoot.
    Capt. M. L. Bowie.
12th Alabama, Col. S. B. Pickens.
26th Alabama, Lieut. Col. John C. Goodgame.

Artillery.

Lieut. Col. THOMAS H. CARTER.

Jeff. Davis (Alabama) Artillery, Capt. W. J. Reese.
King William (Virginia) Artillery, Capt. W. P. Carter.
Morris (Virginia) Artillery, Capt. R. C. M. Page.
Orange (Virginia) Artillery, Capt. C. W. Fry.

---

* The four captains present (West, Robinson, James M. Taylor, Thomas N. Jordan), were reported as wounded July 1 ; Robinson and Taylor as having rejoined July 2, but it does not appear who commanded during Robinson's absence.

† Lieutenant-Colonel Slough and Maj. John S. Brooks reported as wounded at 4 p. m. July 1.

‡ Colonel Christie, Lieut. Col. R. D. Johnston, Maj. C. C. Blacknall, and the senior captain (Abner D. Peace), reported as wounded early in the fight, July 1,

ARTILLERY RESERVE.

Col. J. THOMPSON BROWN.

First Virginia Artillery.

Capt. WILLIS J. DANCE.

2d Richmond (Virginia) Howitzers, Capt. David Watson.
3d Richmond (Virginia) Howitzers, Capt. B. H. Smith, jr.
Powhatan (Virginia) Artillery. Lieut. John M. Cunningham.
Rockbridge (Virginia) Artillery, Capt. A. Graham.
Salem (Virginia) Artillery, Lieut. C. B. Griffin.

Nelson's Battalion.

Lieut. Col. WILLIAM NELSON.

Amherst (Virginia) Artillery, Capt. T. J. Kirkpatrick.
Fluvanna (Virginia) Artillery, Capt. J. L. Massie.
Georgia Battery, Capt. John Milledge, jr.

THIRD ARMY CORPS.

Lieut. Gen. AMBROSE P. HILL.

ANDERSON'S DIVISION.

Maj. Gen. R. H. ANDERSON.

Wilcox's Brigade.

Brig. Gen. CADMUS M. WILCOX.

8th Alabama, Lieut. Col. Hilary A. Herbert.
9th Alabama, Capt. J. H. King.
10th Alabama:
    Col. William H. Forney.
    Lieut. Col. James E. Shelley.
11th Alabama:
    Col. J. C. C. Sanders.
    Lieut. Col. George E. Tayloe.
14th Alabama:
    Col. L. Pinckard.
    Lieut. Col. James A. Broome.

Wright's Brigade.

Brig. Gen. A. R. WRIGHT.
Col. WILLIAM GIBSON.
Brig. Gen. A. R. WRIGHT.

3d Georgia, Col. E. J. Walker.
22d Georgia:
    Col. Joseph Wasden.
    Capt. B. C. McCurry.
48th Georgia:
    Col. William Gibson.
    Capt. M. R. Hall.
    Col. William Gibson.
2d Georgia Battalion:
    Maj. George W. Ross.
    Capt. Charles J. Moffett.

Mahone's Brigade.

Brig. Gen. WILLIAM MAHONE.

6th Virginia, Col. George T. Rogers.
12th Virginia, Col. D. A. Weisiger.
16th Virginia, Col. Joseph H. Ham.
41st Virginia, Col. William A. Parham.
61st Virginia, Col. V. D. Groner.

Perry's Brigade.

Col. DAVID LANG.

2d Florida, Maj. W. R. Moore.
5th Florida, Capt. R. N. Gardner.
8th Florida, Col. David Lang.

Posey's Brigade.

Brig. Gen. CARNOT POSEY.

12th Mississippi, Col. W. H. Taylor.
16th Mississippi, Col. Samuel E. Baker.
19th Mississippi, Col. N. H. Harris.
48th Mississippi, Col. Joseph M. Jayne.

Artillery (Sumter Battalion).

Maj. JOHN LANE.

Company A, Capt. Hugh M. Ross.
Company B, Capt. George M. Patterson.
Company C, Capt. John T. Wingfield.

Maj. Gen. HENRY HETH.
Brig. Gen. J. J. PETTIGREW.

First Brigade.

Brig. Gen. J. J. PETTIGREW.
Col. J. K. MARSHALL.

11th North Carolina, Col. Collett Leventhorpe.
26th North Carolina:
    Col. Henry K. Burgwyn, jr.
    Capt. H. C. Albright.
47th North Carolina, Col. G. H. Faribault.
52d North Carolina:
    Col. J. K. Marshall.
    Lieut. Col. Marcus A. Parks.

Second Brigade.

Col. J. M. BROCKENBROUGH.

40th Virginia:
    Capt. T. E. Betts.
    Capt. R. B. Davis.
47th Virginia, Col. Robert M. Mayo.
55th Virginia, Col. W. S. Christian.
22d Virginia Battalion, Maj. John S. Bowles.

Third Brigade.

Brig. Gen. JAMES J. ARCHER.
Col. B. D. FRY.
Lieut. Col. S. G. SHEPARD.

13th Alabama, Col. B. D. Fry.
5th Alabama Battalion, Maj. A. S. Van de Graaff.
1st Tennessee (Provisional Army), Maj. Felix G. Buchanan.
7th Tennessee, Lieut. Col. S. G. Shepard.
14th Tennessee, Capt. B. L. Phillips.

Fourth Brigade.

Brig. Gen. JOSEPH R. DAVIS.

2d Mississippi, Col. J. M. Stone.
11th Mississippi, Col. F. M. Green.
42d Mississippi, Col. H. R. Miller.
55th North Carolina, Col. J. K. Connally.

Artillery.

Lieut. Col. JOHN J. GARNETT.

Donaldsonville (Louisiana) Artillery, Capt. V. Maurin.
Huger (Virginia) Artillery, Capt. Joseph D. Moore.
Lewis (Virginia) Artillery, Capt. John W. Lewis.
Norfolk Light Artillery Blues, Capt. C. R. Grandy.

PENDER'S DIVISION.

Maj. Gen. WILLIAM D. PENDER.
Brig. Gen. JAMES H. LANE.
Maj. Gen. I. R. TRIMBLE.
Brig. Gen. JAMES H. LANE.

First Brigade.

Col. ABNER PERRIN.

1st South Carolina (Provisional Army), Maj. C. W. McCreary.
1st South Carolina Rifles, Capt. William M. Hadden.
12th South Carolina, Col. John L. Miller.
13th South Carolina, Lieut. Col. B. T. Brockman.
14th South Carolina, Lieut. Col. Joseph N. Brown.

Second Brigade.

Brig. Gen. JAMES H. LANE.
Col. C. M. AVERY.
Brig. Gen. JAMES H. LANE.
Col. C. M. AVERY.

7th North Carolina:
    Capt. J. McLeod Turner.
    Capt. James G. Harris.
18th North Carolina, Col. John D. Barry.
28th North Carolina:
    Col. S. D. Lowe.
    Lieut. Col. W. H. A. Speer.
33d North Carolina, Col. C. M. Avery.
37th North Carolina, Col. W. M. Barbour.

Third Brigade.

Brig. Gen. EDWARD L. THOMAS.

14th Georgia.
35th Georgia.
45th Georgia.
49th Georgia, Col. S. T. Player.

Fourth Brigade.

Brig. Gen. A. M. SCALES.
Lieut. Col. G. T. GORDON.
Col. W. LEE J. LOWRANCE.

13th North Carolina :
 Col. J. H. Hyman.
 Lieut. Col. H. A. Rogers.
16th North Carolina, Capt. L. W. Stowe.
22d North Carolina, Col. James Conner.
34th North Carolina :
 Col. William Lee J. Lowrance.
 Lieut. Col. G. T. Gordon.
38th North Carolina :
 Col. W. J. Hoke.
 Lieut. Col. John Ashford.

Artillery.

Maj. WILLIAM T. POAGUE.

Albemarle (Virginia) Artillery, Capt. James W. Wyatt.
Charlotte (North Carolina) Artillery, Capt. Joseph Graham.
Madison (Mississippi) Light Artillery, Capt. George Ward.
Virginia Battery, Capt. J. V. Brooke.

ARTILLERY RESERVE.
Col. R. LINDSAY WALKER.

McIntosh's Battalion.

Maj. D. G. McINTOSH.

Danville (Virginia) Artillery, Capt. R. S. Rice.
Hardaway (Alabama) Artillery, Capt. W. B. Hurt.
2d Rockbridge (Virginia) Artillery, Lieut. Samuel Wallace.
Virginia Battery, Capt. M. Johnson.

Pegram's Battalion.

Maj. W. J. PEGRAM.
Capt. E. B. BRUNSON.

Crenshaw (Virginia) Battery.
Fredericksburg (Virginia) Artillery, Capt. E. A. Marye.
Letcher (Virginia) Artillery, Capt. T. A. Brander.
Pee Dee (South Carolina) Artillery, Lieut. William E. Zimmerman.
Purcell (Virginia) Artillery, Capt. Joseph McGraw.

CAVALRY.
STUART'S DIVISION.
Maj. Gen. J. E. B. STUART.

Hampton's Brigade.

Brig. Gen. WADE HAMPTON.
Col. L. S. BAKER.

1st North Carolina, Col. L. S. Baker.
1st South Carolina.
2d South Carolina.
Cobb's (Georgia) Legion.
Jeff. Davis Legion.
Phillips (Georgia) Legion.

Robertson's Brigade.

Br'g. Gen. BEVERLY H. ROBERTSON.*

4th North Carolina, Col. D. D. Ferebee.
5th North Carolina.

Fitz. Lee's Brigade.

Brig. Gen. FITZ. LEE.

1st Maryland Battalion : †
 Maj. Harry Gilmor.
 Maj. Ridgely Brown.
1st Virginia, Col. James H. Drake.
2d Virginia, Col. T. T. Munford.
3d Virginia, Col. Thomas H. Owen.
4th Virginia, Col. Williams C. Wickham.
5th Virginia, Col. T. L. Rosser.

Jenkins' Brigade.

Brig. Gen. A. G. JENKINS.
Col. M. J. FERGUSON.

14th Virginia.
16th Virginia.
17th Virginia.
34th Virginia Battalion, Lieut. Col. V. A. Witcher.
36th Virginia Battalion.
Jackson's (Virginia) Battery, Capt. Thomas E. Jackson.

---

* Commanded his own and W. E. Jones' brigade. † Serving with Ewell's corps.

Jones' Brigade.	*W. H. F. Lee's Brigade.*
Brig. Gen. WILLIAM E. JONES.	Col. J. R. CHAMBLISS, Jr.
6th Virginia, Maj. C. E. Flournoy.	2d North Carolina.
7th Virginia, Lieut. Col. Thomas Marshall.	9th Virginia, Col. R. L. T. Beale.
	10th Virginia, Col. J. Lucius Davis.
11th Virginia, Col. L. L. Lomax.	13th Virginia.

Stuart Horse Artillery.

Maj. R. F. BECKHAM.

Breathed's (Virginia) Battery, Capt. James Breathed.
Chew's (Virginia) Battery, Capt. R. P. Chew.
Griffin's (Maryland) Battery, Capt. W. H. Griffin.
Hart's (South Carolina) Battery, Capt. J. F. Hart.
McGregor's (Virginia) Battery, Capt. W. M. McGregor.
Moorman's (Virginia) Battery, Capt. M. N. Moorman.

IMBODEN'S COMMAND.

Brig. Gen. J. D. IMBODEN.

18th Virginia Cavalry, Col. George W. Imboden.
62d Virginia Infantry,* Col. George H. Smith.
Virginia Partisan Rangers, Capt. John H. McNeill.
Virginia Battery, Capt. J. H. McClanahan.

ARTILLERY.†

Brig. Gen. W. N. PENDLETON.

NOTES

ABBREVIATIONS

The following abbreviations are used in the notes and illustration credits.

AAS American Antiquarian Society, Worcester, Massachusetts.

ACHS Adams County Historical Society, Gettysburg, Pennsylvania.

BC Bowdoin College Library, Brunswick, Maine.

BP John B. Bachelder Papers, New Hampshire Historical Society, Concord, New Hampshire.

BPL Bancroft Public Library, Salem, New York.

CC Thomas Clemens Collection, U.S. Army Military History Institute, U.S. Army History Collection, Carlisle Barracks, Pennsylvania.

CCW U.S. Congress. *Report of the Joint Committee on the Conduct of the War at the Second Session, Thirty-Eighth Congress, Army of the Potomac, General Meade.* . . . Washington, D.C.: U.S. Government Printing Office, 1865.

CSL Connecticut State Library, Hartford, Connecticut.

CU Colgate University Archives, Case Library, Hamilton, New York.

CW&M College of William and Mary, Earl Gregg Swem Library, Williamsburg, Virginia.

CWMC Civil War Miscellaneous Collection, U.S. Army Military History Institute, U.S. Army History Collection, Carlisle Barracks, Pennsylvania.

CWTI *Civil War Times Illustrated* Collection, U.S. Army Military History Institute, U.S. Army History Collection, Carlisle Barracks, Pennsylvania.

DAB Allen Johnson and Dumas Malone, eds. *Dictionary of American Biography.* 20 vols. New York: Charles Scribner's Sons, 1928–36.

DU Duke University, Special Collections Library, Durham, North Carolina.

FNMP Fredericksburg and Spotsylvania National Military Park, Fredericksburg, Virginia.

GCC Gregory Coco Collection, Harrisburg Civil War Round Table, U.S. Army Military History Institute, U.S. Army History Collection, Carlisle Barracks, Pennsylvania.

GDAH Georgia Department of Archives and History, Atlanta, Georgia.

GNMP Gettysburg National Military Park, Gettysburg, Pennsylvania.

HLA Handley Library Archives, Winchester, Virginia.

HSP Historical Society of Pennsylvania, Philadelphia, Pennsylvania.

LC Library of Congress, Washington, D.C.

MC   Museum of the Confederacy, Ellen S. Brockenbrough Library, Richmond, Virginia.

ML   George G. Meade Collection, Letters, Meade and Gettysburg, Historical Society of Pennsylvania, Philadelphia, Pennsylvania.

MM   Military Order of the Loyal Legion of the United States, Massachusetts, U.S. Army Military History Institute, Carlisle Barracks, Pennsylvania.

NA   National Archives, Washington, D.C.

NCDAH   North Carolina Department of Cultural Resources, Division of Archives and History, Raleigh, North Carolina.

NCWRTC   Norwich Civil War Round Table Collection, U.S. Army Military History Institute, U.S. Army History Collection, Carlisle Barracks, Pennsylvania.

NSUL   Northwestern State University of Louisiana, Watson Memorial Library, Cammie Henry Research Center, Natchitoches, Louisiana.

NYHS   New-York Historical Society, New York, New York.

NYPL   New York Public Library, Rare Books and Manuscripts Division, New York, New York.

OR   U.S. War Department. *The War of the Rebellion: A Compilation of the Official Records of the Union and Confederate Armies*. 128 vols. Washington, D.C.: U.S. Government Printing Office, 1880–1901. All citations to *OR* are to series 1.

PSA   Pennsylvania Historical and Museum Commission, Pennsylvania State Archives, Harrisburg, Pennsylvania.

PU   Princeton University Library, Rare Books and Special Collections, Princeton, New Jersey.

RBC   Robert L. Brake Collection, U.S. Army Military History Institute, U.S. Army History Collection, Carlisle Barracks, Pennsylvania.

SHC   University of North Carolina, Wilson Library, Southern Historical Collection, Chapel Hill, North Carolina.

TSLA   Tennessee State Library and Archives, Nashville, Tennessee.

TU   Tulane University, Howard Tilton Memorial Library, Louisiana Historical Association Collection, New Orleans, Louisiana.

USAMHI   U.S. Army Military History Institute, U.S. Army History Collection, Carlisle Barracks, Pennsylvania.

UV   University of Virginia, Alderman Library, Charlottesville, Virginia.

VHS   Virginia Historical Society, Richmond, Virginia.

W&L   Washington and Lee University Library, Special Collections and Papers of the Rockbridge Historical Society, Lexington, Virginia.

WLM   War Library and Museum, Military Order of the Loyal Legion of the United States, Philadelphia, U.S. Army Military History Institute, Carlisle Barracks, Pennsylvania.

1. *DAB* 3:229–30; Boatner, *Dictionary*, pp. 268–69. Much of the biographical material on Ewell, here and below, was taken from a draft biography by Donald C. Pfanz.

2. Oath, 19 July 1865, Ewell Papers, LC; *DAB* 3:230.

3. "Memoirs of Clement D. Fishburne," p. 83, UV; Harriet Stoddert Turner to Early, 3 Mar. 1878, J. A. Early Papers, VHS. Harriet Turner, his stepdaughter, cited criticisms of Ewell by Col. Walter Taylor (see Taylor, "Second Paper") and postwar remarks attributed by William Allan to General Lee.

4. Hotchkiss, "Draft Review of *From Manassas to Appomattox*," Hotchkiss Papers, LC.

5. Freeman, *Lee's Lieutenants*, 2:713.

6. Ibid., pp. 701–2.

7. Ibid., pp. 702–6; Boatner, *Dictionary*, pp. 106, 442–43, 849, 884.

8. Robertson, *General A. P. Hill*. Robertson determined that Hill was afflicted with syphilis and that its effects were becoming increasingly debilitating.

9. Coddington, *Gettysburg Campaign*, pp. 41–42; Hunt, "First Day," pp. 259–61. The Army of the Potomac had sixty-seven batteries. See *OR* 27 (1):157–68. A Federal artillery brigade and Confederate battalion were comparable.

10. Carpenter, *Sword*, p. 19; Young, *Gettysburg*, p. 345.

11. *DAB* 4:279; Carpenter, *Sword*, pp. 7–8.

12. Carpenter, *Sword*, p. 19; McFeely, *Yankee Stepfather*, p. 38.

13. Carpenter, *Sword*, pp. 18, 26; McFeely, *Yankee Stepfather*, p. 33; Haskell, *Gettysburg*, p. 35.

14. Harwell and Racine, *Fiery Trail*, p. 100.

15. Carpenter, *Sword*, p. 27.

16. Ibid., pp. 32–33; Boatner, *Dictionary*, p. 413.

17. O. O. Howard, *Autobiography*, 1:349; Carpenter, *Sword*, pp. 42–43.

18. O. O. Howard, *Autobiography*, 1:349, 536–37; Howard to Mother, "Before Gettysburg," C. H. Howard Papers, BC; Hitz, *Winkler*, p. 41; McFeely, *Yankee Stepfather*, p. 14. In his autobiography, Howard wrote that later in the war Gen. Thomas J. Wood kidded him in Gen. William T. Sherman's presence about being a teetotaler. Sherman retorted, "Wood, let Howard alone! I want one officer who don't drink."

19. Howard to Mother, 27 Dec. 1863, O. O. Howard Papers, BC; Doubleday to Bates, 19 Oct. 1875, Bates Papers, PSA.

20. Hitz, *Winkler*, p. 43.

21. Hooker to Bates, 15 Aug. 1876, Bates Papers, PSA; Hunt to Gantt, 1 Nov. 1882, Hunt Papers, LC.

22. Nevins, *Wainwright*, pp. 183, 210. Doubleday, who did not like Howard, repeated a story that was probably told among their colleagues: "At West Point he talked nothing but religion. If a young lady was introduced to him he would ask her if she had reflected on the goodness of God during the past night." Doubleday to Bates, 19 Oct. 1875, Bates Papers, PSA.

23. Hunt, "First Day," p. 256; Hitz, *Winkler*, p. 61. Hunt wrote, "Under the

circumstances no men could have withstood such a sudden attack as that made by 'Stonewall' Jackson on the flank and rear of the Eleventh Corps."

24. *OR* 27 (1):305, 313; Coddington, *Gettysburg Campaign*, pp. 8–9.

25. *OR* 27 (2):305, 313, 439, (3):27.

26. Coddington, *Gettysburg Campaign*, p. 73; *OR* 27 (2):306, 314–15.

27. *OR* 27 (2):307, 443.

28. Ibid., pp. 307, 316, 443, 466–68.

29. *OR* 27 (1):142–44.

30. *OR* 27 (2):443, 551–52; Gallagher, "Ewell," p. 56.

31. *OR* 27 (2):443, 697; Gallagher, "Ewell," p. 56; "Memoirs of Clement D. Fishburne," pp. 90–91, UV.

32. *OR* 27 (2):316, 444, 552.

33. *OR* 27 (1):114, 144.

34. Ibid., pp. 67, 144.

35. O. O. Howard, *Autobiography*, 1:402.

36. *OR* 27 (3):416–21.

CHAPTER TWO

1. *OR* 27 (1):144, (3):414–17. The house that was Moritz Tavern is just north of the interchange of U.S. 15 and the old Emmitsburg Road. In 1863 it was in the southeast corner of a crossroads, but the new highway has severed the road to the east.

2. Schurz, *Reminiscences*, 3:3; Hitz, *Winkler*, pp. 67–68.

3. Pula, *Krzyzanowski*, pp. 91–92.

4. O. O. Howard, *Autobiography*, 1:302–3, and "Campaign," p. 51; Howard to Jacobs, 23 Mar. 1864, O. O. Howard Papers, BC; C. H. Howard, "First Day," p. 313. General Howard thought that Lt. F. W. Gilbreath was the aide who accompanied him, but Maj. Charles H. Howard, his brother, wrote that it was he who rode with the general to see Reynolds. Capt. Daniel Hall wrote in 1877 that he had gone to see Reynolds also. See Hall to Howard, 19 Feb. 1877, O. O. Howard Papers, BC.

5. O. O. Howard, *Autobiography*, 1:402.

6. *OR* 27 (1):701; O. O. Howard, *Autobiography*, 1:403, and "Campaign," p. 52.

7. *OR* 27 (3):414, 417. The reported Confederate advance on Gettysburg must have been that made by Pettigrew's brigade. The colonel to whom Early's note was addressed was probably either Elijah V. White of the 35th Cavalry Battalion or William French of the 17th Virginia Cavalry Regiment.

8. *OR* 27 (1):923–24, (3):417–18; Coddington, *Gettysburg Campaign*, p. 234; Nichols, *Toward Gettysburg*, p. 196.

9. *OR* 27 (3):416.

10. Ibid., pp. 616–17.

11. O. O. Howard, *Autobiography*, 1:408; C. H. Howard, "First Day," pp. 313–14.

12. M. Jacobs, "Meteorology." Michael Jacobs (1808–1871) was born in Waynesboro, Pennsylvania, and attended Jefferson College. He was a Lutheran pastor

and at the time of the battle was a professor of mathematics and natural sciences at Pennsylvania College (now Gettysburg College). In 1845 he had developed a method of preserving fruit by canning. During the battle he recorded weather observations and afterward wrote of his experiences during the battle and authored a book on the campaign. See Law, *Berlin Improvement Society*, p. 209.

13. *OR* 27 (1):244, 265, 418, 701; O. O. Howard, *Autobiography*, 1:408; Nichols, *Toward Gettysburg*, pp. 198–99; Doubleday, *Chancellorsville*, p. 125.

14. Reynolds to Howard, 1 July 1863, Bates Papers, PSA; *OR* 27 (3):457. Reynolds must have written this letter somewhere north of Marsh Creek.

The Peach Orchard is about 1.5 miles from Cemetery Hill. In the discussion of distance below, with respect to the Army of the Potomac, Cemetery Hill will be the measurement point for Gettysburg.

15. O. O. Howard, *Autobiography*, 1:409, and "Campaign," p. 53; Howard to Coppee, 3 Mar. 1864, Howard to Riddle, 22 Mar. 1864, and Howard to Hall, 23 May 1872, O. O. Howard Papers, BC. In both *Autobiography* and "Campaign," Howard stated that when there was no action, "supporting distance" would have been somewhere in the area of four to five miles in the rear—in this case he would have halted his corps near Rock Creek.

16. *OR* 27 (1):114, 727; O. O. Howard, *Autobiography*, 1:410–11, and "Campaign," p. 53. Howard emphasized that both he and Meysenburg meant that it was a "good position" for the whole army. Howard used these quotations in several talks and articles. In his account, Maj. C. H. Howard said that the staff officer O. O. Howard spoke to was Lieutenant Colonel Assmussen and that Assmussen was with Schurz's column. It seems likely that Howard would have made this comment first to Meysenburg, who was with him when he reached the hill, although he might have repeated it to Assmussen later.

Doubleday wrote that it was "probable" that Reynolds ordered Howard to form his corps on Cemetery Hill. He stated that Lt. Joseph G. Rosengarten of Reynolds's staff heard the order given for Howard to occupy Cemetery Ridge. See Doubleday, *Chancellorsville*, pp. 126–27.

17. O. O. Howard, *Autobiography*, 1:411.

18. Ibid., p. 412; O. O. Howard, "Campaign," p. 54. Howard's visit to the Fahnestock building is described in Kiefer, *One Hundred and Fifty-third Regiment*, pp. 120–21, as recalled by Skelly and others. They state that Howard was accompanied to the observatory by Skelly, Mrs. E. G. Fahnestock, Isaac L. Johns, and August Bentley. If so, Howard had more local help than he probably needed. Both the courthouse and the Fahnestock building exist today, but the courthouse has an addition to its rear and right and another floor has been added onto the Fahnestock building.

19. Coddington, *Gettysburg Campaign*, pp. 260–77; Hassler, *Crisis*. Hassler's excellent monograph is devoted solely to the battle of 1 July. *The First Day at Gettysburg*, edited by Gary Gallagher, contains four excellent essays on leadership during the battle of 1 July.

20. O. O. Howard, *Autobiography*, 1:412–13, and "Campaign," p. 54; C. H. Howard, "First Day," pp. 243–44. In his report (*OR* 27 [1]:702), Howard wrote that he had been told of Reynolds's death by Maj. William Riddle, but later he said

his aide Captain Hall told him instead. See Howard to Chaplain Winfield Scott, 20 July 1888, and Howard to Fowler, 20 July 1888, O. O. Howard Papers, BC.

Doubleday probably instructed both Hall and Major Howard to advise General Howard that he was in command. Yet in 1874 he expressed doubts as to Howard's right to succeed to the left wing. Perhaps Doubleday, who could be a nitpicker, saw a technical difference between Howard's taking command of the troops on the field and taking command of the right wing. See Doubleday to Bates, 24 Apr. 1874, Bates Papers, PSA.

Howard remembered the orderly as a Lieutenant Quinn; Skelly wrote that he was Guinn, whom he knew. I could find no Lieutenant Quinn that might have qualified. See Skelly, *A Boy's Experiences*, p. 12.

21. O. O. Howard, *Autobiography*, 1:413, and "Campaign," p. 54; "Address to Graduating Class, Syracuse University, 10 June 1903," Biographical Articles and Addresses, no. 23, O. O. Howard Papers, BC; Skelly, *A Boy's Experiences*, p. 14.

22. O. O. Howard, *Autobiography*, 1:413, and "Campaign," p. 54; *OR* 27 (3):463, 464; C. H. Howard, "First Day," pp. 316, 321–22. In his accounts of the battle, Howard stated that he sent off these dispatches soon after he learned of Reynolds's death. Major Howard wrote that the general was informed of the death between 10:30 and 11:00 A.M., therefore the dispatches should have gotten off by noon. Yet in his dispatch to Meade concerning this, Sickles wrote that Howard's dispatch to him was timed 1:30 P.M. Unfortunately, no copies of these dispatches have been found.

According to Major Howard, Pearson wrote that he had been delayed by looking for Sickles north of Emmitsburg before he found him in Emmitsburg itself.

23. *OR* 27 (1):727; Schurz, *Reminiscences*, 3:4–5; Hartwig, "11th Army Corps," p. 33.

24. Cemetery Hill itself rises from Winebrenner's Run, at the south edge of the town, to a height of about 100 feet. Its crest extends in a southwest-northeast direction for about 700 yards. The Baltimore Pike, approaching Gettysburg from the southeast, crosses a shallow saddle on the crest about 150 yards from its northeast slope and runs down to a junction with the Emmitsburg Road at a point about 400 yards north of the crest. That part of the hill northeast of the pike has been called East Cemetery Hill. Its northeast slope is steep, and near its base was Brickyard Lane, now Wainwright Avenue, which connected the Menchey's Spring area with the south end of the town. The gentler north slope of the hill is from a shoulder that bulges toward the town and parallels the Baltimore Pike on its west slope. The Taneytown Road, which approaches from the south, crosses over the southwest nose of the crest at the side of a saddle that separates Cemetery Hill from Cemetery Ridge. It intersects the Emmitsburg Road about 300 yards southwest of the Baltimore Pike junction. Thus, the largest portion of Cemetery Hill is located within an area bounded by the Taneytown Road on the west, the Emmitsburg Road on the northwest, and the Baltimore Pike on the northeast.

25. Schurz, *Reminiscences*, 3:6.

26. *OR* 27 (1):702–3, 727; O. O. Howard, *Autobiography*, 1:413; Schurz, *Reminiscences*, 3:7. General Wadsworth advised an advance but did not know if the enemy was moving around his right. See *OR* 27 (3):463.

27. *DAB* 8:466–67; Boatner, *Dictionary*, pp. 727, 761.

28. *DAB* 8:470; Howard to Mother, "Before Gettysburg," C. H. Howard Papers, BC. The misfortunes of the Eleventh Corps did not adversely affect Schurz's career, either in the army or as a civilian. After the war, he became a senator from Missouri and was secretary of the interior under Pres. Rutherford B. Hayes.

29. *OR* 27 (1):702, 727, 747, 752; Schurz, *Reminiscences*, 3:7; Wheeler, *In Memorium*, p. 408; T. W. Osborn, "Artillery." Apparently all of the batteries of the Eleventh Corps were marching with Schurz's column and none with Barlow's. Dilger marched with Schurz's division, Wheeler with von Steinwehr's.

30. *OR* 27 (1):702, 728; O. O. Howard, "Campaign," p. 55; Schurz, "Gettysburg," p. 275.

31. Howard's headquarters site is marked by a upright cannon barrel on the crest of East Cemetery Hill.

32. O. O. Howard, "Campaign," pp. 55–56, and *Autobiography*, 1:414. Daniel M. Connor, Company K, 1st Indiana Cavalry, claimed that he carried the first dispatch to Meade and that Meade questioned him about the situation at Gettysburg. See Connor, "At Gettysburg."

33. H. Jacobs, "Eyewitness," GNMP.

34. Butts, *A Gallant Captain*, p. 74; Nicholson, *Pennsylvania*, 1:434; Schurz, *Reminiscences*, 3:8. Von Gilsa, in a letter written to General Howard on 30 June 1863, stated that Barlow on 27 June had sent him an order to rejoin the First Division at Middletown, Maryland, but since it was contrary to an order from Howard, he had disregarded it. See Letters Received, 11th Corps, vol. 1, part 2, RG 393, NA.

Henry Hauschild is buried in Gettysburg National Cemetery.

35. *OR* 27 (1):266, 703, 721, 724, 758, 751; Howard to Bates, 14 Sept. 1875, Bates Papers, PSA; Hartwig, "11th Army Corps," p. 40.

36. Howard to Bates, 14 Sept. 1875, Bates Papers, PSA.

CHAPTER THREE

1. *OR* 27 (2):307, 443–44, 467–68, 503, 552; Trimble to Bachelder, 8 Feb. 1883, BP; Coddington, *Gettysburg Campaign*, pp. 188–92. General Early wrote that Capt. Elliott Johnston carried the recall order to him. Capt. Frank A. Bond and four men of Company A, 1st Maryland Cavalry, escorted Johnston on this potentially dangerous ride. See Bond, "Company A."

2. Freeman, *Lee's Lieutenants*, 2:256–57, 417, 700–701; Trimble, "Battle," pp. 120–21; Boatner, *Dictionary*, p. 849.

3. Trimble, "Battle," p. 122; Trimble to Bachelder, 8 Feb. 1883, BP.

4. Trimble to Bachelder, 8 Feb. 1883, BP; Trimble, "Battle," p. 122; Trimble, "Campaign," p. 211; Coddington, *Gettysburg Campaign*, pp. 192–93, 656. Coddington suggested that Trimble overemphasized Ewell's indecisiveness and his own perceptiveness. Coddington was right!

5. *OR* 27 (2):444, 468. In his accounts, Trimble suggested that no orders were given that night. The reports cited suggest otherwise. The road designations are modern.

6. Trimble to Bachelder, 8 Feb. 1883, BP; "Personal Narrative, C. Brown," Hunt Papers, LC.

7. "Personal Narrative, C. Brown," Hunt Papers, LC; *OR* 27 (2):444.

8. *OR* 27 (1):938, (2):552, 578–79, 596; Nicholson, *Pennsylvania*, 2:877. The cavalry line was posted about three miles north of Gettysburg, possibly at the north end of Oak Ridge proper and on the road south of the run near the Deardorff farm. The low ground, in geological terms, is the "Gettysburg plain." It is a plateau cut by ravines and containing hills such as the Round Tops and Culp's Hill on the battlefield. See Stose, *Geology*, pp. 14–15.

9. *OR* 27 (2):552.

10. Ibid., pp. 444, 552; Trimble to Bachelder, 8 Feb. 1883, BP. Lt. Col. Thomas H. Carter and General Lee were cousins.

11. *OR* 27 (1):248, 289.

12. "Personal Narrative, C. Brown," Hunt Papers, LC; G. C. Brown, "Reminiscences," TSLA. Stuart reached Carlisle on the afternoon of 1 July.

13. *OR* 27 (2):444, 552; Connor, "At Gettysburg."

14. *OR* 27 (2):444; G. C. Brown, "Reminiscences," p. 29, TSLA; "Personal Narrative, C. Brown," Hunt Papers, LC. At First Manassas, General Ewell had not received an important dispatch from Gen. Pierre Beauregard because the courier did not reach him. Thereafter, Ewell often sent important dispatches by two separate riders.

15. *OR* 27 (2):468; E. M. Daniel, *Speeches*, p. 80; J. A. Early, *Memoirs*, p. 266; J. W. Daniel, "Memoir of the Battle of Gettysburg," p. 1, VHS.

16. *OR* 27 (2):468, 495; J. W. Daniel, "Memoir of the Battle of Gettysburg," pp. 2–3, VHS; E. M. Daniel, *Speeches*, pp. 80–81. The position of Jones's battalion is now surrounded by a subdivision, and its character is altered beyond recognition.

17. *OR* 27 (2):607, 638, 656.

18. Ibid., pp. 317, 607, 638; Hassler, *Crisis*, p. 88; Freeman, *Lee's Lieutenants*, 3:86–87, and *R. E. Lee*, 3:70–71. In his report of January 1864, Lee wrote that Hill ordered an advance as soon as Pender's division arrived. In his report, Hill wrote that Pender advanced when Rodes arrived and suggested that at this time Heth was already engaged. Heth said only that he was ordered to advance and was told that Pender would support him. Heth's account, from which the above was taken, was written after the war and does not mention Hill.

19. For a full account of the battle of 1 July, see Hassler, *Crisis*. For an analysis of leadership, see Gallagher, *First Day*.

20. *OR* 27 (2):662.

21. Hitz, *Winkler*, p. 70. For an excellent brief account of the fight of the Eleventh Corps on 1 July, see Hartwig, "11th Army Corps."

22. *OR* 27 (1):703; O. O. Howard, *Autobiography*, 1:416–17, and "Campaign," pp. 56–57; Howard to Bates, 14 Sept. 1875, Bates Papers, PSA.

23. *OR* 27 (1):703, 939; New York Monuments Commission, *Final Report*, 3:1247. Devin's cavalry brigade was supposed to be on the right of the York Pike near the town at this time. If so, it was at about half the distance to Jones's battalion and probably to the right. No cavalrymen were hit.

24. *OR* 27 (1):703–4; O. O. Howard, "Campaign," p. 57, and *Autobiography*, 1:417.

25. Doubleday to Bates, 3 Apr. 1874, Bates Papers, PSA; Doubleday, *Chancellorsville*, p. 146. In his report of the battle (*OR* 27 [1]:246–47), Doubleday wrote that to have fallen back from the position west of Gettysburg without orders from the commanding general "might have inflicted lasting disgrace upon the corps" and that there were abundant reasons for holding on. Certainly Reynolds intended to do so. Yet in this letter Doubleday stated that Howard tried to hold on too long. He claimed that Howard had said that "the misconduct of his corps [at Chancellorsville] forced him always to vote for assaulting the enemy whether it was the best thing to do or not."

26. *OR* 27 (1):704, 934; O. O. Howard, "Campaign," p. 57.

27. *OR* 27 (1):704, 721; Doubleday, *Chancellorsville*, p. 149.

28. Hassler, *Crisis*, pp. 149–50; Coddington, *Gettysburg Campaign*, p. 305. Coddington said that of the Eleventh Corps' 7,500 "ultimately engaged," there were 3,000 casualties or 40 percent.

CHAPTER FOUR

1. Hitz, *Winkler*, p. 71.

2. Ibid.

3. "The Story of Mrs. Jacob Kitzmiller [Anna Garlach]," ACHS; Dawes, *Sixth Wisconsin*, p. 178. The First Corps insignia was a disk, the Eleventh Corps badge a crescent, and the Twelfth Corps a star. The color of the first division of each was red, the second division was white, and the third division was blue. The insignia was usually a piece of flannel sewed to the top of the kepi, but sometimes it was a metal badge worn on the blouse.

4. *OR* 27 (1):251, 730; Doubleday Testimony, *CCW*, p. 308; Schurz to Frank Moore, 6 June 1885, De Coppet Collection, PU; Schurz, *Reminiscences*, 3:12.

5. H. Jacobs, "Eyewitness," GNMP; M. Jacobs, *Notes*, pp. 24–25.

6. *OR* 27 (1):356.

7. Nevins, *Wainwright*, pp. 236–37.

8. Culp, "Gettysburg."

9. Butts, *A Gallant Captain*, pp. 76–77. The sword had been carried by an uncle who had served as a general of cavalry under Napoleon. Von Fritsch belonged to the 68th New York Regiment.

10. Culp, "Gettysburg."

11. *OR* 27 (1):276–77; Dawes, "With the Sixth," pp. 229–32.

12. *OR* 27 (1):735; New York Monuments Commission, *Final Report*, 1:25, 374–76, 380. The legend on the regiment's Gettysburg memorial states that those men captured refused parole, hoping "to encumber the enemy, believing that the Union army would capture the cripple foe and thereby effect their release." Many men were imprisoned at Andersonville. Captain Irsch received a Medal of Honor for his heroism on 1 July.

13. Nevins, *Wainwright*, p. 236; *OR* 27 (1):357.

14. Stewart, "Battery B," p. 370. The more famous railroad cut was at McPherson Ridge 400 yards to the west.

15. Ibid., pp. 371–72.

16. *OR* 27 (1):231; Nevins, *Wainwright*, p. 236. Apparently most of the caissons had been sent ahead to Cemetery Hill. See Nicholson, *Pennsylvania*, 2:899.

17. *OR* 27 (1):357, 363; McKelvey, "George Breck's Civil War Letters," p. 129; Nevins, *Wainwright*, p. 237. Wainwright stated that the gun lost was a three-inch Ordnance rifle whose serial number was "1."

18. Stewart, "Battery B," p. 373.

19. *OR* 27 (1):748, 755.

20. Ibid., pp. 756–57; Hunt, "First Day," p. 281; McCreary, "Gettysburg," GNMP. Lt. Bayard Wilkeson, the commander of Battery G, 4th U.S. Artillery, age nineteen, was mortally wounded near the almshouse on 1 July. Albertus McCreary wrote of seeing a cannon fired in front of his house on Baltimore Street at High Street. It was likely a piece from Wilkeson's battery.

21. *OR* 27 (1):742, 754; T. W. Osborn, "Artillery." One account states that Dilger's battery might have been at the square, but Dilger's report does not support this. The guns at the square were probably from Wilkeson's battery.

22. *OR* 27 (1):281. The source states that McDermott and the flag were hit by canister. This was probably not true. Any Confederate guns that might have been firing would have to have been 600 yards away. Since the flag and McDermott were hit at the same time, a burst of a spherical case would have been more likely.

23. Dawes, *Sixth Wisconsin*, pp. 178–79.

24. Jacob Smith, *Camps and Campaigns*, p. 88. On 2 July Company C, 110th Pennsylvania Regiment, acting as a provost guard, found many stragglers hiding in the fields south of Gettysburg. See Pfanz, *Gettysburg*, p. 92.

25. Culp, "Gettysburg."

26. O. O. Howard, *Autobiography*, 1:419. In O. O. Howard, "Campaign," p. 58, Howard identified the colonel as George von Amsberg of the 45th New York Regiment. This is questionable because Amsberg was the acting commander of Schimmelfennig's brigade. The portion of the 45th that fell back to the hill did so under Capt. Andrew B. Searles. See New York Monuments Commission, *Final Report*, 1:381.

27. *OR* 27 (1):718.

28. Nicholson, *Pennsylvania*, 1:420; *OR* 27 (1):721–22; Ker to Nicholson, 1 May 1894, 73d Pennsylvania Volunteer Infantry Regiment, GNMP.

29. Nevins, *Wainwright*, pp. 237–38; *OR* 27 (1):748; T. W. Osborn, "Artillery." Wainwright suggested that he divided the hill between himself and Osborn; Osborn said that Howard did.

30. *OR* 27 (1):751; Nevins, *Wainwright*, p. 238; Wiedrich to Bachelder, 30 Jan. 1886, BP; Remington, *Battery I*, p. 21; New York Monuments Commission, *Final Report*, 3:1246. The detachment of Schmidt's section is not mentioned in the battery's report or on its memorial. Its location west of the pike was not recorded.

31. *OR* 27 (1):252, 368, 764; Schurz, "Gettysburg," p. 277.

32. *OR* 27 (1):357, 365; Nevins, *Wainwright*, p. 238; Stewart, "Battery B," pp.

373–74; Nicholson, *Pennsylvania*, 2:899. Wainwright's report stated that two of Stewart's Napoleons had been disabled by the loss of their pointing rings—the rings at the end of the guns' trails into which the trail handspikes were inserted in order to shift the trails for aiming.

Stewart wrote that General Hancock had posted three of his guns on the pike and the fourth at right angles to them. Likely, the fourth piece soon was brought in line. Two of the lunettes erected to protect Stewart's guns can be seen in the classic photograph of the cemetery gatehouse.

33. *OR* 27 (1):357; Nevins, *Wainwright*, p. 238; McKelvey, "George Breck's Civil War Letters," p. 129; New York Monuments Commission, *Final Report*, 3:1257.

34. Maine Gettysburg Commission, *Maine at Gettysburg*, pp. 88–89.

35. Ibid., pp. 89–90; For Hunt's time of arrival, see Pfanz, *Gettysburg*, p. 42. Hunt could not have visited the battery at this time for he did not reach the field until about midnight. The officer remembered must have been Wainwright.

36. *OR* 27 (1):357; Nevins, *Wainwright*, pp. 238–39. Major Osborn reported that he supplied ammunition to the First Corps batteries because their train was not at hand. This caused Osborn annoyance later.

Artillerymen were often frustrated because officers in command of brigades and divisions, whose knowledge of artillery was minimal, gave them orders on the use of their guns. Hancock was guilty of this and had a postwar feud with Hunt, particularly over the use of batteries on the Second Corps front just before Pickett's Charge.

37. *OR* 27 (1):360, 748. Hall had three three-inch rifles, Schmidt's section of Wiedrich's battery had two three-inch rifles, Wilkeson (Bancroft) and Dilger each had six Napoleons, and Wheeler had three three-inch rifles.

38. *OR* 27 (1):749; Stubbs to Bachelder, 13 June 1883, BP; McKelvey, "George Breck's Civil War Letters," pp. 131–32.

39. T. W. Osborn, "Artillery."

CHAPTER FIVE

1. E. M. Daniel, *Speeches*, p. 81; J. W. Daniel "Commentary on John B. Gordon's *Reminiscences of the Civil War*," Civil War Material, Gettysburg, J. W. Daniel Papers, UV.

2. *OR* 27 (2):468–69, 477, 493; J. A. Early, *Memoirs*, pp. 268–69, and "Leading Confederates," pp. 254–55; Hartwig, "11th Army Corps," p. 46. Hartwig's article contains a map showing this Federal line. The high ground was the area left by Barlow when he advanced to the knoll.

3. Carrington, "First Day," pp. 330–32. The battery remained in Gettysburg most of the night. It was not engaged again during the battle.

4. Gilmor, *Four Years*, pp. 96–97. The Order of Battle lists Gilmor and then Maj. Ridgely Brown as commanders of the 1st Maryland Cavalry Battalion. Goldsborough wrote that Gilmor had been placed in charge of Companies B, C, and D and that Capt. Frank Bond was placed in command of Company A. Company A came to Gettysburg with Ewell, and Gilmor's companies arrived from Chambers-

burg during the 1 July battle. Major Brown, who had been recovering from a wound, reached Gettysburg on 2 July and resumed command of the battalion. Hindsight suggests that Gilmor and his three companies could have been better used in reconnaissances on the left. See *OR* 27 (2):290; Goldsborough, *Maryland Line*, pp. 177–78.

5. *OR* 27 (2):658, 662–63; Caldwell, *Brigade of South Carolinians*, p. 100.

6. New York Monuments Commission, *Final Report*, 1:24.

7. J. W. Daniel, "Memoir of the Battle of Gettysburg," pp. 5–6, VHS.

8. Ibid., pp. 9–10.

9. Aughinbaugh, *Personal Experience.*

10. H. Jacobs, "Eyewitness," GNMP. Jacobs identified the wounded man as "Burlingame" of the 149th Pennsylvania Volunteer Infantry. There was no one of that name in the 149th, but there was a Cpl. H. L. Burlingame in the 150th. The Confederates returned later for Burlingame.

11. M. Jacobs, *Notes*, p. 25.

12. McCreary, "Gettysburg," pp. 5–6, GNMP.

13. Brodhead, "Diary," 1 July 1863, ACHS; McCreary, "Gettysburg," p. 7, GNMP.

14. McLean, "Days of Terror." McLean identified the officer as a Georgian named Monaghan. There was a Col. William Monaghan of the 6th Louisiana at Winchester, but he was not listed with his regiment at Gettysburg.

15. Fahnestock, "Recollections," p. 2, ACHS.

16. M. Jacobs, *Notes*, p. 25; Fahnestock, "Recollections," p. 2, ACHS; McLean, "Days of Terror"; H. Jacobs, "Eyewitness."

17. *DAB* 3:598; Boatner, *Dictionary*, pp. 268–69.

18. Freeman, *Lee's Lieutenants*, 1:85–86, 3:xxiv, 770; Stiles, *Four Years*, p. 189.

19. E. M. Daniel, *Speeches*, pp. 574–78.

20. Gallagher, "Jubal Early," p. 1; E. M. Daniel, *Speeches*, p. 579.

21. *OR* 27 (2):469; J. A. Early, *Memoirs*, p. 269, and "Leading Confederates," pp. 254–55.

22. *OR* 27 (2):469, 489; J. A. Early, *Autobiographical Sketch*, pp. 268–69, and "Leading Confederates," pp. 254–55; Statement of Lt. C. B. C[oiner], Finley Papers, UV. It seems likely that Smith's brigade followed Shealer Road from the Harrisburg Road to the York Pike.

In his "Leading Confederates," Early stated that Smith's request arrived after he had seen an officer of Pender's division and while he was talking with Colonel Smead as mentioned below. However, in his report Early stated that Smith's request came first. Since the report was written soon after the event I assume that it is correct.

23. *DAB* 9:361; Wakelyn, *Biographical Dictionary*, p. 392; Stiles, *Four Years*, p. 111. See also various references in Freeman, *Lee's Lieutenants*, vols. 2 and 3. Smith served as governor until Lee's surrender. He retired then to his farm near Warrenton. He served from 1877 to 1879 in the Virginia legislature and died in 1887 at the age of ninety.

24. *OR* 27 (2):469; J. A. Early, *Memoirs*, p. 269, and "Leading Confederates," p. 255.

25. J. A. Early, "Leading Confederates," p. 255.

CHAPTER SIX

1. *OR* 27 (2):603; Statement of Capt. W. P. Carter, Jubal Early Material, Gettysburg, and James P. Smith to Daniel, 15 July 1903, Civil War Material, Gettysburg, J. W. Daniel Papers, UV.

2. Douglas to Editor, *Evening Star*, 1 Feb., Ewell Papers, LC; "Letters of John H. Stone," HLA; Goldsborough, "With Lee." Ewell was probably on the high ground north of Stevens's Run on the high point west of the Carlisle Road where Dilger's battery had been.

In his report, Johnson complained that the wagons of Longstreet's corps had obstructed his march; Longstreet in turn complained that his march was delayed by Johnson's division and the wagons of Ewell's corps. See *OR* 27 (2):358, 504. Johnson and his wagons were given precedence over Longstreet. Perhaps it was Hill's train that delayed Johnson.

3. Douglas to Editor, *Evening Post*, 1 Feb., Ewell Papers, LC. It is likely that at this time, insofar as Ewell knew, Lee was still near Cashtown.

This often-quoted remark is usually attributed to Major Pendleton, Ewell's chief of staff. If so, the comment and its implied criticism of his chief were particularly unfortunate. See Freeman, *Lee's Lieutenants*, 3:93.

4. Taylor, "Second Paper," p. 127, and *Four Years*, p. 95.

5. *OR* 27 (2):318, 445. Taylor's account was published five years after Ewell's death; though Ewell could not comment on it, others did. Campbell Brown wrote in a private letter that the account was utterly worthless and that Taylor had carried no such message to Ewell. Jubal Early regarded Taylor's comments, together with some by Henry Heth and William Allan, as an implication that Ewell was remiss in his duty. He denied this and replied by publishing his own version of the operations at Gettysburg by Ewell's corps that refuted the statements of Ewell's critics. See Brown to Hunt, 6 May 1885, Hunt Papers, LC, and J. A. Early, "Leading Confederates," pp. 52–53, 265.

6. James P. Smith to Major Brown, n.d., typescript, J. A. Early Papers, LC; J. P. Smith, "With Stonewall Jackson," p. 57. The high ground that Early and Rodes referred to was probably the north end of Cemetery Ridge rather than the more distant Peach Orchard area.

7. G. C. Brown, "Reminiscences," p. 33, TSLA; J. W. Daniel, "Commentary on John B. Gordon's *Reminiscences of the Civil War*," Civil War Material, Gettysburg, J. W. Daniel Papers, UV. According to Gordon, Ewell was shot in his wooden leg at this time. This is wrong, as will be shown below. Daniel identified the officer shot as a Lieutenant Williamson, but no officer with that name was on any of the staffs present. See Gordon, *Reminiscences*, p. 157.

8. James P. Smith to Major Brown, n.d., typescript, J. A. Early Papers, LC;

J. P. Smith, "With Stonewall Jackson," pp. 57–58; G. C. Brown, "Reminiscences," TSLA. I have pieced this story from the two Smith accounts listed above, using quotations from both. Smith was not clear about Lee's location. He also made no mention of having seen any of Buford's cavalry, which ought to have been in evidence to his right. He also did not note a reconnaissance that was probably being made at this time by Col. A. L. Long of Lee's staff. Long concluded that "an attack made at that time, with the troops at hand, would have been hazardous and of very doubtful success." See Long to Early, 30 Mar. and 5 Apr. 1876, J. A. Early Papers, LC.

9. *OR* 27 (2):445; G. C. Brown, "Reminiscences," p. 34, TSLA. Benner's Hill was beyond Early's left and probably was deemed an ineligible position until after the arrival of Johnson's division.

10. *OR* 27 (2):445.

11. J. A. Early, "Leading Confederates," p. 255; G. C. Brown, "Reminiscences," pp. 33–34, TSLA. It is possible that Capt. Fred Smith carried only one message at this time. Yet the circumstances described surrounding their delivery suggest that there were two. Two trips within the time frame would have required hard riding.

12. *OR* 27 (2):555, 562.

13. Campbell Brown to Hunt, 7 May 1885, Hunt Papers, LC.

14. *OR* 27 (2):489; Statement of Lt. C. B. C[oiner], Finley Papers, UV; Driver, *52d Virginia*, p. 40; Hale and Phillips, *Forty-ninth Virginia*, pp. 77–78. It is possible that some Confederate cavalry, particularly the 17th and 35th Virginia battalions, were also on the left and, if so, that they might have been responsible for some of Smith's alarms.

15. J. A. Early, "Leading Confederates," p. 256.

16. McKim, *Soldier's Recollections*, pp. 295–96; G. Thomas, "Address," p. 444; "Letters of John H. Stone," p. 40, HLA; Goldsborough, *Maryland Line*, p. 102.

17. *OR* 27 (2):504, 509, 526, 530, 531; Goldsborough, "With Lee." A chaplain who was traveling with the portion of Ewell's train escorted by Johnson's division wrote that the train was parked near Cashtown. See Gwaltney Diary, 1 July 1863, SHC.

18. S. Z. Ammen, "Second Maryland Battalion, Fourteenth Paper—Second Series," in Ammen, "Maryland Troops in the Confederacy," p. 130, CC; McKim, "Steuart's Brigade," p. 292.

19. *OR* 27 (2):509, 526, 527, 530, 531. See Bruce to Daniel, 8 Apr. 1904, J. W. Daniel Papers, UV, referring to an article quoted by Bruce entitled, "Would Have Saved Officers," in the *Charlottesville Daily Progress*, 22 Mar. 1904. Bruce wrote that the article had omitted language that "was more forceful than elegant" and that the conversation between Johnson and Early included "words of considerable warmth." According to Bruce the two division commanders argued after Ewell told Early to occupy "the heights beyond the town" and Early said that his division was in no condition to accomplish such a mission. Then, according to Bruce, Ewell ordered Early to "go into camp for the night" (which he did not do) and Johnson to "go into camp in a wood" (which he also did not do). In short, it appears that Bruce

witnessed an argument of some sort, but its subject remains a mystery. It would seem that by this time Early's division would have already been posted.

General Walker, whose brigade was probably in the division rear, remembered its arrival as having been "sooner than sun-set, but not earlier than an hour before sunset." Sunset was at about 7:40 P.M. See J. A. Early, "Leading Confederates," p. 264.

20. Turner's account of the reconnaissance of Culp's Hill is found in at least three places: "Gettysburg, Captain Turner," typescript, J. A. Early Papers, CW&M; "Personal Narrative, C. Brown," Hunt Papers, LC; and H. S. Turner to Early, J. A. Early Papers, VHS.

21. The Johnston reconnaissance is described in Pfanz, *Gettysburg*, pp. 106–7. In a marginal note, Hunt wrote that Wadsworth's line must have been laid out before Turner's reconnaissance and that the division must have been "fortifying." Hunt mused: "I think that from the top of the Ridge Turner, whilst he could see Cemetery Hill and part of the ridge connecting it with Culp's [Hill,] might not see Wadsworth's men who were pretty well concealed by woods. It is hard to reconcile sometimes perfectly true accounts." See "Personal Narrative, C. Brown," p. 4, Hunt Papers, LC.

22. *OR* 27 (2):465, 504, 509, 513, 526, 531. Moonrise was at about 8:09 P.M.

23. *OR* 27 (2):504, 509, 513, 521, 531.

24. Trimble to Bachelder, 8 Feb. 1883, BP.

25. J. A. Early, "Leading Confederates," p. 18.

26. *OR* 27 (2):308, 318. Discussion of this may be found in Hunt, "Second Day," pp. 293–94; Coddington, *Gettysburg Campaign*, pp. 360–63; and Pfanz, *Gettysburg*, pp. 26–29.

27. J. A. Early, "Leading Confederates," p. 271. Tradition holds that the conference site was the Blocher house near the junction of the Carlisle and Table Rock roads about eight-tenths of a mile north of Gettysburg. See Freeman, *Lee's Lieutenants*, 3:94, 101. However, John C. Early wrote many years later that the meeting took place on the porch of the residence of the superintendent of the county almshouse. See J. C. Early, "Southern Boy's Experience," pp. 420–21. Ewell also had meals at the nearby Crawford house. See Shevchuk, "Wounding of Albert Jenkins," p. 59. I am inclined to believe that Ewell's headquarters were somewhere near the almshouse or at or near the Crawford house on the edge of the town.

28. J. A. Early, "Leading Confederates," pp. 271–72.

29. Ibid., pp. 272–73. Early wrote his account of this meeting after all of the other participants were dead, and it cannot be considered the account of a disinterested man.

Maj. Harry Gilmor, who acted as provost marshal for Gettysburg for awhile, wrote that the 2,500 muskets piled in the square were not removed and were recovered by the Federals. See Gilmor, *Four Years*, p. 98.

30. J. A. Early, "Leading Confederates," pp. 273–74.

31. Marshall to Early, 13 Mar. 1878, J. A. Early Papers, LC.

32. Marshall to Early, 23 Mar. 1870 and 13 Mar. 1878, J. A. Early Papers, LC.

33. Marshall to Early, 23 Mar. 1870, J. A. Early Papers, LC; *OR* 27 (2):446.

See also the comments in Freeman, *Lee's Lieutenants*, 3:103, and Coddington, *Gettysburg Campaign*, p. 366.

34. *OR* 27 (2):446; "Gettysburg, Captain Turner," J. A. Early Papers, VHS.

35. *OR* 27 (2):446.

36. *OR* 27 (1):284–85; Hofmann, "Fifty-sixth Regiment"; "At Gettysburg." General Hunt wrote that General Wadsworth had posted the 7th Indiana, that a civil engineer in the regiment had laid out the works, and that the rest of the brigade had tied in with it. See Hunt to Gantt, 20 Mar. 1886, Hunt Papers, LC.

37. *OR* 27 (2):446; "Gettysburg, Captain Turner," J. A. Early Papers, VHS. In his "Reminiscences," p. 36, TSLA, G. Campbell Brown wrote that Ewell had supposed until nearly daylight that Johnson had occupied Culp's Hill. He stated that Johnson, in his report, gave his reason for not doing so, but, in fact, Johnson ignored the matter completely. Brown wrote that Ewell had held Johnson "not altogether free from blame in this matter."

38. *OR* 27 (2):446.

CHAPTER SEVEN

1. *OR* 27 (1):758, (3):416, 458. According to Williams, his division led the corps. See Quaife, *Williams*, p. 224. However, William F. Fox in "General Slocum," p. 79, stated categorically that Geary's division had the lead that day and arrived at Two Taverns at 11:00 A.M. Lockwood's brigade, which would be assigned to Williams's division, did not report to the corps until 2 July.

2. *OR* 27 (3):458–59.

3. *OR* 27 (1):458, 462.

4. *DAB* 9:216–17; New York Monuments Commission, *Final Report*, 3:133–34. Philip Sheridan was a roommate of Slocum's at West Point.

5. New York Monuments Commission, *Final Report*, 3:1334–35; Boatner, *Dictionary*, p. 765.

6. Slocum, *Life and Services*, pp. 292–93; Quaife, *Williams*, p. 141.

7. Slocum left the army in September 1865 and in 1866 set up a successful law practice in Brooklyn. He served three years in Congress before his death in 1894.

8. Tallman, "War of the Rebellion," 66th Ohio Volunteer Infantry Regiment, GNMP; Collins, *149th Regiment*, p. 134; Horton to Bachelder, 23 Jan. 1907, BP; Hinkley, *Third Wisconsin*, p. 82; Mouat, "Three Years," HSP; Slocum to Davis, 8 Sept. 1876, Bates Papers, PSA.

9. Tallman, "War of the Rebellion," 66th Ohio Volunteer Infantry Regiment, GNMP; Horton to Bachelder, 23 Jan. 1907, BP; Brown, *Twenty-seventh Indiana*, pp. 364–65; Hinkley, *Third Wisconsin*, p. 82; Morse, *Second Massachusetts*, p. 6; Stork, "Gettysburg." In his biography, Charles Slocum stated that Henry Slocum had not heard the guns (*Life and Services*, p. 102), but in a letter (Slocum to Davis, 8 Sept. 1876, Bates Papers, PSA), Slocum stated that firing was heard while on the march.

10. *OR* 27 (3):463; C. H. Howard, "First Day," pp. 249–50.

11. In *Life and Services*, Charles Slocum wrote that Howard's first message

came at about the time of the arrival of Williams's division at Two Taverns and that "this call did not give sufficient reason for Slocum to answer it immediately as desired inasmuch as Howard, as well as Slocum, had received a copy of the circular directing retreat on Pipe Creek" (p. 102). Howard, of course, did not receive the circular. William F. Fox in "Twelfth and Twentieth Corps," p. 175, wrote that Slocum and the corps left for Gettysburg in response to Howard's first message received before 2:00 P.M. He stated also that a Mr. Snyder, in whose tavern Slocum was eating, said that Slocum left immediately on getting the message.

12. Bates, *Gettysburg*, pp. 92–93.

13. Slocum to T. H. Davis and Co., 8 Sept. 1875, Bates Papers, PSA; Slocum to Sidney Cooke, 16 May 1886, in Cooke, "First Day," p. 286.

14. Slocum to T. H. Davis and Co., 8 Sept. 1875, Bates Papers, PSA. Doubleday wrote that possibly Slocum had declined to go to Gettysburg without orders from Meade because "he probably thought if any one commander could assume the direction of other corps, he might antagonize the plans of the general in chief." See Doubleday, *Chancellorsville*, p. 137.

15. *OR* 27 (1):771, 773.

16. Ibid., p. 703; O. O. Howard, *Autobiography*, 1:416.

17. C. H. Howard, "First Day," pp. 325–26; Hall to Howard, 19 Feb. 1877, O. O. Howard Papers, BC; Carpenter, "O. O. Howard," p. 267.

18. *OR* 27 (1):126. The time frame was given by Mason. Williams wrote that he heard of Reynolds's death while on the march, perhaps at this time but possibly from Hall or another source. See Williams to Bachelder, 10 Nov. 1865, BP.

19. *OR* 27 (3):465.

20. *OR* 27 (1):704, 758; C. H. Howard, "First Day," p. 330. Whether Howard wanted the Twelfth Corps beyond Wolf Hill or on Culp's Hill was not stated.

21. Tallman, "War of the Rebellion," 66th Ohio Volunteer Infantry Regiment, GNMP; Toombs, *New Jersey Troops*, p. 187.

22. *OR* 27 (1):771, 773; Williams to Bachelder, 10 Nov. 1865, BP.

23. *OR* 27 (1):811. The road followed by Williams's division leaves the Baltimore Pike about a half mile from the Rock Creek crossing and today is immediately northwest of the U.S. 15 interchange. It runs generally northeast from there nearly two miles to the Hanover Road at a point about a mile east of Benner's Hill. Today it reaches the Hanover Road less than a quarter mile east of the U.S. 15 interchange. The road doglegs and connects a half dozen farms. At a point halfway to the Hanover Road on the east slope of Wolf Hill, it connects with a side road that runs southeast to Rock Creek opposite McAllister's Mill. The road is shown on the Cope Map and on the Warren Map.

24. Morse, *Second Massachusetts*, p. 6; Quaife, *Williams*, p. 224.

25. Williams to Bachelder, 10 Nov. 1865, BP; Quaife, *Williams*, pp. 224–25. The source of Williams's information was not given. Only Early's division was near Benner's Hill.

26. *OR* 27 (1):811, 816; Williams to Bachelder, 10 Nov. 1865, BP. Williams's division is shown in this position on Bachelder's draft map for 6:00 P.M. on 2 July at GNMP.

27. Williams to Bachelder, 10 Nov. 1865, BP.

28. Ibid.; Quaife, *Williams*, pp. 224–26; *OR* 27 (1):771, 773, 777, 811; Morse, *Second Massachusetts*, p. 7; Brown, *Twenty-seventh Indiana*, p. 367; Bryant, *Third Regiment*, p. 184.

29. *OR* 27 (1):704; C. H. Howard, "First Day," p. 330. According to Major Howard, Slocum's exact words were: "I'll be damned if I will take the responsibility of this fight."

30. "Col. C. H. Morgan's Statement," typescript, p. 323, BP.

31. Howard to Maj. E. Whittlesday, 9 July 1863, C. H. Howard Papers, BC; Carpenter, "Gettysburg Letter," p. 10; O. O. Howard, "Campaign," p. 60.

32. Doubleday to Bates, 24 Apr. 1874, Bates Papers, PSA.

33. Meade, *Life and Letters*, 2:249.

34. Pfanz, *Gettysburg*, p. 37; Boatner, *Dictionary*, p. 372.

35. Pfanz, *Gettysburg*, p. 38.

36. *OR* 27 (3):461; Hancock Testimony, *CCW*, p. 404; W. S. Hancock, "Gettysburg," p. 821; "Col. C. H. Morgan's Statement," typescript, pp. 318–19, BP. Doubleday believed that Meade had no right to assign Hancock over Howard. See Doubleday to Bates, 4 Apr. 1874, Bates Papers, PSA.

37. A. R. Hancock, *Reminiscences*, pp. 188–89; *OR* 27 (1):367–68; Hancock Testimony, *CCW*, p. 405.

38. H. Osborn, *Trials*, p. 97; Hancock Testimony, *CCW*, p. 405; W. S. Hancock, "Gettysburg," p. 822. The times of Hancock's arrival given in *OR* 27 (1):368, 696, 704 are 3:00 P.M. by Hancock and 4:00 and 4:30 P.M. by Howard. This matter is discussed briefly in Coddington, *Gettysburg Campaign*, p. 700. This controversy is discussed at greater length in appendix B.

39. O. O. Howard, "Campaign," p. 58, and *Autobiography*, 1:418.

40. W. S. Hancock, "Gettysburg," pp. 823–24. Others who might not have heard this conversation gave verbatim versions of it. Capt. E. P. Halstead of the First Corps, who claimed to have been nearby and was no admirer of Howard, wrote that Howard told Hancock that he was the senior. To this, Hancock replied, "I am aware of that, General, but I have written orders in my pocket from General Meade, which I will show you if you wish to see them." Howard responded, "No; I do not doubt your word, General Hancock, but you can give no orders here while I am here." Hancock then answered, "Very well, General Howard, I will second any order that you have to give, but General Meade has also directed me to select a field on which to fight this battle in rear of Pipe Creek. But I think this is the strongest position by nature upon which to fight a battle that I ever saw, and if it meets with your approbation I will select this as the battle-field." Howard replied, "I think it a very strong position, General Hancock; a very strong position!" To this, Hancock replied, "Very well, sir, I select this as the battle-field." This account is hard to believe since it seems unlikely that Hancock would have volunteered to second any order that Howard might have given. We can also wonder how Halstead could have heard all of the conversation that is quoted. See Halstead, "Incidents," p. 285. James S. Wadsworth, Jr., wrote that Howard said, "You cannot issue these orders Hancock for I rank you." Hancock is supposed to have replied, "Then I will go back to Gen'l Meade." Howard reconsidered and replied, "Don't do that

Hancock, but stay here and assist me with your advice." See "Battle of July 1st," Wadsworth Family Papers, LC. This too rings false. Would Hancock have left the field if Howard had not accepted his authority? On the other hand, Colonel Morgan, who was probably with Hancock, wrote that Hancock said, "General, I have been ordered here to take command of all the troops on the field, until General Slocum arrives." He added that he had the order in his pocket and would show it to Howard. Morgan wrote that Howard "waived looking at it and expressed his satisfaction at General Hancock's arrival." See "Col. C. H. Morgan's Statement," typescript, p. 320, BP.

41. *OR* 27 (1):252, 368, 704; Hancock Testimony, *CCW*, p. 405; "Col. C. H. Morgan's Statement," typescript, p. 320, BP. Geary, in his report, wrote that Slocum had told him to leave a brigade and a section of artillery in reserve and to report to Howard, but not finding Howard, he reported to Hancock. He left Kane's brigade in reserve. See *OR* 27 (1):825.

42. *OR* 27 (1):115, 368; Meade Testimony, *CCW*, pp. 330–31; Hancock Testimony, *CCW*, p. 405; Warren Testimony, *CCW*, p. 377. Warren had left Taneytown for Gettysburg before Meade ordered Hancock there, but Warren traveled via Emmitsburg and reached the field after Hancock.

43. *OR* 27 (1):252, 704; Stewart, "Battery B," pp. 189–90; Coddington, *Gettysburg Campaign*, pp. 298, 700–701; Nevins, *Wainwright*, pp. 237–38. Colonel Wainwright wrote that he too had posted Stewart. Perhaps he was concerned with the technicalities and details involved, especially after Hancock had galloped off to other parts of the field.

44. Schurz, *Reminiscences*, 3:15–16, and "Gettysburg," pp. 277–78.

45. Schurz, *Reminiscences*, 3:14; Comte de Paris et al., "Gettysburg," p. 146.

46. *OR* 27 (1):368–69, 704.

47. Ibid., pp. 696–97.

48. "Mrs. Thorn's War Story"; "Wife of Cemetery Caretaker." In a letter to Howard, 2 July 1863, O. O. Howard Papers, BC, John Moeser, who signed his name as "Sexton" of the Evergreen Cemetery, asked for payment of property used or destroyed by the army. In spite of this signature, it was his daughter, Catherine Thorn, who wielded authority in her husband's absence.

Each of the buildings forming the cemetery gate is about sixteen feet deep and twelve feet wide across the front. The legs of the arch proper, each three feet wide, are attached to their inside faces, and the arch spans a drive ten feet wide. Each building has a pair of windows on its front side on each of its two floors. The arch proper extends upward from the bases at the front face and does not cover the entire space between the gatehouse buildings and above the drive. The arch at the top is surmounted by an urn and is decorated with three wreaths. Shortly after the war an extension was added to the north building. In "Mrs. Thorn's War Story," mention is made of there being a thirteen-year-old boy in the Thorn household, but nothing more is said of him.

49. "Mrs. Thorn's War Story," p. 3. "Coon Town," more properly "Kuhn Town," was along Stratton Street north of the railroad and just south of the area where Coster's brigade made its stand.

50. "Wife of Cemetery Caretaker." The Myers house, a short distance toward the town from the gate, was a large frame building that later housed the Soldiers' Orphans Home.

51. O. O. Howard, *Autobiography*, 1:419. In the fall of 1890 Howard, Slocum, and Doubleday visited Gettysburg with the Comte de Paris. In his account of the visit, Howard mentioned going to the cemetery and asking, "Where is that good woman, Mrs. Thorn, who gave us a cup of coffee, the sweetest one ever drunk, the night of the first of July after the battle?" He was told that she had moved toward Baltimore a few miles. See Comte de Paris et al., "Gettysburg," p. 138. Yet in 1883 in a letter to David McConaughy at Gettysburg, Howard wrote of having only a vague recollection of her. See Howard to McConaughy, 7 Feb. 1883, McConaughy Collection, Gettysburg College, Gettysburg, Pennsylvania.

52. "Mrs. Thorn's War Story," pp. 3–4.

CHAPTER EIGHT

1. Hunt, "Second Day," pp. 294–95.

2. Meade's party included Brig. Gen. Henry Hunt, two aides—Capts. George G. Meade, Jr., and Charles Cadwalader—and Sgt. William Waters, the chief of orderlies. See Meade, *With Meade*, p. 69, and *Life and Letters*, 2:62; Waters to Col. George Meade, 21 June 1889, ML; Hunt Testimony, *CCW*, p. 448; Paine to Meade, 20 May 1886, and 16 June 1888, ML; O. O. Howard, *Autobiography*, 1:423; Hunt, "Second Day," p. 291. The times given for Meade's arrival at the cemetery vary from 10:30 P.M. on 1 July to daylight on 2 July. Howard believed that he arrived at 3:00 A.M.; Hunt said after midnight. Captain Paine, who led the party, wrote that they left Taneytown at 10:00 P.M., reached the Second Corps headquarters in fifty-seven minutes, and arrived at the cemetery between 11:30 and midnight. I believe that Paine is correct.

3. O. O. Howard, *Autobiography*, 1:423; Paine to Meade, 20 May 1885, ML.

4. *OR* 27 (1):129–30; O. O. Howard, *Autobiography*, 1:422–23; Schurz, *Reminiscences*, 3:19; Meade, *Life and Letters*, 2:62. Howard had written Butterfield at 10:00 P.M. that "the position is plenty good for a general battle unless you fear it being turned at a considerable distance from Gettysburg." Likely Meade did not see this dispatch before he reached the field. See *OR* 51 (1):1067.

5. *OR* 27 (1):70–71, 115, (3):461, 466; Meade Testimony, *CCW*, p. 438; Hunt Testimony, *CCW*, p. 448; Meade, *With Meade*, p. 65; Hunt, "Second Day," p. 290. See also Coddington, *Gettysburg Campaign*, pp. 323–24; Pfanz, *Gettysburg*, pp. 39–40.

6. Meade, *Life and Letters*, 2:61–62; Paine to Meade, 16 June 1888, ML.

7. Mouat, "Three Years," HSP. Since the regiment had about 485 officers and men and was larger than most at Gettysburg, it seems likely that Meade was referring to Kane's whole brigade, which had only three Pennsylvania regiments including the 29th and numbered only about 890. I have added some punctuation and altered capitalization in this quotation for clarity's sake.

8. Smart, *Radical View*, 2:23.

9. Schurz, *Reminiscences*, 3:20–21.

10. Ibid.

11. *OR* 27 (1):232–33, 749; Hunt, "Second Day," p. 297; Hunt to Meade, 14 Aug. 1888, ML. In later years, Major Osborn wrote that he had discovered this gap early on 2 July. He said that he reported it to General Howard, and when Howard said that he had no troops to send there, he offered to try to cover it with artillery. He then posted ten guns of two batteries to guard it. He wrote nothing of Twelfth Corps batteries being there. See T. W. Osborn, "Experiences," Osborn Papers, CU.

12. The Culp's Hill area is best depicted by the Warren Map. McAllister's Mill was built in 1790 and purchased by the McAllisters in 1822. The mill was used by the Underground Railroad prior to the war. It fell into disuse shortly after the war. See *Miller's Review*, 15 Mar. 1912. For more on Spangler's Spring, see appendix A.

13. *OR* 27 (1):759, 826, 836, 847, 849, 856, 863, 864, 868; New York Monuments Commission, *Final Report*, 1:450, 3:1013. Greene's New York regiments formed in order left to right from the top of the hill: 78th, 60th, 102d, 149th, and 137th. Kane's Pennsylvanians had the 109th and the 111th in the forward line and the 29th in the rear. The deployment of Candy's brigade, the 5th, 7th, 29th, and 66th Ohio and the 147th Pennsylvania regiments, was not described except that the 66th was probably on Candy's right and constructed works overlooking the saddle. See also Alexander to Bachelder, 2 Sept. 1887, BP.

14. Quaife, *Williams*, p. 226; New York Monuments Commission, *Greene*, p. 82; Collins, *149th Regiment*, p. 137; Horton to Bachelder, 23 Jan. 1907, BP; New York Monuments Commission, *Final Report*, 3:1013.

15. Dawes, *Sixth Wisconsin*, p. 179, and "With the Sixth," p. 233; *OR* 27 (1):284; Dawes to Bachelder, Mar. 1868, BP; Curtis, *Twenty-fourth Michigan*, p. 191; Wadsworth Testimony, *CCW*, p. 414.

16. *OR* 27 (1):825, 836, 847, 849, 856, 864; J. H. Jones, "Saved the Day"; Eddy, *Sixtieth Regiment*, p. 260; Collins, *149th Regiment*, p. 144; New York Monuments Commission, *Final Report*, 3:1023; Morse, "Twelfth Corps," p. 822; Nicholson, *Pennsylvania*, 2:715.

17. *OR* 27 (1):856.

18. Quaife, *Williams*, p. 226.

19. *OR* 27 (1):773; Quaife, *Williams*, p. 226; Williams to Bachelder, 10 Nov. 1865, BP.

20. *OR* 27 (1):592, 600, 610, 622, 633, 634, 638, 644, 646; *OR* 27 (2):504, 518, 521; "Culp's Farm, July 3, 1863," Nadenbousch Papers, DU. See also Pfanz, *Gettysburg*, pp. 51–52, 61–62. Crawford's division was the last in the Fifth Corps column and did not reach the Brinkerhoff's Ridge area in time to take position there.

21. *OR* 27 (1):600, 610, 612, 811, 812.

22. Hancock Testimony, *CCW*, p. 406.

23. Ibid.; *OR* 27 (1):381, 407, 413–14, 442.

24. Meade Testimony, *CCW*, pp. 437–38; Warren Testimony, *CCW*, p. 377; *OR* 27 (3):486–87. See also Pfanz, *Gettysburg*, pp. 60–61.

25. Maine Gettysburg Commission, *Maine at Gettysburg*, pp. 521–23. All men

were back by 2:00 P.M. If that time was correct, this exercise had nothing to do with Slocum's morning reply to Meade.

26. *OR* 27 (3):487–88, (1):72.

27. *OR* 27 (2):308, 318–19; Pfanz, *Gettysburg*, pp. 105–11.

28. Venable to Longstreet, 11 May 1875, in Longstreet, "Account," pp. 76–77.

29. Ibid.; J. A. Early, "Supplement," p. 289.

30. G. C. Brown, "Reminiscences," pp. 36–37, TSLA. See also Pfanz, *Gettysburg*, pp. 107, 110.

31. For a discussion of Lee's plan and his conversations with Longstreet and others on the Confederate right, see Pfanz, *Gettysburg*, pp. 104–13.

32. W. C. Storrick Notes, Civil War Sources and Photostats, Freeman Papers, LC. The site of Ewell's headquarters at this time is a matter of conjecture. It was marked as having been at a house just west of Rock Creek on the Hanover Road, but if it was there, and Trimble's account is correct, why did he take Lee all the way back to the almshouse? Probably it was still north of the town near the almshouse.

33. Trimble, "Battle," p. 125.

34. Maurice, *Aide de Camp*, p. 233.

35. *OR* 27 (2):318, 446; G. C. Brown, "Reminiscences," pp. 36–38, TSLA.

36. *DAB* 5:95–96; Boatner, *Dictionary*, pp. 437–38; Patterson, "'Allegheny' Johnson," p. 14.

37. Freeman, *Lee's Lieutenants*, 2:508–9; Patterson, "'Allegheny' Johnson," p. 14.

38. Freeman, *Lee's Lieutenants*, 2:415, 508–9, 525, 666, 701, 711.

39. *OR* 27 (2):454.

40. Rollins, "Going to Gettysburg" and "Playing Cavalry"; Patterson, "'Allegheny' Johnson," p. 14; McH. Howard, *Recollections*, pp. 86, 242, 301; Stiles, *Four Years*, p. 218; Casler, *Four Years*, p. 173; Ted to Sister, 26 May and 8 July 1863, Barclay Papers, W&L. Johnson continued to command the division until his capture at the Mule Shoe at Spotsylvania. After his exchange, he commanded a division in Tennessee under Hood and was captured a second time at Nashville. After the war, he farmed in Chesterfield County, Virginia, until his death in 1873 at the age of fifty-seven. He was so revered that his body lay in state in the capitol at Richmond before its burial in Hollywood Cemetery.

41. G. Thomas, "Address," p. 444; "Paper Read by Co'l David Zable . . . December 12, 1903," TU. In their postwar accounts, several men mentioned the disappointment felt on the night of 1 July and on the morning of 2 July over the failure to attack Culp's Hill then as they believed Stonewall Jackson would have done. This is good hindsight.

42. Rollins, "Playing Cavalry"; Casler, *Four Years*, p. 176.

43. McKim, "Steuart's Brigade," p. 293; David Hunter to Mrs. Edmund Hunter, 2 July 1863, GNMP.

44. *OR* 27 (1):778, 783, 788, 796, 800, 803; Morhous, *123d Regiment*, p. 47; Toombs, "Battle," p. 11; Love, *Wisconsin*, p. 415. The 123d New York, 20th Connecticut, and 46th Pennsylvania regiments were probably in this order from the

left in the first line; the 3d Maryland, 145th New York, and 5th Connecticut were in the rear line behind the wall in this order from the left.

45. "Robert Cruikshank Letters," 2 July 1863, pp. 122–23, BPL.

46. *OR* 27 (1):778, 783, 812, 815, 818, 819, 823; Bryant, *Third Regiment*, pp. 184–85; Morhous, *123d Regiment*, p. 47; Toombs, "Battle," p. 11; Love, *Wisconsin*, p. 415.

47. *OR* 27 (2):470, 480; Eaton Diary, 2 July 1863, SHC; John A. McPherson to J. T. Avery, 3 Aug. 1863, Hoke Papers, NCDAH. The strengths given are from tablets on the field.

48. *OR* 27 (2):480, 484; Clark, *Histories*, 3:415; T. Jones, *Seymour*, p. 73. The slope south of the run's ravine climbed to the nose of East Cemetery Hill on Hays's right, but on the left it was separated from the hill by another ravine containing a rivulet that drained springs at the eastern base of Cemetery Hill. The latter rivulet joined Winebrenner's Run about 700 yards east of Baltimore Street on the North Carolinians' front. The slopes of Winebrenner's Run must have been high enough to afford cover from Cemetery Hill.

49. T. Jones, *Seymour*, p. 73; *OR* 27 (2):480, 484; Reed, "Gettysburg Campaign," p. 188; Clark, *Histories*, 3:414; R. J. Hancock to Daniel, n.d., J. W. Daniel Papers, DU. The above Reed article includes a letter written by Lt. J. Warren Jackson, 8th Louisiana Regiment, to his brother R. Stark Jackson. It was written from Darkesville, Virginia, on 20 July 1863 and is now in the David French Boyd Civil War Papers, Louisiana State University Libraries, Louisiana and Lower Mississippi Valley Collections, Baton Rouge, Louisiana.

50. *OR* 27 (2):456, 555, 569, 573, 575, 577, 580, 582, 584, 585, 590, 593, 596, 601, 604. The 1st Virginia Artillery was commanded by Capt. Willis Dance. Capt. David Watson's battery was just north of the railroad cut, Capt. B. H. Smith's battery was just north of the seminary, and Dance's battery, under Lt. John M. Cunningham, was between the seminary dormitory and the Fairfield Road.

51. *OR* 27 (2):598; Norman, *Portion of My Life*, p. 186; Green Diary, 2 July 1863, SHC; Blackford, *War Years*, p. 231.

52. *OR* 27 (1):358, 361, 365, 751, 753; Boies, *Thirty-third Massachusetts*, p. 33; Butts, *A Gallant Captain*, p. 83.

53. *OR* 27 (1):705, (2):318–19; Wheeler, *In Memorium*, p. 411.

CHAPTER NINE

1. Seth Williams to Howard, 3 July 1863, Letters Received, 11th Corps, RG 393, NA.

2. U.S. War Department, *U.S. Infantry Tactics*, pp. 155, 426, 429.

3. Ibid., pp. 155–89; Gilham, *Manual*, pp. 189–216. The reserve and the chief of section's group of four provided replacements or added strength as needed.

4. *OR* 27 (2):504, 509, 531, 536; Clark, *Histories*, 1:148; Firebaugh Diary, 1 and 2 July 1863, SHC; Packer Diary, 2 July 1863, CSL and RBC.

5. *OR* 27 (1):826, 836, 840, 845, 862; Nicholson, *Pennsylvania*, 1:836. Colonel

Candy reported that Lt. Col. Orrin J. Crane of the 7th Ohio commanded his brigade's skirmishers, that is, the 28th Pennsylvania Regiment. The 28th has a large marker at its forward position.

6. *OR* 27 (1):800; "John Emerson Anderson Reminiscences," AAS. The party seen by Captain Oakey might have been that of General Johnson mentioned in chapter 11.

7. Harris to Brown, 7 Apr. 1864, BP.

8. McPherson to Avery, 3 Aug. 1863, Hoke Papers, SHC.

9. Kiefer, *One Hundred and Fifty-third Regiment*, pp. 141, 250; J. C. Miller, "At Gettysburg."

10. Maine Gettysburg Commission, *Maine at Gettysburg*, p. 91.

11. *OR* 27 (1):705, 716, 721–22, 724, 730; McKay, "Three Years," p. 132. Col. Charles R. Coster was a native of New York City and at the outbreak of the war was a private in the 7th New York Militia Regiment. He received a commission in the 12th U.S. Infantry Regiment in May 1861 and was promoted to captain in August 1862. He served with the regulars on the Peninsula and was wounded at Gaines's Mill. Coster became colonel of the 134th New York Infantry Regiment, which was in Barlow's brigade of the Eleventh Corps at Chancellorsville. After that battle, the regiment was transferred to Buschbeck's brigade. Since Buschbeck was absent with a wound, Coster became brigade commander. After the Eleventh Corps went to Chattanooga, Coster resigned both of his commissions and in May 1864 became provost marshal of New York's Sixth District and administered the draft there. He died in 1888. See Sifakis, *Who Was Who*, p. 146.

The remnants of the 134th and 154th New York were together in the cemetery on 2 and 3 July. See Dunkelman and Winey, "Hardtack Regiment."

12. Nicholson, *Pennsylvania*, 1:420. Rupp's tannery was closest to Cemetery Hill and was probably the one passed.

13. Monath, "Experience at Gettysburg." According to David Blubaugh, the hotel's manager, it lost all of its linen, bedclothes, and silverware.

14. This line of houses is pictured in the accompanying view of Gettysburg of Baltimore Street from Cemetery Hill. See also Frassanito, *Gettysburg*, pp. 96, 116. All three photographs show a tower, probably a smokestack, north of the Rupp house. The names associated with houses were taken from draft maps prepared by Robert Brake in RBC.

15. The Kuhn identification for the brickyard is in the notes with Robert Brake's draft maps in RBC. It is referred to elsewhere as Houck's brickyard.

16. The Study house is gone, but the Myers house is there and has been converted into commercial use. The house is said to have been Howard's headquarters, but its location makes the claim doubtful—at least after 1 July. The headquarters site is marked at the crest of East Cemetery Hill. The house was the site of the Soldiers' Orphans Home from 1866 to 1876.

17. Ker to Nicholson, 1 May 1864, 73d Pennsylvania Volunteer Infantry Regiment, GNMP; Bates, *Pennsylvania Volunteers*, 2:866.

18. Rupp to Sister Anne, 19 July 1863, ACHS.

19. The story of Corporal Poole's death is taken from an old label exhibited

with the table in the present GNMP visitor center. The information was discovered by Frank Rosensteel when he acquired the table, presumably from the John McCreary family in 1878. It states that one of the McCrearys wrapped Poole's body in a blanket and buried it near Long Lane. The label refers to Poole as John Poole. The corrected name, William H. Poole, is from Krick, *Gettysburg Death Roster*, p. 74. Years after the battle, the postmaster of Gettysburg received a letter from a man who described the McCreary house and said that he had shot at a Confederate seen in one of its upper rooms and had seen him drop. See McCreary, "Gettysburg," p. 10, GNMP.

20. Reed, "Gettysburg Campaign," pp. 188–89.

21. Miller to Bachelder, 2 Mar. 1864, BP; "The Story of Mrs. Jacob Kitzmiller [Anna Garlach]," ACHS. Pockmarks made by bullets fired by Union skirmishers are visible on the south sides of these and many other nearby buildings today.

22. Blackford, *War Years*, pp. 231–32; *OR* 27 (2):598. The buildings described by Blackford have not been mentioned by anyone else in this context or identified. In his report, Blackford said that his battalion deployed in the fields west of town on 2 July and in the houses on 3 July.

23. Kiefer, *One Hundred and Fifty-third Regiment*, p. 221.

24. Butts, *A Gallant Captain*, p. 63. Special rifles used for sniping are discussed in Coggins, *Arms*, p. 37.

25. Salomon, "Gettysburg," pp. 11–14; Simonhoff, *Jewish Participation*, pp. 77–78. Sometime between 1911 and 1913, after the Medal of Honor had gained some prestige, Salomon tried to have one awarded to Greenhut for his part in this action. Instead, Secretary of War Henry Stimson sent Greenhut a letter of commendation. It seems likely that the house seized by Greenhut was Welty's or McCreary's.

26. Salomon, "Gettysburg," p. 11. In his own account, Greenhut suggests that Ackermann did not go forward at all. See Meites, *Jews of Chicago*, p. 95.

27. Horn, *Henry Eyster Jacobs*, 1:56; McLean, "Days of Terror." The old label with the bed in the GNMP museum states that Mrs. McLean was in the bed when the bullet struck it. In his account, McLean says she was in the cellar.

28. McCreary, "Gettysburg," p. 10, GNMP.

29. "Reminiscences of John Charles Will," pp. 15–18, GNMP.

30. "The Story of Mrs. Jacob Kitzmiller [Anna Garlach]," ACHS.

31. McCreary, "Gettysburg," p. 8, GNMP.

32. McLean, "Days of Terror."

33. McCreary, "Gettysburg," p. 10, GNMP.

34. *OR* 27 (2):555, 582, 587, 598, 663, 665–66; Norman, *Portion of My Life*, p. 186; Green Diary, 2 July 1863, SHC.

35. New York Monuments Commission, *Final Report*, 3:85–86; Lonn, *Foreigners*, p. 193. Lonn states that von Steinwehr received a commission in an Alabama regiment, but, if so, he did not go to Mexico with it. Kaufmann, in *Die Deutschen*, p. 470, states that he was also a Prussian officer and an instructor at the Kadettenhause in Potsdam.

36. New York Monuments Commission, *Final Report*, 3:85–86; Lonn, *Foreigners*, p. 193; O. O. Howard, "Eleventh Corps," p. 199.

37. Quaife, *Williams*, p. 166; H. Osborn, *Trials*, p. 96; von Steinwehr to Howard, 1 Mar. 1866, O. O. Howard Papers, BC. After Gettysburg, von Steinwehr and his division shared the fortunes of the Eleventh Corps in Tennessee, where he led the division in the battles of Wauhatchie and Missionary Ridge. Unfortunately, in April 1864, when the Eleventh and Twelfth corps were consolidated into the Twentieth Corps, his division was abolished, and he was left without a field command. He resigned his commission in July 1865 and embarked on a distinguished career as a professor of military science at Yale, an architect, a geographer, and a publisher. Although he resided in Cincinnati in his last years, he died in Buffalo and is buried in Albany. See New York Monuments Commission, *Final Report*, 3:1346.

That portion of the Emmitsburg Road within von Steinwehr's sector was named for him. Unfortunately, although von Steinwehr served for two years as a division commander, he was not even brevetted to the grade of major general.

38. Reid, *Ohio in the War*, 1:419, 2:983; Sifakis, *Who Was Who*, p. 606; Talbott and Hobart, *Railway Officials*, p. 225. Orland Smith resigned in February 1864 and returned to railroading. In 1877 he became general superintendent of the Columbus, Hocking Valley, and Toledo Railroad and in 1882 became its president. The army recognized his service as a brigade commander in March 1865 with a brevet to brigadier general.

39. *OR* 27 (1):721, 725; George Metcalf, "Reminiscence," GCC; Hurst, *Seventy-third Ohio*, p. 68; Henry Henney, "55th Ohio, Diary," 2 July 1863, *CWTI*.

40. *OR* 27 (1):722, 724, 726; H. Osborn, *Trials*, p. 96; Hurst, *Seventy-third Ohio*, p. 68; New York Monuments Commission, *Final Report*, 3:931.

41. *OR* 27 (1):724, 726; Hand, "Gettysburg."

42. George Metcalf, "Reminiscence," GCC. Perhaps because of their prominence, church steeples were often believed to shelter snipers.

43. Hand, "Gettysburg." The location of the spring was not given. Probably it was a source of Winebrenner's Run.

44. L. A. Smith, "Recollections," pp. 343–44.

45. George Metcalf, "Reminiscence," GCC.

46. *OR* 27 (2):658, 663, 665; Caldwell, *Brigade of South Carolinians*, p. 100; Hurst, *Seventy-third Ohio*, p. 68.

47. *OR* 27 (2):658, 663.

48. Medal of Honor File, Charles Stacey, 55th Ohio Volunteer Infantry, Box 406, RG 94, NA; Mesnard, "Reminiscence," pp. 35–36, CWMC; H. Osborn, *Trials*, p. 99. The "cut" that concealed the Confederate sharpshooters was probably Long Lane. Mesnard observed that Stacey had done good work but that he had a "better, safer, place than the rest of us."

49. H. Osborn, *Trials*, p. 100.

50. Mesnard, "Reminiscence," pp. 36–37, CWMC.

51. H. Osborn, *Trials*, pp. 257–58.

52. Medal of Honor Application, Richard Enderlin, 73d Ohio Volunteer Infantry, RG 94, NA; *OR* 27 (1):183; *Burke's Presidential Families*, p. 571. Pvt. George Nixon is buried in the Ohio plot at the Gettysburg National Cemetery overlooking the ground on which he fought and fell.

53. *OR* 27 (1):183. The strength figure is the sum of those given on the regimental memorials.

54. Ibid., pp. 722, 724.

CHAPTER TEN

1. *OR* 27 (1):777, 811, 816; Brown, *Twenty-seventh Indiana*, pp. 308–9. Colgrove's report mentions these buildings but does not identify them. It seems likely that the Confederates held the Deardorff or Heck buildings on Colgrove's right. The buildings to his left were probably at the Rosenstiel farmstead, which was in the woods a quarter of a mile from the others. Today this area is bisected by U.S. 15. The Deardorff house and the Lott house north of it still stand.

2. *OR* 27 (1):601, 610, 811; Guiney to Chamberlain, 26 Oct. 1865, Chamberlain Papers, LC; MacNamara, *Irish Ninth*, pp. 195–96.

3. *OR* 27 (2):518, 521, 526, 530; Rollins, "Playing Cavalry." It is not clear whether the skirmishing watched by Rollins was with the 9th Massachusetts or with Twelfth Corps troops from Culp's Hill. The reference to cavalry suggests the former.

4. Evans, *Confederate Military History*, 3:676–78; Freeman, *Lee's Lieutenants*, 3:704; Sifakis, *Who Was Who*, p. 684; Wakelyn, *Biographical Dictionary*, p. 423; Warner, *Generals in Gray*, p. 319; Rollins, "Going to Gettysburg." Walker led his brigade to Spotsylvania, where he was seriously wounded. He commanded what had been Early's division at Appomattox. After the war, he farmed, practiced law, was lieutenant governor of Virginia, and served two terms in the U.S. House of Representatives as a Republican. He died in Wytheville in 1901.

5. Guiney to Chamberlain, 26 Oct. 1865, Chamberlain Papers, LC.

6. *OR* 27 (1):144–45, 916, 956; Shevchuk, "Brinkerhoff's Ridge," pp. 61–62. This excellent article by Shevchuk contains much background and other information on the cavalry's operations on 2 July that will not be covered below.

7. *DAB* 4:596; Boatner, *Dictionary*, p. 357. Gregg served briefly in 1874 as U.S. consul in Prague and for three years as adjutant general of Pennsylvania.

8. Nicholson, *Pennsylvania*, 2:817; W. E. Miller, "Cavalry Battle," p. 399; Rawle, *Third Pennsylvania*, p. 266; Preston, "Campaigning"; Shevchuk, "Brinkerhoff's Ridge," p. 61.

9. *OR* 27 (1):956, 977; Shevchuk, "Brinkerhoff's Ridge," pp. 65, 67.

10. The 10th New York's 1861 campsite is indicated on the Gettysburg map in Preston, *Tenth Regiment*.

11. See the Order of Battle in appendix C. I do not know why Gregg's division had no artillery at this time. Nine batteries were assigned to the Cavalry Corps, and Capt. William D. Fuller's battery, C of the 3d U.S. Artillery, had marched with Gregg's division. Gregg had sent it to Westminster with Huey's brigade. Capt. Alanson M. Randol's batteries, E and G of the 1st U.S. Artillery, were not engaged until 3 July.

12. Boatner, *Dictionary*, p. 534; Warner, *Generals in Blue*, pp. 300–301. After recovering from a fall from his horse, McIntosh served as a brigade commander.

He lost a leg from wounds received at Winchester in 1864. McIntosh received brevets for White Oak Swamp, Gettysburg, Ashland, Opequon, and Winchester. After the war, he served as a lieutenant colonel of infantry in spite of having only one leg, and he retired as a brigadier general and as a brevet major general in 1870. He died in New Brunswick in 1888.

13. Sifakis, *Who Was Who*, pp. 265–66; Boatner, *Dictionary*, pp. 357–58; Nicholson, *Pennsylvania*, 2:861. J. Irvin Gregg continued to serve as a brigade commander in the grade of colonel. Yet he received five brevets, including one as a major general of volunteers for war service. He was wounded at both Deep Bottom and Hatcher's Run and captured at Farmville three days before Lee's surrender. After the war, he reverted to a captaincy in the regular army but received the colonelcy of the 8th U.S. Cavalry in 1866. He retired in 1879.

14. Nicholson, *Pennsylvania*, 2:863–64; Preston, *Tenth Regiment*, pp. 108–9, and "Campaigning"; Shevchuk, "Brinkerhoff's Ridge," p. 67. The accounts of the 16th Pennsylvania Cavalry's participation are very nebulous. Reference is made to a "Ruler House," but it is not shown on extant maps.

The cavalrymen believed that the 9th Massachusetts Regiment was from either the Eleventh or Twelfth Corps but not from the Fifth.

15. Preston, *Tenth Regiment*, p. 108.

16. Nicholson, *Pennsylvania*, 2:817, 923–24; Rawle, "With Gregg." Rank's battery's memorial, which is at its position, is beside the Hanover Road about one and a half miles east of U.S. 15. The battery had been converted to a four-gun light battery in the spring of 1863. Its first section had been sent to Baltimore, leaving only one section of two three-inch rifles in the field. See *OR* 27 (1):238.

17. *OR* 27 (2):518, 521; Draft Report of Battle, Nadenbousch Papers, DU; Preston, *Tenth Regiment*, p. 108; Shevchuk, "Brinkerhoff's Ridge," p. 68.

18. Preston, *Tenth Regiment*, pp. 109, 111.

19. Ibid., p. 110; Busey, *Regimental Strengths and Losses*, p. 208.

20. Preston, *Tenth Regiment*, pp. 109–10; Shevchuk, "Brinkerhoff's Ridge," pp. 68–69; Kempster, "Cavalry," p. 413. The Shriver farm was west of Brinkerhoff's Woods about 300 yards west of Benner's Run and midway between the York Pike and the Hanover Road.

21. Preston, *Tenth Regiment*, p. 111.

22. Ibid., pp. 112–13.

23. Ibid., pp. 115–16; Shevchuk, "The Fight," p. 71.

24. Preston, *Tenth Regiment*, p. 113.

25. Shevchuk, "Brinkerhoff's Ridge," p. 71; W. E. Miller, "Cavalry Battle," pp. 399–401; Rawle, "With Gregg"; Kempster, "Cavalry," p. 415; Preston, *Tenth Regiment*, p. 113.

26. Rawle, "With Gregg"; Gilmore, "With Gregg." Many who saw this incident found it amusing. Because versions of this story appear in several places, it seems likely that it was a favorite among the veterans of this fight.

27. W. E. Miller, "Cavalry Battle," p. 401; Nicholson, *Pennsylvania*, 2:818; Rawle, "With Gregg"; Pyne, *First New Jersey*, p. 164; Maryland Gettysburg Monuments Commission, *Report*, pp. 103–4.

28. Maryland Gettysburg Monuments Commission, *Report*, p. 104; Rawle, "With

Gregg"; Pyne, *First New Jersey*, pp. 164–65; Rawle, *Third Pennsylvania*, p. 296. Pyne stated that another regiment ordered to relieve the 1st New Jersey would not come forward. The unnamed regiment halted 100 yards in the rear of the 1st's line and would advance no further.

29. W. E. Miller, "Cavalry Battle," pp. 400–401; Rawle, "With Gregg"; Gilmore, "With Gregg," pp. 474–75; Nicholson, *Pennsylvania*, 2:811, 818.

30. Rawle, *Third Pennsylvania*, p. 316. Official casualty figures are not broken down by day. See *OR* 27 (1):179, 186.

31. *OR* 27 (2):504, 518–19.

32. Ibid., p. 519; Rawle, *Third Pennsylvania*, p. 296; Preston, *Tenth Regiment*, 114. Colonel Nadenbousch left Companies I and K and a portion of Company A on Brinkerhoff's Ridge to guard the left. They rejoined the regiment on the night of 3 July.

CHAPTER ELEVEN

1. Krick, *Lee's Colonels*, p. 212; Freeman, *Lee's Lieutenants*, 3:197; G. C. Brown, "Reminiscences," pp. 38–39, TSLA; Sifakis, *Who Was Who*, p. 375.

2. *OR* 27 (2):542; "John William Ford Hatton Memoir," p. 452, LC.

3. See Warren Map.

4. E. A. Moore, *Cannoneer*, pp. 195–96. Major Osborn wrote that the battery fired for about an hour shortly after dawn. Perhaps it was determining the ranges to its targets. See T. W. Osborn, "Artillery."

5. *OR* 27 (1):231, 233, 357, 361, 363, 365, 751.

6. Ibid., pp. 233, 748–49.

7. Ibid., pp. 233, 748–49, 756.

8. Ibid., pp. 360, 892–95; Hall to Bachelder, 29 Dec. 1869, BP; Maine Gettysburg Commission, *Maine at Gettysburg*, p. 21; Wheeler, *In Memorium*, p. 410.

9. New York Monuments Commission, *Final Report*, 3:1247.

10. *OR* 27 (1):237, 748–49, 891, 893; New York Monuments Commission, *Final Report*, 3:1297. Battery H, 1st Ohio Light Artillery Regiment, was called "Huntington's Battery" because Capt. James F. Huntington was its assigned commander. At Gettysburg, Huntington commanded the Third Volunteer Brigade of the Artillery Reserve, to which the battery was assigned, and Lt. George W. Norton was the battery's acting commander.

11. Sifakis, *Who Was Who*, p. 682; Nevins, *Wainwright*, pp. v–xvi.

12. Sifakis, *Who Was Who*, pp. 480–81; Wheeler, *In Memorium*, p. 415.

13. *OR* 27 (1):233, 870. Lieutenant Muhlenberg's command of the Twelfth Corps' artillery brigade indicates a deficiency in the Federal artillery system about which Hunt complained, including in his report. See ibid., p. 242. Each of the four batteries of the brigade was commanded by a lieutenant, and Muhlenberg commanded the brigade because he ranked his peers. Ideally the batteries should have been commanded by captains and the brigade by a field officer. Lt. Col. Clermont L. Best had previously commanded the brigade, but he had left to serve on Slocum's staff as the corps inspector general. Yet he apparently continued to be directly

involved with the corps' artillery. Slocum reported that Best posted the corps batteries on the night of 2 July. See ibid., p. 761.

14. *OR* 27 (2):495, 603, 604–5. I have wondered why Colonel Brown did not try posting batteries west of Gettysburg south of Middle Street and, perhaps, somewhere along the Hanover Road west of Rock Creek when intense fire was needed. Guns placed in these areas would have been highly vulnerable to Federal fire but might have done splendid service. Yet we must presume that the artillerymen knew what they were doing.

15. Ibid., p. 604. Dance's three batteries had four guns each; Wallace had ten-pounder Parrotts, and Smith and Cunningham had three-inch rifles.

16. Ibid., p. 675. Hurt's battery had the two 2.75-inch Whitworth rifles and two three-inch Ordnance rifles; Johnson had two Napoleons and two three-inch rifles; Wallace had four three-inch rifles; and Rice had four Napoleons. For information on the Whitworths and other guns, see Hazlett, Olmstead, and Parks, *Field Artillery Weapons*.

17. *OR* 27 (2):652. Richardson had three pieces from Victor Maurin's battery, two from John W. Lewis's, two from Joseph D. Moore's, and two from C. R. Grandy's. Seven were three-inch Ordnance rifles, two were ten-pounder Parrotts.

18. Ibid., p. 678. Brander had two Napoleons and two ten-pounder Parrotts; McGraw had four Napoleons; Zimmerman had four three-inch rifles; Johnson's Crenshaw Battery had two Napoleons and two twelve-pounder howitzers; and Marye had two Napoleons and two ten-pounder Parrotts.

19. Ibid., pp. 610, 678; T. W. Osborn, "Artillery"; Nicholson, *Pennsylvania*, 2:900; New York Monuments Commission, *Final Report*, 3:1257; G. C. Brown, "Reminiscences," p. 37, TSLA.

20. Shevchuk, "Wounding of Albert Jenkins," p. 66. Shevchuk suggests that the wounding of Jenkins may have had great consequences because if his brigade had relieved Smith's and Gordon's brigades, Smith's brigade might also have been available to Early in his assault on Cemetery Hill.

21. T. W. Osborn, "Experiences," pp. 43–45, Osborn Papers, CU. Osborn here no doubt refers to Jennie Wade's death, for which the artillery was not responsible. See chapter 19.

22. *OR* 27 (2):446, 470, 504, 543; G. C. Brown, "Reminiscences," p. 38, TSLA; S. Z. Ammen, "Second Maryland Battalion, Fourteenth Paper—Second Series," in Ammen, "Maryland Troops in the Confederacy," p. 131, CC. Both Union and Confederate sources say that this phase of the battle began at about 4:00 P.M., yet Ewell timed it at 5:00 P.M., which is more likely to be correct.

23. William W. Goldsborough, "The Chesapeake Artillery at Gettysburg," Cronin Papers of the War, NYHS; S. Z. Ammen, "Second Maryland Battalion, Fourteenth Paper—Second Series," in Ammen, "Maryland Troops in the Confederacy," p. 131, CC. Ammen stated that Goldsborough was screened by a growth of cherry trees while on the hill. There is no orchard shown on the Warren Map. Perhaps these were wild cherry trees in one of the clumps at the south end of the crest.

24. *OR* 27 (2):543–44; S. Z. Ammen, "Second Maryland Battalion, Fourteenth Paper—Second Series," in Ammen, "Maryland Troops in the Confederacy," p. 132,

CC. The batteries of Latimer's battalion were armed as follows: Raine had two twenty-pounder Parrotts, one ten-pounder Parrott, and one three-inch Ordnance rifle; Dement had four Napoleons; Carpenter had two Napoleons and two three-inch rifles; and Brown had four ten-pounder Parrotts.

25. C. F. J. [J. F. Cook], "The Chesapeake," in S. Z. Ammen, "Maryland Troops in the Confederacy," p. 182, CC; "John William Ford Hatton Memoir," pp. 454–55, LC.

26. "Washington Hands's Civil War Notebook," p. 95, UV; D. R. Howard, "Left on the Field," in S. Z. Ammen, "Maryland Troops in the Confederacy," p. 139, CC.

27. T. W. Osborn, "Artillery"; O. O. Howard, "Campaign," p. 63.

28. O. O. Howard, "Campaign," p. 63.

29. E. A. Moore, *Cannoneer*, p. 197; Stewart, "Battery B," pp. 374–75. Stewart's battery had thirty-six casualties at Gettysburg.

30. Nevins, *Wainwright*, p. 244.

31. Ibid.; Nicholson, *Pennsylvania*, 2:901. I have not been able to identify the brothers mentioned by Wainwright.

32. Nicholson, *Pennsylvania*, 2:901.

33. Nevins, *Wainwright*, p. 244. Although described as old, Wiedrich was forty-two at Gettysburg. He was born in Hochorville, France. See Raus, *Generation*, p. 87.

A pendulum hausse was a detachable rear sight with an elevation scale.

34. Maine Gettysburg Commission, *Maine at Gettysburg*, pp. 92–93; Whittier, "Left Attack," p. 79. Each gun should have occupied about seventeen yards of frontage; therefore Latimer's fourteen pieces should have needed only 200 yards of space plus an interval of several yards between batteries. Since the crest of Benner's Hill south of the road extends nearly 400 yards, Latimer's guns should not have been crowded.

A cascabel is a knob at the rear end of the barrel of a muzzle-loading cannon used in hoisting the barrel from the carriage.

35. *OR* 27 (1):826, 870; Nicholson, *Pennsylvania*, 2:913.

36. Edward R. Geary to Mother, 17 July 1863, Knap's Battery, GNMP. Lieutenant Geary was killed in the battle of Wauhatchie, Tennessee, in October 1863. See O. O. Howard, *Autobiography*, 1:469.

37. Goldsborough, *Maryland Line*, p. 324; William W. Goldsborough, "The Chesapeake Artillery at Gettysburg," Cronin Papers of the War, NYHS; "Washington Hands's Civil War Notebook," p. 95, UV.

38. C. F. J. [J. F. Cook], "The Chesapeake," in S. Z. Ammen, "Maryland Troops in the Confederacy," p. 182, CC. It seems likely that "Doctor" was Brian's name and not a title.

39. "John William Ford Hatton Memoir," pp. 453–54, LC.

40. Ibid., p. 454; William W. Goldsborough, "The Chesapeake Artillery at Gettysburg," Cronin Papers of the War, NYHS; Goldsborough, *Maryland Line*, p. 325; C. F. J. [J. F. Cook], "The Chesapeake," in S. Z. Ammen, "Maryland Troops in the Confederacy," p. 182, CC.

41. C. F. J. [J. F. Cook], "The Chesapeake," in S. Z. Ammen, "Maryland Troops in the Confederacy," p. 182, CC.

42. "John William Ford Hatton Memoir," p. 455, LC.

43. *OR* (2):456, 504, 554.

44. C. F. J. [J. F. Cook], "The Chesapeake," in S. Z. Ammen, "Maryland Troops in the Confederacy," p. 182, CC.

45. *OR* 27 (2):544; "John William Ford Hatton Memoir," p. 456, LC; Krick, *Lee's Colonels*, p. 456. We can wonder if some of the wounded who, like Latimer, were transported back to Virginia might not have fared a lot better had they been left at Gettysburg.

46. Stiles, *Four Years*, p. 34.

47. *OR* 27 (2):341, 458–59, 543–44.

48. Ibid., p. 456. Some Confederates wrote later that Cemetery Hill dominated Benner's Hill and that Latimer's guns were subjected to a plunging fire. Although Cemetery Hill is as much as forty feet higher than Benner's Hill, the distance between the hills makes this difference in elevation none too obvious, though it might have increased the range of the Union guns a little.

49. Ibid., pp. 344–45, 659, 675–76, 678.

50. Ibid., pp. 233, 858, 872. Batteries B and M of the 1st Connecticut Heavy Artillery were left at Westminster. They belonged to the Artillery Reserve.

51. H. Osborn, *Trials*, pp. 100–101; Mesnard, "Reminiscence," p. 36, CWMC.

52. T. W. Osborn, "Artillery."

53. *OR* 27 (1):360, 365, 753, 892, 895.

CHAPTER TWELVE

1. *OR* 27 (3):458, (1):165, 763, 765, 768, 769–70, 773.

2. *OR* 27 (1):769–70; Slocum to Morgan, 2 Jan. 1864, in Quaife, *Williams*, p. 285.

3. Williams to Bachelder, 10 Nov. 1865, BP; Quaife, *Williams*, pp. 227–28. Henry H. Lockwood, a native of Delaware, graduated from West Point in 1836 and served in the army for a year in campaigns against the Seminoles. He farmed for a time before joining the faculty of the U.S. Naval Academy as an instructor in mathematics. He taught at the academy until the outbreak of the Civil War, except for a period of service during the Mexican War as a navy officer aboard the USS *United States*. When the Civil War broke out, Lockwood joined the army as colonel of the 1st Delaware Regiment. He became a brigadier general in August 1861 and from that time served in Maryland, principally as commander of the District of the Eastern Shore. After Gettysburg, he served in the Potomac Valley, except for a brief period at Cold Harbor, where he commanded a division of the Fifth Corps. He spent the postwar years at the Naval Academy and at the Naval Observatory in Washington, D.C. Shortly after their first meeting, Williams described Lockwood as a "very pleasant gentleman." See Sifakis, *Who Was Who*, pp. 391–92; Boatner, *Dictionary*, p. 486; and Quaife, *Williams*, p. 227.

4. *DAB* 10:247; Quaife, *Williams*, pp. 3–11; Boatner, *Dictionary*, pp. 926–27. After the war, Williams was a minister to El Salvador, an unsuccessful candidate for the governorship of Michigan, and a U.S. congressman. He died during his second term as a Democratic member of Congress in December 1876.

5. Quaife, *Williams*, pp. 8, 204–5, 393. Williams's published letters give interesting insight into the command of a division.

6. Ibid., pp. 163–64, 170, 206, 348–49.

7. Meade, *Life and Letters*, 2:86–87; Slocum to Davis, 8 Sept. 1875, Bates Papers, PSA; Williams to Bachelder, 21 Apr. 1864 and 10 Nov. 1865, BP.

8. Slocum to Davis, 8 Sept. 1875, Bates Papers, PSA. Perhaps General Slocum had a credibility problem at army headquarters. In 1886 Paul Oliver, formerly of General Meade's staff, wrote: "Between you and the post he [Slocum] always exaggerated[;] if he had a good skirmish line in front of him, he had the whole army in front of him, and when he sent for a brigade, I felt it was all bosh and that he could get along without it just as well. But this time I was mistaken, he was really hard pressed." See Oliver to Meade, 21 July 1886, ML.

9. New York Monuments Commission, *Slocum*, pp. 80–81, 178; Slocum, *Life and Services*, pp. 104–5; New York Monuments Commission, *Final Report*, 1:62. In the latter publication's narrative prepared by William F. Fox, the removal of the troops of the Twelfth Corps from Culp's Hill was judged a "grave error" on Meade's part. Fox, at Gettysburg, was an officer of the 107th New York Regiment in McDougall's brigade.

10. Slocum to Davis, 8 Sept. 1875, Bates Papers, PSA.

11. Quaife, *Williams*, p. 228; Williams to Bachelder, 21 Apr. 1864 and 10 Nov. 1865, BP. It is to be assumed that Williams intended that Geary's line extend at least to the swale. In essence, Candy's brigade would have replaced McDougall's in the forward line.

12. Morse, "Twelfth Corps," pp. 25–26, and *Second Massachusetts*, p. 8.

13. Raus, *Generation*, pp. 29, 84; New York Monuments Commission, *Final Report*, 3:1033, 1042; Maryland Gettysburg Monuments Commission, *Report*, p. 56.

14. New York Monuments Commission, *Final Report*, 3:858, 1033; Morhous, *123d Regiment*, p. 48.

15. *OR* 27 (1):774, 804, 806; Williams to Bachelder, 10 Nov. 1865, BP; "My Maryland"; Maryland Gettysburg Monuments Commission, *Report*, pp. 56, 83. It cannot be known with certainty which woods Williams referred to; it might have been the north end of Weikert's Woods. In a letter in Quaife, *Williams*, p. 228, Williams wrote that the Marylanders attacked in column.

16. *OR* 27 (1):774, 804, 805–6, 809; Cook and Benton, *Dutchess County Regiment*, p. 31. For a broader picture of operations in this area, see Pfanz, *Gettysburg*, chaps. 13 and 16.

17. *OR* 27 (1):773–74, 778, 783, 812–13; Morse, *Second Massachusetts*, pp. 8–9.

18. *OR* 27 (1):774, 778, 780, 812–13. Colonel Colgrove in his report stated that his brigade was in position in Weikert's Woods for between forty minutes and an hour. Ruger reported that the division formed "in line of masses."

19. Williams to Bachelder, 21 Apr. 1864 and 10 Nov. 1865, BP. Williams described Owen as being "in not a very clear state of mind." He stated that Owen had just been released from arrest and had no command but "a sort of roving commission." Owen had commanded the Philadelphia Brigade in the Second Corps, which at Gettysburg was commanded by Alexander S. Webb. Owen would soon command another brigade in the Second Corps.

20. Williams to Bachelder, 21 Apr. 1864 and 10 Nov. 1865, BP; *OR* 27 (1):775.

21. *OR* 27 (1):770; Williams to Bachelder, 10 Nov. 1865, BP; Quaife, *Williams*, p. 229.

22. *OR* 27 (1):73; Gibbon, "Council of War," p. 314.

23. Quaife, *Williams*, p. 229.

24. *OR* 27 (1):759, 774.

25. Ibid., p. 826. In 1867 Capt. Charles P. Horton of Greene's staff wrote that the brigade was ordered from its works and to the left at 6:00 P.M. Being on the left of the division it was the last to leave. The brigade was actually leaving its works and its skirmishers were ordered in when it learned from Lieutenant Colonel Redington that the enemy was advancing in heavy force of 5,000 or 6,000. At this, Greene halted the movement, reinforced his skirmish line, and reported the action to Geary. Geary replied that he should follow the division as ordered. At this point, the officer sent to Geary met Lieutenant Colonel Rodgers of Slocum's staff and told him of the Confederate advance. Rodgers told him that Greene should hold his position and said that he would send Geary back with the rest of the division. After the evening's fight was over, Horton reported to Slocum's headquarters and spoke to Rodgers. Rodgers acted surprised that Geary had not returned, said that he had been ordered back, and sent staff members in all directions to find him. Kane's brigade appeared an hour later. See Horton to Bachelder, 23 Jan. 1867, BP.

Lieutenant Colonel Rodgers appears to have been the key man on Slocum's staff. He had started in May 1861 as a captain in the 27th New York Regiment and received assignments as an adjutant general. He advanced in such assignments to the post of adjutant general on the Twelfth Corps staff. He resigned his commission in January 1865 and received a brevet to brigadier general of volunteers for his war service. See Boatner, *Dictionary*, p. 707.

26. *OR* 27 (1):826.

27. *DAB* 4:203–4; Tinkom, *Geary*, pp. 1–6, 35–36, 40–60, 97; Beers, "Geary," pp. 11–16; O. O. Howard, *Autobiography*, 1:469, 616. After Gettysburg, Geary served with the Twelfth and Twentieth corps and was military governor of Savannah. He served two terms as governor of Pennsylvania from 1867 to 1873 and died three weeks after his term ended.

In a letter to Col. Ezra Carman of the 13th New Jersey Regiment written in 1876, General Williams wrote: "Geary always claimed all the fighting. You should not place the least reliance on his Official Reports unless confirmed by others. Almost every official report is full of unintentional errors & mistakes, but Geary's were often premeditated & wicked lies—They were written solely for his own exultation without the least regard for facts." Whether Williams held this opinion at the time of the battle of Gettysburg, I do not know. See Williams to Carman, 13 Aug. 1876, Carman Papers, NYPL.

28. Mouat, "Three Years," HSP.

29. *OR* 27 (1):844, 851; Mouat, "Three Years," HSP; Nicholson, *Pennsylvania*, 1:219; Rickards to Bachelder, 12 Apr. 1864, BP.

30. *OR* 27 (1):828, 836. The few official and personal accounts of this debacle add to the confusion. The Warren Map shows that the west slope of the hill presumably occupied was in wheat and grass. Yet we may presume that there were some trees

and brush along the creek in Candy's front. The 5th Ohio was reported to have been in trees, the 7th in open fields behind a stone wall, and the 29th near a road leading to the pike. See ibid., pp. 839, 840, 842, 846.

31. Ibid., pp. 847, 849; "Notes of a Conversation with Gen. Kane," BP.

CHAPTER THIRTEEN

1. S. Z. Ammen, "Second Maryland Battalion, Fourteenth Paper—Second Series," in Ammen, "Maryland Troops in the Confederacy," p. 132, CC.

2. See chapter 4 and *OR* 27 (2):446.

3. "Paper Read by Co'l David Zable . . . December 12, 1903," p. 2, TU; McKim, *Soldier's Recollections*, p. 193; Goldsborough, "With Lee."

4. *OR* 27 (2):531, 538–39.

5. Sifakis, *Who Was Who*, p. 350; Boatner, *Dictionary*, p. 442; Freeman, *Lee's Lieutenants*, 3:704–5; Warner, *Generals in Gray*, p. 164.

6. *OR* 27 (1):862, (2):536.

7. *OR* 27 (2):536; Rollins, "Playing Cavalry."

8. *OR* 27 (2):504, 513, 532. Col. Jesse Milton Williams (1831–1864) was a resident of Mansfield, Louisiana, who had attended the University of Alabama. He became captain of Company D, 2d Louisiana Regiment, in May 1861 and the regiment's commander in the summer of 1862. He served with the regiment during the Peninsular campaign and commanded it at Cedar Mountain, Second Manassas, and Antietam, where he was wounded. When General Nicholls was wounded at Chancellorsville, Williams took command of the brigade and led it to Gettysburg. Subsequently, when Gen. LeRoy Stafford took command of the brigade in the fall of 1863, Williams resumed command of the regiment. He was killed at Spotsylvania. See Sifakis, *Who Was Who*, p. 717, and Krick, *Lee's Colonels*, p. 371.

9. *OR* 27 (2):504. The strength figures are from the War Department tablets on the battlefield. They are as follows: Jones, 1,600; Nicholls, 1,100; Steuart, 1,700; and Walker, 1,450. Lewis R. Stegman, commander of the 102d New York at Gettysburg, stated that the Confederate attack column was three ranks deep. See New York Monuments Commission, *Greene*, p. 45.

10. *OR* 27 (1):894, (2):537–39.

11. *OR* 27 (2):513; Murphy, "Some Reminiscences," Murphy-Sandlin Collection, NSUL; Note Card, "1st Louisiana Infantry," GNMP. The latter source states that the 1st Regiment was on the right, but "Paper Read by Co'l David Zable . . . December 12, 1903," TU, says it was on the left.

12. *OR* 27 (2):508–10; John Cowan and James I. Metts, "A Sketch of This Gallant Command's Service in Field and Camp," in "Eliza Hall Parsley's Book," Parsley Papers, SHC; McKim, *Soldier's Recollections*, p. 195; Goldsborough, "With Lee"; Roberts, "Keystone Guards," p. 148; Report of the 10th and 23d Virginia Regiments, 8 and 9 July 1863, MC.

13. *DAB* 4:566–67; New York Monuments Commission, *Final Report*, 3:1349–51; Boatner, *Dictionary*, pp. 355–56. In the postwar years, Greene worked at engineering projects in New York City, Washington, D.C., Detroit, and Troy.

He was a president of the American Society of Civil Engineers and of the New York Genealogical and Biographical Society. One son, Samuel D. Greene, was the executive officer on the USS *Monitor*. Greene died in January 1899.

14. Horton to Bachelder, 23 Jan. 1907, BP; Greene, "Breastworks," p. 317. Little is known about the traverse. No one reported specifically who built it, there is no description of it, and no traces of it remain. Greene wrote that it was built to protect his right, yet it could have been built by Candy's brigade rather than his. It is shown in the sketch with the Greene article, and the Warren Map shows a stub at its location. The ground may have been too hard for digging at its site, and it could have consisted primarily of tree trunks and limbs and rocks, which were removed soon after the battle.

15. *OR* 27 (1):845. Company H, 7th Ohio, was also on the skirmish line, and Candy's report states that Lt. Col. Orrin J. Crane of the 7th Ohio commanded the skirmishers of Candy's brigade.

16. Ibid., pp. 856, 862, 863; New York Monuments Commission, *Greene*, p. 43. Greene's brigade had been formed with the 78th New York's 198 officers and men on the left at the peak of the hill immediately right of Wadsworth's division. The 60th New York, 263 men strong, was next in line, with its left at the peak and extending down the steep slope to the right. The 102d New York, with a strength of 248, and the 149th, 319 men strong, extended the line to the right to the depression where the 137th New York had been. The 137th, a large regiment numbering 456 men, had moved beyond the saddle into Kane's brigade's works. Lt. Col. Herbert von Hammerstein, age twenty-nine, had served with the Austrian army and as a captain in the 8th New York Regiment in 1861 and on the staff of General McClellan. After leaving the volunteer army in 1865, he became a sergeant in the 2d U.S. Cavalry. Perhaps he was hoping for a commission. If so, he was disappointed for his legs were frozen and amputated. After leaving the army, he returned to Europe. See Raus, *Generation*, p. 71.

17. *OR* 27 (1):864, 866; New York Monuments Commission, *Final Report*, 3:1013; New York Monuments Commission, *Greene*, p. 44.

18. *OR* 27 (1):731, 735, 856; Dawes, *Sixth Wisconsin*, p. 181. Dawes wrote that he watched the repulse of Early's attack before he went to Greene's aid.

19. *OR* 27 (1):731, 735, 738, (2):506; Salomon, "Gettysburg"; New York Monuments Commission, *Final Report*, 1:452; Elmore, "Courage," p. 88 (which cites A. A. Barlow, *Company G/A Record of the Services of One Company of the 157th New York Volunteers* . . . [Syracuse, 1899]); Report of the 37th Virginia Regiment, 8 July 1863, MC.

20. Schurz to Frank Moore, 6 June 1865, De Coppet Collection, PU.

21. *OR* 27 (1):845, 862, 863; New York Monuments Commission, *Greene*, p. 43; J. H. Jones, "Saved the Day."

22. Collins, *149th Regiment*, pp. 138–39; J. H. Jones, "Saved the Day."

23. Collins, *149th Regiment*, pp. 138–39; J. H. Jones, "Saved the Day" and "A Pair of Breastplates."

24. *OR* 27 (2):536.

25. Ibid., pp. 532, 536, 537, 538; "Memoirs of Benjamin Andrew Jones, Vir-

ginian, Civil War Experiences," VHS. Captain Buckner became a lieutenant colonel and was killed at Spotsylvania.

26. *OR* 27 (2):513; "Paper Read by Co'l David Zable . . . December 12, 1903," TU; Lloyd, "Second Louisiana," p. 417; Murphy, "Reminiscences," Murphy-Sandlin Collection, NSUL; "Memoirs of W. P. Snakenburg, Wilson, North Carolina, Private, 'Louisiana Tigers,'" Bass Collection, Spring Hill, North Carolina.

27. *OR* 27 (2):510; "Washington Hands's Civil War Notebook," p. 96, UV; Report of the 10th Virginia Regiment, 8 July 1863, MC.

28. *OR* 27 (2):510; "Washington Hands's Civil War Notebook," p. 96, UV; Report of the 3d North Carolina Regiment, 10 July 1863, MC. The 1st Maryland Battalion received fire from skirmishers when it reached the creek. See Clemens, "Diary of John H. Stone," p. 132.

29. New York Monuments Commission, *Greene*, pp. 45–46.

30. *OR* 27 (2):510.

31. McKim, "Steuart's Brigade," p. 293; Report of the 1st North Carolina Regiment, 10 July 1863, MC. Even if McKim's part in this unfortunate affair was known within the brigade, the fact that he published an account of it suggests a high degree of moral courage. By the time of the writing he was a priest of the Episcopal church.

32. *OR* 27 (2):510; Goldsborough, *Maryland Line*, p. 103; Clark, *Histories*, 1:195; John Futch to Wife, 6 Aug. 1863, Futch Letters, NCDAH.

33. "Charles Anderson Raines Memoirs," p. 7, FNMP; Report of the 23d Virginia Regiment, 9 July 1863, MC.

34. *OR* 27 (2):510; "Washington Hands's Civil War Notebook," pp. 96–97, UV.

35. *OR* 27 (2):510; "Washington Hands's Civil War Notebook," p. 96, UV; Zollinger, Holliday, and Howard, "Steuart's Brigade," p. 106.

36. S. Z. Ammen, "Second Maryland Battalion, Fourteenth Paper—Second Series," in Ammen, "Maryland Troops in the Confederacy," p. 131, CC; "Egbert at Gettysburg," clipping with William W. Goldsborough, "The Chesapeake Artillery at Gettysburg," Cronin Papers of the War, NYHS.

37. *OR* 27 (1):856, 866.

38. Ibid., p. 432; Horton to Bachelder, 23 Jan. 1867, BP.

39. *OR* 27 (1):427, 432, 856, 866; Horton to Bachelder, 23 Jan. 1867, BP; William J. Burns, "Civil War Diary," 71st Pennsylvania Folder, RBC; Tevis and Marquis, *Fighting Fourteenth*, p. 138; Fowler to Bachelder, 2 Oct. 1899, BP. The 71st Pennsylvania Regiment, the "California Regiment," fought at Ball's Bluff and in subsequent battles with the Army of the Potomac. It participated in the repulse of Wright's Georgia brigade on 2 July and Pickett's Charge on 3 July. There is no reason to believe that Colonel Smith was disciplined for his abrupt departure.

40. *OR* 27 (2):510; Report of the 10th Virginia Regiment, 8 July 1863, MC.

41. *OR* 27 (2):866–67; O. Taylor, "A War Story of a Confederate Soldier Boy," 37th Virginia Folder, RBC.

42. New York Monuments Commission, *Final Report*, 3:1002; Lyman Diary, 2 July 1863, 147th New York Volunteer Infantry Regiment, GNMP.

43. *OR* 27 (1):287, 866; Tevis and Marquis, *Fighting Fourteenth*, pp. 91–92, 138;

New York Monuments Commission, *Final Report*, 2:689; Report of the 10th Virginia Regiment, 8 July 1863, MC; Fowler to Bachelder, 2 Oct. 1889, BP. In the above letter, Fowler wrote that the 71st Pennsylvania was to the 14th's right. If so, this must have been after it left the works. In an undated letter to Bachelder (vol. 3, pp. 244–45, BP), Colonel Fowler stated that the 14th formed in a ravine with its right toward the field, likely the ravine in Greene's rear. He wrote that two lieutenants, E. H. Flavin and A. F. Ackley, went out to reconnoiter.

44. *OR* 27 (1):827, 856; Dawes, *Sixth Wisconsin*, pp. 181–82.

45. Dawes, "With the Sixth," p. 386, and *Sixth Wisconsin*, p. 182; Dawes to Bachelder, Mar. 1868, BP. Dawes gave no specific location for the works that he occupied. However, he stated that the 14th Brooklyn came in on the right of the 6th. If so, and the 14th relieved the 137th New York (see n. 43 above), the 6th would have been in the position of the 149th New York. However, he also suggests that the 6th might have faced the lower hill and been relieved by Kane's returning troops.

46. Goldsborough, *Maryland Line*, p. 104; William W. Goldsborough, "Gettysburg Continued," Cronin Papers of the War, NYHS.

47. *OR* 27 (1):759–61, 774, 827, 857; Horton to Bachelder, 23 Jan. 1887, BP.

48. *OR* 27 (1):827.

49. Sifakis, *Who Was Who*, p. 104.

50. *DAB* 5:258; Quaife, *Williams*, pp. 137, 144; "Notes of a Conversation with Gen. Kane," BP. Kane resigned from the army in November 1863 for health reasons and resided in Philadelphia until his death in 1883. He was active in civic and charitable affairs and authored three books. His wife, Elizabeth D. Wood, was a physician. In spite of his limited service as a brigade commander, he was brevetted a major general in March 1865.

51. Sifakis, *Who Was Who*, p. 130.

52. *OR* 27 (1):851; Mouat, "Three Years," HSP.

53. *OR* 27 (1):851, 853, 854; Rickards to Bachelder, 12 Apr. 1864, BP; Nicholson, *Pennsylvania*, 1:220, 570, 598.

54. *OR* 27 (1):854; Nicholson, *Pennsylvania*, 1:598; Boyle, *Soldiers True*, p. 125. Lt. W. J. Alexander of Geary's staff wrote that the 111th formed on Greene's right and "a little past their refused right regiment." See Alexander to Bachelder, 2 Sept. 1887, BP. Except for a short segment of a wall at its west end and a short segment of its bed near the saddle, there are no obvious traces of this lane extant today. The Warren Map shows it following a straight line except across the low ground behind the house. It is likely that boulders in the area would have prevented it from being straight.

55. *OR* 27 (1):851–53; Nicholson, *Pennsylvania*, 1:220, 570. Captain Johnson escaped captivity in the mountains and soon rejoined his regiment.

56. *OR* 27 (1):827, 847, 852, 855, 857; Nicholson, *Pennsylvania*, 1:220; Tevis and Marquis, *Fighting Fourteenth*, p. 93. In 1887 an officer of Geary's staff wrote that the 111th was moved back to the site of the memorial of the 29th Pennsylvania. See Alexander to Bachelder, 2 Sept. 1887, BP.

57. *OR* 27 (1):855; Nicholson, *Pennsylvania*, 1:598.

58. Mouat, "Three Years," HSP.

59. *OR* 27 (1):827–28, 836.

60. Ibid., p. 840; Nicholson, *Pennsylvania*, 2:717; Company C, 7th Ohio Volunteer Infantry, "Geary."

61. *OR* 27 (1):780; "John Emerson Anderson Reminiscences," AAS. Anderson indicated that Oakey's men had not gone to the works.

62. *DAB* 8:219; Boatner, *Dictionary*, p. 712.

63. Quaife, *Williams*, p. 252; O. O. Howard, *Autobiography*, 1:431–32. After Gettysburg, Ruger went west with the Twelfth Corps and served under Sherman until the capture of Atlanta. He commanded a division in the Twenty-third Corps at the battle of Franklin, Tennessee, and in North Carolina in 1865. Ruger remained in the army after the war, serving in the South, as superintendent at West Point, as commander of the 33d and 18th U.S. Infantry regiments, and at other assignments. He had been brevetted a major general at the end of the war but became a major general in the regular army in 1895. He retired in 1897 and died in Stamford, Connecticut, in 1907. See *DAB* 8:219; Boatner, *Dictionary*, p. 712.

64. *OR* 27 (1):783.

65. Ibid. The 123d New York was in the first line; presumably the 5th Connecticut was also.

In his report of the battle, Col. James L. Selfridge of the 46th Pennsylvania wrote that when he approached his old works he found the enemy there. In the address at the dedication of the 46th's memorial, Capt. Joseph Matchett said that if it were not for the forethought of Colonel Selfridge they would have marched into the enemy lines. He went on to say that Capt. Alexander W. Selfridge of Company H took some canteens to Spangler's Spring to fill them. The captain found "Johnnies" there and backed away. When this was reported to McDougall, it was said that he did not believe it and became angry. Selfridge insisted on sending in a skirmish line and found the enemy "as stated." The 46th Pennsylvania's claims might be correct, at least partially. They are not supported by the brigade and division reports, but Lieutenant Cruikshank in his letters states that Selfridge suggested to McDougall that skirmishers be sent forward and Lieutenant Beadle of the 123d New York was given the task. See *OR* 27 (1):803; Nicholson, *Pennsylvania*, 1:308; and "Robert Cruikshank Letters," 2 July 1863, pp. 124–25, BPL.

Col. Archibald L. McDougall was one of the many unsung brigade commanders in the Army of the Potomac. He was born in 1817 and old for a colonel. Appointed colonel of the 123d New York Regiment on 26 July 1862, he organized the regiment at Camp Washington near Salem, New York, and led it at the battle of Chancellorsville. The regiment was transferred from the Second Brigade to the First Brigade of Williams's division in May 1863, and McDougall received command of the brigade. After Gettysburg, the brigade moved to Sherman's command near Chattanooga. McDougall was wounded in the leg at Dallas Gap, Georgia, on 25 May 1864. His right leg was amputated, and he died of his wound on 23 June. In a resolution adopted by the officers of the 123d New York Regiment on 15 July 1864, McDougall was eulogized as "a warm friend, a genial companion, an ardent patriot, a born soldier & skillful officer." See Personnel Folder, Col. Archibald McDougall, RG 94, NA.

66. *OR* 27 (1):789, 790; Packer Diary, CSL and RBC. In his diary, Capt. Har-

lan P. Rugg wrote that the chaplain had been taken prisoner. See Rugg Diary, CSL and RBC.

67. *OR* 27 (1):798; New York Monuments Commission, *Final Report*, 2:858; "Robert Cruikshank Letters," 2 July 1863, pp. 124–25, BPL.

68. *OR* 27 (1):780, 783, 796, 798, 800; "Robert Cruikshank Letters," 2 July 1863, p. 125, BPL; New York Monuments Commission, *Final Report*, 2:858; Morhous, *123d Regiment*, pp. 48–49; Coy to Sarah, 6 July 1863, Coy Letters, GNMP. Lt. Charles L. Warner of the 145th New York left his regiment and went to Cemetery Hill. He returned to Culp's Hill at the time of the Confederate assault and discovered that McDougall's brigade had gone from its works. He wrote, "I supposed of course that our men had been frightened away, and I then swore to resign provided I got out safe, so completely was I disgusted with their action." He soon learned from an aide that the brigade had gone to the left. He met the brigade as it returned, and his disgust turned to worry that Col. E. Livingstone Price would prefer charges against him for being absent. It did not happen; perhaps the colonel had better things to do. See Warner to Mother, 9 July 1863, Paul W. Bean Collection, 145th New York Folder, RBC.

69. *OR* 27 (1):813, 817, 823; Morse, *Letters*, p. 144.

70. *OR* 27 (1):813, 817, 820; Morse, *Second Massachusetts*, p. 10.

71. Morse, *Letters*, p. 145.

72. *OR* 27 (1):817; Morse, *Letters*, p. 145, and *Second Massachusetts*, p. 11.

73. *OR* 27 (1):820. At the dedication of the 107th's memorial, Capt. H. O. Brigham stated that Colonel Crane had talked with Confederates and quoted their conversation. This seems not to conform with Crane's report. See New York Monuments Commission, *Final Report*, 2:771.

74. *OR* 27 (1):775, 780, 827; Williams to Bachelder, 10 Nov. 1865, BP. Williams stated in the letter to Bachelder that no one knew what had become of Geary and his two brigades.

CHAPTER FOURTEEN

1. *OR* 27 (2):470; J. A. Early, "Leading Confederates," p. 278. Neither Early nor Gordon gave the time of Gordon's recall.

2. *OR* 27 (2):470, 480; J. W. Daniel, "Memoir of the Battle of Gettysburg," pp. 13–14, VHS; T. Jones, *Seymour*, p. 75.

3. R. J. Hancock to Daniel, 4 Apr. 1905, J. W. Daniel Papers, UV; Reed, "Gettysburg Campaign," p. 189.

4. *DAB* 4:462; Wakelyn, *Biographical Dictionary*, p. 298; Evans, *Confederate Military History*, 10:304–5. Hays's brigade inherited the nickname "Louisiana Tigers" from Wheat's Battalion, the original and infamous Tigers, which, until its disbandment in November 1862, had been one of the units of the brigade.

5. T. Jones, *Lee's Tigers*, pp. 236–43; Iobst and Manarin, *Bloody Sixth*, p. 137; *OR* 27 (2):484–85. In his draft map in GNMP, Bachelder shows four unidentified regiments of Hays's brigade on the line and one in support. He did not put this

formation on his published map. Yet from various writings, it seems that the 9th Regiment ought to be on the left and the 7th somewhere near the right.

6. Clark, *Histories*, 1:312, 2:136, 415; Eaton Diary, 2 July 1863, SHC. The strength figure is from the War Department tablet near the Culp farm buildings. The landscape has changed greatly along Winebrenner's Run. We cannot know now what the terrain along Hays's line was like. There are three school buildings there now, the ravine is gone, much of the run is underground, and the buildings sit on bulldozed ground. However, most of the ground occupied by Hoke's brigade seems unchanged.

It is likely that Hoke's left was about twenty-five yards west of the Culp spring-house, for troops closer to it than that would have been visible from Cemetery Hill. If this is so and the brigade had a strength of 900, the line should have extended 100 yards west from there along the stream to a point about 80 yards west of East Confederate Avenue. Major Tate placed the 6th North Carolina's right 1,100 feet directly south of the junction of York Street and the Hanover Road, then to a point 120 feet away at 81 degrees east. See U.S. War Department, Gettysburg Battlefield Commission, "Engineer's Journal," 25 July 1893–31 Jan. 1896, p. 129, GNMP. This would place the right of the line slightly closer to the avenue but in the same area. Hays's brigade was between Hoke's right and Baltimore Street.

7. Phifer, "Saga," pp. 326–28; Krick, *Lee's Colonels*, p. 34.

8. "Pathetic Relic of the Civil War"; "Resolution, Officers of Hoke's Brigade," 20 July 1863, Avery Papers, NCDAH; "Hero's Lost Grave."

9. McPherson to I. T. Avery, 3 Sept. 1863, Hoke Papers, NCDAH; Clark, *Histories*, 1:313, 607, 3:415. The reporter of the 57th's operations wrote of the sun's glinting on its line of bayonets. Most reports state that the sun had set by the time that the brigade advanced.

10. McPherson to I. T. Avery, 3 Aug. 1863, Hoke Papers, NCDAH.

11. Harris to Bachelder, 14 Mar. 1881, and Miller to Bachelder, 2 Mar. 1884, BP. We do not know if the two lines seen by Miller were side by side or one behind the other.

12. Nicholson, *Pennsylvania*, 1:199, 420; New York Monuments Commission, *Final Report*, 2:918, 3:1056. Unfortunately, no one took the trouble to indicate the position of Coster's brigade with accuracy. Schurz wrote that Coster and Ames's division were to his right. See Schurz, *Reminiscences*, 3:15.

13. *OR* 27 (1):729–30.

14. Ames to Howard, 2 July 1863, Letters Received, 11th Corps, RG 393, NA; *OR* 27 (1):713. After the campaign, 344 men of the First Brigade and 161 of the Second Brigade were listed as missing. Colonel Harris stated that Ames had expected more from his weak division than it could accomplish and that he did not make the report that the facts warranted. See Harris to Bachelder, 14 Mar. 1881, BP.

15. Sifakis, *Who Was Who*, p. 8; Boatner, *Dictionary*, pp. 11–12.

16. Nevins, *Wainwright*, p. 242; Becker and Thomas, *Ladley*, p. 147. After the Gettysburg campaign, Ames and his division left the Army of the Potomac for service with the Tenth and Eighteenth corps in Petersburg, Virginia, and along the North Carolina coast. Ames commanded a division of the Twenty-fourth Corps in

the Fort Fisher expeditions, a division in the Tenth Corps at the end of the war, and the corps itself in the summer of 1865. He became lieutenant colonel of the 24th Infantry in the postwar years and military governor of Mississippi. Ames left the army in 1870 for a political career and became a Republican senator from Mississippi. He became governor in 1873 and resigned in 1876 when the carpetbag government lost Federal support. In 1870 he married a daughter of Benjamin Butler. He served as a brigadier general during the war with Spain. When he died in 1933, he was the last surviving Union general of the Civil War. See Sifakis, *Who Was Who*, p. 8, and Boatner, *Dictionary*, pp. 11–12.

17. Reid, *Ohio in the War*, 1:432–38, 2:968; Raus, *Generation*, p. 100; Mercer, *Representative Men*, pp. 118–27; Lowry, *Preble County, Ohio*, pp. 226–27. In the postwar period, Harris practiced law in Preble County, was a judge, served in the Ohio legislature, and was governor of Ohio from 1906 to 1909. He died in Eaton in September 1913.

18. *OR* 27 (1):716, 718, 720; Harris to Bachelder, 7 Apr. 1864, BP. The order of regiments in line at the wall from the left was 75th, 107th, 17th, and 75th. See Young to Bachelder, 12 Aug. 1887, and Vignos to Bachelder, 17 Apr. 1864, BP. I shall refer to this lane as "Brickyard Lane." It is thought to have been an early right-of-way for the road that became the Baltimore Pike. Wainwright Avenue was built beside it, and now there are no traces of Brickyard Lane aboveground.

19. *OR* 27 (1):713; New York Monuments Commission, *Final Report*, 1:308; Martin, *Forty-first New York*, pp. 149–50; Butts, *A Gallant Captain*, p. 80. The 49th New York had only nine companies.

20. New York Monuments Commission, *Final Report*, 1:304, 402–3, 2:506; Nicholson, *Pennsylvania*, 2:1143; Raus, *Generation*, pp. 59, 62, 68, 140. The regiments' strengths before the battle of 1 July were as follows: 41st New York, 218; 54th New York, 216; 68th New York, 264; and 153d Pennsylvania, 569.

21. Lonn, *Foreigners*, p. 217; Sifakis, *Who Was Who*, p. 678; Kaufmann, *Die Deutschen*, p. 503; O. O. Howard, *Autobiography*, 1:349; Schurz, *Reminiscences*, 3:10; Coddington, *Gettysburg Campaign*, p. 704; New York Monuments Commission, *Final Report*, 1:304–7.

22. Report of Col. A. B. Underwood, 33d Massachusetts Volunteer Infantry Regiment, GNMP.

23. Ibid.; *OR* 27 (1):714; Maine Gettysburg Commission, *Maine at Gettysburg*, pp. 93–94.

24. *OR* 27 (1):705, 713; Ricketts to Bachelder, 2 Mar. 1886, BP. Nothing in either Howard's or Ames's reports and writings address this threat and Ames's reaction to it.

25. *OR* 27 (1):716, 718; Harris to Bachelder, 14 Mar. 1881, BP. The wall manned by the Ohio Brigade is the second one from the front in the illustration and in Frassanito, *Gettysburg*, pp. 102–3. The left of the 107th Ohio would have been about where the tall oak tree is shown in ibid., p. 102; the west end of the wall is between the tents and buildings on p. 103.

26. *OR* 27 (1):713.

27. Ibid., p. 716; Harris to Bachelder, 11 Mar. 1881, BP. I have seen no good documentary evidence on the position of the three Ohio regiments. However, flank

markers beside the stone walls show where they were alleged to have been at one stage of the fight. The wall held by the 107th Ohio is between the town's water tanks and a residential area that covers most of the north slope of Cemetery Hill east of Baltimore Street. Whether the 25th Ohio faced north or northeast after its shift is not known. Probably it still faced north.

28. *OR* 27 (1):714; Report of Col. A. B. Underwood, 33d Massachusetts Volunteer Infantry Regiment, GNMP; Harris to Bachelder, 14 Mar. 1881 and 7 Apr. 1864, BP; New York Monuments Commission, *Final Report*, 1:404; Martin, *Forty-first New York*, p. 150. Underwood states that the threat was from Early; von Einsiedel suggests that it was from Johnson.

Lieutenant Miller of the 153d Pennsylvania wrote that on 3 July after von Gilsa's regiments had returned to their old positions, he went to a spring in front of the 54th and 78th New York. But, with the advent of Carroll's brigade, the position occupied on 3 July might not have been that of 2 July. The strengths of these regiments can only be guessed. Possibly the 17th had 250 men in line; the 153d, 420; the 68th, 160; the 54th, 140; and the 41st, 200. The figures for the regiments that fought on 1 July were estimated by taking the numbers brought to the field and subtracting half the number killed and wounded and most of the number missing.

It seems that the memorials located along Wainwright Avenue are placed about 100 yards to the left of the regiments' positions on 2 July and that the 153d memorial ought to be to the right of the 54th. The memorials might have been located to show positions at another stage in the battle.

29. *OR* 27 (1):715, 716; Harris to Bachelder, 14 Mar. 1881, BP. The 107th must have had many stragglers who returned after the battle. On 30 June it had 480 officers and men; out of this number, 23 were killed, 111 wounded, and 77 missing, most undoubtedly from the fight on 1 July. Sgt. Frederick Nussbaum wrote that men began flocking back to the regiment on 2 July and swelled its ranks to 450—a high figure. See Jacob Smith, *Camps and Campaigns*, p. 226.

The 25th Ohio started the battle with 280 and 9 were killed, 100 wounded, and 75 missing. The 75th started with 285 and lost 16 killed, 74 wounded, and 96 missing.

30. Report of Col. A. B. Underwood, 33d Massachusetts Volunteer Infantry Regiment, GNMP; Miller to Bachelder, 2 Mar. 1884, BP; Kiefer, *One Hundred and Fifty-third Regiment*, p. 141.

31. *OR* 27 (2):480; Reed, "Gettysburg Campaign," p. 189; T. Jones, *Seymour*, p. 75; Clark, *Histories*, 1:313, 3:415; Iobst, *Bloody Sixth*, p. 137. Pvt. Reuben S. Ruch of the 153d Pennsylvania, who watched the advance from the German Reformed Church, wrote that the "Johnnies" started out stooped over and scattered until they reached the cover of the little ridge in their front. They formed there, gave the Rebel yell, and advanced at a double-quick. After shells plowed their ranks, the ranks closed like water. See Kiefer, *One Hundred and Fifty-third Regiment*, p. 220.

32. *OR* 27 (2):480; T. Jones, *Seymour*, p. 75; Clark, *Histories*, 1:313.

33. The strength of Hays's brigade, according to the brigade tablet, was initially 1,200, minus the casualties of 1 July, which were few. Therefore, if formed in a single, two-ranked line, its front would not have exceeded 400 yards. If one or more regiments were in a support line, the front would have been narrower.

In his report (*OR* 27 [1]:358), Colonel Wainwright wrote that Hays's right's approach was covered by the houses along Baltimore Street. This is not confirmed by other writings. In a letter to Bachelder, Colonel Harris wrote that Hays's right struck his line between the 107th and 25th regiments. See Harris to Bachelder, 14 Mar. 1881, BP. Possibly Hays deployed troops from his line as skirmishers to hold the attention of Federals in the houses, but nothing was written of this.

34. *OR* 27 (2):484. A regiment would probably have crossed the fence in a body rather than in increments.

35. T. Jones, *Seymour*, p. 75; *OR* 27 (2):480.

36. The fold of high ground extending northeast of Harris's center would have protected that portion of Hays's brigade north of it from all but Wiedrich's four guns.

37. Nevins, *Wainwright*, p. 245; L. E. C. Moore, "Charge of the Louisianians"; Ricketts to Bachelder, 2 Mar. 1866 and 3 Dec. 1883, BP; Nicholson, *Pennsylvania*, 2:921. In the positions occupied by Ricketts's and Cooper's batteries on Cemetery Hill today are ten marking cannons, each with its own lunette. On the evening of 2 July there should have been no more than six lunettes. Therefore, the integrity of the lunettes and the accuracy of the marking is open to question.

38. Maine Gettysburg Commission, *Maine at Gettysburg*, pp. 93–94; Whittier, "Left Attack," p. 86.

39. Whittier, "Left Attack," p. 87.

40. Maine Gettysburg Commission, *Maine at Gettysburg*, p. 94. Colonel Wainwright stated that the Confederate charge began an hour after sundown and was made in the moonlight. He said also that as soon as he saw the column from Cemetery Hill he sent a Lieutenant Matthewson of his staff to Stevens's battery and directed them to open on it. See Nevins, *Wainwright*, p. 245.

41. Maine Gettysburg Commission, *Maine at Gettysburg*, pp. 94–95; Whittier, "Left Attack," p. 87.

42. New York Monuments Commission, *Final Report*, 3:1247.

43. Brockway to McConaughy, 5 Mar. 1864, Rothermel Papers, PSA.

44. Whittier wrote that as the left of Hoke's brigade came under increasing fire from his battery, it tended to refuse its left flank. When it got too far into the valley separating Culp's Hill from Cemetery Hill, Avery, "finding his men too far to the left of the position they had been ordered to assault, ordered a change of front and wheeled his brigade to the right." See Whittier, "Left Attack," p. 88.

45. Ibid.; New York Monuments Commission, *Final Report*, 1:308; Miller to Bachelder, 2 Mar. 1884, BP.

46. Brockway to McConaughy, 5 Mar. 1864, Rothermel Papers, PSA.

47. Whittier, "Left Attack," p. 88; *OR* 27 (1):363. The distances given are mine.

48. *OR* 27 (1):715, 716; Harris to Bachelder, 14 Mar. 1881, BP.

49. Reed, "Gettysburg Campaign," p. 189; Clements, "25th Ohio."

50. Young to Bachelder, 12 Aug. 1887, and Rider to Bachelder, 20 Aug. 1885, BP.

51. *OR* 27 (1):718; Fox to Harris, 14 Nov. 1885, BP; Peck, "Eleventh Corps." The trees appear in the right of the photograph in Frassanito, *Gettysburg*, pp. 102–3.

The terrain in the sector held by the 17th Connecticut was changed by the construction of Wainwright Avenue, which was built across the lower slope of the hill and has a retaining wall on its downhill side. It seems likely that the old road in the area occupied by Harris's right and von Gilsa's left ran in front of the location of the present retaining wall, beginning at a point about fifty yards north of Menchey's Spring.

52. Clark, *Histories*, 1:313, 606, 3:415; Causeby, "Storming the Stone Fence," p. 340.

53. The original note is in the Avery Papers, NCDAH. The text quoted is the accepted version of the words that are on the blood-stained paper. See McPherson to I. T. Avery, 3 Sept. 1863, Hoke Papers, NCDAH.

On 20 June 1896, John A. McPherson, formerly of Avery's staff, marked the site of Avery's fall in the area now occupied by the high school stadium. I and others believe that the site marked is too far to the right and would have been in the zone of Hays's brigade rather than Hoke's.

Avery's body was taken to Hagerstown and buried there. Its location was unknown for many years, but Fred Mende of Charlotte, North Carolina, and others who have taken a great interest in the matter believe that Avery is buried under the name "Col. J. E. Ayres" in the Confederate cemetery at Hagerstown.

54. Underwood, *Thirty-third Massachusetts*, p. 129; Report of Col. A. B. Underwood, 33d Massachusetts Volunteer Infantry Regiment, GNMP.

55. Hatton, "Godwin," p. 153.

56. Miller to Bachelder, 2 Mar. 1884, BP; J. C. Miller, "At Gettysburg"; Kiefer, *One Hundred and Fifty-third Regiment*, p. 87.

57. New York Monuments Commission, *Final Report*, 1:308, 2:568. Information on the 54th and 68th regiments is negligible. Their reports, if written, were not published in the *Official Records*.

58. *OR* 27 (1):714; New York Monuments Commission, *Final Report*, 1:308; Martin, *Forty-first New York*, pp. 152–54. Lt. Col. Detleo von Einsiedel wrote a report for the 41st New York Regiment. Unfortunately, it appears muddled. He seems to have introduced Carroll's brigade too early in his account.

59. Miller to Bachelder, 2 Mar. 1884, BP; Simmers and Bachschmid, *Volunteers' Manual*, p. 30; Kiefer, *One Hundred and Fifty-third Regiment*, pp. 87, 142.

60. Miller to Bachelder, 2 Mar. 1884, BP; Kiefer, *One Hundred and Fifty-third Regiment*, p. 142; *OR* 27 (1):714; Nevins, *Wainwright*, p. 245.

61. Clark, *Histories*, 2:136–38.

CHAPTER FIFTEEN

1. *OR* 27 (1):705, 722, 731; O. O. Howard, *Autobiography*, 1:429; Schurz, *Reminiscences*, 3:25.

2. *OR* 27 (1):372, 706. Just how Carroll received his order is unclear. Howard's version is that given in the text. Hancock wrote that he sent help to Culp's Hill and to Cemetery Hill under his own volition. Of course, both could have been correct. Gibbon, in *Personal Recollections*, p. 138, wrote that Hancock said to him, "We ought to send some help over there," and then ordered him to send a brigade and two regiments to Howard. This was testimony to Hancock's penchant for taking

the initiative. See also Howard to Editors, *Cincinnati Commercial*, 27 Mar. 1864, O. O. Howard Papers, BC; Hancock to Hooker, 27 June 1876, Bates Papers, PSA.

3. Sifakis, *Who Was Who*, p. 108; Boatner, *Dictionary*, p. 129; O. O. Howard, *Autobiography*, 1:101–2, 137.

4. Sifakis, *Who Was Who*, p. 108; Boatner, *Dictionary*, p. 129; Reid, *Ohio in the War*, 1:930; Howard to Editor, *Cincinnati Commercial*, 27 Mar. 1864, O. O. Howard Papers, BC; Fiske, *Dunn Browne's Experiences*, p. 195. Dunn Browne of the 14th Connecticut wrote that Carroll's recommendations for promotion were turned down for lack of political influence. Carroll received three wounds in May 1864, the last of which resulted in the amputation of his arm. He finally became a brigadier general as of May 1864 and in the course of the war received five brevets, including one of major general in the regular army. He served as a lieutenant colonel in the postwar army, and he retired as a major general for health reasons in 1869. He died in 1893.

5. Keppler, *Fourth Regiment*, p. 128; "M," Company E, "14th Indiana"; Carroll to Hancock, 24 July 1876, Bates Papers, PSA; Dickelman, "Fierce Battle." According to Keppler, the 4th Ohio had remained on the division left near The Angle when the 14th and 7th regiments returned to their old positions and had to rejoin them in order to go to the right. Carroll's fourth regiment, the 8th Ohio, was on the skirmish line and remained there.

6. *OR* 27 (2):484, 486; Clark, *Histories*, 1:314.

7. New York Monuments Commission, *Final Report*, 3:1247; Gilmor, *Four Years*, pp. 98–99.

8. Nevins, *Wainwright*, p. 245; Butts, *A Gallant Captain*, pp. 85–86.

9. Simmers and Bachschmid, *Volunteers' Manual*, p. 30.

10. *OR* 27 (1):894; Brockway to McConaughy, 5 Mar. 1864, Rothermel Papers, PSA. Ricketts was vitriolic about the infantry in his front. Although he probably could not have seen Ames's line in the darkness, he wrote Bachelder in order to criticize the behavior of the troops of Ames's division. He termed their conduct "cowardly and disgraceful in the extreme" and charged that they began to run away as soon as the charge commenced. They scarcely fired a shot, he said, "certainly not a volley," and they were so panic-stricken that they ran into his canister. See Ricketts to Bachelder, 2 Mar. 1886, BP.

11. Thurston, "Ricketts Batteryman."

12. Brockway to McConaughy, 5 Mar. 1864, Rothermel Papers, PSA; Nicholson, *Pennsylvania*, 2:922.

13. Brockway to McConaughy, 5 Mar. 1864, Rothermel Papers, PSA.

14. Ibid.; Nicholson, *Pennsylvania*, 2:919; L. E. C. Moore, "Charge of the Louisianians." Four of Ricketts's guns at Gettysburg bore the serial numbers 325, 375, 378, and 379.

15. *OR* 27 (1):720; Young to Bachelder, 12 Aug. 1887, BP; Reed, "Gettysburg Campaign," p. 189; Kiefer, *One Hundred and Fifty-third Regiment*, p. 86. Sergeant Nussbaum's account varies from Young's. According to Nussbaum, the color-bearer shot Young with his revolver, and Young, in turn, jabbed his sword into the man's chest, killing him. Nussbaum wrote that they found seven bullet holes in the Confederate color-bearer and that his canteen contained a mixture of

whiskey and gunpowder. Nussbaum said that he took the man's knapsack, which was leather with a goatskin cover.

16. *OR* 27 (1):480, 485, 486; Clark, *Histories*, 1:313.

17. *OR* 27 (2):480–81; T. Jones, *Seymour*, pp. 75–76.

18. *OR* 27 (1):486; Clark, *Histories*, 1:313, 314.

19. *OR* 27 (1):740, 743; Schurz, *Reminiscences*, 3:25; New York Monuments Commission, *Final Report*, 3:431; Butts, *A Gallant Captain*, p. 85. Apparently the fight was short and Coster's regiments and the 119th New York repulsed the Confederates before the 58th New York could get involved. Col. Wladimir Krzyzanowski, who led this counterattack and the Second Brigade, Third Division, Eleventh Corps, left Poland in 1846 for the United States, where he worked as a civil engineer. He entered the army as colonel of the 58th New York Regiment. He succeeded to the command of his brigade in the fall of 1862 and retained it until the consolidation of the Eleventh and Twelfth corps in 1864. He was nominated to the grade of brigadier general in November 1862 but was not confirmed by Congress. Schurz said that this was because they could not pronounce his name. (In the army, they referred to him as "Kriz.") In March 1865 he was made a brevet brigadier general. He died in 1887 while serving as a treasury agent in New York City. A biography, *For Liberty and Justice: The Life and Times of Wladimir Krzyzanowski*, has been written by James S. Pula. See also Lonn, *Foreigners*, pp. 233–34; Boatner, *Dictionary*, p. 469; and Sifakis, *Who Was Who*, pp. 368–69.

20. *OR* 27 (1):722, 726; Nicholson, *Pennsylvania*, 1:199, 420; Diembach, "Incident on Cemetery Hill," pp. 22–23; George Metcalf, "Reminiscence," p. 92, GCC. The lack of reports from Coster's brigade leaves a huge gap in our knowledge of these events. Both the 27th and 73d Pennsylvania regiments have memorials on Cemetery Hill, the 73d's just behind Wiedrich's battery. It has a bas-relief depicting the fight at the battery.

21. Parmelee, "At Gettysburg"; Carroll to Hancock, 23 July 1876, Bates Papers, PSA; Cavins, "Gettysburg Diary"; "M," Company E, "14th Indiana."

22. *OR* 27 (1):457, 459, 460; Dickelman, "Gibraltar Brigade."

23. *OR* 27 (1):457, 459, 462; Cavins, "Gettysburg Diary"; Dickelman, "Gibraltar Brigade"; Wright, "At Gettysburg."

24. *OR* 27 (1):457; Carroll to Hancock, 23 July 1876, Bates Papers, PSA; "M," Company E, "14th Indiana"; Meyerhoff, "Carroll's Brigade."

25. Keppler, *Fourth Regiment*, p. 129; Dickelman, "Gibraltar Brigade."

26. Carroll to Hancock, 23 July 1876, Bates Papers, PSA. Possibly Ames missed the 17th Connecticut because it was beyond the bulge in the slope to his left, and the 41st New York and 33d Massachusetts were 100 or so yards to his right.

Capt. John M. Brown belonged to the 20th Maine Regiment as had Ames.

In Wright, "At Gettysburg," two quotations attributed to Carroll fall in the context of his reply to Ames. He is quoted as saying: "Well, I can hold this line as long as necessary; but why, in the name of Christ, don't he get his men down here? He's got all night to do it in," and "——, ——, such a speech. Tell him to bring his men back and align them on this wall. If he can't inspire them, by —— I can." Perhaps these remarks were a part of the lore of the 14th Indiana.

27. Carroll to Hancock, 23 July 1876, Bates Papers, PSA.

28. Keppler, *Fourth Regiment*, p. 120. The captured field officers were Lt. Col. William S. Rankin and Maj. Alexander Miller of the 21st North Carolina.

29. William C. Wickham of the 55th Ohio, who was on Ames's staff, wrote that Carroll did not arrive until after the attack had been repulsed and that the "bombastic legend" on the 14th Indiana's memorial was false. See Wickham, "Gettysburg." See also Peck, "At Gettysburg."

In attempting to sort out what happened on the hill, one cannot rely on the artillery marking there. On 2 July Wiedrich's battery had four guns there, yet the battery is marked with six guns in lunettes. Since Ricketts replaced Cooper, there never were more than six guns in that position, yet there are ten marked there today.

The locations of the monuments of the 14th Indiana and 4th Ohio seem to have little relevance to their deeds on 2 July.

30. *OR* 27 (2):481.

31. Ibid., p. 486.

32. Ibid., p. 470; J. W. Daniel, "Memoir of the Battle of Gettysburg," pp. 13–14, VHS; J. A. Early, *Autobiographical Sketch*, p. 274.

33. J. W. Daniel, "Memoir of the Battle of Gettysburg," p. 14, VHS.

34. Freeman, *Lee's Lieutenants*, 1:247–48; Boatner, *Dictionary*, p. 706.

35. Freeman, *Lee's Lieutenants*, 1:lii, 247–48, 2:xxxviii, 3:xliv. Rodes would lead his division in Lee's battles in May 1864 and then in the Shenandoah Valley under Early. He was killed at Winchester on 19 September 1864.

36. *OR* 27 (2):555–56.

37. Ibid., p. 556.

38. Sifakis, *Who Was Who*, p. 529; Boatner, *Dictionary*, p. 677. See also Gallagher, *Ramseur*. General Iverson, whose brigade lost heavily on 1 July, wrote that he had attached the remnants of his brigade to Ramseur's early in the day and would act in concert with him. See *OR* 27 (2):580.

39. *OR* 27 (2):582, 585, 587; Tripp, "North Carolina," p. 41; "Battle of Gettysburg," in Notebook, Gorman Papers, NCDAH.

40. *OR* 27 (2):586.

41. Ibid., pp. 580, 582, 588; "Battle of Gettysburg," in Notebook, Gorman Papers, and "Experiences of B. B. Ross," Hicks Papers, both in NCDAH; Norman, *Portion of My Life*, p. 186.

42. *OR* 27 (1):588; "Battle of Gettysburg," in Notebook, Gorman Papers, NCDAH; Tripp, "North Carolina," p. 42.

43. *OR* 27 (2):556, 581, 582.

44. Phillips to Schenk, 27 Oct. 1891, Ramseur Papers, SHC; Norman, *Portion of My Life*, p. 187; "John J. McLendon Reminiscences," W. A. Smith Papers, DU.

45. *OR* 27 (2):447. Ewell wrote that after he learned that General Lane had no orders to cooperate in Ewell's attack, he had no time to reach General Hill. Coddington discusses this briefly in *Gettysburg Campaign*, pp. 429–30.

46. *OR* 27 (2):470; J. A. Early, "Leading Confederates," p. 280.

47. *OR* 27 (2):447; Brown to Hunt, 7 May 1885, Hunt Papers, LC.

48. *OR* 27 (2):256; J. C. Early, "Southern Boy's Experience," p. 422; Hamlin, *Ewell*, p. 150. Campbell Brown wrote that a bullet had barked Captain Early's

shin, "no doubt a painful wound, but not one to excite our sympathies." He was "groaning horribly & making enough fuss for two or three mortal wounds." See G. C. Brown, "Reminiscences," p. 4, TSLA.

49. J. W. Daniel, "Memoir of the Battle of Gettysburg," pp. 14–15, VHS.

50. "Mrs. Thorn's War Story."

51. "A Battle."

CHAPTER SIXTEEN

1. Williams to Bachelder, 10 Nov. 1865, BP; *OR* 27 (1):775.

2. *OR* 27 (1):775, 780; Williams to Bachelder, 10 Nov. 1865, BP; Quaife, *Williams*, p. 230.

3. *OR* 27 (1):775; Williams to Bachelder, 10 Nov. 1865, BP; Brown, *Twenty-seventh Indiana*, pp. 373–74.

4. *OR* 27 (1):237, 775, 870, 873, 899; Nicholson, *Pennsylvania*, 2:915–16; New York Monuments Commission, *Final Report*, 3:1265.

5. *OR* 27 (1):761, 775, 828, 870.

6. Lockwood's brigade's position was not described in specific terms. The map with Ruger's report showed it as having been along the pike in two segments, one to the left front of the guns, the other to the right front. Yet Cook and Benton, *Dutchess County Regiment*, p. 31, says the 150th New York supported one battery, probably Rugg's, on its left and that the 1st Maryland Regiment, the Potomac Home Brigade, was on the battery's right.

7. Williams to Bachelder, 10 Nov. 1865, BP; Quaife, *Williams*, p. 230.

8. *OR* 27 (2):308, 320, 447, 504–5.

9. Ibid., pp. 533, 535–39.

10. Ibid., p. 513; "Paper Read by Co'l David Zable . . . December 12, 1903," TU.

11. "Washington Hands's Civil War Notebook," p. 98, UV.

12. *OR* 27 (2):519, 526, 528.

13. Ibid., p. 568.

14. Ibid., p. 593.

15. Ibid., p. 489; Driver, *52d Virginia*, p. 40; Hale, *Forty-ninth Virginia*, p. 79; W. O. Johnson, "The 49th Virginia Infantry at Gettysburg," J. W. Daniel Papers, UV.

16. *OR* 27 (2):447.

17. Williams to Bachelder, 10 Nov. 1865, BP; Goldsborough, "With Lee"; "Washington Hands's Civil War Notebook," pp. 98–99, UV. Bates and others have written that the signal to open fire was given by Geary. Slocum denied this. See Slocum to Bates, 8 Sept. 1875, Bates Papers, PSA.

18. Morhous, *123d Regiment*, p. 50; *OR* 27 (1):784–85, 798, 801, 803; New York Monuments Commission, *Final Report*, 3:858; "Robert Cruikshank Letters," 3 July 1863, p. 126, BPL.

19. *OR* 27 (1):871.

20. *OR* 27 (2):447, 504.

21. "Paper Read by Co'l David Zable . . . December 12, 1903," TU.

22. *OR* 27 (2):519, 521.

23. *OR* 27 (1):804, 806; "My Maryland"; Maryland Gettysburg Monuments Commission, *Report*, p. 57.

24. *OR* 27 (2):511; J. W. Thomas Diary, 3 July 1863, FNMP; William W. Goldsborough, "Gettysburg Centennial," p. 4, Cronin Papers of the War, NYHS; "Washington Hands's Civil War Notebook," p. 99, UV. In Clark, *Histories*, 1:196, the 3d North Carolina was said to have entered the battle with 300 men and to be reduced by 223. After the battle, the regiment had seventy-seven muskets in the ranks. According to the "Return of Casualties" in *OR* 27 (2):341, the 3d had 156 casualties; this should have left 144 on duty.

25. "Washington Hands's Civil War Notebook," pp. 93–94, 99, UV; S. Z. Ammen, "Second Maryland Battalion, Fifteenth Paper—Second Series," in Ammen, "Maryland Troops in the Confederacy," p. 135, CC; J. W. Thomas Diary, 3 July 1863, FNMP.

26. "Washington Hands's Civil War Notebook," p. 100, UV; McKim, "Steuart's Brigade," p. 296.

27. Powell to Bachelder, 15 May 1878, and Mitchell et al. to A. E. Lee, 15 Aug. 1887, BP.

28. Powell to Bachelder, 23 Mar. 1886, BP; Powell, "Rebellion's High Tide."

29. Powell, "Rebellion's High Tide."

30. *OR* 27 (1):837, 844; Powell to Bachelder, 15 May 1878, and 15 and 23 Mar. 1886, BP; Raus, *Generation*, p. 99.

31. *OR* 27 (1):861; Eddy, *Sixtieth Regiment*, p. 263; New York Monuments Commission, *Final Report*, 1:452.

32. Camden Diary, FNMP. Camden is mentioned along with some other company commanders in Colonel Higginbotham's report, but the colonel wrote that his sharpshooters were commanded by lieutenants. See *OR* 27 (2):536.

33. *OR* 27 (1):770, (3):498.

34. *OR* 27 (1):863.

35. Ibid., pp. 847, 849, 852, 853, 855; Mouat, "Three Years," HSP. The reports of the 111th and 29th Pennsylvania regiments suggest that each was in the front line when the morning's fight began and was relieved by the other. I believe that the 111th was in the forward line first. The 29th had a strength of 485; the 109th, 149; and the 111th, 259. The 29th could have occupied the space of both of the other regiments. See Raus, *Generation*, pp. 112, 130, 131.

36. *OR* 27 (1):828, 836, 846: Nicholson, *Pennsylvania*, 2:717–18; "Rough Sketch of the War as Seen by Joseph Addison Moore," CWMC. In the brigade report, Candy wrote that the 147th Pennsylvania "were ordered forward, and occupied a stone fence in front of the enemy, and by their fire caused considerable casualties and havoc among them [the enemy]." No mention of this is made in the regiment's report.

37. *OR* 27 (1):839–40.

38. James S. Hyde Diary, 3 July 1863, NCWRTC.

39. New York Monuments Commission, *Final Report*, 3:1011; Raus, *Generation*, p. 84; Boatner, *Dictionary*, p. 46.

40. Collins, *149th Regiment*, pp. 140–49.

41. *OR* 27 (1):863, 865, 866.

42. *OR* 27 (2):593, 595, 601; "Paper Read by Co'l David Zable . . . December 12, 1903," TU.

43. "Reminiscences of the War Between the States by W. H. May in 1886," GDAH.

44. Ibid.; *OR* 27 (2):593.

45. Collins, *149th Regiment*, pp. 149–50.

46. *OR* 27 (1):842, 843; Collins, *149th Regiment*, pp. 140–41.

47. *OR* 27 (1):185, 869; Collins, *149th Regiment*, p. 144.

48. *OR* 27 (1):847, 849, 852, 855; Boyle, *Soldiers True*, p. 126; Nicholson, *Pennsylvania*, 1:571.

49. Mouat, "Three Years," HSP. The white star was the insignia of Geary's division, the Second Division, Twelfth Corps. The remark about Ewell was one that seemed to circulate among units on the Union right, although there seems to be no Confederate substantiation of it. See Kiefer, *One Hundred and Fifty-third Regiment*, p. 100.

50. Boyle, *Soldiers True*, p. 127.

51. Ibid.

52. *OR* 27 (1):184, 841; Norris, "Ohio at Gettysburg."

53. *OR* 27 (1):843, 867; Nicholson, *Pennsylvania*, 1:204.

54. *OR* 27 (1):287.

55. New York Monuments Commission, *Final Report*, 3:1002; Lyman Diary, 3 July 1863, 147th New York Volunteer Infantry Regiment, GNMP.

56. Tevis and Marquis, *Fighting Fourteenth*, pp. 138–39; Grube and Woodbridge, "14th Regiment," p. 83. Fowler wrote that the sergeant major was responsible for the ammunition supply.

57. Collins, *149th Regiment*, pp. 144–45.

58. Cook and Benton, *Dutchess County Regiment*, pp. 34–35.

59. *OR* 27 (1):154, 804–5, 810, 863, 865; W. F. Howard, *Gettysburg Death Roster*, p. 186; Cook and Benton, *Dutchess County Regiment*, p. 35.

60. *OR* 27 (1):808; Rastall, "Union Slave Owners"; Maryland Gettysburg Monuments Commission, *Report*, p. 75. Colonel Wallace resigned in December 1863 over the question of the enlistment of blacks, including some belonging to members of his regiment. See Raus, *Generation*, p. 29.

61. *OR* 27 (1):808–9; Wallace to Bachelder, 4 July 1878, BP; Shane, "Getting into the Fight"; Wallace, "Our March," p. 67. The 149th New York's history said that a Maryland regiment came up in its rear, "fired in the backs of the men and scampered away." It said also that when it was relieved, the 149th stood in the Maryland regiment's rear with fixed bayonets to keep it "from gigging out" a second time. This accusation is not repeated elsewhere. See Collins, *149th Regiment*, p. 143.

The Eastern Shore Regiment wore new uniforms, and probably the regiment's other equipment was relatively new also. Mouat wrote that the 29th Pennsylvania took equipment dropped by the Marylanders. See Mouat, "Three Years," HSP.

62. *OR* 27 (1):808–9; Wallace to Bachelder, 4 July 1878, BP; Shane, "Getting into the Fight." The Eastern Shore Regiment's place in the works is not clear. Colonel Wallace believed that it was at Geary's extreme left, which seems improbable, but

the regiment's memorial is among those at the left center of Greene's line. Still, there is the accusation of the 149th New York in n. 61, and Wallace wrote that the Eastern Shore Regiment opposed the Confederate Marylanders. The alleged poor conduct of the Eastern Shore Regiment was skirted in the reports. Shane, who wrote of it, was a lieutenant in the regiment, and his account was not published until after his death.

63. *OR* 27 (1):806, 807, 865.

64. Ibid., pp. 805, 857.

65. Ibid., pp. 829–30.

CHAPTER SEVENTEEN

1. *OR* 27 (2):447, 504. The reports of Ewell and Johnson do not reveal which of them was responsible for ordering specific assaults. Ewell, of course, in accordance with Lee's plan, directed Johnson to attack the hill.

2. Ibid., p. 511; Goldsborough, *Maryland Line*, p. 106; Clark, *Histories*, 1:195.

3. Evans, *Confederate Military History*, 2:167–68; Boatner, *Dictionary*, p. 766; Freeman, *Lee's Lieutenants*, 2:403–5, 472–79. Steuart was captured at Spotsylvania, was exchanged, and commanded a brigade in Pickett's division at the end of the war. After the war, he farmed in Anne Arundel County, Maryland.

4. McH. Howard, *Recollections*, pp. 60, 224, 352, 417, 426. The 1st Maryland Battalion, C.S.A., became the 2d Maryland Battalion. Because the Order of Battle lists it as the 1st Battalion, I have used that designation here.

5. *OR* 27 (2):568–69, 572, 573, 575, 577, 578; Clark, *Histories*, 3:6; Winston, "A Correction," p. 94; McKim, "Colonel Winston's Correction Corrected," p. 315. The 32d and 53d regiments were in the support line, the 32d probably to the rear of the 45th, which it replaced when the 45th expended its ammunition.

Daniel's brigade had numbered over 2,100 when it reached Gettysburg, but it had lost as much as 30 percent of its strength in the battle of 1 July. In the entire battle, its 2d North Carolina Battalion's 240 men had 199 casualties. Its strength on Culp's Hill can only be guessed. See Busey and Martin, *Regimental Strengths and Losses*.

6. Wakelyn, *Biographical Dictionary*, pp. 158–59; Boatner, *Dictionary*, p. 222.

7. *OR* 27 (2):568; McKim, "Steuart's Brigade," p. 297.

8. *OR* 27 (1):519; Rollins, "A Private's Story."

9. *OR* 27 (2):511; Goldsborough, *Maryland Line*, p. 106; "Washington Hands's Civil War Notebook," p. 100, UV.

10. Goldsborough, *Maryland Line*, p. 106; "Washington Hands's Civil War Notebook," p. 100, UV; D. R. Howard, "Left on the Field," in S. Z. Ammen, "Maryland Troops in the Confederacy," CC. Goldsborough's various narratives are almost identical.

11. *OR* 27 (2):511; S. Z. Ammen, "Second Maryland Battalion, Fifteenth Paper—Second Series," in Ammen, "Maryland Troops in the Confederacy," p. 136, CC; Goldsborough, *Maryland Line*, p. 106; "Washington Hands's Civil War Notebook," p. 100, UV; Reports of the 3d North Carolina Regiment, 10 July 1863, the 23d Virginia Regiment, 9 July 1863, and the 1st North Carolina Regiment, 10 July

1863, MC; Clark, *Histories*, 1:145. The 3d North Carolina had one company and part of another detached, the 23d Virginia had six companies detached, and the 1st North Carolina had at least four companies detached. Thus, the equivalent of more than one regiment of Steuart's brigade was not at hand. The figure 900 probably originated with Goldsborough and is probably rough. Goldsborough states in *Maryland Line*, p. 109, that the 1st Maryland Battalion had 300 men in the charge and the 3d North Carolina only 18. No North Carolinian gave a figure. Since the 3d started the battle with over 500 men and its total casualties were 218, it would seem that a goodly portion of its strength should have been present. Yet this was not the case. See Busey and Martin, *Regimental Strengths and Losses*, p. 285.

12. *OR* 27 (2):511; Report, 10th Virginia Regiment, 8 July 1863, MC. Goldsborough, in *Maryland Line*, p. 103, includes the 10th Virginia in the line but states that the 1st North Carolina was in reserve. McKim, in "Steuart's Brigade," p. 298, includes the whole brigade in the line with the 10th Virginia joining the 1st Maryland.

13. Goldsborough, *Maryland Line*, p. 109; McKim, "Steuart's Brigade," p. 298; D. R. Howard, "Left on the Field," in S. Z. Ammen, "Maryland Troops in the Confederacy," p. 139, CC; G. Thomas, "Address." McKim, Howard, and Thomas all say that Steuart advanced with his brigade.

14. *OR* 27 (2):573.

15. This area was altered by the construction of Williams Avenue in front of the Federal position. The location of the lane is not marked at this time.

16. Goldsborough, *Maryland Line*, p. 109; S. Z. Ammen, "Second Maryland Battalion, Fifteenth Paper—Second Series," in Ammen, "Maryland Troops in the Confederacy," p. 136, CC; J. W. Thomas Diary, 3 July 1863, FNMP; Nicholson, *Pennsylvania*, 2:718.

17. O. Taylor, "A War Story of a Confederate Soldier Boy," 37th Virginia Folder, RBC; Report of the 37th Virginia Regiment, 8 July 1863, MC.

18. Goldsborough, *Maryland Line*, p. 109.

19. "Washington Hands's Civil War Notebook," p. 101, UV.

20. Nicholson, *Pennsylvania*, 1:220; Mouat, "Three Years," HSP.

21. J. W. Thomas Diary, 3 July 1863, FNMP.

22. Ibid.; S. Z. Ammen, "Second Maryland Battalion, Fifteenth Paper—Second Series," in Ammen, "Maryland Troops in the Confederacy," pp. 114, 137, CC.

23. D. R. Howard, "Left on the Field," in S. Z. Ammen, "Maryland Troops in the Confederacy," p. 139, CC.

24. Clark, *Histories*, 1:195–96.

25. Kane to Rothermel, 21 Mar. 1874, Rothermel Papers, PSA. In his fine painting, Rothermel depicted the dog as black and of medium size.

26. Goldsborough, *Maryland Line*, p. 109. Sister Mary Serena (Thadia Klimkiewicz), a member of the Congregation of the Sisters of Charity, was one of the nuns of her order who went to Gettysburg soon after the battle to nurse the wounded there. Soon after arriving on the battlefield, she sponged the blood and grime from the face of an unconscious Confederate soldier who suffered from a severe wound. After she was able to see his face, she recognized him as her brother Thaddeus! Pvt. Thaddeus A. Klimkiewicz, a native of Washington, D.C., and a resident of

Maryland, was a member of Company A, 1st Maryland Battalion, C.S.A., and was one of the casualties mourned by General Steuart. Thaddeus apparently returned to duty and survived the war. See Liquori, "Polish Sisters"; Goldsborough, *Maryland Line*, p. 153; Service Record, Thaddeus Klimkiewicz, 1st Maryland Infantry Battalion, RG 109, NA.

27. *OR* 27 (2):573.

28. "Washington Hands's Civil War Notebook," p. 101, UV.

29. J. W. Thomas Diary, 3 July 1863, FNMP.

30. D. R. Howard, "Left on the Field," in S. Z. Ammen, "Maryland Troops in the Confederacy," p. 140, CC.

31. Wallace to Bachelder, 4 July 1878, BP.

32. Eby to Bachelder, 20 Oct. 1885, BP; Nicholson, *Pennsylvania*, 2:718–19.

33. *OR* 27 (2):519, 568.

34. Ibid., pp. 568–69. Daniel apparently believed that the troops moving from the works to the hollow were "fleeing."

35. Leon, *Diary of a Tarheel*, pp. 36–37.

36. Collins, *149th Regiment*, p. 141.

37. Norris, "Ohio at Gettysburg"; Bean, *Liberty Hall Volunteers*, p. 150; Bertholf, "12th Corps"; Collins, *149th Regiment*, p. 141.

38. *OR* 27 (1):829. Alexander Shaler was born in Haddam, Connecticut, in 1827 but spent his adult years in New York City. He was active in the New York militia and in 1860 was made major of the 7th New York Regiment. His *Manual of Arms for Light Infantry* was published in 1861. He went to Washington, D.C., with the 7th in 1861 and returned to New York with it in forty-five days. He was then commissioned lieutenant colonel in the 65th New York Regiment. He became colonel of the regiment on 17 June 1862. The 65th New York and Shaler participated in the campaigns and battles of the Army of the Potomac in 1862 and 1863. Shaler became commander of the brigade in March 1863 and led it in the assault on Marye's Heights in May. He became a brigadier general on 26 May. He and his brigade were sent to guard the prison camp at Johnson's Island in Lake Erie during the winter of 1864 and returned to Virginia in time to participate in the Battle of the Wilderness. Shaler was captured on 6 May 1864 and was exchanged that fall. He then served in the Department of the Gulf and in Arkansas until he left the army in August 1865. Shaler was brevetted a major general in July 1865. In 1893 he received a Medal of Honor for his assault on Marye's Heights. After the war, Shaler served as a commissioner of the New York Fire Department and as a major general in the New York National Guard. He was an organizer and president of the National Rifle Association. See New York Monuments Commission, *Final Report*, 3:1362–64; Boatner, *Dictionary*, p. 734.

39. *OR* 27 (1):681, 682, 829; Titus to Shaler, 15 Sept. 1886, ML.

40. Sanford Truesdell to Ozia Truesdell, 9 July 1863, 122d New York File, RBC. Shaler stated that the 122d relieved the 111th Pennsylvania Regiment. See *OR* 27 (1):682.

41. Collins, *149th Regiment*, p. 142.

42. Bean, *Liberty Hall Volunteers*, p. 150.

43. *OR* 27 (1):831, 841, 843, 867; Bean, *Liberty Hall Volunteers*, p. 148; Sanford Truesdell to Ozia Truesdell, 9 July 1863, 122d New York File, RBC.

44. *OR* 27 (1):841.

45. Collins, *149th Regiment*, p. 148; Freeman, *Lee's Lieutenants*, 2:572–74.

46. *OR* 27 (2):505.

47. *OR* 27 (1):830, 841, 848, (2):505; Fergus Elliott to Brother, 8 July 1863, *CWTI*; Horton to Bachelder, 23 Jan. 1887, BP.

48. *OR* 27 (2):447–48, 504–5.

49. Ibid., pp. 489, 511, 519, 522, 569; McKim, *Second Maryland*, p. 14.

CHAPTER EIGHTEEN

1. This information came in part from Jessie Meyers, a niece of Wesley Culp, during an interview conducted on 30 August 1961. See Memorandum for the File, Wesley Culp, and Note Card, "J. Wesley Culp," in Culp Folder, GNMP; *Pittsburgh Gazette Times*, 9 November 1913, untitled article on J. Wesley Culp; Douglas, *I Rode with Stonewall*, p. 251.

2. *OR* 27 (2):519, 521; Draft Report of Battle, Nadenbousch Papers, DU.

3. *OR* 27 (2):521; Clark, *Histories*, 1:148, 595–96; Report of the 1st North Carolina Regiment, 10 July 1863, MC. The six companies of the 1st North Carolina that occupied the rocks on the Confederate left near Spangler's Spring early on the morning of 3 July left there in time to participate in Steuart's charge at about 10:00 A.M. They could have been relieved by Smith's brigade or possibly by some units of the 10th Virginia Regiment. The claim is made in Clark, *Histories*, 1:596, and in Boone, "History of Company F, First Regiment, North Carolina Infantry," 1st North Carolina Folder, RBC, that they repelled the charge of the 2d Massachusetts Regiment early in the morning. Likely the charge they repelled was that of the 1st Maryland, Potomac Home Brigade, or a lesser effort by one of Ruger's regiments.

The position of the 1st North Carolina in the boulders is marked by the name of A. Lucian Coble of that regiment, who carved it on a boulder there in 1913 to mark where he had been. This is just south of the stone wall and west of East Confederate Avenue, northeast of Spangler's Spring.

4. *OR* 27 (2):511, 522.

5. *OR* 27 (1):824; Toombs, *New Jersey Troops*, pp. 272–73; Grimes to Bachelder, 2 Apr. 1864, BP; Bryant, *Third Regiment*, pp. 191–92; Morse, *Second Massachusetts*, p. 11, and "Twelfth Corps," p. 828; Brown, *Twenty-seventh Indiana*, p. 377; Rankin, "Gettysburg," 23 June 1892; Hinkley, "At Gettysburg," 12 Oct. 1892.

6. Hinkley, "At Gettysburg," 12 Jan. 1893.

7. Morse, *Second Massachusetts*, p. 12.

8. *OR* 27 (1):818; Toombs, *New Jersey Troops*, pp. 274–75, and "Battle," p. 12; Brown, *Twenty-seventh Indiana*, p. 387; New York Monuments Commission, *Final Report*, 3:1265–66.

9. *OR* 27 (1):522.

10. *OR* 27 (2):680; Maine Gettysburg Commission, *Maine at Gettysburg*, p. 432. Brig. Gen. Thomas Hewson Neill, a Pennsylvanian, graduated from West Point in 1847. He taught there and soldiered in the West with the infantry but did not take part in the war with Mexico. He was colonel of the 23d Pennsylvania Regiment during the Army of the Potomac's campaigns of 1862 and in December 1862 took command of his brigade. His promotion to brigadier general dated from 29 November 1862. He commanded the Second Division, Sixth Corps, for about four months in 1864 and served on Sheridan's staff. After the war, he was brevetted a major general in the regular army and served as commandant of cadets at West Point. He retired in 1883 as colonel of the 5th Cavalry. See Sifakis, *Who Was Who*, p. 468, and Boatner, *Dictionary*, p. 586.

11. Maine Gettysburg Commission, *Maine at Gettysburg*, p. 432; New York Monuments Commission, *Final Report*, 2:623; Connor to Bachelder, 25 Mar. 1864, BP. The brigade's line on Wolf Hill (Sheep Heaven) is marked with the 49th New York on the left near the Taney house followed in turn by the 7th Maine, the 43d New York, and the 61st Pennsylvania. The 33d New York, which was listed in the Order of Battle, had been mustered out on 2 June, but a few of its former members still with the brigade served with the 49th New York. See New York Monuments Commission, *Final Report*, 1:77. Neill's men probably occupied the Taney house immediately in front of the brigade's position, although no reports confirm this. The house is now gone.

Lt. Col. J. Selden Connor became a brigadier general on 19 June 1864 and was governor of Maine from 1876 to 1879. See Boatner, *Dictionary*, p. 172.

12. *OR* 27 (1):680, (2):522; Maine Gettysburg Commission, *Maine at Gettysburg*, p. 433. Neill's casualties were two killed, twelve wounded, and two captured.

13. *OR* 27 (2):522; Connor to Father, 10 July 1863, 7th Maine Folder, RBC; Stevens, *Three Years*, p. 249; New York Monuments Commission, *Final Report*, 1:333.

14. Brown, *Twenty-seventh Indiana*, p. 387; Maine Gettysburg Commission, *Maine at Gettysburg*, pp. 433, 457.

15. Chapman, *Civil War Diary*, pp. 22–23; Storrs, *Twentieth Connecticut*, p. 93. Unfortunately, no landmarks were mentioned in the accounts of the 20th's fight that would tell us just where it took place.

16. *OR* 27 (2):489; Driver, *52d Virginia*, p. 39.

17. O. Wilson Diaries, 3 July 1863, Virginia State Library, Richmond, Virginia; Hale and Phillips, *Forty-ninth Virginia*, p. 80; Hall, *Diary*, p. 83.

18. *OR* 27 (1):781; Ruger to Bachelder, 12 Aug. 1869, BP. Neither Williams nor Slocum mentioned why Slocum became involved in this purely tactical matter.

The time of Ruger's order was recalled differently by many of the men involved. Some remembered it as having been shortly after daybreak, others at different times later in the morning. Major Morse wrote in his report that it was after 5:30 A.M.; Colgrove suggested that it was early in the morning. I have opted to accept Ruger's time for it seems to fit best with the other events of the morning, and he possibly would have been in the best position to know. See ibid., pp. 813, 817.

19. Ibid., p. 781.

20. Ibid.; Ruger to Bachelder, 12 Aug. 1869, BP.

21. Ruger to Bachelder, 12 Aug. 1869, BP; Brown, *Twenty-seventh Indiana*, p. 379.

22. Raus, *Generation*, p. 20; Boatner, *Dictionary*, p. 166; Regimental Histories Folder, 27th Indiana, Love Papers, LC; Ruger to Bachelder, 12 Aug. 1869, BP.

23. *OR* 27 (1):813. In his report, Colgrove stated that the First Brigade was on his right. This was incorrect.

24. Colgrove remembered the 2d and 27th regiments facing across the meadow and the three remaining regiments in a second line. The 107th was back near the pike. See Statement of General Silas Colgrove, BP. The official reports indicate only that the 27th was in the 3d Wisconsin's works of the evening before and that the 3d was aligned perpendicular to its former position across the meadow. See *OR* 27 (1):815, 824. Brown, in *Twenty-seventh Indiana*, p. 380, describes the 27th's position as having been the 3d Wisconsin's on the previous day, "almost at right angle to the line of the charge." He says that the 13th was in the angle between the 27th and the 2d. However, on the sketch on p. 392, the 27th is shown between the 2d and the 13th. In a sketch by Rankin in "Gettysburg," 10 Nov. 1892, the 27th is shown fronting the creek to the right of the 13th. In the sketch in Toombs, *New Jersey Troops*, p. 272, the 27th is shown directly behind both the 2d and the 13th and facing the meadow. Rankin is dogmatic in his articles; however, his description of the 27th's moves corresponds with that of Brown (*Twenty-seventh Indiana*, p. 380), which suggests that the 27th was to the right of the 13th and facing toward the creek. See Rankin, "Gettysburg," 4 Aug. 1892 and 23 June 1893.

For information on the 3d Wisconsin, see Hinkley, "By an Eyewitness" and "At Gettysburg," 12 Oct. 1892 and 12 Jan. 1893. See also Regimental Histories Folder, 3d Wisconsin, Love Papers, LC.

The 13th New Jersey's position is shown on the map in Toombs, *New Jersey Troops*, pp. 267, 272. Here the 13th faces the creek; the two companies on its left connect with the right of the 2d Massachusetts, and the 27th Indiana is behind the 2d. The same position is described by Toombs in "Battle." The 13th's position is hard to reconcile with the 27th's.

25. Regimental Histories Folder, 27th Indiana, Love Papers, LC. The 27th Indiana contained many tall men. Capt. David van Buskirk, at six feet, ten inches, was believed to have been the tallest man in the Union army.

26. *OR* 27 (1):813–14, 815, 817. Mudge was the son of a merchant in Lynn, Massachusetts, and a graduate of Harvard's class of 1860. He was buried in the yard of Saint Stephen's Church in Lynn. See Milano, "Call of Leadership," pp. 69, 74.

27. *OR* 27 (1):813–14, 817; Quint, *Second Massachusetts*, p. 180; Morse, *Second Massachusetts*, p. 13; Fox to Carman, 4 Apr. 1887, Carman Papers, NYPL. Quint, the chaplain of the regiment, was the first to put Mudge's words in print.

28. *OR* 27 (1):815, 818; Brown, *Twenty-seventh Indiana*, p. 380; Rankin, "Gettysburg," 4 Aug. and 10 Nov. 1892. Rankin confirmed Brown's account and stated that the 27th crossed the works occupied by the 2d Massachusetts. Probably if the 27th simply faced about and wheeled right, its file closers would have been in its front rank.

29. *OR* 27 (1):824; Toombs, *New Jersey Troops*, p. 237, and "Battle," p. 12.

30. *OR* (1):814.

31. Ibid., p. 817; Morse, *Second Massachusetts*, pp. 13–14; "John Emerson Anderson Reminiscences," AAS; Hinkley, "By an Eyewitness" and "At Gettysburg," 12 Oct. 1892; A. S. Jones, "Gettysburg."

32. Morse, *Second Massachusetts*, pp. 16–17.

33. A. S. Jones, "Gettysburg."

34. Brown, *Twenty-seventh Indiana*, pp. 381–82. The corpses suggest that the 27th crossed the 2d's works.

35. Ibid., pp. 382, 397–98: Rankin, "Gettysburg," 4 Aug. 1892.

36. Brown, *Twenty-seventh Indiana*, pp. 382–86.

37. Ibid., pp. 385–86.

38. W. O. Johnson, "The 49th Virginia Infantry at Gettysburg," J. W. Daniel Papers, UV. Johnson said that his rifle was a Spencer.

39. *OR* 27 (1):817; Morse, *Second Massachusetts*, pp. 13–14; Milano, "Call of Leadership," p. 74.

40. Morse, *Second Massachusetts*, p. 14; Thayer, "Gettysburg"; Quint, *Second Massachusetts*, p. 183. Morse recalled the wall as being about halfway across the meadow, detached, and nearly parallel to the 2d's former position. The Warren Map shows no such detached wall. However, the extension of the wall between the meadow and McAllister's Woods meets most of the description. The caption below the photograph in Brown, *Twenty-seventh Indiana*, p. 381, states that the wall in the middle ground is that which sheltered the 2d Massachusetts. It is an extension of the wall at the woods.

41. Ashcroft, *31st Virginia*, pp. 54–55; Morse, *Second Massachusetts*, p. 15. Madden was made a corporal.

42. *OR* 27 (1):781; Toombs, *New Jersey Troops*, p. 273, and "Battle," p. 12; Hinkley, "By an Eyewitness"; A. S. Jones, "Gettysburg"; Hinkley, "At Gettysburg," 12 Jan. 1893.

43. *OR* 27 (1):817; Morse, *Second Massachusetts*, pp. 15–16.

44. Morse, *Second Massachusetts*, p. 16; Brown, *Twenty-seventh Indiana*, p. 388.

45. Ruger to Bachelder, 12 Aug. 1869, BP; Fox to Carman, 4 Apr. 1877, Carman Papers, NYPL.

46. *OR* 27 (1):784, 793–94.

47. Ibid., pp. 784, 794.

48. Ibid., pp. 784, 794, 798; Wooster to Bachelder, 11 Dec. 1886, BP.

49. "Robert Cruikshank Letters," 3 July 1862, BPL. Sgt. Lorenzo Coy of the 123d New York wrote his wife that the 123d advanced to a stone wall and found the 46th Pennsylvania (20th Connecticut?) lying there. The 123d went over the wall with a shout and saw Rebels spring over the breastworks. When the 123d reached the works, the Rebels "were on a wild run through the woods beyond." See Lorenzo Coy to Wife, 6 July 1863, Coy Letters, GNMP.

50. *OR* 27 (1):858.

51. Ibid., pp. 185, 833. Busey and Martin in *Regimental Strengths*, p. 285, estimate Johnson's losses at over 1,936.

52. *OR* 27 (2):331, 506. The 1,823 figure was in Johnson's report and included 375 soldiers listed as missing. The adjutant general's later report gave Johnson's

casualties as 1,297, 46 of which were from Andrews's artillery battalion, and it included no missing.

On 30 October 1863, General Johnson told Jed Hotchkiss, the engineer, that he did not want to "go up" the hill at Gettysburg. Unfortunately, he was not more explicit as to what day, why, and why he did go. See McDonald, *Make Me a Map*, p. 180.

CHAPTER NINETEEN

1. *OR* 27 (2):448, 505, 511, 513, 526; O. Taylor, "A War Story of a Confederate Soldier Boy," 37th Virginia Folder, RBC; S. Z. Ammen, "Second Maryland Battalion, Ninth Paper—Second Series," in Ammen, "Maryland Troops in the Confederacy," p. 115, CC.

2. *OR* 27 (2):522; Frye, *2d Virginia*, p. 92. No one wrote where Culp fell, and since we do not know where his company fought on 3 July, we cannot know where he was shot. It could have been somewhere opposite McAllister's Woods, east or west of Rock Creek, or it could have been in front of Neill's brigade. One account states that he was behind a rock with two other soldiers. Against their advice, he climbed to the top of the rock to see what was going on and was shot in the forehead. See Moler, "History Repeated." Although a Confederate soldier, Pvt. Benjamin S. Pendleton, is said to have told someone in the family where Culp was buried, his body was not found. However, a piece of his gun's stock carved with his name was recovered. See J. Wesley Culp Folder, GNMP; *Pittsburgh Gazette Times*, 9 Nov. 1913, untitled article on J. Wesley Culp.

3. *OR* 27 (1):681–83, 829; *OR* 27 (3):500; Glenn, "23d Pennsylvania"; Wray, *Twenty-third Pennsylvania*, p. 94; Horton to Bachelder, 23 Jan. 1867, BP.

4. *OR* 27 (1):831; Mouat, "Three Years," HSP; Bryant, *Third Regiment*, p. 196.

5. *OR* 27 (1):831; "John Emerson Anderson Reminiscences," AAS; Bryant, *Third Regiment*, p. 197; Mouat, "Three Years," HSP; Collins, *149th Regiment*, p. 146.

6. "John Emerson Anderson Reminiscences," AAS.

7. *OR* 27 (1):761, 775, 781, 785, 805, 806, 810. In Williams to Bachelder, 10 Nov. 1865, BP, Williams wrote that only one regiment of Lockwood's brigade went to the center. Williams was probably mistaken.

8. "Robert Cruikshank Letters," 3 July 1863, p. 129, BPL. The captured Confederates might have believed this story, but it does not comport with orders given and actions taken in higher echelons. By the time that the incident probably took place, Johnson was moving his division back across the creek.

9. Wilson, "Charge up Culp's Hill."

10. Nevins, *Wainwright*, p. 248.

11. Harris to Bachelder, 7 Apr. 1864, BP.

12. T. Jones, *Seymour*, p. 79; Gordon, *Reminiscences*, p. 157. Campbell Brown placed the shooting at about noon, but he is not explicit about the date. See G. C. Brown, "Reminiscences," p. 4, TSLA. Both Brown and Seymour differ from Gordon, who states that the shooting occurred on 1 July in the town. Gordon's account is often quoted, but Seymour is more credible as to time and place.

13. Note Card, "Jennie Wade," GNMP. The Jennie Wade story is covered at length in Small, *Jenny Wade*.

Among the Gettysburg civilians wounded were John Burns who fought on 1 July, a Mr. Whetstone at the seminary who was wounded in the foot, a Mr. Lehman at the college who had a leg wound, and a Mr. R. F. McIlhenny who was wounded in the foot. See "Wounded Citizens."

14. *OR* 27 (1):238, 689, 750, 891, 893–95; Raus, *Generation*, 102, 157, 165, 177; Huntington to Bachelder, 6 June 1878, BP; Parmelee, "At Gettysburg." Capt. William H. McCartney reported that he collected from the section of woods in his rear, probably at the south end of the cemetery near the Taneytown Road, forty-eight rounds for a three-inch gun in perfect condition. He stated that the ground had been occupied by Edgell's battery. Edgell had three-inch guns, but his report suggests that his battery was not relieved. See *OR* 27 (1):689, 893. Major Osborn wrote that an Ohio battery had been sent to him from the Artillery Reserve and had taken position near this grove of trees. After being there a few minutes, its men began taking ammunition from their chests and throwing it into the trees so that they could report it exhausted and leave. Osborn wrote that he spoke to the battery commander in "explicit English" and that he then left him. A few minutes later the battery pulled out and went down the Baltimore Pike at full speed. He did not identify the battery further. See T. W. Osborn, "Experiences," Osborn Papers, CU. No Ohio batteries other than those of Dilger and Huntington are known to have been in his line. Heckman's battery was an Eleventh Corps battery, and Osborn would have known it. This leaves only Gibbs's battery of the Fifth Corps, which was on Little Round Top at the time. Hill's West Virginia battery was composed of Ohioans in great part and was in this area, but Osborn mentioned it in his report and knew its identity. Hill stated in his report that his battery occupied its position until 5 July. See *OR* 27 (1):895. Unfortunately, Osborn, in his postwar writing, was careless with the identity of batteries and names of personnel and is not to be trusted in such matters.

15. T. W. Osborn, "Artillery."

16. *OR* 27 (2):456, 603, 604, 606, 675.

17. *OR* 27 (1):689, 750; T. W. Osborn, "Artillery" and "Experiences," Osborn Papers, CU.

18. Schurz to Frank Moore, 6 June 1865, De Coppet Collection, Box 35, Folder 4, PU; Schurz, "Gettysburg," p. 282.

19. Butts, *A Gallant Captain*, pp. 87–89.

20. O. O. Howard, "Campaign," p. 67, and *Autobiography*, 1:437; *OR* 51 (1):1069. Howard erred, of course, in his identification of the four-gun battery. There was no such gun as a twelve-pounder Parrott; they were either ten-pounder Parrotts or twelve-pounder howitzers or Napoleons. Hill's battery had four ten-pounder Parrotts and was the only four-gun battery known to be in the line. If Howard was in front of Hill's battery, he would have been close to the Taneytown Road.

21. "Agate," "Gettysburg," p. 97.

22. George Metcalf, "Reminiscence," p. 94, GCC.

23. T. W. Osborn, "Artillery"; E. A. Moore, *Cannoneer*, pp. 198–99; *OR* 27 (1):891–92.

24. T. W. Osborn, "Artillery" and "Experiences," Osborn Papers, CU.

25. T. W. Osborn, "Experiences," Osborn Papers, CU.

26. Hunt, "Third Day," p. 374; O. O. Howard, "Campaign," p. 67.

27. O. O. Howard, "Campaign," p. 67; T. W. Osborn, "Artillery." Osborn stated that the idea of ceasing fire in order to prompt a Confederate assault was his. Neither Hunt's nor Howard's account supports Osborn's claims. In fact, Hunt's account suggests that the idea was his and that he thought of it before reaching Cemetery Hill. Later Hunt met one of Meade's staff officers who gave him Meade's order for the guns to cease fire. As it happened, General Hancock would not allow the Second Corps batteries to cease fire. This created one of Gettysburg's several postwar disputes. See Hunt, "Third Day," p. 375.

28. George Metcalf, "Reminiscence," pp. 95–96, GCC; O. O. Howard, "Campaign," p. 67.

29. T. W. Osborn, "Artillery"; Schurz, *Reminiscences*, 3:33.

30. J. W. Daniel, "Memoir of the Battle of Gettysburg," p. 16, VHS.

CHAPTER TWENTY

1. *OR* 27 (2):322, 360, 448, 471.

2. Ibid., pp. 471, 482, 505, 511, 513, 522, 557, 597; J. A. Early, *Autobiographical Sketch*, p. 276; Horn, *Henry Eyster Jacobs*, 1:59.

3. J. W. Daniel, "Memoir of the Battle of Gettysburg," p. 19, VHS.

4. Ibid., pp. 18–19; Leon, *Diary of a Tarheel*, p. 37; Reed, "Gettysburg Campaign," p. 190.

5. Spencer, *Civil War Marriage*, p. 187; Ted Barclay to Sister, 13 July 1863, Barclay Papers, W&L.

6. J. W. Daniel, "Memoir of the Battle of Gettysburg," pp. 17–19, VHS; Micajah Woods to Father, 17 July 1863, Woods Papers, UV. Lieutenant Woods belonged to Capt. Thomas E. Jackson's Virginia battery, which supported Jenkins's cavalry brigade.

7. Fox to Harris, 14 Nov. 1885, BP.

8. Harris to Bachelder, 7 Apr. 1864, BP; "Robert Cruikshank Letters," 4 July 1863, p. 120, BPL; Jacob Smith, *Camps and Campaigns*, pp. 227–28; Becker, *Ladley*, p. 146. Colonel Harris wrote that his left was on Baltimore Street (he misnamed it Washington Street) and his right beyond the brick kiln.

9. Simmers and Bachschmid, *Volunteers' Manual*, p. 31; Miller to Bachelder, 2 Mar. 1884, BP; Bloom, *Adams County*, p. 212.

10. *OR* 27 (1):731, 743; New York Monuments Commission, *Final Report*, 1:431.

11. *OR* 27 (1):285; Nicholson, *Pennsylvania*, 1:343; Hofmann, "Fifty-sixth Regiment."

12. *OR* 27 (1):761, 781–82, 786, 791, 816; "Robert Cruikshank Letters," 4 July 1863, p. 130, BPL; Toombs, "Battle," p. 13; New York Monuments Commission, *Slocum*, p. 186.

13. Buckingham to Wife, 17 July 1863, Buckingham Papers, AAS; Mouat, "Three Years," HSP.

14. Norris, "Ohio at Gettysburg."

15. Collins, *149th Regiment*, p. 149; "John Emerson Anderson Reminiscences," AAS.

16. Collins, *149th Regiment*, p. 147; Report of Col. A. B. Underwood, 33d Massachusetts Volunteer Infantry Regiment, and Tallman, "War of the Rebellion," 66th Ohio Volunteer Infantry Regiment, GNMP.

17. "Robert Cruikshank Letters," 4 July 1863, p. 130, BPL.

18. Horn, *Henry Eyster Jacobs*, 1:11.

19. Schurz, *Reminiscences*, 3:34–35.

20. Butts, *A Gallant Captain*, p. 88.

21. *OR* 27 (3):532–33, (1):700–701, 707.

22. Collins, *149th Regiment*, p. 150; Milano, "Call of Leadership," p. 75.

23. "Mrs. Thorn's War Story." On 2 July 1863, John Moeser, who signed his name as "Sexton" of the Evergreen Cemetery, wrote General Howard requesting payment for 5,000 pounds of hay, $25 worth of grass, $15 worth of sundry greens, 25 bushels of potatoes, and one good milch cow. His billing was prompt, but any payment would not have come from Howard. See Moeser to Howard, 2 July 1863, O. O. Howard Papers, BC.

Mrs. Thorn stated that all of the windows in the gatehouse were gone. A post-battle photograph suggests that this was an exaggeration.

24. Unrau, *Administrative History*, pp. 3, 4. This portion of Unrau's study is based on a number of sources but especially on John Russell Bartlett, *The Soldiers' National Cemetery* (Providence, 1874), and Kathleen Georg, "The Great Enterprize," and David McConaughy Correspondence, both at GNMP.

25. Unrau, *Administrative History*, p. 5.

26. Ibid., pp. 7–10; Pfanz, "From Bloody Battlefield to Historic Shrine," pp. 45–46.

27. Unrau, *Administrative History*, p. 6.

APPENDIX A

1. This local lore is from the files of Col. Jacob M. Sheads of Gettysburg. I do not know its origins.

2. Thayer, "Gettysburg," p. 14.

3. Morse, "Twelfth Corps," p. 828.

4. Nicholson, *Pennsylvania*, 1:308.

5. Chapman, *Civil War Diary*, p. 22.

6. "Robert Cruikshank Letters," 2 July 1863, p. 124, BPL.

APPENDIX B

1. Howard to Bates, 14 Sept. 1875, Bates Papers, PSA.

2. *OR* 27 (1):140.

3. "TRUTH," "Congress and General Howard," 20 Feb. 1864; "One Who Knows,"

"Congress and General Howard"; "TRUTH," "Congress and General Howard," 2 Apr. 1864.

4. Howard to Hancock, 25 Feb. 1864, O. O. Howard Papers, BC.

5. Hancock to Howard, 14 Mar. 1864, O. O. Howard Papers, BC.

6. Howard to Coppee, 14 Mar. 1864, O. O. Howard Papers, BC.

7. O. O. Howard, "Campaign," pp. 58–59.

8. W. S. Hancock, "Gettysburg," pp. 821–31; Hancock to Hooker, 23 July 1876, Bates Papers, PSA.

9. Howard to O'Donnell, 11 June 1888, O. O. Howard Papers, BC; O. O. Howard, *Autobiography*, 1:422.

10. Slocum to Howland, 17 July 1863, Howland Manuscripts, NYHS.

11. *OR* 27 (1):769; Quaife, *Williams*, p. 271.

12. *OR* 27 (1):763; Slocum to Morgan, 2 Jan. 1864, in Quaife, *Williams*, pp. 183–85.

13. *OR* 27 (1):769–70.

14. Ibid.

15. Ibid., pp. 117, 770.

16. Ibid., pp. 120–21.

BIBLIOGRAPHY

A bibliography of sources cited appears below. It includes a variety of manuscripts and published items. Almost all of the latter are personal accounts of the battle or unit histories, which might be considered as primary sources.

One primary source is particularly noteworthy. It is the John B. Bachelder Papers, the originals of which are at the New Hampshire Historical Society. They include scores of letters written by participants in the battle to Bachelder when he was making his various maps of the battlefield and when he was the historian for the Gettysburg Battlefield Memorial Association.

Most historians of the battle of Gettysburg mourn the lack of good Confederate accounts. Gen. Jubal A. Early was exceptional in that he wrote extensively of some aspects of the battle. However, in consulting Early's writings it must be remembered that he was often quite partisan.

William W. Goldsborough and some other members of the 1st Maryland Battalion, C.S.A., were also exceptions. One of the Maryland sources is "Washington Hands's Civil War Notebook," the original of which is on file at the library of the University of Virginia. Hands was a corporal in the 1st Maryland Regiment and a private in the Baltimore Light Artillery. I have not read all of Hands's notebook, which is voluminous, but I believe that his Gettysburg section is either copied from Goldsborough's writings or strongly influenced by them. Therefore, I have considered it to be another Goldsborough source.

I have not listed newspapers separately. Most, if not all, newspaper items used identify authors, and it seems unnecessary to list the newspapers in a separate category. One newspaper merits special mention. It is the *National Tribune*, a Washington, D.C., weekly printed for Union veterans. It is rich in Union source materials, but each must be evaluated for its own accuracy.

My most valuable source, of course, was *The War of the Rebellion: A Compilation of the Official Records of the Union and Confederate Armies*, series 1, volumes 27 and 51.

I would also like to call particular attention to the reference books that have been most helpful. They are listed below under their compilers' names. I am especially grateful to Mark M. Boatner III, William F. Howard, Robert K. Krick, Edmund J. Raus, Richard A. Sauers, Stewart Sifakis, Jon L. Wakelyn, and Ezra J. Warner. I must also make special mention of William A. Frassanito, whose photographic study provides unique help.

The battlefield, like the *Official Records*, is an indispensable source that any writer about battles must try to know and appreciate. Unfortunately, however, terrain changes with the passage of time. The important area of the field north, northeast, and northwest of Cemetery Hill has been developed and diminished. Although Culp's Hill itself has not been developed, large areas of its vital historic open spaces have been blanketed with trees and brush so that they are hard to identify on the ground and understand. Nevertheless, such an effort can be interesting and rewarding.

MANUSCRIPT SOURCES

Adams County Historical Society, Gettysburg, Pennsylvania
  Sarah Brodhead, "The Diary of a Lady of Gettysburg," photocopy
  Gates D. Fahnestock, "Recollections of the Battle of Gettysburg"
  "The Story of Mrs. Jacob Kitzmiller [Anna Garlach]"
  Letter, John Rupp to Sister Anne, 19 July 1863
American Antiquarian Society, Worcester, Massachusetts
  "John Emerson Anderson Reminiscences," Civil War Collection
  Philo B. Buckingham Papers
Bancroft Public Library, Salem, New York
  "Robert Cruikshank Letters"
John R. Bass Collection, Spring Hill, North Carolina
  "Memoirs of W. P. Snakenburg, Wilson, North Carolina, Private, 'Louisiana Tigers'"
Bowdoin College Library, Brunswick, Maine
  Charles Henry Howard Papers
  Oliver Otis Howard Papers
Colgate University Archives, Case Library, Hamilton, New York
  Thomas W. Osborn Papers
College of William and Mary, Earl Gregg Swem Library, Williamsburg, Virginia
  Jubal A. Early Papers
Connecticut State Library, Hartford, Connecticut
  Col. Warren Packer Diary, 1861–64
  Capt. Harlan P. Rugg Diary
Duke University, Special Collections Library, Durham, North Carolina
  John W. Daniel Papers
  John Quincy Adams Nadenbousch Papers
  William Alexander Smith Papers
Fredericksburg and Spotsylvania National Military Park, Fredericksburg, Virginia
  Edward D. Camden Diary, 25th Virginia Infantry
  "Charles Anderson Raine Memoirs," 21st Virginia Regiment
  Sgt. J. William Thomas Diary, 1st Maryland Battalion
Georgia Department of Archives and History, Atlanta, Georgia
  "Reminiscences of the War Between the States by W. H. May in 1886"
Gettysburg College, Musselman Library, Gettysburg, Pennsylvania
  McConaughy Collection
Gettysburg National Military Park, Gettysburg, Pennsylvania
  John Badger Bachelder Notes
  Sgt. Lorenzo R. Coy Letters, 123d New York Volunteer Infantry Regiment
  J. Wesley Culp Folder

Note Card, "1st Louisiana Infantry"

Letter, Edward R. Geary to Mother, 17 July 1863, Knap's Battery

Letter, David Hunter to Mrs. Edmund Hunter, 2 July 1863, 2d Virginia
Infantry

Henry Jacobs, "How an Eyewitness Watched the Battle," typescript

Letter, William W. Ker to John P. Nicholson, 1 May 1894, 73d Pennsylvania
Volunteer Infantry Regiment

Henry H. Lyman Diary, 147th New York Volunteer Infantry Regiment

Albertus McCreary, "Gettysburg: A Boy's Experience of the Battle,"
typescript

William Henry Tallman, "The War of the Rebellion," typescript, 66th Ohio
Volunteer Infantry Regiment

Report of Col. A. B. Underwood to the Adjutant General, 9 December 1881,
33d Massachusetts Volunteer Infantry Regiment

U.S. Gettysburg Battlefield Commission, Engineer's Department, "A Record
of the Position of Troops on the Battlefield"

U.S. War Department, Gettysburg Battlefield Commission, "Engineer's Journal," 25 July 1893–31 January 1896

Note Card, "Jennie Wade"

"Reminiscences of John Charles Will," typescript

Handley Library Archives, Winchester, Virginia

"Letters of John H. Stone" (#320)

Historical Society of Pennsylvania, Philadelphia, Pennsylvania

George G. Meade Collection, Letters, Meade and Gettysburg

David Mouat, "Three Years in the 29th Pennsylvania Volunteers," 29th Regiment Pennsylvania Volunteers Papers

Library of Congress, Washington, D.C.

Joshua L. Chamberlain Papers

Jubal A. Early Papers

Richard S. Ewell Papers

Douglas Southall Freeman Papers

"John William Ford Hatton Memoir"

Jedediah Hotchkiss Papers

Henry Jackson Hunt Papers

John J. H. Love Papers

James W. Wadsworth, Jr., Family Papers

Louisiana State University Libraries, Louisiana and Lower Mississippi Valley
Collections, Baton Rouge, Louisiana

Albert A. Batchelor Papers

David French Boyd Civil War Papers

Museum of the Confederacy, Eleanor S. Brockenbrough Library, Richmond,
Virginia

Reports of Units of Steuart's Confederate Brigade for the Battle of Gettysburg

National Archives, Washington, D.C.

Record Groups 94, 109, 393

New Hampshire Historical Society, Concord, New Hampshire
  John B. Bachelder Papers
New-York Historical Society, New York, New York
  David E. Cronin Papers of the War
  Col. Joseph Howland Manuscripts
New York Public Library, Rare Books and Manuscripts Division, New York,
  New York
  Ezra Ayres Carman Papers
North Carolina Department of Cultural Resources, Division of Archives and
  History, Raleigh, North Carolina
  Isaac Erwin Avery Papers
  Futch Letters
  Thomas M. Gorman Papers
  Georgia Hicks Papers, United Daughters of the Confederacy
  Robert F. Hoke Papers
Northwestern State University of Louisiana, Watson Memorial Library, Cammie
  Henry Research Center, Natchitoches, Louisiana
  Murphy-Sandlin Collection
Pennsylvania Historical and Museum Commission, Pennsylvania State Archives,
  Harrisburg, Pennsylvania
  Samuel Penniman Bates Papers (MG-17)
  Peter F. Rothermel Papers (MG-108)
Princeton University Library, Rare Books and Special Collections, Princeton,
  New Jersey
  Andre De Coppet Collection
Tennessee State Library and Archives, Nashville, Tennessee
  G. Campbell Brown, "Reminiscences," Brown-Ewell Papers
Tulane University, Howard Tilton Memorial Library, Louisiana Historical Asso-
  ciation Collection, New Orleans, Louisiana
  "Paper Read by Co'l David Zable . . . December 12, 1903"
University of North Carolina, Wilson Library, Southern Historical Collection,
  Chapel Hill, North Carolina
  Samuel W. Eaton Diary
  Samuel Angus Firebaugh Diary
  James E. Green Diary
  William Robert Gwaltney Diary
  Robert F. Hoke Papers
  Eliza Hall Parsley Papers
  Stephen Dodson Ramseur Papers
University of Virginia, Alderman Library, Charlottesville, Virginia
  John W. Daniel Papers (#158)
  George Williamson Finley Papers (#3528)
  "Memoirs of Clement D. Fishburne" (#2341)
  "Washington Hands's Civil War Notebook" (#10361)
  Micajah Woods Papers (#10279)

U.S. Army Military History Institute, U.S. Army History Collection, Carlisle
Barracks, Pennsylvania
Robert L. Brake Collection
Civil War Miscellaneous Collection
Civil War Times Illustrated Collection
Thomas Clemens Collection
Gregory Coco Collection, Harrisburg Civil War Round Table
Norwich Civil War Round Table Collection
Virginia Historical Society, Richmond, Virginia
John W. Daniel, "Memoir of the Battle of Gettysburg"
Jubal A. Early Papers
"Memoirs of Benjamin Anderson Jones, Virginian, Civil War Experiences"
Virginia State Library, Richmond, Virginia
Osborn Wilson Diaries
Washington and Lee University Library, Special Collections and Papers of the
Rockbridge Historical Society, Lexington, Virginia
Alexander Tedford Barclay Papers

MAPS

Bachelder, John B. *Position of Troops, Second Day's Battle.* New York: Office of
the Chief of Engineers, U.S. Army, 1879.
————. "Position of Troops, Second Day's Battle." Draft Map. Gettysburg
National Military Park, Gettysburg, Pennsylvania.
Gettysburg National Park Commission. *Map of the Battlefield of Gettysburg.*
Gettysburg: Gettysburg National Park Commission, 1901. ("Cope Map"
throughout notes.) (See plate XL of the atlas to U.S. War Department, *The
War of the Rebellion: A Compilation of the Official Records of the Union and
Confederate Armies.*)
U.S. Army. Engineer Department. *Map of the Battlefield of Gettysburg, Sur-
veyed and drawn under the direction of Bvt. Maj. Gen. G. K. Warren.* ("Warren
Map" throughout notes.) (See plate XCV of the atlas to U.S. War Department,
*The War of the Rebellion: A Compilation of the Official Records of the Union
and Confederate Armies.*)

BOOKS, ARTICLES, AND PAMPHLETS

"Agate" [pseud.]. "The Battle of Gettysburg." In *The Rebellion Record: A Diary
of American Events,* edited by Frank Moore, pp. 84–102. New York: D. van
Nostrand Publishers, 1864.
Ashcroft, John M. *31st Virginia Infantry.* Lynchburg: H. E. Howard, 1988.
"At Gettysburg, How a Proposed Night Attack by the Enemy Was Foiled."
National Tribune, 11 February 1886.

Aughinbaugh, Nellie E. *Personal Experience of a Young Girl during the Battle of Gettysburg*. Washington, D.C.: Louis Dale Leeds, n.d.

Bandy, Ken, and Florence Freeland. *The Gettysburg Papers*. 3 vols. Dayton: Morningside, 1978.

Bates, Samuel P. *The Battle of Gettysburg*. Philadelphia: T. H. Davis, 1875.

——. *History of the Pennsylvania Volunteers*. 5 vols. Harrisburg: D. Singerly, State Printer, 1869.

"A Battle, How It Appeared to an Eyewitness." *Gettysburg Compiler*, 12 April 1883.

Bean, William Gleason. *The Liberty Hall Volunteers*. Charlottesville: University Press of Virginia, 1964.

Becker, Carl M., and Ritchie Thomas, eds. *Hearth and Knapsack: The Ladley Letters, 1857–1880*. Athens: Ohio University Press, 1988.

Beers, Paul. "A Profile of John W. Geary." *Civil War Times Illustrated* 9, no. 3 (June 1870): 11–13.

Bertholf, G. D. "The 12th Corps at Gettysburg." *National Tribune*, 11 May 1893.

Blackford, William W. *War Years with Jeb Stuart*. New York: Charles Scribner's Sons, 1945.

Bloom, Robert L. *A History of Adams County, Pennsylvania, 1700–1990*. Gettysburg: Adams County Historical Society, 1992.

Boatner, Mark M., III. *Civil War Dictionary*. New York: David McKay Company, 1959.

Boies, Andrew J. *Record of the Thirty-third Massachusetts Volunteer Infantry*. Fitchburg, Mass.: Sentinel Printing Company, 1880.

Bond, Arthur W. "Company A, First Maryland Cavalry." *Confederate Veteran* 6 (February 1897): 78.

Booth, H. B. "Credit to Whom Credit Is Due." *National Tribune*, 29 January 1909.

Boyle, John Richards. *Soldiers True: The Story of the 111th Regiment, Pennsylvania Volunteers*. New York: Eaton and Mains, 1903.

Brown, Edmund R. *History of the Twenty-seventh Indiana Volunteer Infantry*. Monticello, 1899.

Bryant, Edwin C. *History of the Third Regiment of Wisconsin Veteran Volunteer Infantry*. Madison: Democrat Printing Company, 1891.

Burke's Presidential Families of the United States of America. London: Burke's Peerage Limited, 1975.

Busey, John W., and David G. Martin. *Regimental Strengths and Losses at Gettysburg*. Hightstown, N.J.: Longstreet House, 1986.

Butts, John Tyler, ed. *A Gallant Captain of the Civil War: From the Record of the Extraordinary Adventures of Friederich Otto Baron von Fritsch*. New York: F. Tennyson Neely, 1902.

Caldwell, J. F. C. *The History of a Brigade of South Carolinians*. Marietta, Ga.: Continental Book Company, 1951.

Carpenter, John A. "General O. O. Howard at Gettysburg." *Civil War History* 9 (September 1963): 261–76.

——. "A Gettysburg Letter." *Lincoln Herald* 58, no. 4 (1957): 10–11.

————. *Sword and Olive Branch*. Pittsburgh: University of Pittsburgh Press, 1964.

Carrington, James McD. "First Day at Gettysburg." *Southern Historical Society Papers* 37 (1909): 326–37.

Casler, John O. *Four Years with the Stonewall Brigade*. Guthrie, Okla.: State Capital Printing Company, 1893.

Causeby, Thomas E. "Storming the Stone Fence at Gettysburg." *Southern Historical Society Papers* 29 (1901): 339–41.

Cavins, Elijah H. C. "A Gettysburg Diary." *National Tribune*, 23 December 1909.

Chapman, Horatio Dana. *Civil War Diary of a Forty-niner*. Hartford: Allis, 1929.

Clark, Walter, ed. *Histories of the Several Regiments and Battalions from North Carolina in the Great War, 1861–1865*. 5 vols. Raleigh: State of North Carolina, 1901.

Clemens, Thomas G., ed. "The Diary of John H. Stone." *Maryland Historical Magazine* 85 (Summer 1990): 109–43.

Clements, G. S. "The 25th Ohio at Gettysburg." *National Tribune*, 6 August 1891.

Coddington, Edwin B. *The Gettysburg Campaign*. Dayton: Morningside, 1879.

Coggins, Jack. *Arms and Equipment of the Civil War*. New York: Fairfax Press, 1902.

Collins, George K. *Memories of the 149th Regiment, New York Volunteer Infantry*. Syracuse: Published by the author, 1891.

Company C, 7th Ohio Volunteer Infantry. "Geary at Gettysburg." *Philadelphia Weekly Press*, 24 February 1886.

Comte de Paris et al. "Gettysburg Thirty Years After." *North American Review* 152 (February 1891): 129–47.

Connor, Daniel M. "At Gettysburg: The Experiences and Sights of an Indiana Cavalryman." *National Tribune*, 27 July 1922.

Cook, Stephen G., and Charles E. Benton, eds. *The Dutchess County Regiment in the Civil War*. Danbury: Danbury Medical Printing Company, 1907.

Cooke, Sidney G. "The First Day at Gettysburg." In *The Gettysburg Papers*, edited by Ken Bandy and Florence Freeland, 1:239–54.

Culp, E. A. "Gettysburg." *National Tribune*, 19 March 1885.

Curtis, Orson B. *History of the Twenty-fourth Michigan of the Iron Brigade*. Detroit: Winn and Hammond, 1891.

Daniel, Edward M., ed. *Speeches and Orations of John Warwick Daniel*. Lynchburg: J. P. Bell Company, 1911.

Dawes, Rufus R. *Service with the Sixth Wisconsin Volunteers*. Marietta, Ohio: E. R. Alderman and Sons, 1890.

————. "With the Sixth Wisconsin at Gettysburg." In *The Gettysburg Papers*, edited by Ken Bandy and Florence Freeland, 1:213–38.

"Death of Colonel McDougall." *Salem* (N.Y.) *Press*, 5 July 1864.

Dickelman, J. L. "The Fierce Battle on Cemetery Hill to Recover the Guns." *National Tribune*, 10 June 1909.

————. "Gen. Carroll's Gibraltar Brigade at Gettysburg." *National Tribune*, 10 December 1908.

Diembach, Andrew. "An Incident on Cemetery Hill." *Blue and Gray* 2 (July 1893): 22.

Doubleday, Abner. *Chancellorsville and Gettysburg*. New York: Charles Scribner's Sons, 1882.

Douglas, Henry Kyd. *I Rode with Stonewall*. Atlanta: Mockingbird Books, 1976.

Driver, Robert J., Jr. *52d Virginia Infantry*. Lynchburg: H. E. Howard, 1986.

Dunkelman, Mark H., and Michael J. Winey. "The Hardtack Regiment in the Brickyard Fight." *Gettysburg Magazine*, 1 January 1993.

Early, John C. "A Southern Boy's Experience at Gettysburg." *Journal of the Military Service Institution of the United States* 43 (January–February 1911): 415–23.

Early, Jubal A. *Autobiographical Sketch and Narrative of the War Between the States*. Philadelphia: J. B. Lippincott, 1912.

————. "Leading Confederates on the Battlefield: A Review by General Early." *Southern Historical Society Papers* 4 (1877): 241–81.

————. "Reminiscences of Gettysburg." *National Magazine*, 1913, pp. 634–40.

————. "Supplement to General Early's Review: A Reply to General Longstreet." *Southern Historical Society Papers* 4 (1877): 282–302.

————. *War Memoirs*. Bloomington: Indiana University Press, 1960.

Eddy, Richard. *History of the Sixtieth Regiment, New York State Volunteers*. Philadelphia: Cressy and Markley Printing, 1864.

Elmore, Thomas J. "Courage against the Trenches: The Attack and Repulse of Steuart's Brigade on Culp's Hill." *Gettysburg Magazine*, 1 July 1992.

Evans, Clement A., ed. *Confederate Military History*. 11 vols. Atlanta: Confederate Publishing Company, 1899.

Fiske, Samuel W., ed. *Mr. Dunn Browne's Experiences in the Army*. Boston: Nichols and Noyes, 1886.

Fox, William F. "A History of the Twelfth and Twentieth Corps." In New York Monuments Commission for the Battlefields of Gettysburg and Chattanooga, *In Memorium, Henry Warner Slocum*, pp. 117–316.

————. "Life of General Slocum." In New York Monuments Commission for the Battlefields of Gettysburg and Chattanooga, *In Memorium, Henry Warner Slocum*, pp. 63–116.

Frassanito, William A. *Gettysburg: A Journey in Time*. New York: Charles Scribner's Sons, 1973.

Freeman, Douglas S. *Lee's Lieutenants*. 3 vols. New York: Charles Scribner's Sons, 1949–51.

————. *R. E. Lee: A Biography*. 4 vols. New York: Charles Scribner's Sons, 1934–35.

Frye, Dennis E. *2d Virginia Infantry*. Lynchburg: H. E. Howard, 1984.

Gallagher, Gary W., ed. *The First Day at Gettysburg*. Kent, Ohio: Kent State University Press, 1992.

————. "In the Shadow of Stonewall Jackson: Richard Ewell in the Gettysburg Campaign." *Civil War*, 5:55–59.

————. "Jubal Early and the Myth of the Lost Cause." *Maryland Line* 10, no. 7 (March 1990): 1.

————. *Stephen Dodson Ramseur: Lee's Gallant General*. Chapel Hill: University of North Carolina Press, 1985.

Gibbon, John. "The Council of War on the Second Day." In *Battles and Leaders of the Civil War*, edited by Robert U. Johnson and Clarence C. Buel, 3:313–14.

————. *Personal Recollections of the Civil War*. New York: G. P. Putnam's Sons, 1928.

Gilham, William. *Manual of Instruction for the Volunteers and Militia of the United States*. Philadelphia: Charles DeSilver, 1861.

Gilmor, Harry. *Four Years in the Saddle*. New York: Harper and Brothers, 1866.

Gilmore, D. M. "With Gregg at Gettysburg." In *The Gettysburg Papers*, edited by Ken Bandy and Florence Freeland, 1:465–83.

Glenn, John F. "The 23d Pennsylvania Volunteers." *Philadelphia Weekly Press*, 28 April 1886.

Goldsborough, William W. *The Maryland Line*. Port Washington, N.Y.: Kennikat Press, 1972.

————. "With Lee at Gettysburg." *Philadelphia Record*, 8 July 1900.

Gordon, John B. *Reminiscences of the Civil War*. Dayton: Morningside, 1985.

Greene, George Sears. "The Breastworks at Culp's Hill." In *Battles and Leaders of the Civil War*, edited by Robert U. Johnson and Clarence C. Buel, 3:317.

Grube, Harry T., and George Woodbridge. "14th Regiment New York State Militia." *Military Collector and Historian* 10, no. 3 (Fall 1958): 80–83.

Hale, Laura Virginia, and Stanley S. Phillips. *History of the Forty-ninth Virginia, C.S.A*. Lanham, Md.: S. S. Phillips, 1981.

Hall, James E. *The Diary of a Confederate Soldier*. Edited by Ruth Woods Dayton. N.p.: Elizabeth T. Phillips, 1961.

Halstead, Eminel P. "The First Day of the Battle of Gettysburg." In *The Gettysburg Papers*, edited by Ken Bandy and Florence Freeland, 1:151–58.

————. "Incidents of the First Day at Gettysburg." In *Battles and Leaders of the Civil War*, edited by Robert U. Johnson and Clarence C. Buel, 3:284–85.

Hamlin, Percy G. *"Old Bald Head," General Richard S. Ewell: Portrait of a Soldier*. Strasburg, Va.: Shenandoah Publishing House, 1940.

Hancock, Almira Russell. *Reminiscences of Winfield Scott Hancock*. New York: Charles L. Webster, 1887.

Hancock, Winfield S. "Gettysburg: Reply to General Howard." *Galaxy* 22 (June 1876): 821–31.

Hand, J. W. "Gettysburg." *National Tribune*, 24 July 1890.

Hartwig, D. Scott. "The 11th Army Corps on July 1, 1863." *Gettysburg Magazine*, 1 January 1990.

Harwell, Richard, and Philip N. Racine, eds. *The Fiery Trail: A Union Officer's Account of Sherman's Last Campaigns*. Knoxville: University of Tennessee Press, 1986.

Haskell, Frank A. *The Battle of Gettysburg*. Boston: Massachusetts Commandery, Military Order of the Loyal Legion, 1908.

Hassler, William W. *Crisis at the Crossroads: The First Day at Gettysburg*. Montgomery: University of Alabama Press, 1970.

Hatton, Clarence R. "Gen. Archibald Campbell Godwin." *Confederate Veteran* 28 (April 1920): 133–36.

Hazlett, James C., Edward Olmstead, and M. Hume Parks. *Field Artillery Weapons of the Civil War*. Newark: University of Delaware Press, 1983.

"A Hero's Lost Grave." *Philadelphia Weekly Times*, 20 June 1886.

Hinkley, Julian W. "At Gettysburg." *National Tribune*, 12 October 1892.

———. "At Gettysburg." *National Tribune*, 12 January 1893.

———. "By an Eyewitness." *National Tribune*, 21 July 1892.

———. *A Narrative of Service with the Third Wisconsin Infantry*. Madison: Wisconsin History Commission, 1912.

Hitz, Louise W., ed. *The Letters of Frederick C. Winkler*. N.p.: Privately printed, 1963.

Hofmann, John W. "The Fifty-sixth Regiment Pennsylvania Volunteers in the Gettysburg Campaign." *Philadelphia Weekly Press*, 13 January 1886.

Horn, Henry E., ed. *Memoirs of Henry Eyster Jacobs*. 3 vols. N.p.: Privately printed, 1974.

Howard, Charles H. "The First Day at Gettysburg." In *The Gettysburg Papers*, edited by Ken Bandy and Florence Freeland, 1:310–36.

Howard, McHenry. *Recollections of a Confederate Staff Officer*. Dayton: Morningside, 1975.

Howard, Oliver O. *Autobiography of Oliver Otis Howard*. 2 vols. New York: Baker and Taylor Company, 1902.

———. "Campaign and Battle of Gettysburg." *Atlantic Monthly* 38 (July 1876): 48–71.

———. "The Eleventh Corps at Chancellorsville." In *Battles and Leaders of the Civil War*, edited by Robert U. Johnson and Clarence C. Buel, 3:239–54.

———. "Personal Reminiscences of the War of the Rebellion." *National Tribune*, 1 January 1885.

Howard, William F. *The Gettysburg Death Roster: The Federal Dead at Gettysburg*. Dayton: Morningside, 1990.

Hunt, Henry J. "The First Day at Gettysburg." In *Battles and Leaders of the Civil War*, edited by Robert U. Johnson and Clarence C. Buel, 3:255–84.

———. "The Second Day at Gettysburg." In *Battles and Leaders of the Civil War*, edited by Robert U. Johnson and Clarence C. Buel, 3:290–313.

———. "The Third Day at Gettysburg." In *Battles and Leaders of the Civil War*, edited by Robert U. Johnson and Clarence C. Buel, 3:369–85.

Hurst, Samuel H. *Journal of the Seventy-third Ohio Volunteer Infantry*. Chillicothe, Ohio, 1866.

Iobst, Richard W., and Louis H. Manarin. *The Bloody Sixth: The Sixth North Carolina Regiment, Confederate States of America*. Durham, N.C.: Christian Printing Company, 1965.

Jacobs, Michael. "Meteorology of the Battle." *Gettysburg Star and Sentinel*, 11 August 1885.

————. *Notes on the Rebel Invasion of Maryland and Pennsylvania and the Battle of Gettysburg*. Gettysburg: Times Printing House, 1909.

Johnson, Allen, and Dumas Malone, eds. *Dictionary of American Biography*. 20 vols. New York: Charles Scribner's Sons, 1928–36.

Johnson, Robert U., and Clarence C. Buel, eds. *Battles and Leaders of the Civil War*. 4 vols. New York: Century Company, 1884–89. Reprint. New York: Thomas Yoseloff, 1956.

Jones, A. Sheridan. "Battle of Gettysburg." *National Tribune*, 29 December 1892.

Jones, Jesse H. "A Pair of Breastplates." *National Tribune*, 6 June 1901.

————. "Saved the Day." *National Tribune*, 7 March 1895.

Jones, Terry, ed. *The Civil War Memoirs of Captain William Seymour*. Baton Rouge: Louisiana State University Press, 1991.

————. *Lee's Tigers: The Louisiana Infantry of the Army of Northern Virginia*. Baton Rouge: Louisiana State University Press, 1987.

Kaufmann, Wilhelm. *Die Deutschen im Amerikanishen Buergerkreig*. Munich: R. Oldenbourg, 1911.

Kempster, Walter. "The Cavalry at Gettysburg." In *The Gettysburg Papers*, edited by Ken Bandy and Florence Freeland, 1:427–59.

Keppler, William. *History of the Three Months and Three Years Service . . . of the Fourth Regiment, Ohio Volunteer Infantry*. Cleveland: Leader Printing Company, 1886.

Kiefer, William R. *History of the One Hundred and Fifty-third Regiment Pennsylvania Volunteer Infantry*. Easton, Penn.: Press of the Chemical Publishing Company, 1909.

Krick, Robert K. *The Gettysburg Death Roster*. Dayton: Morningside, 1981.

————. *Lee's Colonels: A Biographical Register of Field Officers of the Army of Northern Virginia*. Dayton: Morningside, 1979.

Law, Wayne E., and Charles B. Wallace. *Berlin Improvement Society*. Harrisburg: McFarland Company, 1977.

Leon, Louis. *Diary of a Tarheel Confederate Soldier*. Charlotte: Stone Publishing Company, 1913.

Liquori, Sister M. "Polish Sisters in the Civil War." *Polish Studies*, January–June 1958.

Lloyd, W. G. "Second Louisiana at Gettysburg." *Confederate Veteran* 6 (September 1898): 417.

Longstreet, James. "General Longstreet's Account of the Campaign and Battle." *Southern Historical Society Papers* 5 (1878): 54–85.

Lonn, Ella. *Foreigners in the Union Army and Navy*. Baton Rouge: Louisiana State University Press, 1952.

Love, William DeLoss. *Wisconsin in the War of the Rebellion*. Chicago: Church and Goodman Publishers, 1886.

Lowry, R. E. *History of Preble County, Ohio*. Owensboro, Ky.: Cook and McDowell Publications, 1981.

Lumbard, J. A. "Geary at Gettysburg." *National Tribune*, 17 March 1886.

"M" [pseud.], Company E. "What the 14th Indiana Did in the Fight." *National Tribune*, 10 September 1885.

McDonald, Archer P., ed. *Make Me a Map of the Valley*. Dallas: Southern Methodist University Press, 1973.

McFeely, William S. *Yankee Stepfather: General O. O. Howard and the Freedmen*. New York: W. W. Norton, 1970.

McKay, Charles W. "Three Years or During the War with Crescent and Star." *National Tribune Scrapbook*, n.d.

McKelvey, Blake, ed. "George Breck's Civil War Letters from Reynolds' Battery." *Rochester Historical Society Publications* 22 (1944): 91–149.

McKim, Randolph H. "Colonel Winston's Correction Corrected." *Southern Historical Society Papers* 7 (1879): 315–16.

———. *The Second Maryland Infantry: An Oration Delivered . . . May 7th 1909*. N.p., 1909.

———. *A Soldier's Recollections*. New York: Longmans, Green, 1910.

———. "Steuart's Brigade at the Battle of Gettysburg." *Southern Historical Society Papers* 5 (1878): 291–300.

McLean, William. "The Days of Terror in 1863." *Gettysburg Compiler*, 1 July 1908.

MacNamara, Michael H. *The Irish Ninth in Bivouac and Battle*. Boston: Lee and Shepard, 1867.

Maine Gettysburg Commission. *Maine at Gettysburg: Report of the Maine Commissioners*. Portland, Maine: Lakeside Press, 1898.

Martin, David G. *Carl Bornemann's Regiment: The Forty-first New York Infantry*. Hightstown, N.J.: Longstreet House, 1987.

Maryland Gettysburg Monuments Commission. *Report . . . to the Governor of Maryland, June 17, 1891*. Baltimore: William K. Boyle and Son, 1891.

Maurice, Frederick, ed. *An Aide de Camp of Lee, Being the Papers of Colonel Charles Marshall*. Boston: Little, Brown, 1927.

Meade, George G., Jr. *The Life and Letters of George Gordon Meade*. 2 vols. New York: Charles Scribner's Sons, 1913.

———. *With Meade at Gettysburg*. Philadelphia: John C. Winston Company, 1930.

Meites, Hyman L. *History of the Jews of Chicago*. Chicago: Jewish Historical Society of Illinois, 1924.

Mercer, James K. *Representative Men of Ohio*. Columbus: Press of Fred J. Heer, 1908.

Meyerhoff, Charles H. "What Troops Did Carroll's Brigade Displace in the Charge?" *National Tribune*, 24 April 1890.

Milano, Anthony. "A Call of Leadership: Lt. Col. Charles Redington Mudge, USV, and the Second Massachusetts Infantry at Gettysburg." *Gettysburg Magazine*, 1 January 1992.

Miller, J. Clyde. "At Gettysburg." *National Tribune*, 22 September 1893.

Miller, William E. "The Cavalry Battle near Gettysburg." In *Battles and Leaders of the Civil War*, edited by Robert U. Johnson and Clarence C. Buel, 3:397–406.

Miller's Review, 15 March 1912. (Untitled article on McAllister's Mill.)

Moler, McClure. "History Repeated." *Shepherdstown Register*, 6 July 1922.

Monath, Henry. "Henry Monath Tells of an Experience at Gettysburg." *Gettysburg Compiler*, 28 December 1897.

Moore, Edward A. *The Story of a Cannoneer under Stonewall Jackson*. Freeport, N.Y.: Books for Libraries Press, 1971.

Moore, L. E. C. "Charge of the Louisianians." *National Tribune*, 5 August 1909.

Morhous, Henry C. *Reminiscences of the 123d Regiment, New York State Volunteers*. Greenwich, N.Y.: People's Journal Book and Job Office, 1879.

Morse, Charles F. *History of the Second Massachusetts Regiment of Infantry*. Boston: George H. Ellis, 1882.

———. *Letters Written during the Civil War*. Boston: T. R. Marvin and Son, 1898.

———. "The Twelfth Corps at Gettysburg." In *The Gettysburg Papers*, edited by Ken Bandy and Florence Freeland, 1:819–40.

"Mrs. Kitzmiller's Story." *Gettysburg Compiler*, 23 August 1905.

"Mrs. Thorn's War Story." *Gettysburg Times*, 2 July 1938.

Myers, Frank M. *The Commanches*. Baltimore: Kelly, Piet, 1871.

"My Maryland." *National Tribune*, 15 February 1883.

Nevins, Allan, ed. *A Diary of Battle: The Personal Journal of Colonel Charles S. Wainwright*. New York: Harcourt Brace and World, 1962.

New York Monuments Commission for the Battlefields of Gettysburg and Chattanooga. *Final Report of the Battlefield of Gettysburg*. 3 vols. Albany: J. B. Lyon Company, 1902.

———. *In Memorium, George Sears Greene*. Albany: J. B. Lyon Company, 1909.

———. *In Memorium, Henry Warner Slocum*. Albany: J. B. Lyon Company, 1904.

Nichols, Edward J. *Toward Gettysburg: A Biography of General John F. Reynolds*. University Park, Penn.: State University Press, 1958.

Nicholson, John P. *Pennsylvania at Gettysburg*. 2 vols. Harrisburg: William Stanley Ray, State Printer, 1904.

Norman, William M. *A Portion of My Life*. Winston-Salem, N.C.: John F. Blair Publisher, 1959.

Norris, S. R. "Ohio at Gettysburg." *National Tribune*, 9 June 1887.

"One Who Knows" [pseud.]. "Congress and General Howard." *Army and Navy Journal*, 19 March 1864.

Osborn, Hartwell. *Trials and Triumphs: The Record of the Fifty-fifth Ohio Volunteer Infantry*. Chicago: A. C. McClurg, 1904.

Osborn, Thomas W. "The Artillery at Gettysburg." *Philadelphia Weekly Times*, 31 May 1879.

Parmelee, W. E. "At Gettysburg: The Experiences of an Ohio Artilleryman." *National Tribune*, 2 September 1886.

"A Pathetic Relic of the Civil War." *Richmond Times Dispatch*, 5 February 1905.

Patterson, Gerard. "'Allegheny' Johnson." *Civil War Times* 5, no. 4 (January 1967): 12–19.

Peck, A. W. "At Gettysburg." *National Tribune*, 24 November 1892.

———. "The Part Taken by the Eleventh Corps." *National Tribune*, 12 December 1889.

Pfanz, Harry W. "From Bloody Battlefield to Historic Shrine." *Civil War Times Illustrated*, July 1963.

———. *Gettysburg—The Second Day*. Chapel Hill: University of North Carolina Press, 1977.

Phifer, Edward W. "Saga of a Burke County Family." *North Carolina Historical Review* 39 (1962): 326–32.

Pittsburgh Gazette Times, 9 November 1913. (Untitled article on J. Wesley Culp.)

Powell, Eugene. "Rebellion's High Tide: The Splendid Work on Culp's Hill by the 12th Corps." *National Tribune*, 5 July 1900.

Preston, Noble D. "Campaigning under Gregg." *Philadelphia Weekly Times*, 29 March 1884.

———. *History of the Tenth Regiment of Cavalry, New York State Volunteers*. New York: D. Appleton, 1892.

Pula, James S. *For Liberty and Justice: The Life and Times of Wladimir Krzyzanowski*. Chicago: Polish-American Congress Charitable Foundation, 1978.

Pyne, Henry R. *The History of the First New Jersey Cavalry*. Trenton, N.J.: J. A. Beecher Publisher, 1871.

Quaife, Milo M. *From the Cannon's Mouth: The Civil War Letters of General Alpheus S. Williams*. Detroit: Wayne State University Press, 1959.

Quint, Alonzo H. *The Record of the Second Massachusetts Infantry, 1861–1865*. Boston: James P. Walker, 1867.

Rankin, John R. "Battle of Gettysburg." *National Tribune*, 4 August and 10 November 1892, 23 June 1893.

Rastall, John E. "Union Slave Owners." *Confederate Veteran* 7 (September 1899): 408.

Raus, Edmund J. *A Generation on the March: The Union Army at Gettysburg*. Lynchburg: H. E. Howard, 1987.

Rawle, William Brooke. *History of the Third Pennsylvania Cavalry*. Philadelphia: Franklin Printing Company, 1905.

———. "With Gregg in Gettysburg Campaign." *Philadelphia Weekly Times*, 2 February 1884.

Reed, Merl E., ed. "The Gettysburg Campaign: A Louisiana Lieutenant's Eyewitness Account." *Pennsylvania History* 30, no. 2 (April 1963): 184–91.

Reid, Whitelaw. *Ohio in the War*. 2 vols. Columbus: Eclectic Publishing Company, 1893.

Remington, Cyrus K. *A Record of Battery I, First New York Light Artillery Volunteers*. Buffalo: Courier Publishing Company, 1891.

Roberts, B. A. "The Keystone Guards." *Southern Historical Society Papers* 30 (1908): 146–51.

Robertson, James I. *General A. P. Hill: The Story of a Confederate Warrior*. New York: Random House, 1987.

———. *The Stonewall Brigade*. Baton Rouge: Louisiana State University Press, 1963.

Rollins, Charles A. "Going to Gettysburg." *Lexington Gazette and Citizen*, 9 August 1888.

———. "Jackson's Foot Cavalry." *Lexington Gazette and Citizen*, 16 August 1888.

———. "Playing Cavalry." *Lexington Gazette and Citizen*, 27 September 1888.

———. "A Private's Story." *Lexington Gazette and Citizen*, 26 July 1888.

Salomon, Edward S. *Gettysburg*. War Paper no. 24, Military Order of the Loyal Legion of the United States, California Commandery. San Francisco: Shannon Conmy Printing Company, 1913.

Sauers, Richard Allen. *The Gettysburg Campaign, June 3–August 1, 1863: A Comprehensive Bibliography*. Westport, Conn.: Greenwood Press, 1982.

Schurz, Carl. "The Battle of Gettysburg." *McClure's Magazine* 29, no. 3 (July 1907): 272–85.

———. *The Reminiscences of Carl Schurz*. 3 vols. New York: McClure Company, 1907–8.

Shane, John H. "Getting into the Fight at Gettysburg." *National Tribune*, 27 November 1924.

Shevchuk, Paul M. "The Fight for Brinkerhoff's Ridge, July 2, 1863." *Gettysburg Magazine*, 1 January 1990.

———. "The Wounding of Albert Jenkins, July 2, 1863." *Gettysburg Magazine*, 1 July 1990.

Sifakis, Stewart. *Who Was Who in the Civil War*. New York: Facts on File Publications, 1986.

Simmers, William, and Paul Bachschmid. *The Volunteers' Manual, or Ten Months with the One Hundred and Fifty-third Pennsylvania Volunteers*. Easton, Penn.: D. H. Neiman, 1863.

Simonhoff, Harry. *Jewish Participation in the Civil War*. New York: Arco Publishing Company, 1963.

Skelly, Daniel A. *A Boy's Experiences during the Battle of Gettysburg*. Gettysburg, 1932.

Slocum, Charles E. *The Life and Services of Major General Henry Warner Slocum*. Toledo: Slocum Publishing Company, 1913.

Small, Cindy L. *The Jenny Wade Story*. Gettysburg: Thomas Publications, 1991.

Smart, James G., ed. *A Radical View: The Agate Dispatches of Whitelaw Reid*. 2 vols. Memphis: Memphis State University Press, 1976.

Smith, Jacob. *Camps and Campaigns of the 107th Regiment Ohio Volunteer Infantry*. N.p., n.d.

Smith, James Power. "With Stonewall Jackson." *Southern Historical Society Papers* 43 (1920): 1–105.

Smith, L. A. "Recollections of Gettysburg." In *The Gettysburg Papers*, edited by Ken Bandy and Florence Freeland, 1:337–50.

Spencer, Carrie Esther. *A Civil War Marriage, Reminiscences, and Letters*. Boyce, Va.: Cass Publishing Company, 1956.

Stevens, George T. *Three Years in the Sixth Corps*. Albany: S. R. Gray, 1866.

Stewart, James. "Battery B, Fourth U.S. Artillery at Gettysburg." In *The Gettysburg Papers*, edited by Ken Bandy and Florence Freeland, 1:364–77.

Stiles, Robert. *Four Years under Marse Robert*. New York: Neale Publishing Company, 1903.

Stork, William L. "Gettysburg." *National Tribune,* 10 September 1891.

Storrs, John. *The Twentieth Connecticut.* Ansonia, Conn.: Press of the Naugatuck Valley Sentinel, 1886.

Stose, George W. *Geology and Mineral Resources in Adams County, Pennsylvania.* Harrisburg: Topographic and Geologic Survey, 1932.

Talbott, E. H., and H. R. Hobart. *The Biographical Directory of the Railway Officials of America.* New York: Railway Age Publishing Company, 1885.

Taylor, Walter H. *Four Years with General Lee.* Bloomington: Indiana University Press, 1962.

———. "Second Paper by Col. Walter H. Taylor." *Southern Historical Society Papers* 4 (1877): 124–39.

Tevis, C. V., and D. R. Marquis. *The History of the Fighting Fourteenth.* New York: Brooklyn Eagle Press, 1911.

Thayer, George A. "Gettysburg as We on the Right Saw It." In Military Order of the Loyal Legion, Ohio Commandery, *Sketches of War History,* 2:24–43. Cincinnati: Robert Clarke, 1888.

Thomas, George. "Address: The Maryland Confederate Monument at Gettysburg." *Southern Historical Society Papers* 14 (1886): 429–46.

Thurston, William H. "A Ricketts Batteryman Supports Carroll's Brigade's Claim." *National Tribune,* 13 October 1892.

Tinkom, Harry Marlin. *John White Geary, Soldier-Statesman.* Philadelphia: University of Pennsylvania Press, 1940.

Toombs, Samuel. "The Battle of Gettysburg." In *Proceedings of the Second Reunion of the Veterans' Association of the Thirteenth Regiment, New Jersey Volunteers, September 14, 1887,* pp. 9–13. Newark: Amzi, Pierson, 1888.

———. *New Jersey Troops in the Gettysburg Campaign.* Orange, N.J.: Evening Mail Publishing House, 1888.

Trimble, Isaac. "The Battle and Campaign of Gettysburg." *Southern Historical Society Papers* 26 (1898): 116–28.

———. "The Campaign and Battle of Gettysburg." *Confederate Veteran* 25 (1917): 204–13.

Tripp, Edward. "North Carolina to the Rescue." In *The Confederate Reveille.* Washington, N.C.: Pamlico Chapter, United Daughters of the Confederacy, 1898.

"TRUTH" [pseud.]. "Congress and General Howard." *Army and Navy Journal,* 20 February and 2 April 1864.

Underwood, Adin B. *The Three Years' Service of the Thirty-third Massachusetts Infantry Regiment.* Boston: A. Williams, 1881.

Unrau, Harlan D. *Administrative History: Gettysburg National Military Park and Gettysburg National Cemetery, Pennsylvania.* Washington, D.C.: National Park Service, 1991.

U.S. Congress. *Report of the Joint Committee on the Conduct of the War at the Second Session, Thirty-Eighth Congress, Army of the Potomac, General Meade. . . .* Washington, D.C.: U.S. Government Printing Office, 1865.

U.S. Department of the Army. *The Medal of Honor of the United States Army.* Washington, D.C.: U.S. Government Printing Office, 1944.

U.S. War Department. *U.S. Infantry Tactics.* . . . Philadelphia: J. B. Lippincott, 1862.

———. *The War of the Rebellion: A Compilation of the Official Records of the Union and Confederate Armies.* 128 vols. Washington, D.C.: U.S. Government Printing Office, 1880–1901.

Wakelyn, Jon L. *Biographical Dictionary of the Confederacy.* Westport, Conn.: Greenwood Press, 1977.

Wallace, James. "Our March to Gettysburg." In Mrs. Lincoln Phelps, *Our Country: Its Relations to the Past, Present, and Future*, pp. 54–69. Baltimore: John D. Toy, 1864.

Warner, Ezra J. *Generals in Blue: Lives of Union Commanders.* Baton Rouge: Louisiana State University Press, 1964.

———. *Generals in Gray: Lives of Confederate Commanders.* Baton Rouge: Louisiana State University Press, 1959.

Wheeler, William. *In Memorium: Letters of William Wheeler of the Class of 1855, YC.* Cambridge: H. G. Houghton, 1873.

Whittier, Edward N. "The Left Attack (Ewell's) at Gettysburg." In *The Gettysburg Papers*, edited by Ken Bandy and Florence Freeland, 2:757–94.

Wickham, W. S. "Gettysburg." *National Tribune*, 7 May 1981.

"Wife of Cemetery Caretaker Relates Horrors of Battle of Gettysburg." In *Hundredth Anniversary of the Battle of Gettysburg*. Gettysburg: Gettysburg Times, 1963.

Wilson, Lawrence. "Charge up Culp's Hill." *Washington Post*, 9 July 1899.

Winston, J. B. "A Correction of Dr. McKim's Paper." *Southern Historical Society Papers* 7 (1879): 94.

"Would Have Saved Officers." *Charlottesville Daily Progress*, 22 March 1894.

"Wounded Citizens in Battle." *Gettysburg Star and Sentinel*, 7 July 1867.

Wray, William W. *History of the Twenty-third Pennsylvania Volunteer Infantry.* N.p., 1903–9.

Wright, Owen. "At Gettysburg." *National Tribune*, 30 June 1892.

Young, Jesse B. *The Battle of Gettysburg: A Comprehensive Narrative.* New York: Harper and Brothers, 1913.

Zollinger, William P., Lamar Holliday, and D. R. Howard. "General George H. Steuart's Brigade at the Battle of Gettysburg." *Southern Historical Society Papers* 2 (1876): 105–7.

Index

Lane's, 40, 148

McGowan's, 60–61, 143, 148

Nicholls's, 5, 78, 79, 80, 180, 210, 216, 217, 287, 288, 290, 292, 296, 300, 314; deployment on 2 July, 209; deployment on 3 July, 288; attack plan, 292; strength, 441 (n. 9)

O'Neal's, 5, 34, 35, 128, 278, 287, 288, 289, 292, 300, 314, 352; to Culp's Hill, 288–89; deployment on 3 July, 300

Pettigrew's, 410 (n. 7)

Ramseur's, 5, 34, 128, 278–79, 454 (n. 38)

Smith's, 38, 67, 77, 78, 235, 281, 287, 327, 334, 352; to York Pike, 67–68, 77–78; to Culp's Hill, 289–90

Steuart's, 5, 80, 205, 210, 214, 217, 218, 221, 227, 287, 288, 290, 292, 298, 310, 313, 314, 316, 317, 327, 350, 377; deployment on 2 July, 210; deployment on 3 July, 288, 310, 315; strength on 3 July, 315, 441 (n. 9), 459 (n. 11); advance, 316–18

Stonewall (Walker's), 5–6, 80, 116, 125, 153, 154, 156, 162, 167, 209, 288, 292, 310, 329, 353; at Hanover Road, 154, 166–67; on Culp's Hill, 288, 293, 298, 314, 322, 323, 325–127; on Wolf Hill, 325; strength, 441 (n. 9)

ARTILLERY BATTALIONS:

Andrews's (Latimer's), 168, 169, 170, 179, 208, 247, 438 (n. 48); on Benner's Hill, 178–80, 183, 185–88, 436 (n. 22), 436–37 (n. 24); damage, 187–88

Carter's, 34, 35, 176, 359

Dance's, 128, 176, 206, 359; deployment, 429 (n. 50); guns, 436 (n. 15)

Garnett's, 177, 188, 436 (n. 17)

Jones's, 39, 414 (n. 23)

Lane's, 178

McIntosh's, 177, 188, 436 (n. 16)

Nelson's, 177, 359, 361

Pegram's, 177–78, 188, 436 (n. 18)

Poague's, 178

ARTILLERY BATTERIES:

Brander's, 177, 436 (n. 18)

Brown's, 179, 185–86

Carpenter's, 179

Carrington's, 59–60, 417 (n. 3)

Carter's, 34, 71

Crenshaw, 177, 436 (n. 18)

Cunningham's, 177, 436 (n. 15)

Dement's, 179, 185, 186

Fry's, 35

Graham's (Rockbridge), 170, 179, 181, 182, 358, 359, 361, 435 (n. 4)

Grandy's, 436 (n. 17)

Griffen's, 359

Hurt's, 177, 359, 436 (n. 16)

Johnson's, 177, 436 (n. 16)

Lewis's, 436 (n. 17)

McGraw's, 177, 436 (n. 18)

Marye's, 177, 436 (n. 18)

Maurin's, 436 (n. 17)

Moore's, 436 (n. 17)

Raine's, 179, 182

Rice's, 177, 436 (n. 16)

Smith's, 177, 359, 436 (n. 15)

Wallace's, 177, 436 (n. 15)

Watson's, 177, 359

Zimmerman's, 177, 436 (n. 18)

Army of the Potomac, 15, 16, 18, 19, 22, 103, 119, 156, 190, 200, 274, 308, 346, 369, 379; organization and Chancellorsville casualties, 6; crosses Potomac, 12; Meade takes command, 14; left wing, 15, 16, 21, 92, 94, 100, 101, 103, 412 (n. 20); orders on 30 June, 18, 19; right wing, 190–91, 382

CORPS:

First, 13, 15, 18, 19, 20, 21, 25, 34, 40, 41, 43, 44, 46, 47, 50, 52, 87, 88, 89, 92, 296, 368, 381; ordered to Cemetery Hill, 41, 44; retreat, 46–47; artillery retreat, 50–52

Second, 18, 100, 102, 117, 194, 363,

Williams, Jesse M., 6, 78, 209, 216; biography, 441 (n. 8)

Williams, Seth, 110

Williamson, George, 314, 318, 327

Wills, David, 373, 374

Wilson, Osborn, 338

Winchester, Va., 11, 123

Winebrenner, John, house, 137, 138, 139

Winebrenner's Run, 134, 137, 235, 237, 275, 276, 429 (n. 48), 432 (n. 43), 447 (n. 6)

Winebrenner tannery, 137, 138

Winegar, Charles E., 96, 331–34

Wing, John P., 307

Winkler, Frederick C., 10, 11, 45, 46

Wisconsin infantry regiments:
3d, 116, 127, 330, 331, 345, 346, 348
6th, 46, 49, 53, 114, 213, 222, 223, 228, 444 (n. 45)

7th, 52

26th, 45, 368

Wolf, George, farm, 80, 159

Wolf Hill, 95, 116, 118–19, 126, 153, 161, 164, 209, 216, 290

Woods, Nicajah, 366–67, 467 (n. 6)

Wooster, William B., 350, 351

Wrightsville, Pa., 12

Yellow jackets, 300–301

York, Pa., 12, 18, 31

York Pike, 67–68, 70, 77, 78, 80, 235, 338

York Street, 368

Young, Peter F., 249, 257, 271, 452–53 (n. 15)

Zable, David, 125, 292, 300

Ziegler's Grove, 203, 268, 364

Zimmerman, William E., 177